Winner, 1996 J**olt Aw**

"This book is a tremend**ous achievem**ent ... *f* to have a copy on your shel**f. The chapter**s ... comprehen**sive and under**standable tr**eatment** ... **I've** seen to date ...

...vens

Contributing Editor, D... Journal

"Eckel's book is the on**ly one** so cl**early ex**plain**s how to ret**hink program constru**ction** for ob**ject orientatio**n. **T**hat the book is also an excellent tutorial on the ins and outs of C++ is an added bonus."

Andrew Binstock
Editor, Unix Review

"Bruce continues to amaze me with his insight into C++, and *Thinking in C++* is his best collection of ideas yet. If you want clear answers to difficult questions about C++, buy this outstanding book."

Gary Entsminger
Author, The Tao of Objects

"*Thinking* in C++ patiently and methodically explores the issues of when and h... inheritanc... as the proper... The entire... philosophy of object and program design. A must for every C++ developer's bookshelf, *Thinking in C++* is the one C++ book you must have if you're doing serious development with C++."

Richard Hale Shaw
Contributing Editor, PC Magazine

Comments from Readers:

Wonderful book ... Great stuff! Andrew Schulman, Doctor Dobbs Journal

An absolute, unqualified must. One of the most-used, most trusted books on my shelf." TUG Lines

This is stuff a programmer can really use. IEEE Computer

A refreshing departure. PJ Plauger, Embedded Systems Programming magazine

...Eckel succeeds ... it's so readable. Unix World

Should definitely be your first buy. C Gazette

A fantastic reference for C++! Michael Brandt, Senior Analyst/Programmer, Sydney, Australia

On our project at HRB Systems we call your book "The Answer Book". It is our C++ Bible for the project. Curt Snyder, HRB Systems

Your book is really great, and I can't thank you enough for making it available for free on the web. It's one of the most thorough and useful references for C++ I've seen. Russell Davis

... the only book out there that even comes close to being actually readable when trying to learn the ropes of C++ (and the basics of good object oriented programming in general). Gunther Schulz, KawaiiSoft

I love the examples in your book. There's stuff there that I never would have thought of (and some things that I didn't know you could do)! Rich Herrick, Senior Associate Software Engineer, Lockheed-Martin Federal Systems, Owego, NY

It's an amazing book. Any questions I have I refer to this online book. Helped in every case. I'm simply happy to have access to a book of this caliber. Wes Kells, Comp Eng. Student, SLC Kingston.

You are an invaluable resource and I greatly appreciate your books, email list etc... It seems every project I have worked on has been successful because of your insights. Justin Voshell

This is the book I have been looking for on C++. Thomas A. Fink, Managing Director, Trepp, LLC

Your books are authoritative yet easy to read. To my colleagues I call you the K&R of C++. Mark Orlassino, Senior Design Engineer, Harmon Industries, Inc., Hauppauge, NY

When I first started learning C++, your book "Thinking in C++" was my shining guide light in a dark tunnel. It has been my endeavor to improve my C++ skills whenever possible, and to that effect, "Thinking in C++" has given me the strong foundation for my continuous improvement. Peter Tran, Senior Systems Analyst (IM), Compaq Computer Corporation

This book is the best general reference in my on-going quest to master C++. Most books explain some topics thoroughly but are deficient in others. "Thinking in C++" 2/E does not pass the buck to another book. When I have questions it has answers. Thomas Michel

I have a whole mountain of books and none of them make sense nor do they explain things properly. I have been dying for a good template and STL book. Then I decided to read your material and I was amazed. What you did was show how to write C++ with templates and STL without bogging down with details. What you did was what I expected of the C++ community, the next generation of C++ authors. As an author I AM IMPRESSED at your writing and explanation skills. You covered topics that nobody has properly covered before. Your approach is one from a person who has actually sat down and went through the material in detail. And then you questioned the sanity of the situation and what would be the problem areas. On my bookshelf, it will definitely be one of the necessary books, right beside Petzold. Christian Gross, consultant/mentor cgross@eusoft.com

I think your book is very, very, VERY good. I have compared it to others in the bookstore, and have found that your book actually teaches me basic C++ fundamentals while I learn the STL... a very nice experience to learn about both at once, hand-in-hand. I think your book is laid out very well, and explains things in an easy-to-understand fashion. Jeff Meininger, Software Developer, boxybutgood.com

Your book is the best by far of any I've seen. Please get it right so that we can all have an excellent and "reliable" reference work! And please hurry! We are desperate for a work of this quality! Steve Strickland, Live Minds (a Puzzle business)

(On Usenet) Unlike most other C++ authors, Eckel has made a career of teaching C++ and Java classes ONLY. He's had the benefit of a GREAT deal of novice feedback, and the books reflect that. His books are not just about writing in C++/Java, but understanding the intent of the languages and the mindset that goes with thinking in them. Eckel's also the best technical writer I've read since Jeff Duntemann. Very clear and easy to read. Don't be put off by the apparent large size of his books. Either can be read in *less* than 21 days. :-} Randy Crawford, MRJ Technology Solutions, Fairfax VA

Your work is greatly appreciated and I thank you for helping me understand both C++ and Java better. Barry Wallin, Math/Computer Science Teacher, Rosemount High School, Rosemount, MN

I would like to thank you for your book "Thinking in C++" which is, with no doubt, the best book I ever read about this subject. Riccardo Tarli - SW Engineer - R&D TXT Ingegneria Informatica - Italy

I have been reading both of your books, Thinking In Java and Thinking In C++. Each of these books is easily the best in its category. Ratnakarprasad H. Tiwari, Mumbai, India

... the "Debugging Hints" section is so valuable, I'm tempted to print it and keep it with me at all times. I think this section should be a mandatory part of any introductory class after the first one or two programming problems. Fred Ballard, Synectics Inc.

Your book is really a treasure trove of C++ knowledge. I feel like you give a good overview and then explain the nuts and bolts. Raymond Pickles, Antenna Section, Radar Division, U.S. Naval Research Laboratory, Washington DC

As an Internal Medicine Specialist and Computer Scientist I spend a great deal of time trying to extract information from books and journals. My experience is that a good author is one who makes difficult concepts accessible, a great one makes it look almost easy. On this score you are certainly one of my top three technical writers. Keep up the good work. Dr. Declan O'Kane, Leicester, England

For my second-level C++ course, "Thinking in C++" is my constant reference and companion, and I urge my students to consult it regularly. I refer to the chapter on Operator Overloading constantly. The examples/code alone are worth the cost of the book many times over. So many books and development environments are predicated on the assumption that the only application for a programming language is for a Windows environment; it's great to find and use a book which concentrates on C++ so we can prepare our students for careers in fields like embedded systems, networking, etc., which require real depth of understanding. Robert Chase, Professor, Sweet Briar College

I think it's a fantastic intro to C++, especially for longtime dabblers like me – I often know "how," but rarely "why," and TIC2 is a godsend. Tony Likhite, System Administrator/DBA, Together Networks

After reading the first 80 pages of this book, I have a better understanding of oop then I've gotten out of the ton of books I've accumulated on the subject. Thanks... Rick Schneewind

Thinking

In

C++

Second Edition

Bruce Eckel
President, MindView Inc.

Prentice Hall
Upper Saddle River, New Jersey 07458
http://www.prenhall.com

Publisher: Alan Apt
Production Editor: Scott Disanno
Executive Managing Editor: Vince O'Brien
Vice President and Editorial Director: Marcia Horton
Vice President of Production and Manufacturing: David W. Riccardi
Project Manager: Ana Terry
Book Design, Cover Design and Cover Line Art:
    Daniel Will-Harris, daniel@will-harris.com
Cover Watercolor: Bruce Eckel
Copy Editor: Stephanie English
Production Coordinator: Lori Bulwin
Editorial Assistant: Toni Holm
Marketing Managers: Jennie Burger, Bryan Gambrel

©2000 by Bruce Eckel, MindView, Inc.

Published by Prentice Hall Inc.
Pearson Higher Education
Upper Saddle River, New Jersey 07632

Printed in the United States of America

10 9 8 7 6 5 4 3 2 1

ISBN 0-13-979809-9

Prentice-Hall International (UK) Limited, *London*
Prentice-Hall of Australia Pty. Limited, *Sydney*
Prentice-Hall Canada, Inc., *Toronto*
Prentice-Hall Hispanoamericana, S.A., *Mexico*
Prentice-Hall of India Private Limited, *New Delhi*
Prentice-Hall of Japan, Inc., *Tokyo*
Pearson Education Asia Ltd., *Singapore*
Editora Prentice-Hall do Brasil, Ltda., *Rio de Janeiro*

10019143273

Dedication

To my parents, my sister, and my brother

What's inside...

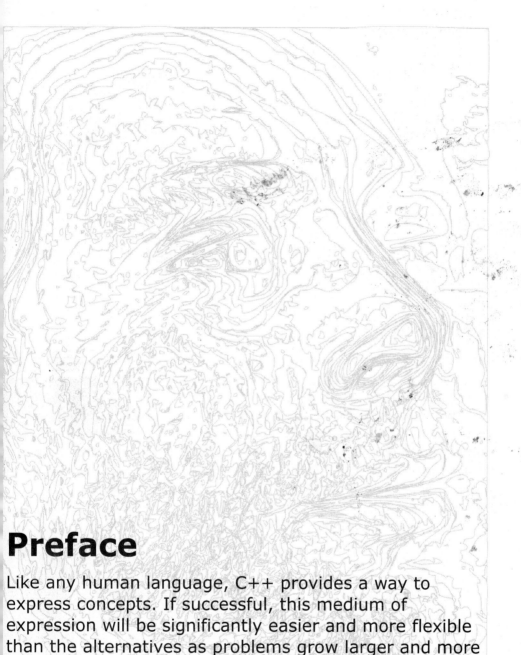

Preface

Like any human language, C++ provides a way to express concepts. If successful, this medium of expression will be significantly easier and more flexible than the alternatives as problems grow larger and more complex.

You can't just look at C++ as a collection of features; some of the features make no sense in isolation. You can only use the sum of the parts if you are thinking about *design*, not simply coding. And to understand C++ this way, you must understand the problems with C and with programming in general. This book discusses programming problems, why they are problems, and the approach C++ has taken to solve such problems. Thus, the set of features I explain in each chapter will be based on the way that I see a particular type of problem being solved with the language. In this way I hope to move you, a little at a time, from understanding C to the point where the C++ mindset becomes your native tongue.

Throughout, I'll be taking the attitude that you want to build a model in your head that allows you to understand the language all the way down to the bare metal; if you encounter a puzzle, you'll be able to feed it to your model and deduce the answer. I will try to convey to you the insights that have rearranged my brain to make me start "thinking in C++."

What's new in the second edition

This book is a thorough rewrite of the first edition to reflect all of the changes introduced in C++ by the finalization of the C++ Standard, and also to reflect what I've learned since writing the first edition. The entire text present in the first edition has been examined and rewritten, sometimes removing old examples, often changing existing examples and adding new ones, and adding many new exercises. Significant rearrangement and re-ordering of the material took place to reflect the availability of better tools and my improved understanding of how people learn C++. A new chapter was added which is a rapid introduction to the C concepts and basic C++ features for those who don't have the C background to tackle the rest of the book. The CD ROM bound into the back of the book contains a seminar that is an even gentler introduction to the C concepts necessary to understand C++ (or Java). It was created by Chuck Allison for my company (MindView, Inc.), and it's called "Thinking in C: Foundations for Java and C++." It introduces you to the aspects of C that are necessary for you to move on to C++ or Java, leaving out the nasty bits that C programmers must deal with on a day-to-day basis but that the C++ and Java languages steer you away from (or even eliminate, in the case of Java).

So the short answer to the question "what's different in the 2nd edition?" is: what isn't brand new has been rewritten, sometimes to the point where you wouldn't recognize the original examples and material.

What's in Volume 2 of this book

The completion of the C++ Standard also added a number of important new libraries, such as **string** and the containers and algorithms in the Standard C++ Library, as well as new complexity in templates. These and other more advanced topics have been relegated to Volume 2 of this book, including issues such as multiple inheritance, exception handling, design patterns, and topics about building and debugging stable systems.

How to get Volume 2

Just like the book you currently hold, *Thinking in C++, Volume 2* is downloadable in its entirety from my Web site at *www.BruceEckel.com*. You can find information on the Web site about the expected print date of Volume 2.

The Web site also contains the source code for both of the books, along with updates and information about other seminars-on-CD ROM that MindView, Inc. offers, public seminars, and in-house training, consulting, mentoring, and walkthroughs.

Prerequisites

In the first edition of this book, I decided to assume that someone else had taught you C and that you have at least a reading level of comfort with it. My primary focus was on simplifying what I found difficult: the C++ language. In this edition I have added a chapter that is a rapid introduction to C, along with the *Thinking in C* seminar-on-CD, but I am still assuming that you already have some kind of programming experience. In addition, just as you learn many new words intuitively by seeing them in context in a novel, it's possible to learn a great deal about C from the context in which it is used in the rest of the book.

Learning C++

I clawed my way into C++ from exactly the same position I expect many of the readers of this book are in: as a programmer with a very no-nonsense, nuts-and-bolts attitude about programming. Worse, my background and experience was in hardware-level embedded programming, in which C has often been considered a high-level language and an inefficient overkill for pushing bits around. I discovered later that I wasn't even a very good C programmer, hiding my ignorance of structures, **malloc( )** and **free( )**, **setjmp( )** and **longjmp( )**, and other "sophisticated" concepts, scuttling away in shame when the subjects came up in conversation instead of reaching out for new knowledge.

When I began my struggle to understand C++, the only decent book was Bjarne Stroustrup's self-professed "expert's guide,[1]" so I was left to simplify the basic concepts on my own. This resulted in my first C++ book,[2] which was essentially a brain dump of my experience. That was designed as a reader's guide to bring programmers into C and C++ at the same time. Both editions[3] of the book garnered enthusiastic response.

At about the same time that *Using C++* came out, I began teaching the language in seminars and presentations. Teaching C++ (and later, Java) became my profession; I've seen nodding heads, blank faces, and puzzled expressions in audiences all over the world since 1989. As I began giving in-house training to smaller groups of people, I discovered something during the exercises. Even those people who were smiling and nodding were confused about many

---

[1] Bjarne Stroustrup, *The C++ Programming Language*, Addison-Wesley, 1986 (first edition).

[2] *Using C++*, Osborne/McGraw-Hill 1989.

[3] *Using C++* and *C++ Inside & Out*, Osborne/McGraw-Hill 1993.

issues. I found out, by creating and chairing the C++ and Java tracks at the Software Development Conference for many years, that I and other speakers tended to give the typical audience too many topics, too fast. So eventually, through both variety in the audience level and the way that I presented the material, I would end up losing some portion of the audience. Maybe it's asking too much, but because I am one of those people resistant to traditional lecturing (and for most people, I believe, such resistance results from boredom), I wanted to try to keep everyone up to speed.

For a time, I was creating a number of different presentations in fairly short order. Thus, I ended up learning by experiment and iteration (a technique that also works well in C++ program design). Eventually I developed a course using everything I had learned from my teaching experience. It tackles the learning problem in discrete, easy-to-digest steps and for a hands-on seminar (the ideal learning situation) there are exercises following each of the presentations. You can find out about my public seminars at *www.BruceEckel.com*, and you can also learn about the seminars that I've turned into CD ROMs.

The first edition of this book developed over the course of two years, and the material in this book has been road-tested in many forms in many different seminars. The feedback that I've gotten from each seminar has helped me change and refocus the material until I feel it works well as a teaching medium. But it isn't just a seminar handout; I tried to pack as much information as I could within these pages, and structure it to draw you through onto the next subject. More than anything, the book is designed to serve the solitary reader who is struggling with a new programming language.

Goals

My goals in this book are to:

1. Present the material one simple step at a time, so the reader can easily digest each concept before moving on.

2.   Use examples that are as simple and short as possible. This often prevents me from tackling "real world" problems, but I've found that beginners are usually happier when they can understand every detail of an example rather than being impressed by the scope of the problem it solves. Also, there's a severe limit to the amount of code that can be absorbed in a classroom situation. For this I sometimes receive criticism for using "toy examples," but I'm willing to accept that in favor of producing something pedagogically useful.

3.   Carefully sequence the presentation of features so that you aren't seeing something you haven't been exposed to. Of course, this isn't always possible; in those situations, a brief introductory description will be given.

4.   Give you what I think is important for you to understand about the language, rather than everything that I know. I believe there is an "information importance hierarchy," and there are some facts that 95 percent of programmers will never need to know and that would just confuse them and add to their perception of the complexity of the language. To take an example from C, if you memorize the operator precedence table (I never did), you can write clever code. But if *you* have to think about it, it will confuse the reader/maintainer of that code. So forget about precedence, and use parentheses when things aren't clear. This same attitude will be taken with some information in the C++ language, which I think is more important for compiler writers than for programmers.

5.   Keep each section focused enough so the lecture time – and the time between exercise periods – is reasonable. Not only does this keep the audience's minds more active and involved during a hands-on seminar, it gives the reader a greater sense of accomplishment.

6.   Provide readers with a solid foundation so they can understand the issues well enough to move on to more difficult coursework and books (in particular, Volume 2 of this book).

7.   I've tried not to use any particular vendor's version of C++ because, for learning the language, I don't think that the details of a particular implementation are as important as the language itself. Most vendors' documentation concerning their own implementation specifics is adequate.

Chapters

C++ is a language in which new and different features are built on top of an existing syntax. (Because of this, it is referred to as a *hybrid* object-oriented programming language.) As more people pass through the learning curve, we've begun to get a feel for the way programmers move through the stages of the C++ language features. Because it appears to be the natural progression of the procedurally-trained mind, I decided to understand and follow this same path and accelerate the process by posing and answering the questions that came to me as I learned the language and those questions that came from audiences as I taught the language.

This course was designed with one thing in mind: to streamline the process of learning C++. Audience feedback helped me understand which parts were difficult and needed extra illumination. In the areas in which I got ambitious and included too many features all at once, I came to know – through the process of presenting the material – that if you include a lot of new features, you have to explain them all, and the student's confusion is easily compounded. As a result, I've taken a great deal of trouble to introduce the features as few at a time as possible; ideally, only one major concept at a time per chapter.

The goal, then, is for each chapter to teach a single concept, or a small group of associated concepts, in such a way that no additional features are relied upon. That way you can digest each piece in the context of your current knowledge before moving on. To accomplish this, I leave some C features in place for longer than I would prefer. The benefit is that you will not be confused by seeing all the C++ features used before they are explained, so your introduction to the language will be gentle and will mirror the way you will assimilate the features if left to your own devices.

Here is a brief description of the chapters contained in this book:

Chapter 1: Introduction to Objects. When projects became too big and complicated to easily maintain, the "software crisis" was born, with programmers saying, "We can't get projects done, and if we can, they're too expensive!" This precipitated a number of responses, which are discussed in this chapter along with the ideas of object-oriented programming (OOP) and how it attempts to solve the software crisis. The chapter walks you through the basic concepts and features of OOP and also introduces the analysis and design process. In addition, you'll learn about the benefits and concerns of adopting the language and suggestions for moving into the world of C++.

Chapter 2: Making and Using Objects. This chapter explains the process of building programs using compilers and libraries. It introduces the first C++ program in the book and shows how programs are constructed and compiled. Then some of the basic libraries of objects available in Standard C++ are introduced. By the time you finish this chapter you'll have a good grasp of what it means to write a C++ program using off-the-shelf object libraries.

Chapter 3: The C in C++. This chapter is a dense overview of the features in C that are used in C++, as well as a number of basic features that are available only in C++. It also introduces the "make" utility that's common in the software development world and that is used to build all the examples in this book (the source code for the book, which is available at *www.BruceEckel.com*, contains makefiles for each chapter). Chapter 3 assumes that you have a solid grounding in some procedural programming language like Pascal, C, or even some flavors of Basic (as long as you've written plenty of code in that language, especially functions). If you find this chapter a bit too much, you should first go through the *Thinking in C* seminar on the CD that's bound with this book (and also available at *www.BruceEckel.com*).

Chapter 4: Data Abstraction. Most features in C++ revolve around the ability to create new data types. Not only does this provide superior code organization, but it lays the groundwork for more powerful OOP abilities. You'll see how this idea is facilitated by the simple act of putting functions inside structures, the details of how to do it, and what kind of code it creates. You'll also learn the best way to organize your code into header files and implementation files.

Chapter 5: Hiding the Implementation. You can decide that some of the data and functions in your structure are unavailable to the user of the new type by making them **private**. This means that you can separate the underlying implementation from the interface that the client programmer sees, and thus allow that implementation to be easily changed without affecting client code. The keyword **class** is also introduced as a fancier way to describe a new data type, and the meaning of the word "object" is demystified (it's a fancy variable).

Chapter 6: Initialization and Cleanup. One of the most common C errors results from uninitialized variables. The *constructor* in C++ allows you to guarantee that variables of your new data type ("objects of your class") will always be initialized properly. If your objects also require some sort of cleanup, you can guarantee that this cleanup will always happen with the C++ *destructor*.

Chapter 7: Function Overloading and Default Arguments. C++ is intended to help you build big, complex projects. While doing this, you may bring in multiple libraries that use the same function name, and you may also choose to use the same name with different meanings within a single library. C++ makes this easy with *function overloading*, which allows you to reuse the same function name as long as the argument lists are different. Default arguments allow you to call the same function in different ways by automatically providing default values for some of your arguments.

Chapter 8: Constants. This chapter covers the **const** and **volatile** keywords, which have additional meaning in C++, especially inside classes. You'll learn what it means to apply **const** to a pointer definition. The chapter also shows how the meaning of **const** varies when used inside and outside of classes and how to create compile-time constants inside classes.

Chapter 9: Inline Functions. Preprocessor macros eliminate function call overhead, but the preprocessor also eliminates valuable C++ type checking. The inline function gives you all the benefits of a preprocessor macro plus all of the benefits of a real function call. This chapter thoroughly explores the implementation and use of inline functions.

Chapter 10: Name Control. Creating names is a fundamental activity in programming, and when a project gets large, the number of names can be overwhelming. C++ allows you a great deal of control over names in terms of their creation, visibility, placement of storage, and linkage. This chapter shows how names are controlled in C++ using two techniques. First, the **static** keyword is used to control visibility and linkage, and its special meaning with classes is explored. A far more useful technique for controlling names at the global scope is C++'s **namespace** feature, which allows you to break up the global name space into distinct regions.

Chapter 11: References and the Copy-Constructor. C++ pointers work like C pointers with the additional benefit of stronger C++ type checking. C++ also provides an additional way to handle addresses: from Algol and Pascal, C++ lifts the *reference,* which lets the compiler handle the address manipulation while you use ordinary notation. You'll also meet the copy-constructor, which controls the way objects are passed into and out of functions by value. Finally, the C++ pointer-to-member is illuminated.

Chapter 12: Operator Overloading. This feature is sometimes called "syntactic sugar;" it lets you sweeten the syntax for using your type by allowing operators as well as function calls. In this chapter you'll learn that operator overloading is just a different type of function call and you'll learn how to write your own, dealing with the sometimes-confusing uses of arguments, return types, and the decision of whether to make an operator a member or friend.

Chapter 13: Dynamic Object Creation. How many planes will an air-traffic system need to manage? How many shapes will a CAD system require? In the general programming problem, you can't know the quantity, lifetime, or type of objects needed by your running program. In this chapter, you'll learn how C++'s **new** and

delete elegantly solve this problem by safely creating objects on the heap. You'll also see how **new** and **delete** can be overloaded in a variety of ways so you can control how storage is allocated and released.

Chapter 14: Inheritance and Composition. Data abstraction allows you to create new types from scratch, but with composition and inheritance, you can create new types from existing types. With composition, you assemble a new type using other types as pieces, and with inheritance, you create a more specific version of an existing type. In this chapter you'll learn the syntax, how to redefine functions, and the importance of construction and destruction for inheritance and composition.

Chapter 15: Polymorphism and virtual Functions. On your own, you might take nine months to discover and understand this cornerstone of OOP. Through small, simple examples, you'll see how to create a family of types with inheritance and manipulate objects in that family through their common base class. The **virtual** keyword allows you to treat all objects in this family generically, which means that the bulk of your code doesn't rely on specific type information. This makes your programs extensible, so building programs and code maintenance is easier and cheaper.

Chapter 16: Introduction to Templates. Inheritance and composition allow you to reuse object code, but that doesn't solve all of your reuse needs. Templates allow you to reuse *source* code by providing the compiler with a way to substitute type names in the body of a class or function. This supports the use of *container class* libraries, which are important tools for the rapid, robust development of object-oriented programs (the Standard C++ Library includes a significant library of container classes). This chapter gives you a thorough grounding in this essential subject.

Additional topics (and more advanced subjects) are available in Volume 2 of this book, which can be downloaded from the Web site *www.BruceEckel.com*.

Exercises

I've discovered that exercises are exceptionally useful during a seminar to complete a student's understanding, so you'll find a set at the end of each chapter. The number of exercises has been greatly increased over the number in the first edition.

Many of the exercises are fairly simple so that they can be finished in a reasonable amount of time in a classroom situation or lab section while the instructor observes, making sure all students are absorbing the material. Some exercises are a bit more challenging to keep advanced students entertained. The bulk of the exercises are designed to be solved in a short time and are intended only to test and polish your knowledge rather than present major challenges (presumably, you'll find those on your own – or more likely, they'll find you).

Exercise solutions

Solutions to selected exercises can be found in the electronic document *The Thinking in C++ Annotated Solution Guide*, available for a small fee from *www.BruceEckel.com*.

Source code

The source code for this book is copyrighted freeware, distributed via the Web site *www.BruceEckel.com*. The copyright prevents you from republishing the code in print media without permission, but you are granted the right to use it in many other situations (see below).

The code is available in a zipped file, designed to be extracted for any platform that has a "zip" utility (most do; you can search the Internet to find a version for your platform if you don't already have one installed). In the starting directory where you unpacked the code you will find the following copyright notice:

```
//:! :Copyright.txt
Copyright (c) 2000, Bruce Eckel
Source code file from the book "Thinking in C++"
```

You may use the code in your projects and in the classroom as long as the copyright notice is retained.

Language standards

Throughout this book, when referring to conformance to the ISO C standard, I will generally just say 'C.' Only if it is necessary to distinguish between Standard C and older, pre-Standard versions of C will I make a distinction.

At this writing the C++ Standards Committee was finished working on the language. Thus, I will use the term *Standard C++* to refer to the standardized language. If I simply refer to C++ you should assume I mean "Standard C++."

There is some confusion over the actual name of the C++ Standards Committee and the name of the standard itself. Steve Clamage, the committee chair, clarified this:

> *There are two C++ standardization committees: The NCITS (formerly X3) J16 committee and the ISO JTC1/SC22/WG14 committee. ANSI charters NCITS to create technical committees for developing American national standards.*

> *J16 was chartered in 1989 to create an American standard for C++. In about 1991 WG14 was chartered to create an international standard. The J16 project was converted to a "Type I" (International) project and subordinated to the ISO standardization effort.*

> *The two committees meet at the same time at the same location, and the J16 vote constitutes the American vote on WG14. WG14 delegates technical work to J16. WG14 votes on the technical work of J16.*

> *The C++ standard was originally created as an ISO standard. ANSI later voted (as recommended by J16) to adopt the ISO C++ standard as the American standard for C++.*

Thus, 'ISO' is the correct way to refer to the C++ Standard.

Language support

Your compiler may not support all of the features discussed in this book, especially if you don't have the newest version of the compiler. Implementing a language like C++ is a Herculean task, and you can expect that the features will appear in pieces rather than all at once. But if you attempt one of the examples in the book and get a lot of errors from the compiler, it's not necessarily a bug in the code or the compiler; it may simply not be implemented in your particular compiler yet.

The book's CD ROM

The primary content of the CD ROM packaged in the back of this book is a "seminar on CD ROM" titled *Thinking in C: Foundations for Java & C++* by Chuck Allison (published by MindView, Inc., and also available in quantities at *www.BruceEckel.com*). This contains many hours of audio lectures and slides, and can be viewed on most computers if you have a CD ROM player and a sound system.

The goal of *Thinking in C* is to take you carefully through the fundamentals of the C language. It focuses on the knowledge necessary for you to be able to move on to the C++ or Java languages instead of trying to make you an expert in all the dark corners of C. (One of the reasons for using a higher-level language like C++ or Java is precisely so we can avoid many of these dark corners.) It also contains exercises and guided solutions. Keep in mind that because Chapter 3 of this book goes beyond the *Thinking in C* CD, the CD is not a replacement for that chapter, but should be used instead as a preparation for this book.

Please note that the CD ROM is browser-based, so you should have a Web browser installed on your machine before using it.

CD ROMs, seminars, and consulting

There are seminars-on-CD-ROM planned to cover Volume 1 and Volume 2 of this book. These comprise many hours of audio lectures by me that accompany slides that cover selected material from each chapter in the book. They can be viewed on most computers if you have a CD ROM player and a sound system. These CDs may be purchased at *www.BruceEckel.com*, where you will find more information and sample lectures.

My company, MindView, Inc., provides public hands-on training seminars based on the material in this book and also on advanced topics. Selected material from each chapter represents a lesson, which is followed by a monitored exercise period so each student receives personal attention. We also provide on-site training, consulting, mentoring, and design and code walkthroughs. Information and sign-up forms for upcoming seminars and other contact information can be found at *www.BruceEckel.com*.

I am sometimes available for design consulting, project evaluation and code walkthroughs. When I first began writing about computers, my primary motivation was to increase my consulting activities, because I find consulting to be challenging, educational, and one of my most enjoyable experiences, professionally. Thus I will try my best to fit you into my schedule, or to provide you with one of my associates (who are people that I know well and trust, and often people who co-develop and teach seminars with me).

Errors

No matter how many tricks a writer uses to detect errors, some always creep in and these often leap off the page to a fresh reader. If you discover anything you believe to be an error, please use the correction form you will find at *www.BruceEckel.com*. Your help is appreciated.

About the cover

The first edition of this book had my face on the cover, but I originally wanted a cover for the second edition that was more of a work of art like the *Thinking in Java* cover. For some reason, C++ seems to me to suggest Art Deco with its simple curves and brushed chrome. I had in mind something like those posters of ships and airplanes with the long sweeping bodies.

My friend Daniel Will-Harris, (*www.Will-Harris.com*) whom I first met in junior high school choir class, went on to become a world-class designer and writer. He has done virtually all of my designs, including the cover for the first edition of this book. During the cover design process, Daniel, unsatisfied with the progress we were making, kept asking "How does this relate people to computers?" We were stuck.

On a whim, with no particular outcome in mind, he asked me to put my face on the scanner. Daniel had one of his graphics programs (Corel Xara, his favorite) "autotrace" the scan of my face. As he describes it, "Autotracing is the computer's way to turn a picture into the kinds of lines and curves it really likes." Then he played with it until he had something that looked like a topographic map of my face, an image that might be the way a computer could see people.

I took this image and photocopied it onto watercolor paper (some color copiers can handle thick stock), and then started creating lots of experiments by adding watercolor to the image. We selected the ones we liked best, then Daniel scanned them back in and arranged them into the cover, adding the text and other design elements. The whole process happened over several months, mostly because of the time it took me to do the watercolors. But I've especially enjoyed it because I got to participate in the art on the cover, and because it gave me incentive to do more watercolors (what they say about practice really is true).

Book design and production

The book's interior design was created by Daniel Will-Harris, who used to play with rub-on letters in junior high school while he awaited the invention of computers and desktop publishing. However, I produced the camera-ready pages myself, so the typesetting errors are mine. Microsoft® Word for Windows Versions 8 and 9 were used to write the book and to create camera-ready pages, including generating the table of contents and index. (I created a COM automation server in Python, called from Word VBA macros, to aid me in index marking.) Python (see *www.Python.org*) was used to create some of the tools for checking the code, and would have been use for the code extraction tool had I discovered it earlier.

I created the diagrams using Visio® – thanks to Visio Corporation for creating a useful tool.

The body typeface is Georgia and the headlines are in Verdana. The final camera-ready version was produced in Adobe® Acrobat 4 and taken directly to press from that file – thanks very much to Adobe for creating a tool that allows e-mailing camera-ready documents, as it enables multiple revisions to be made in a single day rather than relying on my laser printer and overnight express services. (We first tried the Acrobat process with *Thinking in Java*, and I was able to upload the final version of that book to the printer in the U.S. from South Africa.)

The HTML version was created by exporting the Word document to RTF, then using RTF2HTML (see *http://www.sunpack.com/RTF/*) to do most of the work of the HTML conversion. (Thanks to Chris Hector for making such a useful, and especially reliable, tool.) The resulting files were cleaned up using a custom Python program that I hacked together, and the WMFs were converted to GIFs using JASC® PaintShop Pro 6 and its batch conversion tool (thanks to JASC for solving so many problems for me with their excellent product). The color syntax highlighting was added via a Perl script kindly contributed by Zafir Anjum.

Acknowledgements

First, thanks to everyone on the Internet who submitted corrections and suggestions; you've been tremendously helpful in improving the quality of this book, and I couldn't have done it without you. Special thanks to John Cook.

The ideas and understanding in this book have come from many sources: friends like Chuck Allison, Andrea Provaglio, Dan Saks, Scott Meyers, Charles Petzold, and Michael Wilk; pioneers of the language like Bjarne Stroustrup, Andrew Koenig, and Rob Murray; members of the C++ Standards Committee like Nathan Myers (who was particularly helpful and generous with his insights), Bill Plauger, Reg Charney, Tom Penello, Tom Plum, Sam Druker, and Uwe Steinmueller; people who have spoken in my C++ track at the Software Development Conference; and often students in my seminars, who ask the questions I need to hear in order to make the material more clear.

A huge thank-you to my friend Gen Kiyooka, whose company Digigami has provided me with a web server.

My friend Richard Hale Shaw and I have taught C++ together; Richard's insights and support have been very helpful (and Kim's, too). Thanks also to KoAnn Vikoren, Eric Faurot, Jennifer Jessup, Tara Arrowood, Marco Pardi, Nicole Freeman, Barbara Hanscome, Regina Ridley, Alex Dunne, and the rest of the cast and crew at MFI.

A special thanks to all my teachers and all my students (who are my teachers as well).

And for favorite writers, my deep appreciation and sympathy for your efforts: John Irving, Neal Stephenson, Robertson Davies (we shall miss you), Tom Robbins, William Gibson, Richard Bach, Carlos Castaneda, and Gene Wolfe.

To Guido van Rossum, for inventing Python and giving it selflessly to the world. You have enriched my life with your contribution.

Thanks to the people at Prentice Hall: Alan Apt, Ana Terry, Scott Disanno, Toni Holm, and my electronic copy-editor Stephanie English. In marketing, Bryan Gambrel and Jennie Burger.

Sonda Donovan helped with the production of the CD Rom. Daniel Will-Harris (of course) created the silkscreen design that's on the Disc itself.

To all the great folks in Crested Butte, thanks for making it a magical place, especially Al Smith (creator of the wonderful Camp4 Coffee Garden), my neighbors Dave & Erika, Marsha at Heg's Place bookstore, Pat & John at the Teocalli Tamale, Sam at the Bakery Café, and Tiller for his help with audio research. And to all the terrific people that hang out at Camp4 in and make my mornings interesting.

The supporting cast of friends includes, but is not limited to, Zack Urlocker, Andrew Binstock, Neil Rubenking, Kraig Brockschmidt, Steve Sinofsky, JD Hildebrandt, Brian McElhinney, Brinkley Barr, Larry O'Brien, Bill Gates at *Midnight Engineering Magazine*, Larry Constantine, Lucy Lockwood, Tom Keffer, Dan Putterman, Gene Wang, Dave Mayer, David Intersimone, Claire Sawyers, the Italians (Andrea Provaglio, Rossella Gioia, Laura Fallai, Marco & Lella Cantu, Corrado, Ilsa and Christina Giustozzi), Chris and Laura Strand (and Parker), the Almquists, Brad Jerbic, Marilyn Cvitanic, the Mabrys, the Haflingers, the Pollocks, Peter Vinci, the Robbins, the Moelters, Dave Stoner, Laurie Adams, the Cranstons, Larry Fogg, Mike and Karen Sequeira, Gary Entsminger and Allison Brody, Kevin, Sonda, & Ella Donovan, Chester and Shannon Andersen, Joe Lordi, Dave and Brenda Bartlett, the Rentschlers, Lynn and Todd, and their families. And of course, Mom and Dad.

1: Introduction to Objects

The genesis of the computer revolution was in a machine. The genesis of our programming languages thus tends to look like that machine.

But computers are not so much machines as they are mind amplification tools ("bicycles for the mind," as Steve Jobs is fond of saying) and a different kind of expressive medium. As a result, the tools are beginning to look less like machines and more like parts of our minds, and also like other expressive mediums such as writing, painting, sculpture, animation, and filmmaking. Object-oriented programming is part of this movement toward using the computer as an expressive medium.

This chapter will introduce you to the basic concepts of object-oriented programming (OOP), including an overview of OOP development methods. This chapter, and this book, assume that you have had experience in a procedural programming language, although not necessarily C. If you think you need more preparation in programming and the syntax of C before tackling this book, you should work through the "Thinking in C: Foundations for C++ and Java" training CD ROM, bound in with this book and also available at *www.BruceEckel.com*.

This chapter is background and supplementary material. Many people do not feel comfortable wading into object-oriented programming without understanding the big picture first. Thus, there are many concepts that are introduced here to give you a solid overview of OOP. However, many other people don't get the big picture concepts until they've seen some of the mechanics first; these people may become bogged down and lost without some code to get their hands on. If you're part of this latter group and are eager to get to the specifics of the language, feel free to jump past this chapter – skipping it at this point will not prevent you from writing programs or learning the language. However, you will want to come back here eventually to fill in your knowledge so you can understand why objects are important and how to design with them.

The progress of abstraction

All programming languages provide abstractions. It can be argued that the complexity of the problems you're able to solve is directly related to the kind and quality of abstraction. By "kind" I mean, "What is it that you are abstracting?" Assembly language is a small abstraction of the underlying machine. Many so-called "imperative" languages that followed (such as Fortran, BASIC, and C) were abstractions of assembly language. These languages are big improvements over assembly language, but their primary abstraction still requires you to think in terms of the structure of the computer rather than the structure of the problem you are trying to solve. The programmer must establish the association between the machine model (in the "solution space," which is the place where you're modeling that problem, such as a computer) and the model of the problem that is actually being solved (in the "problem space," which is the place where the problem exists). The effort required to perform this mapping, and the fact that it is extrinsic to the programming language, produces programs that are difficult to write and expensive to maintain, and as a side effect created the entire "programming methods" industry.

The alternative to modeling the machine is to model the problem you're trying to solve. Early languages such as LISP and APL chose particular views of the world ("All problems are ultimately lists" or "All problems are algorithmic"). PROLOG casts all problems into chains of decisions. Languages have been created for constraint-based programming and for programming exclusively by manipulating graphical symbols. (The latter proved to be too restrictive.) Each of these approaches is a good solution to the particular class of problem they're designed to solve, but when you step outside of that domain they become awkward.

The object-oriented approach goes a step farther by providing tools for the programmer to represent elements in the problem space. This representation is general enough that the programmer is not constrained to any particular type of problem. We refer to the elements in the problem space and their representations in the solution space as "objects." (Of course, you will also need other objects that don't have problem-space analogs.) The idea is that the program is allowed to adapt itself to the lingo of the problem by adding new types of objects, so when you read the code describing the solution, you're reading words that also express the problem. This is a more flexible and powerful language abstraction than what we've had before. Thus, OOP allows you to describe the problem in terms of the problem, rather than in terms of the computer where

---

the solution will run. There's still a connection back to the computer, though. Each object looks quite a bit like a little computer; it has a state, and it has operations that you can ask it to perform. However, this doesn't seem like such a bad analogy to objects in the real world; they all have characteristics and behaviors.

Some language designers have decided that object-oriented programming by itself is not adequate to easily solve all programming problems, and advocate the combination of various approaches into *multiparadigm* programming languages.[1]

Alan Kay summarized five basic characteristics of Smalltalk, the first successful object-oriented language and one of the languages upon which C++ is based. These characteristics represent a pure approach to object-oriented programming:

1. **Everything is an object.** Think of an object as a fancy variable; it stores data, but you can "make requests" to that object, asking it to perform operations on itself. In theory, you can take any conceptual component in the problem you're trying to solve (dogs, buildings, services, etc.) and represent it as an object in your program.

2. **A program is a bunch of objects telling each other what to do by sending messages**. To make a request of an object, you "send a message" to that object. More concretely, you can think of a message as a request to call a function that belongs to a particular object.

3. **Each object has its own memory made up of other objects**. Put another way, you create a new kind of object by making a package containing existing objects. Thus, you can build complexity in a program while hiding it behind the simplicity of objects.

---

[1] See *Multiparadigm Programming in Leda* by Timothy Budd (Addison-Wesley 1995).

4. **Every object has a type**. Using the parlance, each object is an *instance* of a *class,* in which "class" is synonymous with "type." The most important distinguishing characteristic of a class is "What messages can you send to it?"

5. **All objects of a particular type can receive the same messages**. This is actually a loaded statement, as you will see later. Because an object of type "circle" is also an object of type "shape," a circle is guaranteed to accept shape messages. This means you can write code that talks to shapes and automatically handles anything that fits the description of a shape. This *substitutability* is one of the most powerful concepts in OOP.

An object has an interface

Aristotle was probably the first to begin a careful study of the concept of *type*; he spoke of "the class of fishes and the class of birds." The idea that all objects, while being unique, are also part of a class of objects that have characteristics and behaviors in common was used directly in the first object-oriented language, Simula-67, with its fundamental keyword **class** that introduces a new type into a program.

Simula, as its name implies, was created for developing simulations such as the classic "bank teller problem[2]." In this, you have a bunch of tellers, customers, accounts, transactions, and units of money – a lot of "objects." Objects that are identical except for their state during a program's execution are grouped together into "classes of objects" and that's where the keyword **class** came from. Creating abstract data types (classes) is a fundamental concept in object-oriented programming. Abstract data types work almost exactly like built-in types: You can create variables of a type (called *objects* or *instances* in object-oriented parlance) and manipulate those variables (called *sending messages* or *requests*; you send a message

---

[2] You can find an interesting implementation of this problem in Volume 2 of this book, available at www.BruceEckel.com.

---

and the object figures out what to do with it). The members (elements) of each class share some commonality: every account has a balance, every teller can accept a deposit, etc. At the same time, each member has its own state, each account has a different balance, each teller has a name. Thus, the tellers, customers, accounts, transactions, etc., can each be represented with a unique entity in the computer program. This entity is the object, and each object belongs to a particular class that defines its characteristics and behaviors.

So, although what we really do in object-oriented programming is create new data types, virtually all object-oriented programming languages use the "class" keyword. When you see the word "type" think "class" and vice versa[3].

Since a class describes a set of objects that have identical characteristics (data elements) and behaviors (functionality), a class is really a data type because a floating point number, for example, also has a set of characteristics and behaviors. The difference is that a programmer defines a class to fit a problem rather than being forced to use an existing data type that was designed to represent a unit of storage in a machine. You extend the programming language by adding new data types specific to your needs. The programming system welcomes the new classes and gives them all the care and type-checking that it gives to built-in types.

The object-oriented approach is not limited to building simulations. Whether or not you agree that any program is a simulation of the system you're designing, the use of OOP techniques can easily reduce a large set of problems to a simple solution.

Once a class is established, you can make as many objects of that class as you like, and then manipulate those objects as if they are the elements that exist in the problem you are trying to solve. Indeed, one of the challenges of object-oriented programming is to create a one-to-one mapping between the elements in the problem space and objects in the solution space.

---

[3] Some people make a distinction, stating that type determines the interface while class is a particular implementation of that interface.

But how do you get an object to do useful work for you? There must be a way to make a request of the object so that it will do something, such as complete a transaction, draw something on the screen or turn on a switch. And each object can satisfy only certain requests. The requests you can make of an object are defined by its *interface*, and the type is what determines the interface. A simple example might be a representation of a light bulb:

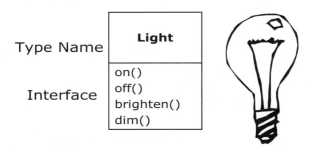

```
Light lt;
lt.on();
```

The interface establishes *what* requests you can make for a particular object. However, there must be code somewhere to satisfy that request. This, along with the hidden data, comprises the *implementation*. From a procedural programming standpoint, it's not that complicated. A type has a function associated with each possible request, and when you make a particular request to an object, that function is called. This process is usually summarized by saying that you "send a message" (make a request) to an object, and the object figures out what to do with that message (it executes code).

Here, the name of the type/class is **Light**, the name of this particular **Light** object is **lt**, and the requests that you can make of a **Light** object are to turn it on, turn it off, make it brighter or make it dimmer. You create a **Light** object by declaring a name (**lt**) for that object. To send a message to the object, you state the name of the object and connect it to the message request with a period (dot). From the standpoint of the user of a pre-defined class, that's pretty much all there is to programming with objects.

The diagram shown above follows the format of the *Unified Modeling Language* (UML). Each class is represented by a box, with the type name in the top portion of the box, any data members that you care to describe in the middle portion of the box, and the *member functions* (the functions that belong to this object, which receive any messages you send to that object) in the bottom portion of the box. Often, only the name of the class and the public member functions are shown in UML design diagrams, and so the middle portion is not shown. If you're interested only in the class name, then the bottom portion doesn't need to be shown, either.

The hidden implementation

It is helpful to break up the playing field into *class creators* (those who create new data types) and *client programmers*[4] (the class consumers who use the data types in their applications). The goal of the client programmer is to collect a toolbox full of classes to use for rapid application development. The goal of the class creator is to build a class that exposes only what's necessary to the client programmer and keeps everything else hidden. Why? Because if it's hidden, the client programmer can't use it, which means that the class creator can change the hidden portion at will without worrying about the impact to anyone else. The hidden portion usually represents the tender insides of an object that could easily be corrupted by a careless or uninformed client programmer, so hiding the implementation reduces program bugs. The concept of implementation hiding cannot be overemphasized.

In any relationship it's important to have boundaries that are respected by all parties involved. When you create a library, you establish a relationship with the client programmer, who is also a programmer, but one who is putting together an application by using your library, possibly to build a bigger library.

If all the members of a class are available to everyone, then the client programmer can do anything with that class and there's no way to enforce rules. Even though you might really prefer that the client programmer not directly manipulate some of the members of

---

[4] I'm indebted to my friend Scott Meyers for this term.

your class, without access control there's no way to prevent it. Everything's naked to the world.

So the first reason for access control is to keep client programmers' hands off portions they shouldn't touch – parts that are necessary for the internal machinations of the data type but not part of the interface that users need in order to solve their particular problems. This is actually a service to users because they can easily see what's important to them and what they can ignore.

The second reason for access control is to allow the library designer to change the internal workings of the class without worrying about how it will affect the client programmer. For example, you might implement a particular class in a simple fashion to ease development, and then later discover that you need to rewrite it in order to make it run faster. If the interface and implementation are clearly separated and protected, you can accomplish this easily and require only a relink by the user.

C++ uses three explicit keywords to set the boundaries in a class: **public**, **private**, and **protected**. Their use and meaning are quite straightforward. These *access specifiers* determine who can use the definitions that follow. **public** means the following definitions are available to everyone. The **private** keyword, on the other hand, means that no one can access those definitions except you, the creator of the type, inside member functions of that type. **private** is a brick wall between you and the client programmer. If someone tries to access a **private** member, they'll get a compile-time error. **protected** acts just like **private**, with the exception that an inheriting class has access to **protected** members, but not **private** members. Inheritance will be introduced shortly.

Reusing the implementation

Once a class has been created and tested, it should (ideally) represent a useful unit of code. It turns out that this reusability is not nearly so easy to achieve as many would hope; it takes experience and insight to produce a good design. But once you have such a design, it begs to be reused. Code reuse is one of the greatest advantages that object-oriented programming languages provide.

The simplest way to reuse a class is to just use an object of that class directly, but you can also place an object of that class inside a new class. We call this "creating a member object." Your new class can be made up of any number and type of other objects, in any combination that you need to achieve the functionality desired in your new class. Because you are composing a new class from existing classes, this concept is called *composition* (or more generally, *aggregation*). Composition is often referred to as a "has-a" relationship, as in "a car has an engine."

(The above UML diagram indicates composition with the filled diamond, which states there is one car. I will typically use a simpler form: just a line, without the diamond, to indicate an association.[5])

Composition comes with a great deal of flexibility. The member objects of your new class are usually private, making them inaccessible to the client programmers who are using the class. This allows you to change those members without disturbing existing client code. You can also change the member objects at runtime, to dynamically change the behavior of your program. Inheritance, which is described next, does not have this flexibility since the compiler must place compile-time restrictions on classes created with inheritance.

Because inheritance is so important in object-oriented programming it is often highly emphasized, and the new programmer can get the idea that inheritance should be used everywhere. This can result in awkward and overly-complicated designs. Instead, you should first look to composition when creating new classes, since it is simpler and more flexible. If you take this approach, your designs will stay cleaner. Once you've had some

---

[5] This is usually enough detail for most diagrams, and you don't need to get specific about whether you're using aggregation or composition.

experience, it will be reasonably obvious when you need inheritance.

Inheritance: reusing the interface

By itself, the idea of an object is a convenient tool. It allows you to package data and functionality together by *concept*, so you can represent an appropriate problem-space idea rather than being forced to use the idioms of the underlying machine. These concepts are expressed as fundamental units in the programming language by using the **class** keyword.

It seems a pity, however, to go to all the trouble to create a class and then be forced to create a brand new one that might have similar functionality. It's nicer if we can take the existing class, clone it, and then make additions and modifications to the clone. This is effectively what you get with *inheritance*, with the exception that if the original class (called the *base* or *super* or *parent* class) is changed, the modified "clone" (called the *derived* or *inherited* or *sub* or *child* class) also reflects those changes.

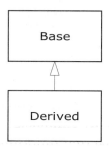

(The arrow in the above UML diagram points from the derived class to the base class. As you will see, there can be more than one derived class.)

A type does more than describe the constraints on a set of objects; it also has a relationship with other types. Two types can have characteristics and behaviors in common, but one type may contain more characteristics than another and may also handle more messages (or handle them differently). Inheritance expresses this similarity between types using the concept of base types and derived types. A base type contains all of the characteristics and behaviors that are shared among the types derived from it. You create a base type to represent the core of your ideas about some objects in your system. From the base type, you derive other types to express the different ways that this core can be realized.

For example, a trash-recycling machine sorts pieces of trash. The base type is "trash," and each piece of trash has a weight, a value, and so on, and can be shredded, melted, or decomposed. From this, more specific types of trash are derived that may have additional characteristics (a bottle has a color) or behaviors (an aluminum can may be crushed, a steel can is magnetic). In addition, some behaviors may be different (the value of paper depends on its type and condition). Using inheritance, you can build a type hierarchy that expresses the problem you're trying to solve in terms of its types.

A second example is the classic "shape" example, perhaps used in a computer-aided design system or game simulation. The base type is "shape," and each shape has a size, a color, a position, and so on. Each shape can be drawn, erased, moved, colored, etc. From this, specific types of shapes are derived (inherited): circle, square, triangle, and so on, each of which may have additional characteristics and behaviors. Certain shapes can be flipped, for example. Some behaviors may be different, such as when you want to calculate the area of a shape. The type hierarchy embodies both the similarities and differences between the shapes.

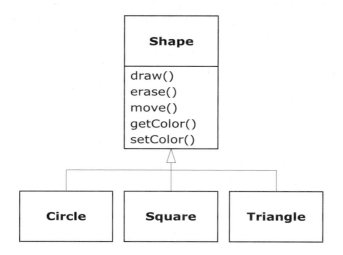

Casting the solution in the same terms as the problem is tremendously beneficial because you don't need a lot of intermediate models to get from a description of the problem to a description of the solution. With objects, the type hierarchy is the primary model, so you go directly from the description of the system in the real world to the description of the system in code. Indeed, one of the difficulties people have with object-oriented design is that it's too simple to get from the beginning to the end. A mind trained to look for complex solutions is often stumped by this simplicity at first.

When you inherit from an existing type, you create a new type. This new type contains not only all the members of the existing type (although the **private** ones are hidden away and inaccessible), but more importantly it duplicates the interface of the base class. That is, all the messages you can send to objects of the base class you can also send to objects of the derived class. Since we know the type of a class by the messages we can send to it, this means that the derived class *is the same type as the base class.* In the previous example, "a circle is a shape." This type equivalence via inheritance is one of the fundamental gateways in understanding the meaning of object-oriented programming.

Since both the base class and derived class have the same interface, there must be some implementation to go along with that interface. That is, there must be some code to execute when an object receives a particular message. If you simply inherit a class and don't do anything else, the methods from the base-class interface come right along into the derived class. That means objects of the derived class have not only the same type, they also have the same behavior, which isn't particularly interesting.

You have two ways to differentiate your new derived class from the original base class. The first is quite straightforward: You simply add brand new functions to the derived class. These new functions are not part of the base class interface. This means that the base class simply didn't do as much as you wanted it to, so you added more functions. This simple and primitive use for inheritance is, at times, the perfect solution to your problem. However, you should look closely for the possibility that your base class might also need these additional functions. This process of discovery and iteration of your design happens regularly in object-oriented programming.

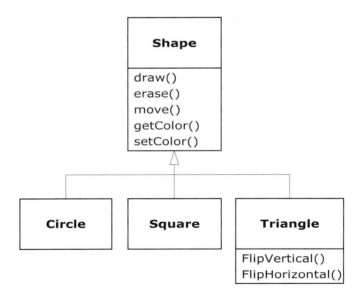

Although inheritance may sometimes imply that you are going to add new functions to the interface, that's not necessarily true. The second and more important way to differentiate your new class is to *change* the behavior of an existing base-class function. This is referred to as *overriding* that function.

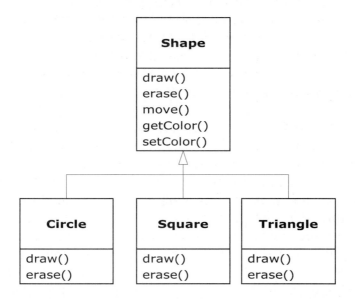

To override a function, you simply create a new definition for the function in the derived class. You're saying, "I'm using the same interface function here, but I want it to do something different for my new type."

Is-a vs. is-like-a relationships

There's a certain debate that can occur about inheritance: Should inheritance override *only* base-class functions (and not add new member functions that aren't in the base class)? This would mean that the derived type is *exactly* the same type as the base class since it has exactly the same interface. As a result, you can exactly substitute an object of the derived class for an object of the base class. This can be thought of as *pure substitution*, and it's often referred to as the *substitution principle*. In a sense, this is the ideal way to treat inheritance. We often refer to the relationship between the base class and derived classes in this case as an *is-a* relationship, because you can say "a circle *is a* shape." A test for inheritance is to determine whether you can state the is-a relationship about the classes and have it make sense.

There are times when you must add new interface elements to a derived type, thus extending the interface and creating a new type. The new type can still be substituted for the base type, but the substitution isn't perfect because your new functions are not accessible from the base type. This can be described as an *is-like-a* relationship; the new type has the interface of the old type but it also contains other functions, so you can't really say it's exactly the same. For example, consider an air conditioner. Suppose your house is wired with all the controls for cooling; that is, it has an interface that allows you to control cooling. Imagine that the air conditioner breaks down and you replace it with a heat pump, which can both heat and cool. The heat pump *is-like-an* air conditioner, but it can do more. Because the control system of your house is designed only to control cooling, it is restricted to communication with the cooling part of the new object. The interface of the new object has been extended, and the existing system doesn't know about anything except the original interface.

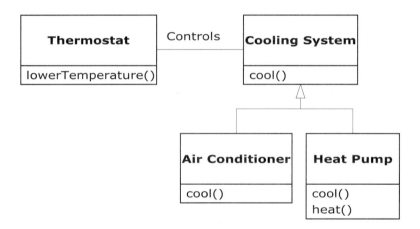

Of course, once you see this design it becomes clear that the base class "cooling system" is not general enough, and should be renamed to "temperature control system" so that it can also include heating – at which point the substitution principle will work. However, the diagram above is an example of what can happen in design and in the real world.

When you see the substitution principle it's easy to feel like this approach (pure substitution) is the only way to do things, and in fact it *is* nice if your design works out that way. But you'll find that there are times when it's equally clear that you must add new functions to the interface of a derived class. With inspection both cases should be reasonably obvious.

Interchangeable objects with polymorphism

When dealing with type hierarchies, you often want to treat an object not as the specific type that it is but instead as its base type. This allows you to write code that doesn't depend on specific types. In the shape example, functions manipulate generic shapes without respect to whether they're circles, squares, triangles, and so on. All shapes can be drawn, erased, and moved, so these functions simply send a message to a shape object; they don't worry about how the object copes with the message.

Such code is unaffected by the addition of new types, and adding new types is the most common way to extend an object-oriented program to handle new situations. For example, you can derive a new subtype of shape called pentagon without modifying the functions that deal only with generic shapes. This ability to extend a program easily by deriving new subtypes is important because it greatly improves designs while reducing the cost of software maintenance.

There's a problem, however, with attempting to treat derived-type objects as their generic base types (circles as shapes, bicycles as vehicles, cormorants as birds, etc.). If a function is going to tell a generic shape to draw itself, or a generic vehicle to steer, or a generic bird to move, the compiler cannot know at compile-time precisely what piece of code will be executed. That's the whole point – when the message is sent, the programmer doesn't *want* to know what piece of code will be executed; the draw function can be applied equally to a circle, a square, or a triangle, and the object will execute the proper code depending on its specific type. If you don't have to know what piece of code will be executed, then when you add a new subtype, the code it executes can be different without requiring changes to the function call. Therefore, the compiler cannot know precisely what piece of code is executed, so what does it do? For example, in the following diagram the **BirdController** object just works with generic **Bird** objects, and does not know what exact type they are. This is convenient from **BirdController**'s perspective, because it doesn't have to write special code to determine the exact type of **Bird** it's working with, or that **Bird**'s behavior. So how does it happen that, when **move( )** is called while ignoring the specific type of **Bird**, the right behavior will occur (a **Goose** runs, flies, or swims, and a **Penguin** runs or swims)?

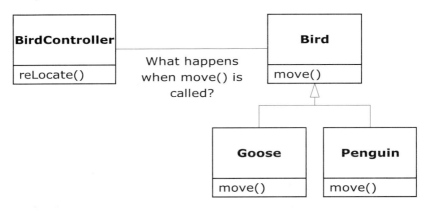

The answer is the primary twist in object-oriented programming: The compiler cannot make a function call in the traditional sense. The function call generated by a non-OOP compiler causes what is called *early binding*, a term you may not have heard before because you've never thought about it any other way. It means the compiler generates a call to a specific function name, and the linker resolves this call to the absolute address of the code to be executed. In OOP, the program cannot determine the address of the code until runtime, so some other scheme is necessary when a message is sent to a generic object.

To solve the problem, object-oriented languages use the concept of *late binding*. When you send a message to an object, the code being called isn't determined until runtime. The compiler does ensure that the function exists and performs type checking on the arguments and return value (a language in which this isn't true is called *weakly typed*), but it doesn't know the exact code to execute.

To perform late binding, the C++ compiler inserts a special bit of code in lieu of the absolute call. This code calculates the address of the function body, using information stored in the object (this process is covered in great detail in Chapter 15). Thus, each object can behave differently according to the contents of that special bit of code. When you send a message to an object, the object actually does figure out what to do with that message.

You state that you want a function to have the flexibility of late-binding properties using the keyword **virtual**. You don't need to understand the mechanics of **virtual** to use it, but without it you can't do object-oriented programming in C++. In C++, you must remember to add the **virtual** keyword because, by default, member functions are *not* dynamically bound. Virtual functions allow you to express the differences in behavior of classes in the same family. Those differences are what cause polymorphic behavior.

Consider the shape example. The family of classes (all based on the same uniform interface) was diagrammed earlier in the chapter. To demonstrate polymorphism, we want to write a single piece of code that ignores the specific details of type and talks only to the base class. That code is *decoupled* from type-specific information, and thus is simpler to write and easier to understand. And, if a new type – a **Hexagon**, for example – is added through inheritance, the code you write will work just as well for the new type of **Shape** as it did on the existing types. Thus, the program is *extensible*.

If you write a function in C++ (as you will soon learn how to do):

```
void doStuff(Shape& s) {
    s.erase();
    // ...
    s.draw();
}
```

This function speaks to any **Shape**, so it is independent of the specific type of object that it's drawing and erasing (the '**&**' means "Take the address of the object that's passed to **doStuff( )**," but it's not important that you understand the details of that right now). If in some other part of the program we use the **doStuff( )** function:

```
Circle c;
```

```
Triangle t;
Line l;
doStuff(c);
doStuff(t);
doStuff(l);
```

The calls to **doStuff( )** automatically work right, regardless of the exact type of the object.

This is actually a pretty amazing trick. Consider the line:

```
doStuff(c);
```

What's happening here is that a **Circle** is being passed into a function that's expecting a **Shape**. Since a **Circle** *is* a **Shape** it can be treated as one by **doStuff( )**. That is, any message that **doStuff( )** can send to a **Shape**, a **Circle** can accept. So it is a completely safe and logical thing to do.

We call this process of treating a derived type as though it were its base type *upcasting*. The name *cast* is used in the sense of casting into a mold and the *up* comes from the way the inheritance diagram is typically arranged, with the base type at the top and the derived classes fanning out downward. Thus, casting to a base type is moving up the inheritance diagram: "upcasting."

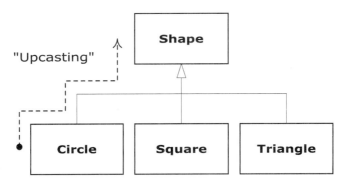

An object-oriented program contains some upcasting somewhere, because that's how you decouple yourself from knowing about the exact type you're working with. Look at the code in **doStuff( )**:

```
s.erase();
// ...
```

```
s.draw();
```

Notice that it doesn't say "If you're a **Circle**, do this, if you're a **Square**, do that, etc." If you write that kind of code, which checks for all the possible types that a **Shape** can actually be, it's messy and you need to change it every time you add a new kind of **Shape**. Here, you just say "You're a shape, I know you can **erase( )** and **draw( )** yourself, do it, and take care of the details correctly."

What's impressive about the code in **doStuff( )** is that, somehow, the right thing happens. Calling **draw( )** for **Circle** causes different code to be executed than when calling **draw( )** for a **Square** or a **Line**, but when the **draw( )** message is sent to an anonymous **Shape**, the correct behavior occurs based on the actual type of the **Shape**. This is amazing because, as mentioned earlier, when the C++ compiler is compiling the code for **doStuff( )**, it cannot know exactly what types it is dealing with. So ordinarily, you'd expect it to end up calling the version of **erase( )** and **draw( )** for **Shape**, and not for the specific **Circle**, **Square**, or **Line**. And yet the right thing happens because of polymorphism. The compiler and runtime system handle the details; all you need to know is that it happens and more importantly how to design with it. If a member function is **virtual**, then when you send a message to an object, the object will do the right thing, even when upcasting is involved.

Creating and destroying objects

Technically, the domain of OOP is abstract data typing, inheritance, and polymorphism, but other issues can be at least as important. This section gives an overview of these issues.

Especially important is the way objects are created and destroyed. Where is the data for an object and how is the lifetime of that object controlled? Different programming languages use different philosophies here. C++ takes the approach that control of efficiency is the most important issue, so it gives the programmer a choice. For maximum runtime speed, the storage and lifetime can be determined while the program is being written, by placing the objects on the stack or in static storage. The stack is an area in memory that is used directly by the microprocessor to store data during program execution. Variables on the stack are sometimes called *automatic* or *scoped* variables. The static storage area is simply a fixed patch of memory that is allocated before the program begins to run. Using the stack or static storage area places a priority on the speed of storage allocation and release, which can be valuable in some situations. However, you sacrifice flexibility because you must know the exact quantity, lifetime, and type of objects *while* you're writing the program. If you are trying to solve a more general problem, such as computer-aided design, warehouse management, or air-traffic control, this is too restrictive.

The second approach is to create objects dynamically in a pool of memory called the *heap*. In this approach you don't know until runtime how many objects you need, what their lifetime is, or what their exact type is. Those decisions are made at the spur of the moment while the program is running. If you need a new object, you simply make it on the heap when you need it, using the **new** keyword. When you're finished with the storage, you must release it using the **delete** keyword.

Because the storage is managed dynamically at runtime, the amount of time required to allocate storage on the heap is significantly longer than the time to create storage on the stack. (Creating storage on the stack is often a single microprocessor instruction to move the stack pointer down, and another to move it back up.) The dynamic approach makes the generally logical assumption that objects tend to be complicated, so the extra overhead of finding storage and releasing that storage will not have an important impact on the creation of an object. In addition, the greater flexibility is essential to solve general programming problems.

There's another issue, however, and that's the lifetime of an object. If you create an object on the stack or in static storage, the compiler determines how long the object lasts and can automatically destroy it. However, if you create it on the heap, the compiler has no knowledge of its lifetime. In C++, the programmer must determine programmatically when to destroy the object, and then perform the destruction using the **delete** keyword. As an alternative, the environment can provide a feature called a *garbage collector* that automatically discovers when an object is no longer in use and destroys it. Of course, writing programs using a garbage collector is much more convenient, but it requires that all applications must be able to tolerate the existence of the garbage collector and the overhead for garbage collection. This does not meet the design requirements of the C++ language and so it was not included, although third-party garbage collectors exist for C++.

Exception handling: dealing with errors

Ever since the beginning of programming languages, error handling has been one of the most difficult issues. Because it's so hard to design a good error-handling scheme, many languages simply ignore the issue, passing the problem on to library designers who come up with halfway measures that can work in many situations but can easily be circumvented, generally by just ignoring them. A major problem with most error-handling schemes is that they rely on programmer vigilance in following an agreed-upon convention that is not enforced by the language. If programmers are not vigilant, which often occurs when they are in a hurry, these schemes can easily be forgotten.

Exception handling wires error handling directly into the programming language and sometimes even the operating system. An exception is an object that is "thrown" from the site of the error and can be "caught" by an appropriate *exception handler* designed to handle that particular type of error. It's as if exception handling is a different, parallel path of execution that can be taken when things go wrong. And because it uses a separate execution path, it doesn't need to interfere with your normally-executing code. This makes that code simpler to write since you aren't constantly forced to check for errors. In addition, a thrown exception is unlike an error value that's returned from a function or a flag that's set by a function in order to indicate an error condition – these can be ignored. An exception cannot be ignored so it's guaranteed to be dealt with at some point. Finally, exceptions provide a way to recover reliably from a bad situation. Instead of just exiting the program, you are often able to set things right and restore the execution of a program, which produces much more robust systems.

It's worth noting that exception handling isn't an object-oriented feature, although in object-oriented languages the exception is normally represented with an object. Exception handling existed before object-oriented languages.

Exception handling is only lightly introduced and used in this Volume; Volume 2 (available from *www.BruceEckel.com*) has thorough coverage of exception handling.

Analysis and design

The object-oriented paradigm is a new and different way of thinking about programming and many folks have trouble at first knowing how to approach an OOP project. Once you know that everything is supposed to be an object, and as you learn to think more in an object-oriented style, you can begin to create "good" designs that take advantage of all the benefits that OOP has to offer.

A *method* (often called a *methodology*) is a set of processes and heuristics used to break down the complexity of a programming problem. Many OOP methods have been formulated since the dawn of object-oriented programming. This section will give you a feel for what you're trying to accomplish when using a method.

Especially in OOP, methodology is a field of many experiments, so it is important to understand what problem the method is trying to solve before you consider adopting one. This is particularly true with C++, in which the programming language is intended to reduce the complexity (compared to C) involved in expressing a program. This may in fact alleviate the need for ever-more-complex methodologies. Instead, simpler ones may suffice in C++ for a much larger class of problems than you could handle using simple methodologies with procedural languages.

It's also important to realize that the term "methodology" is often too grand and promises too much. Whatever you do now when you design and write a program is a method. It may be your own method, and you may not be conscious of doing it, but it is a process you go through as you create. If it is an effective process, it may need only a small tune-up to work with C++. If you are not satisfied with your productivity and the way your programs turn out, you may want to consider adopting a formal method, or choosing pieces from among the many formal methods.

While you're going through the development process, the most important issue is this: Don't get lost. It's easy to do. Most of the analysis and design methods are intended to solve the largest of problems. Remember that most projects don't fit into that category, so you can usually have successful analysis and design with a relatively small subset of what a method recommends[6]. But some sort of process, no matter how limited, will generally get you on your way in a much better fashion than simply beginning to code.

It's also easy to get stuck, to fall into "analysis paralysis," where you feel like you can't move forward because you haven't nailed down every little detail at the current stage. Remember, no matter how much analysis you do, there are some things about a system that won't reveal themselves until design time, and more things that won't reveal themselves until you're coding, or not even until a program is up and running. Because of this, it's crucial to move fairly quickly through analysis and design, and to implement a test of the proposed system.

This point is worth emphasizing. Because of the history we've had with procedural languages, it is commendable that a team will want to proceed carefully and understand every minute detail before moving to design and implementation. Certainly, when creating a DBMS, it pays to understand a customer's needs thoroughly. But a DBMS is in a class of problems that is very well-posed and well-understood; in many such programs, the database structure *is* the problem to be tackled. The class of programming problem discussed in this chapter is of the "wild-card" (my term) variety, in which the solution isn't simply re-forming a well-known solution,

---

[6] An excellent example of this is *UML Distilled*, by Martin Fowler (Addison-Wesley 2000), which reduces the sometimes-overwhelming UML process to a manageable subset.

but instead involves one or more "wild-card factors" – elements for which there is no well-understood previous solution, and for which research is necessary[7]. Attempting to thoroughly analyze a wild-card problem before moving into design and implementation results in analysis paralysis because you don't have enough information to solve this kind of problem during the analysis phase. Solving such a problem requires iteration through the whole cycle, and that requires risk-taking behavior (which makes sense, because you're trying to do something new and the potential rewards are higher). It may seem like the risk is compounded by "rushing" into a preliminary implementation, but it can instead reduce the risk in a wild-card project because you're finding out early whether a particular approach to the problem is viable. Product development is risk management.

It's often proposed that you "build one to throw away." With OOP, you may still throw *part* of it away, but because code is encapsulated into classes, during the first iteration you will inevitably produce some useful class designs and develop some worthwhile ideas about the system design that do not need to be thrown away. Thus, the first rapid pass at a problem not only produces critical information for the next analysis, design, and implementation iteration, it also creates a code foundation for that iteration.

That said, if you're looking at a methodology that contains tremendous detail and suggests many steps and documents, it's still difficult to know when to stop. Keep in mind what you're trying to discover:

1.   What are the objects? (How do you partition your project into its component parts?)

2.   What are their interfaces? (What messages do you need to be able to send to each object?)

---

[7] My rule of thumb for estimating such projects: If there's more than one wild card, don't even try to plan how long it's going to take or how much it will cost until you've created a working prototype. There are too many degrees of freedom.

If you come up with nothing more than the objects and their interfaces, then you can write a program. For various reasons you might need more descriptions and documents than this, but you can't get away with any less.

The process can be undertaken in five phases, and a phase 0 that is just the initial commitment to using some kind of structure.

Phase 0: Make a plan

You must first decide what steps you're going to have in your process. It sounds simple (in fact, *all* of this sounds simple) and yet people often don't make this decision before they start coding. If your plan is "let's jump in and start coding," fine. (Sometimes that's appropriate when you have a well-understood problem.) At least agree that this is the plan.

You might also decide at this phase that some additional process structure is necessary, but not the whole nine yards. Understandably enough, some programmers like to work in "vacation mode" in which no structure is imposed on the process of developing their work; "It will be done when it's done." This can be appealing for awhile, but I've found that having a few milestones along the way helps to focus and galvanize your efforts around those milestones instead of being stuck with the single goal of "finish the project." In addition, it divides the project into more bite-sized pieces and makes it seem less threatening (plus the milestones offer more opportunities for celebration).

When I began to study story structure (so that I will someday write a novel) I was initially resistant to the idea of structure, feeling that when I wrote I simply let it flow onto the page. But I later realized that when I write about computers the structure is clear enough so that I don't think much about it. But I still structure my work, albeit only semi-consciously in my head. So even if you think that your plan is to just start coding, you still somehow go through the subsequent phases while asking and answering certain questions.

The mission statement
Any system you build, no matter how complicated, has a fundamental purpose, the business that it's in, the basic need that it

satisfies. If you can look past the user interface, the hardware- or system-specific details, the coding algorithms and the efficiency problems, you will eventually find the core of its being, simple and straightforward. Like the so-called *high concept* from a Hollywood movie, you can describe it in one or two sentences. This pure description is the starting point.

The high concept is quite important because it sets the tone for your project; it's a mission statement. You won't necessarily get it right the first time (you may be in a later phase of the project before it becomes completely clear), but keep trying until it feels right. For example, in an air-traffic control system you may start out with a high concept focused on the system that you're building: "The tower program keeps track of the aircraft." But consider what happens when you shrink the system to a very small airfield; perhaps there's only a human controller or none at all. A more useful model won't concern the solution you're creating as much as it describes the problem: "Aircraft arrive, unload, service and reload, and depart."

Phase 1: What are we making?

In the previous generation of program design (called *procedural design*), this is called "creating the *requirements analysis* and *system specification*." These, of course, were places to get lost; intimidatingly-named documents that could become big projects in their own right. Their intention was good, however. The requirements analysis says "Make a list of the guidelines we will use to know when the job is done and the customer is satisfied." The system specification says "Here's a description of *what* the program will do (not *how*) to satisfy the requirements." The requirements analysis is really a contract between you and the customer (even if the customer works within your company or is some other object or system). The system specification is a top-level exploration into the problem and in some sense a discovery of whether it can be done and how long it will take. Since both of these will require consensus among people (and because they will usually change over time), I think it's best to keep them as bare as possible – ideally, to lists and basic diagrams – to save time. You might have other constraints that require you to expand them into bigger documents, but by keeping the initial document small and concise, it can be created in a few sessions of group brainstorming with a leader who dynamically creates the description. This not only solicits input from everyone, it also fosters initial buy-in and agreement by everyone on the team. Perhaps most importantly, it can kick off a project with a lot of enthusiasm.

It's necessary to stay focused on the heart of what you're trying to accomplish in this phase: determine what the system is supposed to do. The most valuable tool for this is a collection of what are called "use cases." Use cases identify key features in the system that will reveal some of the fundamental classes you'll be using. These are essentially descriptive answers to questions like[8]:

- "Who will use this system?"
- "What can those actors do with the system?"
- "How does this actor do that with this system?"
- "How else might this work if someone else were doing this, or if the same actor had a different objective?" (to reveal variations)
- "What problems might happen while doing this with the system?" (to reveal exceptions)

If you are designing an auto-teller, for example, the use case for a particular aspect of the functionality of the system is able to describe what the auto-teller does in every possible situation. Each of these "situations" is referred to as a *scenario*, and a use case can be considered a collection of scenarios. You can think of a scenario as a question that starts with: "What does the system do if...?" For example, "What does the auto-teller do if a customer has just deposited a check within 24 hours and there's not enough in the account without the check to provide the desired withdrawal?"

Use case diagrams are intentionally simple to prevent you from getting bogged down in system implementation details prematurely:

---

[8] Thanks for help from James H Jarrett.

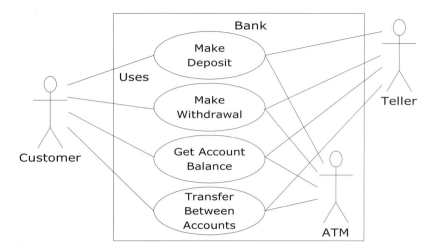

Each stick person represents an "actor," which is typically a human or some other kind of free agent. (These can even be other computer systems, as is the case with "ATM.") The box represents the boundary of your system. The ellipses represent the use cases, which are descriptions of valuable work that can be performed with the system. The lines between the actors and the use cases represent the interactions.

It doesn't matter how the system is actually implemented, as long as it looks like this to the user.

A use case does not need to be terribly complex, even if the underlying system is complex. It is only intended to show the system as it appears to the user. For example:

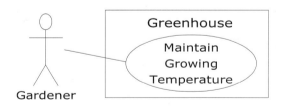

The use cases produce the requirements specifications by determining all the interactions that the user may have with the system. You try to discover a full set of use cases for your system, and once you've done that you have the core of what the system is supposed to do. The nice thing about focusing on use cases is that they always bring you back to the essentials and keep you from drifting off into issues that aren't critical for getting the job done. That is, if you have a full set of use cases you can describe your system and move onto the next phase. You probably won't get it all figured out perfectly on the first try, but that's OK. Everything will reveal itself in time, and if you demand a perfect system specification at this point you'll get stuck.

If you get stuck, you can kick-start this phase by using a rough approximation tool: describe the system in a few paragraphs and then look for nouns and verbs. The nouns can suggest actors, context of the use case (e.g. "lobby"), or artifacts manipulated in the use case. Verbs can suggest interactions between actors and use cases, and specify steps within the use case. You'll also discover that nouns and verbs produce objects and messages during the design phase (and note that use cases describe interactions between subsystems, so the "noun and verb" technique can be used only as a brainstorming tool as it does not generate use cases) [9].

The boundary between a use case and an actor can point out the existence of a user interface, but it does not define such a user interface. For a process of defining and creating user interfaces, see *Software for Use* by Larry Constantine and Lucy Lockwood, (Addison Wesley Longman, 1999) or go to *www.ForUse.com*.

Although it's a black art, at this point some kind of basic scheduling is important. You now have an overview of what you're building so you'll probably be able to get some idea of how long it will take. A lot of factors come into play here. If you estimate a long schedule then the company might decide not to build it (and thus use their resources on something more reasonable – that's a *good* thing). Or a manager might have already decided how long the project should take and will try to influence your estimate. But it's best to have an honest schedule from the beginning and deal with the tough

---

[9] More information on use cases can be found in *Applying Use Cases* by Schneider & Winters (Addison-Wesley 1998) and *Use Case Driven Object Modeling with UML* by Rosenberg (Addison-Wesley 1999).

decisions early. There have been a lot of attempts to come up with accurate scheduling techniques (like techniques to predict the stock market), but probably the best approach is to rely on your experience and intuition. Get a gut feeling for how long it will really take, then double that and add 10 percent. Your gut feeling is probably correct; you *can* get something working in that time. The "doubling" will turn that into something decent, and the 10 percent will deal with the final polishing and details[10]. However you want to explain it, and regardless of the moans and manipulations that happen when you reveal such a schedule, it just seems to work out that way.

Phase 2: How will we build it?

In this phase you must come up with a design that describes what the classes look like and how they will interact. An excellent technique in determining classes and interactions is the *Class-Responsibility-Collaboration* (CRC) card. Part of the value of this tool is that it's so low-tech: you start out with a set of blank 3" by 5" cards, and you write on them. Each card represents a single class, and on the card you write:

1.   The name of the class. It's important that this name capture the essence of what the class does, so that it makes sense at a glance.

2.   The "responsibilities" of the class: what it should do. This can typically be summarized by just stating the names of the member functions (since those names should be descriptive in a good design), but it does not preclude other notes. If you need to seed the process, look at the problem from a lazy programmer's standpoint: What objects would you like to magically appear to solve your problem?

---

[10] My personal take on this has changed lately. Doubling and adding 10 percent will give you a reasonably accurate estimate (assuming there are not too many wild-card factors), but you still have to work quite diligently to finish in that time. If you want time to really make it elegant and to enjoy yourself in the process, the correct multiplier is more like three or four times, I believe.

---

3.   The "collaborations" of the class: what other classes does it interact with? "Interact" is an intentionally broad term; it could mean aggregation or simply that some other object exists that will perform services for an object of the class. Collaborations should also consider the audience for this class. For example, if you create a class **Firecracker**, who is going to observe it, a **Chemist** or a **Spectator**? The former will want to know what chemicals go into the construction, and the latter will respond to the colors and shapes released when it explodes.

You may feel like the cards should be bigger because of all the information you'd like to get on them, but they are intentionally small, not only to keep your classes small but also to keep you from getting into too much detail too early. If you can't fit all you need to know about a class on a small card, the class is too complex (either you're getting too detailed, or you should create more than one class). The ideal class should be understood at a glance. The idea of CRC cards is to assist you in coming up with a first cut of the design so that you can get the big picture and then refine your design.

One of the great benefits of CRC cards is in communication. It's best done real-time, in a group, without computers. Each person takes responsibility for several classes (which at first have no names or other information). You run a live simulation by solving one scenario at a time, deciding which messages are sent to the various objects to satisfy each scenario. As you go through this process, you discover the classes that you need along with their responsibilities and collaborations, and you fill out the cards as you do this. When you've moved through all the use cases, you should have a fairly complete first cut of your design.

Before I began using CRC cards, the most successful consulting experiences I had when coming up with an initial design involved standing in front of a team, who hadn't built an OOP project before, and drawing objects on a whiteboard. We talked about how the objects should communicate with each other, and erased some of them and replaced them with other objects. Effectively, I was managing all the "CRC cards" on the whiteboard. The team (who knew what the project was supposed to do) actually created the design; they "owned" the design rather than having it given to them.

All I was doing was guiding the process by asking the right questions, trying out the assumptions, and taking the feedback from the team to modify those assumptions. The true beauty of the process was that the team learned how to do object-oriented design not by reviewing abstract examples, but by working on the one design that was most interesting to them at that moment: theirs.

Once you've come up with a set of CRC cards, you may want to create a more formal description of your design using UML[11]. You don't need to use UML, but it can be helpful, especially if you want to put up a diagram on the wall for everyone to ponder, which is a good idea. An alternative to UML is a textual description of the objects and their interfaces, or, depending on your programming language, the code itself[12].

UML also provides an additional diagramming notation for describing the dynamic model of your system. This is helpful in situations in which the state transitions of a system or subsystem are dominant enough that they need their own diagrams (such as in a control system). You may also need to describe the data structures, for systems or subsystems in which data is a dominant factor (such as a database).

You'll know you're done with phase 2 when you have described the objects and their interfaces. Well, most of them – there are usually a few that slip through the cracks and don't make themselves known until phase 3. But that's OK. All you are concerned with is that you eventually discover all of your objects. It's nice to discover them early in the process but OOP provides enough structure so that it's not so bad if you discover them later. In fact, the design of an object tends to happen in five stages, throughout the process of program development.

Five stages of object design

The design life of an object is not limited to the time when you're writing the program. Instead, the design of an object appears over a sequence of stages. It's helpful to have this perspective because you

---

[11] For starters, I recommend the aforementioned *UML Distilled*.
[12] Python (www.Python.org) is often used as "executable pseudocode."

stop expecting perfection right away; instead, you realize that the understanding of what an object does and what it should look like happens over time. This view also applies to the design of various types of programs; the pattern for a particular type of program emerges through struggling again and again with that problem (*Design Patterns* are covered in Volume 2). Objects, too, have their patterns that emerge through understanding, use, and reuse.

1. Object discovery. This stage occurs during the initial analysis of a program. Objects may be discovered by looking for external factors and boundaries, duplication of elements in the system, and the smallest conceptual units. Some objects are obvious if you already have a set of class libraries. Commonality between classes suggesting base classes and inheritance may appear right away, or later in the design process.

2. Object assembly. As you're building an object you'll discover the need for new members that didn't appear during discovery. The internal needs of the object may require other classes to support it.

3. System construction. Once again, more requirements for an object may appear at this later stage. As you learn, you evolve your objects. The need for communication and interconnection with other objects in the system may change the needs of your classes or require new classes. For example, you may discover the need for facilitator or helper classes, such as a linked list, that contain little or no state information and simply help other classes function.

4. System extension. As you add new features to a system you may discover that your previous design doesn't support easy system extension. With this new information, you can restructure parts of the system, possibly adding new classes or class hierarchies.

5. Object reuse. This is the real stress test for a class. If someone tries to reuse it in an entirely new situation, they'll probably discover some shortcomings. As you change a class to adapt to more new programs, the general principles of the class will become clearer, until you have a truly reusable type. However, don't expect most objects from a system design to be reusable – it is

---

perfectly acceptable for the bulk of your objects to be system-specific. Reusable types tend to be less common, and they must solve more general problems in order to be reusable.

Guidelines for object development

These stages suggest some guidelines when thinking about developing your classes:

1. Let a specific problem generate a class, then let the class grow and mature during the solution of other problems.

2. Remember, discovering the classes you need (and their interfaces) is the majority of the system design. If you already had those classes, this would be an easy project.

3. Don't force yourself to know everything at the beginning; learn as you go. This will happen anyway.

4. Start programming; get something working so you can prove or disprove your design. Don't fear that you'll end up with procedural-style spaghetti code – classes partition the problem and help control anarchy and entropy. Bad classes do not break good classes.

5. Always keep it simple. Little clean objects with obvious utility are better than big complicated interfaces. When decision points come up, use an Occam's Razor approach: Consider the choices and select the one that is simplest, because simple classes are almost always best. Start small and simple, and you can expand the class interface when you understand it better, but as time goes on, it's difficult to remove elements from a class.

Phase 3: Build the core

This is the initial conversion from the rough design into a compiling and executing body of code that can be tested, and especially that will prove or disprove your architecture. This is not a one-pass process, but rather the beginning of a series of steps that will iteratively build the system, as you'll see in phase 4.

Your goal is to find the core of your system architecture that needs to be implemented in order to generate a running system, no matter how incomplete that system is in this initial pass. You're creating a framework that you can build upon with further iterations. You're also performing the first of many system integrations and tests, and giving the stakeholders feedback about what their system will look like and how it is progressing. Ideally, you are also exposing some of the critical risks. You'll probably also discover changes and improvements that can be made to your original architecture – things you would not have learned without implementing the system.

Part of building the system is the reality check that you get from testing against your requirements analysis and system specification (in whatever form they exist). Make sure that your tests verify the requirements and use cases. When the core of the system is stable, you're ready to move on and add more functionality.

Phase 4: Iterate the use cases

Once the core framework is running, each feature set you add is a small project in itself. You add a feature set during an *iteration*, a reasonably short period of development.

How big is an iteration? Ideally, each iteration lasts one to three weeks (this can vary based on the implementation language). At the end of that period, you have an integrated, tested system with more functionality than it had before. But what's particularly interesting is the basis for the iteration: a single use case. Each use case is a package of related functionality that you build into the system all at once, during one iteration. Not only does this give you a better idea of what the scope of a use case should be, but it also gives more validation to the idea of a use case, since the concept isn't discarded after analysis and design, but instead it is a fundamental unit of development throughout the software-building process.

You stop iterating when you achieve target functionality or an external deadline arrives and the customer can be satisfied with the current version. (Remember, software is a subscription business.) Because the process is iterative, you have many opportunities to ship a product instead of a single endpoint; open-source projects work exclusively in an iterative, high-feedback environment, which is precisely what makes them successful.

An iterative development process is valuable for many reasons. You can reveal and resolve critical risks early, the customers have ample opportunity to change their minds, programmer satisfaction is higher, and the project can be steered with more precision. But an additional important benefit is the feedback to the stakeholders, who can see by the current state of the product exactly where everything lies. This may reduce or eliminate the need for mind-numbing status meetings and increase the confidence and support from the stakeholders.

Phase 5: Evolution

This is the point in the development cycle that has traditionally been called "maintenance," a catch-all term that can mean everything from "getting it to work the way it was really supposed to in the first place" to "adding features that the customer forgot to mention" to the more traditional "fixing the bugs that show up" and "adding new features as the need arises." So many misconceptions have been applied to the term "maintenance" that it has taken on a slightly deceiving quality, partly because it suggests that you've actually built a pristine program and all you need to do is change parts, oil it, and keep it from rusting. Perhaps there's a better term to describe what's going on.

I'll use the term *evolution*[13]. That is, "You won't get it right the first time, so give yourself the latitude to learn and to go back and make changes." You might need to make a lot of changes as you learn and understand the problem more deeply. The elegance you'll produce if you evolve until you get it right will pay off, both in the short and the long term. Evolution is where your program goes from good to great, and where those issues that you didn't really understand in the first pass become clear. It's also where your classes can evolve from single-project usage to reusable resources.

---

[13] At least one aspect of evolution is covered in Martin Fowler's book *Refactoring: improving the design of existing code* (Addison-Wesley 1999). Be forewarned that this book uses Java examples exclusively.

What it means to "get it right" isn't just that the program works according to the requirements and the use cases. It also means that the internal structure of the code makes sense to you, and feels like it fits together well, with no awkward syntax, oversized objects, or ungainly exposed bits of code. In addition, you must have some sense that the program structure will survive the changes that it will inevitably go through during its lifetime, and that those changes can be made easily and cleanly. This is no small feat. You must not only understand what you're building, but also how the program will evolve (what I call the *vector of change*[14]). Fortunately, object-oriented programming languages are particularly adept at supporting this kind of continuing modification – the boundaries created by the objects are what tend to keep the structure from breaking down. They also allow you to make changes – ones that would seem drastic in a procedural program – without causing earthquakes throughout your code. In fact, support for evolution might be the most important benefit of OOP.

With evolution, you create something that at least approximates what you think you're building, and then you kick the tires, compare it to your requirements and see where it falls short. Then you can go back and fix it by redesigning and re-implementing the portions of the program that didn't work right[15]. You might actually need to solve the problem, or an aspect of the problem, several times before you hit on the right solution. (A study of *Design Patterns*, described in Volume 2, is usually helpful here.)

Evolution also occurs when you build a system, see that it matches your requirements, and then discover it wasn't actually what you wanted. When you see the system in operation, you find that you really wanted to solve a different problem. If you think this kind of evolution is going to happen, then you owe it to yourself to build

---

[14] This term is explored in the *Design Patterns* chapter in Volume 2.

[15] This is something like "rapid prototyping," where you were supposed to build a quick-and-dirty version so that you could learn about the system, and then throw away your prototype and build it right. The trouble with rapid prototyping is that people didn't throw away the prototype, but instead built upon it. Combined with the lack of structure in procedural programming, this often produced messy systems that were expensive to maintain.

your first version as quickly as possible so you can find out if it is indeed what you want.

Perhaps the most important thing to remember is that by default – by definition, really – if you modify a class then its super- and subclasses will still function. You need not fear modification (especially if you have a built-in set of unit tests to verify the correctness of your modifications). Modification won't necessarily break the program, and any change in the outcome will be limited to subclasses and/or specific collaborators of the class you change.

Plans pay off

Of course you wouldn't build a house without a lot of carefully-drawn plans. If you build a deck or a dog house, your plans won't be so elaborate but you'll probably still start with some kind of sketches to guide you on your way. Software development has gone to extremes. For a long time, people didn't have much structure in their development, but then big projects began failing. In reaction, we ended up with methodologies that had an intimidating amount of structure and detail, primarily intended for those big projects. These methodologies were too scary to use – it looked like you'd spend all your time writing documents and no time programming. (This was often the case.) I hope that what I've shown you here suggests a middle path – a sliding scale. Use an approach that fits your needs (and your personality). No matter how minimal you choose to make it, *some* kind of plan will make a big improvement in your project as opposed to no plan at all. Remember that, by most estimates, over 50 percent of projects fail (some estimates go up to 70 percent!).

By following a plan – preferably one that is simple and brief – and coming up with design structure before coding, you'll discover that things fall together far more easily than if you dive in and start hacking, and you'll also realize a great deal of satisfaction. It's my experience that coming up with an elegant solution is deeply satisfying at an entirely different level; it feels closer to art than technology. And elegance always pays off; it's not a frivolous pursuit. Not only does it give you a program that's easier to build and debug, but it's also easier to understand and maintain, and that's where the financial value lies.

Extreme programming

I have studied analysis and design techniques, on and off, since I was in graduate school. The concept of *Extreme Programming* (XP) is the most radical, and delightful, that I've seen. You can find it chronicled in *Extreme Programming Explained* by Kent Beck (Addison-Wesley 2000) and on the Web at *www.xprogramming.com*.

XP is both a philosophy about programming work and a set of guidelines to do it. Some of these guidelines are reflected in other recent methodologies, but the two most important and distinct contributions, in my opinion, are "write tests first" and "pair programming." Although he argues strongly for the whole process, Beck points out that if you adopt only these two practices you'll greatly improve your productivity and reliability.

Write tests first

Testing has traditionally been relegated to the last part of a project, after you've "gotten everything working, but just to be sure." It's implicitly had a low priority, and people who specialize in it have not been given a lot of status and have often even been cordoned off in a basement, away from the "real programmers." Test teams have responded in kind, going so far as to wear black clothing and cackling with glee whenever they broke something (to be honest, I've had this feeling myself when breaking C++ compilers).

XP completely revolutionizes the concept of testing by giving it equal (or even greater) priority than the code. In fact, you write the tests *before* you write the code that's being tested, and the tests stay with the code forever. The tests must be executed successfully every time you do an integration of the project (which is often, sometimes more than once a day).

Writing tests first has two extremely important effects.

First, it forces a clear definition of the interface of a class. I've often suggested that people "imagine the perfect class to solve a particular problem" as a tool when trying to design the system. The XP testing strategy goes further than that – it specifies exactly what the class must look like, to the consumer of that class, and exactly how the class must behave. In no uncertain terms. You can write all the prose, or create all the diagrams you want describing how a class should behave and what it looks like, but nothing is as real as a set of tests. The former is a wish list, but the tests are a contract that is enforced by the compiler and the running program. It's hard to imagine a more concrete description of a class than the tests.

While creating the tests, you are forced to completely think out the class and will often discover needed functionality that might be missed during the thought experiments of UML diagrams, CRC cards, use cases, etc.

The second important effect of writing the tests first comes from running the tests every time you do a build of your software. This activity gives you the other half of the testing that's performed by the compiler. If you look at the evolution of programming languages from this perspective, you'll see that the real improvements in the technology have actually revolved around testing. Assembly language checked only for syntax, but C imposed some semantic restrictions, and these prevented you from making certain types of mistakes. OOP languages impose even more semantic restrictions, which if you think about it are actually forms of testing. "Is this data type being used properly? Is this function being called properly?" are the kinds of tests that are being performed by the compiler or run-time system. We've seen the results of having these tests built into the language: people have been able to write more complex systems, and get them to work, with much less time and effort. I've puzzled over why this is, but now I realize it's the tests: you do something wrong, and the safety net of the built-in tests tells you there's a problem and points you to where it is.

But the built-in testing afforded by the design of the language can only go so far. At some point, *you* must step in and add the rest of the tests that produce a full suite (in cooperation with the compiler and run-time system) that verifies all of your program. And, just like having a compiler watching over your shoulder, wouldn't you want these tests helping you right from the beginning? That's why you write them first, and run them automatically with every build of your system. Your tests become an extension of the safety net provided by the language.

One of the things that I've discovered about the use of more and more powerful programming languages is that I am emboldened to try more brazen experiments, because I know that the language will keep me from wasting my time chasing bugs. The XP test scheme does the same thing for your entire project. Because you know your tests will always catch any problems that you introduce (and you regularly add any new tests as you think of them), you can make big changes when you need to without worrying that you'll throw the whole project into complete disarray. This is incredibly powerful.

Pair programming

Pair programming goes against the rugged individualism that we've been indoctrinated into from the beginning, through school (where we succeed or fail on our own, and working with our neighbors is considered "cheating") and media, especially Hollywood movies in which the hero is usually fighting against mindless conformity[16]. Programmers, too, are considered paragons of individuality – "cowboy coders" as Larry Constantine likes to say. And yet XP, which is itself battling against conventional thinking, says that code should be written with two people per workstation. And that this should be done in an area with a group of workstations, without the barriers that the facilities design people are so fond of. In fact, Beck says that the first task of converting to XP is to arrive with screwdrivers and Allen wrenches and take apart everything that gets in the way.[17] (This will require a manager who can deflect the ire of the facilities department.)

---

[16] Although this may be a more American perspective, the stories of Hollywood reach everywhere.

[17] Including (especially) the PA system. I once worked in a company that insisted on broadcasting every phone call that arrived for every executive, and it constantly interrupted our productivity (but the managers couldn't begin to conceive of stifling

The value of pair programming is that one person is actually doing the coding while the other is thinking about it. The thinker keeps the big picture in mind, not only the picture of the problem at hand, but the guidelines of XP. If two people are working, it's less likely that one of them will get away with saying, "I don't want to write the tests first," for example. And if the coder gets stuck, they can swap places. If both of them get stuck, their musings may be overheard by someone else in the work area who can contribute. Working in pairs keeps things flowing and on track. Probably more important, it makes programming a lot more social and fun.

I've begun using pair programming during the exercise periods in some of my seminars and it seems to significantly improve everyone's experience.

Why C++ succeeds

Part of the reason C++ has been so successful is that the goal was not just to turn C into an OOP language (although it started that way), but also to solve many other problems facing developers today, especially those who have large investments in C. Traditionally, OOP languages have suffered from the attitude that you should abandon everything you know and start from scratch with a new set of concepts and a new syntax, arguing that it's better in the long run to lose all the old baggage that comes with procedural languages. This may be true, in the long run. But in the short run, a lot of that baggage was valuable. The most valuable elements may not be the existing code base (which, given adequate tools, could be translated), but instead the existing *mind base*. If you're a functioning C programmer and must drop everything you know about C in order to adopt a new language, you immediately become much less productive for many months, until your mind fits around the new paradigm. Whereas if you can leverage off of your existing C knowledge and expand on it, you can continue to be productive with what you already know while moving into the world of object-oriented programming. As everyone has his or her own

---

such an important service as the PA). Finally, when no one was looking I started snipping speaker wires.

---

mental model of programming, this move is messy enough as it is without the added expense of starting with a new language model from square one. So the reason for the success of C++, in a nutshell, is economic: It still costs to move to OOP, but C++ may cost less[18].

The goal of C++ is improved productivity. This productivity comes in many ways, but the language is designed to aid you as much as possible, while hindering you as little as possible with arbitrary rules or any requirement that you use a particular set of features. C++ is designed to be practical; C++ language design decisions were based on providing the maximum benefits to the programmer (at least, from the world view of C).

A better C

You get an instant win even if you continue to write C code because C++ has closed many holes in the C language and provides better type checking and compile-time analysis. You're forced to declare functions so that the compiler can check their use. The need for the preprocessor has virtually been eliminated for value substitution and macros, which removes a set of difficult-to-find bugs. C++ has a feature called *references* that allows more convenient handling of addresses for function arguments and return values. The handling of names is improved through a feature called *function overloading*, which allows you to use the same name for different functions. A feature called *namespaces* also improves the control of names. There are numerous smaller features that improve the safety of C.

You're already on the learning curve

The problem with learning a new language is productivity. No company can afford to suddenly lose a productive software engineer because he or she is learning a new language. C++ is an extension to C, not a complete new syntax and programming model. It allows you to continue creating useful code, applying the features

---

[18] I say "may" because, due to the complexity of C++, it might actually be cheaper to move to Java. But the decision of which language to choose has many factors, and in this book I'll assume that you've chosen C++.

---

gradually as you learn and understand them. This may be one of the most important reasons for the success of C++.

In addition, all of your existing C code is still viable in C++, but because the C++ compiler is pickier, you'll often find hidden C errors when recompiling the code in C++.

Efficiency

Sometimes it is appropriate to trade execution speed for programmer productivity. A financial model, for example, may be useful for only a short period of time, so it's more important to create the model rapidly than to execute it rapidly. However, most applications require some degree of efficiency, so C++ always errs on the side of greater efficiency. Because C programmers tend to be very efficiency-conscious, this is also a way to ensure that they won't be able to argue that the language is too fat and slow. A number of features in C++ are intended to allow you to tune for performance when the generated code isn't efficient enough.

Not only do you have the same low-level control as in C (and the ability to directly write assembly language within a C++ program), but anecdotal evidence suggests that the program speed for an object-oriented C++ program tends to be within ±10% of a program written in C, and often much closer[19]. The design produced for an OOP program may actually be more efficient than the C counterpart.

Systems are easier to express and understand

Classes designed to fit the problem tend to express it better. This means that when you write the code, you're describing your solution in the terms of the problem space ("Put the grommet in the bin") rather than the terms of the computer, which is the solution space ("Set the bit in the chip that means that the relay will close").

---

[19] However, look at Dan Saks' columns in the *C/C++ User's Journal* for some important investigations into C++ library performance.

You deal with higher-level concepts and can do much more with a single line of code.

The other benefit of this ease of expression is maintenance, which (if reports can be believed) takes a huge portion of the cost over a program's lifetime. If a program is easier to understand, then it's easier to maintain. This can also reduce the cost of creating and maintaining the documentation.

Maximal leverage with libraries

The fastest way to create a program is to use code that's already written: a library. A major goal in C++ is to make library use easier. This is accomplished by casting libraries into new data types (classes), so that bringing in a library means adding new types to the language. Because the C++ compiler takes care of how the library is used – guaranteeing proper initialization and cleanup, and ensuring that functions are called properly – you can focus on what you want the library to do, not how you have to do it.

Because names can be sequestered to portions of your program via C++ namespaces, you can use as many libraries as you want without the kinds of name clashes you'd run into with C.

Source-code reuse with templates

There is a significant class of types that require source-code modification in order to reuse them effectively. The *template* feature in C++ performs the source code modification automatically, making it an especially powerful tool for reusing library code. A type that you design using templates will work effortlessly with many other types. Templates are especially nice because they hide the complexity of this kind of code reuse from the client programmer.

Error handling

Error handling in C is a notorious problem, and one that is often ignored – finger-crossing is usually involved. If you're building a large, complex program, there's nothing worse than having an error buried somewhere with no clue as to where it came from. C++

exception handling (introduced in this Volume, and fully covered in Volume 2, which is downloadable from *www.BruceEckel.com*) is a way to guarantee that an error is noticed and that something happens as a result.

Programming in the large

Many traditional languages have built-in limitations to program size and complexity. BASIC, for example, can be great for pulling together quick solutions for certain classes of problems, but if the program gets more than a few pages long or ventures out of the normal problem domain of that language, it's like trying to swim through an ever-more viscous fluid. C, too, has these limitations. For example, when a program gets beyond perhaps 50,000 lines of code, name collisions start to become a problem – effectively, you run out of function and variable names. Another particularly bad problem is the little holes in the C language – errors buried in a large program can be extremely difficult to find.

There's no clear line that tells you when your language is failing you, and even if there were, you'd ignore it. You don't say, "My BASIC program just got too big; I'll have to rewrite it in C!" Instead, you try to shoehorn a few more lines in to add that one new feature. So the extra costs come creeping up on you.

C++ is designed to aid *programming in the large*, that is, to erase those creeping-complexity boundaries between a small program and a large one. You certainly don't need to use OOP, templates, namespaces, and exception handling when you're writing a hello-world style utility program, but those features are there when you need them. And the compiler is aggressive about ferreting out bug-producing errors for small and large programs alike.

Strategies for transition

If you buy into OOP, your next question is probably, "How can I get my manager/colleagues/department/peers to start using objects?" Think about how you – one independent programmer – would go about learning to use a new language and a new programming paradigm. You've done it before. First comes education and examples; then comes a trial project to give you a feel for the basics without doing anything too confusing. Then comes a "real world" project that actually does something useful. Throughout your first projects you continue your education by reading, asking questions of experts, and trading hints with friends. This is the approach many experienced programmers suggest for the switch from C to C++. Switching an entire company will of course introduce certain group dynamics, but it will help at each step to remember how one person would do it.

Guidelines

Here are some guidelines to consider when making the transition to OOP and C++:

1. Training

The first step is some form of education. Remember the company's investment in plain C code, and try not to throw everything into disarray for six to nine months while everyone puzzles over how multiple inheritance works. Pick a small group for indoctrination, preferably one composed of people who are curious, work well together, and can function as their own support network while they're learning C++.

An alternative approach that is sometimes suggested is the education of all company levels at once, including overview courses for strategic managers as well as design and programming courses for project builders. This is especially good for smaller companies making fundamental shifts in the way they do things, or at the division level of larger companies. Because the cost is higher, however, some may choose to start with project-level training, do a pilot project (possibly with an outside mentor), and let the project team become the teachers for the rest of the company.

2. Low-risk project

Try a low-risk project first and allow for mistakes. Once you've gained some experience, you can either seed other projects from members of this first team or use the team members as an OOP technical support staff. This first project may not work right the first time, so it should not be mission-critical for the company. It

---

should be simple, self-contained, and instructive; this means that it should involve creating classes that will be meaningful to the other programmers in the company when they get their turn to learn C++.

3. Model from success
Seek out examples of good object-oriented design before starting from scratch. There's a good probability that someone has solved your problem already, and if they haven't solved it exactly you can probably apply what you've learned about abstraction to modify an existing design to fit your needs. This is the general concept of *design patterns,* covered in Volume 2.

4. Use existing class libraries
The primary economic motivation for switching to OOP is the easy use of existing code in the form of class libraries (in particular, the Standard C++ libraries, which are covered in depth in Volume two of this book). The shortest application development cycle will result when you don't have to write anything but **main( )**, creating and using objects from off-the-shelf libraries. However, some new programmers don't understand this, are unaware of existing class libraries, or, through fascination with the language, desire to write classes that may already exist. Your success with OOP and C++ will be optimized if you make an effort to seek out and reuse other people's code early in the transition process.

5. Don't rewrite existing code in C++
Although *compiling* your C code with a C++ compiler usually produces (sometimes tremendous) benefits by finding problems in the old code, it is not usually the best use of your time to take existing, functional code and rewrite it in C++. (If you must turn it into objects, you can "wrap" the C code in C++ classes.) There are incremental benefits, especially if the code is slated for reuse. But chances are you aren't going to see the dramatic increases in productivity that you hope for in your first few projects unless that project is a new one. C++ and OOP shine best when taking a project from concept to reality.

Management obstacles

If you're a manager, your job is to acquire resources for your team, to overcome barriers to your team's success, and in general to try to provide the most productive and enjoyable environment so your team is most likely to perform those miracles that are always being asked of you. Moving to C++ falls in all three of these categories, and it would be wonderful if it didn't cost you anything as well. Although moving to C++ may be cheaper – depending on your constraints[20] – than the OOP alternatives for a team of C programmers (and probably for programmers in other procedural languages), it isn't free, and there are obstacles you should be aware of before trying to sell the move to C++ within your company and embarking on the move itself.

Startup costs

The cost of moving to C++ is more than just the acquisition of C++ compilers (the GNU C++ compiler, one of the very best, is free). Your medium- and long-term costs will be minimized if you invest in training (and possibly mentoring for your first project) and also if you identify and purchase class libraries that solve your problem rather than trying to build those libraries yourself. These are hard-money costs that must be factored into a realistic proposal. In addition, there are the hidden costs in loss of productivity while learning a new language and possibly a new programming environment. Training and mentoring can certainly minimize these, but team members must overcome their own struggles to understand the new technology. During this process they will make more mistakes (this is a feature, because acknowledged mistakes are the fastest path to learning) and be less productive. Even then, with some types of programming problems, the right classes, and the right development environment, it's possible to be more productive while you're learning C++ (even considering that you're making more mistakes and writing fewer lines of code per day) than if you'd stayed with C.

---

[20] Because of its productivity improvements, the Java language should also be considered here.

Performance issues

A common question is, "Doesn't OOP automatically make my programs a lot bigger and slower?" The answer is, "It depends." Most traditional OOP languages were designed with experimentation and rapid prototyping in mind rather than lean-and-mean operation. Thus, they virtually guaranteed a significant increase in size and decrease in speed. C++, however, is designed with production programming in mind. When your focus is on rapid prototyping, you can throw together components as fast as possible while ignoring efficiency issues. If you're using any third party libraries, these are usually already optimized by their vendors; in any case it's not an issue while you're in rapid-development mode. When you have a system that you like, if it's small and fast enough, then you're done. If not, you begin tuning with a profiling tool, looking first for speedups that can be done with simple applications of built-in C++ features. If that doesn't help, you look for modifications that can be made in the underlying implementation so no code that uses a particular class needs to be changed. Only if nothing else solves the problem do you need to change the design. The fact that performance is so critical in that portion of the design is an indicator that it must be part of the primary design criteria. You have the benefit of finding this out early using rapid development.

As mentioned earlier, the number that is most often given for the difference in size and speed between C and C++ is ±10%, and often much closer to par. You might even get a significant improvement in size and speed when using C++ rather than C because the design you make for C++ could be quite different from the one you'd make for C.

The evidence for size and speed comparisons between C and C++ tends to be anecdotal and is likely to remain so. Regardless of the number of people who suggest that a company try the same project using C and C++, no company is likely to waste money that way unless it's very big and interested in such research projects. Even then, it seems like the money could be better spent. Almost universally, programmers who have moved from C (or some other procedural language) to C++ (or some other OOP language) have had the personal experience of a great acceleration in their programming productivity, and that's the most compelling argument you can find.

Common design errors

When starting your team into OOP and C++, programmers will typically go through a series of common design errors. This often happens because of too little feedback from experts during the design and implementation of early projects, because no experts have been developed within the company and there may be resistance to retaining consultants. It's easy to feel that you understand OOP too early in the cycle and go off on a bad tangent. Something that's obvious to someone experienced with the language may be a subject of great internal debate for a novice. Much of this trauma can be skipped by using an experienced outside expert for training and mentoring.

On the other hand, the fact that it is easy to make these design errors points to C++'s main drawback: its backward compatibility with C (of course, that's also its main strength). To accomplish the feat of being able to compile C code, the language had to make some compromises, which have resulted in a number of "dark corners." These are a reality, and comprise much of the learning curve for the language. In this book and the subsequent volume (and in other books; see Appendix C), I try to reveal most of the pitfalls you are likely to encounter when working with C++. You should always be aware that there are some holes in the safety net.

Summary

This chapter attempts to give you a feel for the broad issues of object-oriented programming and C++, including why OOP is different, and why C++ in particular is different, concepts of OOP methodologies, and finally the kinds of issues you will encounter when moving your own company to OOP and C++.

OOP and C++ may not be for everyone. It's important to evaluate your own needs and decide whether C++ will optimally satisfy those needs, or if you might be better off with another programming system (including the one you're currently using). If you know that your needs will be very specialized for the foreseeable future and if you have specific constraints that may not be satisfied by C++, then you owe it to yourself to investigate the alternatives[21]. Even if you eventually choose C++ as your language, you'll at least understand what the options were and have a clear vision of why you took that direction.

You know what a procedural program looks like: data definitions and function calls. To find the meaning of such a program you have to work a little, looking through the function calls and low-level concepts to create a model in your mind. This is the reason we need intermediate representations when designing procedural programs – by themselves, these programs tend to be confusing because the terms of expression are oriented more toward the computer than to the problem you're solving.

Because C++ adds many new concepts to the C language, your natural assumption may be that the **main( )** in a C++ program will be far more complicated than for the equivalent C program. Here, you'll be pleasantly surprised: A well-written C++ program is generally far simpler and much easier to understand than the equivalent C program. What you'll see are the definitions of the objects that represent concepts in your problem space (rather than the issues of the computer representation) and messages sent to those objects to represent the activities in that space. One of the delights of object-oriented programming is that, with a well-designed program, it's easy to understand the code by reading it. Usually there's a lot less code, as well, because many of your problems will be solved by reusing existing library code.

---

[21] In particular, I recommend looking at Java (http://java.sun.com) and Python (http://www.Python.org).

2: Making & Using Objects

This chapter will introduce enough C++ syntax and program construction concepts to allow you to write and run some simple object-oriented programs. In the subsequent chapter we will cover the basic syntax of C and C++ in detail.

By reading this chapter first, you'll get the basic flavor of what it is like to program with objects in C++, and you'll also discover some of the reasons for the enthusiasm surrounding this language. This should be enough to carry you through Chapter 3, which can be a bit exhausting since it contains most of the details of the C language.

The user-defined data type, or *class*, is what distinguishes C++ from traditional procedural languages. A class is a new data type that you or someone else creates to solve a particular kind of problem. Once a class is created, anyone can use it without knowing the specifics of how it works, or even how classes are built. This chapter treats classes as if they are just another built-in data type available for use in programs.

Classes that someone else has created are typically packaged into a library. This chapter uses several of the class libraries that come with all C++ implementations. An especially important standard library is iostreams, which (among other things) allow you to read from files and the keyboard, and to write to files and the display. You'll also see the very handy **string** class, and the **vector** container from the Standard C++ Library. By the end of the chapter, you'll see how easy it is to use a pre-defined library of classes.

In order to create your first program you must understand the tools used to build applications.

The process of language translation

All computer languages are translated from something that tends to be easy for a human to understand (*source code*) into something that is executed on a computer (*machine instructions*). Traditionally, translators fall into two classes: *interpreters* and *compilers*.

Interpreters

An interpreter translates source code into activities (which may comprise groups of machine instructions) and immediately executes those activities. BASIC, for example, has been a popular interpreted language. Traditional BASIC interpreters translate and execute one line at a time, and then forget that the line has been translated. This makes them slow, since they must re-translate any repeated code. BASIC has also been compiled, for speed. More modern interpreters, such as those for the Python language, translate the entire program into an intermediate language that is then executed by a much faster interpreter[1].

Interpreters have many advantages. The transition from writing code to executing code is almost immediate, and the source code is always available so the interpreter can be much more specific when an error occurs. The benefits often cited for interpreters are ease of interaction and rapid development (but not necessarily execution) of programs.

Interpreted languages often have severe limitations when building large projects (Python seems to be an exception to this). The interpreter (or a reduced version) must always be in memory to execute the code, and even the fastest interpreter may introduce unacceptable speed restrictions. Most interpreters require that the complete source code be brought into the interpreter all at once. Not only does this introduce a space limitation, it can also cause more difficult bugs if the language doesn't provide facilities to localize the effect of different pieces of code.

Compilers

A compiler translates source code directly into assembly language or machine instructions. The eventual end product is a file or files containing machine code. This is an involved process, and usually

---

[1] The boundary between compilers and interpreters can tend to become a bit fuzzy, especially with Python, which has many of the features and power of a compiled language but the quick turnaround of an interpreted language.

---

takes several steps. The transition from writing code to executing code is significantly longer with a compiler.

Depending on the acumen of the compiler writer, programs generated by a compiler tend to require much less space to run, and they run much more quickly. Although size and speed are probably the most often cited reasons for using a compiler, in many situations they aren't the most important reasons. Some languages (such as C) are designed to allow pieces of a program to be compiled independently. These pieces are eventually combined into a final *executable* program by a tool called the *linker*. This process is called *separate compilation*.

Separate compilation has many benefits. A program that, taken all at once, would exceed the limits of the compiler or the compiling environment can be compiled in pieces. Programs can be built and tested one piece at a time. Once a piece is working, it can be saved and treated as a building block. Collections of tested and working pieces can be combined into *libraries* for use by other programmers. As each piece is created, the complexity of the other pieces is hidden. All these features support the creation of large programs[2].

Compiler debugging features have improved significantly over time. Early compilers only generated machine code, and the programmer inserted print statements to see what was going on. This is not always effective. Modern compilers can insert information about the source code into the executable program. This information is used by powerful *source-level debuggers* to show exactly what is happening in a program by tracing its progress through the source code.

Some compilers tackle the compilation-speed problem by performing *in-memory compilation*. Most compilers work with files, reading and writing them in each step of the compilation process. In-memory compilers keep the compiler program in RAM. For small programs, this can seem as responsive as an interpreter.

---

[2] Python is again an exception, since it also provides separate compilation.

The compilation process

To program in C and C++, you need to understand the steps and tools in the compilation process. Some languages (C and C++, in particular) start compilation by running a *preprocessor* on the source code. The preprocessor is a simple program that replaces patterns in the source code with other patterns the programmer has defined (using *preprocessor directives*). Preprocessor directives are used to save typing and to increase the readability of the code. (Later in the book, you'll learn how the design of C++ is meant to discourage much of the use of the preprocessor, since it can cause subtle bugs.) The pre-processed code is often written to an intermediate file.

Compilers usually do their work in two passes. The first pass *parses* the pre-processed code. The compiler breaks the source code into small units and organizes it into a structure called a *tree*. In the expression "**A + B**" the elements '**A**', '**+**,' and '**B**' are leaves on the parse tree.

A *global optimizer* is sometimes used between the first and second passes to produce smaller, faster code.

In the second pass, the *code generator* walks through the parse tree and generates either assembly language code or machine code for the nodes of the tree. If the code generator creates assembly code, the assembler must then be run. The end result in both cases is an object module (a file that typically has an extension of **.o** or **.obj**). A *peephole optimizer* is sometimes used in the second pass to look for pieces of code containing redundant assembly-language statements.

The use of the word "object" to describe chunks of machine code is an unfortunate artifact. The word came into use before object-oriented programming was in general use. "Object" is used in the same sense as "goal" when discussing compilation, while in object-oriented programming it means "a thing with boundaries."

The *linker* combines a list of object modules into an executable program that can be loaded and run by the operating system. When a function in one object module makes a reference to a function or variable in another object module, the linker resolves these references; it makes sure that all the external functions and data you claimed existed during compilation do exist. The linker also adds a special object module to perform start-up activities.

The linker can search through special files called *libraries* in order to resolve all its references. A library contains a collection of object modules in a single file. A library is created and maintained by a program called a *librarian*.

Static type checking

The compiler performs *type checking* during the first pass. Type checking tests for the proper use of arguments in functions and prevents many kinds of programming errors. Since type checking occurs during compilation instead of when the program is running, it is called *static type checking*.

Some object-oriented languages (notably Java) perform some type checking at runtime (*dynamic type checking*). If combined with static type checking, dynamic type checking is more powerful than static type checking alone. However, it also adds overhead to program execution.

C++ uses static type checking because the language cannot assume any particular runtime support for bad operations. Static type checking notifies the programmer about misuses of types during compilation, and thus maximizes execution speed. As you learn C++, you will see that most of the language design decisions favor the same kind of high-speed, production-oriented programming the C language is famous for.

You can disable static type checking in C++. You can also do your own dynamic type checking – you just need to write the code.

Tools for separate compilation

Separate compilation is particularly important when building large projects. In C and C++, a program can be created in small, manageable, independently tested pieces. The most fundamental tool for breaking a program up into pieces is the ability to create named subroutines or subprograms. In C and C++, a subprogram is called a *function*, and functions are the pieces of code that can be placed in different files, enabling separate compilation. Put another way, the function is the atomic unit of code, since you cannot have part of a function in one file and another part in a different file; the entire function must be placed in a single file (although files can and do contain more than one function).

When you call a function, you typically pass it some *arguments*, which are values you'd like the function to work with during its execution. When the function is finished, you typically get back a *return value*, a value that the function hands back to you as a result. It's also possible to write functions that take no arguments and return no values.

To create a program with multiple files, functions in one file must access functions and data in other files. When compiling a file, the C or C++ compiler must know about the functions and data in the other files, in particular their names and proper usage. The compiler ensures that functions and data are used correctly. This process of "telling the compiler" the names of external functions and data and what they should look like is called *declaration*. Once you declare a function or variable, the compiler knows how to check to make sure it is used properly.

Declarations vs. definitions

It's important to understand the difference between *declarations* and *definitions* because these terms will be used precisely throughout the book. Essentially all C and C++ programs require declarations. Before you can write your first program, you need to understand the proper way to write a declaration.

A *declaration* introduces a name – an identifier – to the compiler. It tells the compiler "This function or this variable exists somewhere, and here is what it should look like." A *definition*, on the other hand, says: "Make this variable here" or "Make this function here." It allocates storage for the name. This meaning works whether you're talking about a variable or a function; in

---

either case, at the point of definition the compiler allocates storage. For a variable, the compiler determines how big that variable is and causes space to be generated in memory to hold the data for that variable. For a function, the compiler generates code, which ends up occupying storage in memory.

You can declare a variable or a function in many different places, but there must be only one definition in C and C++ (this is sometimes called the ODR: *one-definition rule*). When the linker is uniting all the object modules, it will usually complain if it finds more than one definition for the same function or variable.

A definition can also be a declaration. If the compiler hasn't seen the name **x** before and you define **int x;**, the compiler sees the name as a declaration and allocates storage for it all at once.

Function declaration syntax

A function declaration in C and C++ gives the function name, the argument types passed to the function, and the return value of the function. For example, here is a declaration for a function called **func1( )** that takes two integer arguments (integers are denoted in C/C++ with the keyword **int**) and returns an integer:

```
int func1(int,int);
```

The first keyword you see is the return value all by itself: **int**. The arguments are enclosed in parentheses after the function name in the order they are used. The semicolon indicates the end of a statement; in this case, it tells the compiler "that's all – there is no function definition here!"

C and C++ declarations attempt to mimic the form of the item's use. For example, if **a** is another integer the above function might be used this way:

```
a = func1(2,3);
```

Since **func1( )** returns an integer, the C or C++ compiler will check the use of **func1( )** to make sure that **a** can accept the return value and that the arguments are appropriate.

Arguments in function declarations may have names. The compiler ignores the names but they can be helpful as mnemonic devices for the user. For example, we can declare **func1( )** in a different fashion that has the same meaning:

```
int func1(int length, int width);
```

A gotcha

There is a significant difference between C and C++ for functions with empty argument lists. In C, the declaration:

```
int func2();
```

means "a function with any number and type of argument." This prevents type-checking, so in C++ it means "a function with no arguments."

Function definitions

Function definitions look like function declarations except that they have bodies. A body is a collection of statements enclosed in braces. Braces denote the beginning and ending of a block of code. To give **func1( )** a definition that is an empty body (a body containing no code), write:

```
int func1(int length, int width) { }
```

Notice that in the function definition, the braces replace the semicolon. Since braces surround a statement or group of statements, you don't need a semicolon. Notice also that the arguments in the function definition must have names if you want to use the arguments in the function body (since they are never used here, they are optional).

Variable declaration syntax

The meaning attributed to the phrase "variable declaration" has historically been confusing and contradictory, and it's important that you understand the correct definition so you can read code properly. A variable declaration tells the compiler what a variable looks like. It says, "I know you haven't seen this name before, but I promise it exists someplace, and it's a variable of X type."

In a function declaration, you give a type (the return value), the function name, the argument list, and a semicolon. That's enough for the compiler to figure out that it's a declaration and what the function should look like. By inference, a variable declaration might be a type followed by a name. For example:

```
int a;
```

could declare the variable **a** as an integer, using the logic above. Here's the conflict: there is enough information in the code above for the compiler to create space for an integer called **a**, and that's what happens. To resolve this dilemma, a keyword was necessary for C and C++ to say "This is only a declaration; it's defined elsewhere." The keyword is **extern**. It can mean the definition is **extern**al to the file, or that the definition occurs later in the file.

Declaring a variable without defining it means using the **extern** keyword before a description of the variable, like this:

```
extern int a;
```

extern can also apply to function declarations. For **func1( )**, it looks like this:

```
extern int func1(int length, int width);
```

This statement is equivalent to the previous **func1( )** declarations. Since there is no function body, the compiler must treat it as a function declaration rather than a function definition. The **extern** keyword is thus superfluous and optional for function declarations. It is probably unfortunate that the designers of C did not require the use of **extern** for function declarations; it would have been more consistent and less confusing (but would have required more typing, which probably explains the decision).

Here are some more examples of declarations:

```
//: C02:Declare.cpp
// Declaration & definition examples
extern int i; // Declaration without definition
extern float f(float); // Function declaration
```

```
float b;   // Declaration & definition
float f(float a) {   // Definition
  return a + 1.0;
}

int i; // Definition
int h(int x) { // Declaration & definition
  return x + 1;
}

int main() {
  b = 1.0;
  i = 2;
  f(b);
  h(i);
} ///:~
```

In the function declarations, the argument identifiers are optional. In the definitions, they are required (the identifiers are required only in C, not C++).

Including headers

Most libraries contain significant numbers of functions and variables. To save work and ensure consistency when making the external declarations for these items, C and C++ use a device called the *header file*. A header file is a file containing the external declarations for a library; it conventionally has a file name extension of 'h', such as **headerfile.h**. (You may also see some older code using different extensions, such as **.hxx** or **.hpp**, but this is becoming rare.)

The programmer who creates the library provides the header file. To declare the functions and external variables in the library, the user simply includes the header file. To include a header file, use the **#include** preprocessor directive. This tells the preprocessor to open the named header file and insert its contents where the **#include** statement appears. A **#include** may name a file in two ways: in angle brackets (< >) or in double quotes.

File names in angle brackets, such as:

```
#include <header>
```

cause the preprocessor to search for the file in a way that is particular to your implementation, but typically there's some kind of "include search path" that you specify in your environment or on the compiler command line. The mechanism for setting the search path varies between machines, operating systems, and C++ implementations, and may require some investigation on your part.

File names in double quotes, such as:

```
#include "local.h"
```

tell the preprocessor to search for the file in (according to the specification) an "implementation-defined way." What this typically means is to search for the file relative to the current directory. If the file is not found, then the include directive is reprocessed as if it had angle brackets instead of quotes.

To include the iostream header file, you write:

```
#include <iostream>
```

The preprocessor will find the iostream header file (often in a subdirectory called "include") and insert it.

Standard C++ include format

As C++ evolved, different compiler vendors chose different extensions for file names. In addition, various operating systems have different restrictions on file names, in particular on name length. These issues caused source code portability problems. To smooth over these rough edges, the standard uses a format that allows file names longer than the notorious eight characters and eliminates the extension. For example, instead of the old style of including **iostream.h**, which looks like this:

```
#include <iostream.h>
```

you can now write:

```
#include <iostream>
```

The translator can implement the include statements in a way that suits the needs of that particular compiler and operating system, if

---

necessary truncating the name and adding an extension. Of course, you can also copy the headers given you by your compiler vendor to ones without extensions if you want to use this style before a vendor has provided support for it.

The libraries that have been inherited from C are still available with the traditional '**.h**' extension. However, you can also use them with the more modern C++ include style by prepending a "**c**" before the name. Thus:

```
#include <stdio.h>
#include <stdlib.h>
```

become:

```
#include <cstdio>
#include <cstdlib>
```

And so on, for all the Standard C headers. This provides a nice distinction to the reader indicating when you're using C versus C++ libraries.

The effect of the new include format is not identical to the old: using the **.h** gives you the older, non-template version, and omitting the **.h** gives you the new templatized version. You'll usually have problems if you try to intermix the two forms in a single program.

Linking

The linker collects object modules (which often use file name extensions like **.o** or **.obj**), generated by the compiler, into an executable program the operating system can load and run. It is the last phase of the compilation process.

Linker characteristics vary from system to system. In general, you just tell the linker the names of the object modules and libraries you want linked together, and the name of the executable, and it goes to work. Some systems require you to invoke the linker yourself. With most C++ packages you invoke the linker through the C++ compiler. In many situations, the linker is invoked for you invisibly.

Some older linkers won't search object files and libraries more than once, and they search through the list you give them from left to right. This means that the order of object files and libraries can be important. If you have a mysterious problem that doesn't show up until link time, one possibility is the order in which the files are given to the linker.

Using libraries

Now that you know the basic terminology, you can understand how to use a library. To use a library:

1.   Include the library's header file.

2.   Use the functions and variables in the library.

3.   Link the library into the executable program.

These steps also apply when the object modules aren't combined into a library. Including a header file and linking the object modules are the basic steps for separate compilation in both C and C++.

How the linker searches a library

When you make an external reference to a function or variable in C or C++, the linker, upon encountering this reference, can do one of two things. If it has not already encountered the definition for the function or variable, it adds the identifier to its list of "unresolved references." If the linker has already encountered the definition, the reference is resolved.

If the linker cannot find the definition in the list of object modules, it searches the libraries. Libraries have some sort of indexing so the linker doesn't need to look through all the object modules in the library – it just looks in the index. When the linker finds a definition in a library, the entire object module, not just the function definition, is linked into the executable program. Note that the whole library isn't linked, just the object module in the library that contains the definition you want (otherwise programs would be unnecessarily large). If you want to minimize executable program size, you might consider putting a single function in each source code file when you build your own libraries. This requires more editing[3], but it can be helpful to the user.

Because the linker searches files in the order you give them, you can pre-empt the use of a library function by inserting a file with your own function, using the same function name, into the list before the library name appears. Since the linker will resolve any references to this function by using your function before it searches the library, your function is used instead of the library function. Note that this can also be a bug, and the kind of thing C++ namespaces prevent.

Secret additions

When a C or C++ executable program is created, certain items are secretly linked in. One of these is the startup module, which contains initialization routines that must be run any time a C or C++ program begins to execute. These routines set up the stack and initialize certain variables in the program.

The linker always searches the standard library for the compiled versions of any "standard" functions called in the program. Because the standard library is always searched, you can use anything in that library by simply including the appropriate header file in your program; you don't have to tell it to search the standard library. The iostream functions, for example, are in the Standard C++ library. To use them, you just include the **<iostream>** header file.

If you are using an add-on library, you must explicitly add the library name to the list of files handed to the linker.

Using plain C libraries

Just because you are writing code in C++, you are not prevented from using C library functions. In fact, the entire C library is included by default into Standard C++. There has been a tremendous amount of work done for you in these functions, so they can save you a lot of time.

---

[3] I would recommend using Perl or Python to automate this task as part of your library-packaging process (see www.Perl.org or www.Python.org).

This book will use Standard C++ (and thus also Standard C) library functions when convenient, but only *standard* library functions will be used, to ensure the portability of programs. In the few cases in which library functions must be used that are not in the C++ standard, all attempts will be made to use POSIX-compliant functions. POSIX is a standard based on a Unix standardization effort that includes functions that go beyond the scope of the C++ library. You can generally expect to find POSIX functions on Unix (in particular, Linux) platforms, and often under DOS/Windows. For example, if you're using multithreading you are better off using the POSIX thread library because your code will then be easier to understand, port and maintain (and the POSIX thread library will usually just use the underlying thread facilities of the operating system, if these are provided).

Your first C++ program

You now know almost enough of the basics to create and compile a program. The program will use the Standard C++ iostream classes. These read from and write to files and "standard" input and output (which normally comes from and goes to the console, but may be redirected to files or devices). In this simple program, a stream object will be used to print a message on the screen.

Using the iostreams class

To declare the functions and external data in the iostreams class, include the header file with the statement

```
#include <iostream>
```

The first program uses the concept of standard output, which means "a general-purpose place to send output." You will see other examples using standard output in different ways, but here it will just go to the console. The iostream package automatically defines a variable (an object) called **cout** that accepts all data bound for standard output.

To send data to standard output, you use the operator <<. C programmers know this operator as the "bitwise left shift," which will be described in the next chapter. Suffice it to say that a bitwise left shift has nothing to do with output. However, C++ allows operators to be *overloaded*. When you overload an operator, you give it a new meaning when that operator is used with an object of a particular type. With iostream objects, the operator << means "send to." For example:

```
cout << "howdy!";
```

sends the string "howdy!" to the object called **cout** (which is short for "console output").

That's enough operator overloading to get you started. Chapter 12 covers operator overloading in detail.

Namespaces

As mentioned in Chapter 1, one of the problems encountered in the C language is that you "run out of names" for functions and identifiers when your programs reach a certain size. Of course, you don't really run out of names; it does, however, become harder to think of new ones after awhile. More importantly, when a program reaches a certain size it's typically broken up into pieces, each of which is built and maintained by a different person or group. Since C effectively has a single arena where all the identifier and function names live, this means that all the developers must be careful not to accidentally use the same names in situations where they can conflict. This rapidly becomes tedious, time-wasting, and, ultimately, expensive.

Standard C++ has a mechanism to prevent this collision: the **namespace** keyword. Each set of C++ definitions in a library or program is "wrapped" in a namespace, and if some other definition has an identical name, but is in a different namespace, then there is no collision.

Namespaces are a convenient and helpful tool, but their presence means that you must be aware of them before you can write any programs. If you simply include a header file and use some functions or objects from that header, you'll probably get strange-sounding errors when you try to compile the program, to the effect that the compiler cannot find any of the declarations for the items that you just included in the header file! After you see this message a few times you'll become familiar with its meaning (which is "You included the header file but all the declarations are within a namespace and you didn't tell the compiler that you wanted to use the declarations in that namespace").

There's a keyword that allows you to say "I want to use the declarations and/or definitions in this namespace." This keyword, appropriately enough, is **using**. All of the Standard C++ libraries are wrapped in a single namespace, which is **std** (for "standard"). As this book uses the standard libraries almost exclusively, you'll see the following *using directive* in almost every program:

```
using namespace std;
```

This means that you want to expose all the elements from the namespace called **std**. After this statement, you don't have to worry that your particular library component is inside a namespace, since the **using** directive makes that namespace available throughout the file where the **using** directive was written.

Exposing all the elements from a namespace after someone has gone to the trouble to hide them may seem a bit counterproductive, and in fact you should be careful about thoughtlessly doing this (as you'll learn later in the book). However, the **using** directive exposes only those names for the current file, so it is not quite as drastic as it first sounds. (But think twice about doing it in a header file – that *is* reckless.)

There's a relationship between namespaces and the way header files are included. Before the modern header file inclusion was standardized (without the trailing '**.h**', as in **<iostream>**), the typical way to include a header file was with the '**.h**', such as **<iostream.h>**. At that time, namespaces were not part of the language either. So to provide backward compatibility with existing code, if you say

```
#include <iostream.h>
```

it means

```
#include <iostream>
using namespace std;
```

However, in this book the standard include format will be used (without the '.h') and so the **using** directive must be explicit.

For now, that's all you need to know about namespaces, but in Chapter 10 the subject is covered much more thoroughly.

Fundamentals of program structure

A C or C++ program is a collection of variables, function definitions, and function calls. When the program starts, it executes initialization code and calls a special function, "**main( )**." You put the primary code for the program here.

As mentioned earlier, a function definition consists of a return type (which must be specified in C++), a function name, an argument list in parentheses, and the function code contained in braces. Here is a sample function definition:

```
int function() {
  // Function code here (this is a comment)
}
```

The function above has an empty argument list and a body that contains only a comment.

There can be many sets of braces within a function definition, but there must always be at least one set surrounding the function body. Since **main( )** is a function, it must follow these rules. In C++, **main( )** always has return type of **int**.

C and C++ are free form languages. With few exceptions, the compiler ignores newlines and white space, so it must have some way to determine the end of a statement. Statements are delimited by semicolons.

C comments start with /* and end with */. They can include newlines. C++ uses C-style comments and has an additional type of comment: //. The // starts a comment that terminates with a newline. It is more convenient than /* */ for one-line comments, and is used extensively in this book.

"Hello, world!"

And now, finally, the first program:

```
//: C02:Hello.cpp
// Saying Hello with C++
#include <iostream> // Stream declarations
using namespace std;

int main() {
  cout << "Hello, World! I am "
       << 8 << " Today!" << endl;
} ///:~
```

The **cout** object is handed a series of arguments via the '<<' operators. It prints out these arguments in left-to-right order. The special iostream function **endl** outputs the line and a newline. With iostreams, you can string together a series of arguments like this, which makes the class easy to use.

In C, text inside double quotes is traditionally called a "string." However, the Standard C++ library has a powerful class called **string** for manipulating text, and so I shall use the more precise term *character array* for text inside double quotes.

The compiler creates storage for character arrays and stores the ASCII equivalent for each character in this storage. The compiler automatically terminates this array of characters with an extra piece of storage containing the value 0 to indicate the end of the character array.

Inside a character array, you can insert special characters by using *escape sequences*. These consist of a backslash (\) followed by a special code. For example **\n** means newline. Your compiler manual or local C guide gives a complete set of escape sequences; others include **\t** (tab), **** (backslash), and **\b** (backspace).

Notice that the statement can continue over multiple lines, and that the entire statement terminates with a semicolon

Character array arguments and constant numbers are mixed together in the above **cout** statement. Because the operator **<<** is overloaded with a variety of meanings when used with **cout**, you can send **cout** a variety of different arguments and it will "figure out what to do with the message."

Throughout this book you'll notice that the first line of each file will be a comment that starts with the characters that start a comment (typically //), followed by a colon, and the last line of the listing will end with a comment followed by '/:~'. This is a technique I use to allow easy extraction of information from code files (the program to do this can be found in volume two of this book, at *www.BruceEckel.com*). The first line also has the name and location of the file, so it can be referred to in text and in other files, and so you can easily locate it in the source code for this book (which is downloadable from *www.BruceEckel.com*).

Running the compiler

After downloading and unpacking the book's source code, find the program in the subdirectory **CO2**. Invoke the compiler with **Hello.cpp** as the argument. For simple, one-file programs like this one, most compilers will take you all the way through the process. For example, to use the GNU C++ compiler (which is freely available on the Internet), you write:

```
g++ Hello.cpp
```

Other compilers will have a similar syntax; consult your compiler's documentation for details.

More about iostreams

So far you have seen only the most rudimentary aspect of the iostreams class. The output formatting available with iostreams also includes features such as number formatting in decimal, octal, and hexadecimal. Here's another example of the use of iostreams:

```
//: C02:Stream2.cpp
// More streams features
#include <iostream>
using namespace std;

int main() {
  // Specifying formats with manipulators:
  cout << "a number in decimal: "
       << dec << 15 << endl;
  cout << "in octal: " << oct << 15 << endl;
  cout << "in hex: " << hex << 15 << endl;
  cout << "a floating-point number: "
       << 3.14159 << endl;
  cout << "non-printing char (escape): "
       << char(27) << endl;
} ///:~
```

This example shows the iostreams class printing numbers in decimal, octal, and hexadecimal using iostream *manipulators* (which don't print anything, but change the state of the output stream). The formatting of floating-point numbers is determined automatically by the compiler. In addition, any character can be sent to a stream object using a *cast* to a **char** (a **char** is a data type that holds single characters). This *cast* looks like a function call: **char( )**, along with the character's ASCII value. In the program above, the **char(27)** sends an "escape" to **cout**.

Character array concatenation

An important feature of the C preprocessor is *character array concatenation*. This feature is used in some of the examples in this book. If two quoted character arrays are adjacent, and no punctuation is between them, the compiler will paste the character arrays together into a single character array. This is particularly useful when code listings have width restrictions:

```
//: C02:Concat.cpp
// Character array Concatenation
#include <iostream>
using namespace std;

int main() {
  cout << "This is far too long to put on a "
    "single line but it can be broken up with "
    "no ill effects\nas long as there is no "
    "punctuation separating adjacent character "
    "arrays.\n";
} ///:~
```

At first, the code above can look like an error because there's no familiar semicolon at the end of each line. Remember that C and C++ are free-form languages, and although you'll usually see a semicolon at the end of each line, the actual requirement is for a semicolon at the end of each statement, and it's possible for a statement to continue over several lines.

Reading input

The iostreams classes provide the ability to read input. The object used for standard input is **cin** (for "console input"). **cin** normally expects input from the console, but this input can be redirected from other sources. An example of redirection is shown later in this chapter.

The iostreams operator used with **cin** is **>>**. This operator waits for the same kind of input as its argument. For example, if you give it an integer argument, it waits for an integer from the console. Here's an example:

```
//: C02:Numconv.cpp
// Converts decimal to octal and hex
#include <iostream>
using namespace std;

int main() {
  int number;
  cout << "Enter a decimal number: ";
  cin >> number;
  cout << "value in octal = 0"
```

```
        << oct << number << endl;
  cout << "value in hex = 0x"
        << hex << number << endl;
} ///:~
```

This program converts a number typed in by the user into octal and hexadecimal representations.

Calling other programs

While the typical way to use a program that reads from standard input and writes to standard output is within a Unix shell script or DOS batch file, any program can be called from inside a C or C++ program using the Standard C **system( )** function, which is declared in the header file **<cstdlib>**:

```
//: C02:CallHello.cpp
// Call another program
#include <cstdlib> // Declare "system()"
using namespace std;

int main() {
  system("Hello");
} ///:~
```

To use the **system( )** function, you give it a character array that you would normally type at the operating system command prompt. This can also include command-line arguments, and the character array can be one that you fabricate at run time (instead of just using a static character array as shown above). The command executes and control returns to the program.

This program shows you how easy it is to use plain C library functions in C++; just include the header file and call the function. This upward compatibility from C to C++ is a big advantage if you are learning the language starting from a background in C.

Introducing strings

While a character array can be fairly useful, it is quite limited. It's simply a group of characters in memory, but if you want to do anything with it you must manage all the little details. For example, the size of a quoted character array is fixed at compile time. If you have a character array and you want to add some more characters to it, you'll need to understand quite a lot (including dynamic memory management, character array copying, and concatenation) before you can get your wish. This is exactly the kind of thing we'd like to have an object do for us.

The Standard C++ **string** class is designed to take care of (and hide) all the low-level manipulations of character arrays that were previously required of the C programmer. These manipulations have been a constant source of time-wasting and errors since the inception of the C language. So, although an entire chapter is devoted to the **string** class in Volume 2 of this book, the **string** is so important and it makes life so much easier that it will be introduced here and used in much of the early part of the book.

To use **string**s you include the C++ header file **<string>**. The **string** class is in the namespace **std** so a **using** directive is necessary. Because of operator overloading, the syntax for using **string**s is quite intuitive:

```
//: C02:HelloStrings.cpp
// The basics of the Standard C++ string class
#include <string>
#include <iostream>
using namespace std;

int main() {
  string s1, s2; // Empty strings
  string s3 = "Hello, World."; // Initialized
  string s4("I am"); // Also initialized
  s2 = "Today"; // Assigning to a string
  s1 = s3 + " " + s4; // Combining strings
  s1 += " 8 "; // Appending to a string
  cout << s1 + s2 + "!" << endl;
} ///:~
```

The first two **string**s, **s1** and **s2**, start out empty, while **s3** and **s4** show two equivalent ways to initialize **string** objects from character arrays (you can just as easily initialize **string** objects from other **string** objects).

You can assign to any **string** object using '='. This replaces the previous contents of the string with whatever is on the right-hand side, and you don't have to worry about what happens to the previous contents – that's handled automatically for you. To combine **string**s you simply use the '+' operator, which also allows you to combine character arrays with **string**s. If you want to append either a **string** or a character array to another **string**, you can use the operator '+='. Finally, note that iostreams already know what to do with **string**s, so you can just send a **string** (or an expression that produces a **string**, which happens with **s1 + s2 + "!"**) directly to **cout** in order to print it.

Reading and writing files

In C, the process of opening and manipulating files requires a lot of language background to prepare you for the complexity of the operations. However, the C++ iostream library provides a simple way to manipulate files, and so this functionality can be introduced much earlier than it would be in C.

To open files for reading and writing, you must include **<fstream>**. Although this will automatically include **<iostream>**, it's generally prudent to explicitly include **<iostream>** if you're planning to use **cin**, **cout**, etc.

To open a file for reading, you create an **ifstream** object, which then behaves like **cin**. To open a file for writing, you create an **ofstream** object, which then behaves like **cout**. Once you've opened the file, you can read from it or write to it just as you would with any other iostream object. It's that simple (which is, of course, the whole point).

One of the most useful functions in the iostream library is **getline( )**, which allows you to read one line (terminated by a newline) into a **string** object[4]. The first argument is the **ifstream**

---

[4] There are actually a number of variants of **getline( )**, which will be discussed thoroughly in the iostreams chapter in Volume 2.

---

object you're reading from and the second argument is the **string** object. When the function call is finished, the **string** object will contain the line.

Here's a simple example, which copies the contents of one file into another:

```
//: C02:Scopy.cpp
// Copy one file to another, a line at a time
#include <string>
#include <fstream>
using namespace std;

int main() {
  ifstream in("Scopy.cpp"); // Open for reading
  ofstream out("Scopy2.cpp"); // Open for writing
  string s;
  while(getline(in, s)) // Discards newline char
    out << s << "\n"; // ... must add it back
} ///:~
```

To open the files, you just hand the **ifstream** and **ofstream** objects the file names you want to create, as seen above.

There is a new concept introduced here, which is the **while** loop. Although this will be explained in detail in the next chapter, the basic idea is that the expression in parentheses following the **while** controls the execution of the subsequent statement (which can also be multiple statements, wrapped inside curly braces). As long as the expression in parentheses (in this case, **getline(in, s)**) produces a "true" result, then the statement controlled by the **while** will continue to execute. It turns out that **getline( )** will return a value that can be interpreted as "true" if another line has been read successfully, and "false" upon reaching the end of the input. Thus, the above **while** loop reads every line in the input file and sends each line to the output file.

getline( ) reads in the characters of each line until it discovers a newline (the termination character can be changed, but that won't be an issue until the iostreams chapter in Volume 2). However, it discards the newline and doesn't store it in the resulting **string**

---

object. Thus, if we want the copied file to look just like the source file, we must add the newline back in, as shown.

Another interesting example is to copy the entire file into a single **string** object:

```
//: C02:FillString.cpp
// Read an entire file into a single string
#include <string>
#include <iostream>
#include <fstream>
using namespace std;

int main() {
  ifstream in("FillString.cpp");
  string s, line;
  while(getline(in, line))
    s += line + "\n";
  cout << s;
} ///:~
```

Because of the dynamic nature of **string**s, you don't have to worry about how much storage to allocate for a **string**; you can just keep adding things and the **string** will keep expanding to hold whatever you put into it.

One of the nice things about putting an entire file into a **string** is that the **string** class has many functions for searching and manipulation that would then allow you to modify the file as a single string. However, this has its limitations. For one thing, it is often convenient to treat a file as a collection of lines instead of just a big blob of text. For example, if you want to add line numbering it's much easier if you have each line as a separate **string** object. To accomplish this, we'll need another approach.

Introducing vector

With **string**s, we can fill up a **string** object without knowing how much storage we're going to need. The problem with reading lines from a file into individual **string** objects is that you don't know up front how many **string**s you're going to need – you only know after you've read the entire file. To solve this problem, we need some sort of holder that will automatically expand to contain as many **string** objects as we care to put into it.

In fact, why limit ourselves to holding **string** objects? It turns out that this kind of problem – not knowing how many of something you have while you're writing a program – happens a lot. And this "container" object sounds like it would be more useful if it would hold *any kind of object at all!* Fortunately, the Standard C++ Library has a ready-made solution: the standard container classes. The container classes are one of the real powerhouses of Standard C++.

There is often a bit of confusion between the containers and algorithms in the Standard C++ Library, and the entity known as the STL. The Standard Template Library was the name Alex Stepanov (who was working at Hewlett-Packard at the time) used when he presented his library to the C++ Standards Committee at the meeting in San Diego, California in Spring 1994. The name stuck, especially after HP decided to make it available for public downloads. Meanwhile, the committee integrated it into the Standard C++ Library, making a large number of changes. STL's development continues at Silicon Graphics (SGI; see *http://www.sgi.com/Technology/STL*). The SGI STL diverges from the Standard C++ Library on many subtle points. So although it's a popular misconception, the C++ Standard does not "include" the STL. It can be a bit confusing since the containers and algorithms in the Standard C++ Library have the same root (and usually the same names) as the SGI STL. In this book, I will say "The Standard C++ Library" or "The Standard Library containers," or something similar and will avoid the term "STL."

Even though the implementation of the Standard C++ Library containers and algorithms uses some advanced concepts and the full coverage takes two large chapters in Volume 2 of this book, this library can also be potent without knowing a lot about it. It's so useful that the most basic of the standard containers, the **vector**, is introduced in this early chapter and used throughout the book. You'll find that you can do a tremendous amount just by using the basics of **vector** and not worrying about the underlying implementation (again, an important goal of OOP). Since you'll learn much more about this and the other containers when you reach the Standard Library chapters in Volume 2, it seems forgivable if the programs that use **vector** in the early portion of the book aren't exactly what an experienced C++ programmer would do. You'll find that in most cases, the usage shown here is adequate.

The **vector** class is a *template*, which means that it can be efficiently applied to different types. That is, we can create a **vector** of **shape**s, a **vector** of **cat**s, a **vector** of **string**s, etc. Basically, with a template you can create a "class of anything." To tell the compiler what it is that the class will work with (in this case, what the **vector** will hold), you put the name of the desired type in "angle brackets," which means '<' and '>'. So a **vector** of **string** would be denoted **vector<string>**. When you do this, you end up with a customized vector that will hold only **string** objects, and you'll get an error message from the compiler if you try to put anything else into it.

Since **vector** expresses the concept of a "container," there must be a way to put things into the container and get things back out of the container. To add a brand-new element on the end of a **vector**, you use the member function **push_back( ).** (Remember that, since it's a member function, you use a '.' to call it for a particular object.) The reason the name of this member function might seem a bit verbose – **push_back( )** instead of something simpler like "put" – is because there are other containers and other member functions for putting new elements into containers. For example, there is an **insert( )** member function to put something in the middle of a container. **vector** supports this but its use is more complicated and we won't need to explore it until Volume 2 of the book. There's also a **push_front( )** (not part of **vector**) to put things at the beginning. There are many more member functions in **vector** and many more containers in the Standard C++ Library, but you'll be surprised at how much you can do just knowing about a few simple features.

So you can put new elements into a **vector** with **push_back( )**, but how do you get these elements back out again? This solution is more clever and elegant – operator overloading is used to make the **vector** look like an *array*. The array (which will be described more fully in the next chapter) is a data type that is available in virtually every programming language so you should already be somewhat familiar with it. Arrays are *aggregates*, which mean they consist of a number of elements clumped together. The distinguishing characteristic of an array is that these elements are the same size and are arranged to be one right after the other. Most importantly, these elements can be selected by "indexing," which means you can say "I want element number n" and that element will be produced, usually quickly. Although there are exceptions in programming languages, the indexing is normally achieved using square brackets, so if you have an array **a** and you want to produce element five, you say **a[4]** (note that indexing always starts at zero).

This very compact and powerful indexing notation is incorporated into the **vector** using operator overloading, just like '<<' and '>>' were incorporated into iostreams. Again, you don't need to know how the overloading was implemented – that's saved for a later chapter – but it's helpful if you're aware that there's some magic going on under the covers in order to make the **[ ]** work with **vector**.

With that in mind, you can now see a program that uses **vector**. To use a **vector**, you include the header file **<vector>**:

```
//: C02:Fillvector.cpp
// Copy an entire file into a vector of string
#include <string>
#include <iostream>
#include <fstream>
#include <vector>
using namespace std;

int main() {
  vector<string> v;
  ifstream in("Fillvector.cpp");
  string line;
  while(getline(in, line))
    v.push_back(line); // Add the line to the end
  // Add line numbers:
```

```
  for(int i = 0; i < v.size(); i++)
    cout << i << ": " << v[i] << endl;
} ///:~
```

Much of this program is similar to the previous one; a file is opened and lines are read into **string** objects one at a time. However, these **string** objects are pushed onto the back of the **vector v**. Once the **while** loop completes, the entire file is resident in memory, inside **v**.

The next statement in the program is called a **for** loop. It is similar to a **while** loop except that it adds some extra control. After the **for**, there is a "control expression" inside of parentheses, just like the **while** loop. However, this control expression is in three parts: a part which initializes, one that tests to see if we should exit the loop, and one that changes something, typically to step through a sequence of items. This program shows the **for** loop in the way you'll see it most commonly used: the initialization part **int i = 0** creates an integer **i** to use as a loop counter and gives it an initial value of zero. The testing portion says that to stay in the loop, **i** should be less than the number of elements in the **vector v**. (This is produced using the member function **size( )**, which I just sort of slipped in here, but you must admit it has a fairly obvious meaning.) The final portion uses a shorthand for C and C++, the "auto-increment" operator, to add one to the value of **i**. Effectively, **i++** says "get the value of **i**, add one to it, and put the result back into **i**. Thus, the total effect of the **for** loop is to take a variable **i** and march it through the values from zero to one less than the size of the **vector**. For each value of **i**, the **cout** statement is executed and this builds a line that consists of the value of **i** (magically converted to a character array by **cout**), a colon and a space, the line from the file, and a newline provided by **endl**. When you compile and run it you'll see the effect is to add line numbers to the file.

Because of the way that the '>>' operator works with iostreams, you can easily modify the program above so that it breaks up the input into whitespace-separated words instead of lines:

```
//: C02:GetWords.cpp
// Break a file into whitespace-separated words
#include <string>
```

```
#include <iostream>
#include <fstream>
#include <vector>
using namespace std;

int main() {
  vector<string> words;
  ifstream in("GetWords.cpp");
  string word;
  while(in >> word)
    words.push_back(word);
  for(int i = 0; i < words.size(); i++)
    cout << words[i] << endl;
} ///:~
```

The expression

```
while(in >> word)
```

is what gets the input one "word" at a time, and when this
expression evaluates to "false" it means the end of the file has been
reached. Of course, delimiting words by whitespace is quite crude,
but it makes for a simple example. Later in the book you'll see more
sophisticated examples that let you break up input just about any
way you'd like.

To demonstrate how easy it is to use a **vector** with any type, here's
an example that creates a **vector<int>**:

```
//: C02:Intvector.cpp
// Creating a vector that holds integers
#include <iostream>
#include <vector>
using namespace std;

int main() {
  vector<int> v;
  for(int i = 0; i < 10; i++)
    v.push_back(i);
  for(int i = 0; i < v.size(); i++)
    cout << v[i] << ", ";
  cout << endl;
  for(int i = 0; i < v.size(); i++)
    v[i] = v[i] * 10; // Assignment
```

```
    for(int i = 0; i < v.size(); i++)
      cout << v[i] << ", ";
    cout << endl;
} ///:~
```

To create a **vector** that holds a different type, you just put that type in as the template argument (the argument in angle brackets). Templates and well-designed template libraries are intended to be exactly this easy to use.

This example goes on to demonstrate another essential feature of **vector**. In the expression

```
v[i] = v[i] * 10;
```

you can see that the **vector** is not limited to only putting things in and getting things out. You also have the ability to *assign* (and thus to change) to any element of a **vector**, also through the use of the square-brackets indexing operator. This means that **vector** is a general-purpose, flexible "scratchpad" for working with collections of objects, and we will definitely make use of it in coming chapters.

Summary

The intent of this chapter is to show you how easy object-oriented programming can be – *if* someone else has gone to the work of defining the objects for you. In that case, you include a header file, create the objects, and send messages to them. If the types you are using are powerful and well-designed, then you won't have to do much work and your resulting program will also be powerful.

In the process of showing the ease of OOP when using library classes, this chapter also introduced some of the most basic and useful types in the Standard C++ library: the family of iostreams (in particular, those that read from and write to the console and files), the **string** class, and the **vector** template. You've seen how straightforward it is to use these and can now probably imagine many things you can accomplish with them, but there's actually a lot more that they're capable of[5]. Even though we'll only be using a limited subset of the functionality of these tools in the early part of the book, they nonetheless provide a large step up from the primitiveness of learning a low-level language like C. and while learning the low-level aspects of C is educational, it's also time consuming. In the end, you'll be much more productive if you've got objects to manage the low-level issues. After all, the whole *point* of OOP is to hide the details so you can "paint with a bigger brush."

However, as high-level as OOP tries to be, there are some fundamental aspects of C that you can't avoid knowing, and these will be covered in the next chapter.

Exercises

Solutions to selected exercises can be found in the electronic document *The Thinking in C++ Annotated Solution Guide*, available for a small fee from http://www.BruceEckel.com

1.   Modify **Hello.cpp** so that it prints out your name and age (or shoe size, or your dog's age, if that makes you feel better). Compile and run the program.

2.   Using **Stream2.cpp** and **Numconv.cpp** as guidelines, create a program that asks for the radius of a circle and prints the area of that circle. You can just use the '*' operator to square the radius. Do not try to print out the value as octal or hex (these only work with integral types).

3.   Create a program that opens a file and counts the whitespace-separated words in that file.

4.   Create a program that counts the occurrence of a particular word in a file (use the **string** class' operator '==' to find the word).

5.   Change **Fillvector.cpp** so that it prints the lines (backwards) from last to first.

---

[5] If you're particularly eager to see all the things that can be done with these and other Standard library components, see Volume 2 of this book at www.BruceEckel.com, and also www.dinkumware.com.

6. Change **Fillvector.cpp** so that it concatenates all the elements in the **vector** into a single string before printing it out, but don't try to add line numbering.

7. Display a file a line at a time, waiting for the user to press the "Enter" key after each line.

8. Create a **vector<float>** and put 25 floating-point numbers into it using a **for** loop. Display the **vector**.

9. Create three **vector<float>** objects and fill the first two as in the previous exercise. Write a **for** loop that adds each corresponding element in the first two **vector**s and puts the result in the corresponding element of the third **vector**. Display all three **vector**s.

10. Create a **vector<float>** and put 25 numbers into it as in the previous exercises. Now square each number and put the result back into the same location in the **vector**. Display the **vector** before and after the multiplication.

3: The C in C++

Since C++ is based on C, you must be familiar with the syntax of C in order to program in C++, just as you must be reasonably fluent in algebra in order to tackle calculus.

If you've never seen C before, this chapter will give you a decent background in the style of C used in C++. If you are familiar with the style of C described in the first edition of Kernighan & Ritchie (often called K&R C), you will find some new and different features in C++ as well as in Standard C. If you are familiar with Standard C, you should skim through this chapter looking for features that are particular to C++. Note that there are some fundamental C++ features introduced here, which are basic ideas that are akin to the features in C or often modifications to the way that C does things. The more sophisticated C++ features will not be introduced until later chapters.

This chapter is a fairly fast coverage of C constructs and introduction to some basic C++ constructs, with the understanding that you've had some experience programming in another language. A more gentle introduction to C is found in the CD ROM packaged in the back of this book, titled *Thinking in C: Foundations for Java & C++* by Chuck Allison (published by MindView, Inc., and also available at www.MindView.net). This is a seminar on a CD ROM with the goal of taking you carefully through the fundamentals of the C language. It focuses on the knowledge necessary for you to be able to move on to the C++ or Java languages rather than trying to make you an expert in all the dark corners of C (one of the reasons for using a higher-level language like C++ or Java is precisely so we can avoid many of these dark corners). It also contains exercises and guided solutions. Keep in mind that because this chapter goes beyond the *Thinking in C* CD, the CD is not a replacement for this chapter, but should be used instead as a preparation for this chapter and for the book.

Creating functions

In old (pre-Standard) C, you could call a function with any number or type of arguments and the compiler wouldn't complain. Everything seemed fine until you ran the program. You got mysterious results (or worse, the program crashed) with no hints as to why. The lack of help with argument passing and the enigmatic bugs that resulted is probably one reason why C was dubbed a "high-level assembly language." Pre-Standard C programmers just adapted to it.

Standard C and C++ use a feature called *function prototyping*. With function prototyping, you must use a description of the types of arguments when declaring and defining a function. This description is the "prototype." When the function is called, the compiler uses the prototype to ensure that the proper arguments are passed in and that the return value is treated correctly. If the programmer makes a mistake when calling the function, the compiler catches the mistake.

Essentially, you learned about function prototyping (without naming it as such) in the previous chapter, since the form of function declaration in C++ requires proper prototyping. In a function prototype, the argument list contains the types of arguments that must be passed to the function and (optionally for the declaration) identifiers for the arguments. The order and type of the arguments must match in the declaration, definition, and function call. Here's an example of a function prototype in a declaration:

```
int translate(float x, float y, float z);
```

You do not use the same form when declaring variables in function prototypes as you do in ordinary variable definitions. That is, you cannot say: **float x, y, z**. You must indicate the type of *each* argument. In a function declaration, the following form is also acceptable:

```
int translate(float, float, float);
```

Since the compiler doesn't do anything but check for types when the function is called, the identifiers are only included for clarity when someone is reading the code.

In the function definition, names are required because the arguments are referenced inside the function:

```
int translate(float x, float y, float z) {
```

```
    x = y = z;
    // ...
}
```

It turns out this rule applies only to C. In C++, an argument may be unnamed in the argument list of the function definition. Since it is unnamed, you cannot use it in the function body, of course. Unnamed arguments are allowed to give the programmer a way to "reserve space in the argument list." Whoever uses the function must still call the function with the proper arguments. However, the person creating the function can then use the argument in the future without forcing modification of code that calls the function. This option of ignoring an argument in the list is also possible if you leave the name in, but you will get an annoying warning message about the value being unused every time you compile the function. The warning is eliminated if you remove the name.

C and C++ have two other ways to declare an argument list. If you have an empty argument list, you can declare it as **func( )** in C++, which tells the compiler there are exactly zero arguments. You should be aware that this only means an empty argument list in C++. In C it means "an indeterminate number of arguments (which is a "hole" in C since it disables type checking in that case). In both C and C++, the declaration **func(void);** means an empty argument list. The **void** keyword means "nothing" in this case (it can also mean "no type" in the case of pointers, as you'll see later in this chapter).

The other option for argument lists occurs when you don't know how many arguments or what type of arguments you will have; this is called a *variable argument list*. This "uncertain argument list" is represented by ellipses (**...**). Defining a function with a variable argument list is significantly more complicated than defining a regular function. You can use a variable argument list for a function that has a fixed set of arguments if (for some reason) you want to disable the error checks of function prototyping. Because of this, you should restrict your use of variable argument lists to C and avoid them in C++ (in which, as you'll learn, there are much better alternatives). Handling variable argument lists is described in the library section of your local C guide.

Function return values

A C++ function prototype must specify the return value type of the function (in C, if you leave off the return value type it defaults to **int**). The return type specification precedes the function name. To specify that no value is returned, use the **void** keyword. This will generate an error if you try to return a value from the function. Here are some complete function prototypes:

```
int f1(void); // Returns an int, takes no arguments
int f2(); // Like f1() in C++ but not in Standard C!
float f3(float, int, char, double); // Returns a float
void f4(void); // Takes no arguments, returns nothing
```

To return a value from a function, you use the **return** statement. **return** exits the function back to the point right after the function call. If **return** has an argument, that argument becomes the return value of the function. If a function says that it will return a particular type, then each **return** statement must return that type. You can have more than one **return** statement in a function definition:

```
//: C03:Return.cpp
// Use of "return"
#include <iostream>
using namespace std;

char cfunc(int i) {
  if(i == 0)
    return 'a';
  if(i == 1)
    return 'g';
  if(i == 5)
    return 'z';
  return 'c';
}

int main() {
  cout << "type an integer: ";
  int val;
  cin >> val;
  cout << cfunc(val) << endl;
} ///:~
```

In **cfunc( )**, the first **if** that evaluates to **true** exits the function via the **return** statement. Notice that a function declaration is not necessary because the function definition appears before it is used in **main( )**, so the compiler knows about it from that function definition.

Using the C function library

All the functions in your local C function library are available while you are programming in C++. You should look hard at the function library before defining your own function – there's a good chance that someone has already solved your problem for you, and probably given it a lot more thought and debugging.

A word of caution, though: many compilers include a lot of extra functions that make life even easier and are tempting to use, but are not part of the Standard C library. If you are certain you will never want to move the application to another platform (and who is certain of that?), go ahead –use those functions and make your life easier. If you want your application to be portable, you should restrict yourself to Standard library functions. If you must perform platform-specific activities, try to isolate that code in one spot so it can be changed easily when porting to another platform. In C++, platform-specific activities are often encapsulated in a class, which is the ideal solution.

The formula for using a library function is as follows: first, find the function in your programming reference (many programming references will index the function by category as well as alphabetically). The description of the function should include a section that demonstrates the syntax of the code. The top of this section usually has at least one **#include** line, showing you the header file containing the function prototype. Duplicate this **#include** line in your file so the function is properly declared. Now you can call the function in the same way it appears in the syntax section. If you make a mistake, the compiler will discover it by comparing your function call to the function prototype in the header and tell you about your error. The linker searches the Standard library by default, so that's all you need to do: include the header file and call the function.

Creating your own libraries with the librarian

You can collect your own functions together into a library. Most programming packages come with a librarian that manages groups of object modules. Each librarian has its own commands, but the general idea is this: if you want to create a library, make a header file containing the function prototypes for all the functions in your library. Put this header file somewhere in the preprocessor's search path, either in the local directory (so it can be found by **#include "header"**) or in the include directory (so it can be found by **#include <header>**). Now take all the object modules and hand them to the librarian along with a name for the finished library (most librarians require a common extension, such as **.lib** or **.a**). Place the finished library where the other libraries reside so the linker can find it. When you use your library, you will have to add something to the command line so the linker knows to search the library for the functions you call. You must find all the details in your local manual, since they vary from system to system.

Controlling execution

This section covers the execution control statements in C++. You must be familiar with these statements before you can read and write C or C++ code.

C++ uses all of C's execution control statements. These include **if-else**, **while**, **do-while**, **for**, and a selection statement called **switch**. C++ also allows the infamous **goto**, which will be avoided in this book.

True and false

All conditional statements use the truth or falsehood of a conditional expression to determine the execution path. An example of a conditional expression is **A == B**. This uses the conditional operator **==** to see if the variable **A** is equivalent to the variable **B**. The expression produces a Boolean **true** or **false** (these are keywords only in C++; in C an expression is "true" if it evaluates to a nonzero value). Other conditional operators are >, <, >=, etc. Conditional statements are covered more fully later in this chapter.

if-else

The **if-else** statement can exist in two forms: with or without the **else**. The two forms are:

```
if(expression)
    statement
```

or

```
if(expression)
    statement
else
    statement
```

The "expression" evaluates to **true** or **false**. The "statement" means either a simple statement terminated by a semicolon or a compound statement, which is a group of simple statements enclosed in braces. Any time the word "statement" is used, it always implies that the statement is simple or compound. Note that this statement can also be another **if**, so they can be strung together.

```cpp
//: C03:Ifthen.cpp
// Demonstration of if and if-else conditionals
#include <iostream>
using namespace std;

int main() {
  int i;
  cout << "type a number and 'Enter'" << endl;
  cin >> i;
  if(i > 5)
    cout << "It's greater than 5" << endl;
  else
    if(i < 5)
      cout << "It's less than 5 " << endl;
    else
      cout << "It's equal to 5 " << endl;

  cout << "type a number and 'Enter'" << endl;
```

```
    cin >> i;
    if(i < 10)
      if(i > 5)   // "if" is just another statement
        cout << "5 < i < 10" << endl;
      else
        cout << "i <= 5" << endl;
    else // Matches "if(i < 10)"
      cout << "i >= 10" << endl;
  } ///:~
```

It is conventional to indent the body of a control flow statement so the reader may easily determine where it begins and ends[1].

while

while, do-while, and for control looping. A statement repeats until the controlling expression evaluates to **false**. The form of a **while** loop is

```
while(expression)
    statement
```

The expression is evaluated once at the beginning of the loop and again before each further iteration of the statement.

This example stays in the body of the **while** loop until you type the secret number or press control-C.

```
//: C03:Guess.cpp
// Guess a number (demonstrates "while")
#include <iostream>
using namespace std;

int main() {
  int secret = 15;
  int guess = 0;
  // "!=" is the "not-equal" conditional:
  while(guess != secret) { // Compound statement
    cout << "guess the number: ";
```

---

[1] Note that all conventions seem to end after the agreement that some sort of indentation take place. The feud between styles of code formatting is unending. See Appendix A for the description of this book's coding style.

```
    cin >> guess;
  }
  cout << "You guessed it!" << endl;
} ///:~
```

The **while**'s conditional expression is not restricted to a simple test as in the example above; it can be as complicated as you like as long as it produces a **true** or **false** result. You will even see code where the loop has no body, just a bare semicolon:

```
while(/* Do a lot here */)
  ;
```

In these cases, the programmer has written the conditional expression not only to perform the test but also to do the work.

do-while

The form of **do-while** is

```
do
    statement
while(expression);
```

The **do-while** is different from the while because the statement always executes at least once, even if the expression evaluates to false the first time. In a regular **while**, if the conditional is false the first time the statement never executes.

If a **do-while** is used in **Guess.cpp**, the variable **guess** does not need an initial dummy value, since it is initialized by the **cin** statement before it is tested:

```
//: C03:Guess2.cpp
// The guess program using do-while
#include <iostream>
using namespace std;

int main() {
  int secret = 15;
  int guess; // No initialization needed here
  do {
    cout << "guess the number: ";
```

```
    cin >> guess; // Initialization happens
  }   while(guess != secret);
  cout << "You got it!" << endl;
} ///:~
```

For some reason, most programmers tend to avoid **do-while** and just work with **while**.

for

A **for** loop performs initialization before the first iteration. Then it performs conditional testing and, at the end of each iteration, some form of "stepping." The form of the **for** loop is:

```
for(initialization; conditional; step)
    statement
```

Any of the expressions *initialization, conditional,* or *step* may be empty. The *initialization* code executes once at the very beginning. The *conditional* is tested before each iteration (if it evaluates to false at the beginning, the statement never executes). At the end of each loop, the *step* executes.

for loops are usually used for "counting" tasks:

```
//: C03:Charlist.cpp
// Display all the ASCII characters
// Demonstrates "for"
#include <iostream>
using namespace std;

int main() {
  for(int i = 0; i < 128; i = i + 1)
    if (i != 26)  // ANSI Terminal Clear screen
      cout << " value: " << i
           << " character: "
           << char(i) // Type conversion
           << endl;
} ///:~
```

You may notice that the variable **i** is defined at the point where it is used, instead of at the beginning of the block denoted by the open curly brace '**{**'. This is in contrast to traditional procedural languages (including C), which require that all variables be defined at the beginning of the block. This will be discussed later in this chapter.

The break and continue keywords

Inside the body of any of the looping constructs **while, do-while, or for**, you can control the flow of the loop using **break** and **continue**. **break** quits the loop without executing the rest of the statements in the loop. **continue** stops the execution of the current iteration and goes back to the beginning of the loop to begin a new iteration.

As an example of **break** and **continue**, this program is a very simple menu system:

```
//: C03:Menu.cpp
// Simple menu program demonstrating
// the use of "break" and "continue"
#include <iostream>
using namespace std;

int main() {
  char c; // To hold response
  while(true) {
    cout << "MAIN MENU:" << endl;
    cout << "l: left, r: right, q: quit -> ";
    cin >> c;
    if(c == 'q')
      break; // Out of "while(1)"
    if(c == 'l') {
      cout << "LEFT MENU:" << endl;
      cout << "select a or b: ";
      cin >> c;
      if(c == 'a') {
        cout << "you chose 'a'" << endl;
        continue; // Back to main menu
      }
      if(c == 'b') {
        cout << "you chose 'b'" << endl;
        continue; // Back to main menu
      }
      else {
```

```
        cout << "you didn't choose a or b!"
            << endl;
        continue; // Back to main menu
      }
    }
    if(c == 'r') {
      cout << "RIGHT MENU:" << endl;
      cout << "select c or d: ";
      cin >> c;
      if(c == 'c') {
        cout << "you chose 'c'" << endl;
        continue; // Back to main menu
      }
      if(c == 'd') {
        cout << "you chose 'd'" << endl;
        continue; // Back to main menu
      }
      else {
        cout << "you didn't choose c or d!"
            << endl;
        continue; // Back to main menu
      }
    }
    cout << "you must type l or r or q!" << endl;
  }
  cout << "quitting menu..." << endl;
} ///:~
```

If the user selects 'q' in the main menu, the **break** keyword is used to quit, otherwise the program just continues to execute indefinitely. After each of the sub-menu selections, the **continue** keyword is used to pop back up to the beginning of the while loop.

The **while(true)** statement is the equivalent of saying "do this loop forever." The **break** statement allows you to break out of this infinite while loop when the user types a 'q.'

switch

A **switch** statement selects from among pieces of code based on the value of an integral expression. Its form is:

```
switch(selector) {
```

```
      case integral-value1 : statement; break;
      case integral-value2 : statement; break;
      case integral-value3 : statement; break;
      case integral-value4 : statement; break;
      case integral-value5 : statement; break;
      (...)
      default: statement;
}
```

Selector is an expression that produces an integral value. The
switch compares the result of *selector* to each *integral value*. If it
finds a match, the corresponding statement (simple or compound)
executes. If no match occurs, the **default** statement executes.

You will notice in the definition above that each **case** ends with a
break, which causes execution to jump to the end of the **switch**
body (the closing brace that completes the **switch**). This is the
conventional way to build a **switch** statement, but the **break** is
optional. If it is missing, your **case** "drops through" to the one after
it. That is, the code for the following **case** statements execute until
a **break** is encountered. Although you don't usually want this kind
of behavior, it can be useful to an experienced programmer.

The **switch** statement is a clean way to implement multi-way
selection (i.e., selecting from among a number of different
execution paths), but it requires a selector that evaluates to an
integral value at compile-time. If you want to use, for example, a
string object as a selector, it won't work in a **switch** statement.
For a **string** selector, you must instead use a series of **if** statements
and compare the **string** inside the conditional.

The menu example shown above provides a particularly nice
example of a **switch**:

```
//: C03:Menu2.cpp
// A menu using a switch statement
#include <iostream>
using namespace std;

int main() {
  bool quit = false;   // Flag for quitting
  while(quit == false) {
```

```
    cout << "Select a, b, c or q to quit: ";
    char response;
    cin >> response;
    switch(response) {
      case 'a' : cout << "you chose 'a'" << endl;
                 break;
      case 'b' : cout << "you chose 'b'" << endl;
                 break;
      case 'c' : cout << "you chose 'c'" << endl;
                 break;
      case 'q' : cout << "quitting menu" << endl;
                 quit = true;
                 break;
      default  : cout << "Please use a,b,c or q!"
                 << endl;
    }
  }
} ///:~
```

The **quit** flag is a **bool**, short for "Boolean," which is a type you'll find only in C++. It can have only the keyword values **true** or **false**. Selecting 'q' sets the **quit** flag to **true**. The next time the selector is evaluated, **quit == false** returns **false** so the body of the **while** does not execute.

Using and misusing goto

The **goto** keyword is supported in C++, since it exists in C. Using **goto** is often dismissed as poor programming style, and most of the time it is. Anytime you use **goto**, look at your code and see if there's another way to do it. On rare occasions, you may discover **goto** can solve a problem that can't be solved otherwise, but still, consider it carefully. Here's an example that might make a plausible candidate:

```
//: C03:gotoKeyword.cpp
// The infamous goto is supported in C++
#include <iostream>
using namespace std;

int main() {
  long val = 0;
  for(int i = 1; i < 1000; i++) {
    for(int j = 1; j < 100; j += 10) {
```

```
      val = i * j;
      if(val > 47000)
        goto bottom;
        // Break would only go to the outer 'for'
    }
  }
  bottom: // A label
  cout << val << endl;
} ///:~
```

The alternative would be to set a Boolean that is tested in the outer **for** loop, and then do a **break** from the inner for loop. However, if you have several levels of **for** or **while** this could get awkward.

Recursion

Recursion is an interesting and sometimes useful programming technique whereby you call the function that you're in. Of course, if this is all you do, you'll keep calling the function you're in until you run out of memory, so there must be some way to "bottom out" the recursive call. In the following example, this "bottoming out" is accomplished by simply saying that the recursion will go only until the **cat** exceeds 'Z':[2]

```
//: C03:CatsInHats.cpp
// Simple demonstration of recursion
#include <iostream>
using namespace std;

void removeHat(char cat) {
  for(char c = 'A'; c < cat; c++)
    cout << "   ";
  if(cat <= 'Z') {
    cout << "cat " << cat << endl;
    removeHat(cat + 1); // Recursive call
  } else
    cout << "VOOM!!!" << endl;
}

int main() {
```

---

[2] Thanks to Kris C. Matson for suggesting this exercise topic.

```
    removeHat('A');
} ///:~
```

In **removeHat( )**, you can see that as long as **cat** is less than 'Z',
removeHat( ) will be called from *within* **removeHat( )**, thus
effecting the recursion. Each time **removeHat( )** is called, its
argument is one greater than the current **cat** so the argument keeps
increasing.

Recursion is often used when evaluating some sort of arbitrarily
complex problem, since you aren't restricted to a particular "size"
for the solution – the function can just keep recursing until it's
reached the end of the problem.

Introduction to operators

You can think of operators as a special type of function (you'll learn
that C++ operator overloading treats operators precisely that way).
An operator takes one or more arguments and produces a new
value. The arguments are in a different form than ordinary function
calls, but the effect is the same.

From your previous programming experience, you should be
reasonably comfortable with the operators that have been used so
far. The concepts of addition (+), subtraction and unary minus (-),
multiplication (*), division (/), and assignment(=) all have
essentially the same meaning in any programming language. The
full set of operators is enumerated later in this chapter.

Precedence

Operator precedence defines the order in which an expression
evaluates when several different operators are present. C and C++
have specific rules to determine the order of evaluation. The easiest
to remember is that multiplication and division happen before
addition and subtraction. After that, if an expression isn't
transparent to you it probably won't be for anyone reading the code,
so you should use parentheses to make the order of evaluation
explicit. For example:

```
A = X + Y - 2/2 + Z;
```

has a very different meaning from the same statement with a particular grouping of parentheses:

```
A = X + (Y - 2)/(2 + Z);
```

(Try evaluating the result with X = 1, Y = 2, and Z = 3.)

Auto increment and decrement

C, and therefore C++, is full of shortcuts. Shortcuts can make code much easier to type, and sometimes much harder to read. Perhaps the C language designers thought it would be easier to understand a tricky piece of code if your eyes didn't have to scan as large an area of print.

One of the nicer shortcuts is the auto-increment and auto-decrement operators. You often use these to change loop variables, which control the number of times a loop executes.

The auto-decrement operator is '--' and means "decrease by one unit." The auto-increment operator is '++' and means "increase by one unit." If **A** is an **int**, for example, the expression **++A** is equivalent to (**A** = **A** + **1**). Auto-increment and auto-decrement operators produce the value of the variable as a result. If the operator appears before the variable, (i.e., **++A**), the operation is first performed and the resulting value is produced. If the operator appears after the variable (i.e. **A++**), the current value is produced, and then the operation is performed. For example:

```
//: C03:AutoIncrement.cpp
// Shows use of auto-increment
// and auto-decrement operators.
#include <iostream>
using namespace std;

int main() {
  int i = 0;
  int j = 0;
  cout << ++i << endl; // Pre-increment
  cout << j++ << endl; // Post-increment
```

```
  cout << --i << endl; // Pre-decrement
  cout << j-- << endl; // Post decrement
} ///:~
```

If you've been wondering about the name "C++," now you understand. It implies "one step beyond C."

Introduction to data types

Data types define the way you use storage (memory) in the programs you write. By specifying a data type, you tell the compiler how to create a particular piece of storage, and also how to manipulate that storage.

Data types can be built-in or abstract. A built-in data type is one that the compiler intrinsically understands, one that is wired directly into the compiler. The types of built-in data are almost identical in C and C++. In contrast, a user-defined data type is one that you or another programmer create as a class. These are commonly referred to as abstract data types. The compiler knows how to handle built-in types when it starts up; it "learns" how to handle abstract data types by reading header files containing class declarations (you'll learn about this in later chapters).

Basic built-in types

The Standard C specification for built-in types (which C++ inherits) doesn't say how many bits each of the built-in types must contain. Instead, it stipulates the minimum and maximum values that the built-in type must be able to hold. When a machine is based on binary, this maximum value can be directly translated into a minimum number of bits necessary to hold that value. However, if a machine uses, for example, binary-coded decimal (BCD) to represent numbers, then the amount of space in the machine required to hold the maximum numbers for each data type will be different. The minimum and maximum values that can be stored in the various data types are defined in the system header files **limits.h** and **float.h** (in C++ you will generally **#include <climits>** and **<cfloat>** instead).

C and C++ have four basic built-in data types, described here for binary-based machines. A **char** is for character storage and uses a minimum of 8 bits (one byte) of storage, although it may be larger. An **int** stores an integral number and uses a minimum of two bytes of storage. The **float** and **double** types store floating-point numbers, usually in IEEE floating-point format. **float** is for single-precision floating point and **double** is for double-precision floating point.

As mentioned previously, you can define variables anywhere in a scope, and you can define and initialize them at the same time. Here's how to define variables using the four basic data types:

```
//: C03:Basic.cpp
// Defining the four basic data
// types in C and C++

int main() {
  // Definition without initialization:
  char protein;
  int carbohydrates;
  float fiber;
  double fat;
  // Simultaneous definition & initialization:
  char pizza = 'A', pop = 'Z';
  int dongdings = 100, twinkles = 150,
    heehos = 200;
  float chocolate = 3.14159;
  // Exponential notation:
  double fudge_ripple = 6e-4;
} ///:~
```

The first part of the program defines variables of the four basic data types without initializing them. If you don't initialize a variable, the Standard says that its contents are undefined (usually, this means they contain garbage). The second part of the program defines and initializes variables at the same time (it's always best, if possible, to provide an initialization value at the point of definition). Notice the use of exponential notation in the constant 6e-4, meaning "6 times 10 to the minus fourth power."

bool, true, & false

Before **bool** became part of Standard C++, everyone tended to use different techniques in order to produce Boolean-like behavior. These produced portability problems and could introduce subtle errors.

The Standard C++ **bool** type can have two states expressed by the built-in constants **true** (which converts to an integral one) and **false** (which converts to an integral zero). All three names are keywords. In addition, some language elements have been adapted:

Element	Usage with bool
&& || !	Take bool arguments and produce **bool** results.
< > <= >= == !=	Produce **bool** results.
if, **for**, **while**, **do**	Conditional expressions convert to **bool** values.
? :	First operand converts to **bool** value.

Because there's a lot of existing code that uses an **int** to represent a flag, the compiler will implicitly convert from an **int** to a **bool** (nonzero values will produce **true** while zero values produce **false**). Ideally, the compiler will give you a warning as a suggestion to correct the situation.

An idiom that falls under "poor programming style" is the use of ++ to set a flag to true. This is still allowed, but *deprecated*, which means that at some time in the future it will be made illegal. The problem is that you're making an implicit type conversion from **bool** to **int**, incrementing the value (perhaps beyond the range of the normal **bool** values of zero and one), and then implicitly converting it back again.

Pointers (which will be introduced later in this chapter) will also be automatically converted to **bool** when necessary.

Specifiers

Specifiers modify the meanings of the basic built-in types and expand them to a much larger set. There are four specifiers: **long**, **short**, **signed**, and **unsigned**.

long and **short** modify the maximum and minimum values that a data type will hold. A plain **int** must be at least the size of a **short**. The size hierarchy for integral types is: **short int**, **int**, **long int**. All the sizes could conceivably be the same, as long as they satisfy the minimum/maximum value requirements. On a machine with a 64-bit word, for instance, all the data types might be 64 bits.

The size hierarchy for floating point numbers is: **float, double,** and **long double**. "long float" is not a legal type. There are no **short** floating-point numbers.

The **signed** and **unsigned** specifiers tell the compiler how to use the sign bit with integral types and characters (floating-point numbers always contain a sign). An **unsigned** number does not keep track of the sign and thus has an extra bit available, so it can store positive numbers twice as large as the positive numbers that can be stored in a **signed** number. **signed** is the default and is only necessary with **char**; **char** may or may not default to **signed**. By specifying **signed char**, you force the sign bit to be used.

The following example shows the size of the data types in bytes by using the **sizeof** operator, introduced later in this chapter:

```
//: C03:Specify.cpp
// Demonstrates the use of specifiers
#include <iostream>
using namespace std;

int main() {
  char c;
  unsigned char cu;
  int i;
  unsigned int iu;
  short int is;
  short iis; // Same as short int
  unsigned short int isu;
```

```
unsigned short iisu;
long int il;
long iil;    // Same as long int
unsigned long int ilu;
unsigned long iilu;
float f;
double d;
long double ld;
cout
  << "\n char= " << sizeof(c)
  << "\n unsigned char = " << sizeof(cu)
  << "\n int = " << sizeof(i)
  << "\n unsigned int = " << sizeof(iu)
  << "\n short = " << sizeof(is)
  << "\n unsigned short = " << sizeof(isu)
  << "\n long = " << sizeof(il)
  << "\n unsigned long = " << sizeof(ilu)
  << "\n float = " << sizeof(f)
  << "\n double = " << sizeof(d)
  << "\n long double = " << sizeof(ld)
  << endl;
} ///:~
```

Be aware that the results you get by running this program will
probably be different from one machine/operating system/compiler
to the next, since (as mentioned previously) the only thing that
must be consistent is that each different type hold the minimum
and maximum values specified in the Standard.

When you are modifying an **int** with **short** or **long**, the keyword
int is optional, as shown above.

Introduction to pointers

Whenever you run a program, it is first loaded (typically from disk)
into the computer's memory. Thus, all elements of your program
are located somewhere in memory. Memory is typically laid out as a
sequential series of memory locations; we usually refer to these
locations as eight-bit *bytes* but actually the size of each space
depends on the architecture of the particular machine and is usually
called that machine's *word size*. Each space can be uniquely
distinguished from all other spaces by its *address*. For the purposes

---

of this discussion, we'll just say that all machines use bytes that have sequential addresses starting at zero and going up to however much memory you have in your computer.

Since your program lives in memory while it's being run, every element of your program has an address. Suppose we start with a simple program:

```
//: C03:YourPets1.cpp
#include <iostream>
using namespace std;

int dog, cat, bird, fish;

void f(int pet) {
  cout << "pet id number: " << pet << endl;
}

int main() {
  int i, j, k;
} ///:~
```

Each of the elements in this program has a location in storage when the program is running. Even the function occupies storage. As you'll see, it turns out that what an element is and the way you define it usually determines the area of memory where that element is placed.

There is an operator in C and C++ that will tell you the address of an element. This is the '&' operator. All you do is precede the identifier name with '&' and it will produce the address of that identifier. **YourPets1.cpp** can be modified to print out the addresses of all its elements, like this:

```
//: C03:YourPets2.cpp
#include <iostream>
using namespace std;

int dog, cat, bird, fish;

void f(int pet) {
  cout << "pet id number: " << pet << endl;
}
```

```
int main() {
  int i, j, k;
  cout << "f(): " << (long)&f << endl;
  cout << "dog: " << (long)&dog << endl;
  cout << "cat: " << (long)&cat << endl;
  cout << "bird: " << (long)&bird << endl;
  cout << "fish: " << (long)&fish << endl;
  cout << "i: " << (long)&i << endl;
  cout << "j: " << (long)&j << endl;
  cout << "k: " << (long)&k << endl;
} ///:~
```

The **(long)** is a *cast*. It says "Don't treat this as if it's normal type, instead treat it as a **long**." The cast isn't essential, but if it wasn't there, the addresses would have been printed out in hexadecimal instead, so casting to a **long** makes things a little more readable.

The results of this program will vary depending on your computer, OS, and all sorts of other factors, but it will always give you some interesting insights. For a single run on my computer, the results looked like this:

```
f(): 4198736
dog: 4323632
cat: 4323636
bird: 4323640
fish: 4323644
i: 6684160
j: 6684156
k: 6684152
```

You can see how the variables that are defined inside **main( )** are in a different area than the variables defined outside of **main( )**; you'll understand why as you learn more about the language. Also, **f( )** appears to be in its own area; code is typically separated from data in memory.

Another interesting thing to note is that variables defined one right after the other appear to be placed contiguously in memory. They are separated by the number of bytes that are required by their data type. Here, the only data type used is **int**, and **cat** is four bytes away

---

from **dog**, **bird** is four bytes away from **cat**, etc. So it would appear that, on this machine, an **int** is four bytes long.

Other than this interesting experiment showing how memory is mapped out, what can you do with an address? The most important thing you can do is store it inside another variable for later use. C and C++ have a special type of variable that holds an address. This variable is called a *pointer*.

The operator that defines a pointer is the same as the one used for multiplication: '*'. The compiler knows that it isn't multiplication because of the context in which it is used, as you will see.

When you define a pointer, you must specify the type of variable it points to. You start out by giving the type name, then instead of immediately giving an identifier for the variable, you say "Wait, it's a pointer" by inserting a star between the type and the identifier. So a pointer to an **int** looks like this:

```
int* ip; // ip points to an int variable
```

The association of the '*' with the type looks sensible and reads easily, but it can actually be a bit deceiving. Your inclination might be to say "intpointer" as if it is a single discrete type. However, with an **int** or other basic data type, it's possible to say:

```
int a, b, c;
```

whereas with a pointer, you'd *like* to say:

```
int* ipa, ipb, ipc;
```

C syntax (and by inheritance, C++ syntax) does not allow such sensible expressions. In the definitions above, only **ipa** is a pointer, but **ipb** and **ipc** are ordinary **int**s (you can say that "* binds more tightly to the identifier"). Consequently, the best results can be achieved by using only one definition per line; you still get the sensible syntax without the confusion:

```
int* ipa;
int* ipb;
int* ipc;
```

Since a general guideline for C++ programming is that you should always initialize a variable at the point of definition, this form actually works better. For example, the variables above are not initialized to any particular value; they hold garbage. It's much better to say something like:

```
int a = 47;
int* ipa = &a;
```

Now both **a** and **ipa** have been initialized, and **ipa** holds the address of **a**.

Once you have an initialized pointer, the most basic thing you can do with it is to use it to modify the value it points to. To access a variable through a pointer, you *dereference* the pointer using the same operator that you used to define it, like this:

```
*ipa = 100;
```

Now **a** contains the value 100 instead of 47.

These are the basics of pointers: you can hold an address, and you can use that address to modify the original variable. But the question still remains: why do you want to modify one variable using another variable as a proxy?

For this introductory view of pointers, we can put the answer into two broad categories:

1.   To change "outside objects" from within a function. This is perhaps the most basic use of pointers, and it will be examined here.

2.   To achieve many other clever programming techniques, which you'll learn about in portions of the rest of the book.

Modifying the outside object

Ordinarily, when you pass an argument to a function, a copy of that argument is made inside the function. This is referred to as *pass-*

by-value. You can see the effect of pass-by-value in the following program:

```
//: C03:PassByValue.cpp
#include <iostream>
using namespace std;

void f(int a) {
  cout << "a = " << a << endl;
  a = 5;
  cout << "a = " << a << endl;
}

int main() {
  int x = 47;
  cout << "x = " << x << endl;
  f(x);
  cout << "x = " << x << endl;
} ///:~
```

In **f( )**, **a** is a *local variable*, so it exists only for the duration of the function call to **f( )**. Because it's a function argument, the value of **a** is initialized by the arguments that are passed when the function is called; in **main( )** the argument is **x,** which has a value of 47, so this value is copied into **a** when **f( )** is called.

When you run this program you'll see:

```
x = 47
a = 47
a = 5
x = 47
```

Initially, of course, **x** is 47. When **f( )** is called, temporary space is created to hold the variable **a** for the duration of the function call, and **a** is initialized by copying the value of **x**, which is verified by printing it out. Of course, you can change the value of **a** and show that it is changed. But when **f( )** is completed, the temporary space that was created for **a** disappears, and we see that the only connection that ever existed between **a** and **x** happened when the value of **x** was copied into **a**.

When you're inside **f( )**, **x** is the *outside object* (my terminology), and changing the local variable does not affect the outside object, naturally enough, since they are two separate locations in storage. But what if you *do* want to modify the outside object? This is where pointers come in handy. In a sense, a pointer is an alias for another variable. So if we pass a *pointer* into a function instead of an ordinary value, we are actually passing an alias to the outside object, enabling the function to modify that outside object, like this:

```
//: C03:PassAddress.cpp
#include <iostream>
using namespace std;

void f(int* p) {
  cout << "p = " << p << endl;
  cout << "*p = " << *p << endl;
  *p = 5;
  cout << "p = " << p << endl;
}

int main() {
  int x = 47;
  cout << "x = " << x << endl;
  cout << "&x = " << &x << endl;
  f(&x);
  cout << "x = " << x << endl;
} ///:~
```

Now **f( )** takes a pointer as an argument and dereferences the pointer during assignment, and this causes the outside object **x** to be modified. The output is:

```
x = 47
&x = 0065FE00
p = 0065FE00
*p = 47
p = 0065FE00
x = 5
```

Notice that the value contained in **p** is the same as the address of **x** – the pointer **p** does indeed point to **x**. If that isn't convincing enough, when **p** is dereferenced to assign the value 5, we see that the value of **x** is now changed to 5 as well.

Thus, passing a pointer into a function will allow that function to modify the outside object. You'll see plenty of other uses for pointers later, but this is arguably the most basic and possibly the most common use.

Introduction to C++ references

Pointers work roughly the same in C and in C++, but C++ adds an additional way to pass an address into a function. This is *pass-by-reference* and it exists in several other programming languages so it was not a C++ invention.

Your initial perception of references may be that they are unnecessary, that you could write all your programs without references. In general, this is true, with the exception of a few important places that you'll learn about later in the book. You'll also learn more about references later, but the basic idea is the same as the demonstration of pointer use above: you can pass the address of an argument using a reference. The difference between references and pointers is that *calling* a function that takes references is cleaner, syntactically, than calling a function that takes pointers (and it is exactly this syntactic difference that makes references essential in certain situations). If **PassAddress.cpp** is modified to use references, you can see the difference in the function call in **main( )**:

```
//: C03:PassReference.cpp
#include <iostream>
using namespace std;

void f(int& r) {
  cout << "r = " << r << endl;
  cout << "&r = " << &r << endl;
  r = 5;
  cout << "r = " << r << endl;
}

int main() {
  int x = 47;
  cout << "x = " << x << endl;
  cout << "&x = " << &x << endl;
  f(x); // Looks like pass-by-value,
```

```
          // is actually pass by reference
    cout << "x = " << x << endl;
} ///:~
```

In **f( )**'s argument list, instead of saying **int*** to pass a pointer, you say **int&** to pass a reference. Inside **f( )**, if you just say '**r**' (which would produce the address if **r** were a pointer) you get *the value in the variable that* **r** *references*. If you assign to **r**, you actually assign to the variable that **r** references. In fact, the only way to get the address that's held inside **r** is with the '**&**' operator.

In **main( )**, you can see the key effect of references in the syntax of the call to **f( )**, which is just **f(x)**. Even though this looks like an ordinary pass-by-value, the effect of the reference is that it actually takes the address and passes it in, rather than making a copy of the value. The output is:

```
x = 47
&x = 0065FE00
r = 47
&r = 0065FE00
r = 5
x = 5
```

So you can see that pass-by-reference allows a function to modify the outside object, just like passing a pointer does (you can also observe that the reference obscures the fact that an address is being passed; this will be examined later in the book). Thus, for this simple introduction you can assume that references are just a syntactically different way (sometimes referred to as "syntactic sugar") to accomplish the same thing that pointers do: allow functions to change outside objects.

Pointers and references as modifiers

So far, you've seen the basic data types **char, int, float,** and **double**, along with the specifiers **signed, unsigned, short,** and **long**, which can be used with the basic data types in almost any combination. Now we've added pointers and references that are orthogonal to the basic data types and specifiers, so the possible combinations have just tripled:

```
//: C03:AllDefinitions.cpp
// All possible combinations of basic data types,
// specifiers, pointers and references
#include <iostream>
using namespace std;

void f1(char c, int i, float f, double d);
void f2(short int si, long int li, long double ld);
void f3(unsigned char uc, unsigned int ui,
  unsigned short int usi, unsigned long int uli);
void f4(char* cp, int* ip, float* fp, double* dp);
void f5(short int* sip, long int* lip,
  long double* ldp);
void f6(unsigned char* ucp, unsigned int* uip,
  unsigned short int* usip,
  unsigned long int* ulip);
void f7(char& cr, int& ir, float& fr, double& dr);
void f8(short int& sir, long int& lir,
  long double& ldr);
void f9(unsigned char& ucr, unsigned int& uir,
  unsigned short int& usir,
  unsigned long int& ulir);

int main() {} ///:~
```

Pointers and references also work when passing objects into and out of functions; you'll learn about this in a later chapter.

There's one other type that works with pointers: **void**. If you state that a pointer is a **void***, it means that any type of address at all can be assigned to that pointer (whereas if you have an **int***, you can assign only the address of an **int** variable to that pointer). For example:

```
//: C03:VoidPointer.cpp
int main() {
  void* vp;
  char c;
  int i;
  float f;
  double d;
  // The address of ANY type can be
  // assigned to a void pointer:
  vp = &c;
```

```
  vp = &i;
  vp = &f;
  vp = &d;
} ///:~
```

Once you assign to a **void*** you lose any information about what type it is. This means that before you can use the pointer, you must cast it to the correct type:

```
//: C03:CastFromVoidPointer.cpp
int main() {
  int i = 99;
  void* vp = &i;
  // Can't dereference a void pointer:
  // *vp = 3; // Compile-time error
  // Must cast back to int before dereferencing:
  *((int*)vp) = 3;
} ///:~
```

The cast **(int*)vp** takes the **void*** and tells the compiler to treat it as an **int***, and thus it can be successfully dereferenced. You might observe that this syntax is ugly, and it is, but it's worse than that – the **void*** introduces a hole in the language's type system. That is, it allows, or even promotes, the treatment of one type as another type. In the example above, I treat an **int** as an **int** by casting **vp** to an **int***, but there's nothing that says I can't cast it to a **char*** or **double***, which would modify a different amount of storage that had been allocated for the **int**, possibly crashing the program. In general, **void** pointers should be avoided, and used only in rare special cases, the likes of which you won't be ready to consider until significantly later in the book.

You cannot have a **void** reference, for reasons that will be explained in Chapter 11.

Scoping

Scoping rules tell you where a variable is valid, where it is created, and where it gets destroyed (i.e., goes out of scope). The scope of a variable extends from the point where it is defined to the first closing brace that matches the closest opening brace before the variable was defined. That is, a scope is defined by its "nearest" set of braces. To illustrate:

```cpp
//: C03:Scope.cpp
// How variables are scoped
int main() {
  int scp1;
  // scp1 visible here
  {
    // scp1 still visible here
    //.....
    int scp2;
    // scp2 visible here
    //.....
    {
      // scp1 & scp2 still visible here
      //..
      int scp3;
      // scp1, scp2 & scp3 visible here
      // ...
    } // <-- scp3 destroyed here
    // scp3 not available here
    // scp1 & scp2 still visible here
    // ...
  } // <-- scp2 destroyed here
  // scp3 & scp2 not available here
  // scp1 still visible here
  //..
} // <-- scp1 destroyed here
///:~
```

The example above shows when variables are visible and when they are unavailable (that is, when they *go out of scope*). A variable can be used only when inside its scope. Scopes can be nested, indicated by matched pairs of braces inside other matched pairs of braces. Nesting means that you can access a variable in a scope that encloses the scope you are in. In the example above, the variable **scp1** is available inside all of the other scopes, while **scp3** is available only in the innermost scope.

Defining variables on the fly

As noted earlier in this chapter, there is a significant difference between C and C++ when defining variables. Both languages require that variables be defined before they are used, but C (and many other traditional procedural languages) forces you to define all the variables at the beginning of a scope, so that when the compiler creates a block it can allocate space for those variables.

While reading C code, a block of variable definitions is usually the first thing you see when entering a scope. Declaring all variables at the beginning of the block requires the programmer to write in a particular way because of the implementation details of the language. Most people don't know all the variables they are going to use before they write the code, so they must keep jumping back to the beginning of the block to insert new variables, which is awkward and causes errors. These variable definitions don't usually mean much to the reader, and they actually tend to be confusing because they appear apart from the context in which they are used.

C++ (not C) allows you to define variables anywhere in a scope, so you can define a variable right before you use it. In addition, you can initialize the variable at the point you define it, which prevents a certain class of errors. Defining variables this way makes the code much easier to write and reduces the errors you get from being forced to jump back and forth within a scope. It makes the code easier to understand because you see a variable defined in the context of its use. This is especially important when you are defining and initializing a variable at the same time – you can see the meaning of the initialization value by the way the variable is used.

You can also define variables inside the control expressions of **for** loops and **while** loops, inside the conditional of an **if** statement, and inside the selector statement of a **switch**. Here's an example showing on-the-fly variable definitions:

```
//: C03:OnTheFly.cpp
// On-the-fly variable definitions
#include <iostream>
using namespace std;
```

```
int main() {
  //..
  { // Begin a new scope
    int q = 0; // C requires definitions here
    //..
    // Define at point of use:
    for(int i = 0; i < 100; i++) {
      q++; // q comes from a larger scope
      // Definition at the end of the scope:
      int p = 12;
    }
    int p = 1;   // A different p
  } // End scope containing q & outer p
  cout << "Type characters:" << endl;
  while(char c = cin.get() != 'q') {
    cout << c << " wasn't it" << endl;
    if(char x = c == 'a' || c == 'b')
      cout << "You typed a or b" << endl;
    else
      cout << "You typed " << x << endl;
  }
  cout << "Type A, B, or C" << endl;
  switch(int i = cin.get()) {
    case 'A': cout << "Snap" << endl; break;
    case 'B': cout << "Crackle" << endl; break;
    case 'C': cout << "Pop" << endl; break;
    default: cout << "Not A, B or C!" << endl;
  }
} ///:~
```

In the innermost scope, **p** is defined right before the scope ends, so it is really a useless gesture (but it shows you can define a variable anywhere). The **p** in the outer scope is in the same situation.

The definition of **i** in the control expression of the **for** loop is an example of being able to define a variable *exactly* at the point you need it (you can do this only in C++). The scope of **i** is the scope of the expression controlled by the **for** loop, so you can turn around and re-use **i** in the next **for** loop. This is a convenient and commonly-used idiom in C++; **i** is the classic name for a loop counter and you don't have to keep inventing new names.

Although the example also shows variables defined within **while**, **if,** and **switch** statements, this kind of definition is much less common than those in **for** expressions, possibly because the syntax is so constrained. For example, you cannot have any parentheses. That is, you cannot say:

```
while((char c = cin.get()) != 'q')
```

The addition of the extra parentheses would seem like an innocent and useful thing to do, and because you cannot use them, the results are not what you might like. The problem occurs because '!=' has a higher precedence than '=', so the **char c** ends up containing a **bool** converted to **char**. When that's printed, on many terminals you'll see a smiley-face character.

In general, you can consider the ability to define variables within **while**, **if**, and **switch** statements as being there for completeness, but the only place you're likely to use this kind of variable definition is in a **for** loop (where you'll use it quite often).

Specifying storage allocation

When creating a variable, you have a number of options to specify the lifetime of the variable, how the storage is allocated for that variable, and how the variable is treated by the compiler.

Global variables

Global variables are defined outside all function bodies and are available to all parts of the program (even code in other files). Global variables are unaffected by scopes and are always available (i.e., the lifetime of a global variable lasts until the program ends). If the existence of a global variable in one file is declared using the **extern** keyword in another file, the data is available for use by the second file. Here's an example of the use of global variables:

```
//: C03:Global.cpp
//{L} Global2
// Demonstration of global variables
#include <iostream>
```

```
using namespace std;

int globe;
void func();
int main() {
  globe = 12;
  cout << globe << endl;
  func(); // Modifies globe
  cout << globe << endl;
} ///:~
```

Here's a file that accesses **globe** as an **extern**:

```
//: C03:Global2.cpp {O}
// Accessing external global variables
extern int globe;
// (The linker resolves the reference)
void func() {
  globe = 47;
} ///:~
```

Storage for the variable **globe** is created by the definition in **Global.cpp**, and that same variable is accessed by the code in **Global2.cpp**. Since the code in **Global2.cpp** is compiled separately from the code in **Global.cpp**, the compiler must be informed that the variable exists elsewhere by the declaration

```
extern int globe;
```

When you run the program, you'll see that the call to **func( )** does indeed affect the single global instance of **globe**.

In **Global.cpp**, you can see the special comment tag (which is my own design):

```
//{L} Global2
```

This says that to create the final program, the object file with the name **Global2** must be linked in (there is no extension because the extension names of object files differ from one system to the next). In **Global2.cpp**, the first line has another special comment tag {O}, which says "Don't try to create an executable out of this file, it's being compiled so that it can be linked into some other

```
```

executable." The **ExtractCode.cpp** program in Volume 2 of this book (downloadable at *www.BruceEckel.com*) reads these tags and creates the appropriate **makefile** so everything compiles properly (you'll learn about **makefile**s at the end of this chapter).

Local variables

Local variables occur within a scope; they are "local" to a function. They are often called *automatic* variables because they automatically come into being when the scope is entered and automatically go away when the scope closes. The keyword **auto** makes this explicit, but local variables default to **auto** so it is never necessary to declare something as an **auto**.

Register variables

A register variable is a type of local variable. The **register** keyword tells the compiler "Make accesses to this variable as fast as possible." Increasing the access speed is implementation dependent, but, as the name suggests, it is often done by placing the variable in a register. There is no guarantee that the variable will be placed in a register or even that the access speed will increase. It is a hint to the compiler.

There are restrictions to the use of **register** variables. You cannot take or compute the address of a **register** variable. A **register** variable can be declared only within a block (you cannot have global or **static register** variables). You can, however, use a **register** variable as a formal argument in a function (i.e., in the argument list).

In general, you shouldn't try to second-guess the compiler's optimizer, since it will probably do a better job than you can. Thus, the **register** keyword is best avoided.

static

The **static** keyword has several distinct meanings. Normally, variables defined local to a function disappear at the end of the function scope. When you call the function again, storage for the variables is created anew and the values are re-initialized. If you want a value to be extant throughout the life of a program, you can define a function's local variable to be **static** and give it an initial value. The initialization is performed only the first time the function is called, and the data retains its value between function calls. This way, a function can "remember" some piece of information between function calls.

You may wonder why a global variable isn't used instead. The beauty of a **static** variable is that it is unavailable outside the scope of the function, so it can't be inadvertently changed. This localizes errors.

Here's an example of the use of **static** variables:

```
//: C03:Static.cpp
// Using a static variable in a function
#include <iostream>
using namespace std;

void func() {
  static int i = 0;
  cout << "i = " << ++i << endl;
}

int main() {
  for(int x = 0; x < 10; x++)
    func();
} ///:~
```

Each time **func( )** is called in the for loop, it prints a different value. If the keyword **static** is not used, the value printed will always be '1'.

The second meaning of **static** is related to the first in the "unavailable outside a certain scope" sense. When **static** is applied to a function name or to a variable that is outside of all functions, it means "This name is unavailable outside of this file." The function name or variable is local to the file; we say it has *file scope*. As a demonstration, compiling and linking the following two files will cause a linker error:

```
//: C03:FileStatic.cpp
```

```
// File scope demonstration. Compiling and
// linking this file with FileStatic2.cpp
// will cause a linker error

// File scope means only available in this file:
static int fs;

int main() {
  fs = 1;
} ///:~
```

Even though the variable **fs** is claimed to exist as an **extern** in the following file, the linker won't find it because it has been declared **static** in **FileStatic.cpp**.

```
//: C03:FileStatic2.cpp {O}
// Trying to reference fs
extern int fs;
void func() {
  fs = 100;
} ///:~
```

The **static** specifier may also be used inside a **class**. This explanation will be delayed until you learn to create classes, later in the book.

extern

The **extern** keyword has already been briefly described and demonstrated. It tells the compiler that a variable or a function exists, even if the compiler hasn't yet seen it in the file currently being compiled. This variable or function may be defined in another file or further down in the current file. As an example of the latter:

```
//: C03:Forward.cpp
// Forward function & data declarations
#include <iostream>
using namespace std;

// This is not actually external, but the
// compiler must be told it exists somewhere:
extern int i;
extern void func();
```

```
int main() {
  i = 0;
  func();
}
int i; // The data definition
void func() {
  i++;
  cout << i;
} ///:~
```

When the compiler encounters the declaration 'extern int i', it knows that the definition for i must exist somewhere as a global variable. When the compiler reaches the definition of i, no other declaration is visible, so it knows it has found the same i declared earlier in the file. If you were to define i as static, you would be telling the compiler that i is defined globally (via the extern), but it also has file scope (via the static), so the compiler will generate an error.

Linkage

To understand the behavior of C and C++ programs, you need to know about *linkage*. In an executing program, an identifier is represented by storage in memory that holds a variable or a compiled function body. Linkage describes this storage as it is seen by the linker. There are two types of linkage: *internal linkage* and *external linkage*.

Internal linkage means that storage is created to represent the identifier only for the file being compiled. Other files may use the same identifier name with internal linkage, or for a global variable, and no conflicts will be found by the linker – separate storage is created for each identifier. Internal linkage is specified by the keyword static in C and C++.

External linkage means that a single piece of storage is created to represent the identifier for all files being compiled. The storage is created once, and the linker must resolve all other references to that storage. Global variables and function names have external linkage. These are accessed from other files by declaring them with the keyword extern. Variables defined outside all functions (with the exception of const in C++) and function definitions default to external linkage. You can specifically force them to have internal linkage using the **static** keyword. You can explicitly state that an identifier has external linkage by defining it with the **extern** keyword. Defining a variable or function with **extern** is not necessary in C, but it is sometimes necessary for **const** in C++.

Automatic (local) variables exist only temporarily, on the stack, while a function is being called. The linker doesn't know about automatic variables, and so these have *no linkage.*

Constants

In old (pre-Standard) C, if you wanted to make a constant, you had to use the preprocessor:

```
#define PI 3.14159
```

Everywhere you used **PI**, the value 3.14159 was substituted by the preprocessor (you can still use this method in C and C++).

When you use the preprocessor to create constants, you place control of those constants outside the scope of the compiler. No type checking is performed on the name **PI** and you can't take the address of **PI** (so you can't pass a pointer or a reference to **PI**). **PI** cannot be a variable of a user-defined type. The meaning of **PI** lasts from the point it is defined to the end of the file; the preprocessor doesn't recognize scoping.

C++ introduces the concept of a named constant that is just like a variable, except that its value cannot be changed. The modifier **const** tells the compiler that a name represents a constant. Any data type, built-in or user-defined, may be defined as **const**. If you define something as **const** and then attempt to modify it, the compiler will generate an error.

You must specify the type of a **const**, like this:

```
const int x = 10;
```

In Standard C and C++, you can use a named constant in an argument list, even if the argument it fills is a pointer or a reference

---

(i.e., you can take the address of a **const**). A **const** has a scope, just like a regular variable, so you can "hide" a **const** inside a function and be sure that the name will not affect the rest of the program.

The **const** was taken from C++ and incorporated into Standard C, albeit quite differently. In C, the compiler treats a **const** just like a variable that has a special tag attached that says "Don't change me." When you define a **const** in C, the compiler creates storage for it, so if you define more than one **const** with the same name in two different files (or put the definition in a header file), the linker will generate error messages about conflicts. The intended use of **const** in C is quite different from its intended use in C++ (in short, it's nicer in C++).

Constant values

In C++, a **const** must always have an initialization value (in C, this is not true). Constant values for built-in types are expressed as decimal, octal, hexadecimal, or floating-point numbers (sadly, binary numbers were not considered important), or as characters.

In the absence of any other clues, the compiler assumes a constant value is a decimal number. The numbers 47, 0, and 1101 are all treated as decimal numbers.

A constant value with a leading 0 is treated as an octal number (base 8). Base 8 numbers can contain only digits 0-7; the compiler flags other digits as an error. A legitimate octal number is 017 (15 in base 10).

A constant value with a leading 0x is treated as a hexadecimal number (base 16). Base 16 numbers contain the digits 0-9 and a-f or A-F. A legitimate hexadecimal number is 0x1fe (510 in base 10).

Floating point numbers can contain decimal points and exponential powers (represented by e, which means "10 to the power of"). Both the decimal point and the **e** are optional. If you assign a constant to a floating-point variable, the compiler will take the constant value and convert it to a floating-point number (this process is one form of what's called *implicit type conversion*). However, it is a good idea to use either a decimal point or an **e** to remind the reader that you are using a floating-point number; some older compilers also need the hint.

Legitimate floating-point constant values are: 1e4, 1.0001, 47.0, 0.0, and -1.159e-77. You can add suffixes to force the type of floating-point number: **f** or **F** forces a **float**, **L** or **l** forces a **long double**; otherwise the number will be a **double**.

Character constants are characters surrounded by single quotes, as: '**A**', '**O**', ' '. Notice there is a big difference between the character '**O**' (ASCII 96) and the value **O**. Special characters are represented with the "backslash escape": '**\n**' (newline), '**\t**' (tab), '****' (backslash), '**\r**' (carriage return), '**\"**' (double quotes), '**\'**' (single quote), etc. You can also express char constants in octal: '**\17**' or hexadecimal: '**\xff**'.

volatile

Whereas the qualifier **const** tells the compiler "This never changes" (which allows the compiler to perform extra optimizations), the qualifier **volatile** tells the compiler "You never know when this will change," and prevents the compiler from performing any optimizations based on the stability of that variable. Use this keyword when you read some value outside the control of your code, such as a register in a piece of communication hardware. A **volatile** variable is always read whenever its value is required, even if it was just read the line before.

A special case of some storage being "outside the control of your code" is in a multithreaded program. If you're watching a particular flag that is modified by another thread or process, that flag should be **volatile** so the compiler doesn't make the assumption that it can optimize away multiple reads of the flag.

Note that **volatile** may have no effect when a compiler is not optimizing, but may prevent critical bugs when you start optimizing the code (which is when the compiler will begin looking for redundant reads).

The **const** and **volatile** keywords will be further illuminated in a later chapter.

Operators and their use

This section covers all the operators in C and C++.

All operators produce a value from their operands. This value is produced without modifying the operands, except with the assignment, increment, and decrement operators. Modifying an operand is called a *side effect*. The most common use for operators that modify their operands is to generate the side effect, but you should keep in mind that the value produced is available for your use just as in operators without side effects.

Assignment

Assignment is performed with the operator =. It means "Take the right-hand side (often called the *rvalue*) and copy it into the left-hand side (often called the *lvalue*)." An rvalue is any constant, variable, or expression that can produce a value, but an lvalue must be a distinct, named variable (that is, there must be a physical space in which to store data). For instance, you can assign a constant value to a variable (**A = 4;**), but you cannot assign anything to constant value – it cannot be an lvalue (you can't say **4 = A;**).

Mathematical operators

The basic mathematical operators are the same as the ones available in most programming languages: addition (**+**), subtraction (**-**), division (**/**), multiplication (*****), and modulus (**%**; this produces the remainder from integer division). Integer division truncates the result (it doesn't round). The modulus operator cannot be used with floating-point numbers.

C and C++ also use a shorthand notation to perform an operation and an assignment at the same time. This is denoted by an operator followed by an equal sign, and is consistent with all the operators in the language (whenever it makes sense). For example, to add 4 to the variable **x** and assign **x** to the result, you say: **x += 4;**.

This example shows the use of the mathematical operators:

```
//: C03:Mathops.cpp
// Mathematical operators
#include <iostream>
using namespace std;

// A macro to display a string and a value.
#define PRINT(STR, VAR) \
  cout << STR " = " << VAR << endl

int main() {
  int i, j, k;
  float u, v, w;  // Applies to doubles, too
  cout << "enter an integer: ";
  cin >> j;
  cout << "enter another integer: ";
  cin >> k;
  PRINT("j",j);  PRINT("k",k);
  i = j + k; PRINT("j + k",i);
  i = j - k; PRINT("j - k",i);
  i = k / j; PRINT("k / j",i);
  i = k * j; PRINT("k * j",i);
  i = k % j; PRINT("k % j",i);
  // The following only works with integers:
  j %= k; PRINT("j %= k", j);
  cout << "Enter a floating-point number: ";
  cin >> v;
  cout << "Enter another floating-point number:";
  cin >> w;
  PRINT("v",v); PRINT("w",w);
  u = v + w; PRINT("v + w", u);
  u = v - w; PRINT("v - w", u);
  u = v * w; PRINT("v * w", u);
  u = v / w; PRINT("v / w", u);
  // The following works for ints, chars,
  // and doubles too:
  PRINT("u", u); PRINT("v", v);
  u += v; PRINT("u += v", u);
  u -= v; PRINT("u -= v", u);
  u *= v; PRINT("u *= v", u);
  u /= v; PRINT("u /= v", u);
} ///:~
```

The rvalues of all the assignments can, of course, be much more complex.

Introduction to preprocessor macros

Notice the use of the macro **PRINT( )** to save typing (and typing errors!). Preprocessor macros are traditionally named with all uppercase letters so they stand out – you'll learn later that macros can quickly become dangerous (and they can also be very useful).

The arguments in the parenthesized list following the macro name are substituted in all the code following the closing parenthesis. The preprocessor removes the name **PRINT** and substitutes the code wherever the macro is called, so the compiler cannot generate any error messages using the macro name, and it doesn't do any type checking on the arguments (the latter can be beneficial, as shown in the debugging macros at the end of the chapter).

Relational operators

Relational operators establish a relationship between the values of the operands. They produce a Boolean (specified with the **bool** keyword in C++) **true** if the relationship is true, and **false** if the relationship is false. The relational operators are: less than (<), greater than (>), less than or equal to (<=), greater than or equal to (>=), equivalent (==), and not equivalent (!=). They may be used with all built-in data types in C and C++. They may be given special definitions for user-defined data types in C++ (you'll learn about this in Chapter 12, which covers operator overloading).

Logical operators

The logical operators *and* (**&&**) and *or* (**||**) produce a **true** or **false** based on the logical relationship of its arguments. Remember that in C and C++, a statement is **true** if it has a non-zero value, and **false** if it has a value of zero. If you print a **bool**, you'll typically see a '**1**' for **true** and '**0**' for **false**.

This example uses the relational and logical operators:

```
//: C03:Boolean.cpp
// Relational and logical operators.
#include <iostream>
using namespace std;
```

```
int main() {
  int i,j;
  cout << "Enter an integer: ";
  cin >> i;
  cout << "Enter another integer: ";
  cin >> j;
  cout << "i > j is " << (i > j) << endl;
  cout << "i < j is " << (i < j) << endl;
  cout << "i >= j is " << (i >= j) << endl;
  cout << "i <= j is " << (i <= j) << endl;
  cout << "i == j is " << (i == j) << endl;
  cout << "i != j is " << (i != j) << endl;
  cout << "i && j is " << (i && j) << endl;
  cout << "i || j is " << (i || j) << endl;
  cout << " (i < 10) && (j < 10) is "
       << ((i < 10) && (j < 10))  << endl;
} ///:~
```

You can replace the definition for **int** with **float** or **double** in the
program above. Be aware, however, that the comparison of a
floating-point number with the value of zero is strict; a number that
is the tiniest fraction different from another number is still "not
equal." A floating-point number that is the tiniest bit above zero is
still true.

Bitwise operators

The bitwise operators allow you to manipulate individual bits in a
number (since floating point values use a special internal format,
the bitwise operators work only with integral types: **char**, **int** and
long). Bitwise operators perform Boolean algebra on the
corresponding bits in the arguments to produce the result.

The bitwise *and* operator (**&**) produces a one in the output bit if
both input bits are one; otherwise it produces a zero. The bitwise or
operator (**|**) produces a one in the output bit if either input bit is a
one and produces a zero only if both input bits are zero. The bitwise
exclusive or, or *xor* (**^**) produces a one in the output bit if one or
the other input bit is a one, but not both. The bitwise *not* (**~**, also
called the *ones complement* operator) is a unary operator – it only
takes one argument (all other bitwise operators are binary

operators). Bitwise *not* produces the opposite of the input bit – a one if the input bit is zero, a zero if the input bit is one.

Bitwise operators can be combined with the = sign to unite the operation and assignment: &=, |=, and ^= are all legitimate operations (since ~ is a unary operator it cannot be combined with the = sign).

Shift operators

The shift operators also manipulate bits. The left-shift operator (<<) produces the operand to the left of the operator shifted to the left by the number of bits specified after the operator. The right-shift operator (>>) produces the operand to the left of the operator shifted to the right by the number of bits specified after the operator. If the value after the shift operator is greater than the number of bits in the left-hand operand, the result is undefined. If the left-hand operand is unsigned, the right shift is a logical shift so the upper bits will be filled with zeros. If the left-hand operand is signed, the right shift may or may not be a logical shift (that is, the behavior is undefined).

Shifts can be combined with the equal sign (<<= and >>=). The lvalue is replaced by the lvalue shifted by the rvalue.

What follows is an example that demonstrates the use of all the operators involving bits. First, here's a general-purpose function that prints a byte in binary format, created separately so that it may be easily reused. The header file declares the function:

```
//: C03:printBinary.h
// Display a byte in binary
void printBinary(const unsigned char val);
///:~
```

Here's the implementation of the function:

```
//: C03:printBinary.cpp {O}
#include <iostream>
void printBinary(const unsigned char val) {
  for(int i = 7; i >= 0; i--)
```

```
    if(val & (1 << i))
      std::cout << "1";
    else
      std::cout << "0";
} ///:~
```

The **printBinary( )** function takes a single byte and displays it bit-by-bit. The expression

```
(1 << i)
```

produces a one in each successive bit position; in binary: 00000001, 00000010, etc. If this bit is bitwise *and*ed with **val** and the result is nonzero, it means there was a one in that position in **val**.

Finally, the function is used in the example that shows the bit-manipulation operators:

```
//: C03:Bitwise.cpp
//{L} printBinary
// Demonstration of bit manipulation
#include "printBinary.h"
#include <iostream>
using namespace std;

// A macro to save typing:
#define PR(STR, EXPR) \
  cout << STR; printBinary(EXPR); cout << endl;

int main() {
  unsigned int getval;
  unsigned char a, b;
  cout << "Enter a number between 0 and 255: ";
  cin >> getval; a = getval;
  PR("a in binary: ", a);
  cout << "Enter a number between 0 and 255: ";
  cin >> getval; b = getval;
  PR("b in binary: ", b);
  PR("a | b = ", a | b);
  PR("a & b = ", a & b);
  PR("a ^ b = ", a ^ b);
  PR("~a = ", ~a);
  PR("~b = ", ~b);
```

```
  // An interesting bit pattern:
  unsigned char c = 0x5A;
  PR("c in binary: ", c);
  a |= c;
  PR("a |= c; a = ", a);
  b &= c;
  PR("b &= c; b = ", b);
  b ^= a;
  PR("b ^= a; b = ", b);
} ///:~
```

Once again, a preprocessor macro is used to save typing. It prints the string of your choice, then the binary representation of an expression, then a newline.

In **main( )**, the variables are **unsigned**. This is because, in general, you don't want signs when you are working with bytes. An **int** must be used instead of a **char** for **getval** because the "**cin >>**" statement will otherwise treat the first digit as a character. By assigning **getval** to **a** and **b**, the value is converted to a single byte (by truncating it).

The << and >> provide bit-shifting behavior, but when they shift bits off the end of the number, those bits are lost (it's commonly said that they fall into the mythical *bit bucket*, a place where discarded bits end up, presumably so they can be reused...). When manipulating bits you can also perform *rotation*, which means that the bits that fall off one end are inserted back at the other end, as if they're being rotated around a loop. Even though most computer processors provide a machine-level rotate command (so you'll see it in the assembly language for that processor), there is no direct support for "rotate" in C or C++. Presumably the designers of C felt justified in leaving "rotate" off (aiming, as they said, for a minimal language) because you can build your own rotate command. For example, here are functions to perform left and right rotations:

```
//: C03:Rotation.cpp {O}
// Perform left and right rotations

unsigned char rol(unsigned char val) {
  int highbit;
  if(val & 0x80) // 0x80 is the high bit only
```

```
      highbit = 1;
   else
      highbit = 0;
   // Left shift (bottom bit becomes 0):
   val <<= 1;
   // Rotate the high bit onto the bottom:
   val |= highbit;
   return val;
}

unsigned char ror(unsigned char val) {
   int lowbit;
   if(val & 1) // Check the low bit
      lowbit = 1;
   else
      lowbit = 0;
   val >>= 1; // Right shift by one position
   // Rotate the low bit onto the top:
   val |= (lowbit << 7);
   return val;
} ///:~
```

Try using these functions in **Bitwise.cpp**. Notice the definitions (or at least declarations) of **rol( )** and **ror( )** must be seen by the compiler in **Bitwise.cpp** before the functions are used.

The bitwise functions are generally extremely efficient to use because they translate directly into assembly language statements. Sometimes a single C or C++ statement will generate a single line of assembly code.

Unary operators

Bitwise *not* isn't the only operator that takes a single argument. Its companion, the *logical not* (!), will take a **true** value and produce a **false** value. The unary minus (-) and unary plus (+) are the same operators as binary minus and plus; the compiler figures out which usage is intended by the way you write the expression. For instance, the statement

```
x = -a;
```

has an obvious meaning. The compiler can figure out:

```
x = a * -b;
```

but the reader might get confused, so it is safer to say:

```
x = a * (-b);
```

The unary minus produces the negative of the value. Unary plus provides symmetry with unary minus, although it doesn't actually do anything.

The increment and decrement operators (++ and --) were introduced earlier in this chapter. These are the only operators other than those involving assignment that have side effects. These operators increase or decrease the variable by one unit, although "unit" can have different meanings according to the data type – this is especially true with pointers.

The last unary operators are the address-of (**&**), dereference (* and ->), and cast operators in C and C++, and **new** and **delete** in C++. Address-of and dereference are used with pointers, described in this chapter. Casting is described later in this chapter, and **new** and **delete** are introduced in Chapter 4.

The ternary operator

The ternary **if-else** is unusual because it has three operands. It is truly an operator because it produces a value, unlike the ordinary **if-else** statement. It consists of three expressions: if the first expression (followed by a **?**) evaluates to **true**, the expression following the **?** is evaluated and its result becomes the value produced by the operator. If the first expression is **false**, the third expression (following a **:**) is executed and its result becomes the value produced by the operator.

The conditional operator can be used for its side effects or for the value it produces. Here's a code fragment that demonstrates both:

```
a = --b ? b : (b = -99);
```

Here, the conditional produces the rvalue. **a** is assigned to the value of **b** if the result of decrementing **b** is nonzero. If **b** became zero, **a** and **b** are both assigned to -99. **b** is always decremented, but it is assigned to -99 only if the decrement causes **b** to become 0. A similar statement can be used without the "**a =**" just for its side effects:

```
--b ? b : (b = -99);
```

Here the second B is superfluous, since the value produced by the operator is unused. An expression is required between the **?** and **:**. In this case, the expression could simply be a constant that might make the code run a bit faster.

The comma operator

The comma is not restricted to separating variable names in multiple definitions, such as

```
int i, j, k;
```

Of course, it's also used in function argument lists. However, it can also be used as an operator to separate expressions – in this case it produces only the value of the last expression. All the rest of the expressions in the comma-separated list are evaluated only for their side effects. This example increments a list of variables and uses the last one as the rvalue:

```
//: C03:CommaOperator.cpp
#include <iostream>
using namespace std;
int main() {
  int a = 0, b = 1, c = 2, d = 3, e = 4;
  a = (b++, c++, d++, e++);
  cout << "a = " << a << endl;
  // The parentheses are critical here. Without
  // them, the statement will evaluate to:
  (a = b++), c++, d++, e++;
  cout << "a = " << a << endl;
} ///:~
```

In general, it's best to avoid using the comma as anything other than a separator, since people are not used to seeing it as an operator.

Common pitfalls when using operators

As illustrated above, one of the pitfalls when using operators is trying to get away without parentheses when you are even the least bit uncertain about how an expression will evaluate (consult your local C manual for the order of expression evaluation).

Another extremely common error looks like this:

```
//: C03:Pitfall.cpp
// Operator mistakes

int main() {
  int a = 1, b = 1;
  while(a = b) {
    // ....
  }
} ///:~
```

The statement **a = b** will always evaluate to true when **b** is non-zero. The variable **a** is assigned to the value of **b**, and the value of **b** is also produced by the operator =. In general, you want to use the equivalence operator == inside a conditional statement, not assignment. This one bites a lot of programmers (however, some compilers will point out the problem to you, which is helpful).

A similar problem is using bitwise *and* and *or* instead of their logical counterparts. Bitwise *and* and *or* use one of the characters (**&** or **|**), while logical *and* and *or* use two (**&&** and **||**). Just as with = and ==, it's easy to just type one character instead of two. A useful mnemonic device is to observe that "Bits are smaller, so they don't need as many characters in their operators."

Casting operators

The word *cast* is used in the sense of "casting into a mold." The compiler will automatically change one type of data into another if it makes sense. For instance, if you assign an integral value to a floating-point variable, the compiler will secretly call a function (or more probably, insert code) to convert the **int** to a **float**. Casting allows you to make this type conversion explicit, or to force it when it wouldn't normally happen.

To perform a cast, put the desired data type (including all modifiers) inside parentheses to the left of the value. This value can be a variable, a constant, the value produced by an expression, or the return value of a function. Here's an example:

```
//: C03:SimpleCast.cpp
int main() {
  int b = 200;
  unsigned long a = (unsigned long int)b;
} ///:~
```

Casting is powerful, but it can cause headaches because in some situations it forces the compiler to treat data as if it were (for instance) larger than it really is, so it will occupy more space in memory; this can trample over other data. This usually occurs when casting pointers, not when making simple casts like the one shown above.

C++ has an additional casting syntax, which follows the function call syntax. This syntax puts the parentheses around the argument, like a function call, rather than around the data type:

```
//: C03:FunctionCallCast.cpp
int main() {
  float a = float(200);
  // This is equivalent to:
  float b = (float)200;
} ///:~
```

Of course in the case above you wouldn't really need a cast; you could just say **200f** (in effect, that's typically what the compiler will do for the above expression). Casts are generally used instead with variables, rather than constants.

C++ explicit casts

Casts should be used carefully, because what you are actually doing is saying to the compiler "Forget type checking – treat it as this other type instead." That is, you're introducing a hole in the C++ type system and preventing the compiler from telling you that you're doing something wrong with a type. What's worse, the compiler believes you implicitly and doesn't perform any other checking to catch errors. Once you start casting, you open yourself up for all kinds of problems. In fact, any program that uses a lot of casts should be viewed with suspicion, no matter how much you are told it simply "must" be done that way. In general, casts should be few and isolated to the solution of very specific problems.

Once you understand this and are presented with a buggy program, your first inclination may be to look for casts as culprits. But how do you locate C-style casts? They are simply type names inside of parentheses, and if you start hunting for such things you'll discover that it's often hard to distinguish them from the rest of your code.

Standard C++ includes an explicit cast syntax that can be used to completely replace the old C-style casts (of course, C-style casts cannot be outlawed without breaking code, but compiler writers could easily flag old-style casts for you). The explicit cast syntax is such that you can easily find them, as you can see by their names:

static_cast	For "well-behaved" and "reasonably well-behaved" casts, including things you might now do without a cast (such as an automatic type conversion).
const_cast	To cast away **const** and/or **volatile**.
reinterpret_cast	To cast to a completely different meaning. The key is that you'll need to cast back to the original type to use it safely. The type you cast to is typically used only for bit twiddling or some other mysterious purpose. This is the most dangerous of all the casts.
dynamic_cast	For type-safe downcasting (this cast will be described in Chapter 15).

The first three explicit casts will be described more completely in the following sections, while the last one can be demonstrated only after you've learned more, in Chapter 15.

static_cast

A **static_cast** is used for all conversions that are well-defined. These include "safe" conversions that the compiler would allow you to do without a cast and less-safe conversions that are nonetheless well-defined. The types of conversions covered by **static_cast** include typical castless conversions, narrowing (information-losing) conversions, forcing a conversion from a **void***, implicit type conversions, and static navigation of class hierarchies (since you haven't seen classes and inheritance yet, this last topic will be delayed until Chapter 15):

```
//: C03:static_cast.cpp
void func(int) {}

int main() {
  int i = 0x7fff; // Max pos value = 32767
  long l;
  float f;
  // (1) Typical castless conversions:
  l = i;
  f = i;
  // Also works:
  l = static_cast<long>(i);
  f = static_cast<float>(i);

  // (2) Narrowing conversions:
  i = l; // May lose digits
  i = f; // May lose info
  // Says "I know," eliminates warnings:
  i = static_cast<int>(l);
  i = static_cast<int>(f);
  char c = static_cast<char>(i);

  // (3) Forcing a conversion from void* :
  void* vp = &i;
  // Old way produces a dangerous conversion:
  float* fp = (float*)vp;
  // The new way is equally dangerous:
  fp = static_cast<float*>(vp);
```

```
// (4) Implicit type conversions, normally
// performed by the compiler:
double d = 0.0;
int x = d; // Automatic type conversion
x = static_cast<int>(d); // More explicit
func(d); // Automatic type conversion
func(static_cast<int>(d)); // More explicit
} ///:~
```

In Section (1), you see the kinds of conversions you're used to doing in C, with or without a cast. Promoting from an **int** to a **long** or **float** is not a problem because the latter can always hold every value that an **int** can contain. Although it's unnecessary, you can use **static_cast** to highlight these promotions.

Converting back the other way is shown in (2). Here, you can lose data because an **int** is not as "wide" as a **long** or a **float**; it won't hold numbers of the same size. Thus these are called *narrowing conversions*. The compiler will still perform these, but will often give you a warning. You can eliminate this warning and indicate that you really did mean it using a cast.

Assigning from a **void*** is not allowed without a cast in C++ (unlike C), as seen in (3). This is dangerous and requires that programmers know what they're doing. The **static_cast**, at least, is easier to locate than the old standard cast when you're hunting for bugs.

Section (4) of the program shows the kinds of implicit type conversions that are normally performed automatically by the compiler. These are automatic and require no casting, but again **static_cast** highlights the action in case you want to make it clear what's happening or hunt for it later.

const_cast

If you want to convert from a **const** to a non**const** or from a **volatile** to a non**volatile**, you use **const_cast**. This is the *only* conversion allowed with **const_cast**; if any other conversion is involved it must be done using a separate expression or you'll get a compile-time error.

```
//: C03:const_cast.cpp
```

```
int main() {
  const int i = 0;
  int* j = (int*)&i; // Deprecated form
  j = const_cast<int*>(&i); // Preferred
  // Can't do simultaneous additional casting:
//! long* l = const_cast<long*>(&i); // Error
  volatile int k = 0;
  int* u = const_cast<int*>(&k);
} ///:~
```

If you take the address of a **const** object, you produce a pointer to a **const**, and this cannot be assigned to a non**const** pointer without a cast. The old-style cast will accomplish this, but the **const_cast** is the appropriate one to use. The same holds true for **volatile**.

reinterpret_cast

This is the least safe of the casting mechanisms, and the one most likely to produce bugs. A **reinterpret_cast** pretends that an object is just a bit pattern that can be treated (for some dark purpose) as if it were an entirely different type of object. This is the low-level bit twiddling that C is notorious for. You'll virtually always need to **reinterpret_cast** back to the original type (or otherwise treat the variable as its original type) before doing anything else with it.

```
//: C03:reinterpret_cast.cpp
#include <iostream>
using namespace std;
const int sz = 100;

struct X { int a[sz]; };

void print(X* x) {
  for(int i = 0; i < sz; i++)
    cout << x->a[i] << ' ';
  cout << endl << "--------------------" << endl;
}

int main() {
  X x;
  print(&x);
  int* xp = reinterpret_cast<int*>(&x);
  for(int* i = xp; i < xp + sz; i++)
```

```
    *i = 0;
  // Can't use xp as an X* at this point
  // unless you cast it back:
  print(reinterpret_cast<X*>(xp));
  // In this example, you can also just use
  // the original identifier:
  print(&x);
} ///:~
```

In this simple example, **struct X** just contains an array of **int**, but when you create one on the stack as in **X x**, the values of each of the **int**s are garbage (this is shown using the **print( )** function to display the contents of the **struct**). To initialize them, the address of the **X** is taken and cast to an **int** pointer, which is then walked through the array to set each **int** to zero. Notice how the upper bound for **i** is calculated by "adding" **sz** to **xp**; the compiler knows that you actually want **sz** pointer locations greater than **xp** and it does the correct pointer arithmetic for you.

The idea of **reinterpret_cast** is that when you use it, what you get is so foreign that it cannot be used for the type's original purpose unless you cast it back. Here, we see the cast back to an **X*** in the call to print, but of course since you still have the original identifier you can also use that. But the **xp** is only useful as an **int***, which is truly a "reinterpretation" of the original **X**.

A **reinterpret_cast** often indicates inadvisable and/or nonportable programming, but it's available when you decide you have to use it.

sizeof – an operator by itself

The **sizeof** operator stands alone because it satisfies an unusual need. **sizeof** gives you information about the amount of memory allocated for data items. As described earlier in this chapter, **sizeof** tells you the number of bytes used by any particular variable. It can also give the size of a data type (with no variable name):

```
//: C03:sizeof.cpp
#include <iostream>
using namespace std;
int main() {
```

```
  cout << "sizeof(double) = " << sizeof(double);
  cout << ", sizeof(char) = " << sizeof(char);
} ///:~
```

By definition, the **sizeof** any type of **char** (**signed**, **unsigned** or plain) is always one, regardless of whether the underlying storage for a **char** is actually one byte. For all other types, the result is the size in bytes.

Note that **sizeof** is an operator, not a function. If you apply it to a type, it must be used with the parenthesized form shown above, but if you apply it to a variable you can use it without parentheses:

```
//: C03:sizeofOperator.cpp
int main() {
  int x;
  int i = sizeof x;
} ///:~
```

sizeof can also give you the sizes of user-defined data types. This is used later in the book.

The asm keyword

This is an escape mechanism that allows you to write assembly code for your hardware within a C++ program. Often you're able to reference C++ variables within the assembly code, which means you can easily communicate with your C++ code and limit the assembly code to that necessary for efficiency tuning or to use special processor instructions. The exact syntax that you must use when writing the assembly language is compiler-dependent and can be discovered in your compiler's documentation.

Explicit operators

These are keywords for bitwise and logical operators. Non-U.S. programmers without keyboard characters like **&**, **|**, **^**, and so on, were forced to use C's horrible *trigraphs*, which were not only annoying to type, but obscure when reading. This is repaired in C++ with additional keywords:

Keyword	Meaning
and	**&&** (logical *and*)
or	**||** (logical *or*)
not	**!** (logical NOT)
not_eq	**!=** (logical not-equivalent)
bitand	**&** (bitwise *and*)
and_eq	**&=** (bitwise *and*-assignment)
bitor	**|** (bitwise *or*)
or_eq	**|=** (bitwise or-assignment)
xor	**^** (bitwise exclusive-or)
xor_eq	**^=** (bitwise exclusive-or-assignment)
compl	**~** (ones complement)

If your compiler complies with Standard C++, it will support these keywords.

Composite type creation

The fundamental data types and their variations are essential, but rather primitive. C and C++ provide tools that allow you to compose more sophisticated data types from the fundamental data types. As you'll see, the most important of these is **struct**, which is the foundation for **class** in C++. However, the simplest way to create more sophisticated types is simply to alias a name to another name via **typedef**.

Aliasing names with typedef

This keyword promises more than it delivers: **typedef** suggests "type definition" when "alias" would probably have been a more accurate description, since that's what it really does. The syntax is:

typedef existing-type-description alias-name

People often use **typedef** when data types get slightly complicated, just to prevent extra keystrokes. Here is a commonly-used **typedef**:

```
typedef unsigned long ulong;
```

Now if you say **ulong** the compiler knows that you mean **unsigned long**. You might think that this could as easily be accomplished using preprocessor substitution, but there are key situations in which the compiler must be aware that you're treating a name as if it were a type, so **typedef** is essential.

One place where **typedef** comes in handy is for pointer types. As previously mentioned, if you say:

```
int* x, y;
```

This actually produces an **int*** which is **x** and an **int** (not an **int***) which is **y**. That is, the '*' binds to the right, not the left. However, if you use a **typedef**:

```
typedef int* IntPtr;
IntPtr x, y;
```

Then both **x** and **y** are of type **int***.

You can argue that it's more explicit and therefore more readable to avoid **typedef**s for primitive types, and indeed programs rapidly become difficult to read when many **typedef**s are used. However, **typedef**s become especially important in C when used with **struct**.

Combining variables with struct

A **struct** is a way to collect a group of variables into a structure. Once you create a **struct**, then you can make many instances of this "new" type of variable you've invented. For example:

```
//: C03:SimpleStruct.cpp
struct Structure1 {
  char c;
  int i;
```

```
    float f;
    ·double d;
};

int main() {
    struct Structure1 s1, s2;
    s1.c = 'a'; // Select an element using a '.'
    s1.i = 1;
    s1.f = 3.14;
    s1.d = 0.00093;
    s2.c = 'a';
    s2.i = 1;
    s2.f = 3.14;
    s2.d = 0.00093;
} ///:~
```

The **struct** declaration must end with a semicolon. In **main( )**, two instances of **Structure1** are created: **s1** and **s2**. Each of these has their own separate versions of **c**, **i**, **f**, and **d**. So **s1** and **s2** represent clumps of completely independent variables. To select one of the elements within **s1** or **s2**, you use a '.', syntax you've seen in the previous chapter when using C++ **class** objects – since **class**es evolved from **struct**s, this is where that syntax arose from.

One thing you'll notice is the awkwardness of the use of **Structure1** (as it turns out, this is only required by C, not C++). In C, you can't just say **Structure1** when you're defining variables, you must say **struct Structure1**. This is where **typedef** becomes especially handy in C:

```
//: C03:SimpleStruct2.cpp
// Using typedef with struct
typedef struct {
    char c;
    int i;
    float f;
    double d;
} Structure2;

int main() {
    Structure2 s1, s2;
    s1.c = 'a';
    s1.i = 1;
```

```
  s1.f = 3.14;
  s1.d = 0.00093;
  s2.c = 'a';
  s2.i = 1;
  s2.f = 3.14;
  s2.d = 0.00093;
} ///:~
```

By using **typedef** in this way, you can pretend (in C; try removing
the **typedef** for C++) that **Structure2** is a built-in type, like **int** or
float, when you define **s1** and **s2** (but notice it only has data –
characteristics – and does not include behavior, which is what we
get with real objects in C++). You'll notice that the **struct** identifier
has been left off at the beginning, because the goal is to create the
typedef. However, there are times when you might need to refer to
the **struct** during its definition. In those cases, you can actually
repeat the name of the **struct** as the **struct** name and as the
typedef:

```
//: C03:SelfReferential.cpp
// Allowing a struct to refer to itself

typedef struct SelfReferential {
  int i;
  SelfReferential* sr; // Head spinning yet?
} SelfReferential;

int main() {
  SelfReferential sr1, sr2;
  sr1.sr = &sr2;
  sr2.sr = &sr1;
  sr1.i = 47;
  sr2.i = 1024;
} ///:~
```

If you look at this for awhile, you'll see that **sr1** and **sr2** point to
each other, as well as each holding a piece of data.

Actually, the **struct** name does not have to be the same as the
typedef name, but it is usually done this way as it tends to keep
things simpler.

Pointers and structs

In the examples above, all the **struct**s are manipulated as objects. However, like any piece of storage, you can take the address of a **struct** object (as seen in **SelfReferential.cpp** above). To select the elements of a particular **struct** object, you use a '.', as seen above. However, if you have a pointer to a **struct** object, you must select an element of that object using a different operator: the '->'. Here's an example:

```
//: C03:SimpleStruct3.cpp
// Using pointers to structs
typedef struct Structure3 {
  char c;
  int i;
  float f;
  double d;
} Structure3;

int main() {
  Structure3 s1, s2;
  Structure3* sp = &s1;
  sp->c = 'a';
  sp->i = 1;
  sp->f = 3.14;
  sp->d = 0.00093;
  sp = &s2; // Point to a different struct object
  sp->c = 'a';
  sp->i = 1;
  sp->f = 3.14;
  sp->d = 0.00093;
} ///:~
```

In **main( )**, the **struct** pointer **sp** is initially pointing to **s1**, and the members of **s1** are initialized by selecting them with the '->' (and you use this same operator in order to read those members). But then **sp** is pointed to **s2**, and those variables are initialized the same way. So you can see that another benefit of pointers is that they can be dynamically redirected to point to different objects; this provides more flexibility in your programming, as you will learn.

For now, that's all you need to know about **struct**s, but you'll become much more comfortable with them (and especially their more potent successors, **class**es) as the book progresses.

Clarifying programs with enum

An enumerated data type is a way of attaching names to numbers, thereby giving more meaning to anyone reading the code. The **enum** keyword (from C) automatically enumerates any list of identifiers you give it by assigning them values of 0, 1, 2, etc. You can declare **enum** variables (which are always represented as integral values). The declaration of an **enum** looks similar to a **struct** declaration.

An enumerated data type is useful when you want to keep track of some sort of feature:

```
//: C03:Enum.cpp
// Keeping track of shapes

enum ShapeType {
  circle,
  square,
  rectangle
};   // Must end with a semicolon like a struct

int main() {
  ShapeType shape = circle;
  // Activities here....
  // Now do something based on what the shape is:
  switch(shape) {
    case circle:  /* circle stuff */ break;
    case square:  /* square stuff */ break;
    case rectangle:  /* rectangle stuff */ break;
  }
} ///:~
```

shape is a variable of the **ShapeType** enumerated data type, and its value is compared with the value in the enumeration. Since **shape** is really just an **int**, however, it can be any value an **int** can hold (including a negative number). You can also compare an **int** variable with a value in the enumeration.

You should be aware that the example above of switching on type turns out to be a problematic way to program. C++ has a much better way to code this sort of thing, the explanation of which must be delayed until much later in the book.

If you don't like the way the compiler assigns values, you can do it yourself, like this:

```
enum ShapeType {
  circle = 10, square = 20, rectangle = 50
};
```

If you give values to some names and not to others, the compiler will use the next integral value. For example,

```
enum snap { crackle = 25, pop };
```

The compiler gives **pop** the value 26.

You can see how much more readable the code is when you use enumerated data types. However, to some degree this is still an attempt (in C) to accomplish the things that we can do with a **class** in C++, so you'll see **enum** used less in C++.

Type checking for enumerations

C's enumerations are fairly primitive, simply associating integral values with names, but they provide no type checking. In C++, as you may have come to expect by now, the concept of type is fundamental, and this is true with enumerations. When you create a named enumeration, you effectively create a new type just as you do with a class: The name of your enumeration becomes a reserved word for the duration of that translation unit.

In addition, there's stricter type checking for enumerations in C++ than in C. You'll notice this in particular if you have an instance of an enumeration **color** called **a**. In C you can say **a++,** but in C++ you can't. This is because incrementing an enumeration is performing two type conversions, one of them legal in C++ and one of them illegal. First, the value of the enumeration is implicitly cast from a **color** to an **int**, then the value is incremented, then the **int** is cast back into a **color**. In C++ this isn't allowed, because **color** is a distinct type and not equivalent to an **int**. This makes sense, because how do you know the increment of **blue** will even be in the list of colors? If you want to increment a **color**, then it should be a class (with an increment operation) and not an **enum**, because the class can be made to be much safer. Any time you write code that assumes an implicit conversion to an **enum** type, the compiler will flag this inherently dangerous activity.

Unions (described next) have similar additional type checking in C++.

Saving memory with union

Sometimes a program will handle different types of data using the same variable. In this situation, you have two choices: you can create a **struct** containing all the possible different types you might need to store, or you can use a **union**. A **union** piles all the data into a single space; it figures out the amount of space necessary for the largest item you've put in the **union**, and makes that the size of the **union**. Use a **union** to save memory.

Anytime you place a value in a **union**, the value always starts in the same place at the beginning of the **union**, but only uses as much space as is necessary. Thus, you create a "super-variable" capable of holding any of the **union** variables. All the addresses of the **union** variables are the same (in a class or **struct**, the addresses are different).

Here's a simple use of a **union**. Try removing various elements and see what effect it has on the size of the **union**. Notice that it makes no sense to declare more than one instance of a single data type in a **union** (unless you're just doing it to use a different name).

```
//: C03:Union.cpp
// The size and simple use of a union
#include <iostream>
using namespace std;

union Packed { // Declaration similar to a class
  char i;
  short j;
```

```
    int k;
    long l;
    float f;
    double d;
    // The union will be the size of a
    // double, since that's the largest element
};   // Semicolon ends a union, like a struct

int main() {
    cout << "sizeof(Packed) = "
         << sizeof(Packed) << endl;
    Packed x;
    x.i = 'c';
    cout << x.i << endl;
    x.d = 3.14159;
    cout << x.d << endl;
} ///:~
```

The compiler performs the proper assignment according to the union member you select.

Once you perform an assignment, the compiler doesn't care what you do with the union. In the example above, you could assign a floating-point value to **x**:

```
x.f = 2.222;
```

and then send it to the output as if it were an **int**:

```
cout << x.i;
```

This would produce garbage.

Arrays

Arrays are a kind of composite type because they allow you to clump a lot of variables together, one right after the other, under a single identifier name. If you say:

```
int a[10];
```

You create storage for 10 **int** variables stacked on top of each other, but without unique identifier names for each variable. Instead, they are all lumped under the name **a**.

To access one of these *array elements*, you use the same square-bracket syntax that you use to define an array:

```
a[5] = 47;
```

However, you must remember that even though the *size* of **a** is 10, you select array elements starting at zero (this is sometimes called *zero indexing*), so you can select only the array elements 0-9, like this:

```
//: C03:Arrays.cpp
#include <iostream>
using namespace std;

int main() {
  int a[10];
  for(int i = 0; i < 10; i++) {
    a[i] = i * 10;
    cout << "a[" << i << "] = " << a[i] << endl;
  }
} ///:~
```

Array access is extremely fast. However, if you index past the end of the array, there is no safety net – you'll step on other variables. The other drawback is that you must define the size of the array at compile time; if you want to change the size at runtime you can't do it with the syntax above (C does have a way to create an array dynamically, but it's significantly messier). The C++ **vector**, introduced in the previous chapter, provides an array-like object that automatically resizes itself, so it is usually a much better solution if your array size cannot be known at compile time.

You can make an array of any type, even of **struct**s:

```
//: C03:StructArray.cpp
// An array of struct

typedef struct {
  int i, j, k;
} ThreeDpoint;

int main() {
  ThreeDpoint p[10];
```

```
  for(int i = 0; i < 10; i++) {
    p[i].i = i + 1;
    p[i].j = i + 2;
    p[i].k = i + 3;
  }
} ///:~
```

Notice how the **struct** identifier **i** is independent of the **for** loop's **i**.

To see that each element of an array is contiguous with the next, you can print out the addresses like this:

```
//: C03:ArrayAddresses.cpp
#include <iostream>
using namespace std;

int main() {
  int a[10];
  cout << "sizeof(int) = "<< sizeof(int) << endl;
  for(int i = 0; i < 10; i++)
    cout << "&a[" << i << "] = "
         << (long)&a[i] << endl;
} ///:~
```

When you run this program, you'll see that each element is one **int** size away from the previous one. That is, they are stacked one on top of the other.

Pointers and arrays

The identifier of an array is unlike the identifiers for ordinary variables. For one thing, an array identifier is not an lvalue; you cannot assign to it. It's really just a hook into the square-bracket syntax, and when you give the name of an array, without square brackets, what you get is the starting address of the array:

```
//: C03:ArrayIdentifier.cpp
#include <iostream>
using namespace std;

int main() {
  int a[10];
  cout << "a = " << a << endl;
  cout << "&a[0] =" << &a[0] << endl;
```

```
} ///:~
```

When you run this program you'll see that the two addresses (which
will be printed in hexadecimal, since there is no cast to **long**) are
the same.

So one way to look at the array identifier is as a read-only pointer to
the beginning of an array. And although we can't change the array
identifier to point somewhere else, we *can* create another pointer
and use that to move around in the array. In fact, the square-
bracket syntax works with regular pointers as well:

```cpp
//: C03:PointersAndBrackets.cpp
int main() {
  int a[10];
  int* ip = a;
  for(int i = 0; i < 10; i++)
    ip[i] = i * 10;
} ///:~
```

The fact that naming an array produces its starting address turns
out to be quite important when you want to pass an array to a
function. If you declare an array as a function argument, what
you're really declaring is a pointer. So in the following example,
func1( ) and **func2( )** effectively have the same argument lists:

```cpp
//: C03:ArrayArguments.cpp
#include <iostream>
#include <string>
using namespace std;

void func1(int a[], int size) {
  for(int i = 0; i < size; i++)
    a[i] = i * i - i;
}

void func2(int* a, int size) {
  for(int i = 0; i < size; i++)
    a[i] = i * i + i;
}

void print(int a[], string name, int size) {
  for(int i = 0; i < size; i++)
```

```
    cout << name << "[" << i << "] = "
        << a[i] << endl;
}

int main() {
  int a[5], b[5];
  // Probably garbage values:
  print(a, "a", 5);
  print(b, "b", 5);
  // Initialize the arrays:
  func1(a, 5);
  func1(b, 5);
  print(a, "a", 5);
  print(b, "b", 5);
  // Notice the arrays are always modified:
  func2(a, 5);
  func2(b, 5);
  print(a, "a", 5);
  print(b, "b", 5);
} ///:~
```

Even though **func1( )** and **func2( )** declare their arguments differently, the usage is the same inside the function. There are some other issues that this example reveals: arrays cannot be passed by value[3], that is, you never automatically get a local copy of the array that you pass into a function. Thus, when you modify an array, you're always modifying the outside object. This can be a bit confusing at first, if you're expecting the pass-by-value provided with ordinary arguments.

You'll notice that **print( )** uses the square-bracket syntax for array arguments. Even though the pointer syntax and the square-bracket syntax are effectively the same when passing arrays as arguments, the square-bracket syntax makes it clearer to the reader that you mean for this argument to be an array.

---

[3] Unless you take the very strict approach that "all argument passing in C/C++ is by value, and the 'value' of an array is what is produced by the array identifier: it's address." This can be seen as true from the assembly-language standpoint, but I don't think it helps when trying to work with higher-level concepts. The addition of references in C++ makes the "all passing is by value" argument more confusing, to the point where I feel it's more helpful to think in terms of "passing by value" vs. "passing addresses."

Also note that the **size** argument is passed in each case. Just passing the address of an array isn't enough information; you must always be able to know how big the array is inside your function, so you don't run off the end of that array.

Arrays can be of any type, including arrays of pointers. In fact, when you want to pass command-line arguments into your program, C and C++ have a special argument list for **main( )**, which looks like this:

```
int main(int argc, char* argv[]) { // ...
```

The first argument is the number of elements in the array, which is the second argument. The second argument is always an array of **char***, because the arguments are passed from the command line as character arrays (and remember, an array can be passed only as a pointer). Each whitespace-delimited cluster of characters on the command line is turned into a separate array argument. The following program prints out all its command-line arguments by stepping through the array:

```
//: C03:CommandLineArgs.cpp
#include <iostream>
using namespace std;

int main(int argc, char* argv[]) {
  cout << "argc = " << argc << endl;
  for(int i = 0; i < argc; i++)
    cout << "argv[" << i << "] = "
         << argv[i] << endl;
} ///:~
```

You'll notice that **argv[0]** is the path and name of the program itself. This allows the program to discover information about itself. It also adds one more to the array of program arguments, so a common error when fetching command-line arguments is to grab **argv[0]** when you want **argv[1]**.

You are not forced to use **argc** and **argv** as identifiers in **main( )**; those identifiers are only conventions (but it will confuse people if you don't use them). Also, there is an alternate way to declare **argv**:

```
int main(int argc, char** argv) { // ...
```

Both forms are equivalent, but I find the version used in this book to be the most intuitive when reading the code, since it says, directly, "This is an array of character pointers."

All you get from the command-line is character arrays; if you want to treat an argument as some other type, you are responsible for converting it inside your program. To facilitate the conversion to numbers, there are some helper functions in the Standard C library, declared in **<cstdlib>**. The simplest ones to use are **atoi( )**, **atol( ),** and **atof( )** to convert an ASCII character array to an **int**, **long,** and **double** floating-point value, respectively. Here's an example using **atoi( )** (the other two functions are called the same way):

```
//: C03:ArgsToInts.cpp
// Converting command-line arguments to ints
#include <iostream>
#include <cstdlib>
using namespace std;

int main(int argc, char* argv[]) {
  for(int i = 1; i < argc; i++)
    cout << atoi(argv[i]) << endl;
} ///:~
```

In this program, you can put any number of arguments on the command line. You'll notice that the **for** loop starts at the value **1** to skip over the program name at **argv[0]**. Also, if you put a floating-point number containing a decimal point on the command line, **atoi( )** takes only the digits up to the decimal point. If you put non-numbers on the command line, these come back from **atoi( )** as zero.

Exploring floating-point format
The **printBinary( )** function introduced earlier in this chapter is handy for delving into the internal structure of various data types. The most interesting of these is the floating-point format that allows C and C++ to store numbers representing very large and very small values in a limited amount of space. Although the details can't

be completely exposed here, the bits inside of **float**s and **double**s are divided into three regions: the exponent, the mantissa, and the sign bit; thus it stores the values using scientific notation. The following program allows you to play around by printing out the binary patterns of various floating point numbers so you can deduce for yourself the scheme used in your compiler's floating-point format (usually this is the IEEE standard for floating point numbers, but your compiler may not follow that):

```cpp
//: C03:FloatingAsBinary.cpp
//{L} printBinary
//{T} 3.14159
#include "printBinary.h"
#include <cstdlib>
#include <iostream>
using namespace std;

int main(int argc, char* argv[]) {
  if(argc != 2) {
    cout << "Must provide a number" << endl;
    exit(1);
  }
  double d = atof(argv[1]);
  unsigned char* cp =
    reinterpret_cast<unsigned char*>(&d);
  for(int i = sizeof(double); i > 0 ; i -= 2) {
    printBinary(cp[i-1]);
    printBinary(cp[i]);
  }
} ///:~
```

First, the program guarantees that you've given it an argument by checking the value of **argc**, which is two if there's a single argument (it's one if there are no arguments, since the program name is always the first element of **argv**). If this fails, a message is printed and the Standard C Library function **exit( )** is called to terminate the program.

The program grabs the argument from the command line and converts the characters to a **double** using **atof( )**. Then the double is treated as an array of bytes by taking the address and casting it to

an **unsigned char***. Each of these bytes is passed to
printBinary( ) for display.

This example has been set up to print the bytes in an order such
that the sign bit appears first – on my machine. Yours may be
different, so you might want to re-arrange the way things are
printed. You should also be aware that floating-point formats are
not trivial to understand; for example, the exponent and mantissa
are not generally arranged on byte boundaries, but instead a
number of bits is reserved for each one and they are packed into the
memory as tightly as possible. To truly see what's going on, you'd
need to find out the size of each part of the number (sign bits are
always one bit, but exponents and mantissas are of differing sizes)
and print out the bits in each part separately.

Pointer arithmetic

If all you could do with a pointer that points at an array is treat it as
if it were an alias for that array, pointers into arrays wouldn't be
very interesting. However, pointers are more flexible than this,
since they can be modified to point somewhere else (but remember,
the array identifier cannot be modified to point somewhere else).

Pointer arithmetic refers to the application of some of the
arithmetic operators to pointers. The reason pointer arithmetic is a
separate subject from ordinary arithmetic is that pointers must
conform to special constraints in order to make them behave
properly. For example, a common operator to use with pointers is
++, which "adds one to the pointer." What this actually means is
that the pointer is changed to move to "the next value," whatever
that means. Here's an example:

```
//: C03:PointerIncrement.cpp
#include <iostream>
using namespace std;

int main() {
  int i[10];
  double d[10];
  int* ip = i;
  double* dp = d;
  cout << "ip = " << (long)ip << endl;
```

```
  ip++;
  cout << "ip = " << (long)ip << endl;
  cout << "dp = " << (long)dp << endl;
  dp++;
  cout << "dp = " << (long)dp << endl;
} ///:~
```

For one run on my machine, the output is:

```
ip = 6684124
ip = 6684128
dp = 6684044
dp = 6684052
```

What's interesting here is that even though the operation ++ appears to be the same operation for both the **int*** and the **double***, you can see that the pointer has been changed only 4 bytes for the **int*** but 8 bytes for the **double***. Not coincidentally, these are the sizes of **int** and **double** on my machine. And that's the trick of pointer arithmetic: the compiler figures out the right amount to change the pointer so that it's pointing to the next element in the array (pointer arithmetic is only meaningful within arrays). This even works with arrays of **struct**s:

```
//: C03:PointerIncrement2.cpp
#include <iostream>
using namespace std;

typedef struct {
  char c;
  short s;
  int i;
  long l;
  float f;
  double d;
  long double ld;
} Primitives;

int main() {
  Primitives p[10];
  Primitives* pp = p;
  cout << "sizeof(Primitives) = "
       << sizeof(Primitives) << endl;
  cout << "pp = " << (long)pp << endl;
```

```
  pp++;
  cout << "pp = " << (long)pp << endl;
} ///:~
```

The output for one run on my machine was:

```
sizeof(Primitives) = 40
pp = 6683764
pp = 6683804
```

So you can see the compiler also does the right thing for pointers to **struct**s (and **class**es and **union**s).

Pointer arithmetic also works with the operators --, +, and -, but the latter two operators are limited: you cannot add two pointers, and if you subtract pointers the result is the number of elements between the two pointers. However, you can add or subtract an integral value and a pointer. Here's an example demonstrating the use of pointer arithmetic:

```
//: C03:PointerArithmetic.cpp
#include <iostream>
using namespace std;

#define P(EX) cout << #EX << ": " << EX << endl;

int main() {
  int a[10];
  for(int i = 0; i < 10; i++)
    a[i] = i; // Give it index values
  int* ip = a;
  P(*ip);
  P(*++ip);
  P(*(ip + 5));
  int* ip2 = ip + 5;
  P(*ip2);
  P(*(ip2 - 4));
  P(*--ip2);
  P(ip2 - ip); // Yields number of elements
} ///:~
```

It begins with another macro, but this one uses a preprocessor feature called *stringizing* (implemented with the '#' sign before an expression) that takes any expression and turns it into a character array. This is quite convenient, since it allows the expression to be printed, followed by a colon, followed by the value of the expression. In **main( )** you can see the useful shorthand that is produced.

Although pre- and postfix versions of ++ and -- are valid with pointers, only the prefix versions are used in this example because they are applied before the pointers are dereferenced in the expressions above, so they allow us to see the effects of the operations. Note that only integral values are being added and subtracted; if two pointers were combined this way the compiler would not allow it.

Here is the output of the program above:

```
*ip: 0
*++ip: 1
*(ip + 5): 6
*ip2: 6
*(ip2 - 4): 2
*--ip2: 5
```

In all cases, the pointer arithmetic results in the pointer being adjusted to point to the "right place," based on the size of the elements being pointed to.

If pointer arithmetic seems a bit overwhelming at first, don't worry. Most of the time you'll only need to create arrays and index into them with [ ], and the most sophisticated pointer arithmetic you'll usually need is ++ and --. Pointer arithmetic is generally reserved for more clever and complex programs, and many of the containers in the Standard C++ library hide most of these clever details so you don't have to worry about them.

Debugging hints

In an ideal environment, you have an excellent debugger available that easily makes the behavior of your program transparent so you can quickly discover errors. However, most debuggers have blind spots, and these will require you to embed code snippets in your program to help you understand what's going on. In addition, you may be developing in an environment (such as an embedded system, which is where I spent my formative years) that has no debugger available, and perhaps very limited feedback (i.e. a one-line LED display). In these cases you become creative in the ways you discover and display information about the execution of your program. This section suggests some techniques for doing this.

Debugging flags

If you hard-wire debugging code into a program, you can run into problems. You start to get too much information, which makes the bugs difficult to isolate. When you think you've found the bug you start tearing out debugging code, only to find you need to put it back in again. You can solve these problems with two types of flags: preprocessor debugging flags and runtime debugging flags.

Preprocessor debugging flags

By using the preprocessor to **#define** one or more debugging flags (preferably in a header file), you can test a flag using an **#ifdef** statement and conditionally include debugging code. When you think your debugging is finished, you can simply **#undef** the flag(s) and the code will automatically be removed (and you'll reduce the size and runtime overhead of your executable file).

It is best to decide on names for debugging flags before you begin building your project so the names will be consistent. Preprocessor flags are traditionally distinguished from variables by writing them in all upper case. A common flag name is simply **DEBUG** (but be careful you don't use **NDEBUG**, which is reserved in C). The sequence of statements might be:

```
#define DEBUG // Probably in a header file
//...
#ifdef DEBUG // Check to see if flag is defined
/* debugging code here */
#endif // DEBUG
```

Most C and C++ implementations will also let you **#define** and **#undef** flags from the compiler command line, so you can re-compile code and insert debugging information with a single command (preferably via the makefile, a tool that will be described shortly). Check your local documentation for details.

Runtime debugging flags

In some situations it is more convenient to turn debugging flags on and off during program execution, especially by setting them when the program starts up using the command line. Large programs are tedious to recompile just to insert debugging code.

To turn debugging code on and off dynamically, create **bool** flags:

```
//: C03:DynamicDebugFlags.cpp
#include <iostream>
#include <string>
using namespace std;
// Debug flags aren't necessarily global:
bool debug = false;

int main(int argc, char* argv[]) {
  for(int i = 0; i < argc; i++)
    if(string(argv[i]) == "--debug=on")
      debug = true;
  bool go = true;
  while(go) {
    if(debug) {
      // Debugging code here
      cout << "Debugger is now on!" << endl;
    } else {
      cout << "Debugger is now off." << endl;
    }
    cout << "Turn debugger [on/off/quit]: ";
    string reply;
    cin >> reply;
    if(reply == "on") debug = true; // Turn it on
    if(reply == "off") debug = false; // Off
    if(reply == "quit") break; // Out of 'while'
  }
} ///:~
```

This program continues to allow you to turn the debugging flag on and off until you type "quit" to tell it you want to exit. Notice it requires that full words are typed in, not just letters (you can shorten it to letter if you wish). Also, a command-line argument can optionally be used to turn debugging on at startup – this argument can appear anyplace in the command line, since the startup code in **main( )** looks at all the arguments. The testing is quite simple because of the expression:

```
string(argv[i])
```

This takes the **argv[i]** character array and creates a **string**, which then can be easily compared to the right-hand side of the ==. The program above searches for the entire string **--debug=on**. You can also look for **--debug=** and then see what's after that, to provide more options. Volume 2 (available from *www.BruceEckel.com*) devotes a chapter to the Standard C++ **string** class.

Although a debugging flag is one of the relatively few areas where it makes a lot of sense to use a global variable, there's nothing that says it must be that way. Notice that the variable is in lower case letters to remind the reader it isn't a preprocessor flag.

Turning variables and expressions into strings

When writing debugging code, it is tedious to write print expressions consisting of a character array containing the variable name, followed by the variable. Fortunately, Standard C includes the *stringize* operator '#', which was used earlier in this chapter. When you put a # before an argument in a preprocessor macro, the preprocessor turns that argument into a character array. This, combined with the fact that character arrays with no intervening punctuation are concatenated into a single character array, allows you to make a very convenient macro for printing the values of variables during debugging:

```
#define PR(x) cout << #x " = " << x << "\n";
```

If you print the variable **a** by calling the macro **PR(a)**, it will have the same effect as the code:

```
cout << "a = " << a << "\n";
```

This same process works with entire expressions. The following program uses a macro to create a shorthand that prints the stringized expression and then evaluates the expression and prints the result:

```
//: C03:StringizingExpressions.cpp
#include <iostream>
using namespace std;

#define P(A) cout << #A << ": " << (A) << endl;

int main() {
    int a = 1, b = 2, c = 3;
    P(a); P(b); P(c);
    P(a + b);
    P((c - a)/b);
} ///:~
```

You can see how a technique like this can quickly become indispensable, especially if you have no debugger (or must use multiple development environments). You can also insert an **#ifdef** to cause **P(A)** to be defined as "nothing" when you want to strip out debugging.

The C assert( ) macro

In the standard header file **<cassert>** you'll find **assert( )**, which is a convenient debugging macro. When you use **assert( )**, you give it an argument that is an expression you are "asserting to be true." The preprocessor generates code that will test the assertion. If the assertion isn't true, the program will stop after issuing an error message telling you what the assertion was and that it failed. Here's a trivial example:

```
//: C03:Assert.cpp
// Use of the assert() debugging macro
#include <cassert>   // Contains the macro
using namespace std;

int main() {
    int i = 100;
    assert(i != 100); // Fails
} ///:~
```

The macro originated in Standard C, so it's also available in the header file **assert.h**.

When you are finished debugging, you can remove the code generated by the macro by placing the line:

```
#define NDEBUG
```

in the program before the inclusion of **<cassert>**, or by defining NDEBUG on the compiler command line. NDEBUG is a flag used in **<cassert>** to change the way code is generated by the macros.

Later in this book, you'll see some more sophisticated alternatives to **assert( )**.

Function addresses

Once a function is compiled and loaded into the computer to be executed, it occupies a chunk of memory. That memory, and thus the function, has an address.

C has never been a language to bar entry where others fear to tread. You can use function addresses with pointers just as you can use variable addresses. The declaration and use of function pointers looks a bit opaque at first, but it follows the format of the rest of the language.

Defining a function pointer

To define a pointer to a function that has no arguments and no return value, you say:

```
void (*funcPtr)();
```

When you are looking at a complex definition like this, the best way to attack it is to start in the middle and work your way out. "Starting in the middle" means starting at the variable name, which is **funcPtr**. "Working your way out" means looking to the right for the nearest item (nothing in this case; the right parenthesis stops you short), then looking to the left (a pointer denoted by the

---

asterisk), then looking to the right (an empty argument list indicating a function that takes no arguments), then looking to the left (**void,** which indicates the function has no return value). This right-left-right motion works with most declarations.

To review, "start in the middle" ("**funcPtr** is a ..."), go to the right (nothing there – you're stopped by the right parenthesis), go to the left and find the '*' ("... pointer to a ..."), go to the right and find the empty argument list ("... function that takes no arguments ... "), go to the left and find the **void** ("**funcPtr** is a pointer to a function that takes no arguments and returns **void**").

You may wonder why ***funcPtr** requires parentheses. If you didn't use them, the compiler would see:

```
void *funcPtr();
```

You would be declaring a function (that returns a **void***) rather than defining a variable. You can think of the compiler as going through the same process you do when it figures out what a declaration or definition is supposed to be. It needs those parentheses to "bump up against" so it goes back to the left and finds the '*', instead of continuing to the right and finding the empty argument list.

Complicated declarations & definitions

As an aside, once you figure out how the C and C++ declaration syntax works you can create much more complicated items. For instance:

```
//: C03:ComplicatedDefinitions.cpp

/* 1. */    void * (*(*fp1)(int))[10];

/* 2. */    float (*(*fp2)(int,int,float))(int);

/* 3. */    typedef double (*(*(*fp3)())[10])();
            fp3 a;

/* 4. */    int (*(*f4())[10])();
```

```
int main() {} ///:~
```

Walk through each one and use the right-left guideline to figure it out. Number 1 says "**fp1** is a pointer to a function that takes an integer argument and returns a pointer to an array of 10 **void** pointers."

Number 2 says "**fp2** is a pointer to a function that takes three arguments (**int, int,** and **float**) and returns a pointer to a function that takes an integer argument and returns a **float**."

If you are creating a lot of complicated definitions, you might want to use a **typedef**. Number 3 shows how a **typedef** saves typing the complicated description every time. It says "An **fp3** is a pointer to a function that takes no arguments and returns a pointer to an array of 10 pointers to functions that take no arguments and return doubles." Then it says "**a** is one of these **fp3** types." **typedef** is generally useful for building complicated descriptions from simple ones.

Number 4 is a function declaration instead of a variable definition. It says "**f4** is a function that returns a pointer to an array of 10 pointers to functions that return integers."

You will rarely if ever need such complicated declarations and definitions as these. However, if you go through the exercise of figuring them out you will not even be mildly disturbed with the slightly complicated ones you may encounter in real life.

Using a function pointer

Once you define a pointer to a function, you must assign it to a function address before you can use it. Just as the address of an array **arr[10]** is produced by the array name without the brackets (**arr**), the address of a function **func()** is produced by the function name without the argument list (**func**). You can also use the more explicit syntax **&func()**. To call the function, you dereference the pointer in the same way that you declared it (remember that C and C++ always try to make definitions look the same as the way they are used). The following example shows how a pointer to a function is defined and used:

```
//: C03:PointerToFunction.cpp
// Defining and using a pointer to a function
#include <iostream>
using namespace std;

void func() {
  cout << "func() called..." << endl;
}

int main() {
  void (*fp)();   // Define a function pointer
  fp = func;   // Initialize it
  (*fp)();      // Dereferencing calls the function
  void (*fp2)() = func;   // Define and initialize
  (*fp2)();
} ///:~
```

After the pointer to function **fp** is defined, it is assigned to the address of a function **func()** using **fp = func** (notice the argument list is missing on the function name). The second case shows simultaneous definition and initialization.

Arrays of pointers to functions

One of the more interesting constructs you can create is an array of pointers to functions. To select a function, you just index into the array and dereference the pointer. This supports the concept of *table-driven code*; instead of using conditionals or case statements, you select functions to execute based on a state variable (or a combination of state variables). This kind of design can be useful if you often add or delete functions from the table (or if you want to create or change such a table dynamically).

The following example creates some dummy functions using a preprocessor macro, then creates an array of pointers to those functions using automatic aggregate initialization. As you can see, it is easy to add or remove functions from the table (and thus, functionality from the program) by changing a small amount of code:

```
//: C03:FunctionTable.cpp
// Using an array of pointers to functions
#include <iostream>
using namespace std;

// A macro to define dummy functions:
#define DF(N) void N() { \
    cout << "function " #N " called..." << endl; }

DF(a); DF(b); DF(c); DF(d); DF(e); DF(f); DF(g);

void (*func_table[])() = { a, b, c, d, e, f, g };

int main() {
  while(1) {
    cout << "press a key from 'a' to 'g' "
      "or q to quit" << endl;
    char c, cr;
    cin.get(c); cin.get(cr); // second one for CR
    if ( c == 'q' )
      break; // ... out of while(1)
    if ( c < 'a' || c > 'g' )
      continue;
    (*func_table[c - 'a'])();
  }
} ///:~
```

At this point, you might be able to imagine how this technique could be useful when creating some sort of interpreter or list processing program.

Make: managing separate compilation

When using *separate compilation* (breaking code into a number of translation units), you need some way to automatically compile each file and to tell the linker to build all the pieces – along with the appropriate libraries and startup code – into an executable file. Most compilers allow you to do this with a single command-line statement. For the GNU C++ compiler, for example, you might say

```
g++ SourceFile1.cpp SourceFile2.cpp
```

The problem with this approach is that the compiler will first compile each individual file, regardless of whether that file *needs* to be rebuilt or not. With many files in a project, it can become prohibitive to recompile everything if you've changed only a single file.

The solution to this problem, developed on Unix but available everywhere in some form, is a program called **make**. The **make** utility manages all the individual files in a project by following the instructions in a text file called a **makefile**. When you edit some of the files in a project and type **make**, the **make** program follows the guidelines in the **makefile** to compare the dates on the source code files to the dates on the corresponding target files, and if a source code file date is more recent than its target file, **make** invokes the compiler on the source code file. **make** only recompiles the source code files that were changed, and any other source-code files that are affected by the modified files. By using **make**, you don't have to re-compile all the files in your project every time you make a change, nor do you have to check to see that everything was built properly. The **makefile** contains all the commands to put your project together. Learning to use **make** will save you a lot of time and frustration. You'll also discover that **make** is the typical way that you install new software on a Linux/Unix machine (although those **makefile**s tend to be far more complicated than the ones presented in this book, and you'll often automatically generate a **makefile** for your particular machine as part of the installation process).

Because **make** is available in some form for virtually all C++ compilers (and even if it isn't, you can use freely-available **make**s with any compiler), it will be the tool used throughout this book. However, compiler vendors have also created their own project building tools. These tools ask you which files are in your project and determine all the relationships themselves. These tools use something similar to a **makefile**, generally called a *project file*, but the programming environment maintains this file so you don't have to worry about it. The configuration and use of project files varies from one development environment to another, so you must find the appropriate documentation on how to use them (although project file tools provided by compiler vendors are usually so simple to use that you can learn them by playing around – my favorite form of education).

The **makefile**s used within this book should work even if you are also using a specific vendor's project-building tool.

Make activities

When you type **make** (or whatever the name of your "make" program happens to be), the **make** program looks in the current directory for a file named **makefile**, which you've created if it's your project. This file lists dependencies between source code files. **make** looks at the dates on files. If a dependent file has an older date than a file it depends on, **make** executes the *rule* given after the dependency.

All comments in **makefile**s start with a # and continue to the end of the line.

As a simple example, the **makefile** for a program called "hello" might contain:

```
# A comment
hello.exe: hello.cpp
        mycompiler hello.cpp
```

This says that **hello.exe** (the target) depends on **hello.cpp**. When **hello.cpp** has a newer date than **hello.exe**, **make** executes the "rule" **mycompiler hello.cpp**. There may be multiple dependencies and multiple rules. Many **make** programs require that all the rules begin with a tab. Other than that, whitespace is generally ignored so you can format for readability.

The rules are not restricted to being calls to the compiler; you can call any program you want from within **make**. By creating groups of interdependent dependency-rule sets, you can modify your source code files, type **make** and be certain that all the affected files will be rebuilt correctly.

Macros

A **makefile** may contain *macros* (note that these are completely different from C/C++ preprocessor macros). Macros allow convenient string replacement. The **makefile**s in this book use a macro to invoke the C++ compiler. For example,

```
CPP = mycompiler
hello.exe: hello.cpp
        $(CPP) hello.cpp
```

The = is used to identify **CPP** as a macro, and the **$** and parentheses expand the macro. In this case, the expansion means that the macro call **$(CPP)** will be replaced with the string **mycompiler**. With the macro above, if you want to change to a different compiler called **cpp**, you just change the macro to:

```
CPP = cpp
```

You can also add compiler flags, etc., to the macro, or use separate macros to add compiler flags.

Suffix Rules

It becomes tedious to tell **make** how to invoke the compiler for every single **cpp** file in your project, when you know it's the same basic process each time. Since **make** is designed to be a time-saver, it also has a way to abbreviate actions, as long as they depend on file name suffixes. These abbreviations are called *suffix rules*. A suffix rule is the way to teach **make** how to convert a file with one type of extension (**.cpp**, for example) into a file with another type of extension (**.obj** or **.exe**). Once you teach **make** the rules for producing one kind of file from another, all you have to do is tell **make** which files depend on which other files. When **make** finds a file with a date earlier than the file it depends on, it uses the rule to create a new file.

The suffix rule tells **make** that it doesn't need explicit rules to build everything, but instead it can figure out how to build things based on their file extension. In this case it says "To build a file that ends in **exe** from one that ends in **cpp**, invoke the following command." Here's what it looks like for the example above:

```
CPP = mycompiler
.SUFFIXES: .exe .cpp
.cpp.exe:
        $(CPP) $<
```

The **.SUFFIXES** directive tells **make** that it should watch out for any of the following file-name extensions because they have special meaning for this particular makefile. Next you see the suffix rule **.cpp.exe,** which says "Here's how to convert any file with an extension of **cpp** to one with an extension of **exe**" (when the **cpp** file is more recent than the **exe** file). As before, the **$(CPP)** macro is used, but then you see something new: **$<**. Because this begins with a '**$**' it's a macro, but this is one of **make**'s special built-in macros. The **$<** can be used only in suffix rules, and it means "whatever prerequisite triggered the rule" (sometimes called the *dependent*), which in this case translates to "the **cpp** file that needs to be compiled."

Once the suffix rules have been set up, you can simply say, for example, "**make Union.exe,**" and the suffix rule will kick in, even though there's no mention of "Union" anywhere in the **makefile**.

Default targets
After the macros and suffix rules, **make** looks for the first "target" in a file, and builds that, unless you specify differently. So for the following **makefile**:

```
CPP = mycompiler
.SUFFIXES: .exe .cpp
.cpp.exe:
        $(CPP) $<
target1.exe:
target2.exe:
```

If you just type '**make**', then **target1.exe** will be built (using the default suffix rule) because that's the first target that **make** encounters. To build **target2.exe** you'd have to explicitly say '**make target2.exe**'. This becomes tedious, so you normally create a default "dummy" target that depends on all the rest of the targets, like this:

```
CPP = mycompiler
```

```
.SUFFIXES:  .exe  .cpp
.cpp.exe:
        $(CPP) $<
all: target1.exe target2.exe
```

Here, '**all**' does not exist and there's no file called '**all**', so every time you type **make**, the program sees '**all**' as the first target in the list (and thus the default target), then it sees that '**all**' does not exist so it had better make it by checking all the dependencies. So it looks at **target1.exe** and (using the suffix rule) sees whether (1) **target1.exe** exists and (2) whether **target1.cpp** is more recent than **target1.exe**, and if so runs the suffix rule (if you provide an explicit rule for a particular target, that rule is used instead). Then it moves on to the next file in the default target list. Thus, by creating a default target list (typically called '**all**' by convention, but you can call it anything) you can cause every executable in your project to be made simply by typing '**make**'. In addition, you can have other non-default target lists that do other things – for example, you could set it up so that typing '**make debug**' rebuilds all your files with debugging wired in.

Makefiles in this book

Using the program **ExtractCode.cpp** from Volume 2 of this book, all the code listings in this book are automatically extracted from the ASCII text version of this book and placed in subdirectories according to their chapters. In addition, **ExtractCode.cpp** creates several **makefile**s in each subdirectory (with different names) so you can simply move into that subdirectory and type **make -f mycompiler.makefile** (substituting the name of your compiler for '**mycompiler**', the '**-f**' flag says "use what follows as the makefile"). Finally, **ExtractCode.cpp** creates a "master" **makefile** in the root directory where the book's files have been expanded, and this **makefile** descends into each subdirectory and calls **make** with the appropriate **makefile**. This way you can compile all the code in the book by invoking a single **make** command, and the process will stop whenever your compiler is unable to handle a particular file (note that a Standard C++ conforming compiler should be able to compile all the files in this book). Because implementations of **make** vary from system to system, only the most basic, common features are used in the generated **makefile**s.

An example makefile

As mentioned, the code-extraction tool **ExtractCode.cpp** automatically generates **makefile**s for each chapter. Because of this, the **makefile**s for each chapter will not be placed in the book (all the makefiles are packaged with the source code, which you can download from *www.BruceEckel.com*). However, it's useful to see an example of a **makefile**. What follows is a shortened version of the one that was automatically generated for this chapter by the book's extraction tool. You'll find more than one **makefile** in each subdirectory (they have different names; you invoke a specific one with '**make -f**'). This one is for GNU C++:

```
CPP = g++
OFLAG = -o
.SUFFIXES : .o .cpp .c
.cpp.o :
  $(CPP) $(CPPFLAGS) -c $<
.c.o :
  $(CPP) $(CPPFLAGS) -c $<

all: \
  Return \
  Declare \
  Ifthen \
  Guess \
  Guess2
# Rest of the files for this chapter not shown

Return: Return.o
  $(CPP) $(OFLAG)Return Return.o

Declare: Declare.o
  $(CPP) $(OFLAG)Declare Declare.o

Ifthen: Ifthen.o
  $(CPP) $(OFLAG)Ifthen Ifthen.o

Guess: Guess.o
  $(CPP) $(OFLAG)Guess Guess.o
```

```
Guess2: Guess2.o
  $(CPP) $(OFLAG)Guess2 Guess2.o

Return.o: Return.cpp
Declare.o: Declare.cpp
Ifthen.o: Ifthen.cpp
Guess.o: Guess.cpp
Guess2.o: Guess2.cpp
```

The macro CPP is set to the name of the compiler. To use a different compiler, you can either edit the **makefile** or change the value of the macro on the command line, like this:

```
make CPP=cpp
```

Note, however, that **ExtractCode.cpp** has an automatic scheme to automatically build **makefiles** for additional compilers.

The second macro **OFLAG** is the flag that's used to indicate the name of the output file. Although many compilers automatically assume the output file has the same base name as the input file, others don't (such as Linux/Unix compilers, which default to creating a file called **a.out**).

You can see that there are two suffix rules here, one for **cpp** files and one for **.c** files (in case any C source code needs to be compiled). The default target is **all**, and each line for this target is "continued" by using the backslash, up until **Guess2**, which is the last one in the list and thus has no backslash. There are many more files in this chapter, but only these are shown here for the sake of brevity.

The suffix rules take care of creating object files (with a **.o** extension) from **cpp** files, but in general you need to explicitly state rules for creating the executable, because normally an executable is created by linking many different object files and **make** cannot guess what those are. Also, in this case (Linux/Unix) there is no standard extension for executables so a suffix rule won't work for these simple situations. Thus, you see all the rules for building the final executables explicitly stated.

This **makefile** takes the absolute safest route of using as few **make** features as possible; it only uses the basic **make** concepts of targets and dependencies, as well as macros. This way it is virtually assured of working with as many **make** programs as possible. It tends to produce a larger **makefile**, but that's not so bad since it's automatically generated by **ExtractCode.cpp**.

There are lots of other **make** features that this book will not use, as well as newer and cleverer versions and variations of **make** with advanced shortcuts that can save a lot of time. Your local documentation may describe the further features of your particular **make**, and you can learn more about **make** from *Managing Projects with Make* by Oram and Talbott (O'Reilly, 1993). Also, if your compiler vendor does not supply a **make** or it uses a non-standard **make**, you can find GNU make for virtually any platform in existence by searching the Internet for GNU archives (of which there are many).

Summary

This chapter was a fairly intense tour through all the fundamental features of C++ syntax, most of which are inherited from and in common with C (and result in C++'s vaunted backwards compatibility with C). Although some C++ features were introduced here, this tour is primarily intended for people who are conversant in programming, and simply need to be given an introduction to the syntax basics of C and C++. If you're already a C programmer, you may have even seen one or two things about C here that were unfamiliar, aside from the C++ features that were most likely new to you. However, if this chapter has still seemed a bit overwhelming, you should go through the CD ROM course *Thinking in C: Foundations for C++ and Java* (which contains lectures, exercises, and guided solutions), which is bound into this book, and also available at *www.BruceEckel.com*.

Exercises

Solutions to selected exercises can be found in the electronic document *The Thinking in C++ Annotated Solution Guide*, available for a small fee from www.BruceEckel.com.

1. Create a header file (with an extension of '**.h**'). In this file, declare a group of functions by varying the argument lists and return values from among the following: **void**, **char**, **int**, and **float**. Now create a **.cpp** file that includes your header file and creates definitions for all of these functions. Each definition should simply print out the function name, argument list, and return type so you know it's been called. Create a second **.cpp** file that includes your header file and defines **int main( )**, containing calls to all of your functions. Compile and run your program.

2. Write a program that uses two nested **for** loops and the modulus operator (**%**) to detect and print prime numbers (integral numbers that are not evenly divisible by any other numbers except for themselves and 1).

3. Write a program that uses a **while** loop to read words from standard input (**cin**) into a **string**. This is an "infinite" **while** loop, which you break out of (and exit the program) using a **break** statement. For each word that is read, evaluate it by first using a sequence of **if** statements to "map" an integral value to the word, and then use a **switch** statement that uses that integral value as its selector (this sequence of events is not meant to be good programming style; it's just supposed to give you exercise with control flow). Inside each **case**, print something meaningful. You must decide what the "interesting" words are and what the meaning is. You must also decide what word will signal the end of the program. Test the program by redirecting a file into the program's standard input (if you want to save typing, this file can be your program's source file).

4. Modify **Menu.cpp** to use **switch** statements instead of **if** statements.

5. Write a program that evaluates the two expressions in the section labeled "precedence."

6. Modify **YourPets2.cpp** so that it uses various different data types (**char**, **int**, **float**, **double,** and their variants). Run the program and create a map of the resulting memory layout. If you have access to more than one kind

of machine, operating system, or compiler, try this experiment with as many variations as you can manage.

7. Create two functions, one that takes a **string*** and one that takes a **string&**. Each of these functions should modify the outside **string** object in its own unique way. In **main( )**, create and initialize a **string** object, print it, then pass it to each of the two functions, printing the results.

8. Write a program that uses all the trigraphs to see if your compiler supports them.

9. Compile and run **Static.cpp**. Remove the **static** keyword from the code, compile and run it again, and explain what happens.

10. Try to compile and link **FileStatic.cpp** with **FileStatic2.cpp**. What does the resulting error message mean?

11. Modify **Boolean.cpp** so that it works with **double** values instead of **int**s.

12. Modify **Boolean.cpp** and **Bitwise.cpp** so they use the explicit operators (if your compiler is conformant to the C++ Standard it will support these).

13. Modify **Bitwise.cpp** to use the functions from **Rotation.cpp**. Make sure you display the results in such a way that it's clear what's happening during rotations.

14. Modify **Ifthen.cpp** to use the ternary **if-else** operator (**?:**).

15. Create a **struct** that holds two **string** objects and one **int**. Use a **typedef** for the **struct** name. Create an instance of the **struct**, initialize all three values in your instance, and print them out. Take the address of your instance and assign it to a pointer to your **struct** type. Change the three values in your instance and print them out, all using the pointer.

16. Create a program that uses an enumeration of colors. Create a variable of this **enum** type and print out all the numbers that correspond with the color names, using a **for** loop.

17. Experiment with **Union.cpp** by removing various **union** elements to see the effects on the size of the resulting **union**. Try assigning to one element (thus one type) of the **union** and printing out a via a different element (thus a different type) to see what happens.

18. Create a program that defines two **int** arrays, one right after the other. Index off the end of the first array into the second, and make an assignment. Print out the second array to see the changes cause by this. Now try defining a **char** variable between the first array definition and the second, and repeat the experiment. You may want to create an array printing function to simplify your coding.

19. Modify **ArrayAddresses.cpp** to work with the data types **char**, **long int**, **float**, and **double**.

20. Apply the technique in **ArrayAddresses.cpp** to print out the size of the **struct** and the addresses of the array elements in **StructArray.cpp**.

21. Create an array of **string** objects and assign a string to each element. Print out the array using a **for** loop.

22. Create two new programs starting from **ArgsToInts.cpp** so they use **atol( )** and **atof( )**, respectively.

23. Modify **PointerIncrement2.cpp** so it uses a **union** instead of a **struct**.

24. Modify **PointerArithmetic.cpp** to work with **long** and **long double**.

25. Define a **float** variable. Take its address, cast that address to an **unsigned char**, and assign it to an **unsigned char** pointer. Using this pointer and **[ ]**, index into the **float** variable and use the **printBinary( )** function defined in this chapter to print out a map of the **float** (go from 0 to **sizeof(float)**). Change the value of the **float** and see if you can figure out what's going on (the **float** contains encoded data).

26. Define an array of **int**. Take the starting address of that array and use **static_cast** to convert it into an **void***. Write a function that takes a **void***, a number (indicating a number of bytes), and a value (indicating the value to which each byte should be set) as arguments. The

function should set each byte in the specified range to the specified value. Try out the function on your array of **int**.

27. Create a **const** array of **double** and a **volatile** array of **double**. Index through each array and use **const_cast** to cast each element to non-**const** and non-**volatile**, respectively, and assign a value to each element.

28. Create a function that takes a pointer to an array of **double** and a value indicating the size of that array. The function should print each element in the array. Now create an array of **double** and initialize each element to zero, then use your function to print the array. Next use **reinterpret_cast** to cast the starting address of your array to an **unsigned char***, and set each byte of the array to 1 (hint: you'll need to use **sizeof** to calculate the number of bytes in a **double**). Now use your array-printing function to print the results. Why do you think each element was not set to the value 1.0?

29. (Challenging) Modify **FloatingAsBinary.cpp** so that it prints out each part of the **double** as a separate group of bits. You'll have to replace the calls to **printBinary( )** with your own specialized code (which you can derive from **printBinary( )**) in order to do this, and you'll also have to look up and understand the floating-point format along with the byte ordering for your compiler (this is the challenging part).

30. Create a makefile that not only compiles **YourPets1.cpp** and **YourPets2.cpp** (for your particular compiler) but also executes both programs as part of the default target behavior. Make sure you use suffix rules.

31. Modify **StringizingExpressions.cpp** so that **P(A)** is conditionally **#ifdef**ed to allow the debugging code to be automatically stripped out by setting a command-line flag. You will need to consult your compiler's documentation to see how to define and undefine preprocessor values on the compiler command line.

32. Define a function that takes a **double** argument and returns an **int**. Create and initialize a pointer to this function, and call the function through your pointer.

33. Declare a pointer to a function taking an **int** argument and returning a pointer to a function that takes a **char** argument and returns a **float**.

34. Modify **FunctionTable.cpp** so that each function returns a **string** (instead of printing out a message) and so that this value is printed inside of **main( )**.

35. Create a **makefile** for one of the previous exercises (of your choice) that allows you to type **make** for a production build of the program, and **make debug** for a build of the program including debugging information.

4: Data Abstraction

C++ is a productivity enhancement tool. Why else
would you make the effort (and it is an effort,
regardless of how easy we attempt to make the
transition)

to switch from some language that you already know and are productive with to a new language in which you're going to be *less* productive for a while, until you get the hang of it? It's because you've become convinced that you're going to get big gains by using this new tool.

Productivity, in computer programming terms, means that fewer people can make much more complex and impressive programs in less time. There are certainly other issues when it comes to choosing a language, such as efficiency (does the nature of the language cause slowdown and code bloat?), safety (does the language help you ensure that your program will always do what you plan, and handle errors gracefully?), and maintenance (does the language help you create code that is easy to understand, modify, and extend?). These are certainly important factors that will be examined in this book.

But raw productivity means a program that formerly took three of you a week to write now takes one of you a day or two. This touches several levels of economics. You're happy because you get the rush of power that comes from building something, your client (or boss) is happy because products are produced faster and with fewer people, and the customers are happy because they get products more cheaply. The only way to get massive increases in productivity is to leverage off other people's code. That is, to use libraries.

A library is simply a bunch of code that someone else has written and packaged together. Often, the most minimal package is a file with an extension like **lib** and one or more header files to tell your compiler what's in the library. The linker knows how to search through the library file and extract the appropriate compiled code. But that's only one way to deliver a library. On platforms that span many architectures, such as Linux/Unix, often the only sensible way to deliver a library is with source code, so it can be reconfigured and recompiled on the new target.

Thus, libraries are probably the most important way to improve productivity, and one of the primary design goals of C++ is to make library use easier. This implies that there's something hard about using libraries in C. Understanding this factor will give you a first insight into the design of C++, and thus insight into how to use it.

A tiny C-like library

A library usually starts out as a collection of functions, but if you have used third-party C libraries you know there's usually more to it than that because there's more to life than behavior, actions, and functions. There are also characteristics (blue, pounds, texture, luminance), which are represented by data. And when you start to deal with a set of characteristics in C, it is very convenient to clump them together into a **struct**, especially if you want to represent more than one similar thing in your problem space. Then you can make a variable of this **struct** for each thing.

Thus, most C libraries have a set of **struct**s and a set of functions that act on those **struct**s. As an example of what such a system looks like, consider a programming tool that acts like an array, but whose size can be established at runtime, when it is created. I'll call it a **CStash**. Although it's written in C++, it has the style of what you'd write in C:

```
//: C04:CLib.h
// Header file for a C-like library
// An array-like entity created at runtime

typedef struct CStashTag {
  int size;       // Size of each space
  int quantity;   // Number of storage spaces
  int next;       // Next empty space
  // Dynamically allocated array of bytes:
  unsigned char* storage;
} CStash;

void initialize(CStash* s, int size);
void cleanup(CStash* s);
int add(CStash* s, const void* element);
void* fetch(CStash* s, int index);
int count(CStash* s);
void inflate(CStash* s, int increase);
///:~
```

A tag name like **CStashTag** is generally used for a **struct** in case you need to reference the **struct** inside itself. For example, when creating a *linked list* (each element in your list contains a pointer to the next element), you need a pointer to the next **struct** variable, so you need a way to identify the type of that pointer within the **struct** body. Also, you'll almost universally see the **typedef** as shown above for every **struct** in a C library. This is done so you can treat the **struct** as if it were a new type and define variables of that **struct** like this:

```
CStash A, B, C;
```

The **storage** pointer is an **unsigned char***. An **unsigned char** is the smallest piece of storage a C compiler supports, although on some machines it can be the same size as the largest. It's implementation dependent, but is often one byte long. You might think that because the **CStash** is designed to hold any type of variable, a **void*** would be more appropriate here. However, the purpose is not to treat this storage as a block of some unknown type, but rather as a block of contiguous bytes.

The source code for the implementation file (which you may not get if you buy a library commercially – you might get only a compiled **obj** or **lib** or **dll**, etc.) looks like this:

```
//: C04:CLib.cpp {O}
// Implementation of example C-like library
// Declare structure and functions:
#include "CLib.h"
#include <iostream>
#include <cassert>
using namespace std;
// Quantity of elements to add
// when increasing storage:
const int increment = 100;

void initialize(CStash* s, int sz) {
  s->size = sz;
  s->quantity = 0;
  s->storage = 0;
  s->next = 0;
}
```

```cpp
int add(CStash* s, const void* element) {
  if(s->next >= s->quantity) //Enough space left?
    inflate(s, increment);
  // Copy element into storage,
  // starting at next empty space:
  int startBytes = s->next * s->size;
  unsigned char* e = (unsigned char*)element;
  for(int i = 0; i < s->size; i++)
    s->storage[startBytes + i] = e[i];
  s->next++;
  return(s->next - 1); // Index number
}

void* fetch(CStash* s, int index) {
  // Check index boundaries:
  assert(0 <= index);
  if(index >= s->next)
    return 0; // To indicate the end
  // Produce pointer to desired element:
  return &(s->storage[index * s->size]);
}

int count(CStash* s) {
  return s->next;   // Elements in CStash
}

void inflate(CStash* s, int increase) {
  assert(increase > 0);
  int newQuantity = s->quantity + increase;
  int newBytes = newQuantity * s->size;
  int oldBytes = s->quantity * s->size;
  unsigned char* b = new unsigned char[newBytes];
  for(int i = 0; i < oldBytes; i++)
    b[i] = s->storage[i]; // Copy old to new
  delete [](s->storage); // Old storage
  s->storage = b; // Point to new memory
  s->quantity = newQuantity;
}

void cleanup(CStash* s) {
  if(s->storage != 0) {
   cout << "freeing storage" << endl;
   delete []s->storage;
  }
```

```
} ///:~
```

initialize( ) performs the necessary setup for **struct CStash** by setting the internal variables to appropriate values. Initially, the **storage** pointer is set to zero – no initial storage is allocated.

The **add( )** function inserts an element into the **CStash** at the next available location. First, it checks to see if there is any available space left. If not, it expands the storage using the **inflate( )** function, described later.

Because the compiler doesn't know the specific type of the variable being stored (all the function gets is a **void***), you can't just do an assignment, which would certainly be the convenient thing. Instead, you must copy the variable byte-by-byte. The most straightforward way to perform the copying is with array indexing. Typically, there are already data bytes in **storage**, and this is indicated by the value of **next**. To start with the right byte offset, **next** is multiplied by the size of each element (in bytes) to produce **startBytes**. Then the argument **element** is cast to an **unsigned char*** so that it can be addressed byte-by-byte and copied into the available **storage** space. **next** is incremented so that it indicates the next available piece of storage, and the "index number" where the value was stored so that value can be retrieved using this index number with **fetch( )**.

fetch( ) checks to see that the index isn't out of bounds and then returns the address of the desired variable, calculated using the **index** argument. Since **index** indicates the number of elements to offset into the **CStash**, it must be multiplied by the number of bytes occupied by each piece to produce the numerical offset in bytes. When this offset is used to index into **storage** using array indexing, you don't get the address, but instead the byte at the address. To produce the address, you must use the address-of operator **&**.

count( ) may look a bit strange at first to a seasoned C programmer. It seems like a lot of trouble to go through to do something that would probably be a lot easier to do by hand. If you have a **struct CStash** called **intStash**, for example, it would seem much more straightforward to find out how many elements it has by saying **intStash.next** instead of making a function call (which has overhead), such as **count(&intStash)**. However, if you wanted to change the internal representation of **CStash** and thus the way the count was calculated, the function call interface allows the necessary flexibility. But alas, most programmers won't bother to find out about your "better" design for the library. They'll look at the **struct** and grab the **next** value directly, and possibly even change **next** without your permission. If only there were some way for the library designer to have better control over things like this! (Yes, that's foreshadowing.)

Dynamic storage allocation

You never know the maximum amount of storage you might need for a **CStash**, so the memory pointed to by **storage** is allocated from the *heap*. The heap is a big block of memory used for allocating smaller pieces at runtime. You use the heap when you don't know the size of the memory you'll need while you're writing a program. That is, only at runtime will you find out that you need space to hold 200 **Airplane** variables instead of 20. In Standard C, dynamic-memory allocation functions include **malloc( )**, **calloc( )**, **realloc( )**, and **free( )**. Instead of library calls, however, C++ has a more sophisticated (albeit simpler to use) approach to dynamic memory that is integrated into the language via the keywords **new** and **delete**.

The **inflate( )** function uses **new** to get a bigger chunk of space for the **CStash**. In this situation, we will only expand memory and not shrink it, and the **assert( )** will guarantee that a negative number is not passed to **inflate( )** as the **increase** value. The new number of elements that can be held (after **inflate( )** completes) is calculated as **newQuantity**, and this is multiplied by the number of bytes per element to produce **newBytes**, which will be the number of bytes in the allocation. So that we know how many bytes to copy over from the old location, **oldBytes** is calculated using the old **quantity**.

The actual storage allocation occurs in the *new-expression*, which is the expression involving the **new** keyword:

```
new unsigned char[newBytes];
```

The general form of the new-expression is:

new Type;

in which **Type** describes the type of variable you want allocated on the heap. In this case, we want an array of **unsigned char** that is **newBytes** long, so that is what appears as the **Type**. You can also allocate something as simple as an **int** by saying:

```
new int;
```

and although this is rarely done, you can see that the form is consistent.

A new-expression returns a *pointer* to an object of the exact type that you asked for. So if you say **new Type**, you get back a pointer to a **Type**. If you say **new int**, you get back a pointer to an **int**. If you want a **new unsigned char** array, you get back a pointer to the first element of that array. The compiler will ensure that you assign the return value of the new-expression to a pointer of the correct type.

Of course, any time you request memory it's possible for the request to fail, if there is no more memory. As you will learn, C++ has mechanisms that come into play if the memory-allocation operation is unsuccessful.

Once the new storage is allocated, the data in the old storage must be copied to the new storage; this is again accomplished with array indexing, copying one byte at a time in a loop. After the data is copied, the old storage must be released so that it can be used by other parts of the program if they need new storage. The **delete** keyword is the complement of **new**, and must be applied to release any storage that is allocated with **new** (if you forget to use **delete**, that storage remains unavailable, and if this so-called *memory leak* happens enough, you'll run out of memory). In addition, there's a special syntax when you're deleting an array. It's as if you must remind the compiler that this pointer is not just pointing to one object, but to an array of objects: you put a set of empty square brackets in front of the pointer to be deleted:

```
delete []myArray;
```

Once the old storage has been deleted, the pointer to the new storage can be assigned to the **storage** pointer, the quantity is adjusted, and **inflate( )** has completed its job.

Note that the heap manager is fairly primitive. It gives you chunks of memory and takes them back when you **delete** them. There's no inherent facility for *heap compaction*, which compresses the heap to provide bigger free chunks. If a program allocates and frees heap storage for a while, you can end up with a *fragmented* heap that has lots of memory free, but without any pieces that are big enough to allocate the size you're looking for at the moment. A heap compactor complicates a program because it moves memory chunks around, so your pointers won't retain their proper values. Some operating environments have heap compaction built in, but they require you to use special memory *handles* (which can be temporarily converted to pointers, after locking the memory so the heap compactor can't move it) instead of pointers. You can also build your own heap-compaction scheme, but this is not a task to be undertaken lightly.

When you create a variable on the stack at compile-time, the storage for that variable is automatically created and freed by the compiler. The compiler knows exactly how much storage is needed, and it knows the lifetime of the variables because of scoping. With dynamic memory allocation, however, the compiler doesn't know how much storage you're going to need, *and* it doesn't know the lifetime of that storage. That is, the storage doesn't get cleaned up automatically. Therefore, you're responsible for releasing the storage using **delete**, which tells the heap manager that storage can be used by the next call to **new**. The logical place for this to happen in the library is in the **cleanup( )** function because that is where all the closing-up housekeeping is done.

To test the library, two **CStash**es are created. The first holds **int**s and the second holds arrays of 80 **char**s:

```
//: C04:CLibTest.cpp
//{L} CLib
// Test the C-like library
#include "CLib.h"
#include <fstream>
#include <iostream>
#include <string>
#include <cassert>
using namespace std;

int main() {
  // Define variables at the beginning
  // of the block, as in C:
  CStash intStash, stringStash;
  int i;
  char* cp;
  ifstream in;
  string line;
  const int bufsize = 80;
  // Now remember to initialize the variables:
  initialize(&intStash, sizeof(int));
  for(i = 0; i < 100; i++)
    add(&intStash, &i);
  for(i = 0; i < count(&intStash); i++)
    cout << "fetch(&intStash, " << i << ") = "
         << *(int*)fetch(&intStash, i)
         << endl;
  // Holds 80-character strings:
  initialize(&stringStash, sizeof(char)*bufsize);
  in.open("CLibTest.cpp");
  assert(in);
  while(getline(in, line))
    add(&stringStash, line.c_str());
  i = 0;
  while((cp = (char*)fetch(&stringStash,i++))!=0)
    cout << "fetch(&stringStash, " << i << ") = "
         << cp << endl;
  cleanup(&intStash);
  cleanup(&stringStash);
} ///:~
```

Following the form required by C, all the variables are created at the beginning of the scope of **main( )**. Of course, you must remember to initialize the **CStash** variables later in the block by calling

initialize( ). One of the problems with C libraries is that you must carefully convey to the user the importance of the initialization and cleanup functions. If these functions aren't called, there will be a lot of trouble. Unfortunately, the user doesn't always wonder if initialization and cleanup are mandatory. They know what *they* want to accomplish, and they're not as concerned about you jumping up and down saying, "Hey, wait, you have to do *this* first!" Some users have even been known to initialize the elements of a structure themselves. There's certainly no mechanism in C to prevent it (more foreshadowing).

The **intStash** is filled up with integers, and the **stringStash** is filled with character arrays. These character arrays are produced by opening the source code file, **CLibTest.cpp**, and reading the lines from it into a **string** called **line**, and then producing a pointer to the character representation of **line** using the member function **c_str( )**.

After each **Stash** is loaded, it is displayed. The **intStash** is printed using a **for** loop, which uses **count( )** to establish its limit. The **stringStash** is printed with a **while**, which breaks out when **fetch( )** returns zero to indicate it is out of bounds.

You'll also notice an additional cast in

```
cp = (char*)fetch(&stringStash,i++)
```

This is due to the stricter type checking in C++, which does not allow you to simply assign a **void*** to any other type (C allows this).

Bad guesses

There is one more important issue you should understand before we look at the general problems in creating a C library. Note that the **CLib.h** header file *must* be included in any file that refers to **CStash** because the compiler can't even guess at what that structure looks like. However, it *can* guess at what a function looks like; this sounds like a feature but it turns out to be a major C pitfall.

Although you should always declare functions by including a header file, function declarations aren't essential in C. It's possible in C (but *not* in C++) to call a function that you haven't declared. A good compiler will warn you that you probably ought to declare a function first, but it isn't enforced by the C language standard. This is a dangerous practice, because the C compiler can assume that a function that you call with an **int** argument has an argument list containing **int**, even if it may actually contain a **float**. This can produce bugs that are very difficult to find, as you will see.

Each separate C implementation file (with an extension of **.c**) is a *translation unit*. That is, the compiler is run separately on each translation unit, and when it is running it is aware of only that unit. Thus, any information you provide by including header files is quite important because it determines the compiler's understanding of the rest of your program. Declarations in header files are particularly important, because everywhere the header is included, the compiler will know exactly what to do. If, for example, you have a declaration in a header file that says **void func(float)**, the compiler knows that if you call that function with an integer argument, it should convert the **int** to a **float** as it passes the argument (this is called *promotion*). Without the declaration, the C compiler would simply assume that a function **func(int)** existed, it wouldn't do the promotion, and the wrong data would quietly be passed into **func( )**.

For each translation unit, the compiler creates an object file, with an extension of **.o** or **.obj** or something similar. These object files, along with the necessary start-up code, must be collected by the linker into the executable program. During linking, all the external references must be resolved. For example, in **CLibTest.cpp**, functions such as **initialize( )** and **fetch( )** are declared (that is, the compiler is told what they look like) and used, but not defined. They are defined elsewhere, in **CLib.cpp**. Thus, the calls in **CLib.cpp** are external references. The linker must, when it puts all the object files together, take the unresolved external references and find the addresses they actually refer to. Those addresses are put into the executable program to replace the external references.

It's important to realize that in C, the external references that the linker searches for are simply function names, generally with an underscore in front of them. So all the linker has to do is match up the function name where it is called and the function body in the object file, and it's done. If you accidentally made a call that the compiler interpreted as **func(int)** and there's a function body for **func(float)** in some other object file, the linker will see _**func** in one place and _**func** in another, and it will think everything's OK. The **func( )** at the calling location will push an **int** onto the stack, and the **func( )** function body will expect a **float** to be on the stack. If the function only reads the value and doesn't write to it, it won't blow up the stack. In fact, the **float** value it reads off the stack might even make some kind of sense. That's worse because it's harder to find the bug.

What's wrong?

We are remarkably adaptable, even in situations in which perhaps we *shouldn't* adapt. The style of the **CStash** library has been a staple for C programmers, but if you look at it for a while, you might notice that it's rather . . . awkward. When you use it, you have to pass the address of the structure to every single function in the library. When reading the code, the mechanism of the library gets mixed with the meaning of the function calls, which is confusing when you're trying to understand what's going on.

One of the biggest obstacles, however, to using libraries in C is the problem of *name clashes*. C has a single name space for functions; that is, when the linker looks for a function name, it looks in a single master list. In addition, when the compiler is working on a translation unit, it can work only with a single function with a given name.

Now suppose you decide to buy two libraries from two different vendors, and each library has a structure that must be initialized and cleaned up. Both vendors decided that **initialize( )** and **cleanup( )** are good names. If you include both their header files in a single translation unit, what does the C compiler do? Fortunately, C gives you an error, telling you there's a type mismatch in the two different argument lists of the declared functions. But even if you don't include them in the same translation unit, the linker will still have problems. A good linker will detect that there's a name clash, but some linkers take the first function name they find, by searching through the list of object files in the order you give them in the link list. (This can even be thought of as a feature because it allows you to replace a library function with your own version.)

In either event, you can't use two C libraries that contain a function with the identical name. To solve this problem, C library vendors will often prepend a sequence of unique characters to the beginning of all their function names. So **initialize( )** and **cleanup( )** might become **CStash_initialize( )** and **CStash_cleanup( )**. This is a logical thing to do because it "decorates" the name of the **struct** the function works on with the name of the function.

Now it's time to take the first step toward creating classes in C++. Variable names inside a **struct** do not clash with global variable names. So why not take advantage of this for function names, when those functions operate on a particular **struct**? That is, why not make functions members of **struct**s?

The basic object

Step one is exactly that. C++ functions can be placed inside **struct**s as "member functions." Here's what it looks like after converting the C version of **CStash** to the C++ **Stash**:

```
//: C04:CppLib.h
// C-like library converted to C++

struct Stash {
  int size;        // Size of each space
  int quantity;    // Number of storage spaces
  int next;        // Next empty space
   // Dynamically allocated array of bytes:
  unsigned char* storage;
  // Functions!
  void initialize(int size);
```

```
  void cleanup();
  int add(const void* element);
  void* fetch(int index);
  int count();
  void inflate(int increase);
}; ///:~
```

First, notice there is no **typedef**. Instead of requiring you to create a **typedef**, the C++ compiler turns the name of the structure into a new type name for the program (just as **int**, **char**, **float** and **double** are type names).

All the data members are exactly the same as before, but now the functions are inside the body of the **struct**. In addition, notice that the first argument from the C version of the library has been removed. In C++, instead of forcing you to pass the address of the structure as the first argument to all the functions that operate on that structure, the compiler secretly does this for you. Now the only arguments for the functions are concerned with what the function *does*, not the mechanism of the function's operation.

It's important to realize that the function code is effectively the same as it was with the C version of the library. The number of arguments is the same (even though you don't see the structure address being passed in, it's still there), and there's only one function body for each function. That is, just because you say

```
Stash A, B, C;
```

doesn't mean you get a different **add( )** function for each variable.

So the code that's generated is almost identical to what you would have written for the C version of the library. Interestingly enough, this includes the "name decoration" you probably would have done to produce **Stash_initialize( )**, **Stash_cleanup( )**, and so on. When the function name is inside the **struct**, the compiler effectively does the same thing. Therefore, **initialize( )** inside the structure **Stash** will not collide with a function named **initialize( )** inside any other structure, or even a global function named **initialize( )**. Most of the time you don't have to worry about the function name decoration – you use the undecorated name. But sometimes you do need to be able to specify that this **initialize( )** belongs to the **struct Stash**, and not to any other **struct**. In particular, when you're defining the function you need to fully specify which one it is. To accomplish this full specification, C++ has an operator (**::**) called the *scope resolution operator* (named so because names can now be in different scopes: at global scope or within the scope of a **struct**). For example, if you want to specify **initialize( )**, which belongs to **Stash**, you say **Stash::initialize(int size)**. You can see how the scope resolution operator is used in the function definitions:

```cpp
//: C04:CppLib.cpp {O}
// C library converted to C++
// Declare structure and functions:
#include "CppLib.h"
#include <iostream>
#include <cassert>
using namespace std;
// Quantity of elements to add
// when increasing storage:
const int increment = 100;

void Stash::initialize(int sz) {
  size = sz;
  quantity = 0;
  storage = 0;
  next = 0;
}

int Stash::add(const void* element) {
  if(next >= quantity) // Enough space left?
    inflate(increment);
  // Copy element into storage,
  // starting at next empty space:
  int startBytes = next * size;
  unsigned char* e = (unsigned char*)element;
  for(int i = 0; i < size; i++)
    storage[startBytes + i] = e[i];
  next++;
  return(next - 1); // Index number
}

void* Stash::fetch(int index) {
```

```
  // Check index boundaries:
  assert(0 <= index);
  if(index >= next)
    return 0; // To indicate the end
  // Produce pointer to desired element:
  return &(storage[index * size]);
}

int Stash::count() {
  return next; // Number of elements in CStash
}

void Stash::inflate(int increase) {
  assert(increase > 0);
  int newQuantity = quantity + increase;
  int newBytes = newQuantity * size;
  int oldBytes = quantity * size;
  unsigned char* b = new unsigned char[newBytes];
  for(int i = 0; i < oldBytes; i++)
    b[i] = storage[i]; // Copy old to new
  delete []storage; // Old storage
  storage = b; // Point to new memory
  quantity = newQuantity;
}

void Stash::cleanup() {
  if(storage != 0) {
    cout << "freeing storage" << endl;
    delete []storage;
  }
} ///:~
```

There are several other things that are different between C and
C++. First, the declarations in the header files are *required* by the
compiler. In C++ you cannot call a function without declaring it
first. The compiler will issue an error message otherwise. This is an
important way to ensure that function calls are consistent between
the point where they are called and the point where they are
defined. By forcing you to declare the function before you call it, the
C++ compiler virtually ensures that you will perform this
declaration by including the header file. If you also include the
same header file in the place where the functions are defined, then
the compiler checks to make sure that the declaration in the header

and the function definition match up. This means that the header file becomes a validated repository for function declarations and ensures that functions are used consistently throughout all translation units in the project.

Of course, global functions can still be declared by hand every place where they are defined and used. (This is so tedious that it becomes very unlikely.) However, structures must always be declared before they are defined or used, and the most convenient place to put a structure definition is in a header file, except for those you intentionally hide in a file.

You can see that all the member functions look almost the same as when they were C functions, except for the scope resolution and the fact that the first argument from the C version of the library is no longer explicit. It's still there, of course, because the function has to be able to work on a particular **struct** variable. But notice, inside the member function, that the member selection is also gone! Thus, instead of saying **s−>size = sz;** you say **size = sz;** and eliminate the tedious **s−>**, which didn't really add anything to the meaning of what you were doing anyway. The C++ compiler is apparently doing this for you. Indeed, it is taking the "secret" first argument (the address of the structure that we were previously passing in by hand) and applying the member selector whenever you refer to one of the data members of a **struct**. This means that whenever you are inside the member function of another **struct**, you can refer to any member (including another member function) by simply giving its name. The compiler will search through the local structure's names before looking for a global version of that name. You'll find that this feature means that not only is your code easier to write, it's a lot easier to read.

But what if, for some reason, you *want* to be able to get your hands on the address of the structure? In the C version of the library it was easy because each function's first argument was a **CStash*** called **s**. In C++, things are even more consistent. There's a special keyword, called **this**, which produces the address of the **struct**. It's the equivalent of the 's' in the C version of the library. So we can revert to the C style of things by saying

```
this->size = Size;
```

The code generated by the compiler is exactly the same, so you don't need to use **this** in such a fashion; occasionally, you'll see code where people explicitly use **this->** everywhere but it doesn't add anything to the meaning of the code and often indicates an inexperienced programmer. Usually, you don't use **this** often, but when you need it, it's there (some of the examples later in the book will use **this**).

There's one last item to mention. In C, you could assign a **void*** to any other pointer like this:

```
int i = 10;
void* vp = &i; // OK in both C and C++
int* ip = vp; // Only acceptable in C
```

and there was no complaint from the compiler. But in C++, this statement is not allowed. Why? Because C is not so particular about type information, so it allows you to assign a pointer with an unspecified type to a pointer with a specified type. Not so with C++. Type is critical in C++, and the compiler stamps its foot when there are any violations of type information. This has always been important, but it is especially important in C++ because you have member functions in **struct**s. If you could pass pointers to **struct**s around with impunity in C++, then you could end up calling a member function for a **struct** that doesn't even logically exist for that **struct**! A real recipe for disaster. Therefore, while C++ allows the assignment of any type of pointer to a **void*** (this was the original intent of **void***, which is required to be large enough to hold a pointer to any type), it will *not* allow you to assign a **void** pointer to any other type of pointer. A cast is always required to tell the reader and the compiler that you really do want to treat it as the destination type.

This brings up an interesting issue. One of the important goals for C++ is to compile as much existing C code as possible to allow for an easy transition to the new language. However, this doesn't mean any code that C allows will automatically be allowed in C++. There are a number of things the C compiler lets you get away with that are dangerous and error-prone. (We'll look at them as the book progresses.) The C++ compiler generates warnings and errors for these situations. This is often much more of an advantage than a hindrance. In fact, there are many situations in which you are trying to run down an error in C and just can't find it, but as soon as you recompile the program in C++, the compiler points out the problem! In C, you'll often find that you can get the program to compile, but then you have to get it to work. In C++, when the program compiles correctly, it often works, too! This is because the language is a lot stricter about type.

You can see a number of new things in the way the C++ version of **Stash** is used in the following test program:

```
//: C04:CppLibTest.cpp
//{L} CppLib
// Test of C++ library
#include "CppLib.h"
#include "../require.h"
#include <fstream>
#include <iostream>
#include <string>
using namespace std;

int main() {
  Stash intStash;
  intStash.initialize(sizeof(int));
  for(int i = 0; i < 100; i++)
    intStash.add(&i);
  for(int j = 0; j < intStash.count(); j++)
    cout << "intStash.fetch(" << j << ") = "
         << *(int*)intStash.fetch(j)
         << endl;
  // Holds 80-character strings:
  Stash stringStash;
  const int bufsize = 80;
  stringStash.initialize(sizeof(char) * bufsize);
  ifstream in("CppLibTest.cpp");
  assure(in, "CppLibTest.cpp");
  string line;
  while(getline(in, line))
    stringStash.add(line.c_str());
  int k = 0;
  char* cp;
```

```
  while((cp =(char*)stringStash.fetch(k++)) != 0)
    cout << "stringStash.fetch(" << k << ") = "
        << cp << endl;
  intStash.cleanup();
  stringStash.cleanup();
} ///:~
```

One thing you'll notice is that the variables are all defined "on the fly" (as introduced in the previous chapter). That is, they are defined at any point in the scope, rather than being restricted – as in C – to the beginning of the scope.

The code is quite similar to **CLibTest.cpp**, but when a member function is called, the call occurs using the member selection operator '**.**' preceded by the name of the variable. This is a convenient syntax because it mimics the selection of a data member of the structure. The difference is that this is a function member, so it has an argument list.

Of course, the call that the compiler *actually* generates looks much more like the original C library function. Thus, considering name decoration and the passing of **this**, the C++ function call **intStash.initialize(sizeof(int), 100)** becomes something like **Stash_initialize(&intStash, sizeof(int), 100)**. If you ever wonder what's going on underneath the covers, remember that the original C++ compiler **cfront** from AT&T produced C code as its output, which was then compiled by the underlying C compiler. This approach meant that **cfront** could be quickly ported to any machine that had a C compiler, and it helped to rapidly disseminate C++ compiler technology. But because the C++ compiler had to generate C, you know that there must be some way to represent C++ syntax in C (some compilers still allow you to produce C code).

There's one other change from **ClibTest.cpp**, which is the introduction of the **require.h** header file. This is a header file that I created for this book to perform more sophisticated error checking than that provided by **assert( )**. It contains several functions, including the one used here called **assure( ),** which is used for files. This function checks to see if the file has successfully been opened, and if not it reports to standard error that the file could not be opened (thus it needs the name of the file as the second

---

argument) and exits the program. The **require.h** functions will be used throughout the book, in particular to ensure that there are the right number of command-line arguments and that files are opened properly. The **require.h** functions replace repetitive and distracting error-checking code, and yet they provide essentially useful error messages. These functions will be fully explained later in the book.

What's an object?

Now that you've seen an initial example, it's time to step back and take a look at some terminology. The act of bringing functions inside structures is the root of what C++ adds to C, and it introduces a new way of thinking about structures: as concepts. In C, a **struct** is an agglomeration of data, a way to package data so you can treat it in a clump. But it's hard to think about it as anything but a programming convenience. The functions that operate on those structures are elsewhere. However, with functions in the package, the structure becomes a new creature, capable of describing both characteristics (like a C **struct** does) *and* behaviors. The concept of an object, a free-standing, bounded entity that can remember *and* act, suggests itself.

In C++, an object is just a variable, and the purest definition is "a region of storage" (this is a more specific way of saying, "an object must have a unique identifier," which in the case of C++ is a unique memory address). It's a place where you can store data, and it's implied that there are also operations that can be performed on this data.

Unfortunately, there's not complete consistency across languages when it comes to these terms, although they are fairly well-accepted. You will also sometimes encounter disagreement about what an object-oriented language is, although that seems to be reasonably well sorted out by now. There are languages that are *object-based*, which means that they have objects like the C++ structures-with-functions that you've seen so far. This, however, is only part of the picture when it comes to an object-oriented language, and languages that stop at packaging functions inside data structures are object-based, not object-oriented.

Abstract data typing

The ability to package data with functions allows you to create a new data type. This is often called *encapsulation*[1]. An existing data type may have several pieces of data packaged together. For example, a **float** has an exponent, a mantissa, and a sign bit. You can tell it to do things: add to another **float** or to an **int**, and so on. It has characteristics and behavior.

The definition of **Stash** creates a new data type. You can **add( )**, **fetch( )**, and **inflate( )**. You create one by saying **Stash s**, just as you create a **float** by saying **float f**. A **Stash** also has characteristics and behavior. Even though it acts like a real, built-in data type, we refer to it as an *abstract data type*, perhaps because it allows us to abstract a concept from the problem space into the solution space. In addition, the C++ compiler treats it like a new data type, and if you say a function expects a **Stash**, the compiler makes sure you pass a **Stash** to that function. So the same level of type checking happens with abstract data types (sometimes called *user-defined types*) as with built-in types.

You can immediately see a difference, however, in the way you perform operations on objects. You say **object.memberFunction(arglist)**. This is "calling a member function for an object." But in object-oriented parlance, this is also referred to as "sending a message to an object." So for a **Stash s**, the statement **s.add(&i)** "sends a message to **s**" saying, "**add( )** this to yourself." In fact, object-oriented programming can be summed up in a single phrase: *sending messages to objects*. Really, that's all you do – create a bunch of objects and send messages to them. The trick, of course, is figuring out what your objects and

---

[1] This term can cause debate. Some people use it as defined here; others use it to describe *access control*, discussed in the following chapter.

---

messages *are*, but once you accomplish this the implementation in C++ is surprisingly straightforward.

Object details

A question that often comes up in seminars is, "How big is an object, and what does it look like?" The answer is "about what you expect from a C **struct**." In fact, the code the C compiler produces for a C **struct** (with no C++ adornments) will usually look *exactly* the same as the code produced by a C++ compiler. This is reassuring to those C programmers who depend on the details of size and layout in their code, and for some reason directly access structure bytes instead of using identifiers (relying on a particular size and layout for a structure is a nonportable activity).

The size of a **struct** is the combined size of all of its members. Sometimes when the compiler lays out a **struct**, it adds extra bytes to make the boundaries come out neatly – this may increase execution efficiency. In Chapter 15, you'll see how in some cases "secret" pointers are added to the structure, but you don't need to worry about that right now.

You can determine the size of a **struct** using the **sizeof** operator. Here's a small example:

```
//: C04:Sizeof.cpp
// Sizes of structs
#include "CLib.h"
#include "CppLib.h"
#include <iostream>
using namespace std;

struct A {
  int i[100];
};

struct B {
  void f();
};

void B::f() {}
```

```
int main() {
  cout << "sizeof struct A = " << sizeof(A)
       << " bytes" << endl;
  cout << "sizeof struct B = " << sizeof(B)
       << " bytes" << endl;
  cout << "sizeof CStash in C = "
       << sizeof(CStash) << " bytes" << endl;
  cout << "sizeof Stash in C++ = "
       << sizeof(Stash) << " bytes" << endl;
} ///:~
```

On my machine (your results may vary) the first print statement produces 200 because each **int** occupies two bytes. **struct B** is something of an anomaly because it is a **struct** with no data members. In C, this is illegal, but in C++ we need the option of creating a **struct** whose sole task is to scope function names, so it is allowed. Still, the result produced by the second print statement is a somewhat surprising nonzero value. In early versions of the language, the size was zero, but an awkward situation arises when you create such objects: They have the same address as the object created directly after them, and so are not distinct. One of the fundamental rules of objects is that each object must have a unique address, so structures with no data members will always have some minimum nonzero size.

The last two **sizeof** statements show you that the size of the structure in C++ is the same as the size of the equivalent version in C. C++ tries not to add any unnecessary overhead.

Header file etiquette

When you create a **struct** containing member functions, you are creating a new data type. In general, you want this type to be easily accessible to yourself and others. In addition, you want to separate the interface (the declaration) from the implementation (the definition of the member functions) so the implementation can be changed without forcing a re-compile of the entire system. You achieve this end by putting the declaration for your new type in a header file.

When I first learned to program in C, the header file was a mystery to me. Many C books don't seem to emphasize it, and the compiler didn't enforce function declarations, so it seemed optional most of the time, except when structures were declared. In C++ the use of header files becomes crystal clear. They are virtually mandatory for easy program development, and you put very specific information in them: declarations. The header file tells the compiler what is available in your library. You can use the library even if you only possess the header file along with the object file or library file; you don't need the source code for the **cpp** file. The header file is where the interface specification is stored.

Although it is not enforced by the compiler, the best approach to building large projects in C is to use libraries; collect associated functions into the same object module or library, and use a header file to hold all the declarations for the functions. It is *de rigueur* in C++; you could throw any function into a C library, but the C++ abstract data type determines the functions that are associated by dint of their common access to the data in a **struct**. Any member function must be declared in the **struct** declaration; you cannot put it elsewhere. The use of function libraries was encouraged in C and institutionalized in C++.

Importance of header files

When using a function from a library, C allows you the option of ignoring the header file and simply declaring the function by hand. In the past, people would sometimes do this to speed up the compiler just a bit by avoiding the task of opening and including the file (this is usually not an issue with modern compilers). For example, here's an extremely lazy declaration of the C function **printf( )** (from **<stdio.h>**):

```
printf(...);
```

The ellipses specify a *variable argument list*[2], which says: **printf( )** has some arguments, each of which has a type, but ignore that. Just take whatever arguments you see and accept them. By using this kind of declaration, you suspend all error checking on the arguments.

This practice can cause subtle problems. If you declare functions by hand, in one file you may make a mistake. Since the compiler sees only your hand-declaration in that file, it may be able to adapt to your mistake. The program will then link correctly, but the use of the function in that one file will be faulty. This is a tough error to find, and is easily avoided by using a header file.

If you place all your function declarations in a header file, and include that header everywhere you use the function and where you define the function, you ensure a consistent declaration across the whole system. You also ensure that the declaration and the definition match by including the header in the definition file.

If a **struct** is declared in a header file in C++, you *must* include the header file everywhere a **struct** is used and where **struct** member functions are defined. The C++ compiler will give an error message if you try to call a regular function, or to call or define a member function, without declaring it first. By enforcing the proper use of header files, the language ensures consistency in libraries, and reduces bugs by forcing the same interface to be used everywhere.

The header is a contract between you and the user of your library. The contract describes your data structures, and states the arguments and return values for the function calls. It says, "Here's what my library does." The user needs some of this information to develop the application and the compiler needs all of it to generate proper code. The user of the **struct** simply includes the header file, creates objects (instances) of that **struct**, and links in the object module or library (i.e.: the compiled code).

---

[2] To write a function definition for a function that takes a true variable argument list, you must use *varargs*, although these should be avoided in C++. You can find details about the use of varargs in your C manual.

The compiler enforces the contract by requiring you to declare all structures and functions before they are used and, in the case of member functions, before they are defined. Thus, you're forced to put the declarations in the header and to include the header in the file where the member functions are defined and the file(s) where they are used. Because a single header file describing your library is included throughout the system, the compiler can ensure consistency and prevent errors.

There are certain issues that you must be aware of in order to organize your code properly and write effective header files. The first issue concerns what you can put into header files. The basic rule is "only declarations," that is, only information to the compiler but nothing that allocates storage by generating code or creating variables. This is because the header file will typically be included in several translation units in a project, and if storage for one identifier is allocated in more than one place, the linker will come up with a multiple definition error (this is C++'s *one definition rule*: You can declare things as many times as you want, but there can be only one actual definition for each thing).

This rule isn't completely hard and fast. If you define a variable that is "file static" (has visibility only within a file) inside a header file, there will be multiple instances of that data across the project, but the linker won't have a collision[3]. Basically, you don't want to do anything in the header file that will cause an ambiguity at link time.

The multiple-declaration problem

The second header-file issue is this: when you put a **struct** declaration in a header file, it is possible for the file to be included more than once in a complicated program. Iostreams are a good example. Any time a **struct** does I/O it may include one of the iostream headers. If the **cpp** file you are working on uses more than one kind of **struct** (typically including a header file for each one), you run the risk of including the **<iostream>** header more than once and re-declaring iostreams.

---

[3] However, in Standard C++ file static is a deprecated feature.

The compiler considers the redeclaration of a structure (this includes both **struct**s and **class**es) to be an error, since it would otherwise allow you to use the same name for different types. To prevent this error when multiple header files are included, you need to build some intelligence into your header files using the preprocessor (Standard C++ header files like **<iostream>** already have this "intelligence").

Both C and C++ allow you to redeclare a function, as long as the two declarations match, but neither will allow the redeclaration of a structure. In C++ this rule is especially important because if the compiler allowed you to redeclare a structure and the two declarations differed, which one would it use?

The problem of redeclaration comes up quite a bit in C++ because each data type (structure with functions) generally has its own header file, and you have to include one header in another if you want to create another data type that uses the first one. In any **cpp** file in your project, it's likely that you'll include several files that include the same header file. During a single compilation, the compiler can see the same header file several times. Unless you do something about it, the compiler will see the redeclaration of your structure and report a compile-time error. To solve the problem, you need to know a bit more about the preprocessor.

The preprocessor directives
#define, #ifdef, and #endif

The preprocessor directive **#define** can be used to create compile-time flags. You have two choices: you can simply tell the preprocessor that the flag is defined, without specifying a value:

```
#define FLAG
```

or you can give it a value (which is the typical C way to define a constant):

```
#define PI 3.14159
```

In either case, the label can now be tested by the preprocessor to see if it has been defined:

```
#ifdef FLAG
```

This will yield a true result, and the code following the **#ifdef** will be included in the package sent to the compiler. This inclusion stops when the preprocessor encounters the statement

```
#endif
```

or

```
#endif // FLAG
```

Any non-comment after the **#endif** on the same line is illegal, even though some compilers may accept it. The **#ifdef**/**#endif** pairs may be nested within each other.

The complement of **#define** is **#undef** (short for "un-define"), which will make an **#ifdef** statement using the same variable yield a false result. **#undef** will also cause the preprocessor to stop using a macro. The complement of **#ifdef** is **#ifndef**, which will yield a true if the label has not been defined (this is the one we will use in header files).

There are other useful features in the C preprocessor. You should check your local documentation for the full set.

A standard for header files

In each header file that contains a structure, you should first check to see if this header has already been included in this particular **cpp** file. You do this by testing a preprocessor flag. If the flag isn't set, the file wasn't included and you should set the flag (so the structure can't get re-declared) and declare the structure. If the flag was set then that type has already been declared so you should just ignore the code that declares it. Here's how the header file should look:

```
#ifndef HEADER_FLAG
#define HEADER_FLAG
// Type declaration here...
#endif // HEADER_FLAG
```

As you can see, the first time the header file is included, the contents of the header file (including your type declaration) will be included by the preprocessor. All the subsequent times it is included – in a single compilation unit – the type declaration will be ignored. The name HEADER_FLAG can be any unique name, but a reliable standard to follow is to capitalize the name of the header file and replace periods with underscores (leading underscores, however, are reserved for system names). Here's an example:

```
//: C04:Simple.h
// Simple header that prevents re-definition
#ifndef SIMPLE_H
#define SIMPLE_H

struct Simple {
  int i,j,k;
  initialize() { i = j = k = 0; }
};
#endif // SIMPLE_H ///:~
```

Although the **SIMPLE_H** after the **#endif** is commented out and thus ignored by the preprocessor, it is useful for documentation.

These preprocessor statements that prevent multiple inclusion are often referred to as *include guards*.

Namespaces in headers

You'll notice that *using directives* are present in nearly all the **cpp** files in this book, usually in the form:

```
using namespace std;
```

Since **std** is the namespace that surrounds the entire Standard C++ library, this particular using directive allows the names in the Standard C++ library to be used without qualification. However, you'll virtually never see a using directive in a header file (at least, not outside of a scope). The reason is that the using directive eliminates the protection of that particular namespace, and the effect lasts until the end of the current compilation unit. If you put a using directive (outside of a scope) in a header file, it means that this loss of "namespace protection" will occur with any file that includes this header, which often means other header files. Thus, if you start putting using directives in header files, it's very easy to end up "turning off" namespaces practically everywhere, and thereby neutralizing the beneficial effects of namespaces.

In short: don't put using directives in header files.

Using headers in projects

When building a project in C++, you'll usually create it by bringing together a lot of different types (data structures with associated functions). You'll usually put the declaration for each type or group of associated types in a separate header file, then define the functions for that type in a translation unit. When you use that type, you must include the header file to perform the declarations properly.

Sometimes that pattern will be followed in this book, but more often the examples will be very small, so everything – the structure declarations, function definitions, and the **main( )** function – may appear in a single file. However, keep in mind that you'll want to use separate files and header files in practice.

Nested structures

The convenience of taking data and function names out of the global name space extends to structures. You can nest a structure within another structure, and therefore keep associated elements together. The declaration syntax is what you would expect, as you can see in the following structure, which implements a push-down stack as a simple linked list so it "never" runs out of memory:

```
//: C04:Stack.h
// Nested struct in linked list
#ifndef STACK_H
#define STACK_H

struct Stack {
  struct Link {
```

```
    void* data;
    Link* next;
    void initialize(void* dat, Link* nxt);
  }* head;
  void initialize();
  void push(void* dat);
  void* peek();
  void* pop();
  void cleanup();
};
#endif // STACK_H ///:~
```

The nested **struct** is called **Link**, and it contains a pointer to the next **Link** in the list and a pointer to the data stored in the **Link**. If the **next** pointer is zero, it means you're at the end of the list.

Notice that the **head** pointer is defined right after the declaration for **struct Link**, instead of a separate definition **Link* head**. This is a syntax that came from C, but it emphasizes the importance of the semicolon after the structure declaration; the semicolon indicates the end of the comma-separated list of definitions of that structure type. (Usually the list is empty.)

The nested structure has its own **initialize( )** function, like all the structures presented so far, to ensure proper initialization. **Stack** has both an **initialize( )** and **cleanup( )** function, as well as **push( )**, which takes a pointer to the data you wish to store (it assumes this has been allocated on the heap), and **pop( )**, which returns the **data** pointer from the top of the **Stack** and removes the top element. (When you **pop( )** an element, you are responsible for destroying the object pointed to by the **data**.) The **peek( )** function also returns the **data** pointer from the top element, but it leaves the top element on the **Stack**.

Here are the definitions for the member functions:

```
//: C04:Stack.cpp {O}
// Linked list with nesting
#include "Stack.h"
#include "../require.h"
using namespace std;
```

```
void
Stack::Link::initialize(void* dat, Link* nxt) {
  data = dat;
  next = nxt;
}

void Stack::initialize() { head = 0; }

void Stack::push(void* dat) {
  Link* newLink = new Link;
  newLink->initialize(dat, head);
  head = newLink;
}

void* Stack::peek() {
  require(head != 0, "Stack empty");
  return head->data;
}

void* Stack::pop() {
  if(head == 0) return 0;
  void* result = head->data;
  Link* oldHead = head;
  head = head->next;
  delete oldHead;
  return result;
}

void Stack::cleanup() {
  require(head == 0, "Stack not empty");
} ///:~
```

The first definition is particularly interesting because it shows you
how to define a member of a nested structure. You simply use an
additional level of scope resolution to specify the name of the
enclosing **struct**. **Stack::Link::initialize( )** takes the arguments
and assigns them to its members.

Stack::initialize( ) sets **head** to zero, so the object knows it has
an empty list.

Stack::push( ) takes the argument, which is a pointer to the
variable you want to keep track of, and pushes it on the **Stack**.

First, it uses **new** to allocate storage for the **Link** it will insert at the top. Then it calls **Link**'s **initialize( )** function to assign the appropriate values to the members of the **Link**. Notice that the **next** pointer is assigned to the current **head**; then **head** is assigned to the new **Link** pointer. This effectively pushes the **Link** in at the top of the list.

Stack::pop( ) captures the **data** pointer at the current top of the **Stack**; then it moves the **head** pointer down and deletes the old top of the **Stack**, finally returning the captured pointer. When **pop( )** removes the last element, then **head** again becomes zero, meaning the **Stack** is empty.

Stack::cleanup( ) doesn't actually do any cleanup. Instead, it establishes a firm policy that "you (the client programmer using this **Stack** object) are responsible for popping all the elements off this **Stack** and deleting them." The **require( )** is used to indicate that a programming error has occurred if the **Stack** is not empty.

Why couldn't the **Stack** destructor be responsible for all the objects that the client programmer didn't **pop( )**? The problem is that the **Stack** is holding **void** pointers, and you'll learn in Chapter 13 that calling **delete** for a **void*** doesn't clean things up properly. The subject of "who's responsible for the memory" is not even *that* simple, as we'll see in later chapters.

Here's an example to test the **Stack**:

```
//: C04:StackTest.cpp
//{L} Stack
//{T} StackTest.cpp
// Test of nested linked list
#include "Stack.h"
#include "../require.h"
#include <fstream>
#include <iostream>
#include <string>
using namespace std;

int main(int argc, char* argv[]) {
  requireArgs(argc, 1); // File name is argument
```

```
ifstream in(argv[1]);
assure(in, argv[1]);
Stack textlines;
textlines.initialize();
string line;
// Read file and store lines in the Stack:
while(getline(in, line))
  textlines.push(new string(line));
// Pop the lines from the Stack and print them:
string* s;
while((s = (string*)textlines.pop()) != 0) {
  cout << *s << endl;
  delete s;
}
textlines.cleanup();
} ///:~
```

This is similar to the earlier example, but it pushes lines from a file (as **string** pointers) on the **Stack** and then pops them off, which results in the file being printed out in reverse order. Note that the **pop( )** member function returns a **void*** and this must be cast back to a **string*** before it can be used. To print the **string**, the pointer is dereferenced.

As **textlines** is being filled, the contents of **line** is "cloned" for each **push( )** by making a **new string(line)**. The value returned from the new-expression is a pointer to the new **string** that was created and that copied the information from **line**. If you had simply passed the address of **line** to **push( )**, you would end up with a **Stack** filled with identical addresses, all pointing to **line**. You'll learn more about this "cloning" process later in the book.

The file name is taken from the command line. To guarantee that there are enough arguments on the command line, you see a second function used from the **require.h** header file: **requireArgs( )**, which compares **argc** to the desired number of arguments and prints an appropriate error message and exits the program if there aren't enough arguments.

Global scope resolution

The scope resolution operator gets you out of situations in which the name the compiler chooses by default (the "nearest" name) isn't what you want. For example, suppose you have a structure with a local identifier **a**, and you want to select a global identifier **a** from inside a member function. The compiler would default to choosing the local one, so you must tell it to do otherwise. When you want to specify a global name using scope resolution, you use the operator with nothing in front of it. Here's an example that shows global scope resolution for both a variable and a function:

```
//: C04:Scoperes.cpp
// Global scope resolution
int a;
void f() {}

struct S {
  int a;
  void f();
};

void S::f() {
  ::f();   // Would be recursive otherwise!
  ::a++;   // Select the global a
  a--;     // The a at struct scope
}
int main() { S s; f(); } ///:~
```

Without scope resolution in **S::f( )**, the compiler would default to selecting the member versions of **f( )** and **a**.

Summary

In this chapter, you've learned the fundamental "twist" of C++: that you can place functions inside of structures. This new type of structure is called an *abstract data type*, and variables you create using this structure are called *objects*, or *instances*, of that type. Calling a member function for an object is called *sending a message* to that object. The primary action in object-oriented programming is sending messages to objects.

Although packaging data and functions together is a significant benefit for code organization and makes library use easier because it prevents name clashes by hiding the names, there's a lot more you can do to make programming safer in C++. In the next chapter, you'll learn how to protect some members of a **struct** so that only you can manipulate them. This establishes a clear boundary between what the user of the structure can change and what only the programmer may change.

Exercises

Solutions to selected exercises can be found in the electronic document *The Thinking in C++ Annotated Solution Guide*, available for a small fee from http://www.BruceEckel.com.

1. In the Standard C library, the function **puts( )** prints a char array to the console (so you can say **puts("hello")**). Write a C program that uses **puts( )** but does not include **<stdio.h>** or otherwise declare the function. Compile this program with your C compiler. (Some C++ compilers are not distinct from their C compilers; in this case you may need to discover a command-line flag that forces a C compilation.) Now compile it with the C++ compiler and note the difference.

2. Create a **struct** declaration with a single member function, then create a definition for that member function. Create an object of your new data type, and call the member function.

3. Change your solution to Exercise 2 so the **struct** is declared in a properly "guarded" header file, with the definition in one **cpp** file and your **main( )** in another.

4. Create a **struct** with a single **int** data member, and two global functions, each of which takes a pointer to that **struct**. The first function has a second **int** argument and sets the **struct**'s **int** to the argument value, the second displays the **int** from the **struct**. Test the functions.

5. Repeat Exercise 4 but move the functions so they are member functions of the **struct**, and test again.

6. Create a class that (redundantly) performs data member selection and a member function call using the **this**

keyword (which refers to the address of the current object).

7. Make a **Stash** that holds **double**s. Fill it with 25 **double** values, then print them out to the console.

8. Repeat Exercise 7 with **Stack**.

9. Create a file containing a function **f( )** that takes an **int** argument and prints it to the console using the **printf( )** function in **<stdio.h>** by saying: **printf("%d\n", i)** in which **i** is the **int** you wish to print. Create a separate file containing **main( )**, and in this file declare **f( )** to take a **float** argument. Call **f( )** from inside **main( )**. Try to compile and link your program with the C++ compiler and see what happens. Now compile and link the program using the C compiler, and see what happens when it runs. Explain the behavior.

10. Find out how to produce assembly language from your C and C++ compilers. Write a function in C and a **struct** with a single member function in C++. Produce assembly language from each and find the function names that are produced by your C function and your C++ member function, so you can see what sort of name decoration occurs inside the compiler.

11. Write a program with conditionally-compiled code in **main( )**, so that when a preprocessor value is defined one message is printed, but when it is not defined another message is printed. Compile this code experimenting with a **#define** within the program, then discover the way your compiler takes preprocessor definitions on the command line and experiment with that.

12. Write a program that uses **assert( )** with an argument that is always false (zero) to see what happens when you run it. Now compile it with **#define NDEBUG** and run it again to see the difference.

13. Create an abstract data type that represents a videotape in a video rental store. Try to consider all the data and operations that may be necessary for the **Video** type to work well within the video rental management system.

Include a **print( )** member function that displays information about the **Video**.

14. Create a **Stack** object to hold the **Video** objects from Exercise 13. Create several **Video** objects, store them in the **Stack**, then display them using **Video::print( )**.

15. Write a program that prints out all the sizes for the fundamental data types on your computer using **sizeof**.

16. Modify **Stash** to use a **vector<char>** as its underlying data structure.

17. Dynamically create pieces of storage of the following types, using **new**: **int**, **long**, an array of 100 **char**s, an array of 100 **float**s. Print the addresses of these and then free the storage using **delete**.

18. Write a function that takes a **char*** argument. Using **new**, dynamically allocate an array of **char** that is the size of the **char** array that's passed to the function. Using array indexing, copy the characters from the argument to the dynamically allocated array (don't forget the null terminator) and return the pointer to the copy. In your **main( )**, test the function by passing a static quoted character array, then take the result of that and pass it back into the function. Print both strings and both pointers so you can see they are different storage. Using **delete**, clean up all the dynamic storage.

19. Show an example of a structure declared within another structure (a *nested structure*). Declare data members in both **struct**s, and declare and define member functions in both **struct**s. Write a **main( )** that tests your new types.

20. How big is a structure? Write a piece of code that prints the size of various structures. Create structures that have data members only and ones that have data members and function members. Then create a structure that has no members at all. Print out the sizes of all these. Explain the reason for the result of the structure with no data members at all.

21. C++ automatically creates the equivalent of a **typedef** for **struct**s, as you've seen in this chapter. It also does this

for enumerations and unions. Write a small program that demonstrates this.

22. Create a **Stack** that holds **Stash**es. Each **Stash** will hold five lines from an input file. Create the **Stash**es using **new**. Read a file into your **Stack**, then reprint it in its original form by extracting it from the **Stack**.

23. Modify Exercise 22 so that you create a **struct** that encapsulates the **Stack** of **Stash**es. The user should only add and get lines via member functions, but under the covers the **struct** happens to use a **Stack** of **Stash**es.

24. Create a **struct** that holds an **int** and a pointer to another instance of the same **struct**. Write a function that takes the address of one of these **struct**s and an **int** indicating the length of the list you want created. This function will make a whole chain of these **struct**s (a *linked list*), starting from the argument (the *head* of the list), with each one pointing to the next. Make the new **struct**s using **new**, and put the count (which object number this is) in the **int**. In the last **struct** in the list, put a zero value in the pointer to indicate that it's the end. Write a second function that takes the head of your list and moves through to the end, printing out both the pointer value and the **int** value for each one.

25. Repeat Exercise 24, but put the functions inside a **struct** instead of using "raw" **struct**s and functions.

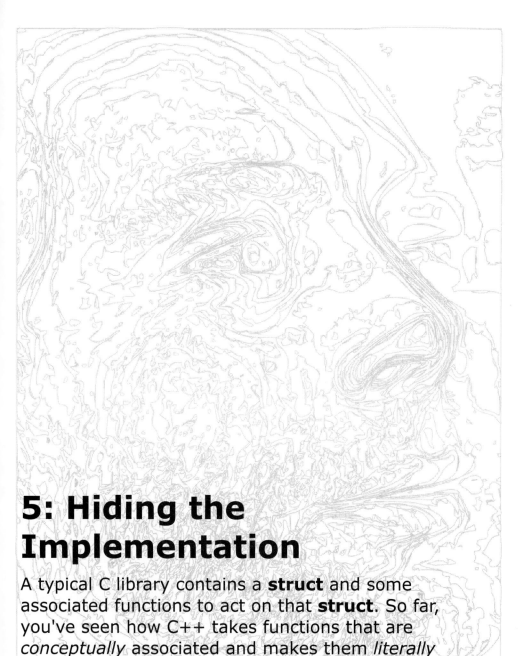

5: Hiding the Implementation

A typical C library contains a **struct** and some associated functions to act on that **struct**. So far, you've seen how C++ takes functions that are *conceptually* associated and makes them *literally* associated by putting the function declarations inside the scope of the **struct**, changing the way functions are called for the **struct**, eliminating the passing of the structure address as the first argument, and adding a new type name to the program (so you don't have to create a **typedef** for the **struct** tag).

These are all convenient – they help you organize your code and make it easier to write and read. However, there are other important issues when making libraries easier in C++, especially the issues of safety and control. This chapter looks at the subject of boundaries in structures.

Setting limits

In any relationship it's important to have boundaries that are respected by all parties involved. When you create a library, you establish a relationship with the *client programmer* who uses that library to build an application or another library.

In a C **struct**, as with most things in C, there are no rules. Client programmers can do anything they want with that **struct**, and there's no way to force any particular behaviors. For example, even though you saw in the last chapter the importance of the functions named **initialize( )** and **cleanup( )**, the client programmer has the option not to call those functions. (We'll look at a better approach in the next chapter.) And even though you would really prefer that the client programmer not directly manipulate some of the members of your **struct**, in C there's no way to prevent it. Everything's naked to the world.

There are two reasons for controlling access to members. The first is to keep the client programmer's hands off tools they shouldn't touch, tools that are necessary for the internal machinations of the data type, but not part of the interface the client programmer needs to solve their particular problems. This is actually a service to client programmers because they can easily see what's important to them and what they can ignore.

The second reason for access control is to allow the library designer to change the internal workings of the structure without worrying about how it will affect the client programmer. In the **Stack** example in the last chapter, you might want to allocate the storage in big chunks, for speed, rather than creating new storage each time an element is added. If the interface and implementation are clearly separated and protected, you can accomplish this and require only a relink by the client programmer.

C++ access control

C++ introduces three new keywords to set the boundaries in a structure: **public**, **private**, and **protected**. Their use and meaning are remarkably straightforward. These *access specifiers* are used only in a structure declaration, and they change the boundary for all the declarations that follow them. Whenever you use an access specifier, it must be followed by a colon.

public means all member declarations that follow are available to everyone. **public** members are like **struct** members. For example, the following **struct** declarations are identical:

```
//: C05:Public.cpp
// Public is just like C's struct

struct A {
  int i;
  char j;
  float f;
  void func();
};

void A::func() {}

struct B {
public:
  int i;
  char j;
  float f;
  void func();
};
```

```
void B::func() {}

int main() {
  A a; B b;
  a.i = b.i = 1;
  a.j = b.j = 'c';
  a.f = b.f = 3.14159;
  a.func();
  b.func();
} ///:~
```

The **private** keyword, on the other hand, means that no one can access that member except you, the creator of the type, inside function members of that type. **private** is a brick wall between you and the client programmer; if someone tries to access a **private** member, they'll get a compile-time error. In **struct B** in the example above, you may want to make portions of the representation (that is, the data members) hidden, accessible only to you:

```
//: C05:Private.cpp
// Setting the boundary

struct B {
private:
  char j;
  float f;
public:
  int i;
  void func();
};

void B::func() {
  i = 0;
  j = '0';
  f = 0.0;
};

int main() {
  B b;
  b.i = 1;      // OK, public
//!  b.j = '1';  // Illegal, private
//!  b.f = 1.0;  // Illegal, private
```

```
} ///:~
```

Although **func( )** can access any member of **B** (because **func( )** is a member of **B**, thus automatically granting it permission), an ordinary global function like **main( )** cannot. Of course, neither can member functions of other structures. Only the functions that are clearly stated in the structure declaration (the "contract") can have access to **private** members.

There is no required order for access specifiers, and they may appear more than once. They affect all the members declared after them and before the next access specifier.

protected

The last access specifier is **protected**. **protected** acts just like **private**, with one exception that we can't really talk about right now: "Inherited" structures (which cannot access **private** members) are granted access to **protected** members. This will become clearer in Chapter 14 when inheritance is introduced. For current purposes, consider **protected** to be just like **private**.

Friends

What if you want to explicitly grant access to a function that isn't a member of the current structure? This is accomplished by declaring that function a **friend** *inside* the structure declaration. It's important that the **friend** declaration occurs inside the structure declaration because you (and the compiler) must be able to read the structure declaration and see every rule about the size and behavior of that data type. And a very important rule in any relationship is, "Who can access my private implementation?"

The class controls which code has access to its members. There's no magic way to "break in" from the outside if you aren't a **friend**; you can't declare a new class and say, "Hi, I'm a friend of **Bob**!" and expect to see the **private** and **protected** members of **Bob**.

You can declare a global function as a **friend**, and you can also declare a member function of another structure, or even an entire structure, as a **friend**. Here's an example :

```
//: C05:Friend.cpp
// Friend allows special access

// Declaration (incomplete type specification):
struct X;

struct Y {
  void f(X*);
};

struct X { // Definition
private:
  int i;
public:
  void initialize();
  friend void g(X*, int); // Global friend
  friend void Y::f(X*);   // Struct member friend
  friend struct Z; // Entire struct is a friend
  friend void h();
};

void X::initialize() {
  i = 0;
}

void g(X* x, int i) {
  x->i = i;
}

void Y::f(X* x) {
  x->i = 47;
}

struct Z {
private:
  int j;
public:
  void initialize();
  void g(X* x);
};
```

```
void Z::initialize() {
  j = 99;
}

void Z::g(X* x) {
  x->i += j;
}

void h() {
  X x;
  x.i = 100; // Direct data manipulation
}

int main() {
  X x;
  Z z;
  z.g(&x);
} ///:~
```

struct Y has a member function **f( )** that will modify an object of type **X**. This is a bit of a conundrum because the C++ compiler requires you to declare everything before you can refer to it, so **struct Y** must be declared before its member **Y::f(X*)** can be declared as a friend in **struct X**. But for **Y::f(X*)** to be declared, **struct X** must be declared first!

Here's the solution. Notice that **Y::f(X*)** takes the *address* of an **X** object. This is critical because the compiler always knows how to pass an address, which is of a fixed size regardless of the object being passed, even if it doesn't have full information about the size of the type. If you try to pass the whole object, however, the compiler must see the entire structure definition of **X**, to know the size and how to pass it, before it allows you to declare a function such as **Y::g(X)**.

By passing the address of an **X**, the compiler allows you to make an *incomplete type specification* of **X** prior to declaring **Y::f(X*)**. This is accomplished in the declaration:

```
struct X;
```

This declaration simply tells the compiler there's a **struct** by that name, so it's OK to refer to it as long as you don't require any more knowledge than the name.

Now, in **struct X**, the function **Y::f(X*)** can be declared as a **friend** with no problem. If you tried to declare it before the compiler had seen the full specification for **Y**, it would have given you an error. This is a safety feature to ensure consistency and eliminate bugs.

Notice the two other **friend** functions. The first declares an ordinary global function **g( )** as a **friend**. But **g( )** has not been previously declared at the global scope! It turns out that **friend** can be used this way to simultaneously declare the function *and* give it **friend** status. This extends to entire structures:

```
friend struct Z;
```

is an incomplete type specification for **Z**, and it gives the entire structure **friend** status.

Nested friends

Making a structure nested doesn't automatically give it access to **private** members. To accomplish this, you must follow a particular form: first, declare (without defining) the nested structure, then declare it as a **friend**, and finally define the structure. The structure definition must be separate from the **friend** declaration, otherwise it would be seen by the compiler as a non-member. Here's an example:

```
//: C05:NestFriend.cpp
// Nested friends
#include <iostream>
#include <cstring> // memset()
using namespace std;
const int sz = 20;

struct Holder {
private:
  int a[sz];
public:
```

```
    void initialize();
    struct Pointer;
    friend Pointer;
    struct Pointer {
    private:
      Holder* h;
      int* p;
    public:
      void initialize(Holder* h);
      // Move around in the array:
      void next();
      void previous();
      void top();
      void end();
      // Access values:
      int read();
      void set(int i);
    };
};

void Holder::initialize() {
  memset(a, 0, sz * sizeof(int));
}

void Holder::Pointer::initialize(Holder* rv) {
  h = rv;
  p = rv->a;
}

void Holder::Pointer::next() {
  if(p < &(h->a[sz - 1])) p++;
}

void Holder::Pointer::previous() {
  if(p > &(h->a[0])) p--;
}

void Holder::Pointer::top() {
  p = &(h->a[0]);
}

void Holder::Pointer::end() {
  p = &(h->a[sz - 1]);
}
```

```
int Holder::Pointer::read() {
  return *p;
}

void Holder::Pointer::set(int i) {
  *p = i;
}

int main() {
  Holder h;
  Holder::Pointer hp, hp2;
  int i;

  h.initialize();
  hp.initialize(&h);
  hp2.initialize(&h);
  for(i = 0; i < sz; i++) {
    hp.set(i);
    hp.next();
  }
  hp.top();
  hp2.end();
  for(i = 0; i < sz; i++) {
    cout << "hp = " << hp.read()
         << ", hp2 = " << hp2.read() << endl;
    hp.next();
    hp2.previous();
  }
} ///:~
```

Once **Pointer** is declared, it is granted access to the private members of **Holder** by saying:

```
friend Pointer;
```

The **struct Holder** contains an array of **int**s and the **Pointer** allows you to access them. Because **Pointer** is strongly associated with **Holder**, it's sensible to make it a member structure of **Holder**. But because **Pointer** is a separate class from **Holder**, you can make more than one of them in **main( )** and use them to select different parts of the array. **Pointer** is a structure instead of a raw C pointer, so you can guarantee that it will always safely point inside the **Holder**.

The Standard C library function **memset( )** (in **<cstring>**) is used for convenience in the program above. It sets all memory starting at a particular address (the first argument) to a particular value (the second argument) for **n** bytes past the starting address (**n** is the third argument). Of course, you could have simply used a loop to iterate through all the memory, but **memset( )** is available, well-tested (so it's less likely you'll introduce an error), and probably more efficient than if you coded it by hand.

Is it pure?

The class definition gives you an audit trail, so you can see from looking at the class which functions have permission to modify the private parts of the class. If a function is a **friend**, it means that it isn't a member, but you want to give permission to modify private data anyway, and it must be listed in the class definition so everyone can see that it's one of the privileged functions.

C++ is a hybrid object-oriented language, not a pure one, and **friend** was added to get around practical problems that crop up. It's fine to point out that this makes the language less "pure," because C++ *is* designed to be pragmatic, not to aspire to an abstract ideal.

Object layout

Chapter 4 stated that a **struct** written for a C compiler and later compiled with C++ would be unchanged. This referred primarily to the object layout of the **struct**, that is, where the storage for the individual variables is positioned in the memory allocated for the object. If the C++ compiler changed the layout of C **struct**s, then any C code you wrote that inadvisably took advantage of knowledge of the positions of variables in the **struct** would break.

When you start using access specifiers, however, you've moved completely into the C++ realm, and things change a bit. Within a particular "access block" (a group of declarations delimited by access specifiers), the variables are guaranteed to be laid out contiguously, as in C. However, the access blocks may not appear in the object in the order that you declare them. Although the compiler will *usually* lay the blocks out exactly as you see them, there is no rule about it, because a particular machine architecture and/or operating environment may have explicit support for **private** and **protected** that might require those blocks to be placed in special memory locations. The language specification doesn't want to restrict this kind of advantage.

Access specifiers are part of the structure and don't affect the objects created from the structure. All of the access specification information disappears before the program is run; generally this happens during compilation. In a running program, objects become "regions of storage" and nothing more. If you really want to, you can break all the rules and access the memory directly, as you can in C. C++ is not designed to prevent you from doing unwise things. It just provides you with a much easier, highly desirable alternative.

In general, it's not a good idea to depend on anything that's implementation-specific when you're writing a program. When you must have implementation-specific dependencies, encapsulate them inside a structure so that any porting changes are focused in one place.

The class

Access control is often referred to as *implementation hiding*. Including functions within structures (often referred to as encapsulation[1]) produces a data type with characteristics and behaviors, but access control puts boundaries within that data type, for two important reasons. The first is to establish what the client programmers can and can't use. You can build your internal mechanisms into the structure without worrying that client programmers will think that these mechanisms are part of the interface they should be using.

---

[1] As noted before, sometimes access control is referred to as encapsulation.

This feeds directly into the second reason, which is to separate the interface from the implementation. If the structure is used in a set of programs, but the client programmers can't do anything but send messages to the **public** interface, then you can change anything that's **private** without requiring modifications to their code.

Encapsulation and access control, taken together, invent something more than a C **struct**. We're now in the world of object-oriented programming, where a structure is describing a class of objects as you would describe a class of fishes or a class of birds: Any object belonging to this class will share these characteristics and behaviors. That's what the structure declaration has become, a description of the way all objects of this type will look and act.

In the original OOP language, Simula-67, the keyword **class** was used to describe a new data type. This apparently inspired Stroustrup to choose the same keyword for C++, to emphasize that this was the focal point of the whole language: the creation of new data types that are more than just C **struct**s with functions. This certainly seems like adequate justification for a new keyword.

However, the use of **class** in C++ comes close to being an unnecessary keyword. It's identical to the **struct** keyword in absolutely every way except one: **class** defaults to **private**, whereas **struct** defaults to **public**. Here are two structures that produce the same result:

```
//: C05:Class.cpp
// Similarity of struct and class

struct A {
private:
  int i, j, k;
public:
  int f();
  void g();
};

int A::f() {
  return i + j + k;
}
```

```
void A::g() {
  i = j = k = 0;
}

// Identical results are produced with:

class B {
  int i, j, k;
public:
  int f();
  void g();
};

int B::f() {
  return i + j + k;
}

void B::g() {
  i = j = k = 0;
}

int main() {
  A a;
  B b;
  a.f(); a.g();
  b.f(); b.g();
} ///:~
```

The **class** is the fundamental OOP concept in C++. It is one of the keywords that will *not* be set in bold in this book – it becomes annoying with a word repeated as often as "class." The shift to classes is so important that I suspect Stroustrup's preference would have been to throw **struct** out altogether, but the need for backwards compatibility with C wouldn't allow that.

Many people prefer a style of creating classes that is more **struct**-like than class-like, because you override the "default-to-**private**" behavior of the class by starting out with **public** elements:

```
class X {
public:
  void interface_function();
private:
```

```
  void private_function();
  int internal_representation;
};
```

The logic behind this is that it makes more sense for the reader to see the members of interest first, then they can ignore anything that says **private**. Indeed, the only reasons all the other members must be declared in the class at all are so the compiler knows how big the objects are and can allocate them properly, and so it can guarantee consistency.

The examples in this book, however, will put the **private** members first, like this:

```
class X {
  void private_function();
  int internal_representation;
public:
  void interface_function();
};
```

Some people even go to the trouble of decorating their own private names:

```
class Y {
public:
  void f();
private:
  int mX;  // "Self-decorated" name
};
```

Because **mX** is already hidden in the scope of **Y**, the **m** (for "member") is unnecessary. However, in projects with many global variables (something you should strive to avoid, but which is sometimes inevitable in existing projects), it is helpful to be able to distinguish inside a member function definition which data is global and which is a member.

Modifying Stash to use access control

It makes sense to take the examples from Chapter 4 and modify them to use classes and access control. Notice how the client programmer portion of the interface is now clearly distinguished, so there's no possibility of client programmers accidentally manipulating a part of the class that they shouldn't.

```
//: C05:Stash.h
// Converted to use access control
#ifndef STASH_H
#define STASH_H

class Stash {
  int size;        // Size of each space
  int quantity;    // Number of storage spaces
  int next;        // Next empty space
  // Dynamically allocated array of bytes:
  unsigned char* storage;
  void inflate(int increase);
public:
  void initialize(int size);
  void cleanup();
  int add(void* element);
  void* fetch(int index);
  int count();
};
#endif // STASH_H ///:~
```

The **inflate( )** function has been made **private** because it is used only by the **add( )** function and is thus part of the underlying implementation, not the interface. This means that, sometime later, you can change the underlying implementation to use a different system for memory management.

Other than the name of the include file, the header above is the only thing that's been changed for this example. The implementation file and test file are the same.

Modifying Stack to use access control

As a second example, here's the **Stack** turned into a class. Now the nested data structure is **private**, which is nice because it ensures that the client programmer will neither have to look at it nor be able to depend on the internal representation of the **Stack**:

```
//: C05:Stack2.h
// Nested structs via linked list
```

```
#ifndef STACK2_H
#define STACK2_H

class Stack {
  struct Link {
    void* data;
    Link* next;
    void initialize(void* dat, Link* nxt);
  }* head;
public:
  void initialize();
  void push(void* dat);
  void* peek();
  void* pop();
  void cleanup();
};
#endif // STACK2_H ///:~
```

As before, the implementation doesn't change and so it is not repeated here. The test, too, is identical. The only thing that's been changed is the robustness of the class interface. The real value of access control is to prevent you from crossing boundaries during development. In fact, the compiler is the only thing that knows about the protection level of class members. There is no access control information mangled into the member name that carries through to the linker. All the protection checking is done by the compiler; it has vanished by runtime.

Notice that the interface presented to the client programmer is now truly that of a push-down stack. It happens to be implemented as a linked list, but you can change that without affecting what the client programmer interacts with, or (more importantly) a single line of client code.

Handle classes

Access control in C++ allows you to separate interface from implementation, but the implementation hiding is only partial. The compiler must still see the declarations for all parts of an object in order to create and manipulate it properly. You could imagine a programming language that requires only the public interface of an object and allows the private implementation to be hidden, but C++ performs type checking statically (at compile time) as much as possible. This means that you'll learn as early as possible if there's an error. It also means that your program is more efficient. However, including the private implementation has two effects: the implementation is visible even if you can't easily access it, and it can cause needless recompilation.

Hiding the implementation

Some projects cannot afford to have their implementation visible to the client programmer. It may show strategic information in a library header file that the company doesn't want available to competitors. You may be working on a system where security is an issue – an encryption algorithm, for example – and you don't want to expose any clues in a header file that might help people to crack the code. Or you may be putting your library in a "hostile" environment, where the programmers will directly access the private components anyway, using pointers and casting. In all these situations, it's valuable to have the actual structure compiled inside an implementation file rather than exposed in a header file.

Reducing recompilation

The project manager in your programming environment will cause a recompilation of a file if that file is touched (that is, modified) *or* if another file it's dependent upon – that is, an included header file – is touched. This means that any time you make a change to a class, whether it's to the public interface or to the private member declarations, you'll force a recompilation of anything that includes that header file. This is often referred to as the *fragile base-class problem*. For a large project in its early stages this can be very unwieldy because the underlying implementation may change often; if the project is very big, the time for compiles can prohibit rapid turnaround.

The technique to solve this is sometimes called *handle classes* or the "Cheshire cat"[2] – everything about the implementation disappears except for a single pointer, the "smile." The pointer refers to a structure whose definition is in the implementation file along with all the member function definitions. Thus, as long as the interface is unchanged, the header file is untouched. The implementation can change at will, and only the implementation file needs to be recompiled and relinked with the project.

Here's a simple example demonstrating the technique. The header file contains only the public interface and a single pointer of an incompletely specified class:

```
//: C05:Handle.h
// Handle classes
#ifndef HANDLE_H
#define HANDLE_H

class Handle {
  struct Cheshire; // Class declaration only
  Cheshire* smile;
public:
  void initialize();
  void cleanup();
  int read();
  void change(int);
};
#endif // HANDLE_H ///:~
```

This is all the client programmer is able to see. The line

```
struct Cheshire;
```

is an *incomplete type specification* or a *class declaration* (A *class definition* includes the body of the class.) It tells the compiler that **Cheshire** is a structure name, but it doesn't give any details about the **struct**. This is only enough information to create a pointer to the **struct**; you can't create an object until the structure body has

---

[2] This name is attributed to John Carolan, one of the early pioneers in C++, and of course, Lewis Carroll. This technique can also be seen as a form of the "bridge" design pattern, described in Volume 2.

---

been provided. In this technique, that structure body is hidden away in the implementation file:

```
//: C05:Handle.cpp {O}
// Handle implementation
#include "Handle.h"
#include "../require.h"

// Define Handle's implementation:
struct Handle::Cheshire {
  int i;
};

void Handle::initialize() {
  smile = new Cheshire;
  smile->i = 0;
}

void Handle::cleanup() {
  delete smile;
}

int Handle::read() {
  return smile->i;
}

void Handle::change(int x) {
  smile->i = x;
} ///:~
```

Cheshire is a nested structure, so it must be defined with scope resolution:

```
struct Handle::Cheshire {
```

In **Handle::initialize( )**, storage is allocated for a **Cheshire** structure, and in **Handle::cleanup( )** this storage is released. This storage is used in lieu of all the data elements you'd normally put into the **private** section of the class. When you compile **Handle.cpp**, this structure definition is hidden away in the object file where no one can see it. If you change the elements of **Cheshire**, the only file that must be recompiled is **Handle.cpp** because the header file is untouched.

The use of **Handle** is like the use of any class: include the header, create objects, and send messages.

```
//: C05:UseHandle.cpp
//{L} Handle
// Use the Handle class
#include "Handle.h"

int main() {
  Handle u;
  u.initialize();
  u.read();
  u.change(1);
  u.cleanup();
} ///:~
```

The only thing the client programmer can access is the public interface, so as long as the implementation is the only thing that changes, the file above never needs recompilation. Thus, although this isn't perfect implementation hiding, it's a big improvement.

Summary

Access control in C++ gives valuable control to the creator of a class. The users of the class can clearly see exactly what they can use and what to ignore. More important, though, is the ability to ensure that no client programmer becomes dependent on any part of the underlying implementation of a class. If you know this as the creator of the class, you can change the underlying implementation with the knowledge that no client programmer will be affected by the changes because they can't access that part of the class.

When you have the ability to change the underlying implementation, you can not only improve your design at some later time, but you also have the freedom to make mistakes. No matter how carefully you plan and design, you'll make mistakes. Knowing that it's relatively safe to make these mistakes means you'll be more experimental, you'll learn faster, and you'll finish your project sooner.

The public interface to a class is what the client programmer *does* see, so that is the most important part of the class to get "right" during analysis and design. But even that allows you some leeway for change. If you don't get the interface right the first time, you can *add* more functions, as long as you don't remove any that client programmers have already used in their code.

Exercises

Solutions to selected exercises can be found in the electronic document *The Thinking in C++ Annotated Solution Guide*, available for a small fee from www.BruceEckel.com.

1. Create a class with **public**, **private**, and **protected** data members and function members. Create an object of this class and see what kind of compiler messages you get when you try to access all the class members.

2. Write a **struct** called **Lib** that contains three **string** objects **a**, **b**, and **c**. In **main( )** create a **Lib** object called **x** and assign to **x.a**, **x.b**, and **x.c**. Print out the values. Now replace **a**, **b**, and **c** with an array of **string s[3]**. Show that your code in **main( )** breaks as a result of the change. Now create a **class** called **Libc**, with **private** **string** objects **a**, **b**, and **c**, and member functions **seta( )**, **geta( )**, **setb( )**, **getb( )**, **setc( )**, and **getc( )** to set and get the values. Write **main( )** as before. Now change the **private string** objects **a**, **b**, and **c** to a **private** array of **string s[3]**. Show that the code in **main( )** does *not* break as a result of the change.

3. Create a class and a global **friend** function that manipulates the **private** data in the class.

4. Write two classes, each of which has a member function that takes a pointer to an object of the other class. Create instances of both objects in **main( )** and call the aforementioned member function in each class.

5. Create three classes. The first class contains **private** data, and grants friendship to the entire second class and to a member function of the third class. In **main( )**, demonstrate that all of these work correctly.

6. Create a **Hen** class. Inside this, nest a **Nest** class. Inside **Nest**, place an **Egg** class. Each class should have a **display( )** member function. In **main( )**, create an instance of each class and call the **display( )** function for each one.

7. Modify Exercise 6 so that **Nest** and **Egg** each contain **private** data. Grant friendship to allow the enclosing classes access to this **private** data.

8. Create a class with data members distributed among numerous **public**, **private,** and **protected** sections. Add a member function **showMap( )** that prints the names of each of these data members and their addresses. If possible, compile and run this program on more than one compiler and/or computer and/or operating system to see if there are layout differences in the object.

9. Copy the implementation and test files for **Stash** in Chapter 4 so that you can compile and test **Stash.h** in this chapter.

10. Place objects of the **Hen** class from Exercise 6 in a **Stash**. Fetch them out and print them (if you have not already done so, you will need to add **Hen::print( )**).

11. Copy the implementation and test files for **Stack** in Chapter 4 so that you can compile and test **Stack2.h** in this chapter.

12. Place objects of the **Hen** class from Exercise 6 in a **Stack**. Fetch them out and print them (if you have not already done so, you will need to add **Hen::print( )**).

13. Modify **Cheshire** in **Handle.cpp**, and verify that your project manager recompiles and relinks only this file, but doesn't recompile **UseHandle.cpp**.

14. Create a **StackOfInt** class (a stack that holds **int**s) using the "Cheshire cat" technique that hides the low-level data structure you use to store the elements in a class called **StackImp**. Implement two versions of **StackImp**: one that uses a fixed-length array of **int**, and one that uses a **vector<int>**. Have a preset maximum size for the stack so you don't have to worry about expanding the array in

the first version. Note that the **StackOfInt.h** class doesn't have to change with **StackImp**.

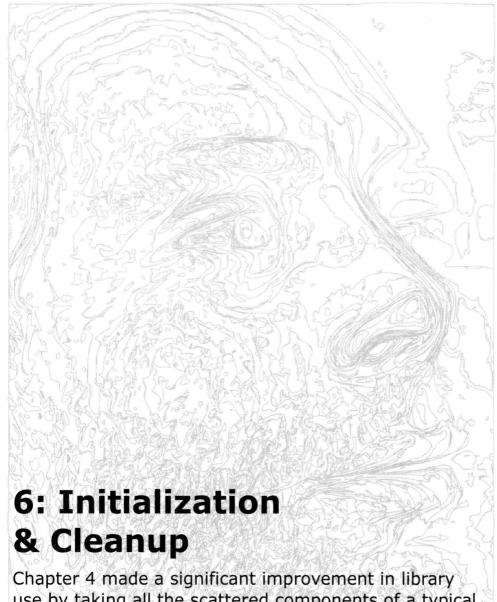

6: Initialization & Cleanup

Chapter 4 made a significant improvement in library use by taking all the scattered components of a typical C library and encapsulating them into a structure (an abstract data type, called a *class* from now on).

This not only provides a single unified point of entry into a library component, but it also hides the names of the functions within the class name. In Chapter 5, access control (implementation hiding) was introduced. This gives the class designer a way to establish clear boundaries for determining what the client programmer is allowed to manipulate and what is off limits. It means the internal mechanisms of a data type's operation are under the control and discretion of the class designer, and it's clear to client programmers what members they can and should pay attention to.

Together, encapsulation and access control make a significant step in improving the ease of library use. The concept of "new data type" they provide is better in some ways than the existing built-in data types from C. The C++ compiler can now provide type-checking guarantees for that data type and thus ensure a level of safety when that data type is being used.

When it comes to safety, however, there's a lot more the compiler can do for us than C provides. In this and future chapters, you'll see additional features that have been engineered into C++ that make the bugs in your program almost leap out and grab you, sometimes before you even compile the program, but usually in the form of compiler warnings and errors. For this reason, you will soon get used to the unlikely-sounding scenario that a C++ program that compiles often runs right the first time.

Two of these safety issues are initialization and cleanup. A large segment of C bugs occur when the programmer forgets to initialize or clean up a variable. This is especially true with C libraries, when client programmers don't know how to initialize a **struct**, or even that they must. (Libraries often do not include an initialization function, so the client programmer is forced to initialize the **struct** by hand.) Cleanup is a special problem because C programmers are comfortable with forgetting about variables once they are finished, so any cleaning up that may be necessary for a library's **struct** is often missed.

In C++, the concept of initialization and cleanup is essential for easy library use and to eliminate the many subtle bugs that occur when the client programmer forgets to perform these activities.

This chapter examines the features in C++ that help guarantee proper initialization and cleanup.

Guaranteed initialization with the constructor

Both the **Stash** and **Stack** classes defined previously have a function called **initialize( )**, which hints by its name that it should be called before using the object in any other way. Unfortunately, this means the client programmer must ensure proper initialization. Client programmers are prone to miss details like initialization in their headlong rush to make your amazing library solve their problem. In C++, initialization is too important to leave to the client programmer. The class designer can guarantee initialization of every object by providing a special function called the *constructor*. If a class has a constructor, the compiler automatically calls that constructor at the point an object is created, before client programmers can get their hands on the object. The constructor call isn't even an option for the client programmer; it is performed by the compiler at the point the object is defined.

The next challenge is what to name this function. There are two issues. The first is that any name you use is something that can potentially clash with a name you might like to use as a member in the class. The second is that because the compiler is responsible for calling the constructor, it must always know which function to call. The solution Stroustrup chose seems the easiest and most logical: the name of the constructor is the same as the name of the class. It makes sense that such a function will be called automatically on initialization.

Here's a simple class with a constructor:

```
class X {
  int i;
public:
  X();  // Constructor
};
```

Now, when an object is defined,

```
void f() {
  X a;
  // ...
}
```

the same thing happens as if **a** were an **int**: storage is allocated for the object. But when the program reaches the *sequence point* (point of execution) where **a** is defined, the constructor is called automatically. That is, the compiler quietly inserts the call to **X::X( )** for the object **a** at the point of definition. Like any member function, the first (secret) argument to the constructor is the **this** pointer – the address of the object for which it is being called. In the case of the constructor, however, **this** is pointing to an un-initialized block of memory, and it's the job of the constructor to initialize this memory properly.

Like any function, the constructor can have arguments to allow you to specify how an object is created, give it initialization values, and so on. Constructor arguments provide you with a way to guarantee that all parts of your object are initialized to appropriate values. For example, if a class **Tree** has a constructor that takes a single integer argument denoting the height of the tree, then you must create a tree object like this:

```
Tree t(12);   // 12-foot tree
```

If **Tree(int)** is your only constructor, the compiler won't let you create an object any other way. (We'll look at multiple constructors and different ways to call constructors in the next chapter.)

That's really all there is to a constructor; it's a specially named function that is called automatically by the compiler for every object at the point of that object's creation. Despite it's simplicity, it is exceptionally valuable because it eliminates a large class of problems and makes the code easier to write and read. In the preceding code fragment, for example, you don't see an explicit function call to some **initialize( )** function that is conceptually separate from definition. In C++, definition and initialization are unified concepts – you can't have one without the other.

Both the constructor and destructor are very unusual types of functions: they have no return value. This is distinctly different from a **void** return value, in which the function returns nothing but you still have the option to make it something else. Constructors and destructors return nothing and you don't have an option. The acts of bringing an object into and out of the program are special, like birth and death, and the compiler always makes the function calls itself, to make sure they happen. If there were a return value, and if you could select your own, the compiler would somehow have to know what to do with the return value, or the client programmer would have to explicitly call constructors and destructors, which would eliminate their safety.

Guaranteed cleanup with the destructor

As a C programmer, you often think about the importance of initialization, but it's rarer to think about cleanup. After all, what do you need to do to clean up an **int**? Just forget about it. However, with libraries, just "letting go" of an object once you're done with it is not so safe. What if it modifies some piece of hardware, or puts something on the screen, or allocates storage on the heap? If you just forget about it, your object never achieves closure upon its exit from this world. In C++, cleanup is as important as initialization and is therefore guaranteed with the destructor.

The syntax for the destructor is similar to that for the constructor: the class name is used for the name of the function. However, the destructor is distinguished from the constructor by a leading tilde (~). In addition, the destructor never has any arguments because destruction never needs any options. Here's the declaration for a destructor:

```
class Y {
public:
  ~Y();
};
```

The destructor is called automatically by the compiler when the object goes out of scope. You can see where the constructor gets called by the point of definition of the object, but the only evidence for a destructor call is the closing brace of the scope that surrounds the object. Yet the destructor is still called, even when you use **goto** to jump out of a scope. (**goto** still exists in C++ for backward compatibility with C and for the times when it comes in handy.) You should note that a *nonlocal goto*, implemented by the Standard C library functions **setjmp( )** and **longjmp( )**, doesn't cause destructors to be called. (This is the specification, even if your compiler doesn't implement it that way. Relying on a feature that isn't in the specification means your code is nonportable.)

Here's an example demonstrating the features of constructors and destructors you've seen so far:

```cpp
//: C06:Constructor1.cpp
// Constructors & destructors
#include <iostream>
using namespace std;

class Tree {
  int height;
public:
  Tree(int initialHeight);   // Constructor
  ~Tree();   // Destructor
  void grow(int years);
  void printsize();
};

Tree::Tree(int initialHeight) {
  height = initialHeight;
}

Tree::~Tree() {
  cout << "inside Tree destructor" << endl;
  printsize();
}

void Tree::grow(int years) {
  height += years;
}
```

```
void Tree::printsize() {
  cout << "Tree height is " << height << endl;
}

int main() {
  cout << "before opening brace" << endl;
  {
    Tree t(12);
    cout << "after Tree creation" << endl;
    t.printsize();
    t.grow(4);
    cout << "before closing brace" << endl;
  }
  cout << "after closing brace" << endl;
} ///:~
```

Here's the output of the above program:

```
before opening brace
after Tree creation
Tree height is 12
before closing brace
inside Tree destructor
Tree height is 16
after closing brace
```

You can see that the destructor is automatically called at the closing brace of the scope that encloses it.

Elimination of the definition block

In C, you must always define all the variables at the beginning of a block, after the opening brace. This is not an uncommon requirement in programming languages, and the reason given has often been that it's "good programming style." On this point, I have my suspicions. It has always seemed inconvenient to me, as a programmer, to pop back to the beginning of a block every time I need a new variable. I also find code more readable when the variable definition is close to its point of use.

Perhaps these arguments are stylistic. In C++, however, there's a significant problem in being forced to define all objects at the

---

beginning of a scope. If a constructor exists, it must be called when the object is created. However, if the constructor takes one or more initialization arguments, how do you know you will have that initialization information at the beginning of a scope? In the general programming situation, you won't. Because C has no concept of **private**, this separation of definition and initialization is no problem. However, C++ guarantees that when an object is created, it is simultaneously initialized. This ensures that you will have no uninitialized objects running around in your system. C doesn't care; in fact, C *encourages* this practice by requiring you to define variables at the beginning of a block before you necessarily have the initialization information[1].

In general, C++ will not allow you to create an object before you have the initialization information for the constructor. Because of this, the language wouldn't be feasible if you had to define variables at the beginning of a scope. In fact, the style of the language seems to encourage the definition of an object as close to its point of use as possible. In C++, any rule that applies to an "object" automatically refers to an object of a built-in type as well. This means that any class object or variable of a built-in type can also be defined at any point in a scope. It also means that you can wait until you have the information for a variable before defining it, so you can always define and initialize at the same time:

```
//: C06:DefineInitialize.cpp
// Defining variables anywhere
#include "../require.h"
#include <iostream>
#include <string>
using namespace std;

class G {
  int i;
public:
  G(int ii);
};
```

---

[1] C99, The updated version of Standard C, allows variables to be defined at any point in a scope, like C++.

```
G::G(int ii) { i = ii; }

int main() {
  cout << "initialization value? ";
  int retval = 0;
  cin >> retval;
  require(retval != 0);
  int y = retval + 3;
  G g(y);
} ///:~
```

You can see that some code is executed, then **retval** is defined,
initialized, and used to capture user input, and then **y** and **g** are
defined. C, on the other hand, does not allow a variable to be
defined anywhere except at the beginning of the scope.

In general, you should define variables as close to their point of use
as possible, and always initialize them when they are defined. (This
is a stylistic suggestion for built-in types, where initialization is
optional.) This is a safety issue. By reducing the duration of the
variable's availability within the scope, you are reducing the chance
it will be misused in some other part of the scope. In addition,
readability is improved because the reader doesn't have to jump
back and forth to the beginning of the scope to know the type of a
variable.

for loops

In C++, you will often see a **for** loop counter defined right inside
the **for** expression:

```
for(int j = 0; j < 100; j++) {
    cout << "j = " << j << endl;
}
for(int i = 0; i < 100; i++)
    cout << "i = " << i << endl;
```

The statements above are important special cases, which cause
confusion to new C++ programmers.

The variables **i** and **j** are defined directly inside the **for** expression (which you cannot do in C). They are then available for use in the **for** loop. It's a very convenient syntax because the context removes all question about the purpose of **i** and **j**, so you don't need to use such ungainly names as **i_loop_counter** for clarity.

However, some confusion may result if you expect the lifetimes of the variables **i** and **j** to extend beyond the scope of the for loop – they do not[2].

Chapter 3 points out that **while** and **switch** statements also allow the definition of objects in their control expressions, although this usage seems far less important than with the **for** loop.

Watch out for local variables that hide variables from the enclosing scope. In general, using the same name for a nested variable and a variable that is global to that scope is confusing and error prone[3].

I find small scopes an indicator of good design. If you have several pages for a single function, perhaps you're trying to do too much with that function. More granular functions are not only more useful, but it's also easier to find bugs.

Storage allocation

A variable can now be defined at any point in a scope, so it might seem that the storage for a variable may not be defined until its point of definition. It's actually more likely that the compiler will follow the practice in C of allocating all the storage for a scope at the opening brace of that scope. It doesn't matter because, as a programmer, you can't access the storage (a.k.a. the object) until it has been defined[4]. Although the storage is allocated at the beginning of the block, the constructor call doesn't happen until the

---

[2] An earlier iteration of the C++ draft standard said the variable lifetime extended to the end of the scope that enclosed the **for** loop. Some compilers still implement that, but it is not correct so your code will only be portable if you limit the scope to the **for** loop.

[3] The Java language considers this such a bad idea that it flags such code as an error.

[4] OK, you probably could by fooling around with pointers, but you'd be very, very bad.

sequence point where the object is defined because the identifier isn't available until then. The compiler even checks to make sure that you don't put the object definition (and thus the constructor call) where the sequence point only conditionally passes through it, such as in a **switch** statement or somewhere a **goto** can jump past it. Uncommenting the statements in the following code will generate a warning or an error:

```
//: C06:Nojump.cpp
// Can't jump past constructors

class X {
public:
  X();
};

X::X() {}

void f(int i) {
  if(i < 10) {
    //! goto jump1; // Error: goto bypasses init
  }
  X x1;   // Constructor called here
 jump1:
  switch(i) {
    case 1 :
      X x2;   // Constructor called here
      break;
  //! case 2 : // Error: case bypasses init
      X x3;   // Constructor called here
      break;
  }
}

int main() {
  f(9);
  f(11);
}///:~
```

In the code above, both the **goto** and the **switch** can potentially jump past the sequence point where a constructor is called. That object will then be in scope even if the constructor hasn't been called, so the compiler gives an error message. This once again guarantees that an object cannot be created unless it is also initialized.

All the storage allocation discussed here happens, of course, on the stack. The storage is allocated by the compiler by moving the stack pointer "down" (a relative term, which may indicate an increase or decrease of the actual stack pointer value, depending on your machine). Objects can also be allocated on the heap using **new**, which is something we'll explore further in Chapter 13.

Stash with constructors and destructors

The examples from previous chapters have obvious functions that map to constructors and destructors: **initialize( )** and **cleanup( )**. Here's the **Stash** header using constructors and destructors:

```
//: C06:Stash2.h
// With constructors & destructors
#ifndef STASH2_H
#define STASH2_H

class Stash {
  int size;       // Size of each space
  int quantity;   // Number of storage spaces
  int next;       // Next empty space
  // Dynamically allocated array of bytes:
  unsigned char* storage;
  void inflate(int increase);
public:
  Stash(int size);
  ~Stash();
  int add(void* element);
  void* fetch(int index);
  int count();
};
#endif // STASH2_H ///:~
```

The only member function definitions that are changed are **initialize( )** and **cleanup( )**, which have been replaced with a constructor and destructor:

```
//: C06:Stash2.cpp {O}
// Constructors & destructors
#include "Stash2.h"
#include "../require.h"
#include <iostream>
#include <cassert>
using namespace std;
const int increment = 100;

Stash::Stash(int sz) {
  size = sz;
  quantity = 0;
  storage = 0;
  next = 0;
}

int Stash::add(void* element) {
  if(next >= quantity) // Enough space left?
    inflate(increment);
  // Copy element into storage,
  // starting at next empty space:
  int startBytes = next * size;
  unsigned char* e = (unsigned char*)element;
  for(int i = 0; i < size; i++)
    storage[startBytes + i] = e[i];
  next++;
  return(next - 1); // Index number
}

void* Stash::fetch(int index) {
  require(0 <= index, "Stash::fetch (-)index");
  if(index >= next)
    return 0; // To indicate the end
  // Produce pointer to desired element:
  return &(storage[index * size]);
}

int Stash::count() {
  return next; // Number of elements in CStash
}

void Stash::inflate(int increase) {
  require(increase > 0,
    "Stash::inflate zero or negative increase");
  int newQuantity = quantity + increase;
```

```
    int newBytes = newQuantity * size;
    int oldBytes = quantity * size;
    unsigned char* b = new unsigned char[newBytes];
    for(int i = 0; i < oldBytes; i++)
      b[i] = storage[i]; // Copy old to new
    delete [](storage); // Old storage
    storage = b; // Point to new memory
    quantity = newQuantity;
}

Stash::~Stash() {
  if(storage != 0) {
    cout << "freeing storage" << endl;
    delete []storage;
  }
} ///:~
```

You can see that the **require.h** functions are being used to watch for programmer errors, instead of **assert( )**. The output of a failed **assert( )** is not as useful as that of the **require.h** functions (which will be shown later in the book).

Because **inflate( )** is private, the only way a **require( )** could fail is if one of the other member functions accidentally passed an incorrect value to **inflate( )**. If you are certain this can't happen, you could consider removing the **require( )**, but you might keep in mind that until the class is stable, there's always the possibility that new code might be added to the class that could cause errors. The cost of the **require( )** is low (and could be automatically removed using the preprocessor) and the value of code robustness is high.

Notice in the following test program how the definitions for **Stash** objects appear right before they are needed, and how the initialization appears as part of the definition, in the constructor argument list:

```
//: C06:Stash2Test.cpp
//{L} Stash2
// Constructors & destructors
#include "Stash2.h"
#include "../require.h"
#include <fstream>
#include <iostream>
```

```
#include <string>
using namespace std;

int main() {
  Stash intStash(sizeof(int));
  for(int i = 0; i < 100; i++)
    intStash.add(&i);
  for(int j = 0; j < intStash.count(); j++)
    cout << "intStash.fetch(" << j << ") = "
         << *(int*)intStash.fetch(j)
         << endl;
  const int bufsize = 80;
  Stash stringStash(sizeof(char) * bufsize);
  ifstream in("Stash2Test.cpp");
  assure(in, " Stash2Test.cpp");
  string line;
  while(getline(in, line))
    stringStash.add((char*)line.c_str());
  int k = 0;
  char* cp;
  while((cp = (char*)stringStash.fetch(k++)) !=0)
    cout << "stringStash.fetch(" << k << ") = "
         << cp << endl;
} ///:~
```

Also notice how the **cleanup( )** calls have been eliminated, but the
destructors are still automatically called when **intStash** and
stringStash go out of scope.

One thing to be aware of in the **Stash** examples: I'm being very
careful to use only built-in types; that is, those without destructors.
If you were to try to copy class objects into the **Stash**, you'd run
into all kinds of problems and it wouldn't work right. The Standard
C++ Library can actually make correct copies of objects into its
containers, but this is a rather messy and complicated process. In
the following **Stack** example, you'll see that pointers are used to
sidestep this issue, and in a later chapter the **Stash** will be
converted so that it uses pointers.

Stack with constructors & destructors

Reimplementing the linked list (inside **Stack**) with constructors and destructors shows how neatly constructors and destructors work with **new** and **delete**. Here's the modified header file:

```
//: C06:Stack3.h
// With constructors/destructors
#ifndef STACK3_H
#define STACK3_H

class Stack {
  struct Link {
    void* data;
    Link* next;
    Link(void* dat, Link* nxt);
    ~Link();
  }* head;
public:
  Stack();
  ~Stack();
  void push(void* dat);
  void* peek();
  void* pop();
};
#endif // STACK3_H ///:~
```

Not only does **Stack** have a constructor and destructor, but so does the nested class **Link**:

```
//: C06:Stack3.cpp {O}
// Constructors/destructors
#include "Stack3.h"
#include "../require.h"
using namespace std;

Stack::Link::Link(void* dat, Link* nxt) {
  data = dat;
  next = nxt;
}

Stack::Link::~Link() { }
```

```
Stack::Stack() { head = 0; }

void Stack::push(void* dat) {
  head = new Link(dat,head);
}

void* Stack::peek() {
  require(head != 0, "Stack empty");
  return head->data;
}

void* Stack::pop() {
  if(head == 0) return 0;
  void* result = head->data;
  Link* oldHead = head;
  head = head->next;
  delete oldHead;
  return result;
}

Stack::~Stack() {
  require(head == 0, "Stack not empty");
} ///:~
```

The **Link::Link( )** constructor simply initializes the **data** and **next** pointers, so in **Stack::push( )** the line

```
head = new Link(dat,head);
```

not only allocates a new link (using dynamic object creation with the keyword **new**, introduced in Chapter 4), but it also neatly initializes the pointers for that link.

You may wonder why the destructor for **Link** doesn't do anything – in particular, why doesn't it **delete** the **data** pointer? There are two problems. In Chapter 4, where the **Stack** was introduced, it was pointed out that you cannot properly **delete** a **void** pointer if it points to an object (an assertion that will be proven in Chapter 13). But in addition, if the **Link** destructor deleted the **data** pointer, **pop( )** would end up returning a pointer to a deleted object, which would definitely be a bug. This is sometimes referred to as the issue of *ownership*: the **Link** and thus the **Stack** only holds the pointers,

---

but is not responsible for cleaning them up. This means that you must be very careful that you know who *is* responsible. For example, if you don't **pop( )** and **delete** all the pointers on the **Stack**, they won't get cleaned up automatically by the **Stack**'s destructor. This can be a sticky issue and leads to memory leaks, so knowing who is responsible for cleaning up an object can make the difference between a successful program and a buggy one – that's why **Stack::~Stack( )** prints an error message if the **Stack** object isn't empty upon destruction.

Because the allocation and cleanup of the **Link** objects are hidden within **Stack** – it's part of the underlying implementation – you don't see it happening in the test program, although you *are* responsible for deleting the pointers that come back from **pop( )**:

```
//: C06:Stack3Test.cpp
//{L} Stack3
//{T} Stack3Test.cpp
// Constructors/destructors
#include "Stack3.h"
#include "../require.h"
#include <fstream>
#include <iostream>
#include <string>
using namespace std;

int main(int argc, char* argv[]) {
  requireArgs(argc, 1); // File name is argument
  ifstream in(argv[1]);
  assure(in, argv[1]);
  Stack textlines;
  string line;
  // Read file and store lines in the stack:
  while(getline(in, line))
    textlines.push(new string(line));
  // Pop the lines from the stack and print them:
  string* s;
  while((s = (string*)textlines.pop()) != 0) {
    cout << *s << endl;
    delete s;
  }
} ///:~
```

In this case, all the lines in **textlines** are popped and deleted, but if they weren't, you'd get a **require( )** message that would mean there was a memory leak.

Aggregate initialization

An *aggregate* is just what it sounds like: a bunch of things clumped together. This definition includes aggregates of mixed types, like **struct**s and **class**es. An array is an aggregate of a single type.

Initializing aggregates can be error-prone and tedious. C++ *aggregate initialization* makes it much safer. When you create an object that's an aggregate, all you must do is make an assignment, and the initialization will be taken care of by the compiler. This assignment comes in several flavors, depending on the type of aggregate you're dealing with, but in all cases the elements in the assignment must be surrounded by curly braces. For an array of built-in types this is quite simple:

```
int a[5] = { 1, 2, 3, 4, 5 };
```

If you try to give more initializers than there are array elements, the compiler gives an error message. But what happens if you give *fewer* initializers? For example:

```
int b[6] = {0};
```

Here, the compiler will use the first initializer for the first array element, and then use zero for all the elements without initializers. Notice this initialization behavior doesn't occur if you define an array without a list of initializers. So the expression above is a succinct way to initialize an array to zero, without using a **for** loop, and without any possibility of an off-by-one error (Depending on the compiler, it may also be more efficient than the **for** loop.)

A second shorthand for arrays is *automatic counting*, in which you let the compiler determine the size of the array based on the number of initializers:

```
int c[] = { 1, 2, 3, 4 };
```

Now if you decide to add another element to the array, you simply add another initializer. If you can set your code up so it needs to be changed in only one spot, you reduce the chance of errors during modification. But how do you determine the size of the array? The expression **sizeof c / sizeof *c** (size of the entire array divided by the size of the first element) does the trick in a way that doesn't need to be changed if the array size changes[5]:

```
for(int i = 0; i < sizeof c / sizeof *c; i++)
   c[i]++;
```

Because structures are also aggregates, they can be initialized in a similar fashion. Because a C-style **struct** has all of its members **public**, they can be assigned directly:

```
struct X {
   int i;
   float f;
   char c;
};

X x1 = { 1, 2.2, 'c' };
```

If you have an array of such objects, you can initialize them by using a nested set of curly braces for each object:

```
X x2[3] = { {1, 1.1, 'a'}, {2, 2.2, 'b'} };
```

Here, the third object is initialized to zero.

If any of the data members are **private** (which is typically the case for a well-designed class in C++), or even if everything's **public** but there's a constructor, things are different. In the examples above, the initializers are assigned directly to the elements of the aggregate, but constructors are a way of forcing initialization to occur through a formal interface. Here, the constructors must be called to perform the initialization. So if you have a **struct** that looks like this,

---

[5] In Volume 2 of this book (freely available at www.BruceEckel.com), you'll see a more succinct calculation of an array size using templates.

```
struct Y {
  float f;
  int i;
  Y(int a);
};
```

You must indicate constructor calls. The best approach is the explicit one as follows:

```
Y y1[] = { Y(1), Y(2), Y(3) };
```

You get three objects and three constructor calls. Any time you have a constructor, whether it's a **struct** with all members **public** or a **class** with **private** data members, all the initialization must go through the constructor, even if you're using aggregate initialization.

Here's a second example showing multiple constructor arguments:

```
//: C06:Multiarg.cpp
// Multiple constructor arguments
// with aggregate initialization
#include <iostream>
using namespace std;

class Z {
  int i, j;
public:
  Z(int ii, int jj);
  void print();
};

Z::Z(int ii, int jj) {
  i = ii;
  j = jj;
}

void Z::print() {
  cout << "i = " << i << ", j = " << j << endl;
}

int main() {
  Z zz[] = { Z(1,2), Z(3,4), Z(5,6), Z(7,8) };
  for(int i = 0; i < sizeof zz / sizeof *zz; i++)
```

```
      zz[i].print();
} ///:~
```

Notice that it looks like an explicit constructor is called for each object in the array.

Default constructors

A *default constructor* is one that can be called with no arguments. A default constructor is used to create a "vanilla object," but it's also important when the compiler is told to create an object but isn't given any details. For example, if you take the **struct Y** defined previously and use it in a definition like this,

```
Y y2[2] = { Y(1) };
```

the compiler will complain that it cannot find a default constructor. The second object in the array wants to be created with no arguments, and that's where the compiler looks for a default constructor. In fact, if you simply define an array of **Y** objects,

```
Y y3[7];
```

the compiler will complain because it must have a default constructor to initialize every object in the array.

The same problem occurs if you create an individual object like this:

```
Y y4;
```

Remember, if you have a constructor, the compiler ensures that construction *always* happens, regardless of the situation.

 The default constructor is so important that *if* (and only if) there are no constructors for a structure (**struct** or **class**), the compiler will automatically create one for you. So this works:

```
//: C06:AutoDefaultConstructor.cpp
// Automatically-generated default constructor

class V {
  int i;  // private
```

```
};  // No constructor

int main() {
  V v, v2[10];
} ///:~
```

If any constructors are defined, however, and there's no default constructor, the instances of **V** above will generate compile-time errors.

You might think that the compiler-synthesized constructor should do some intelligent initialization, like setting all the memory for the object to zero. But it doesn't – that would add extra overhead but be out of the programmer's control. If you want the memory to be initialized to zero, you must do it yourself by writing the default constructor explicitly.

Although the compiler will create a default constructor for you, the behavior of the compiler-synthesized constructor is rarely what you want. You should treat this feature as a safety net, but use it sparingly. In general, you should define your constructors explicitly and not allow the compiler to do it for you.

Summary

The seemingly elaborate mechanisms provided by C++ should give you a strong hint about the critical importance placed on initialization and cleanup in the language. As Stroustrup was designing C++, one of the first observations he made about productivity in C was that a significant portion of programming problems are caused by improper initialization of variables. These kinds of bugs are hard to find, and similar issues apply to improper cleanup. Because constructors and destructors allow you to *guarantee* proper initialization and cleanup (the compiler will not allow an object to be created and destroyed without the proper constructor and destructor calls), you get complete control and safety.

Aggregate initialization is included in a similar vein – it prevents you from making typical initialization mistakes with aggregates of built-in types and makes your code more succinct.

Safety during coding is a big issue in C++. Initialization and cleanup are an important part of this, but you'll also see other safety issues as the book progresses.

Exercises

Solutions to selected exercises can be found in the electronic document *The Thinking in C++ Annotated Solution Guide*, available for a small fee from www.BruceEckel.com.

1. Write a simple class called **Simple** with a constructor that prints something to tell you that it's been called. In **main( )** make an object of your class.

2. Add a destructor to Exercise 1 that prints out a message to tell you that it's been called.

3. Modify Exercise 2 so that the class contains an **int** member. Modify the constructor so that it takes an **int** argument that it stores in the class member. Both the constructor and destructor should print out the **int** value as part of their message, so you can see the objects as they are created and destroyed.

4. Demonstrate that destructors are still called even when **goto** is used to jump out of a loop.

5. Write two **for** loops that print out values from zero to 10. In the first, define the loop counter before the **for** loop, and in the second, define the loop counter in the control expression of the **for** loop. For the second part of this exercise, modify the identifier in the second **for** loop so that it as the same name as the loop counter for the first and see what your compiler does.

6. Modify the **Handle.h**, **Handle.cpp**, and **UseHandle.cpp** files at the end of Chapter 5 to use constructors and destructors.

7. Use aggregate initialization to create an array of **double** in which you specify the size of the array but do not provide enough elements. Print out this array using

sizeof to determine the size of the array. Now create an array of **double** using aggregate initialization *and* automatic counting. Print out the array.

8. Use aggregate initialization to create an array of **string** objects. Create a **Stack** to hold these **string**s and step through your array, pushing each **string** on your **Stack**. Finally, **pop** the **string**s off your **Stack** and print each one.

9. Demonstrate automatic counting and aggregate initialization with an array of objects of the class you created in Exercise 3. Add a member function to that class that prints a message. Calculate the size of the array and move through it, calling your new member function.

10. Create a class without any constructors, and show that you can create objects with the default constructor. Now create a nondefault constructor (one with an argument) for the class, and try compiling again. Explain what happened.

7: Function Overloading & Default Arguments

One of the important features in any programming language is the convenient use of names.

When you create an object (a variable), you give a name to a region of storage. A function is a name for an action. By making up names to describe the system at hand, you create a program that is easier for people to understand and change. It's a lot like writing prose – the goal is to communicate with your readers.

A problem arises when mapping the concept of nuance in human language onto a programming language. Often, the same word expresses a number of different meanings, depending on context. That is, a single word has multiple meanings – it's *overloaded*. This is very useful, especially when it comes to trivial differences. You say "wash the shirt, wash the car." It would be silly to be forced to say, "shirt_wash the shirt, car_wash the car" just so the listener doesn't have to make any distinction about the action performed. Human languages have built-in redundancy, so even if you miss a few words, you can still determine the meaning. We don't need unique identifiers – we can deduce meaning from context.

Most programming languages, however, require that you have a unique identifier for each function. If you have three different types of data that you want to print: **int**, **char**, and **float**, you generally have to create three different function names, for example, **print_int( )**, **print_char( )**, and **print_float( )**. This loads extra work on you as you write the program, and on readers as they try to understand it.

In C++, another factor forces the overloading of function names: the constructor. Because the constructor's name is predetermined by the name of the class, it would seem that there can be only one constructor. But what if you want to create an object in more than one way? For example, suppose you build a class that can initialize itself in a standard way and also by reading information from a file. You need two constructors, one that takes no arguments (the default constructor) and one that takes a **string** as an argument, which is the name of the file to initialize the object. Both are constructors, so they must have the same name: the name of the class. Thus, function overloading is essential to allow the same function name – the constructor in this case – to be used with different argument types.

Although function overloading is a must for constructors, it's a general convenience and can be used with any function, not just class member functions. In addition, function overloading means that if you have two libraries that contain functions of the same name, they won't conflict as long as the argument lists are different. We'll look at all these factors in detail throughout this chapter.

The theme of this chapter is convenient use of function names. Function overloading allows you to use the same name for different functions, but there's a second way to make calling a function more convenient. What if you'd like to call the same function in different ways? When functions have long argument lists, it can become tedious to write (and confusing to read) the function calls when most of the arguments are the same for all the calls. A commonly used feature in C++ is called *default arguments*. A default argument is one the compiler inserts if it isn't specified in the function call. Thus, the calls **f("hello")**, **f("hi", 1)**, and **f("howdy", 2, 'c')** can all be calls to the same function. They could also be calls to three overloaded functions, but when the argument lists are this similar, you'll usually want similar behavior, which calls for a single function.

Function overloading and default arguments really aren't very complicated. By the time you reach the end of this chapter, you'll understand when to use them and the underlying mechanisms that implement them during compiling and linking.

More name decoration

In Chapter 4, the concept of *name decoration* was introduced. In the code

```
void f();
class X { void f(); };
```

the function **f( )** inside the scope of **class X** does not clash with the global version of **f( )**. The compiler performs this scoping by manufacturing different internal names for the global version of **f( )** and **X::f( )**. In Chapter 4, it was suggested that the names are simply the class name "decorated" together with the function name, so the internal names the compiler uses might be **_f** and **_X_f**. However, it turns out that function name decoration involves more than the class name.

Here's why. Suppose you want to overload two function names

```
void print(char);
void print(float);
```

It doesn't matter whether they are both inside a class or at the global scope. The compiler can't generate unique internal identifiers if it uses only the scope of the function names. You'd end up with **_print** in both cases. The idea of an overloaded function is that you use the same function name, but different argument lists. Thus, for overloading to work the compiler must decorate the function name with the names of the argument types. The functions above, defined at global scope, produce internal names that might look something like **_print_char** and **_print_float**. It's worth noting there is no standard for the way names must be decorated by the compiler, so you will see very different results from one compiler to another. (You can see what it looks like by telling the compiler to generate assembly-language output.) This, of course, causes problems if you want to buy compiled libraries for a particular compiler and linker – but even if name decoration were standardized, there would be other roadblocks because of the way different compilers generate code.

That's really all there is to function overloading: you can use the same function name for different functions as long as the argument lists are different. The compiler decorates the name, the scope, and the argument lists to produce internal names for it and the linker to use.

Overloading on return values

It's common to wonder, "Why just scopes and argument lists? Why not return values?" It seems at first that it would make sense to also decorate the return value with the internal function name. Then you could overload on return values, as well:

```
void f();
```

```
int f();
```

This works fine when the compiler can unequivocally determine the meaning from the context, as in **int x = f( );**. However, in C you've always been able to call a function and ignore the return value (that is, you can call the function for its *side effects*). How can the compiler distinguish which call is meant in this case? Possibly worse is the difficulty the reader has in knowing which function call is meant. Overloading solely on return value is a bit too subtle, and thus isn't allowed in C++.

Type-safe linkage

There is an added benefit to all of this name decoration. A particularly sticky problem in C occurs when the client programmer misdeclares a function, or, worse, a function is called without declaring it first, and the compiler infers the function declaration from the way it is called. Sometimes this function declaration is correct, but when it isn't, it can be a difficult bug to find.

Because all functions *must* be declared before they are used in C++, the opportunity for this problem to pop up is greatly diminished. The C++ compiler refuses to declare a function automatically for you, so it's likely that you will include the appropriate header file. However, if for some reason you still manage to misdeclare a function, either by declaring by hand or including the wrong header file (perhaps one that is out of date), the name decoration provides a safety net that is often referred to as *type-safe linkage*.

Consider the following scenario. In one file is the definition for a function:

```
//: C07:Def.cpp {O}
// Function definition
void f(int) {}
///:~
```

In the second file, the function is misdeclared and then called:

```
//: C07:Use.cpp
//{L} Def
```

```
// Function misdeclaration
void f(char);

int main() {
//!  f(1); // Causes a linker error
} ///:~
```

Even though you can see that the function is actually **f(int)**, the compiler doesn't know this because it was told – through an explicit declaration – that the function is **f(char)**. Thus, the compilation is successful. In C, the linker would also be successful, but *not* in C++. Because the compiler decorates the names, the definition becomes something like **f_int**, whereas the use of the function is **f_char**. When the linker tries to resolve the reference to **f_char**, it can only find **f_int**, and it gives you an error message. This is type-safe linkage. Although the problem doesn't occur all that often, when it does it can be incredibly difficult to find, especially in a large project. This is one of the cases where you can easily find a difficult error in a C program simply by running it through the C++ compiler.

Overloading example

We can now modify earlier examples to use function overloading. As stated before, an immediately useful place for overloading is in constructors. You can see this in the following version of the **Stash** class:

```
//: C07:Stash3.h
// Function overloading
#ifndef STASH3_H
#define STASH3_H

class Stash {
  int size;       // Size of each space
  int quantity;   // Number of storage spaces
  int next;       // Next empty space
  // Dynamically allocated array of bytes:
  unsigned char* storage;
  void inflate(int increase);
public:
```

```
   Stash(int size); // Zero quantity
   Stash(int size, int initQuantity);
   ~Stash();
   int add(void* element);
   void* fetch(int index);
   int count();
};
#endif // STASH3_H ///:~
```

The first **Stash( )** constructor is the same as before, but the second one has a **Quantity** argument to indicate the initial number of storage places to be allocated. In the definition, you can see that the internal value of **quantity** is set to zero, along with the **storage** pointer. In the second constructor, the call to **inflate(initQuantity)** increases **quantity** to the allocated size:

```
//: C07:Stash3.cpp {O}
// Function overloading
#include "Stash3.h"
#include "../require.h"
#include <iostream>
#include <cassert>
using namespace std;
const int increment = 100;

Stash::Stash(int sz) {
  size = sz;
  quantity = 0;
  next = 0;
  storage = 0;
}

Stash::Stash(int sz, int initQuantity) {
  size = sz;
  quantity = 0;
  next = 0;
  storage = 0;
  inflate(initQuantity);
}

Stash::~Stash() {
  if(storage != 0) {
    cout << "freeing storage" << endl;
    delete []storage;
```

```
    }
}

int Stash::add(void* element) {
  if(next >= quantity) // Enough space left?
    inflate(increment);
  // Copy element into storage,
  // starting at next empty space:
  int startBytes = next * size;
  unsigned char* e = (unsigned char*)element;
  for(int i = 0; i < size; i++)
    storage[startBytes + i] = e[i];
  next++;
  return(next - 1); // Index number
}

void* Stash::fetch(int index) {
  require(0 <= index, "Stash::fetch (-)index");
  if(index >= next)
    return 0; // To indicate the end
  // Produce pointer to desired element:
  return &(storage[index * size]);
}

int Stash::count() {
  return next; // Number of elements in CStash
}

void Stash::inflate(int increase) {
  assert(increase >= 0);
  if(increase == 0) return;
  int newQuantity = quantity + increase;
  int newBytes = newQuantity * size;
  int oldBytes = quantity * size;
  unsigned char* b = new unsigned char[newBytes];
  for(int i = 0; i < oldBytes; i++)
    b[i] = storage[i]; // Copy old to new
  delete [](storage); // Release old storage
  storage = b; // Point to new memory
  quantity = newQuantity; // Adjust the size
} ///:~
```

When you use the first constructor no memory is allocated for
storage. The allocation happens the first time you try to **add( )** an

object and any time the current block of memory is exceeded inside
add( ).

Both constructors are exercised in the test program:

```
//: C07:Stash3Test.cpp
//{L} Stash3
// Function overloading
#include "Stash3.h"
#include "../require.h"
#include <fstream>
#include <iostream>
#include <string>
using namespace std;

int main() {
  Stash intStash(sizeof(int));
  for(int i = 0; i < 100; i++)
    intStash.add(&i);
  for(int j = 0; j < intStash.count(); j++)
    cout << "intStash.fetch(" << j << ") = "
         << *(int*)intStash.fetch(j)
         << endl;
  const int bufsize = 80;
  Stash stringStash(sizeof(char) * bufsize, 100);
  ifstream in("Stash3Test.cpp");
  assure(in, "Stash3Test.cpp");
  string line;
  while(getline(in, line))
    stringStash.add((char*)line.c_str());
  int k = 0;
  char* cp;
  while((cp = (char*)stringStash.fetch(k++))!=0)
    cout << "stringStash.fetch(" << k << ") = "
         << cp << endl;
} ///:~
```

The constructor call for **stringStash** uses a second argument;
presumably you know something special about the specific problem
you're solving that allows you to choose an initial size for the **Stash**.

unions

As you've seen, the only difference between **struct** and **class** in C++ is that **struct** defaults to **public** and **class** defaults to **private**. A **struct** can also have constructors and destructors, as you might expect. But it turns out that a **union** can also have a constructor, destructor, member functions, and even access control. You can again see the use and benefit of overloading in the following example:

```
//: C07:UnionClass.cpp
// Unions with constructors and member functions
#include<iostream>
using namespace std;

union U {
private: // Access control too!
  int i;
  float f;
public:
  U(int a);
  U(float b);
  ~U();
  int read_int();
  float read_float();
};

U::U(int a) { i = a; }

U::U(float b) { f = b;}

U::~U() { cout << "U::~U()\n"; }

int U::read_int() { return i; }

float U::read_float() { return f; }

int main() {
  U X(12), Y(1.9F);
  cout << X.read_int() << endl;
  cout << Y.read_float() << endl;
} ///:~
```

You might think from the code above that the only difference between a **union** and a **class** is the way the data is stored (that is, the **int** and **float** are overlaid on the same piece of storage). However, a **union** cannot be used as a base class during inheritance, which is quite limiting from an object-oriented design standpoint (you'll learn about inheritance in Chapter 14).

Although the member functions civilize access to the **union** somewhat, there is still no way to prevent the client programmer from selecting the wrong element type once the **union** is initialized. In the example above, you could say **X.read_float( )** even though it is inappropriate. However, a "safe" **union** can be encapsulated in a class. In the following example, notice how the **enum** clarifies the code, and how overloading comes in handy with the constructors:

```cpp
//: C07:SuperVar.cpp
// A super-variable
#include <iostream>
using namespace std;

class SuperVar {
  enum {
    character,
    integer,
    floating_point
  } vartype;  // Define one
  union {  // Anonymous union
    char c;
    int i;
    float f;
  };
public:
  SuperVar(char ch);
  SuperVar(int ii);
  SuperVar(float ff);
  void print();
};

SuperVar::SuperVar(char ch) {
  vartype = character;
  c = ch;
}
```

```
SuperVar::SuperVar(int ii) {
  vartype = integer;
  i = ii;
}

SuperVar::SuperVar(float ff) {
  vartype = floating_point;
  f = ff;
}

void SuperVar::print() {
  switch (vartype) {
    case character:
      cout << "character: " << c << endl;
      break;
    case integer:
      cout << "integer: " << i << endl;
      break;
    case floating_point:
      cout << "float: " << f << endl;
      break;
  }
}

int main() {
  SuperVar A('c'), B(12), C(1.44F);
  A.print();
  B.print();
  C.print();
} ///:~
```

In the code above, the **enum** has no type name (it is an untagged enumeration). This is acceptable if you are going to immediately define instances of the **enum**, as is done here. There is no need to refer to the **enum's** type name in the future, so the type name is optional.

The **union** has no type name and no variable name. This is called an *anonymous union*, and creates space for the **union** but doesn't require accessing the **union** elements with a variable name and the dot operator. For instance, if your anonymous **union** is:

```
//: C07:AnonymousUnion.cpp
```

```
int main() {
  union {
    int i;
    float f;
  };
  // Access members without using qualifiers:
  i = 12;
  f = 1.22;
} ///:~
```

Note that you access members of an anonymous union just as if they were ordinary variables. The only difference is that both variables occupy the same space. If the anonymous **union** is at file scope (outside all functions and classes) then it must be declared **static** so it has internal linkage.

Although **SuperVar** is now safe, its usefulness is a bit dubious because the reason for using a **union** in the first place is to save space, and the addition of **vartype** takes up quite a bit of space relative to the data in the **union**, so the savings are effectively eliminated. There are a couple of alternatives to make this scheme workable. If the **vartype** controlled more than one **union** instance – if they were all the same type – then you'd only need one for the group and it wouldn't take up more space. A more useful approach is to have **#ifdef**s around all the **vartype** code, which can then guarantee things are being used correctly during development and testing. For shipping code, the extra space and time overhead can be eliminated.

Default arguments

In **Stash3.h**, examine the two constructors for **Stash( )**. They don't seem all that different, do they? In fact, the first constructor seems to be a special case of the second one with the initial **size** set to zero. It's a bit of a waste of effort to create and maintain two different versions of a similar function.

C++ provides a remedy with *default arguments*. A default argument is a value given in the declaration that the compiler

---

automatically inserts if you don't provide a value in the function call. In the **Stash** example, we can replace the two functions:

```
Stash(int size); // Zero quantity
Stash(int size, int initQuantity);
```

with the single function:

```
Stash(int size, int initQuantity = 0);
```

The **Stash(int)** definition is simply removed – all that is necessary is the single **Stash(int, int)** definition.

Now, the two object definitions

```
Stash A(100), B(100, 0);
```

will produce exactly the same results. The identical constructor is called in both cases, but for **A**, the second argument is automatically substituted by the compiler when it sees the first argument is an **int** and that there is no second argument. The compiler has seen the default argument, so it knows it can still make the function call if it substitutes this second argument, which is what you've told it to do by making it a default.

Default arguments are a convenience, as function overloading is a convenience. Both features allow you to use a single function name in different situations. The difference is that with default arguments the compiler is substituting arguments when you don't want to put them in yourself. The preceding example is a good place to use default arguments instead of function overloading; otherwise you end up with two or more functions that have similar signatures and similar behaviors. If the functions have very different behaviors, it doesn't usually make sense to use default arguments (for that matter, you might want to question whether two functions with very different behaviors should have the same name).

There are two rules you must be aware of when using default arguments. First, only trailing arguments may be defaulted. That is, you can't have a default argument followed by a non-default argument. Second, once you start using default arguments in a particular function call, all the subsequent arguments in that function's argument list must be defaulted (this follows from the first rule).

Default arguments are only placed in the declaration of a function (typically placed in a header file). The compiler must see the default value before it can use it. Sometimes people will place the commented values of the default arguments in the function definition, for documentation purposes

```cpp
void fn(int x /* = 0 */) { // ...
```

Placeholder arguments

Arguments in a function declaration can be declared without identifiers. When these are used with default arguments, it can look a bit funny. You can end up with

```cpp
void f(int x, int = 0, float = 1.1);
```

In C++ you don't need identifiers in the function definition, either:

```cpp
void f(int x, int, float flt) { /* ... */ }
```

In the function body, **x** and **flt** can be referenced, but not the middle argument, because it has no name. Function calls must still provide a value for the placeholder, though: **f(1)** or **f(1,2,3.0)**. This syntax allows you to put the argument in as a placeholder without using it. The idea is that you might want to change the function definition to use the placeholder later, without changing all the code where the function is called. Of course, you can accomplish the same thing by using a named argument, but if you define the argument for the function body without using it, most compilers will give you a warning message, assuming you've made a logical error. By intentionally leaving the argument name out, you suppress this warning.

More important, if you start out using a function argument and later decide that you don't need it, you can effectively remove it without generating warnings, and yet not disturb any client code that was calling the previous version of the function.

Choosing overloading vs. default arguments

Both function overloading and default arguments provide a convenience for calling function names. However, it can seem confusing at times to know which technique to use. For example, consider the following tool that is designed to automatically manage blocks of memory for you:

```
//: C07:Mem.h
#ifndef MEM_H
#define MEM_H
typedef unsigned char byte;

class Mem {
  byte* mem;
  int size;
  void ensureMinSize(int minSize);
public:
  Mem();
  Mem(int sz);
  ~Mem();
  int msize();
  byte* pointer();
  byte* pointer(int minSize);
};
#endif // MEM_H ///:~
```

A **Mem** object holds a block of **byte**s and makes sure that you have enough storage. The default constructor doesn't allocate any storage, and the second constructor ensures that there is **sz** storage in the **Mem** object. The destructor releases the storage, **msize( )** tells you how many bytes there are currently in the **Mem** object, and **pointer( )** produces a pointer to the starting address of the storage (**Mem** is a fairly low-level tool). There's an overloaded version of **pointer( )** in which client programmers can say that they want a pointer to a block of bytes that is at least **minSize** large, and the member function ensures this.

Both the constructor and the **pointer( )** member function use the **private ensureMinSize( )** member function to increase the size

of the memory block (notice that it's not safe to hold the result of
pointer( ) if the memory is resized).

Here's the implementation of the class:

```
//: C07:Mem.cpp {O}
#include "Mem.h"
#include <cstring>
using namespace std;

Mem::Mem() { mem = 0; size = 0; }

Mem::Mem(int sz) {
  mem = 0;
  size = 0;
  ensureMinSize(sz);
}

Mem::~Mem() { delete []mem; }

int Mem::msize() { return size; }

void Mem::ensureMinSize(int minSize) {
  if(size < minSize) {
    byte* newmem = new byte[minSize];
    memset(newmem + size, 0, minSize - size);
    memcpy(newmem, mem, size);
    delete []mem;
    mem = newmem;
    size = minSize;
  }
}

byte* Mem::pointer() { return mem; }

byte* Mem::pointer(int minSize) {
  ensureMinSize(minSize);
  return mem;
} ///:~
```

You can see that **ensureMinSize( )** is the only function
responsible for allocating memory, and that it is used from the
second constructor and the second overloaded form of **pointer( )**.
Inside **ensureMinSize( )**, nothing needs to be done if the **size** is

large enough. If new storage must be allocated in order to make the block bigger (which is also the case when the block is of size zero after default construction), the new "extra" portion is set to zero using the Standard C library function **memset( )**, which was introduced in Chapter 5. The subsequent function call is to the Standard C library function **memcpy( )**, which in this case copies the existing bytes from **mem** to **newmem** (typically in an efficient fashion). Finally, the old memory is deleted and the new memory and sizes are assigned to the appropriate members.

The **Mem** class is designed to be used as a tool within other classes to simplify their memory management (it could also be used to hide a more sophisticated memory-management system provided, for example, by the operating system). Appropriately, it is tested here by creating a simple "string" class:

```cpp
//: C07:MemTest.cpp
// Testing the Mem class
//{L} Mem
#include "Mem.h"
#include <cstring>
#include <iostream>
using namespace std;

class MyString {
  Mem* buf;
public:
  MyString();
  MyString(char* str);
  ~MyString();
  void concat(char* str);
  void print(ostream& os);
};

MyString::MyString() {  buf = 0;  }

MyString::MyString(char* str) {
  buf = new Mem(strlen(str) + 1);
  strcpy((char*)buf->pointer(), str);
}

void MyString::concat(char* str) {
  if(!buf) buf = new Mem;
```

```
   strcat((char*)buf->pointer(
     buf->msize() + strlen(str) + 1), str);
}

void MyString::print(ostream& os) {
  if(!buf) return;
  os << buf->pointer() << endl;
}

MyString::~MyString() { delete buf; }

int main() {
  MyString s("My test string");
  s.print(cout);
  s.concat(" some additional stuff");
  s.print(cout);
  MyString s2;
  s2.concat("Using default constructor");
  s2.print(cout);
} ///:~
```

All you can do with this class is to create a **MyString**, concatenate text, and print to an **ostream**. The class only contains a pointer to a **Mem**, but note the distinction between the default constructor, which sets the pointer to zero, and the second constructor, which creates a **Mem** and copies data into it. The advantage of the default constructor is that you can create, for example, a large array of empty **MyString** objects very cheaply, since the size of each object is only one pointer and the only overhead of the default constructor is that of assigning to zero. The cost of a **MyString** only begins to accrue when you concatenate data; at that point the **Mem** object is created if it hasn't been already. However, if you use the default constructor and never concatenate any data, the destructor call is still safe because calling **delete** for zero is defined such that it does not try to release storage or otherwise cause problems.

If you look at these two constructors it might at first seem like this is a prime candidate for default arguments. However, if you drop the default constructor and write the remaining constructor with a default argument:

```
MyString(char* str = "");
```

everything will work correctly, but you'll lose the previous efficiency benefit since a **Mem** object will always be created. To get the efficiency back, you must modify the constructor:

```
MyString::MyString(char* str) {
  if(!*str) { // Pointing at an empty string
    buf = 0;
    return;
  }
  buf = new Mem(strlen(str) + 1);
  strcpy((char*)buf->pointer(), str);
}
```

This means, in effect, that the default value becomes a flag that causes a separate piece of code to be executed than if a non-default value is used. Although it seems innocent enough with a small constructor like this one, in general this practice can cause problems. If you have to *look* for the default rather than treating it as an ordinary value, that should be a clue that you will end up with effectively two different functions inside a single function body: one version for the normal case and one for the default. You might as well split it up into two distinct function bodies and let the compiler do the selection. This results in a slight (but usually invisible) increase in efficiency, because the extra argument isn't passed and the extra code for the conditional isn't executed. More importantly, you are keeping the code for two separate functions *in* two separate functions rather than combining them into one using default arguments, which will result in easier maintainability, especially if the functions are large.

On the other hand, consider the **Mem** class. If you look at the definitions of the two constructors and the two **pointer( )** functions, you can see that using default arguments in both cases will not cause the member function definitions to change at all. Thus, the class could easily be:

```
//: C07:Mem2.h
#ifndef MEM2_H
#define MEM2_H
typedef unsigned char byte;

class Mem {
```

```
  byte* mem;
  int size;
  void ensureMinSize(int minSize);
public:
  Mem(int sz = 0);
  ~Mem();
  int msize();
  byte* pointer(int minSize = 0);
};
#endif // MEM2_H ///:~
```

Notice that a call to **ensureMinSize(0)** will always be quite efficient.

Although in both of these cases I based some of the decision-making process on the issue of efficiency, you must be careful not to fall into the trap of thinking only about efficiency (fascinating as it is). The most important issue in class design is the interface of the class (its **public** members, which are available to the client programmer). If these produce a class that is easy to use and reuse, then you have a success; you can always tune for efficiency if necessary but the effect of a class that is designed badly because the programmer is over-focused on efficiency issues can be dire. Your primary concern should be that the interface makes sense to those who use it and who read the resulting code. Notice that in **MemTest.cpp** the usage of **MyString** does not change regardless of whether a default constructor is used or whether the efficiency is high or low.

Summary

As a guideline, you shouldn't use a default argument as a flag upon which to conditionally execute code. You should instead break the function into two or more overloaded functions if you can. A default argument should be a value you would ordinarily put in that position. It's a value that is more likely to occur than all the rest, so client programmers can generally ignore it or use it only if they want to change it from the default value.

The default argument is included to make function calls easier, especially when those functions have many arguments with typical values. Not only is it much easier to write the calls, it's easier to read them, especially if the class creator can order the arguments so the least-modified defaults appear latest in the list.

An especially important use of default arguments is when you start out with a function with a set of arguments, and after it's been used for a while you discover you need to add arguments. By defaulting all the new arguments, you ensure that all client code using the previous interface is not disturbed.

Exercises

Solutions to selected exercises can be found in the electronic document *The Thinking in C++ Annotated Solution Guide*, available for a small fee from www.BruceEckel.com.

1. Create a **Text** class that contains a **string** object to hold the text of a file. Give it two constructors: a default constructor and a constructor that takes a **string** argument that is the name of the file to open. When the second constructor is used, open the file and read the contents into the **string** member object. Add a member function **contents( )** to return the **string** so (for example) it can be printed. In **main( )**, open a file using **Text** and print the contents.

2. Create a **Message** class with a constructor that takes a single **string** with a default value. Create a private member **string**, and in the constructor simply assign the argument **string** to your internal **string**. Create two overloaded member functions called **print( )**: one that takes no arguments and simply prints the message stored in the object, and one that takes a **string** argument, which it prints in addition to the internal message. Does it make sense to use this approach instead of the one used for the constructor?

3. Determine how to generate assembly output with your compiler, and run experiments to deduce the name-decoration scheme.

4. Create a class that contains four member functions, with 0, 1, 2, and 3 **int** arguments, respectively. Create a **main( )** that makes an object of your class and calls each of the member functions. Now modify the class so it has instead a single member function with all the arguments defaulted. Does this change your **main( )**?

5. Create a function with two arguments and call it from **main( )**. Now make one of the arguments a "placeholder" (no identifier) and see if your call in **main( )** changes.

6. Modify **Stash3.h** and **Stash3.cpp** to use default arguments in the constructor. Test the constructor by making two different versions of a **Stash** object.

7. Create a new version of the **Stack** class (from Chapter 6) that contains the default constructor as before, and a second constructor that takes as its arguments an array of pointers to objects and the size of that array. This constructor should move through the array and push each pointer onto the **Stack**. Test your class with an array of **string**.

8. Modify **SuperVar** so that there are **#ifdef**s around all the **vartype** code as described in the section on **enum**. Make **vartype** a regular and **public** enumeration (with no instance) and modify **print( )** so that it requires a **vartype** argument to tell it what to do.

9. Implement **Mem2.h** and make sure that the modified class still works with **MemTest.cpp**.

10. Use **class Mem** to implement **Stash**. Note that because the implementation is **private** and thus hidden from the client programmer, the test code does not need to be modified.

11. In **class Mem**, add a **bool moved( )** member function that takes the result of a call to **pointer( )** and tells you whether the pointer has moved (due to reallocation). Write a **main( )** that tests your **moved( )** member function. Does it make more sense to use something like **moved( )** or to simply call **pointer( )** every time you need to access the memory in **Mem**?

8: Constants

The concept of *constant* (expressed by the **const** keyword) was created to allow the programmer to draw a line between what changes and what doesn't. This provides safety and control in a C++ programming project.

Since its origin, **const** has taken on a number of different purposes. In the meantime it trickled back into the C language where its meaning was changed. All this can seem a bit confusing at first, and in this chapter you'll learn when, why, and how to use the **const** keyword. At the end there's a discussion of **volatile**, which is a near cousin to **const** (because they both concern change) and has identical syntax.

The first motivation for **const** seems to have been to eliminate the use of preprocessor **#define**s for value substitution. It has since been put to use for pointers, function arguments, return types, class objects and member functions. All of these have slightly different but conceptually compatible meanings and will be looked at in separate sections in this chapter.

Value substitution

When programming in C, the preprocessor is liberally used to create macros and to substitute values. Because the preprocessor simply does text replacement and has no concept nor facility for type checking, preprocessor value substitution introduces subtle problems that can be avoided in C++ by using **const** values.

The typical use of the preprocessor to substitute values for names in C looks like this:

```
#define BUFSIZE 100
```

BUFSIZE is a name that only exists during preprocessing, therefore it doesn't occupy storage and can be placed in a header file to provide a single value for all translation units that use it. It's very important for code maintenance to use value substitution instead of so-called "magic numbers." If you use magic numbers in your code, not only does the reader have no idea where the numbers come from or what they represent, but if you decide to change a value, you must perform hand editing, and you have no trail to follow to ensure you don't miss one of your values (or accidentally change one you shouldn't).

Most of the time, **BUFSIZE** will behave like an ordinary variable, but not all the time. In addition, there's no type information. This can hide bugs that are very difficult to find. C++ uses **const** to eliminate these problems by bringing value substitution into the domain of the compiler. Now you can say

```
const int bufsize = 100;
```

You can use **bufsize** anyplace where the compiler must know the value at compile time. The compiler can use **bufsize** to perform *constant folding*, which means the compiler will reduce a complicated constant expression to a simple one by performing the necessary calculations at compile time. This is especially important in array definitions:

```
char buf[bufsize];
```

You can use **const** for all the built-in types (**char**, **int**, **float**, and **double**) and their variants (as well as class objects, as you'll see later in this chapter). Because of subtle bugs that the preprocessor might introduce, you should always use **const** instead of **#define** value substitution.

const in header files

To use **const** instead of **#define**, you must be able to place **const** definitions inside header files as you can with **#define**. This way, you can place the definition for a **const** in a single place and distribute it to translation units by including the header file. A **const** in C++ defaults to *internal linkage*; that is, it is visible only within the file where it is defined and cannot be seen at link time by other translation units. You must always assign a value to a **const** when you define it, *except* when you make an explicit declaration using **extern**:

```
extern const int bufsize;
```

Normally, the C++ compiler avoids creating storage for a **const**, but instead holds the definition in its symbol table. When you use **extern** with **const**, however, you force storage to be allocated (this is also true for certain other cases, such as taking the address of a

const). Storage must be allocated because **extern** says "use external linkage," which means that several translation units must be able to refer to the item, which requires it to have storage.

In the ordinary case, when **extern** is not part of the definition, no storage is allocated. When the **const** is used, it is simply folded in at compile time.

The goal of never allocating storage for a **const** also fails with complicated structures. Whenever the compiler must allocate storage, constant folding is prevented (since there's no way for the compiler to know for sure what the value of that storage is – if it could know that, it wouldn't need to allocate the storage).

Because the compiler cannot always avoid allocating storage for a **const**, **const** definitions *must* default to internal linkage, that is, linkage only *within* that particular translation unit. Otherwise, linker errors would occur with complicated **const**s because they cause storage to be allocated in multiple **cpp** files. The linker would then see the same definition in multiple object files, and complain. Because a **const** defaults to internal linkage, the linker doesn't try to link those definitions across translation units, and there are no collisions. With built-in types, which are used in the majority of cases involving constant expressions, the compiler can always perform constant folding.

Safety consts

The use of **const** is not limited to replacing **#define**s in constant expressions. If you initialize a variable with a value that is produced at runtime and you know it will not change for the lifetime of that variable, it is good programming practice to make it a **const** so the compiler will give you an error message if you accidentally try to change it. Here's an example:

```
//: C08:Safecons.cpp
// Using const for safety
#include <iostream>
using namespace std;

const int i = 100;  // Typical constant
```

```
const int j = i + 10; // Value from const expr
long address = (long)&j; // Forces storage
char buf[j + 10]; // Still a const expression

int main() {
  cout << "type a character & CR:";
  const char c = cin.get(); // Can't change
  const char c2 = c + 'a';
  cout << c2;
  // ...
} ///:~
```

You can see that **i** is a compile-time **const**, but **j** is calculated from
i. However, because **i** is a **const**, the calculated value for **j** still
comes from a constant expression and is itself a compile-time
constant. The very next line requires the address of **j** and therefore
forces the compiler to allocate storage for **j**. Yet this doesn't prevent
the use of **j** in the determination of the size of **buf** because the
compiler knows **j** is **const** and that the value is valid even if storage
was allocated to hold that value at some point in the program.

In **main( )**, you see a different kind of **const** in the identifier **c**
because the value cannot be known at compile time. This means
storage is required, and the compiler doesn't attempt to keep
anything in its symbol table (the same behavior as in C). The
initialization must still happen at the point of definition, and once
the initialization occurs, the value cannot be changed. You can see
that **c2** is calculated from **c** and also that scoping works for **const**s
as it does for any other type – yet another improvement over the
use of **#define**.

As a matter of practice, if you think a value shouldn't change, you
should make it a **const**. This not only provides insurance against
inadvertent changes, it also allows the compiler to generate more
efficient code by eliminating storage and memory reads.

Aggregates

It's possible to use **const** for aggregates, but you're virtually
assured that the compiler will not be sophisticated enough to keep
an aggregate in its symbol table, so storage will be allocated. In

these situations, **const** means "a piece of storage that cannot be changed." However, the value cannot be used at compile time because the compiler is not required to know the contents of the storage at compile time. In the following code, you can see the statements that are illegal:

```
//: C08:Constag.cpp
// Constants and aggregates
const int i[] = { 1, 2, 3, 4 };
//! float f[i[3]]; // Illegal
struct S { int i, j; };
const S s[] = { { 1, 2 }, { 3, 4 } };
//! double d[s[1].j]; // Illegal
int main() {} ///:~
```

In an array definition, the compiler must be able to generate code that moves the stack pointer to accommodate the array. In both of the illegal definitions above, the compiler complains because it cannot find a constant expression in the array definition.

Differences with C

Constants were introduced in early versions of C++ while the Standard C specification was still being finished. Although the C committee then decided to include **const** in C, somehow it came to mean for them "an ordinary variable that cannot be changed." In C, a **const** always occupies storage and its name is global. The C compiler cannot treat a **const** as a compile-time constant. In C, if you say

```
const int bufsize = 100;
char buf[bufsize];
```

you will get an error, even though it seems like a rational thing to do. Because **bufsize** occupies storage somewhere, the C compiler cannot know the value at compile time. You can optionally say

```
const int bufsize;
```

in C, but not in C++, and the C compiler accepts it as a declaration indicating there is storage allocated elsewhere. Because C defaults to external linkage for **const**s, this makes sense. C++ defaults to internal linkage for **const**s so if you want to accomplish the same thing in C++, you must explicitly change the linkage to external using **extern**:

```
extern const int bufsize; // Declaration only
```

This line also works in C.

In C++, a **const** doesn't necessarily create storage. In C a **const** always creates storage. Whether or not storage is reserved for a **const** in C++ depends on how it is used. In general, if a **const** is used simply to replace a name with a value (just as you would use a **#define**), then storage doesn't have to be created for the **const**. If no storage is created (this depends on the complexity of the data type and the sophistication of the compiler), the values may be folded into the code for greater efficiency after type checking, not before, as with **#define**. If, however, you take an address of a **const** (even unknowingly, by passing it to a function that takes a reference argument) or you define it as **extern**, then storage is created for the **const**.

In C++, a **const** that is outside all functions has file scope (i.e., it is invisible outside the file). That is, it defaults to internal linkage. This is very different from all other identifiers in C++ (and from **const** in C!) that default to external linkage. Thus, if you declare a **const** of the same name in two different files and you don't take the address or define that name as **extern**, the ideal C++ compiler won't allocate storage for the **const**, but simply fold it into the code. Because **const** has implied file scope, you can put it in C++ header files with no conflicts at link time.

Since a **const** in C++ defaults to internal linkage, you can't just define a **const** in one file and reference it as an **extern** in another file. To give a **const** external linkage so it can be referenced from another file, you must explicitly define it as **extern**, like this:

```
extern const int x = 1;
```

Notice that by giving it an initializer and saying it is **extern**, you force storage to be created for the **const** (although the compiler still has the option of doing constant folding here). The initialization establishes this as a definition, not a declaration. The declaration:

```
extern const int x;
```

in C++ means that the definition exists elsewhere (again, this is not necessarily true in C). You can now see why C++ requires a **const** definition to have an initializer: the initializer distinguishes a declaration from a definition (in C it's always a definition, so no initializer is necessary). With an **extern const** declaration, the compiler cannot do constant folding because it doesn't know the value.

The C approach to **const** is not very useful, and if you want to use a named value inside a constant expression (one that must be evaluated at compile time), C almost *forces* you to use **#define** in the preprocessor.

Pointers

Pointers can be made **const**. The compiler will still endeavor to prevent storage allocation and do constant folding when dealing with **const** pointers, but these features seem less useful in this case. More importantly, the compiler will tell you if you attempt to change a **const** pointer, which adds a great deal of safety.

When using **const** with pointers, you have two options: **const** can be applied to what the pointer is pointing to, or the **const** can be applied to the address stored in the pointer itself. The syntax for these is a little confusing at first but becomes comfortable with practice.

Pointer to const

The trick with a pointer definition, as with any complicated definition, is to read it starting at the identifier and work your way out. The **const** specifier binds to the thing it is "closest to." So if you want to prevent any changes to the element you are pointing to, you write a definition like this:

```
const int* u;
```

Starting from the identifier, we read "**u** is a pointer, which points to a **const int**." Here, no initialization is required because you're saying that **u** can point to anything (that is, it is not **const**), but the thing it points to cannot be changed.

Here's the mildly confusing part. You might think that to make the pointer itself unchangeable, that is, to prevent any change to the address contained inside **u**, you would simply move the **const** to the other side of the **int** like this:

```
int const* v;
```

It's not all that crazy to think that this should read "**v** is a **const** pointer to an **int**." However, the way it *actually* reads is "**v** is an ordinary pointer to an **int** that happens to be **const**." That is, the **const** has bound itself to the **int** again, and the effect is the same as the previous definition. The fact that these two definitions are the same is the confusing point; to prevent this confusion on the part of your reader, you should probably stick to the first form.

const pointer

To make the pointer itself a **const**, you must place the **const** specifier to the right of the *, like this:

```
int d = 1;
int* const w = &d;
```

Now it reads: "**w** is a pointer, which is **const**, that points to an **int**." Because the pointer itself is now the **const**, the compiler requires that it be given an initial value that will be unchanged for the life of that pointer. It's OK, however, to change what that value points to by saying

```
*w = 2;
```

You can also make a **const** pointer to a **const** object using either of two legal forms:

```
int d = 1;
```

```
const int* const x = &d;   // (1)
int const* const x2 = &d;  // (2)
```

Now neither the pointer nor the object can be changed.

Some people argue that the second form is more consistent because the **const** is always placed to the right of what it modifies. You'll have to decide which is clearer for your particular coding style.

Here are the above lines in a compileable file:

```
//: C08:ConstPointers.cpp
const int* u;
int const* v;
int d = 1;
int* const w = &d;
const int* const x = &d;   // (1)
int const* const x2 = &d;  // (2)
int main() {} ///:~
```

Formatting

This book makes a point of only putting one pointer definition on a line, and initializing each pointer at the point of definition whenever possible. Because of this, the formatting style of "attaching" the '*' to the data type is possible:

```
int* u = &i;
```

as if **int*** were a discrete type unto itself. This makes the code easier to understand, but unfortunately that's not actually the way things work. The '*' in fact binds to the identifier, not the type. It can be placed anywhere between the type name and the identifier. So you could do this:

```
int *u = &i, v = 0;
```

which creates an **int* u**, as before, and a non-pointer **int v**. Because readers often find this confusing, it is best to follow the form shown in this book.

Assignment and type checking

C++ is very particular about type checking, and this extends to pointer assignments. You can assign the address of a non-**const** object to a **const** pointer because you're simply promising not to change something that is OK to change. However, you can't assign the address of a **const** object to a non-**const** pointer because then you're saying you might change the object via the pointer. Of course, you can always use a cast to force such an assignment, but this is bad programming practice because you are then breaking the **const**ness of the object, along with any safety promised by the **const**. For example:

```
//: C08:PointerAssignment.cpp
int d = 1;
const int e = 2;
int* u = &d; // OK -- d not const
//! int* v = &e; // Illegal -- e const
int* w = (int*)&e; // Legal but bad practice
int main() {} ///:~
```

Although C++ helps prevent errors it does not protect you from yourself if you want to break the safety mechanisms.

Character array literals

The place where strict **const**ness is not enforced is with character array literals. You can say

```
char* cp = "howdy";
```

and the compiler will accept it without complaint. This is technically an error because a character array literal (**"howdy"** in this case) is created by the compiler as a constant character array, and the result of the quoted character array is its starting address in memory. Modifying any of the characters in the array is a runtime error, although not all compilers enforce this correctly.

So character array literals are actually constant character arrays. Of course, the compiler lets you get away with treating them as non-**const** because there's so much existing C code that relies on this. However, if you try to change the values in a character array literal,

---

the behavior is undefined, although it will probably work on many machines.

If you want to be able to modify the string, put it in an array:

```
char cp[] = "howdy";
```

Since compilers often don't enforce the difference you won't be reminded to use this latter form and so the point becomes rather subtle.

Function arguments & return values

The use of **const** to specify function arguments and return values is another place where the concept of constants can be confusing. If you are passing objects *by value*, specifying **const** has no meaning to the client (it means that the passed argument cannot be modified inside the function). If you are returning an object of a user-defined type by value as a **const**, it means the returned value cannot be modified. If you are passing and returning *addresses*, **const** is a promise that the destination of the address will not be changed.

Passing by const value

You can specify that function arguments are **const** when passing them by value, such as

```
void f1(const int i) {
  i++; // Illegal -- compile-time error
}
```

but what does this mean? You're making a promise that the original value of the variable will not be changed by the function **f1( )**. However, because the argument is passed by value, you immediately make a copy of the original variable, so the promise to the client is implicitly kept.

Inside the function, the **const** takes on meaning: the argument cannot be changed. So it's really a tool for the creator of the function, and not the caller.

To avoid confusion to the caller, you can make the argument a **const** *inside* the function, rather than in the argument list. You could do this with a pointer, but a nicer syntax is achieved with the *reference*, a subject that will be fully developed in Chapter 11. Briefly, a reference is like a constant pointer that is automatically dereferenced, so it has the effect of being an alias to an object. To create a reference, you use the **&** in the definition. So the non-confusing function definition looks like this:

```
void f2(int ic) {
  const int& i = ic;
  i++;  // Illegal -- compile-time error
}
```

Again, you'll get an error message, but this time the **const**ness of the local object is not part of the function signature; it only has meaning to the implementation of the function and therefore it's hidden from the client.

Returning by const value

A similar truth holds for the return value. If you say that a function's return value is **const**:

```
const int g();
```

you are promising that the original variable (inside the function frame) will not be modified. And again, because you're returning it by value, it's copied so the original value could never be modified via the return value.

At first, this can make the specification of **const** seem meaningless. You can see the apparent lack of effect of returning **const**s by value in this example:

```
//: C08:Constval.cpp
// Returning consts by value
// has no meaning for built-in types
```

```
int f3() { return 1; }
const int f4() { return 1; }

int main() {
  const int j = f3(); // Works fine
  int k = f4(); // But this works fine too!
} ///:~
```

For built-in types, it doesn't matter whether you return by value as a **const**, so you should avoid confusing the client programmer and leave off the **const** when returning a built-in type by value.

Returning by value as a **const** becomes important when you're dealing with user-defined types. If a function returns a class object by value as a **const**, the return value of that function cannot be an lvalue (that is, it cannot be assigned to or otherwise modified). For example:

```
//: C08:ConstReturnValues.cpp
// Constant return by value
// Result cannot be used as an lvalue

class X {
  int i;
public:
  X(int ii = 0);
  void modify();
};

X::X(int ii) { i = ii; }

void X::modify() { i++; }

X f5() {
  return X();
}

const X f6() {
  return X();
}

void f7(X& x) { // Pass by non-const reference
  x.modify();
```

```
  }

int main() {
  f5() = X(1); // OK -- non-const return value
  f5().modify(); // OK
//!  f7(f5()); // Causes warning
// Causes compile-time errors:
//!  f6() = X(1);
//!  f6().modify();
//!  f7(f6());
} ///:~
```

f5( ) returns a non-**const X** object, while **f6( )** returns a **const X** object. Only the non-**const** return value can be used as an lvalue. Thus, it's important to use **const** when returning an object by value if you want to prevent its use as an lvalue.

The reason **const** has no meaning when you're returning a built-in type by value is that the compiler already prevents it from being an lvalue (because it's always a value, and not a variable). Only when you're returning objects of user-defined types by value does it become an issue.

The function **f7( )** takes its argument as a non-**const** *reference* (an additional way of handling addresses in C++ and the subject of Chapter 11). This is effectively the same as taking a non-**const** pointer; it's just that the syntax is different. The reason this won't compile in C++ is because of the creation of a temporary.

Temporaries

Sometimes, during the evaluation of an expression, the compiler must create *temporary objects*. These are objects like any other: they require storage and they must be constructed and destroyed. The difference is that you never see them – the compiler is responsible for deciding that they're needed and the details of their existence. But there is one thing about temporaries: they're automatically **const**. Because you usually won't be able to get your hands on a temporary object, telling it to do something that will change that temporary is almost certainly a mistake because you won't be able to use that information. By making all temporaries

---

automatically **const**, the compiler informs you when you make that mistake.

In the above example, **f5( )** returns a non-**const X** object. But in the expression:

```
f7(f5());
```

the compiler must manufacture a temporary object to hold the return value of **f5( )** so it can be passed to **f7( )**. This would be fine if **f7( )** took its argument by value; then the temporary would be copied into **f7( )** and it wouldn't matter what happened to the temporary **X**. However, **f7( )** takes its argument *by reference*, which means in this example takes the address of the temporary **X**. Since **f7( )** doesn't take its argument by **const** reference, it has permission to modify the temporary object. But the compiler knows that the temporary will vanish as soon as the expression evaluation is complete, and thus any modifications you make to the temporary **X** will be lost. By making all temporary objects automatically **const**, this situation causes a compile-time message so you don't get caught by what would be a very difficult bug to find.

However, notice the expressions that are legal:

```
f5() = X(1);
f5().modify();
```

Although these pass muster for the compiler, they are actually problematic. **f5( )** returns an **X** object, and for the compiler to satisfy the above expressions it must create a temporary to hold that return value. So in both expressions the temporary object is being modified, and as soon as the expression is over the temporary is cleaned up. As a result, the modifications are lost so this code is probably a bug – but the compiler doesn't tell you anything about it. Expressions like these are simple enough for you to detect the problem, but when things get more complex it's possible for a bug to slip through these cracks.

The way the **const**ness of class objects is preserved is shown later in the chapter.

Passing and returning addresses

If you pass or return an address (either a pointer or a reference), it's possible for the client programmer to take it and modify the original value. If you make the pointer or reference a **const**, you prevent this from happening, which may save you some grief. In fact, whenever you're passing an address into a function, you should make it a **const** if at all possible. If you don't, you're excluding the possibility of using that function with anything that is a **const**.

The choice of whether to return a pointer or reference to a **const** depends on what you want to allow your client programmer to do with it. Here's an example that demonstrates the use of **const** pointers as function arguments and return values:

```
//: C08:ConstPointer.cpp
// Constant pointer arg/return

void t(int*) {}

void u(const int* cip) {
//!  *cip = 2; // Illegal -- modifies value
   int i = *cip; // OK -- copies value
//!  int* ip2 = cip; // Illegal: non-const
}

const char* v() {
  // Returns address of static character array:
  return "result of function v()";
}

const int* const w() {
  static int i;
  return &i;
}

int main() {
  int x = 0;
  int* ip = &x;
  const int* cip = &x;
  t(ip);   // OK
//!  t(cip); // Not OK
  u(ip);   // OK
```

```
  u(cip); // Also OK
//!  char* cp = v(); // Not OK
  const char* ccp = v(); // OK
//!  int* ip2 = w(); // Not OK
  const int* const ccip = w(); // OK
  const int* cip2 = w(); // OK
//!  *w() = 1; // Not OK
} ///:~
```

The function **t( )** takes an ordinary non-**const** pointer as an argument, and **u( )** takes a **const** pointer. Inside **u( )** you can see that attempting to modify the destination of the **const** pointer is illegal, but you can of course copy the information out into a non-**const** variable. The compiler also prevents you from creating a non-**const** pointer using the address stored inside a **const** pointer.

The functions **v( )** and **w( )** test return value semantics. **v( )** returns a **const char*** that is created from a character array literal. This statement actually produces the address of the character array literal, after the compiler creates it and stores it in the static storage area. As mentioned earlier, this character array is technically a constant, which is properly expressed by the return value of **v( )**.

The return value of **w( )** requires that both the pointer and what it points to must be **const**. As with **v( )**, the value returned by **w( )** is valid after the function returns only because it is **static**. You never want to return pointers to local stack variables because they will be invalid after the function returns and the stack is cleaned up. (Another common pointer you might return is the address of storage allocated on the heap, which is still valid after the function returns.)

In **main( )**, the functions are tested with various arguments. You can see that **t( )** will accept a non-**const** pointer argument, but if you try to pass it a pointer to a **const**, there's no promise that **t( )** will leave the pointer's destination alone, so the compiler gives you an error message. **u( )** takes a **const** pointer, so it will accept both types of arguments. Thus, a function that takes a **const** pointer is more general than one that does not.

As expected, the return value of **v( )** can be assigned only to a pointer to a **const**. You would also expect that the compiler refuses to assign the return value of **w( )** to a non-**const** pointer, and accepts a **const int* const**, but it might be a bit surprising to see that it also accepts a **const int***, which is not an exact match to the return type. Once again, because the value (which is the address contained in the pointer) is being copied, the promise that the original variable is untouched is automatically kept. Thus, the second **const** in **const int* const** is only meaningful when you try to use it as an lvalue, in which case the compiler prevents you.

Standard argument passing

In C it's very common to pass by value, and when you want to pass an address your only choice is to use a pointer[1]. However, neither of these approaches is preferred in C++. Instead, your first choice when passing an argument is to pass by reference, and by **const** reference at that. To the client programmer, the syntax is identical to that of passing by value, so there's no confusion about pointers – they don't even have to think about pointers. For the creator of the function, passing an address is virtually always more efficient than passing an entire class object, and if you pass by **const** reference it means your function will not change the destination of that address, so the effect from the client programmer's point of view is exactly the same as pass-by-value (only more efficient).

Because of the syntax of references (it looks like pass-by-value to the caller) it's possible to pass a temporary object to a function that takes a **const** reference, whereas you can never pass a temporary object to a function that takes a pointer – with a pointer, the address must be explicitly taken. So passing by reference produces a new situation that never occurs in C: a temporary, which is always **const**, can have its *address* passed to a function. This is why, to allow temporaries to be passed to functions by reference, the argument must be a **const** reference. The following example demonstrates this:

---

[1] Some folks go as far as saying that *everything* in C is pass by value, since when you pass a pointer a copy is made (so you're passing the pointer by value). However precise this might be, I think it actually confuses the issue.

```
//: C08:ConstTemporary.cpp
// Temporaries are const

class X {};

X f() { return X(); } // Return by value

void g1(X&) {} // Pass by non-const reference
void g2(const X&) {} // Pass by const reference

int main() {
  // Error: const temporary created by f():
//!  g1(f());
  // OK: g2 takes a const reference:
  g2(f());
} ///:~
```

f( ) returns an object of **class X** *by value.* That means when you immediately take the return value of **f( )** and pass it to another function as in the calls to **g1( )** and **g2( )**, a temporary is created and that temporary is **const**. Thus, the call in **g1( )** is an error because **g1( )** doesn't take a **const** reference, but the call to **g2( )** is OK.

Classes

This section shows the ways you can use **const** with classes. You may want to create a local **const** in a class to use inside constant expressions that will be evaluated at compile time. However, the meaning of **const** is different inside classes, so you must understand the options in order to create **const** data members of a class.

You can also make an entire object **const** (and as you've just seen, the compiler always makes temporary objects **const**). But preserving the **const**ness of an object is more complex. The compiler can ensure the **const**ness of a built-in type but it cannot monitor the intricacies of a class. To guarantee the **const**ness of a class object, the **const** member function is introduced: only a **const** member function may be called for a **const** object.

const in classes

One of the places you'd like to use a **const** for constant expressions is inside classes. The typical example is when you're creating an array inside a class and you want to use a **const** instead of a **#define** to establish the array size and to use in calculations involving the array. The array size is something you'd like to keep hidden inside the class, so if you used a name like **size**, for example, you could use that name in another class without a clash. The preprocessor treats all **#define**s as global from the point they are defined, so this will not achieve the desired effect.

You might assume that the logical choice is to place a **const** inside the class. This doesn't produce the desired result. Inside a class, **const** partially reverts to its meaning in C. It allocates storage within each object and represents a value that is initialized once and then cannot change. The use of **const** inside a class means "This is constant for the lifetime of the object." However, each different object may contain a different value for that constant.

Thus, when you create an ordinary (non-**static**) **const** inside a class, you cannot give it an initial value. This initialization must occur in the constructor, of course, but in a special place in the constructor. Because a **const** must be initialized at the point it is created, inside the main body of the constructor the **const** must *already* be initialized. Otherwise you're left with the choice of waiting until some point later in the constructor body, which means the **const** would be un-initialized for a while. Also, there would be nothing to keep you from changing the value of the **const** at various places in the constructor body.

The constructor initializer list

The special initialization point is called the *constructor initializer list*, and it was originally developed for use in inheritance (covered in Chapter 14). The constructor initializer list – which, as the name implies, occurs only in the definition of the constructor – is a list of "constructor calls" that occur after the function argument list and a colon, but before the opening brace of the constructor body. This is to remind you that the initialization in the list occurs before any of the main constructor code is executed. This is the place to put all

---

const initializations. The proper form for **const** inside a class is shown here:

```
//: C08:ConstInitialization.cpp
// Initializing const in classes
#include <iostream>
using namespace std;

class Fred {
  const int size;
public:
  Fred(int sz);
  void print();
};

Fred::Fred(int sz) : size(sz) {}
void Fred::print() { cout << size << endl; }

int main() {
  Fred a(1), b(2), c(3);
  a.print(), b.print(), c.print();
} ///:~
```

The form of the constructor initializer list shown above is confusing at first because you're not used to seeing a built-in type treated as if it has a constructor.

"Constructors" for built-in types

As the language developed and more effort was put into making user-defined types look like built-in types, it became apparent that there were times when it was helpful to make built-in types look like user-defined types. In the constructor initializer list, you can treat a built-in type as if it has a constructor, like this:

```
//: C08:BuiltInTypeConstructors.cpp
#include <iostream>
using namespace std;

class B {
  int i;
public:
  B(int ii);
  void print();
```

```
};

B::B(int ii) : i(ii) {}
void B::print() { cout << i << endl; }

int main() {
  B a(1), b(2);
  float pi(3.14159);
  a.print(); b.print();
  cout << pi << endl;
} ///:~
```

This is especially critical when initializing **const** data members because they must be initialized before the function body is entered.

It made sense to extend this "constructor" for built-in types (which simply means assignment) to the general case, which is why the **float pi(3.14159)** definition works in the above code.

It's often useful to encapsulate a built-in type inside a class to guarantee initialization with the constructor. For example, here's an **Integer** class:

```
//: C08:EncapsulatingTypes.cpp
#include <iostream>
using namespace std;

class Integer {
  int i;
public:
  Integer(int ii = 0);
  void print();
};

Integer::Integer(int ii) : i(ii) {}
void Integer::print() { cout << i << ' '; }

int main() {
  Integer i[100];
  for(int j = 0; j < 100; j++)
    i[j].print();
} ///:~
```

The array of **Integer**s in **main( )** are all automatically initialized to zero. This initialization isn't necessarily more costly than a **for** loop or **memset( )**. Many compilers easily optimize this to a very fast process.

Compile-time constants in classes

The above use of **const** is interesting and probably useful in cases, but it does not solve the original problem which is: "how do you make a compile-time constant inside a class?" The answer requires the use of an additional keyword which will not be fully introduced until Chapter 10: **static**. The **static** keyword, in this situation, means "there's only one instance, regardless of how many objects of the class are created," which is precisely what we need here: a member of a class which is constant, and which cannot change from one object of the class to another. Thus, a **static const** of a built-in type can be treated as a compile-time constant.

There is one feature of **static const** when used inside classes which is a bit unusual: you must provide the initializer at the point of definition of the **static const**. This is something that only occurs with the **static const**; as much as you might like to use it in other situations it won't work because all other data members must be initialized in the constructor or in other member functions.

Here's an example that shows the creation and use of a **static const** called **size** inside a class that represents a stack of string pointers[2]:

```
//: C08:StringStack.cpp
// Using static const to create a
// compile-time constant inside a class
#include <string>
#include <iostream>
using namespace std;

class StringStack {
  static const int size = 100;
```

---

[2] At the time of this writing, not all compilers supported this feature.

```
  const string* stack[size];
  int index;
public:
  StringStack();
  void push(const string* s);
  const string* pop();
};

StringStack::StringStack() : index(0) {
  memset(stack, 0, size * sizeof(string*));
}

void StringStack::push(const string* s) {
  if(index < size)
    stack[index++] = s;
}

const string* StringStack::pop() {
  if(index > 0) {
    const string* rv = stack[--index];
    stack[index] = 0;
    return rv;
  }
  return 0;
}

string iceCream[] = {
  "pralines & cream",
  "fudge ripple",
  "jamocha almond fudge",
  "wild mountain blackberry",
  "raspberry sorbet",
  "lemon swirl",
  "rocky road",
  "deep chocolate fudge"
};

const int iCsz =
  sizeof iceCream / sizeof *iceCream;

int main() {
  StringStack ss;
  for(int i = 0; i < iCsz; i++)
    ss.push(&iceCream[i]);
  const string* cp;
```

```
  while((cp = ss.pop()) != 0)
    cout << *cp << endl;
} ///:~
```

Since **size** is used to determine the size of the array **stack**, it is indeed a compile-time constant, but one that is hidden inside the class.

Notice that **push( )** takes a **const string*** as an argument, **pop( )** returns a **const string***, and **StringStack** holds **const string***. If this were not true, you couldn't use a **StringStack** to hold the pointers in **iceCream**. However, it also prevents you from doing anything that will change the objects contained by **StringStack**. Of course, not all containers are designed with this restriction.

The "enum hack" in old code

In older versions of C++, **static const** was not supported inside classes. This meant that **const** was useless for constant expressions inside classes. However, people still wanted to do this so a typical solution (usually referred to as the "enum hack") was to use an untagged **enum** with no instances. An enumeration must have all its values established at compile time, it's local to the class, and its values are available for constant expressions. Thus, you will commonly see:

```
//: C08:EnumHack.cpp
#include <iostream>
using namespace std;

class Bunch {
  enum { size = 1000 };
  int i[size];
};

int main() {
  cout << "sizeof(Bunch) = " << sizeof(Bunch)
       << ", sizeof(i[1000]) = "
       << sizeof(int[1000]) << endl;
} ///:~
```

The use of **enum** here is guaranteed to occupy no storage in the object, and the enumerators are all evaluated at compile time. You can also explicitly establish the values of the enumerators:

```
enum { one = 1, two = 2, three };
```

With integral **enum** types, the compiler will continue counting from the last value, so the enumerator **three** will get the value 3.

In the **StringStack.cpp** example above, the line:

```
static const int size = 100;
```

would be instead:

```
enum { size = 100 };
```

Although you'll often see the **enum** technique in legacy code, the **static const** feature was added to the language to solve just this problem. However, there is no overwhelming reason that you *must* choose **static const** over the **enum** hack, and in this book the **enum** hack is used because it is supported by more compilers at the time this book was written.

const objects & member functions

Class member functions can be made **const**. What does this mean? To understand, you must first grasp the concept of **const** objects.

A **const** object is defined the same for a user-defined type as a built-in type. For example:

```
const int i = 1;
const blob b(2);
```

Here, **b** is a **const** object of type **blob**. Its constructor is called with an argument of two. For the compiler to enforce **const**ness, it must ensure that no data members of the object are changed during the object's lifetime. It can easily ensure that no public data is modified, but how is it to know which member functions will change the data and which ones are "safe" for a **const** object?

If you declare a member function **const**, you tell the compiler the function can be called for a **const** object. A member function that is not specifically declared **const** is treated as one that will modify data members in an object, and the compiler will not allow you to call it for a **const** object.

It doesn't stop there, however. Just *claiming* a member function is **const** doesn't guarantee it will act that way, so the compiler forces you to reiterate the **const** specification when defining the function. (The **const** becomes part of the function signature, so both the compiler and linker check for **const**ness.) Then it enforces **const**ness during the function definition by issuing an error message if you try to change any members of the object *or* call a non-**const** member function. Thus, any member function you declare **const** is guaranteed to behave that way in the definition.

To understand the syntax for declaring **const** member functions, first notice that preceding the function declaration with **const** means the return value is **const**, so that doesn't produce the desired results. Instead, you must place the **const** specifier *after* the argument list. For example,

```
//: C08:ConstMember.cpp
class X {
   int i;
public:
   X(int ii);
   int f() const;
};

X::X(int ii) : i(ii) {}
int X::f() const { return i; }

int main() {
   X x1(10);
   const X x2(20);
   x1.f();
   x2.f();
} ///:~
```

Note that the **const** keyword must be repeated in the definition or the compiler sees it as a different function. Since **f( )** is a **const** member function, if it attempts to change **i** in any way *or* to call another member function that is not **const**, the compiler flags it as an error.

You can see that a **const** member function is safe to call with both **const** and non-**const** objects. Thus, you could think of it as the most general form of a member function (and because of this, it is unfortunate that member functions do not automatically default to **const**). Any function that doesn't modify member data should be declared as **const**, so it can be used with **const** objects.

Here's an example that contrasts a **const** and non-**const** member function:

```cpp
//: C08:Quoter.cpp
// Random quote selection
#include <iostream>
#include <cstdlib> // Random number generator
#include <ctime> // To seed random generator
using namespace std;

class Quoter {
  int lastquote;
public:
  Quoter();
  int lastQuote() const;
  const char* quote();
};

Quoter::Quoter() {
  lastquote = -1;
  srand(time(0)); // Seed random number generator
}

int Quoter::lastQuote() const {
  return lastquote;
}

const char* Quoter::quote() {
  static const char* quotes[] = {
    "Are we having fun yet?",
    "Doctors always know best",
    "Is it ... Atomic?",
```

```
    "Fear is obscene",
    "There is no scientific evidence "
    "to support the idea "
    "that life is serious",
    "Things that make us happy, make us wise",
  };
  const int qsize = sizeof quotes/sizeof *quotes;
  int qnum = rand() % qsize;
  while(lastquote >= 0 && qnum == lastquote)
    qnum = rand() % qsize;
  return quotes[lastquote = qnum];
}

int main() {
  Quoter q;
  const Quoter cq;
  cq.lastQuote(); // OK
//!  cq.quote(); // Not OK; non const function
  for(int i = 0; i < 20; i++)
    cout << q.quote() << endl;
} ///:~
```

Neither constructors nor destructors can be **const** member
functions because they virtually always perform some modification
on the object during initialization and cleanup. The **quote( )**
member function also cannot be **const** because it modifies the data
member **lastquote** (see the **return** statement). However,
lastQuote( ) makes no modifications, and so it can be **const** and
can be safely called for the **const** object **cq**.

mutable: bitwise vs. logical const

What if you want to create a **const** member function, but you'd still
like to change some of the data in the object? This is sometimes
referred to as the difference between *bitwise* **const** and *logical*
const (also sometimes called *memberwise* **const**). Bitwise **const**
means that every bit in the object is permanent, so a bit image of
the object will never change. Logical **const** means that, although
the entire object is conceptually constant, there may be changes on
a member-by-member basis. However, if the compiler is told that
an object is **const**, it will jealously guard that object to ensure
bitwise **const**ness. To effect logical **const**ness, there are two ways
to change a data member from within a **const** member function.

The first approach is the historical one and is called *casting away constness*. It is performed in a rather odd fashion. You take **this** (the keyword that produces the address of the current object) and cast it to a pointer to an object of the current type. It would seem that **this** is *already* such a pointer. However, inside a **const** member function it's actually a **const** pointer, so by casting it to an ordinary pointer, you remove the **const**ness for that operation. Here's an example:

```
//: C08:Castaway.cpp
// "Casting away" constness

class Y {
  int i;
public:
  Y();
  void f() const;
};

Y::Y() { i = 0; }

void Y::f() const {
//!  i++; // Error -- const member function
  ((Y*)this)->i++; // OK: cast away const-ness
  // Better: use C++ explicit cast syntax:
  (const_cast<Y*>(this))->i++;
}

int main() {
  const Y yy;
  yy.f(); // Actually changes it!
} ///:~
```

This approach works and you'll see it used in legacy code, but it is not the preferred technique. The problem is that this lack of **const**ness is hidden away in a member function definition, and you have no clue from the class interface that the data of the object is actually being modified unless you have access to the source code (and you must suspect that **const**ness is being cast away, and look for the cast). To put everything out in the open, you should use the **mutable** keyword in the class declaration to specify that a particular data member may be changed inside a **const** object:

```
//: C08:Mutable.cpp
// The "mutable" keyword

class Z {
  int i;
  mutable int j;
public:
  Z();
  void f() const;
};

Z::Z() : i(0), j(0) {}

void Z::f() const {
//! i++; // Error -- const member function
    j++; // OK: mutable
}

int main() {
  const Z zz;
  zz.f(); // Actually changes it!
} ///:~
```

This way, the user of the class can see from the declaration which members are likely to be modified in a **const** member function.

ROMability

If an object is defined as **const**, it is a candidate to be placed in read-only memory (ROM), which is often an important consideration in embedded systems programming. Simply making an object **const**, however, is not enough – the requirements for ROMability are much stricter. Of course, the object must be bitwise-**const**, rather than logical-**const**. This is easy to see if logical **const**ness is implemented only through the **mutable** keyword, but probably not detectable by the compiler if **const**ness is cast away inside a **const** member function. In addition,

1.   The **class** or **struct** must have no user-defined constructors or destructor.

2.   There can be no base classes (covered in Chapter 14) or member objects with user-defined constructors or destructors.

The effect of a write operation on any part of a **const** object of a ROMable type is undefined. Although a suitably formed object may be placed in ROM, no objects are ever *required* to be placed in ROM.

volatile

The syntax of **volatile** is identical to that for **const**, but **volatile** means "This data may change outside the knowledge of the compiler." Somehow, the environment is changing the data (possibly through multitasking, multithreading or interrupts), and **volatile** tells the compiler not to make any assumptions about that data, especially during optimization.

If the compiler says, "I read this data into a register earlier, and I haven't touched that register," normally it wouldn't need to read the data again. But if the data is **volatile**, the compiler cannot make such an assumption because the data may have been changed by another process, and it must reread that data rather than optimizing the code to remove what would normally be a redundant read.

You create **volatile** objects using the same syntax that you use to create **const** objects. You can also create **const volatile** objects, which can't be changed by the client programmer but instead change through some outside agency. Here is an example that might represent a class associated with some piece of communication hardware:

```
//: C08:Volatile.cpp
// The volatile keyword

class Comm {
  const volatile unsigned char byte;
  volatile unsigned char flag;
  enum { bufsize = 100 };
  unsigned char buf[bufsize];
  int index;
public:
  Comm();
```

```
  void isr() volatile;
  char read(int index) const;
};

Comm::Comm() : index(0), byte(0), flag(0) {}

// Only a demo; won't actually work
// as an interrupt service routine:
void Comm::isr() volatile {
  flag = 0;
  buf[index++] = byte;
  // Wrap to beginning of buffer:
  if(index >= bufsize) index = 0;
}

char Comm::read(int index) const {
  if(index < 0 || index >= bufsize)
    return 0;
  return buf[index];
}

int main() {
  volatile Comm Port;
  Port.isr(); // OK
//! Port.read(0); // Error, read() not volatile
} ///:~
```

As with **const**, you can use **volatile** for data members, member
functions, and objects themselves. You can only call **volatile**
member functions for **volatile** objects.

The reason that **isr( )** can't actually be used as an interrupt service
routine is that in a member function, the address of the current
object (**this**) must be secretly passed, and an ISR generally wants
no arguments at all. To solve this problem, you can make **isr( )** a
static member function, a subject covered in Chapter 10.

The syntax of **volatile** is identical to **const**, so discussions of the
two are often treated together. The two are referred to in
combination as the *c-v qualifier*.

Summary

The **const** keyword gives you the ability to define objects, function arguments, return values and member functions as constants, and to eliminate the preprocessor for value substitution without losing any preprocessor benefits. All this provides a significant additional form of type checking and safety in your programming. The use of so-called *const correctness* (the use of **const** anywhere you possibly can) can be a lifesaver for projects.

Although you can ignore **const** and continue to use old C coding practices, it's there to help you. Chapters 11 and on begin using references heavily, and there you'll see even more about how critical it is to use **const** with function arguments.

Exercises

Solutions to selected exercises can be found in the electronic document *The Thinking in C++ Annotated Solution Guide*, available for a small fee from www.BruceEckel.com.

1. Create three **const int** values, then add them together to produce a value that determines the size of an array in an array definition. Try to compile the same code in C and see what happens (you can generally force your C++ compiler to run as a C compiler by using a command-line flag).
2. Prove to yourself that the C and C++ compilers really do treat constants differently. Create a global **const** and use it in a global constant expression; then compile it under both C and C++.
3. Create example **const** definitions for all the built-in types and their variants. Use these in expressions with other **const**s to make new **const** definitions. Make sure they compile successfully.
4. Create a **const** definition in a header file, include that header file in two **.cpp** files, then compile those files and link them. You should not get any errors. Now try the same experiment with C.

---

5.   Create a **const** whose value is determined at runtime by reading the time when the program starts (you'll have to use the **<ctime>** standard header). Later in the program, try to read a second value of the time into your **const** and see what happens.

6.   Create a **const** array of **char**, then try to change one of the **char**s.

7.   Create an **extern const** declaration in one file, and put a **main( )** in that file that prints the value of the **extern const**. Provide an **extern const** definition in a second file, then compile and link the two files together.

8.   Write two pointers to **const long** using both forms of the declaration. Point one of them to an array of **long**. Demonstrate that you can increment or decrement the pointer, but you can't change what it points to.

9.   Write a **const** pointer to a **double**, and point it at an array of **double**. Show that you can change what the pointer points to, but you can't increment or decrement the pointer.

10.   Write a **const** pointer to a **const** object. Show that you can only read the value that the pointer points to, but you can't change the pointer or what it points to.

11.   Remove the comment on the error-generating line of code in **PointerAssignment.cpp** to see the error that your compiler generates.

12.   Create a character array literal with a pointer that points to the beginning of the array. Now use the pointer to modify elements in the array. Does your compiler report this as an error? Should it? If it doesn't, why do you think that is?

13.   Create a function that takes an argument by value as a **const**; then try to change that argument in the function body.

14.   Create a function that takes a **float** by value. Inside the function, bind a **const float&** to the argument, and only use the reference from then on to ensure that the argument is not changed.

15. Modify **ConstReturnValues.cpp** removing comments on the error-causing lines one at a time, to see what error messages your compiler generates.

16. Modify **ConstPointer.cpp** removing comments on the error-causing lines one at a time, to see what error messages your compiler generates.

17. Make a new version of **ConstPointer.cpp** called **ConstReference.cpp** which demonstrates references instead of pointers (you may need to look forward to Chapter 11).

18. Modify **ConstTemporary.cpp** removing the comment on the error-causing line to see what error messages your compiler generates.

19. Create a class containing both a **const** and a non-**const** **float**. Initialize these using the constructor initializer list.

20. Create a class called **MyString** which contains a **string** and has a constructor that initializes the **string**, and a **print( )** function. Modify **StringStack.cpp** so that the container holds **MyString** objects, and **main( )** so it prints them.

21. Create a class containing a **const** member that you initialize in the constructor initializer list and an untagged enumeration that you use to determine an array size.

22. In **ConstMember.cpp**, remove the **const** specifier on the member function definition, but leave it on the declaration, to see what kind of compiler error message you get.

23. Create a class with both **const** and non-**const** member functions. Create **const** and non-**const** objects of this class, and try calling the different types of member functions for the different types of objects.

24. Create a class with both **const** and non-**const** member functions. Try to call a non-**const** member function from a **const** member function to see what kind of compiler error message you get.

---

25. In **Mutable.cpp**, remove the comment on the error-causing line to see what sort of error message your compiler produces.

26. Modify **Quoter.cpp** by making **quote( )** a **const** member function and **lastquote mutable**.

27. Create a class with a **volatile** data member. Create both **volatile** and non-**volatile** member functions that modify the **volatile** data member, and see what the compiler says. Create both **volatile** and non-**volatile** objects of your class and try calling both the **volatile** and non-**volatile** member functions to see what is successful and what kind of error messages the compiler produces.

28. Create a class called **bird** that can **fly( )** and a class **rock** that can't. Create a **rock** object, take its address, and assign that to a **void***. Now take the **void***, assign it to a **bird*** (you'll have to use a cast), and call **fly( )** through that pointer. Is it clear why C's permission to openly assign via a **void*** (without a cast) is a "hole" in the language, which couldn't be propagated into C++?

9: Inline Functions

One of the important features C++ inherits from C is efficiency. If the efficiency of C++ were dramatically less than C, there would be a significant contingent of programmers who couldn't justify its use.

In C, one of the ways to preserve efficiency is through the use of *macros*, which allow you to make what looks like a function call without the normal function call overhead. The macro is implemented with the preprocessor instead of the compiler proper, and the preprocessor replaces all macro calls directly with the macro code, so there's no cost involved from pushing arguments, making an assembly-language CALL, returning arguments, and performing an assembly-language RETURN. All the work is performed by the preprocessor, so you have the convenience and readability of a function call but it doesn't cost you anything.

There are two problems with the use of preprocessor macros in C++. The first is also true with C: a macro looks like a function call, but doesn't always act like one. This can bury difficult-to-find bugs. The second problem is specific to C++: the preprocessor has no permission to access class member data. This means preprocessor macros cannot be used as class member functions.

To retain the efficiency of the preprocessor macro, but to add the safety and class scoping of true functions, C++ has the *inline function*. In this chapter, we'll look at the problems of preprocessor macros in C++, how these problems are solved with inline functions, and guidelines and insights on the way inlines work.

Preprocessor pitfalls

The key to the problems of preprocessor macros is that you can be fooled into thinking that the behavior of the preprocessor is the same as the behavior of the compiler. Of course, it was intended that a macro look and act like a function call, so it's quite easy to fall into this fiction. The difficulties begin when the subtle differences appear.

As a simple example, consider the following:

```
#define F (x) (x + 1)
```

Now, if a call is made to **F** like this

```
F(1)
```

the preprocessor expands it, somewhat unexpectedly, to the following:

```
(x)  (x + 1)(1)
```

The problem occurs because of the gap between **F** and its opening parenthesis in the macro definition. When this gap is removed, you can actually *call* the macro with the gap

```
F (1)
```

and it will still expand properly to

```
(1 + 1)
```

The example above is fairly trivial and the problem will make itself evident right away. The real difficulties occur when using expressions as arguments in macro calls.

There are two problems. The first is that expressions may expand inside the macro so that their evaluation precedence is different from what you expect. For example,

```
#define FLOOR(x,b)  x>=b?0:1
```

Now, if expressions are used for the arguments

```
if(FLOOR(a&0x0f,0x07)) // ...
```

the macro will expand to

```
if(a&0x0f>=0x07?0:1)
```

The precedence of **&** is lower than that of **>=**, so the macro evaluation will surprise you. Once you discover the problem, you can solve it by putting parentheses around everything in the macro definition. (This is a good practice to use when creating preprocessor macros.) Thus,

```
#define FLOOR(x,b)  ((x)>=(b)?0:1)
```

Discovering the problem may be difficult, however, and you may not find it until after you've taken the proper macro behavior for

---

granted. In the un-parenthesized version of the preceding macro, *most* expressions will work correctly because the precedence of >= is lower than most of the operators like +, /, − −, and even the bitwise shift operators. So you can easily begin to think that it works with all expressions, including those using bitwise logical operators.

The preceding problem can be solved with careful programming practice: parenthesize everything in a macro. However, the second difficulty is subtler. Unlike a normal function, every time you use an argument in a macro, that argument is evaluated. As long as the macro is called only with ordinary variables, this evaluation is benign, but if the evaluation of an argument has side effects, then the results can be surprising and will definitely not mimic function behavior.

For example, this macro determines whether its argument falls within a certain range:

```
#define BAND(x)  (((x)>5 && (x)<10) ? (x) : 0)
```

As long as you use an "ordinary" argument, the macro works very much like a real function. But as soon as you relax and start believing it *is* a real function, the problems start. Thus:

```
//: C09:MacroSideEffects.cpp
#include "../require.h"
#include <fstream>
using namespace std;

#define BAND(x)  (((x)>5 && (x)<10) ? (x) : 0)

int main() {
  ofstream out("macro.out");
  assure(out, "macro.out");
  for(int i = 4; i < 11; i++) {
    int a = i;
    out << "a = " << a << endl << '\t';
    out << "BAND(++a)=" << BAND(++a) << endl;
    out << "\t a = " << a << endl;
  }
} ///:~
```

Notice the use of all upper-case characters in the name of the macro. This is a helpful practice because it tells the reader this is a macro and not a function, so if there are problems, it acts as a little reminder.

Here's the output produced by the program, which is not at all what you would have expected from a true function:

```
a = 4
   BAND(++a)=0
     a = 5
a = 5
   BAND(++a)=8
     a = 8
a = 6
   BAND(++a)=9
     a = 9
a = 7
   BAND(++a)=10
     a = 10
a = 8
   BAND(++a)=0
     a = 10
a = 9
   BAND(++a)=0
     a = 11
a = 10
   BAND(++a)=0
     a = 12
```

When **a** is four, only the first part of the conditional occurs, so the expression is evaluated only once, and the side effect of the macro call is that **a** becomes five, which is what you would expect from a normal function call in the same situation. However, when the number is within the band, both conditionals are tested, which results in two increments. The result is produced by evaluating the argument again, which results in a third increment. Once the number gets out of the band, both conditionals are still tested so you get two increments. The side effects are different, depending on the argument.

This is clearly not the kind of behavior you want from a macro that looks like a function call. In this case, the obvious solution is to make it a true function, which of course adds the extra overhead and may reduce efficiency if you call that function a lot. Unfortunately, the problem may not always be so obvious, and you can unknowingly get a library that contains functions and macros mixed together, so a problem like this can hide some very difficult-to-find bugs. For example, the **putc( )** macro in **cstdio** may evaluate its second argument twice. This is specified in Standard C. Also, careless implementations of **toupper( )** as a macro may evaluate the argument more than once, which will give you unexpected results with **toupper(*p++)**.[1]

Macros and access

Of course, careful coding and use of preprocessor macros is required with C, and we could certainly get away with the same thing in C++ if it weren't for one problem: a macro has no concept of the scoping required with member functions. The preprocessor simply performs text substitution, so you cannot say something like

```
class X {
  int i;
public:
#define VAL(X::i) // Error
```

or anything even close. In addition, there would be no indication of which object you were referring to. There is simply no way to express class scope in a macro. Without some alternative to preprocessor macros, programmers will be tempted to make some data members **public** for the sake of efficiency, thus exposing the underlying implementation and preventing changes in that implementation, as well as eliminating the guarding that **private** provides.

---

[1]Andrew Koenig goes into more detail in his book *C Traps & Pitfalls* (Addison-Wesley, 1989).

Inline functions

In solving the C++ problem of a macro with access to **private** class members, *all* the problems associated with preprocessor macros were eliminated. This was done by bringing the concept of macros under the control of the compiler where they belong. C++ implements the macro as *inline function*, which is a true function in every sense. Any behavior you expect from an ordinary function, you get from an inline function. The only difference is that an inline function is expanded in place, like a preprocessor macro, so the overhead of the function call is eliminated. Thus, you should (almost) never use macros, only inline functions.

Any function defined within a class body is automatically inline, but you can also make a non-class function inline by preceding it with the **inline** keyword. However, for it to have any effect, you must include the function body with the declaration, otherwise the compiler will treat it as an ordinary function declaration. Thus,

```
inline int plusOne(int x);
```

has no effect at all other than declaring the function (which may or may not get an inline definition sometime later). The successful approach provides the function body:

```
inline int plusOne(int x) { return ++x; }
```

Notice that the compiler will check (as it always does) for the proper use of the function argument list and return value (performing any necessary conversions), something the preprocessor is incapable of. Also, if you try to write the above as a preprocessor macro, you get an unwanted side effect.

You'll almost always want to put inline definitions in a header file. When the compiler sees such a definition, it puts the function type (the signature combined with the return value) *and* the function body in its symbol table. When you use the function, the compiler checks to ensure the call is correct and the return value is being used correctly, and then substitutes the function body for the function call, thus eliminating the overhead. The inline code does occupy space, but if the function is small, this can actually take less space than the code generated to do an ordinary function call (pushing arguments on the stack and doing the CALL).

An inline function in a header file has a special status, since you must include the header file containing the function *and* its definition in every file where the function is used, but you don't end up with multiple definition errors (however, the definition must be identical in all places where the inline function is included).

Inlines inside classes

To define an inline function, you must ordinarily precede the function definition with the **inline** keyword. However, this is not necessary inside a class definition. Any function you define inside a class definition is automatically an inline. For example:

```cpp
//: C09:Inline.cpp
// Inlines inside classes
#include <iostream>
#include <string>
using namespace std;

class Point {
  int i, j, k;
public:
  Point(): i(0), j(0), k(0) {}
  Point(int ii, int jj, int kk)
    : i(ii), j(jj), k(kk) {}
  void print(const string& msg = "") const {
    if(msg.size() != 0) cout << msg << endl;
    cout << "i = " << i << ", "
         << "j = " << j << ", "
         << "k = " << k << endl;
  }
};

int main() {
  Point p, q(1,2,3);
  p.print("value of p");
  q.print("value of q");
} ///:~
```

Here, the two constructors and the **print( )** function are all inlines by default. Notice in **main( )** that the fact you are using inline functions is transparent, as it should be. The logical behavior of a function must be identical regardless of whether it's an inline (otherwise your compiler is broken). The only difference you'll see is in performance.

Of course, the temptation is to use inlines everywhere inside class declarations because they save you the extra step of making the external member function definition. Keep in mind, however, that the idea of an inline is to provide improved opportunities for optimization by the compiler. But inlining a big function will cause that code to be duplicated everywhere the function is called, producing code bloat that may mitigate the speed benefit (the only reliable course of action is to experiment to discover the effects of inlining on your program with your compiler).

Access functions

One of the most important uses of inlines inside classes is the *access function*. This is a small function that allows you to read or change part of the state of an object – that is, an internal variable or variables. The reason inlines are so important for access functions can be seen in the following example:

```
//: C09:Access.cpp
// Inline access functions

class Access {
  int i;
public:
  int read() const { return i; }
  void set(int ii) { i = ii; }
};

int main() {
  Access A;
  A.set(100);
  int x = A.read();
} ///:~
```

Here, the class user never has direct contact with the state variables inside the class, and they can be kept **private**, under the control of the class designer. All the access to the **private** data members can be controlled through the member function interface. In addition, access is remarkably efficient. Consider the **read( )**, for example. Without inlines, the code generated for the call to **read( )** would typically include pushing **this** on the stack and making an assembly language CALL. With most machines, the size of this code would be larger than the code created by the inline, and the execution time would certainly be longer.

Without inline functions, an efficiency-conscious class designer will be tempted to simply make **i** a public member, eliminating the overhead by allowing the user to directly access **i**. From a design standpoint, this is disastrous because **i** then becomes part of the public interface, which means the class designer can never change it. You're stuck with an **int** called **i**. This is a problem because you may learn sometime later that it would be much more useful to represent the state information as a **float** rather than an **int**, but because **int i** is part of the public interface, you can't change it. Or you may want to perform some additional calculation as part of reading or setting **i**, which you can't do if it's **public**. If, on the other hand, you've always used member functions to read and change the state information of an object, you can modify the underlying representation of the object to your heart's content.

In addition, the use of member functions to control data members allows you to add code to the member function to detect when that data is being changed, which can be very useful during debugging. If a data member is **public**, anyone can change it anytime without you knowing about it.

Accessors and mutators

Some people further divide the concept of access functions into *accessors* (to read state information from an object) and *mutators* (to change the state of an object). In addition, function overloading may be used to provide the same function name for both the accessor and mutator; how you call the function determines whether you're reading or modifying state information. Thus,

```
//: C09:Rectangle.cpp
// Accessors & mutators

class Rectangle {
  int wide, high;
public:
  Rectangle(int w = 0, int h = 0)
    : wide(w), high(h) {}
  int width() const { return wide; } // Read
  void width(int w) { wide = w; } // Set
  int height() const { return high; } // Read
  void height(int h) { high = h; } // Set
};

int main() {
  Rectangle r(19, 47);
  // Change width & height:
  r.height(2 * r.width());
  r.width(2 * r.height());
} ///:~
```

The constructor uses the constructor initializer list (briefly introduced in Chapter 8 and covered fully in Chapter 14) to initialize the values of **wide** and **high** (using the pseudoconstructor form for built-in types).

You cannot have member function names using the same identifiers as data members, so you might be tempted to distinguish the data members with a leading underscore. However, identifiers with leading underscores are reserved so you should not use them.

You may choose instead to use "get" and "set" to indicate accessors and mutators:

```
//: C09:Rectangle2.cpp
// Accessors & mutators with "get" and "set"

class Rectangle {
  int width, height;
public:
  Rectangle(int w = 0, int h = 0)
    : width(w), height(h) {}
  int getWidth() const { return width; }
```

```
  void setWidth(int w) { width = w; }
  int getHeight() const { return height; }
  void setHeight(int h) { height = h; }
};

int main() {
  Rectangle r(19, 47);
  // Change width & height:
  r.setHeight(2 * r.getWidth());
  r.setWidth(2 * r.getHeight());
} ///:~
```

Of course, accessors and mutators don't have to be simple pipelines to an internal variable. Sometimes they can perform more sophisticated calculations. The following example uses the Standard C library time functions to produce a simple **Time** class:

```
//: C09:Cpptime.h
// A simple time class
#ifndef CPPTIME_H
#define CPPTIME_H
#include <ctime>
#include <cstring>

class Time {
  std::time_t t;
  std::tm local;
  char asciiRep[26];
  unsigned char lflag, aflag;
  void updateLocal() {
    if(!lflag) {
      local = *std::localtime(&t);
      lflag++;
    }
  }
  void updateAscii() {
    if(!aflag) {
      updateLocal();
      std::strcpy(asciiRep, std::asctime(&local));
      aflag++;
    }
  }
public:
  Time() { mark(); }
```

```cpp
  void mark() {
    lflag = aflag = 0;
    std::time(&t);
  }
  const char* ascii() {
    updateAscii();
    return asciiRep;
  }
  // Difference in seconds:
  int delta(Time* dt) const {
    return int(std::difftime(t, dt->t));
  }
  int daylightSavings() {
    updateLocal();
    return local.tm_isdst;
  }
  int dayOfYear() { // Since January 1
    updateLocal();
    return local.tm_yday;
  }
  int dayOfWeek() { // Since Sunday
    updateLocal();
    return local.tm_wday;
  }
  int since1900() { // Years since 1900
    updateLocal();
    return local.tm_year;
  }
  int month() { // Since January
    updateLocal();
    return local.tm_mon;
  }
  int dayOfMonth() {
    updateLocal();
    return local.tm_mday;
  }
  int hour() { // Since midnight, 24-hour clock
    updateLocal();
    return local.tm_hour;
  }
  int minute() {
    updateLocal();
    return local.tm_min;
  }
  int second() {
```

```
    updateLocal();
    return local.tm_sec;
  }
};
#endif // CPPTIME_H ///:~
```

The Standard C library functions have multiple representations for
time, and these are all part of the **Time** class. However, it isn't
necessary to update all of them, so instead the **time_t t** is used as
the base representation, and the **tm local** and ASCII character
representation **asciiRep** each have flags to indicate if they've been
updated to the current **time_t**. The two **private** functions
updateLocal( ) and **updateAscii( )** check the flags and
conditionally perform the update.

The constructor calls the **mark( )** function (which the user can also
call to force the object to represent the current time), and this clears
the two flags to indicate that the local time and ASCII
representation are now invalid. The **ascii( )** function calls
updateAscii( ), which copies the result of the Standard C library
function **asctime( )** into a local buffer because **asctime( )** uses a
static data area that is overwritten if the function is called
elsewhere. The **ascii( )** function return value is the address of this
local buffer.

All the functions starting with **daylightSavings( )** use the
updateLocal( ) function, which causes the resulting composite
inlines to be fairly large. This doesn't seem worthwhile, especially
considering you probably won't call the functions very much.
However, this doesn't mean all the functions should be made non-
inline. If you make other functions non-inline, at least keep
updateLocal( ) inline so that its code will be duplicated in the
non-inline functions, eliminating extra function-call overhead.

Here's a small test program:

```
//: C09:Cpptime.cpp
// Testing a simple time class
#include "Cpptime.h"
#include <iostream>
using namespace std;
```

```
int main() {
  Time start;
  for(int i = 1; i < 1000; i++) {
    cout << i << ' ';
    if(i%10 == 0) cout << endl;
  }
  Time end;
  cout << endl;
  cout << "start = " << start.ascii();
  cout << "end = " << end.ascii();
  cout << "delta = " << end.delta(&start);
} ///:~
```

A **Time** object is created, then some time-consuming activity is performed, then a second **Time** object is created to mark the ending time. These are used to show starting, ending, and elapsed times.

Stash & Stack with inlines

Armed with inlines, we can now convert the **Stash** and **Stack** classes to be more efficient:

```
//: C09:Stash4.h
// Inline functions
#ifndef STASH4_H
#define STASH4_H
#include "../require.h"

class Stash {
  int size;       // Size of each space
  int quantity;   // Number of storage spaces
  int next;       // Next empty space
  // Dynamically allocated array of bytes:
  unsigned char* storage;
  void inflate(int increase);
public:
  Stash(int sz) : size(sz), quantity(0),
    next(0), storage(0) {}
  Stash(int sz, int initQuantity) : size(sz),
    quantity(0), next(0), storage(0) {
    inflate(initQuantity);
```

```
  }
  Stash::~Stash() {
    if(storage != 0)
      delete []storage;
  }
  int add(void* element);
  void* fetch(int index) const {
    require(0 <= index, "Stash::fetch (-)index");
    if(index >= next)
      return 0; // To indicate the end
    // Produce pointer to desired element:
    return &(storage[index * size]);
  }
  int count() const { return next; }
};
#endif // STASH4_H ///:~
```

The small functions obviously work well as inlines, but notice that
the two largest functions are still left as non-inlines, since inlining
them probably wouldn't cause any performance gains:

```
//: C09:Stash4.cpp {O}
#include "Stash4.h"
#include <iostream>
#include <cassert>
using namespace std;
const int increment = 100;

int Stash::add(void* element) {
  if(next >= quantity) // Enough space left?
    inflate(increment);
  // Copy element into storage,
  // starting at next empty space:
  int startBytes = next * size;
  unsigned char* e = (unsigned char*)element;
  for(int i = 0; i < size; i++)
    storage[startBytes + i] = e[i];
  next++;
  return(next - 1); // Index number
}

void Stash::inflate(int increase) {
  assert(increase >= 0);
  if(increase == 0) return;
```

```
  int newQuantity = quantity + increase;
  int newBytes = newQuantity * size;
  int oldBytes = quantity * size;
  unsigned char* b = new unsigned char[newBytes];
  for(int i = 0; i < oldBytes; i++)
    b[i] = storage[i]; // Copy old to new
  delete [](storage); // Release old storage
  storage = b; // Point to new memory
  quantity = newQuantity; // Adjust the size
} ///:~
```

Once again, the test program verifies that everything is working correctly:

```
//: C09:Stash4Test.cpp
//{L} Stash4
#include "Stash4.h"
#include "../require.h"
#include <fstream>
#include <iostream>
#include <string>
using namespace std;

int main() {
  Stash intStash(sizeof(int));
  for(int i = 0; i < 100; i++)
    intStash.add(&i);
  for(int j = 0; j < intStash.count(); j++)
    cout << "intStash.fetch(" << j << ") = "
         << *(int*)intStash.fetch(j)
         << endl;
  const int bufsize = 80;
  Stash stringStash(sizeof(char) * bufsize, 100);
  ifstream in("Stash4Test.cpp");
  assure(in, "Stash4Test.cpp");
  string line;
  while(getline(in, line))
    stringStash.add((char*)line.c_str());
  int k = 0;
  char* cp;
  while((cp = (char*)stringStash.fetch(k++))!=0)
    cout << "stringStash.fetch(" << k << ") = "
         << cp << endl;
} ///:~
```

This is the same test program that was used before, so the output should be basically the same.

The **Stack** class makes even better use of inlines:

```
//: C09:Stack4.h
// With inlines
#ifndef STACK4_H
#define STACK4_H
#include "../require.h"

class Stack {
  struct Link {
    void* data;
    Link* next;
    Link(void* dat, Link* nxt) :
      data(dat), next(nxt) {}
  }* head;
public:
  Stack() : head(0) {}
  ~Stack() {
    require(head == 0, "Stack not empty");
  }
  void push(void* dat) {
    head = new Link(dat, head);
  }
  void* peek() const {
    return head ? head->data : 0;
  }
  void* pop() {
    if(head == 0) return 0;
    void* result = head->data;
    Link* oldHead = head;
    head = head->next;
    delete oldHead;
    return result;
  }
};
#endif // STACK4_H ///:~
```

Notice that the **Link** destructor that was present but empty in the previous version of **Stack** has been removed. In **pop( )**, the expression **delete oldHead** simply releases the memory used by

---

that **Link** (it does not destroy the **data** object pointed to by the
Link).

Most of the functions inline quite nicely and obviously, especially
for **Link**. Even **pop( )** seems legitimate, although anytime you have
conditionals or local variables it's not clear that inlines will be that
beneficial. Here, the function is small enough that it probably won't
hurt anything.

If all your functions *are* inlined, using the library becomes quite
simple because there's no linking necessary, as you can see in the
test example (notice that there's no **Stack4.cpp**):

```
//: C09:Stack4Test.cpp
//{T} Stack4Test.cpp
#include "Stack4.h"
#include "../require.h"
#include <fstream>
#include <iostream>
#include <string>
using namespace std;

int main(int argc, char* argv[]) {
  requireArgs(argc, 1); // File name is argument
  ifstream in(argv[1]);
  assure(in, argv[1]);
  Stack textlines;
  string line;
  // Read file and store lines in the stack:
  while(getline(in, line))
    textlines.push(new string(line));
  // Pop the lines from the stack and print them:
  string* s;
  while((s = (string*)textlines.pop()) != 0) {
    cout << *s << endl;
    delete s;
  }
} ///:~
```

People will sometimes write classes with all inline functions so that
the whole class will be in the header file (you'll see in this book that
I step over the line myself). During program development this is
probably harmless, although sometimes it can make for longer

compilations. Once the program stabilizes a bit, you'll probably want to go back and make functions non-inline where appropriate.

Inlines & the compiler

To understand when inlining is effective, it's helpful to know what the compiler does when it encounters an inline. As with any function, the compiler holds the function *type* (that is, the function prototype including the name and argument types, in combination with the function return value) in its symbol table. In addition, when the compiler sees that the inline's function type *and* the function body parses without error, the code for the function body is also brought into the symbol table. Whether the code is stored in source form, compiled assembly instructions, or some other representation is up to the compiler.

When you make a call to an inline function, the compiler first ensures that the call can be correctly made. That is, all the argument types must either be the exact types in the function's argument list, or the compiler must be able to make a type conversion to the proper types and the return value must be the correct type (or convertible to the correct type) in the destination expression. This, of course, is exactly what the compiler does for any function and is markedly different from what the preprocessor does because the preprocessor cannot check types or make conversions.

If all the function type information fits the context of the call, then the inline code is substituted directly for the function call, eliminating the call overhead and allowing for further optimizations by the compiler. Also, if the inline is a member function, the address of the object (**this**) is put in the appropriate place(s), which of course is another action the preprocessor is unable to perform.

Limitations

There are two situations in which the compiler cannot perform inlining. In these cases, it simply reverts to the ordinary form of a function by taking the inline definition and creating storage for the function just as it does for a non-inline. If it must do this in multiple translation units (which would normally cause a multiple definition error), the linker is told to ignore the multiple definitions.

The compiler cannot perform inlining if the function is too complicated. This depends upon the particular compiler, but at the point most compilers give up, the inline probably wouldn't gain you any efficiency. In general, any sort of looping is considered too complicated to expand as an inline, and if you think about it, looping probably entails much more time inside the function than what is required for the function call overhead. If the function is just a collection of simple statements, the compiler probably won't have any trouble inlining it, but if there are a lot of statements, the overhead of the function call will be much less than the cost of executing the body. And remember, every time you call a big inline function, the entire function body is inserted in place of each call, so you can easily get code bloat without any noticeable performance improvement. (Note that some of the examples in this book may exceed reasonable inline sizes in favor of conserving screen real estate.)

The compiler also cannot perform inlining if the address of the function is taken implicitly or explicitly. If the compiler must produce an address, then it will allocate storage for the function code and use the resulting address. However, where an address is not required, the compiler will probably still inline the code.

It is important to understand that an inline is just a suggestion to the compiler; the compiler is not forced to inline anything at all. A good compiler will inline small, simple functions while intelligently ignoring inlines that are too complicated. This will give you the results you want – the true semantics of a function call with the efficiency of a macro.

Forward references

If you're imagining what the compiler is doing to implement inlines, you can confuse yourself into thinking there are more limitations than actually exist. In particular, if an inline makes a forward reference to a function that hasn't yet been declared in the class (whether that function is inline or not), it can seem like the compiler won't be able to handle it:

```
//: C09:EvaluationOrder.cpp
// Inline evaluation order

class Forward {
  int i;
public:
  Forward() : i(0) {}
  // Call to undeclared function:
  int f() const { return g() + 1; }
  int g() const { return i; }
};

int main() {
  Forward frwd;
  frwd.f();
} ///:~
```

In **f( )**, a call is made to **g( )**, although **g( )** has not yet been declared. This works because the language definition states that no inline functions in a class shall be evaluated until the closing brace of the class declaration.

Of course, if **g( )** in turn called **f( )**, you'd end up with a set of recursive calls, which are too complicated for the compiler to inline. (Also, you'd have to perform some test in **f( )** or **g( )** to force one of them to "bottom out," or the recursion would be infinite.)

Hidden activities in constructors & destructors

Constructors and destructors are two places where you can be fooled into thinking that an inline is more efficient than it actually is. Constructors and destructors may have hidden activities, because the class can contain subobjects whose constructors and destructors must be called. These subobjects may be member objects, or they may exist because of inheritance (covered in Chapter 14). As an example of a class with member objects:

```
//: C09:Hidden.cpp
// Hidden activities in inlines
```

```
#include <iostream>
using namespace std;

class Member {
  int i, j, k;
public:
  Member(int x = 0) : i(x), j(x), k(x) {}
  ~Member() { cout << "~Member" << endl; }
};

class WithMembers {
  Member q, r, s; // Have constructors
  int i;
public:
  WithMembers(int ii) : i(ii) {} // Trivial?
  ~WithMembers() {
    cout << "~WithMembers" << endl;
  }
};

int main() {
  WithMembers wm(1);
} ///:~
```

The constructor for **Member** is simple enough to inline, since
there's nothing special going on – no inheritance or member objects
are causing extra hidden activities. But in **class WithMembers**
there's more going on than meets the eye. The constructors and
destructors for the member objects **q**, **r**, and **s** are being called
automatically, and *those* constructors and destructors are also
inline, so the difference is significant from normal member
functions. This doesn't necessarily mean that you should always
make constructor and destructor definitions non-inline; there are
cases in which it makes sense. Also, when you're making an initial
"sketch" of a program by quickly writing code, it's often more
convenient to use inlines. But if you're concerned about efficiency,
it's a place to look.

Reducing clutter

In a book like this, the simplicity and terseness of putting inline
definitions inside classes is very useful because more fits on a page

or screen (in a seminar). However, Dan Saks[2] has pointed out that in a real project this has the effect of needlessly cluttering the class interface and thereby making the class harder to use. He refers to member functions defined within classes using the Latin *in situ* (in place) and maintains that all definitions should be placed outside the class to keep the interface clean. Optimization, he argues, is a separate issue. If you want to optimize, use the **inline** keyword. Using this approach, the earlier **Rectangle.cpp** example becomes:

```
//: C09:Noinsitu.cpp
// Removing in situ functions

class Rectangle {
  int width, height;
public:
  Rectangle(int w = 0, int h = 0);
  int getWidth() const;
  void setWidth(int w);
  int getHeight() const;
  void setHeight(int h);
};

inline Rectangle::Rectangle(int w, int h)
  : width(w), height(h) {}

inline int Rectangle::getWidth() const {
  return width;
}

inline void Rectangle::setWidth(int w) {
  width = w;
}

inline int Rectangle::getHeight() const {
  return height;
}

inline void Rectangle::setHeight(int h) {
  height = h;
}
```

---

[2] Co-author with Tom Plum of *C++ Programming Guidelines*, Plum Hall, 1991.

```
int main() {
    Rectangle r(19, 47);
    // Transpose width & height:
    int iHeight = r.getHeight();
    r.setHeight(r.getWidth());
    r.setWidth(iHeight);
} ///:~
```

Now if you want to compare the effect of inline functions to non-inline functions, you can simply remove the **inline** keyword. (Inline functions should normally be put in header files, however, while non-inline functions must reside in their own translation unit.) If you want to put the functions into documentation, it's a simple cut-and-paste operation. *In situ* functions require more work and have greater potential for errors. Another argument for this approach is that you can always produce a consistent formatting style for function definitions, something that doesn't always occur with *in situ* functions.

More preprocessor features

Earlier, I said that you *almost* always want to use **inline** functions instead of preprocessor macros. The exceptions are when you need to use three special features in the C preprocessor (which is also the C++ preprocessor): stringizing, string concatenation, and token pasting. Stringizing, introduced earlier in the book, is performed with the # directive and allows you to take an identifier and turn it into a character array. String concatenation takes place when two adjacent character arrays have no intervening punctuation, in which case they are combined. These two features are especially useful when writing debug code. Thus,

```
#define DEBUG(x) cout << #x " = " << x << endl
```

This prints the value of any variable. You can also get a trace that prints out the statements as they execute:

```
#define TRACE(s) cerr << #s << endl; s
```

The **#s** stringizes the statement for output, and the second **s** reiterates the statement so it is executed. Of course, this kind of thing can cause problems, especially in one-line **for** loops:

```
for(int i = 0; i < 100; i++)
    TRACE(f(i));
```

Because there are actually two statements in the **TRACE( )** macro, the one-line **for** loop executes only the first one. The solution is to replace the semicolon with a comma in the macro.

Token pasting

Token pasting, implemented with the ## directive, is very useful when you are manufacturing code. It allows you to take two identifiers and paste them together to automatically create a new identifier. For example,

```
#define FIELD(a) char* a##_string; int a##_size
class Record {
    FIELD(one);
    FIELD(two);
    FIELD(three);
    // ...
};
```

Each call to the **FIELD( )** macro creates an identifier to hold a character array and another to hold the length of that array. Not only is it easier to read, it can eliminate coding errors and make maintenance easier.

Improved error checking

The **require.h** functions have been used up to this point without defining them (although **assert( )** has also been used to help detect programmer errors where it's appropriate). Now it's time to define this header file. Inline functions are convenient here because they allow everything to be placed in a header file, which simplifies the process of using the package. You just include the header file and you don't need to worry about linking an implementation file.

You should note that exceptions (presented in detail in Volume 2 of this book) provide a much more effective way of handling many kinds of errors – especially those that you'd like to recover from – instead of just halting the program. The conditions that **require.h** handles, however, are ones which prevent the continuation of the program, such as if the user doesn't provide enough command-line arguments or if a file cannot be opened. Thus, it's acceptable that they call the Standard C Library function **exit( )**.

The following header file is placed in the book's root directory so it's easily accessed from all chapters.

```
//: :require.h
// Test for error conditions in programs
// Local "using namespace std" for old compilers
#ifndef REQUIRE_H
#define REQUIRE_H
#include <cstdio>
#include <cstdlib>
#include <fstream>
#include <string>

inline void require(bool requirement,
  const std::string& msg = "Requirement failed"){
  using namespace std;
  if (!requirement) {
    fputs(msg.c_str(), stderr);
    fputs("\n", stderr);
    exit(1);
  }
}

inline void requireArgs(int argc, int args,
  const std::string& msg =
    "Must use %d arguments") {
  using namespace std;
   if (argc != args + 1) {
     fprintf(stderr, msg.c_str(), args);
     fputs("\n", stderr);
     exit(1);
   }
}
```

```
inline void requireMinArgs(int argc, int minArgs,
  const std::string& msg =
    "Must use at least %d arguments") {
  using namespace std;
  if(argc < minArgs + 1) {
    fprintf(stderr, msg.c_str(), minArgs);
    fputs("\n", stderr);
    exit(1);
  }
}

inline void assure(std::ifstream& in,
  const std::string& filename = "") {
  using namespace std;
  if(!in) {
    fprintf(stderr, "Could not open file %s\n",
      filename.c_str());
    exit(1);
  }
}

inline void assure(std::ofstream& out,
  const std::string& filename = "") {
  using namespace std;
  if(!out) {
    fprintf(stderr, "Could not open file %s\n",
      filename.c_str());
    exit(1);
  }
}
#endif // REQUIRE_H ///:~
```

The default values provide reasonable messages that can be
changed if necessary.

You'll notice that instead of using **char*** arguments, **const
string&** arguments are used. This allows both **char*** and **string**s
as arguments to these functions, and thus is more generally useful
(you may want to follow this form in your own coding).

In the definitions for **requireArgs( )** and **requireMinArgs( )**,
one is added to the number of arguments you need on the
command line because **argc** always includes the name of the

program being executed as argument zero, and so always has a value that is one more than the number of actual arguments on the command line.

Note the use of local "**using namespace std**" declarations within each function. This is because some compilers at the time of this writing incorrectly did not include the C standard library functions in **namespace std**, so explicit qualification would cause a compile-time error. The local declaration allows **require.h** to work with both correct and incorrect libraries without opening up the namespace **std** for anyone who includes this header file.

Here's a simple program to test **require.h**:

```
//: C09:ErrTest.cpp
//{T} ErrTest.cpp
// Testing require.h
#include "../require.h"
#include <fstream>
using namespace std;

int main(int argc, char* argv[]) {
  int i = 1;
  require(i, "value must be nonzero");
  requireArgs(argc, 1);
  requireMinArgs(argc, 1);
  ifstream in(argv[1]);
  assure(in, argv[1]); // Use the file name
  ifstream nofile("nofile.xxx");
  // Fails:
//!  assure(nofile); // The default argument
  ofstream out("tmp.txt");
  assure(out);
} ///:~
```

You might be tempted to go one step further for opening files and add a macro to **require.h**:

```
#define IFOPEN(VAR, NAME) \
  ifstream VAR(NAME); \
  assure(VAR, NAME);
```

Which could then be used like this:

```
IFOPEN(in, argv[1])
```

At first, this might seem appealing since it means there's less to type. It's not terribly unsafe, but it's a road best avoided. Note that, once again, a macro looks like a function but behaves differently; it's actually creating an object (**in**) whose scope persists beyond the macro. You may understand this, but for new programmers and code maintainers it's just one more thing they have to puzzle out. C++ is complicated enough without adding to the confusion, so try to talk yourself out of using preprocessor macros whenever you can.

Summary

It's critical that you be able to hide the underlying implementation of a class because you may want to change that implementation sometime later. You'll make these changes for efficiency, or because you get a better understanding of the problem, or because some new class becomes available that you want to use in the implementation. Anything that jeopardizes the privacy of the underlying implementation reduces the flexibility of the language. Thus, the inline function is very important because it virtually eliminates the need for preprocessor macros and their attendant problems. With inlines, member functions can be as efficient as preprocessor macros.

The inline function can be overused in class definitions, of course. The programmer is tempted to do so because it's easier, so it will happen. However, it's not that big of an issue because later, when looking for size reductions, you can always change the functions to non-inlines with no effect on their functionality. The development guideline should be "First make it work, then optimize it."

Exercises

Solutions to selected exercises can be found in the electronic document *The Thinking in C++ Annotated Solution Guide*, available for a small fee from www.BruceEckel.com.

1. Write a program that uses the **F( )** macro shown at the beginning of the chapter and demonstrates that it does

not expand properly, as described in the text. Repair the macro and show that it works correctly.

2. Write a program that uses the **FLOOR( )** macro shown at the beginning of the chapter. Show the conditions under which it does not work properly.

3. Modify **MacroSideEffects.cpp** so that **BAND( )** works properly.

4. Create two identical functions, **f1( )** and **f2( )**. Inline **f1( )** and leave **f2( )** as an non-inline function. Use the Standard C Library function **clock( )** that is found in **<ctime>** to mark the starting point and ending points and compare the two functions to see which one is faster. You may need to make repeated calls to the functions inside your timing loop in order to get useful numbers.

5. Experiment with the size and complexity of the code inside the functions in Exercise 4 to see if you can find a break-even point where the inline function and the non-inline function take the same amount of time. If you have them available, try this with different compilers and note the differences.

6. Prove that inline functions default to internal linkage.

7. Create a class that contains an array of **char**. Add an inline constructor that uses the Standard C library function **memset( )** to initialize the array to the constructor argument (default this to ' '), and an inline member function called **print( )** to print out all the characters in the array.

8. Take the **NestFriend.cpp** example from Chapter 5 and replace all the member functions with inlines. Make them non-*in situ* inline functions. Also change the **initialize( )** functions to constructors.

9. Modify **StringStack.cpp** from Chapter 8 to use inline functions.

10. Create an **enum** called **Hue** containing **red, blue**, and **yellow**. Now create a class called **Color** containing a data member of type **Hue** and a constructor that sets the **Hue** from its argument. Add access functions to "get" and "set" the **Hue**. Make all of the functions inlines.

11. Modify Exercise 10 to use the "accessor" and "mutator" approach.

12. Modify **Cpptime.cpp** so that it measures the time from the time that the program begins running to the time when the user presses the "Enter" or "Return" key.

13. Create a class with two inline member functions, such that the first function that's defined in the class calls the second function, without the need for a forward declaration. Write a main that creates an object of the class and calls the first function.

14. Create a class **A** with an inline default constructor that announces itself. Now make a new class **B** and put an object of **A** as a member of **B**, and give **B** an inline constructor. Create an array of **B** objects and see what happens.

15. Create a large quantity of the objects from the previous Exercise, and use the **Time** class to time the difference between non-inline constructors and inline constructors. (If you have a profiler, also try using that.)

16. Write a program that takes a **string** as the command-line argument. Write a **for** loop that removes one character from the **string** with each pass, and use the **DEBUG( )** macro from this chapter to print the **string** each time.

17. Correct the **TRACE( )** macro as specified in this chapter, and prove that it works correctly.

18. Modify the **FIELD( )** macro so that it also contains an **index** number. Create a class whose members are composed of calls to the **FIELD( )** macro. Add a member function that allows you to look up a field using its index number. Write a **main( )** to test the class.

19. Modify the **FIELD( )** macro so that it automatically generates access functions for each field (the data should still be private, however). Create a class whose members are composed of calls to the **FIELD( )** macro. Write a **main( )** to test the class.

20. Write a program that takes two command-line arguments: the first is an **int** and the second is a file name. Use **require.h** to ensure that you have the right

number of arguments, that the **int** is between 5 and 10, and that the file can successfully be opened.

21. Write a program that uses the **IFOPEN( )** macro to open a file as an input stream. Note the creation of the **ifstream** object and its scope.

22. (Challenging) Determine how to get your compiler to generate assembly code. Create a file containing a very small function and a **main( )** that calls the function. Generate assembly code when the function is inlined and not inlined, and demonstrate that the inlined version does not have the function call overhead.

10: Name Control

Creating names is a fundamental activity in programming, and when a project gets large, the number of names can easily be overwhelming.

C++ allows you a great deal of control over the creation and visibility of names, where storage for those names is placed, and linkage for names.

The **static** keyword was overloaded in C before people knew what the term "overload" meant, and C++ has added yet another meaning. The underlying concept with all uses of **static** seems to be "something that holds its position" (like static electricity), whether that means a physical location in memory or visibility within a file.

In this chapter, you'll learn how **static** controls storage and visibility, and an improved way to control access to names via C++'s *namespace* feature. You'll also find out how to use functions that were written and compiled in C.

Static elements from C

In both C and C++ the keyword **static** has two basic meanings, which unfortunately often step on each other's toes:

1.   Allocated once at a fixed address; that is, the object is created in a special *static data area* rather than on the stack each time a function is called. This is the concept of *static storage*.

2.   Local to a particular translation unit (and local to a class scope in C++, as you will see later). Here, **static** controls the *visibility* of a name, so that name cannot be seen outside the translation unit or class. This also describes the concept of *linkage*, which determines what names the linker will see.

This section will look at the above meanings of **static** as they were inherited from C.

static variables inside functions

When you create a local variable inside a function, the compiler allocates storage for that variable each time the function is called by moving the stack pointer down an appropriate amount. If there is an initializer for the variable, the initialization is performed each time that sequence point is passed.

Sometimes, however, you want to retain a value between function calls. You could accomplish this by making a global variable, but then that variable would not be under the sole control of the function. C and C++ allow you to create a **static** object inside a function; the storage for this object is not on the stack but instead in the program's static data area. This object is initialized only once, the first time the function is called, and then retains its value between function invocations. For example, the following function returns the next character in the array each time the function is called:

```
//: C10:StaticVariablesInfunctions.cpp
#include "../require.h"
#include <iostream>
using namespace std;

char oneChar(const char* charArray = 0) {
  static const char* s;
  if(charArray) {
    s = charArray;
    return *s;
  }
  else
    require(s, "un-initialized s");
  if(*s == '\0')
    return 0;
  return *s++;
}

char* a = "abcdefghijklmnopqrstuvwxyz";

int main() {
  // oneChar(); // require() fails
  oneChar(a); // Initializes s to a
  char c;
  while((c = oneChar()) != 0)
    cout << c << endl;
} ///:~
```

The **static char* s** holds its value between calls of **oneChar( )** because its storage is not part of the stack frame of the function, but is in the static storage area of the program. When you call **oneChar( )** with a **char*** argument, s is assigned to that argument, and the first character of the array is returned. Each subsequent call to **oneChar( )** *without* an argument produces the default value of zero for **charArray**, which indicates to the function that you are still extracting characters from the previously initialized value of **s**. The function will continue to produce characters until it reaches the null terminator of the character array, at which point it stops incrementing the pointer so it doesn't overrun the end of the array.

But what happens if you call **oneChar( )** with no arguments and without previously initializing the value of **s**? In the definition for **s**, you could have provided an initializer,

```
static char* s = 0;
```

but if you do not provide an initializer for a static variable of a built-in type, the compiler guarantees that variable will be initialized to zero (converted to the proper type) at program start-up. So in **oneChar( )**, the first time the function is called, **s** is zero. In this case, the **if(!s)** conditional will catch it.

The initialization above for **s** is very simple, but initialization for static objects (like all other objects) can be arbitrary expressions involving constants and previously declared variables and functions.

You should be aware that the function above is very vulnerable to multithreading problems; whenever you design functions containing static variables you should keep multithreading issues in mind.

static class objects inside functions
The rules are the same for static objects of user-defined types, including the fact that some initialization is required for the object. However, assignment to zero has meaning only for built-in types; user-defined types must be initialized with constructor calls. Thus, if you don't specify constructor arguments when you define the static object, the class must have a default constructor. For example,

```
//: C10:StaticObjectsInFunctions.cpp
#include <iostream>
using namespace std;

class X {
  int i;
public:
  X(int ii = 0) : i(ii) {} // Default
  ~X() { cout << "X::~X()" << endl; }
};

void f() {
  static X x1(47);
  static X x2; // Default constructor required
}

int main() {
  f();
} ///:~
```

The static objects of type **X** inside **f( )** can be initialized either with
the constructor argument list or with the default constructor. This
construction occurs the first time control passes through the
definition, and only the first time.

Static object destructors

Destructors for static objects (that is, all objects with static storage,
not just local static objects as in the example above) are called when
main( ) exits or when the Standard C library function **exit( )** is
explicitly called. In most implementations, **main( )** just calls
exit( ) when it terminates. This means that it can be dangerous to
call **exit( )** inside a destructor because you can end up with infinite
recursion. Static object destructors are *not* called if you exit the
program using the Standard C library function **abort( )**.

You can specify actions to take place when leaving **main( )** (or
calling **exit( )**) by using the Standard C library function **atexit( )**.
In this case, the functions registered by **atexit( )** may be called
before the destructors for any objects constructed before leaving
main( ) (or calling **exit( )**).

Like ordinary destruction, destruction of static objects occurs in the reverse order of initialization. However, only objects that have been constructed are destroyed. Fortunately, the C++ development tools keep track of initialization order and the objects that have been constructed. Global objects are always constructed before **main( )** is entered and destroyed as **main( )** exits, but if a function containing a local static object is never called, the constructor for that object is never executed, so the destructor is also not executed. For example,

```
//: C10:StaticDestructors.cpp
// Static object destructors
#include <fstream>
using namespace std;
ofstream out("statdest.out"); // Trace file

class Obj {
  char c; // Identifier
public:
  Obj(char cc) : c(cc) {
    out << "Obj::Obj() for " << c << endl;
  }
  ~Obj() {
    out << "Obj::~Obj() for " << c << endl;
  }
};

Obj a('a'); // Global (static storage)
// Constructor & destructor always called

void f() {
  static Obj b('b');
}

void g() {
  static Obj c('c');
}

int main() {
  out << "inside main()" << endl;
  f(); // Calls static constructor for b
  // g() not called
  out << "leaving main()" << endl;
```

```
} ///:~
```

In **Obj**, the **char c** acts as an identifier so the constructor and destructor can print out information about the object they're working on. The **Obj a** is a global object, so the constructor is always called for it before **main( )** is entered, but the constructors for the **static Obj b** inside **f( )** and the **static Obj c** inside **g( )** are called only if those functions are called.

To demonstrate which constructors and destructors are called, only **f( )** is called. The output of the program is

```
Obj::Obj() for a
inside main()
Obj::Obj() for b
leaving main()
Obj::~Obj() for b
Obj::~Obj() for a
```

The constructor for **a** is called before **main( )** is entered, and the constructor for **b** is called only because **f( )** is called. When **main( )** exits, the destructors for the objects that have been constructed are called in reverse order of their construction. This means that if **g( )** *is* called, the order in which the destructors for **b** and **c** are called depends on whether **f( )** or **g( )** is called first.

Notice that the trace file **ofstream** object **out** is also a static object – since it is defined outside of all functions, it lives in the static storage area. It is important that its definition (as opposed to an **extern** declaration) appear at the beginning of the file, before there is any possible use of **out**. Otherwise, you'll be using an object before it is properly initialized.

In C++, the constructor for a global static object is called before **main( )** is entered, so you now have a simple and portable way to execute code before entering **main( )** and to execute code with the destructor after exiting **main( )**. In C, this was always a trial that required you to root around in the compiler vendor's assembly-language startup code.

Controlling linkage

Ordinarily, any name at *file scope* (that is, not nested inside a class or function) is visible throughout all translation units in a program. This is often called *external linkage* because at link time the name is visible to the linker everywhere, external to that translation unit. Global variables and ordinary functions have external linkage.

There are times when you'd like to limit the visibility of a name. You might like to have a variable at file scope so all the functions in that file can use it, but you don't want functions outside that file to see or access that variable, or to inadvertently cause name clashes with identifiers outside the file.

An object or function name at file scope that is explicitly declared **static** is local to its translation unit (in the terms of this book, the **cpp** file where the declaration occurs). That name has *internal linkage*. This means that you can use the same name in other translation units without a name clash.

One advantage to internal linkage is that the name can be placed in a header file without worrying that there will be a clash at link time. Names that are commonly placed in header files, such as **const** definitions and **inline** functions, default to internal linkage. (However, **const** defaults to internal linkage only in C++; in C it defaults to external linkage.) Note that linkage refers only to elements that have addresses at link/load time; thus, class declarations and local variables have no linkage.

Confusion

Here's an example of how the two meanings of **static** can cross over each other. All global objects implicitly have static storage class, so if you say (at file scope),

```
int a = 0;
```

then storage for **a** will be in the program's static data area, and the initialization for **a** will occur once, before **main( )** is entered. In addition, the visibility of **a** is global across all translation units. In terms of visibility, the opposite of **static** (visible only in this translation unit) is **extern**, which explicitly states that the visibility of the name is across all translation units. So the definition above is equivalent to saying

```
extern int a = 0;
```

But if you say instead,

```
static int a = 0;
```

all you've done is change the visibility, so **a** has internal linkage. The storage class is unchanged – the object resides in the static data area whether the visibility is **static** or **extern**.

Once you get into local variables, **static** stops altering the visibility and instead alters the storage class.

If you declare what appears to be a local variable as **extern**, it means that the storage exists elsewhere (so the variable is actually global to the function). For example:

```
//: C10:LocalExtern.cpp
//{L} LocalExtern2
#include <iostream>

int main() {
  extern int i;
  std::cout << i;
} ///:~

//: C10:LocalExtern2.cpp {O}
int i = 5;
///:~
```

With function names (for non-member functions), **static** and **extern** can only alter visibility, so if you say

```
extern void f();
```

it's the same as the unadorned declaration

```
void f();
```

and if you say,

```
static void f();
```

it means **f( )** is visible only within this translation unit – this is sometimes called *file static.*

Other storage class specifiers

You will see **static** and **extern** used commonly. There are two other storage class specifiers that occur less often. The **auto** specifier is almost never used because it tells the compiler that this is a local variable. **auto** is short for "automatic" and it refers to the way the compiler automatically allocates storage for the variable. The compiler can always determine this fact from the context in which the variable is defined, so **auto** is redundant.

A **register** variable is a local (**auto**) variable, along with a hint to the compiler that this particular variable will be heavily used so the compiler ought to keep it in a register if it can. Thus, it is an optimization aid. Various compilers respond differently to this hint; they have the option to ignore it. If you take the address of the variable, the **register** specifier will almost certainly be ignored. You should avoid using **register** because the compiler can usually do a better job of optimization than you.

Namespaces

Although names can be nested inside classes, the names of global functions, global variables, and classes are still in a single global name space. The **static** keyword gives you some control over this by allowing you to give variables and functions internal linkage (that is, to make them file static). But in a large project, lack of control over the global name space can cause problems. To solve these problems for classes, vendors often create long complicated names that are unlikely to clash, but then you're stuck typing those names. (A **typedef** is often used to simplify this.) It's not an elegant, language-supported solution.

You can subdivide the global name space into more manageable pieces using the *namespace* feature of C++. The **namespace** keyword, similar to **class**, **struct**, **enum**, and **union**, puts the names of its members in a distinct space. While the other keywords have additional purposes, the creation of a new name space is the only purpose for **namespace**.

Creating a namespace

The creation of a namespace is notably similar to the creation of a **class**:

```
//: C10:MyLib.cpp
namespace MyLib {
  // Declarations
}
int main() {} ///:~
```

This produces a new namespace containing the enclosed declarations. There are significant differences from **class**, **struct**, **union** and **enum**, however:

- A namespace definition can appear only at global scope, or nested within another namespace.

- No terminating semicolon is necessary after the closing brace of a namespace definition.

- A namespace definition can be "continued" over multiple header files using a syntax that, for a class, would appear to be a redefinition:

```
//: C10:Header1.h
#ifndef HEADER1_H
#define HEADER1_H
namespace MyLib {
  extern int x;
  void f();
  // ...
}
```

```
#endif // HEADER1_H ///:~
//: C10:Header2.h
#ifndef HEADER2_H
#define HEADER2_H
#include "Header1.h"
```

```
// Add more names to MyLib
namespace MyLib { // NOT a redefinition!
  extern int y;
  void g();
  // ...
}

#endif // HEADER2_H ///:~
//: C10:Continuation.cpp
#include "Header2.h"
int main() {} ///:~
```

- A namespace name can be *aliased* to another name, so you don't have to type an unwieldy name created by a library vendor:

```
//: C10:BobsSuperDuperLibrary.cpp
namespace BobsSuperDuperLibrary {
  class Widget { /* ... */ };
  class Poppit { /* ... */ };
  // ...
}
// Too much to type! I'll alias it:
namespace Bob = BobsSuperDuperLibrary;
int main() {} ///:~
```

- You cannot create an instance of a namespace as you can with a class.

Unnamed namespaces

Each translation unit contains an unnamed namespace that you can add to by saying "**namespace**" without an identifier:

```
//: C10:UnnamedNamespaces.cpp
namespace {
  class Arm  { /* ... */ };
  class Leg  { /* ... */ };
  class Head { /* ... */ };
  class Robot {
    Arm arm[4];
    Leg leg[16];
    Head head[3];
    // ...
  } xanthan;
```

```
    int i, j, k;
}
int main() {} ///:~
```

The names in this space are automatically available in that translation unit without qualification. It is guaranteed that an unnamed space is unique for each translation unit. If you put local names in an unnamed namespace, you don't need to give them internal linkage by making them **static**.

C++ deprecates the use of file statics in favor of the unnamed namespace.

Friends

You can *inject* a **friend** declaration into a namespace by declaring it within an enclosed class:

```
//: C10:FriendInjection.cpp
namespace Me {
  class Us {
    //...
    friend void you();
  };
}
int main() {} ///:~
```

Now the function **you( )** is a member of the namespace **Me**.

If you introduce a friend within a class in the global namespace, the friend is injected globally.

Using a namespace

You can refer to a name within a namespace in three ways: by specifying the name using the scope resolution operator, with a **using** directive to introduce all names in the namespace, or with a **using** declaration to introduce names one at a time.

Scope resolution

Any name in a namespace can be explicitly specified using the scope resolution operator in the same way that you can refer to the names within a class:

```
//: C10:ScopeResolution.cpp
namespace X {
  class Y {
    static int i;
  public:
    void f();
  };
  class Z;
  void func();
}
int X::Y::i = 9;
class X::Z {
  int u, v, w;
public:
  Z(int i);
  int g();
};
X::Z::Z(int i) { u = v = w = i; }
int X::Z::g() { return u = v = w = 0; }
void X::func() {
  X::Z a(1);
  a.g();
}
int main(){} ///:~
```

Notice that the definition **X::Y::i** could just as easily be referring to a data member of a class **Y** nested in a class **X** instead of a namespace **X**.

So far, namespaces look very much like classes.

The using directive

Because it can rapidly get tedious to type the full qualification for an identifier in a namespace, the **using** keyword allows you to import an entire namespace at once. When used in conjunction with the **namespace** keyword this is called a *using directive*. The **using** directive makes names appear as if they belong to the nearest enclosing namespace scope, so you can conveniently use the unqualified names. Consider a simple namespace:

```
//: C10:NamespaceInt.h
#ifndef NAMESPACEINT_H
```

```
#define NAMESPACEINT_H
namespace Int {
  enum sign { positive, negative };
  class Integer {
    int i;
    sign s;
  public:
    Integer(int ii = 0)
      : i(ii),
        s(i >= 0 ? positive : negative)
    {}
    sign getSign() const { return s; }
    void setSign(sign sgn) { s = sgn; }
    // ...
  };
}
#endif // NAMESPACEINT_H ///:~
```

One use of the **using** directive is to bring all of the names in **Int** into another namespace, leaving those names nested within the namespace:

```
//: C10:NamespaceMath.h
#ifndef NAMESPACEMATH_H
#define NAMESPACEMATH_H
#include "NamespaceInt.h"
namespace Math {
  using namespace Int;
  Integer a, b;
  Integer divide(Integer, Integer);
  // ...
}
#endif // NAMESPACEMATH_H ///:~
```

You can also declare all of the names in **Int** inside a function, but leave those names nested within the function:

```
//: C10:Arithmetic.cpp
#include "NamespaceInt.h"
void arithmetic() {
  using namespace Int;
  Integer x;
  x.setSign(positive);
}
```

```
int main(){} ///:~
```

Without the **using** directive, all the names in the namespace would need to be fully qualified.

One aspect of the **using** directive may seem slightly counterintuitive at first. The visibility of the names introduced with a **using** directive is the scope in which the directive is made. But you can override the names from the **using** directive as if they've been declared globally to that scope!

```
//: C10:NamespaceOverriding1.cpp
#include "NamespaceMath.h"
int main() {
  using namespace Math;
  Integer a; // Hides Math::a;
  a.setSign(negative);
  // Now scope resolution is necessary
  // to select Math::a :
  Math::a.setSign(positive);
} ///:~
```

Suppose you have a second namespace that contains some of the names in **namespace Math**:

```
//: C10:NamespaceOverriding2.h
#ifndef NAMESPACEOVERRIDING2_H
#define NAMESPACEOVERRIDING2_H
#include "NamespaceInt.h"
namespace Calculation {
  using namespace Int;
  Integer divide(Integer, Integer);
  // ...
}
#endif // NAMESPACEOVERRIDING2_H ///:~
```

Since this namespace is also introduced with a **using** directive, you have the possibility of a collision. However, the ambiguity appears at the point of *use* of the name, not at the **using** directive:

```
//: C10:OverridingAmbiguity.cpp
#include "NamespaceMath.h"
#include "NamespaceOverriding2.h"
void s() {
```

```
  using namespace Math;
  using namespace Calculation;
  // Everything's ok until:
  //! divide(1, 2); // Ambiguity
}
int main() {} ///:~
```

Thus, it's possible to write **using** directives to introduce a number of namespaces with conflicting names without ever producing an ambiguity.

The using declaration
You can inject names one at a time into the current scope with a *using declaration*. Unlike the **using** directive, which treats names as if they were declared globally to the scope, a **using** declaration is a declaration within the current scope. This means it can override names from a **using** directive:

```
//: C10:UsingDeclaration.h
#ifndef USINGDECLARATION_H
#define USINGDECLARATION_H
namespace U {
  inline void f() {}
  inline void g() {}
}
namespace V {
  inline void f() {}
  inline void g() {}
}
#endif // USINGDECLARATION_H ///:~
```

```
//: C10:UsingDeclaration1.cpp
#include "UsingDeclaration.h"
void h() {
  using namespace U; // Using directive
  using V::f; // Using declaration
  f(); // Calls V::f();
  U::f(); // Must fully qualify to call
}
int main() {} ///:~
```

The **using** declaration just gives the fully specified name of the identifier, but no type information. This means that if the namespace contains a set of overloaded functions with the same

---

name, the **using** declaration declares all the functions in the overloaded set.

You can put a **using** declaration anywhere a normal declaration can occur. A **using** declaration works like a normal declaration in all ways but one: because you don't give an argument list, it's possible for a **using** declaration to cause the overload of a function with the same argument types (which isn't allowed with normal overloading). This ambiguity, however, doesn't show up until the point of use, rather than the point of declaration.

A **using** declaration can also appear within a namespace, and it has the same effect as anywhere else – that name is declared within the space:

```
//: C10:UsingDeclaration2.cpp
#include "UsingDeclaration.h"
namespace Q {
  using U::f;
  using V::g;
  // ...
}
void m() {
  using namespace Q;
  f(); // Calls U::f();
  g(); // Calls V::g();
}
int main() {} ///:~
```

A **using** declaration is an alias, and it allows you to declare the same function in separate namespaces. If you end up re-declaring the same function by importing different namespaces, it's OK – there won't be any ambiguities or duplications.

The use of namespaces

Some of the rules above may seem a bit daunting at first, especially if you get the impression that you'll be using them all the time. In general, however, you can get away with very simple usage of namespaces as long as you understand how they work. The key thing to remember is that when you introduce a global **using** directive (via a "**using namespace**" outside of any scope) you have thrown open the namespace for that file. This is usually fine for an implementation file (a "**cpp**" file) because the **using** directive is only in effect until the end of the compilation of that file. That is, it doesn't affect any other files, so you can adjust the control of the namespaces one implementation file at a time. For example, if you discover a name clash because of too many **using** directives in a particular implementation file, it is a simple matter to change that file so that it uses explicit qualifications or **using** declarations to eliminate the clash, without modifying other implementation files.

Header files are a different issue. You virtually never want to introduce a global **using** directive into a header file, because that would mean that any other file that included your header would also have the namespace thrown open (and header files can include other header files).

So, in header files you should either use explicit qualification or scoped **using** directives and **using** declarations. This is the practice that you will find in this book, and by following it you will not "pollute" the global namespace and throw yourself back into the pre-namespace world of C++.

Static members in C++

There are times when you need a single storage space to be used by all objects of a class. In C, you would use a global variable, but this is not very safe. Global data can be modified by anyone, and its name can clash with other identical names in a large project. It would be ideal if the data could be stored as if it were global, but be hidden inside a class, and clearly associated with that class.

This is accomplished with **static** data members inside a class. There is a single piece of storage for a **static** data member, regardless of how many objects of that class you create. All objects share the same **static** storage space for that data member, so it is a way for them to "communicate" with each other. But the **static** data belongs to the class; its name is scoped inside the class and it can be **public**, **private**, or **protected**.

Defining storage for static data members

Because **static** data has a single piece of storage regardless of how many objects are created, that storage must be defined in a single place. The compiler will not allocate storage for you. The linker will report an error if a **static** data member is declared but not defined.

The definition must occur outside the class (no inlining is allowed), and only one definition is allowed. Thus, it is common to put it in the implementation file for the class. The syntax sometimes gives people trouble, but it is actually quite logical. For example, if you create a static data member inside a class like this:

```
class A {
  static int i;
public:
  //...
};
```

Then you must define storage for that static data member in the definition file like this:

```
int A::i = 1;
```

If you were to define an ordinary global variable, you would say

```
int i = 1;
```

but here, the scope resolution operator and the class name are used to specify **A::i**.

Some people have trouble with the idea that **A::i** is **private**, and yet here's something that seems to be manipulating it right out in the open. Doesn't this break the protection mechanism? It's a completely safe practice for two reasons. First, the only place this initialization is legal is in the definition. Indeed, if the **static** data were an object with a constructor, you would call the constructor instead of using the = operator. Second, once the definition has been made, the end-user cannot make a second definition – the linker will report an error. And the class creator is forced to create the definition or the code won't link during testing. This ensures that the definition happens only once and that it's in the hands of the class creator.

The entire initialization expression for a static member is in the scope of the class. For example,

```
//: C10:Statinit.cpp
// Scope of static initializer
#include <iostream>
using namespace std;

int x = 100;

class WithStatic {
  static int x;
  static int y;
public:
  void print() const {
    cout << "WithStatic::x = " << x << endl;
    cout << "WithStatic::y = " << y << endl;
  }
};

int WithStatic::x = 1;
int WithStatic::y = x + 1;
// WithStatic::x NOT ::x

int main() {
  WithStatic ws;
  ws.print();
} ///:~
```

Here, the qualification **WithStatic::** extends the scope of **WithStatic** to the entire definition.

static array initialization

Chapter 8 introduced the **static const** variable that allows you to define a constant value inside a class body. It's also possible to create arrays of **static** objects, both **const** and non-**const**. The syntax is reasonably consistent:

```
//: C10:StaticArray.cpp
// Initializing static arrays in classes
```

```
class Values {
  // static consts are initialized in-place:
  static const int scSize = 100;
  static const long scLong = 100;
  // Automatic counting works with static arrays.
  // Arrays, Non-integral and non-const statics
  // must be initialized externally:
  static const int scInts[];
  static const long scLongs[];
  static const float scTable[];
  static const char scLetters[];
  static int size;
  static const float scFloat;
  static float table[];
  static char letters[];
};

int Values::size = 100;
const float Values::scFloat = 1.1;

const int Values::scInts[] = {
  99, 47, 33, 11, 7
};

const long Values::scLongs[] = {
  99, 47, 33, 11, 7
};

const float Values::scTable[] = {
  1.1, 2.2, 3.3, 4.4
};

const char Values::scLetters[] = {
  'a', 'b', 'c', 'd', 'e',
  'f', 'g', 'h', 'i', 'j'
};

float Values::table[4] = {
  1.1, 2.2, 3.3, 4.4
};

char Values::letters[10] = {
  'a', 'b', 'c', 'd', 'e',
  'f', 'g', 'h', 'i', 'j'
};
```

```
int main() { Values v; } ///:~
```

With **static const**s of integral types you can provide the definitions inside the class, but for everything else (including arrays of integral types, even if they are **static const**) you must provide a single external definition for the member. These definitions have internal linkage, so they can be placed in header files. The syntax for initializing static arrays is the same as for any aggregate, including automatic counting.

You can also create **static const** objects of class types and arrays of such objects. However, you cannot initialize them using the "inline syntax" allowed for **static const**s of integral built-in types:

```
//: C10:StaticObjectArrays.cpp
// Static arrays of class objects
class X {
  int i;
public:
  X(int ii) : i(ii) {}
};

class Stat {
  // This doesn't work, although
  // you might want it to:
//!   static const X x(100);
  // Both const and non-const static class
  // objects must be initialized externally:
  static X x2;
  static X xTable2[];
  static const X x3;
  static const X xTable3[];
};

X Stat::x2(100);

X Stat::xTable2[] = {
  X(1), X(2), X(3), X(4)
};

const X Stat::x3(100);
```

```
const X Stat::xTable3[] = {
  X(1), X(2), X(3), X(4)
};

int main() { Stat v; } ///:~
```

The initialization of both **const** and non-**const static** arrays of
class objects must be performed the same way, following the typical
static definition syntax.

Nested and local classes

You can easily put static data members in classes that are nested
inside other classes. The definition of such members is an intuitive
and obvious extension – you simply use another level of scope
resolution. However, you cannot have **static** data members inside
local classes (a local class is a class defined inside a function). Thus,

```
//: C10:Local.cpp
// Static members & local classes
#include <iostream>
using namespace std;

// Nested class CAN have static data members:
class Outer {
  class Inner {
    static int i; // OK
  };
};

int Outer::Inner::i = 47;

// Local class cannot have static data members:
void f() {
  class Local {
  public:
//! static int i;  // Error
    // (How would you define i?)
  } x;
}

int main() { Outer x; f(); } ///:~
```

You can see the immediate problem with a **static** member in a local class: How do you describe the data member at file scope in order to define it? In practice, local classes are used very rarely.

static member functions

You can also create **static** member functions that, like **static** data members, work for the class as a whole rather than for a particular object of a class. Instead of making a global function that lives in and "pollutes" the global or local namespace, you bring the function inside the class. When you create a **static** member function, you are expressing an association with a particular class.

You can call a **static** member function in the ordinary way, with the dot or the arrow, in association with an object. However, it's more typical to call a **static** member function by itself, without any specific object, using the scope-resolution operator, like this:

```
//: C10:SimpleStaticMemberFunction.cpp
class X {
public:
  static void f(){};
};

int main() {
  X::f();
} ///:~
```

When you see static member functions in a class, remember that the designer intended that function to be conceptually associated with the class as a whole.

A **static** member function cannot access ordinary data members, only **static** data members. It can call only other **static** member functions. Normally, the address of the current object (**this**) is quietly passed in when any member function is called, but a **static** member has no **this**, which is the reason it cannot access ordinary members. Thus, you get the tiny increase in speed afforded by a global function because a **static** member function doesn't have the extra overhead of passing **this**. At the same time you get the benefits of having the function inside the class.

For data members, **static** indicates that only one piece of storage for member data exists for all objects of a class. This parallels the use of **static** to define objects *inside* a function to mean that only one copy of a local variable is used for all calls of that function.

Here's an example showing **static** data members and **static** member functions used together:

```
//: C10:StaticMemberFunctions.cpp
class X {
  int i;
  static int j;
public:
  X(int ii = 0) : i(ii) {
     // Non-static member function can access
     // static member function or data:
    j = i;
  }
  int val() const { return i; }
  static int incr() {
    //! i++; // Error: static member function
    // cannot access non-static member data
    return ++j;
  }
  static int f() {
    //! val(); // Error: static member function
    // cannot access non-static member function
    return incr(); // OK -- calls static
  }
};

int X::j = 0;

int main() {
  X x;
  X* xp = &x;
  x.f();
  xp->f();
  X::f(); // Only works with static members
} ///:~
```

Because they have no **this** pointer, **static** member functions can neither access non-**static** data members nor call non-**static** member functions.

Notice in **main( )** that a **static** member can be selected using the usual dot or arrow syntax, associating that function with an object, but also with no object (because a **static** member is associated with a class, not a particular object), using the class name and scope resolution operator.

Here's an interesting feature: Because of the way initialization happens for **static** member objects, you can put a **static** data member of the same class *inside* that class. Here's an example that allows only a single object of type **Egg** to exist by making the constructor private. You can access that object, but you can't create any new **Egg** objects:

```
//: C10:Singleton.cpp
// Static member of same type, ensures that
// only one object of this type exists.
// Also referred to as the "singleton" pattern.
#include <iostream>
using namespace std;

class Egg {
  static Egg e;
  int i;
  Egg(int ii) : i(ii) {}
  Egg(const Egg&); // Prevent copy-construction
public:
  static Egg* instance() { return &e; }
  int val() const { return i; }
};

Egg Egg::e(47);

int main() {
//!  Egg x(1); // Error -- can't create an Egg
  // You can access the single instance:
  cout << Egg::instance()->val() << endl;
} ///:~
```

The initialization for **E** happens after the class declaration is complete, so the compiler has all the information it needs to allocate storage and make the constructor call.

To completely prevent the creation of any other objects, something else has been added: a second private constructor called the *copy-constructor*. At this point in the book, you cannot know why this is necessary since the copy constructor will not be introduced until the next chapter. However, as a sneak preview, if you were to remove the copy-constructor defined in the example above, you'd be able to create an **Egg** object like this:

```
Egg e = *Egg::instance();
Egg e2(*Egg::instance());
```

Both of these use the copy-constructor, so to seal off that possibility the copy-constructor is declared as private (no definition is necessary because it never gets called). A large portion of the next chapter is a discussion of the copy-constructor so it should become clear to you then.

Static initialization dependency

Within a specific translation unit, the order of initialization of static objects is guaranteed to be the order in which the object definitions appear in that translation unit. The order of destruction is guaranteed to be the reverse of the order of initialization.

However, there is no guarantee concerning the order of initialization of static objects *across* translation units, and the language provides no way to specify this order. This can cause significant problems. As an example of an instant disaster (which will halt primitive operating systems and kill the process on sophisticated ones), if one file contains

```
// First file
#include <fstream>
std::ofstream out("out.txt");
```

and another file uses the **out** object in one of its initializers

```
// Second file
#include <fstream>
extern std::ofstream out;
class Oof {
```

```
public:
  Oof() { std::out << "ouch"; }
} oof;
```

the program may work, and it may not. If the programming environment builds the program so that the first file is initialized before the second file, then there will be no problem. However, if the second file is initialized before the first, the constructor for **Oof** relies upon the existence of **out**, which hasn't been constructed yet and this causes chaos.

This problem only occurs with static object initializers *that depend* on each other. The statics in a translation unit are initialized before the first invocation of a function in that unit – but it could be after **main( )**. You can't be sure about the order of initialization of static objects if they're in different files.

A subtler example can be found in the ARM.[1] In one file you have at the global scope:

```
extern int y;
int x = y + 1;
```

and in a second file you have at the global scope:

```
extern int x;
int y = x + 1;
```

For all static objects, the linking-loading mechanism guarantees a static initialization to zero before the dynamic initialization specified by the programmer takes place. In the previous example, zeroing of the storage occupied by the **fstream out** object has no special meaning, so it is truly undefined until the constructor is called. However, with built-in types, initialization to zero *does* have meaning, and if the files are initialized in the order they are shown above, **y** begins as statically initialized to zero, so **x** becomes one, and **y** is dynamically initialized to two. However, if the files are

---

[1] Bjarne Stroustrup and Margaret Ellis, *The Annotated C++ Reference Manual*, Addison-Wesley, 1990, pp. 20-21.

---

initialized in the opposite order, **x** is statically initialized to zero, **y** is dynamically initialized to one, and **x** then becomes two.

Programmers must be aware of this because they can create a program with static initialization dependencies and get it working on one platform, but move it to another compiling environment where it suddenly, mysteriously, doesn't work.

What to do

There are three approaches to dealing with this problem:

1.   Don't do it. Avoiding static initialization dependencies is the best solution.

2.   If you must do it, put the critical static object definitions in a single file, so you can portably control their initialization by putting them in the correct order.

3.   If you're convinced it's unavoidable to scatter static objects across translation units – as in the case of a library, where you can't control the programmer who uses it – there are two programmatic techniques to solve the problem.

Technique one

This technique was pioneered by Jerry Schwarz while creating the iostream library (because the definitions for **cin**, **cout**, and **cerr** are **static** and live in a separate file). It's actually inferior to the second technique but it's been around a long time and so you may come across code that uses it; thus it's important that you understand how it works.

This technique requires an additional class in your library header file. This class is responsible for the dynamic initialization of your library's static objects. Here is a simple example:

```
//: C10:Initializer.h
// Static initialization technique
#ifndef INITIALIZER_H
#define INITIALIZER_H
#include <iostream>
```

```
extern int x; // Declarations, not definitions
extern int y;

class Initializer {
  static int initCount;
public:
  Initializer() {
    std::cout << "Initializer()" << std::endl;
    // Initialize first time only
    if(initCount++ == 0) {
      std::cout << "performing initialization"
                << std::endl;
      x = 100;
      y = 200;
    }
  }
  ~Initializer() {
    std::cout << "~Initializer()" << std::endl;
    // Clean up last time only
    if(--initCount == 0) {
      std::cout << "performing cleanup"
                << std::endl;
      // Any necessary cleanup here
    }
  }
};

// The following creates one object in each
// file where Initializer.h is included, but that
// object is only visible within that file:
static Initializer init;
#endif // INITIALIZER_H ///:~
```

The declarations for **x** and **y** announce only that these objects exist, but they don't allocate storage for the objects. However, the definition for the **Initializer init** allocates storage for that object in every file where the header is included. But because the name is **static** (controlling visibility this time, not the way storage is allocated; storage is at file scope by default), it is visible only within that translation unit, so the linker will not complain about multiple definition errors.

Here is the file containing the definitions for **x**, **y**, and **initCount**:

```
//: C10:InitializerDefs.cpp {O}
// Definitions for Initializer.h
#include "Initializer.h"
// Static initialization will force
// all these values to zero:
int x;
int y;
int Initializer::initCount;
///:~
```

(Of course, a file static instance of **init** is also placed in this file when the header is included.) Suppose that two other files are created by the library user:

```
//: C10:Initializer.cpp {O}
// Static initialization
#include "Initializer.h"
///:~
```

and

```
//: C10:Initializer2.cpp
//{L} InitializerDefs Initializer
// Static initialization
#include "Initializer.h"
using namespace std;

int main() {
  cout << "inside main()" << endl;
  cout << "leaving main()" << endl;
} ///:~
```

Now it doesn't matter which translation unit is initialized first. The first time a translation unit containing **Initializer.h** is initialized, **initCount** will be zero so the initialization will be performed. (This depends heavily on the fact that the static storage area is set to zero before any dynamic initialization takes place.) For all the rest of the translation units, **initCount** will be nonzero and the initialization will be skipped. Cleanup happens in the reverse order, and **~Initializer( )** ensures that it will happen only once.

This example used built-in types as the global static objects. The technique also works with classes, but those objects must then be dynamically initialized by the **Initializer** class. One way to do this is to create the classes without constructors and destructors, but instead with initialization and cleanup member functions using different names. A more common approach, however, is to have pointers to objects and to create them using **new** inside **Initializer( )**.

Technique two

Long after technique one was in use, someone (I don't know who) came up with the technique explained in this section, which is much simpler and cleaner than technique one. The fact that it took so long to discover is a tribute to the complexity of C++.

This technique relies on the fact that static objects inside functions are initialized the first time (only) that the function is called. Keep in mind that the problem we're really trying to solve here is not *when* the static objects are initialized (that can be controlled separately) but rather making sure that the initialization happens in the proper order.

This technique is very neat and clever. For any initialization dependency, you place a static object inside a function that returns a reference to that object. This way, the only way you can access the static object is by calling the function, and if that object needs to access other static objects on which it is dependent it must call *their* functions. And the first time a function is called, it forces the initialization to take place. The order of static initialization is guaranteed to be correct because of the design of the code, not because of an arbitrary order established by the linker.

To set up an example, here are two classes that depend on each other. The first one contains a **bool** that is initialized only by the constructor, so you can tell if the constructor has been called for a static instance of the class (the static storage area is initialized to zero at program startup, which produces a **false** value for the **bool** if the constructor has not been called):

```
//: C10:Dependency1.h
#ifndef DEPENDENCY1_H
#define DEPENDENCY1_H
```

```
#include <iostream>

class Dependency1 {
  bool init;
public:
  Dependency1() : init(true) {
    std::cout << "Dependency1 construction"
              << std::endl;
  }
  void print() const {
    std::cout << "Dependency1 init: "
              << init << std::endl;
  }
};
#endif // DEPENDENCY1_H ///:~
```

The constructor also announces when it is being called, and you can
print( ) the state of the object to find out if it has been initialized.

The second class is initialized from an object of the first class, which
is what will cause the dependency:

```
//: C10:Dependency2.h
#ifndef DEPENDENCY2_H
#define DEPENDENCY2_H
#include "Dependency1.h"

class Dependency2 {
  Dependency1 d1;
public:
  Dependency2(const Dependency1& dep1): d1(dep1){
    std::cout << "Dependency2 construction ";
    print();
  }
  void print() const { d1.print(); }
};
#endif // DEPENDENCY2_H ///:~
```

The constructor announces itself and prints the state of the **d1**
object so you can see if it has been initialized by the time the
constructor is called.

To demonstrate what can go wrong, the following file first puts the
static object definitions in the wrong order, as they would occur if

---

the linker happened to initialize the **Dependency2** object before the **Dependency1** object. Then the order is reversed to show how it works correctly if the order happens to be "right." Lastly, technique two is demonstrated.

To provide more readable output, the function **separator( )** is created. The trick is that you can't call a function globally unless that function is being used to perform the initialization of a variable, so **separator( )** returns a dummy value that is used to initialize a couple of global variables.

```cpp
//: C10:Technique2.cpp
#include "Dependency2.h"
using namespace std;

// Returns a value so it can be called as
// a global initializer:
int separator() {
  cout << "---------------------" << endl;
  return 1;
}

// Simulate the dependency problem:
extern Dependency1 dep1;
Dependency2 dep2(dep1);
Dependency1 dep1;
int x1 = separator();

// But if it happens in this order it works OK:
Dependency1 dep1b;
Dependency2 dep2b(dep1b);
int x2 = separator();

// Wrapping static objects in functions succeeds
Dependency1& d1() {
  static Dependency1 dep1;
  return dep1;
}

Dependency2& d2() {
  static Dependency2 dep2(d1());
  return dep2;
}
```

```
int main() {
  Dependency2& dep2 = d2();
} ///:~
```

The functions **d1( )** and **d2( )** wrap static instances of
Dependency1 and **Dependency2** objects. Now, the only way you
can get to the static objects is by calling the functions and that
forces static initialization on the first function call. This means that
initialization is guaranteed to be correct, which you'll see when you
run the program and look at the output.

Here's how you would actually organize the code to use the
technique. Ordinarily, the static objects would be defined in
separate files (because you're forced to for some reason; remember
that defining the static objects in separate files is what causes the
problem), so instead you define the wrapping functions in separate
files. But they'll need to be declared in header files:

```
//: C10:Dependency1StatFun.h
#ifndef DEPENDENCY1STATFUN_H
#define DEPENDENCY1STATFUN_H
#include "Dependency1.h"
extern Dependency1& d1();
#endif // DEPENDENCY1STATFUN_H ///:~
```

Actually, the "extern" is redundant for the function declaration.
Here's the second header file:

```
//: C10:Dependency2StatFun.h
#ifndef DEPENDENCY2STATFUN_H
#define DEPENDENCY2STATFUN_H
#include "Dependency2.h"
extern Dependency2& d2();
#endif // DEPENDENCY2STATFUN_H ///:~
```

Now, in the implementation files where you would previously have
placed the static object definitions, you instead place the wrapping
function definitions:

```
//: C10:Dependency1StatFun.cpp {O}
#include "Dependency1StatFun.h"
Dependency1& d1() {
```

```
  static Dependency1 dep1;
  return dep1;
} ///:~
```

Presumably, other code might also be placed in these files. Here's the other file:

```
//: C10:Dependency2StatFun.cpp {O}
#include "Dependency1StatFun.h"
#include "Dependency2StatFun.h"
Dependency2& d2() {
  static Dependency2 dep2(d1());
  return dep2;
} ///:~
```

So now there are two files that could be linked in any order and if they contained ordinary static objects could produce any order of initialization. But since they contain the wrapping functions, there's no threat of incorrect initialization:

```
//: C10:Technique2b.cpp
//{L} Dependency1StatFun Dependency2StatFun
#include "Dependency2StatFun.h"
int main() { d2(); } ///:~
```

When you run this program you'll see that the initialization of the **Dependency1** static object always happens before the initialization of the **Dependency2** static object. You can also see that this is a much simpler approach than technique one.

You might be tempted to write **d1( )** and **d2( )** as inline functions inside their respective header files, but this is something you must definitely not do. An inline function can be duplicated in every file in which it appears – and this duplication *includes* the static object definition. Because inline functions automatically default to internal linkage, this would result in having multiple static objects across the various translation units, which would certainly cause problems. So you must ensure that there is only one definition of each wrapping function, and this means not making the wrapping functions inline.

Alternate linkage specifications

What happens if you're writing a program in C++ and you want to use a C library? If you make the C function declaration,

```
float f(int a, char b);
```

the C++ compiler will decorate this name to something like **_f_int_char** to support function overloading (and type-safe linkage). However, the C compiler that compiled your C library has most definitely *not* decorated the name, so its internal name will be **_f**. Thus, the linker will not be able to resolve your C++ calls to **f( )**.

The escape mechanism provided in C++ is the *alternate linkage specification*, which was produced in the language by overloading the **extern** keyword. The **extern** is followed by a string that specifies the linkage you want for the declaration, followed by the declaration:

```
extern "C" float f(int a, char b);
```

This tells the compiler to give C linkage to **f( )** so that the compiler doesn't decorate the name. The only two types of linkage specifications supported by the standard are **"C"** and **"C++,"** but compiler vendors have the option of supporting other languages in the same way.

If you have a group of declarations with alternate linkage, put them inside braces, like this:

```
extern "C" {
  float f(int a, char b);
  double d(int a, char b);
}
```

Or, for a header file,

```
extern "C" {
#include "Myheader.h"
}
```

Most C++ compiler vendors handle the alternate linkage specifications inside their header files that work with both C and C++, so you don't have to worry about it.

Summary

The **static** keyword can be confusing because in some situations it controls the location of storage, and in others it controls visibility and linkage of a name.

With the introduction of C++ namespaces, you have an improved and more flexible alternative to control the proliferation of names in large projects.

The use of **static** inside classes is one more way to control names in a program. The names do not clash with global names, and the visibility and access is kept within the program, giving you greater control in the maintenance of your code.

Exercises

Solutions to selected exercises can be found in the electronic document *The Thinking in C++ Annotated Solution Guide*, available for a small fee from www.BruceEckel.com.

1. Create a function with a static variable that is a pointer (with a default argument of zero). When the caller provides a value for this argument it is used to point at the beginning of an array of **int**. If you call the function with a zero argument (using the default argument), the function returns the next value in the array, until it sees a "-1" value in the array (to act as an end-of-array indicator). Exercise this function in **main( )**.

2. Create a function that returns the next value in a Fibonacci sequence every time you call it. Add an argument that is a **bool** with a default value of **false** such that when you give the argument with **true** it "resets" the function to the beginning of the Fibonacci sequence. Exercise this function in **main( )**.

3. Create a class that holds an array of **ints**. Set the size of the array using **static const int** inside the class. Add a **const int** variable, and initialize it in the constructor initializer list; make the constructor **inline**. Add a **static int** member variable and initialize it to a specific value. Add a **static** member function that prints the **static** data member. Add an **inline** member function called **print( )** to print out all the values in the array and to call the **static** member function. Exercise this class in **main( )**.

4. Create a class called **Monitor** that keeps track of the number of times that its **incident( )** member function has been called. Add a **print( )** member function that displays the number of incidents. Now create a global function (not a member function) containing a **static Monitor** object. Each time you call the function it should call **incident( )**, then **print( )** to display the incident count. Exercise the function in **main( )**.

5. Modify the **Monitor** class from Exercise 4 so that you can **decrement( )** the incident count. Make a class **Monitor2** that takes as a constructor argument a pointer to a **Monitor1**, and which stores that pointer and calls **incident( )** and **print( )**. In the destructor for **Monitor2**, call **decrement( )** and **print( )**. Now make a **static** object of **Monitor2** inside a function. Inside **main( )**, experiment with calling the function and not calling the function to see what happens with the destructor of **Monitor2**.

6. Make a global object of **Monitor2** and see what happens.

7. Create a class with a destructor that prints a message and then calls **exit( )**. Create a global object of this class and see what happens.

8. In **StaticDestructors.cpp**, experiment with the order of constructor and destructor calls by calling **f( )** and **g( )** inside **main( )** in different orders. Does your compiler get it right?

9. In **StaticDestructors.cpp**, test the default error handling of your implementation by turning the original definition of **out** into an **extern** declaration and putting the actual definition after the definition of **a** (whose **Obj**

constructor sends information to **out**). Make sure there's nothing else important running on your machine when you run the program or that your machine will handle faults robustly.

10. Prove that file static variables in header files don't clash with each other when included in more than one **cpp** file.

11. Create a simple class containing an **int**, a constructor that initializes the **int** from its argument, a member function to set the **int** from its argument, and a **print( )** function that prints the **int**. Put your class in a header file, and include the header file in two **cpp** files. In one **cpp** file make an instance of your class, and in the other declare that identifier **extern** and test it inside **main( )**. Remember, you'll have to link the two object files or else the linker won't find the object.

12. Make the instance of the object in Exercise 11 **static** and verify that it cannot be found by the linker because of this.

13. Declare a function in a header file. Define the function in one **cpp** file and call it inside **main( )** in a second **cpp** file. Compile and verify that it works. Now change the function definition so that it is **static** and verify that the linker cannot find it.

14. Modify **Volatile.cpp** from Chapter 8 to make **comm::isr( )** something that could actually work as an interrupt service routine. Hint: an interrupt service routine doesn't take any arguments.

15. Write and compile a simple program that uses the **auto** and **register** keywords.

16. Create a header file containing a **namespace**. Inside the **namespace** create several function declarations. Now create a second header file that includes the first one and continues the **namespace**, adding several more function declarations. Now create a **cpp** file that includes the second header file. Alias your namespace to another (shorter) name. Inside a function definition, call one of your functions using scope resolution. Inside a separate function definition, write a **using** directive to introduce your namespace into that function scope, and show that

you don't need scope resolution to call the functions from your namespace.

17. Create a header file with an unnamed namespace. Include the header in two separate **cpp** files and show that an unnamed space is unique for each translation unit.

18. Using the header file from Exercise 17, show that the names in an unnamed namespace are automatically available in a translation unit without qualification.

19. Modify **FriendInjection.cpp** to add a definition for the friend function and to call the function inside **main( )**.

20. In **Arithmetic.cpp**, demonstrate that the **using** directive does not extend outside the function in which the directive was made.

21. Repair the problem in **OverridingAmbiguity.cpp**, first with scope resolution, then instead with a **using** declaration that forces the compiler to choose one of the identical function names.

22. In two header files, create two namespaces, each containing a class (with all inline definitions) with a name identical to that in the other namespace. Create a **cpp** file that includes both header files. Create a function, and inside the function use the **using** directive to introduce both namespaces. Try creating an object of the class and see what happens. Make the **using** directives global (outside of the function) to see if it makes any difference. Repair the problem using scope resolution, and create objects of both classes.

23. Repair the problem in Exercise 22 with a **using** declaration that forces the compiler to choose one of the identical class names.

24. Extract the namespace declarations in **BobsSuperDuperLibrary.cpp** and **UnnamedNamespaces.cpp** and put them in separate header files, giving the unnamed namespace a name in the process. In a third header file create a new namespace that combines the elements of the other two namespaces with **using** declarations. In **main( )**, introduce your new

namespace with a **using** directive and access all the elements of your namespace.

25. Create a header file that includes **<string>** and **<iostream>** but does not use any **using** directives or **using** declarations. Add "include guards" as you've seen in the header files in this book. Create a class with all inline functions that contains a **string** member, with a constructor that initializes that **string** from its argument and a **print( )** function that displays the **string**. Create a **cpp** file and exercise your class in **main( )**.

26. Create a class containing a **static double** and **long**. Write a **static** member function that prints out the values.

27. Create a class containing an **int**, a constructor that initializes the **int** from its argument, and a **print( )** function to display the **int**. Now create a second class that contains a **static** object of the first one. Add a **static** member function that calls the **static** object's **print( )** function. Exercise your class in **main( )**.

28. Create a class containing both a **const** and a non-**const** **static** array of **int**. Write **static** methods to print out the arrays. Exercise your class in **main( )**.

29. Create a class containing a **string**, with a constructor that initializes the **string** from its argument, and a **print( )** function to display the **string**. Create another class that contains both **const** and non-**const static** arrays of objects of the first class, and **static** methods to print out these arrays. Exercise this second class in **main( )**.

30. Create a **struct** that contains an **int** and a default constructor that initializes the **int** to zero. Make this **struct** local to a function. Inside that function, create an array of objects of your **struct** and demonstrate that each **int** in the array has automatically been initialized to zero.

31. Create a class that represents a printer connection, and that only allows you to have one printer.

32. In a header file, create a class **Mirror** that contains two data members: a pointer to a **Mirror** object and a **bool**. Give it two constructors: the default constructor

initializes the **bool** to **true** and the **Mirror** pointer to zero. The second constructor takes as an argument a pointer to a **Mirror** object, which it assigns to the object's internal pointer; it sets the **bool** to **false**. Add a member function **test( )**: if the object's pointer is nonzero, it returns the value of **test( )** called through the pointer. If the pointer is zero, it returns the **bool**. Now create five **cpp** files, each of which includes the **Mirror** header. The first **cpp** file defines a global **Mirror** object using the default constructor. The second file declares the object in the first file as **extern**, and defines a global **Mirror** object using the second constructor, with a pointer to the first object. Keep doing this until you reach the last file, which will also contain a global object definition. In that file, **main( )** should call the **test( )** function and report the result. If the result is **true**, find out how to change the linking order for your linker and change it until the result is **false**.

33. Repair the problem in Exercise 32 using technique one shown in this book.

34. Repair the problem in Exercise 32 using technique two shown in this book.

35. Without including a header file, declare the function **puts( )** from the Standard C Library. Call this function from **main( )**.

11: References & the Copy-Constructor

References are like constant pointers that are automatically dereferenced by the compiler.

Although references also exist in Pascal, the C++ version was taken from the Algol language. They are essential in C++ to support the syntax of operator overloading (see Chapter 12), but they are also a general convenience to control the way arguments are passed into and out of functions.

This chapter will first look briefly at the differences between pointers in C and C++, then introduce references. But the bulk of the chapter will delve into a rather confusing issue for the new C++ programmer: the copy-constructor, a special constructor (requiring references) that makes a new object from an existing object of the same type. The copy-constructor is used by the compiler to pass and return objects *by value* into and out of functions.

Finally, the somewhat obscure C++ *pointer-to-member* feature is illuminated.

Pointers in C++

The most important difference between pointers in C and those in C++ is that C++ is a more strongly typed language. This stands out where **void*** is concerned. C doesn't let you casually assign a pointer of one type to another, but it *does* allow you to accomplish this through a **void***. Thus,

```
bird* b;
rock* r;
void* v;
v = r;
b = v;
```

Because this "feature" of C allows you to quietly treat any type like any other type, it leaves a big hole in the type system. C++ doesn't allow this; the compiler gives you an error message, and if you really want to treat one type as another, you must make it explicit, both to the compiler and to the reader, using a cast. (Chapter 3 introduced C++'s improved "explicit" casting syntax.)

References in C++

A *reference* (**&**) is like a constant pointer that is automatically dereferenced. It is usually used for function argument lists and function return values. But you can also make a free-standing reference. For example,

```cpp
//: C11:FreeStandingReferences.cpp
#include <iostream>
using namespace std;

// Ordinary free-standing reference:
int y;
int& r = y;
// When a reference is created, it must
// be initialized to a live object.
// However, you can also say:
const int& q = 12;   // (1)
// References are tied to someone else's storage:
int x = 0;            // (2)
int& a = x;           // (3)
int main() {
  cout << "x = " << x << ", a = " << a << endl;
  a++;
  cout << "x = " << x << ", a = " << a << endl;
} ///:~
```

In line (1), the compiler allocates a piece of storage, initializes it with the value 12, and ties the reference to that piece of storage. The point is that any reference must be tied to someone *else's* piece of storage. When you access a reference, you're accessing that storage. Thus, if you write lines like (2) and (3), then incrementing **a** is actually incrementing **x**, as is shown in **main( )**. Again, the easiest way to think about a reference is as a fancy pointer. One advantage of this "pointer" is that you never have to wonder whether it's been initialized (the compiler enforces it) and how to dereference it (the compiler does it).

There are certain rules when using references:

1.   A reference must be initialized when it is created. (Pointers can be initialized at any time.)

2. Once a reference is initialized to an object, it cannot be changed to refer to another object. (Pointers can be pointed to another object at any time.)

3. You cannot have NULL references. You must always be able to assume that a reference is connected to a legitimate piece of storage.

References in functions

The most common place you'll see references is as function arguments and return values. When a reference is used as a function argument, any modification to the reference *inside* the function will cause changes to the argument *outside* the function. Of course, you could do the same thing by passing a pointer, but a reference has much cleaner syntax. (You can think of a reference as nothing more than a syntax convenience, if you want.)

If you return a reference from a function, you must take the same care as if you return a pointer from a function. Whatever the reference is connected to shouldn't go away when the function returns, otherwise you'll be referring to unknown memory.

Here's an example:

```
//: C11:Reference.cpp
// Simple C++ references

int* f(int* x) {
  (*x)++;
  return x; // Safe, x is outside this scope
}

int& g(int& x) {
  x++; // Same effect as in f()
  return x; // Safe, outside this scope
}

int& h() {
  int q;
//!  return q;   // Error
  static int x;
```

```
  return x; // Safe, x lives outside this scope
}

int main() {
  int a = 0;
  f(&a); // Ugly (but explicit)
  g(a);  // Clean (but hidden)
} ///:~
```

The call to **f( )** doesn't have the convenience and cleanliness of using references, but it's clear that an address is being passed. In the call to **g( )**, an address is being passed (via a reference), but you don't see it.

const references

The reference argument in **Reference.cpp** works only when the argument is a non-**const** object. If it is a **const** object, the function **g( )** will not accept the argument, which is actually a good thing, because the function *does* modify the outside argument. If you know the function will respect the **const**ness of an object, making the argument a **const** reference will allow the function to be used in all situations. This means that, for built-in types, the function will not modify the argument, and for user-defined types, the function will call only **const** member functions, and won't modify any **public** data members.

The use of **const** references in function arguments is especially important because your function may receive a temporary object. This might have been created as a return value of another function or explicitly by the user of your function. Temporary objects are always **const**, so if you don't use a **const** reference, that argument won't be accepted by the compiler. As a very simple example,

```
//: C11:ConstReferenceArguments.cpp
// Passing references as const

void f(int&) {}
void g(const int&) {}

int main() {
//!  f(1); // Error
  g(1);
```

```
} ///:~
```

The call to **f(1)** causes a compile-time error because the compiler must first create a reference. It does so by allocating storage for an **int**, initializing it to one and producing the address to bind to the reference. The storage *must* be a **const** because changing it would make no sense – you can never get your hands on it again. With all temporary objects you must make the same assumption: that they're inaccessible. It's valuable for the compiler to tell you when you're changing such data because the result would be lost information.

Pointer references

In C, if you want to modify the *contents* of the pointer rather than what it points to, your function declaration looks like:

```
void f(int**);
```

and you'd have to take the address of the pointer when passing it in:

```
int i = 47;
int* ip = &i;
f(&ip);
```

With references in C++, the syntax is cleaner. The function argument becomes a reference to a pointer, and you no longer have to take the address of that pointer. Thus,

```
//: C11:ReferenceToPointer.cpp
#include <iostream>
using namespace std;

void increment(int*& i) { i++; }

int main() {
  int* i = 0;
  cout << "i = " << i << endl;
  increment(i);
  cout << "i = " << i << endl;
} ///:~
```

By running this program, you'll prove to yourself that the pointer is incremented, not what it points to.

Argument-passing guidelines

Your normal habit when passing an argument to a function should be to pass by **const** reference. Although at first this may seem like only an efficiency concern (and you normally don't want to concern yourself with efficiency tuning while you're designing and assembling your program), there's more at stake: as you'll see in the remainder of the chapter, a copy-constructor is required to pass an object by value, and this isn't always available.

The efficiency savings can be substantial for such a simple habit: to pass an argument by value requires a constructor and destructor call, but if you're not going to modify the argument then passing by **const** reference only needs an address pushed on the stack.

In fact, virtually the only time passing an address *isn't* preferable is when you're going to do such damage to an object that passing by value is the only safe approach (rather than modifying the outside object, something the caller doesn't usually expect). This is the subject of the next section.

The copy-constructor

Now that you understand the basics of the reference in C++, you're ready to tackle one of the more confusing concepts in the language: the copy-constructor, often called **X(X&)** ("X of X ref"). This constructor is essential to control passing and returning of user-defined types by value during function calls. It's so important, in fact, that the compiler will automatically synthesize a copy-constructor if you don't provide one yourself, as you will see.

Passing & returning by value

To understand the need for the copy-constructor, consider the way C handles passing and returning variables by value during function calls. If you declare a function and make a function call,

```
int f(int x, char c);
int g = f(a, b);
```

how does the compiler know how to pass and return those variables? It just knows! The range of the types it must deal with is so small – **char**, **int**, **float**, **double**, and their variations – that this information is built into the compiler.

If you figure out how to generate assembly code with your compiler and determine the statements generated by the function call to **f( )**, you'll get the equivalent of:

```
push  b
push  a
call  f()
add   sp,4
mov   g, register a
```

This code has been cleaned up significantly to make it generic; the expressions for **b** and **a** will be different depending on whether the variables are global (in which case they will be _**b** and _**a**) or local (the compiler will index them off the stack pointer). This is also true for the expression for **g**. The appearance of the call to **f( )** will depend on your name-decoration scheme, and "register a" depends on how the CPU registers are named within your assembler. The logic behind the code, however, will remain the same.

In C and C++, arguments are first pushed on the stack from right to left, then the function call is made. The calling code is responsible for cleaning the arguments off the stack (which accounts for the **add sp,4**). But notice that to pass the arguments by value, the compiler simply pushes copies on the stack – it knows how big they are and that pushing those arguments makes accurate copies of them.

The return value of **f( )** is placed in a register. Again, the compiler knows everything there is to know about the return value type because that type is built into the language, so the compiler can return it by placing it in a register. With the primitive data types in C, the simple act of copying the bits of the value is equivalent to copying the object.

Passing & returning large objects

But now consider user-defined types. If you create a class and you want to pass an object of that class by value, how is the compiler supposed to know what to do? This is not a type built into the compiler; it's a type you have created.

To investigate this, you can start with a simple structure that is clearly too large to return in registers:

```
//: C11:PassingBigStructures.cpp
struct Big {
  char buf[100];
  int i;
  long d;
} B, B2;

Big bigfun(Big b) {
  b.i = 100; // Do something to the argument
  return b;
}

int main() {
  B2 = bigfun(B);
} ///:~
```

Decoding the assembly output is a little more complicated here because most compilers use "helper" functions instead of putting all functionality inline. In **main( )**, the call to **bigfun( )** starts as you might guess – the entire contents of **B** is pushed on the stack. (Here, you might see some compilers load registers with the address of the **Big** and its size, then call a helper function to push the **Big** onto the stack.)

In the previous code fragment, pushing the arguments onto the stack was all that was required before making the function call. In **PassingBigStructures.cpp**, however, you'll see an additional action: the address of **B2** is pushed before making the call, even though it's obviously not an argument. To comprehend what's going on here, you need to understand the constraints on the compiler when it's making a function call.

Function-call stack frame

When the compiler generates code for a function call, it first pushes all the arguments on the stack, then makes the call. Inside the function, code is generated to move the stack pointer down even farther to provide storage for the function's local variables. ("Down" is relative here; your machine may increment or decrement the stack pointer during a push.) But during the assembly-language CALL, the CPU pushes the address in the program code where the function call *came from*, so the assembly-language RETURN can use that address to return to the calling point. This address is of course sacred, because without it your program will get completely lost. Here's what the stack frame looks like after the CALL and the allocation of local variable storage in the function:

Function arguments
Return address
Local variables

The code generated for the rest of the function expects the memory to be laid out exactly this way, so that it can carefully pick from the function arguments and local variables without touching the return address. I shall call this block of memory, which is everything used by a function in the process of the function call, the *function frame*.

You might think it reasonable to try to return values on the stack. The compiler could simply push it, and the function could return an offset to indicate how far down in the stack the return value begins.

Re-entrancy

The problem occurs because functions in C and C++ support interrupts; that is, the languages are *re-entrant*. They also support recursive function calls. This means that at any point in the execution of a program an interrupt can occur without breaking the program. Of course, the person who writes the interrupt service routine (ISR) is responsible for saving and restoring all the registers that are used in the ISR, but if the ISR needs to use any memory further down on the stack, this must be a safe thing to do. (You can think of an ISR as an ordinary function with no arguments and **void** return value that saves and restores the CPU state. An ISR function call is triggered by some hardware event instead of an explicit call from within a program.)

Now imagine what would happen if an ordinary function tried to return values on the stack. You can't touch any part of the stack that's above the return address, so the function would have to push the values below the return address. But when the assembly-language RETURN is executed, the stack pointer must be pointing to the return address (or right below it, depending on your machine), so right before the RETURN, the function must move the stack pointer up, thus clearing off all its local variables. If you're trying to return values on the stack below the return address, you become vulnerable at that moment because an interrupt could come along. The ISR would move the stack pointer down to hold its return address and its local variables and overwrite your return value.

To solve this problem, the caller *could* be responsible for allocating the extra storage on the stack for the return values before calling the function. However, C was not designed this way, and C++ must be compatible. As you'll see shortly, the C++ compiler uses a more efficient scheme.

Your next idea might be to return the value in some global data area, but this doesn't work either. Reentrancy means that any function can be an interrupt routine for any other function, *including the same function you're currently inside*. Thus, if you put the return value in a global area, you might return into the same function, which would overwrite that return value. The same logic applies to recursion.

The only safe place to return values is in the registers, so you're back to the problem of what to do when the registers aren't large enough to hold the return value. The answer is to push the address of the return value's destination on the stack as one of the function arguments, and let the function copy the return information directly into the destination. This not only solves all the problems,

it's more efficient. It's also the reason that, in
PassingBigStructures.cpp, the compiler pushes the address of
B2 before the call to **bigfun( )** in **main( )**. If you look at the
assembly output for **bigfun( )**, you can see it expects this hidden
argument and performs the copy to the destination *inside* the
function.

Bitcopy versus initialization

So far, so good. There's a workable process for passing and
returning large simple structures. But notice that all you have is a
way to copy the bits from one place to another, which certainly
works fine for the primitive way that C looks at variables. But in
C++ objects can be much more sophisticated than a patch of bits;
they have meaning. This meaning may not respond well to having
its bits copied.

Consider a simple example: a class that knows how many objects of
its type exist at any one time. From Chapter 10, you know the way
to do this is by including a **static** data member:

```
//: C11:HowMany.cpp
// A class that counts its objects
#include <fstream>
#include <string>
using namespace std;
ofstream out("HowMany.out");

class HowMany {
  static int objectCount;
public:
  HowMany() { objectCount++; }
  static void print(const string& msg = "") {
    if(msg.size() != 0) out << msg << ": ";
    out << "objectCount = "
        << objectCount << endl;
  }
  ~HowMany() {
    objectCount--;
    print("~HowMany()");
  }
};
```

```
int HowMany::objectCount = 0;

// Pass and return BY VALUE:
HowMany f(HowMany x) {
  x.print("x argument inside f()");
  return x;
}

int main() {
  HowMany h;
  HowMany::print("after construction of h");
  HowMany h2 = f(h);
  HowMany::print("after call to f()");
} ///:~
```

The class **HowMany** contains a **static int objectCount** and a **static** member function **print( )** to report the value of that **objectCount**, along with an optional message argument. The constructor increments the count each time an object is created, and the destructor decrements it.

The output, however, is not what you would expect:

```
after construction of h: objectCount = 1
x argument inside f(): objectCount = 1
~HowMany(): objectCount = 0
after call to f(): objectCount = 0
~HowMany(): objectCount = -1
~HowMany(): objectCount = -2
```

After **h** is created, the object count is one, which is fine. But after the call to **f( )** you would expect to have an object count of two, because **h2** is now in scope as well. Instead, the count is zero, which indicates something has gone horribly wrong. This is confirmed by the fact that the two destructors at the end make the object count go negative, something that should never happen.

Look at the point inside **f( )**, which occurs after the argument is passed by value. This means the original object **h** exists outside the function frame, and there's an additional object *inside* the function frame, which is the copy that has been passed by value. However, the argument has been passed using C's primitive notion of bitcopying, whereas the C++ **HowMany** class requires true initialization to maintain its integrity, so the default bitcopy fails to produce the desired effect.

When the local object goes out of scope at the end of the call to **f( )**, the destructor is called, which decrements **objectCount**, so outside the function, **objectCount** is zero. The creation of **h2** is also performed using a bitcopy, so the constructor isn't called there either, and when **h** and **h2** go out of scope, their destructors cause the negative values of **objectCount**.

Copy-construction

The problem occurs because the compiler makes an assumption about how to create *a new object from an existing object*. When you pass an object by value, you create a new object, the passed object inside the function frame, from an existing object, the original object outside the function frame. This is also often true when returning an object from a function. In the expression

```
HowMany h2 = f(h);
```

h2, a previously unconstructed object, is created from the return value of **f( )**, so again a new object is created from an existing one.

The compiler's assumption is that you want to perform this creation using a bitcopy, and in many cases this may work fine, but in **HowMany** it doesn't fly because the meaning of initialization goes beyond simply copying. Another common example occurs if the class contains pointers – what do they point to, and should you copy them or should they be connected to some new piece of memory?

Fortunately, you can intervene in this process and prevent the compiler from doing a bitcopy. You do this by defining your own function to be used whenever the compiler needs to make a new object from an existing object. Logically enough, you're making a new object, so this function is a constructor, and also logically enough, the single argument to this constructor has to do with the object you're constructing from. But that object can't be passed into the constructor by value because you're trying to *define* the function that handles passing by value, and syntactically it doesn't make sense to pass a pointer because, after all, you're creating the new object from an existing object. Here, references come to the rescue, so you take the reference of the source object. This function is called the *copy-constructor* and is often referred to as **X(X&)**, which is its appearance for a class called **X**.

If you create a copy-constructor, the compiler will not perform a bitcopy when creating a new object from an existing one. It will always call your copy-constructor. So, if you don't create a copy-constructor, the compiler will do something sensible, but you have the choice of taking over complete control of the process.

Now it's possible to fix the problem in **HowMany.cpp**:

```cpp
//: C11:HowMany2.cpp
// The copy-constructor
#include <fstream>
#include <string>
using namespace std;
ofstream out("HowMany2.out");

class HowMany2 {
  string name; // Object identifier
  static int objectCount;
public:
  HowMany2(const string& id = "") : name(id) {
    ++objectCount;
    print("HowMany2()");
  }
  ~HowMany2() {
    --objectCount;
    print("~HowMany2()");
  }
  // The copy-constructor:
  HowMany2(const HowMany2& h) : name(h.name) {
    name += " copy";
    ++objectCount;
    print("HowMany2(const HowMany2&)");
  }
  void print(const string& msg = "") const {
    if(msg.size() != 0)
      out << msg << endl;
```

```
      out << '\t' << name << ": "
          << "objectCount = "
          << objectCount << endl;
  }
};

int HowMany2::objectCount = 0;

// Pass and return BY VALUE:
HowMany2 f(HowMany2 x) {
  x.print("x argument inside f()");
  out << "Returning from f()" << endl;
  return x;
}

int main() {
  HowMany2 h("h");
  out << "Entering f()" << endl;
  HowMany2 h2 = f(h);
  h2.print("h2 after call to f()");
  out << "Call f(), no return value" << endl;
  f(h);
  out << "After call to f()" << endl;
} ///:~
```

There are a number of new twists thrown in here so you can get a
better idea of what's happening. First, the **string name** acts as an
object identifier when information about that object is printed. In
the constructor, you can put an identifier string (usually the name
of the object) that is copied to **name** using the **string** constructor.
The default = "" creates an empty **string**. The constructor
increments the **objectCount** as before, and the destructor
decrements it.

Next is the copy-constructor, **HowMany2(const HowMany2&)**.
The copy-constructor can create a new object only from an existing
one, so the existing object's name is copied to **name**, followed by
the word "copy" so you can see where it came from. If you look
closely, you'll see that the call **name(h.name)** in the constructor
initializer list is actually calling the **string** copy-constructor.

Inside the copy-constructor, the object count is incremented just as it is inside the normal constructor. This means you'll now get an accurate object count when passing and returning by value.

The **print( )** function has been modified to print out a message, the object identifier, and the object count. It must now access the **name** data of a particular object, so it can no longer be a **static** member function.

Inside **main( )**, you can see that a second call to **f( )** has been added. However, this call uses the common C approach of ignoring the return value. But now that you know how the value is returned (that is, code *inside* the function handles the return process, putting the result in a destination whose address is passed as a hidden argument), you might wonder what happens when the return value is ignored. The output of the program will throw some illumination on this.

Before showing the output, here's a little program that uses iostreams to add line numbers to any file:

```
//: C11:Linenum.cpp
//{T} Linenum.cpp
// Add line numbers
#include "../require.h"
#include <vector>
#include <string>
#include <fstream>
#include <iostream>
#include <cmath>
using namespace std;

int main(int argc, char* argv[]) {
  requireArgs(argc, 1, "Usage: linenum file\n"
    "Adds line numbers to file");
  ifstream in(argv[1]);
  assure(in, argv[1]);
  string line;
  vector<string> lines;
  while(getline(in, line)) // Read in entire file
    lines.push_back(line);
  if(lines.size() == 0) return 0;
```

```
    int num = 0;
    // Number of lines in file determines width:
    const int width = int(log10(lines.size())) + 1;
    for(int i = 0; i < lines.size(); i++) {
      cout.setf(ios::right, ios::adjustfield);
      cout.width(width);
      cout << ++num << ") " << lines[i] << endl;
    }
  } ///:~
```

The entire file is read into a **vector<string>**, using the same code that you've seen earlier in the book. When printing the line numbers, we'd like all the lines to be aligned with each other, and this requires adjusting for the number of lines in the file so that the width allowed for the line numbers is consistent. We can easily determine the number of lines using **vector::size( )**, but what we really need to know is whether there are more than 10 lines, 100 lines, 1,000 lines, etc. If you take the logarithm, base 10, of the number of lines in the file, truncate it to an **int** and add one to the value, you'll find out the maximum width that your line count will be.

You'll notice a couple of strange calls inside the **for** loop: **setf( )** and **width( )**. These are **ostream** calls that allow you to control, in this case, the justification and width of the output. However, they must be called each time a line is output and that is why they are inside the **for** loop. Volume 2 of this book has an entire chapter explaining iostreams that will tell you more about these calls as well as other ways to control iostreams.

When **Linenum.cpp** is applied to **HowMany2.out**, the result is

```
 1) HowMany2()
 2)   h: objectCount = 1
 3) Entering f()
 4) HowMany2(const HowMany2&)
 5)   h copy: objectCount = 2
 6) x argument inside f()
 7)   h copy: objectCount = 2
 8) Returning from f()
 9) HowMany2(const HowMany2&)
10)   h copy copy: objectCount = 3
```

```
11)  ~HowMany2()
12)     h copy: objectCount = 2
13) h2 after call to f()
14)     h copy copy: objectCount = 2
15) Call f(), no return value
16) HowMany2(const HowMany2&)
17)     h copy: objectCount = 3
18) x argument inside f()
19)     h copy: objectCount = 3
20) Returning from f()
21) HowMany2(const HowMany2&)
22)     h copy copy: objectCount = 4
23) ~HowMany2()
24)     h copy: objectCount = 3
25) ~HowMany2()
26)     h copy copy: objectCount = 2
27) After call to f()
28) ~HowMany2()
29)     h copy copy: objectCount = 1
30) ~HowMany2()
31)     h: objectCount = 0
```

As you would expect, the first thing that happens is that the normal constructor is called for **h**, which increments the object count to one. But then, as **f( )** is entered, the copy-constructor is quietly called by the compiler to perform the pass-by-value. A new object is created, which is the copy of **h** (thus the name "h copy") inside the function frame of **f( )**, so the object count becomes two, courtesy of the copy-constructor.

Line eight indicates the beginning of the return from **f( )**. But before the local variable "h copy" can be destroyed (it goes out of scope at the end of the function), it must be copied into the return value, which happens to be **h2**. A previously unconstructed object (**h2**) is created from an existing object (the local variable inside **f( )**), so of course the copy-constructor is used again in line nine. Now the name becomes "h copy copy" for **h2**'s identifier because it's being copied from the copy that is the local object inside **f( )**. After the object is returned, but before the function ends, the object count becomes temporarily three, but then the local object "h copy" is destroyed. After the call to **f( )** completes in line 13, there are only two objects, **h** and **h2**, and you can see that **h2** did indeed end up as "h copy copy."

Temporary objects

Line 15 begins the call to **f(h)**, this time ignoring the return value. You can see in line 16 that the copy-constructor is called just as before to pass the argument in. And also, as before, line 21 shows the copy-constructor is called for the return value. But the copy-constructor must have an address to work on as its destination (a **this** pointer). Where does this address come from?

It turns out the compiler can create a temporary object whenever it needs one to properly evaluate an expression. In this case it creates one you don't even see to act as the destination for the ignored return value of **f( )**. The lifetime of this temporary object is as short as possible so the landscape doesn't get cluttered up with temporaries waiting to be destroyed and taking up valuable resources. In some cases, the temporary might immediately be passed to another function, but in this case it isn't needed after the function call, so as soon as the function call ends by calling the destructor for the local object (lines 23 and 24), the temporary object is destroyed (lines 25 and 26).

Finally, in lines 28-31, the **h2** object is destroyed, followed by **h**, and the object count goes correctly back to zero.

Default copy-constructor

Because the copy-constructor implements pass and return by value, it's important that the compiler creates one for you in the case of simple structures – effectively, the same thing it does in C. However, all you've seen so far is the default primitive behavior: a bitcopy.

When more complex types are involved, the C++ compiler will still automatically create a copy-constructor if you don't make one. Again, however, a bitcopy doesn't make sense, because it doesn't necessarily implement the proper meaning.

Here's an example to show the more intelligent approach the compiler takes. Suppose you create a new class composed of objects of several existing classes. This is called, appropriately enough, *composition*, and it's one of the ways you can make new classes from existing classes. Now take the role of a naive user who's trying to solve a problem quickly by creating a new class this way. You don't know about copy-constructors, so you don't create one. The example demonstrates what the compiler does while creating the default copy-constructor for your new class:

```cpp
//: C11:DefaultCopyConstructor.cpp
// Automatic creation of the copy-constructor
#include <iostream>
#include <string>
using namespace std;

class WithCC { // With copy-constructor
public:
  // Explicit default constructor required:
  WithCC() {}
  WithCC(const WithCC&) {
    cout << "WithCC(WithCC&)" << endl;
  }
};

class WoCC { // Without copy-constructor
  string id;
public:
  WoCC(const string& ident = "") : id(ident) {}
  void print(const string& msg = "") const {
    if(msg.size() != 0) cout << msg << ": ";
    cout << id << endl;
  }
};

class Composite {
  WithCC withcc; // Embedded objects
  WoCC wocc;
public:
  Composite() : wocc("Composite()") {}
  void print(const string& msg = "") const {
    wocc.print(msg);
  }
```

```
};

int main() {
  Composite c;
  c.print("Contents of c");
  cout << "Calling Composite copy-constructor"
       << endl;
  Composite c2 = c;  // Calls copy-constructor
  c2.print("Contents of c2");
} ///:~
```

The class **WithCC** contains a copy-constructor, which simply announces that it has been called, and this brings up an interesting issue. In the class **Composite**, an object of **WithCC** is created using a default constructor. If there were no constructors at all in **WithCC**, the compiler would automatically create a default constructor, which would do nothing in this case. However, if you add a copy-constructor, you've told the compiler you're going to handle constructor creation, so it no longer creates a default constructor for you and will complain unless you explicitly create a default constructor as was done for **WithCC**.

The class **WoCC** has no copy-constructor, but its constructor will store a message in an internal **string** that can be printed out using **print( )**. This constructor is explicitly called in **Composite**'s constructor initializer list (briefly introduced in Chapter 8 and covered fully in Chapter 14). The reason for this becomes apparent later.

The class **Composite** has member objects of both **WithCC** and **WoCC** (note the embedded object **wocc** is initialized in the constructor-initializer list, as it must be), and no explicitly defined copy-constructor. However, in **main( )** an object is created using the copy-constructor in the definition:

```
Composite c2 = c;
```

The copy-constructor for **Composite** is created automatically by the compiler, and the output of the program reveals the way that it is created:

```
Contents of c: Composite()
```

```
Calling Composite copy-constructor
WithCC(WithCC&)
Contents of c2: Composite()
```

To create a copy-constructor for a class that uses composition (and inheritance, which is introduced in Chapter 14), the compiler recursively calls the copy-constructors for all the member objects and base classes. That is, if the member object also contains another object, its copy-constructor is also called. So in this case, the compiler calls the copy-constructor for **WithCC**. The output shows this constructor being called. Because **WoCC** has no copy-constructor, the compiler creates one for it that just performs a bitcopy, and calls that inside the **Composite** copy-constructor. The call to **Composite::print( )** in main shows that this happens because the contents of **c2.wocc** are identical to the contents of **c.wocc**. The process the compiler goes through to synthesize a copy-constructor is called *memberwise initialization*.

It's always best to create your own copy-constructor instead of letting the compiler do it for you. This guarantees that it will be under your control.

Alternatives to copy-construction

At this point your head may be swimming, and you might be wondering how you could have possibly written a working class without knowing about the copy-constructor. But remember: You need a copy-constructor only if you're going to pass an object of your class *by value*. If that never happens, you don't need a copy-constructor.

Preventing pass-by-value

"But," you say, "if I don't make a copy-constructor, the compiler will create one for me. So how do I know that an object will never be passed by value?"

There's a simple technique for preventing pass-by-value: declare a **private** copy-constructor. You don't even need to create a definition, unless one of your member functions or a **friend** function needs to perform a pass-by-value. If the user tries to pass or return the object by value, the compiler will produce an error message because the copy-constructor is **private**. It can no longer create a default copy-constructor because you've explicitly stated that you're taking over that job.

Here's an example:

```
//: C11:NoCopyConstruction.cpp
// Preventing copy-construction

class NoCC {
  int i;
  NoCC(const NoCC&); // No definition
public:
  NoCC(int ii = 0) : i(ii) {}
};

void f(NoCC);

int main() {
  NoCC n;
//! f(n); // Error: copy-constructor called
//! NoCC n2 = n; // Error: c-c called
//! NoCC n3(n); // Error: c-c called
} ///:~
```

Notice the use of the more general form

```
NoCC(const NoCC&);
```

using the **const**.

Functions that modify outside objects

Reference syntax is nicer to use than pointer syntax, yet it clouds the meaning for the reader. For example, in the iostreams library one overloaded version of the **get( )** function takes a **char&** as an argument, and the whole point of the function is to modify its argument by inserting the result of the **get( )**. However, when you read code using this function it's not immediately obvious to you that the outside object is being modified:

```
char c;
cin.get(c);
```

Instead, the function call looks like a pass-by-value, which suggests the outside object is *not* modified.

Because of this, it's probably safer from a code maintenance standpoint to use pointers when you're passing the address of an argument to modify. If you *always* pass addresses as **const** references *except* when you intend to modify the outside object via the address, where you pass by non-**const** pointer, then your code is far easier for the reader to follow.

Pointers to members

A pointer is a variable that holds the address of some location. You can change what a pointer selects at runtime, and the destination of the pointer can be either data or a function. The C++ *pointer-to-member* follows this same concept, except that what it selects is a location inside a class. The dilemma here is that a pointer needs an address, but there is no "address" inside a class; selecting a member of a class means offsetting into that class. You can't produce an actual address until you combine that offset with the starting address of a particular object. The syntax of pointers to members requires that you select an object at the same time you're dereferencing the pointer to member.

To understand this syntax, consider a simple structure, with a pointer **sp** and an object **so** for this structure. You can select members with the syntax shown:

```
//: C11:SimpleStructure.cpp
struct Simple { int a; };
int main() {
  Simple so, *sp = &so;
  sp->a;
  so.a;
} ///:~
```

Now suppose you have an ordinary pointer to an integer, **ip**. To access what **ip** is pointing to, you dereference the pointer with a '*':

```
*ip = 4;
```

Finally, consider what happens if you have a pointer that happens to point to something inside a class object, even if it does in fact represent an offset into the object. To access what it's pointing at, you must dereference it with *. But it's an offset into an object, so you must also refer to that particular object. Thus, the * is combined with the object dereference. So the new syntax becomes −>* for a pointer to an object, and .* for the object or a reference, like this:

```
objectPointer->*pointerToMember = 47;
object.*pointerToMember = 47;
```

Now, what is the syntax for defining **pointerToMember**? Like any pointer, you have to say what type it's pointing at, and you use a * in the definition. The only difference is that you must say what class of objects this pointer-to-member is used with. Of course, this is accomplished with the name of the class and the scope resolution operator. Thus,

```
int ObjectClass::*pointerToMember;
```

defines a pointer-to-member variable called **pointerToMember** that points to any **int** inside **ObjectClass**. You can also initialize the pointer-to-member when you define it (or at any other time):

```
int ObjectClass::*pointerToMember = &ObjectClass::a;
```

There is actually no "address" of **ObjectClass::a** because you're just referring to the class and not an object of that class. Thus, **&ObjectClass::a** can be used only as pointer-to-member syntax.

Here's an example that shows how to create and use pointers to data members:

```
//: C11:PointerToMemberData.cpp
#include <iostream>
using namespace std;

class Data {
public:
  int a, b, c;
  void print() const {
```

```
      cout << "a = " << a << ", b = " << b
           << ", c = " << c << endl;
  }
};

int main() {
  Data d, *dp = &d;
  int Data::*pmInt = &Data::a;
  dp->*pmInt = 47;
  pmInt = &Data::b;
  d.*pmInt = 48;
  pmInt = &Data::c;
  dp->*pmInt = 49;
  dp->print();
} ///:~
```

Obviously, these are too awkward to use anywhere except for special cases (which is exactly what they were intended for).

Also, pointers to members are quite limited: they can be assigned only to a specific location inside a class. You could not, for example, increment or compare them as you can with ordinary pointers.

Functions

A similar exercise produces the pointer-to-member syntax for member functions. A pointer to a function (introduced at the end of Chapter 3) is defined like this:

```
int (*fp)(float);
```

The parentheses around **(*fp)** are necessary to force the compiler to evaluate the definition properly. Without them this would appear to be a function that returns an **int***.

Parentheses also play an important role when defining and using pointers to member functions. If you have a function inside a class, you define a pointer to that member function by inserting the class name and scope resolution operator into an ordinary function pointer definition:

```
//: C11:PmemFunDefinition.cpp
class Simple2 {
```

```
public:
  int f(float) const { return 1; }
};
int (Simple2::*fp)(float) const;
int (Simple2::*fp2)(float) const = &Simple2::f;
int main() {
  fp = &Simple2::f;
} ///:~
```

In the definition for **fp2** you can see that a pointer to member
function can also be initialized when it is created, or at any other
time. Unlike non-member functions, the **&** is *not* optional when
taking the address of a member function. However, you can give the
function identifier without an argument list, because overload
resolution can be determined by the type of the pointer to member.

An example

The value of a pointer is that you can change what it points to at
runtime, which provides an important flexibility in your
programming because through a pointer you can select or change
behavior at runtime. A pointer-to-member is no different; it allows
you to choose a member at runtime. Typically, your classes will only
have member functions publicly visible (data members are usually
considered part of the underlying implementation), so the following
example selects member functions at runtime.

```
//: C11:PointerToMemberFunction.cpp
#include <iostream>
using namespace std;

class Widget {
public:
  void f(int) const { cout << "Widget::f()\n"; }
  void g(int) const { cout << "Widget::g()\n"; }
  void h(int) const { cout << "Widget::h()\n"; }
  void i(int) const { cout << "Widget::i()\n"; }
};

int main() {
  Widget w;
  Widget* wp = &w;
  void (Widget::*pmem)(int) const = &Widget::h;
  (w.*pmem)(1);
```

```
    (wp->*pmem)(2);
} ///:~
```

Of course, it isn't particularly reasonable to expect the casual user
to create such complicated expressions. If the user must directly
manipulate a pointer-to-member, then a **typedef** is in order. To
really clean things up, you can use the pointer-to-member as part of
the internal implementation mechanism. Here's the preceding
example using a pointer-to-member *inside* the class. All the user
needs to do is pass a number in to select a function.[1]

```
//: C11:PointerToMemberFunction2.cpp
#include <iostream>
using namespace std;

class Widget {
  void f(int) const { cout << "Widget::f()\n"; }
  void g(int) const { cout << "Widget::g()\n"; }
  void h(int) const { cout << "Widget::h()\n"; }
  void i(int) const { cout << "Widget::i()\n"; }
  enum { cnt = 4 };
  void (Widget::*fptr[cnt])(int) const;
public:
  Widget() {
    fptr[0] = &Widget::f; // Full spec required
    fptr[1] = &Widget::g;
    fptr[2] = &Widget::h;
    fptr[3] = &Widget::i;
  }
  void select(int i, int j) {
    if(i < 0 || i >= cnt) return;
    (this->*fptr[i])(j);
  }
  int count() { return cnt; }
};

int main() {
  Widget w;
  for(int i = 0; i < w.count(); i++)
    w.select(i, 47);
} ///:~
```

---

[1] Thanks to Owen Mortensen for this example

In the class interface and in **main( )**, you can see that the entire implementation, including the functions, has been hidden away. The code must even ask for the **count( )** of functions. This way, the class implementer can change the quantity of functions in the underlying implementation without affecting the code where the class is used.

The initialization of the pointers-to-members in the constructor may seem overspecified. Shouldn't you be able to say

```
fptr[1] = &g;
```

because the name **g** occurs in the member function, which is automatically in the scope of the class? The problem is this doesn't conform to the pointer-to-member syntax, which is required so everyone, especially the compiler, can figure out what's going on. Similarly, when the pointer-to-member is dereferenced, it seems like

```
(this->*fptr[i])(j);
```

is also over-specified; **this** looks redundant. Again, the syntax requires that a pointer-to-member always be bound to an object when it is dereferenced.

Summary

Pointers in C++ are almost identical to pointers in C, which is good. Otherwise, a lot of C code wouldn't compile properly under C++. The only compile-time errors you will produce occur with dangerous assignments. If these are in fact what are intended, the compile-time errors can be removed with a simple (and explicit!) cast.

C++ also adds the *reference* from Algol and Pascal, which is like a constant pointer that is automatically dereferenced by the compiler. A reference holds an address, but you treat it like an object. References are essential for clean syntax with operator overloading (the subject of the next chapter), but they also add syntactic convenience for passing and returning objects for ordinary functions.

The copy-constructor takes a reference to an existing object of the same type as its argument, and it is used to create a new object from an existing one. The compiler automatically calls the copy-constructor when you pass or return an object by value. Although the compiler will automatically create a copy-constructor for you, if you think one will be needed for your class, you should always define it yourself to ensure that the proper behavior occurs. If you don't want the object passed or returned by value, you should create a private copy-constructor.

Pointers-to-members have the same functionality as ordinary pointers: You can choose a particular region of storage (data or function) at runtime. Pointers-to-members just happen to work with class members instead of with global data or functions. You get the programming flexibility that allows you to change behavior at runtime.

Exercises

Solutions to selected exercises can be found in the electronic document *The Thinking in C++ Annotated Solution Guide*, available for a small fee from www.BruceEckel.com.

1. Turn the "bird & rock" code fragment at the beginning of this chapter into a C program (using **struct**s for the data types), and show that it compiles. Now try to compile it with the C++ compiler and see what happens.
2. Take the code fragments in the beginning of the section titled "References in C++" and put them into a **main( )**. Add statements to print output so that you can prove to yourself that references are like pointers that are automatically dereferenced.
3. Write a program in which you try to (1) Create a reference that is not initialized when it is created. (2) Change a reference to refer to another object after it is initialized. (3) Create a NULL reference.

4. Write a function that takes a pointer argument, modifies what the pointer points to, and then returns the destination of the pointer as a reference.

5. Create a class with some member functions, and make that the object that is pointed to by the argument of Exercise 4. Make the pointer a **const** and make some of the member functions **const** and prove that you can only call the **const** member functions inside your function. Make the argument to your function a reference instead of a pointer.

6. Take the code fragments at the beginning of the section titled "Pointer references" and turn them into a program.

7. Create a function that takes an argument of a reference to a pointer to a pointer and modifies that argument. In **main( )**, call the function.

8. Create a function that takes a **char&** argument and modifies that argument. In **main( )**, print out a **char** variable, call your function for that variable, and print it out again to prove to yourself that it has been changed. How does this affect program readability?

9. Write a class that has a **const** member function and a non-**const** member function. Write three functions that take an object of that class as an argument; the first takes it by value, the second by reference, and the third by **const** reference. Inside the functions, try to call both member functions of your class and explain the results.

10. (Somewhat challenging) Write a simple function that takes an **int** as an argument, increments the value, and returns it. In **main( )**, call your function. Now discover how your compiler generates assembly code and trace through the assembly statements so that you understand how arguments are passed and returned, and how local variables are indexed off the stack.

11. Write a function that takes as its arguments a **char**, **int**, **float**, and **double**. Generate assembly code with your compiler and find the statements that push the arguments on the stack before a function call.

12. Write a function that returns a **double**. Generate assembly code and determine how the value is returned.

13. Produce assembly code for
    PassingBigStructures.cpp. Trace through and
    demystify the way your compiler generates code to pass
    and return large structures.

14. Write a simple recursive function that decrements its
    argument and returns zero if the argument becomes zero,
    otherwise it calls itself. Generate assembly code for this
    function and explain how the way that the assembly code
    is created by the compiler supports recursion.

15. Write code to prove that the compiler automatically
    synthesizes a copy-constructor if you don't create one
    yourself. Prove that the synthesized copy-constructor
    performs a bitcopy of primitive types and calls the copy-
    constructor of user-defined types.

16. Write a class with a copy-constructor that announces
    itself to **cout**. Now create a function that passes an object
    of your new class in by value and another one that creates
    a local object of your new class and returns it by value.
    Call these functions to prove to yourself that the copy-
    constructor is indeed quietly called when passing and
    returning objects by value.

17. Create a class that contains a **double***. The constructor
    initializes the **double*** by calling **new double** and
    assigning a value to the resulting storage from the
    constructor argument. The destructor prints the value
    that's pointed to, assigns that value to -1, calls **delete** for
    the storage, and then sets the pointer to zero. Now create
    a function that takes an object of your class by value, and
    call this function in **main( )**. What happens? Fix the
    problem by writing a copy-constructor.

18. Create a class with a constructor that looks like a copy-
    constructor, but that has an extra argument with a
    default value. Show that this is still used as the copy-
    constructor.

19. Create a class with a copy-constructor that announces
    itself. Make a second class containing a member object of
    the first class, but do not create a copy-constructor. Show
    that the synthesized copy-constructor in the second class
    automatically calls the copy-constructor of the first class.

---

20. Create a very simple class, and a function that returns an object of that class by value. Create a second function that takes a reference to an object of your class. Call the first function as the argument of the second function, and demonstrate that the second function must use a **const** reference as its argument.

21. Create a simple class without a copy-constructor, and a simple function that takes an object of that class by value. Now change your class by adding a **private** declaration (only) for the copy-constructor. Explain what happens when your function is compiled.

22. This exercise creates an alternative to using the copy-constructor. Create a class **X** and declare (but don't define) a **private** copy-constructor. Make a public **clone( )** function as a **const** member function that returns a copy of the object that is created using **new**. Now write a function that takes as an argument a **const X&** and clones a local copy that can be modified. The drawback to this approach is that you are responsible for explicitly destroying the cloned object (using **delete**) when you're done with it.

23. Explain what's wrong with both **Mem.cpp** and **MemTest.cpp** from Chapter 7. Fix the problem.

24. Create a class containing a **double** and a **print( )** function that prints the **double**. In **main( )**, create pointers to members for both the data member and the function in your class. Create an object of your class and a pointer to that object, and manipulate both class elements via your pointers to members, using both the object and the pointer to the object.

25. Create a class containing an array of **int**. Can you index through this array using a pointer to member?

26. Modify **PmemFunDefinition.cpp** by adding an overloaded member function **f( )** (you can determine the argument list that causes the overload). Now make a second pointer to member, assign it to the overloaded version of **f( )**, and call the function through that pointer. How does the overload resolution happen in this case?

27. Start with **FunctionTable.cpp** from Chapter 3. Create a class that contains a **vector** of pointers to functions, with **add( )** and **remove( )** member functions to add and remove pointers to functions. Add a **run( )** function that moves through the **vector** and calls all of the functions.

28. Modify the above Exercise 27 so that it works with pointers to member functions instead.

12: Operator Overloading

Operator overloading is just "syntactic sugar," which means it is simply another way for you to make a function call.

The difference is that the arguments for this function don't appear inside parentheses, but instead they surround or are next to characters you've always thought of as immutable operators.

There are two differences between the use of an operator and an ordinary function call. The syntax is different; an operator is often "called" by placing it between or sometimes after the arguments. The second difference is that the compiler determines which "function" to call. For instance, if you are using the operator + with floating-point arguments, the compiler "calls" the function to perform floating-point addition (this "call" is typically the act of inserting in-line code, or a floating-point-processor instruction). If you use operator + with a floating-point number and an integer, the compiler "calls" a special function to turn the **int** into a **float**, and then "calls" the floating-point addition code.

But in C++, it's possible to define new operators that work with classes. This definition is just like an ordinary function definition except that the name of the function consists of the keyword **operator** followed by the operator. That's the only difference, and it becomes a function like any other function, which the compiler calls when it sees the appropriate pattern.

Warning & reassurance

It's tempting to become overenthusiastic with operator overloading. It's a fun toy, at first. But remember it's *only* syntactic sugar, another way of calling a function. Looking at it this way, you have no reason to overload an operator except if it will make the code involving your class easier to write and especially easier to *read*. (Remember, code is read much more than it is written.) If this isn't the case, don't bother.

Another common response to operator overloading is panic; suddenly, C operators have no familiar meaning anymore. "Everything's changed and all my C code will do different things!" This isn't true. All the operators used in expressions that contain only built-in data types cannot be changed. You can never overload operators such that

```
1 << 4;
```

behaves differently, or

```
1.414 << 2;
```

has meaning. Only an expression containing a user-defined type can have an overloaded operator.

Syntax

Defining an overloaded operator is like defining a function, but the name of that function is **operator@**, in which @ represents the operator that's being overloaded. The number of arguments in the overloaded operator's argument list depends on two factors:

1. Whether it's a unary operator (one argument) or a binary operator (two arguments).

2. Whether the operator is defined as a global function (one argument for unary, two for binary) or a member function (zero arguments for unary, one for binary – the object becomes the left-hand argument).

Here's a small class that shows the syntax for operator overloading:

```
//: C12:OperatorOverloadingSyntax.cpp
#include <iostream>
using namespace std;

class Integer {
  int i;
public:
  Integer(int ii) : i(ii) {}
  const Integer
  operator+(const Integer& rv) const {
    cout << "operator+" << endl;
    return Integer(i + rv.i);
  }
  Integer&
  operator+=(const Integer& rv) {
    cout << "operator+=" << endl;
```

```
      i += rv.i;
      return *this;
  }
};

int main() {
  cout << "built-in types:" << endl;
  int i = 1, j = 2, k = 3;
  k += i + j;
  cout << "user-defined types:" << endl;
  Integer ii(1), jj(2), kk(3);
  kk += ii + jj;
} ///:~
```

The two overloaded operators are defined as inline member functions that announce when they are called. The single argument is what appears on the right-hand side of the operator for binary operators. Unary operators have no arguments when defined as member functions. The member function is called for the object on the left-hand side of the operator.

For non-conditional operators (conditionals usually return a Boolean value), you'll almost always want to return an object or reference of the same type you're operating on if the two arguments are the same type. (If they're not the same type, the interpretation of what it should produce is up to you.) This way, complicated expressions can be built up:

```
kk += ii + jj;
```

The **operator+** produces a new **Integer** (a temporary) that is used as the **rv** argument for the **operator+=**. This temporary is destroyed as soon as it is no longer needed.

Overloadable operators

Although you can overload almost all the operators available in C, the use of operator overloading is fairly restrictive. In particular, you cannot combine operators that currently have no meaning in C (such as ** to represent exponentiation), you cannot change the evaluation precedence of operators, and you cannot change the number of arguments required by an operator. This makes sense – all of these actions would produce operators that confuse meaning rather than clarify it.

The next two subsections give examples of all the "regular" operators, overloaded in the form that you'll most likely use.

Unary operators

The following example shows the syntax to overload all the unary operators, in the form of both global functions (non-member **friend** functions) and as member functions. These will expand upon the **Integer** class shown previously and add a new **byte** class. The meaning of your particular operators will depend on the way you want to use them, but consider the client programmer before doing something unexpected.

Here is a catalog of all the unary functions:

```
//: C12:OverloadingUnaryOperators.cpp
#include <iostream>
using namespace std;

// Non-member functions:
class Integer {
  long i;
  Integer* This() { return this; }
public:
  Integer(long ll = 0) : i(ll) {}
  // No side effects takes const& argument:
  friend const Integer&
    operator+(const Integer& a);
  friend const Integer
    operator-(const Integer& a);
  friend const Integer
    operator~(const Integer& a);
  friend Integer*
    operator&(Integer& a);
  friend int
    operator!(const Integer& a);
  // Side effects have non-const& argument:
  // Prefix:
  friend const Integer&
```

```
    operator++(Integer& a);
  // Postfix:
  friend const Integer
    operator++(Integer& a, int);
  // Prefix:
  friend const Integer&
    operator--(Integer& a);
  // Postfix:
  friend const Integer
    operator--(Integer& a, int);
};

// Global operators:
const Integer& operator+(const Integer& a) {
  cout << "+Integer\n";
  return a; // Unary + has no effect
}
const Integer operator-(const Integer& a) {
  cout << "-Integer\n";
  return Integer(-a.i);
}
const Integer operator~(const Integer& a) {
  cout << "~Integer\n";
  return Integer(~a.i);
}
Integer* operator&(Integer& a) {
  cout << "&Integer\n";
  return a.This(); // &a is recursive!
}
int operator!(const Integer& a) {
  cout << "!Integer\n";
  return !a.i;
}
// Prefix; return incremented value
const Integer& operator++(Integer& a) {
  cout << "++Integer\n";
  a.i++;
  return a;
}
// Postfix; return the value before increment:
const Integer operator++(Integer& a, int) {
  cout << "Integer++\n";
  Integer before(a.i);
  a.i++;
  return before;
```

```
}
// Prefix; return decremented value
const Integer& operator--(Integer& a) {
  cout << "--Integer\n";
  a.i--;
  return a;
}
// Postfix; return the value before decrement:
const Integer operator--(Integer& a, int) {
  cout << "Integer--\n";
  Integer before(a.i);
  a.i--;
  return before;
}

// Show that the overloaded operators work:
void f(Integer a) {
  +a;
  -a;
  ~a;
  Integer* ip = &a;
  !a;
  ++a;
  a++;
  --a;
  a--;
}

// Member functions (implicit "this"):
class Byte {
  unsigned char b;
public:
  Byte(unsigned char bb = 0) : b(bb) {}
  // No side effects: const member function:
  const Byte& operator+() const {
    cout << "+Byte\n";
    return *this;
  }
  const Byte operator-() const {
    cout << "-Byte\n";
    return Byte(-b);
  }
  const Byte operator~() const {
    cout << "~Byte\n";
    return Byte(~b);
```

```
  }
  Byte operator!() const {
    cout << "!Byte\n";
    return Byte(!b);
  }
  Byte* operator&() {
    cout << "&Byte\n";
    return this;
  }
  // Side effects: non-const member function:
  const Byte& operator++() { // Prefix
    cout << "++Byte\n";
    b++;
    return *this;
  }
  const Byte operator++(int) { // Postfix
    cout << "Byte++\n";
    Byte before(b);
    b++;
    return before;
  }
  const Byte& operator--() { // Prefix
    cout << "--Byte\n";
    --b;
    return *this;
  }
  const Byte operator--(int) { // Postfix
    cout << "Byte--\n";
    Byte before(b);
    --b;
    return before;
  }
};

void g(Byte b) {
  +b;
  -b;
  ~b;
  Byte* bp = &b;
  !b;
  ++b;
  b++;
  --b;
  b--;
}
```

```
int main() {
  Integer a;
  f(a);
  Byte b;
  g(b);
} ///:~
```

The functions are grouped according to the way their arguments are passed. Guidelines for how to pass and return arguments are given later. The forms above (and the ones that follow in the next section) are typically what you'll use, so start with them as a pattern when overloading your own operators.

Increment & decrement

The overloaded ++ and − − operators present a dilemma because you want to be able to call different functions depending on whether they appear before (prefix) or after (postfix) the object they're acting upon. The solution is simple, but people sometimes find it a bit confusing at first. When the compiler sees, for example, **++a** (a pre-increment), it generates a call to **operator++(a)**; but when it sees **a++**, it generates a call to **operator++(a, int)**. That is, the compiler differentiates between the two forms by making calls to different overloaded functions. In **OverloadingUnaryOperators.cpp** for the member function versions, if the compiler sees **++b**, it generates a call to **B::operator++( )**; if it sees **b++** it calls **B::operator++(int)**.

All the user sees is that a different function gets called for the prefix and postfix versions. Underneath, however, the two functions calls have different signatures, so they link to two different function bodies. The compiler passes a dummy constant value for the **int** argument (which is never given an identifier because the value is never used) to generate the different signature for the postfix version.

Binary operators

The following listing repeats the example of **OverloadingUnaryOperators.cpp** for binary operators so you have an example of all the operators you might want to overload.

Again, both global versions and member function versions are shown.

```
//: C12:Integer.h
// Non-member overloaded operators
#ifndef INTEGER_H
#define INTEGER_H
#include <iostream>

// Non-member functions:
class Integer {
  long i;
public:
  Integer(long ll = 0) : i(ll) {}
  // Operators that create new, modified value:
  friend const Integer
    operator+(const Integer& left,
              const Integer& right);
  friend const Integer
    operator-(const Integer& left,
              const Integer& right);
  friend const Integer
    operator*(const Integer& left,
              const Integer& right);
  friend const Integer
    operator/(const Integer& left,
              const Integer& right);
  friend const Integer
    operator%(const Integer& left,
              const Integer& right);
  friend const Integer
    operator^(const Integer& left,
              const Integer& right);
  friend const Integer
    operator&(const Integer& left,
              const Integer& right);
  friend const Integer
    operator|(const Integer& left,
              const Integer& right);
  friend const Integer
    operator<<(const Integer& left,
               const Integer& right);
  friend const Integer
    operator>>(const Integer& left,
```

```
                  const Integer& right);
// Assignments modify & return lvalue:
friend Integer&
  operator+=(Integer& left,
             const Integer& right);
friend Integer&
  operator-=(Integer& left,
             const Integer& right);
friend Integer&
  operator*=(Integer& left,
             const Integer& right);
friend Integer&
  operator/=(Integer& left,
             const Integer& right);
friend Integer&
  operator%=(Integer& left,
             const Integer& right);
friend Integer&
  operator^=(Integer& left,
             const Integer& right);
friend Integer&
  operator&=(Integer& left,
             const Integer& right);
friend Integer&
  operator|=(Integer& left,
             const Integer& right);
friend Integer&
  operator>>=(Integer& left,
              const Integer& right);
friend Integer&
  operator<<=(Integer& left,
              const Integer& right);
// Conditional operators return true/false:
friend int
  operator==(const Integer& left,
             const Integer& right);
friend int
  operator!=(const Integer& left,
             const Integer& right);
friend int
  operator<(const Integer& left,
            const Integer& right);
friend int
  operator>(const Integer& left,
            const Integer& right);
```

```cpp
  friend int
    operator<=(const Integer& left,
               const Integer& right);
  friend int
    operator>=(const Integer& left,
               const Integer& right);
  friend int
    operator&&(const Integer& left,
               const Integer& right);
  friend int
    operator||(const Integer& left,
               const Integer& right);
  // Write the contents to an ostream:
  void print(std::ostream& os) const { os << i; }
};
#endif // INTEGER_H ///:~
```

```cpp
//: C12:Integer.cpp {O}
// Implementation of overloaded operators
#include "Integer.h"
#include "../require.h"

const Integer
  operator+(const Integer& left,
            const Integer& right) {
  return Integer(left.i + right.i);
}
const Integer
  operator-(const Integer& left,
            const Integer& right) {
  return Integer(left.i - right.i);
}
const Integer
  operator*(const Integer& left,
            const Integer& right) {
  return Integer(left.i * right.i);
}
const Integer
  operator/(const Integer& left,
            const Integer& right) {
  require(right.i != 0, "divide by zero");
  return Integer(left.i / right.i);
}
const Integer
  operator%(const Integer& left,
```

```
                  const Integer& right) {
    require(right.i != 0, "modulo by zero");
    return Integer(left.i % right.i);
}
const Integer
  operator^(const Integer& left,
            const Integer& right) {
    return Integer(left.i ^ right.i);
}
const Integer
  operator&(const Integer& left,
            const Integer& right) {
    return Integer(left.i & right.i);
}
const Integer
  operator|(const Integer& left,
            const Integer& right) {
    return Integer(left.i | right.i);
}
const Integer
  operator<<(const Integer& left,
             const Integer& right) {
    return Integer(left.i << right.i);
}
const Integer
  operator>>(const Integer& left,
             const Integer& right) {
    return Integer(left.i >> right.i);
}
// Assignments modify & return lvalue:
Integer& operator+=(Integer& left,
                    const Integer& right) {
    if(&left == &right) {/* self-assignment */}
    left.i += right.i;
    return left;
}
Integer& operator-=(Integer& left,
                    const Integer& right) {
    if(&left == &right) {/* self-assignment */}
    left.i -= right.i;
    return left;
}
Integer& operator*=(Integer& left,
                    const Integer& right) {
    if(&left == &right) {/* self-assignment */}
```

```
      left.i *= right.i;
      return left;
   }
   Integer& operator/=(Integer& left,
                       const Integer& right) {
      require(right.i != 0, "divide by zero");
      if(&left == &right) {/* self-assignment */}
      left.i /= right.i;
      return left;
   }
   Integer& operator%=(Integer& left,
                       const Integer& right) {
      require(right.i != 0, "modulo by zero");
      if(&left == &right) {/* self-assignment */}
      left.i %= right.i;
      return left;
   }
   Integer& operator^=(Integer& left,
                       const Integer& right) {
      if(&left == &right) {/* self-assignment */}
      left.i ^= right.i;
      return left;
   }
   Integer& operator&=(Integer& left,
                       const Integer& right) {
      if(&left == &right) {/* self-assignment */}
      left.i &= right.i;
      return left;
   }
   Integer& operator|=(Integer& left,
                       const Integer& right) {
      if(&left == &right) {/* self-assignment */}
      left.i |= right.i;
      return left;
   }
   Integer& operator>>=(Integer& left,
                       const Integer& right) {
      if(&left == &right) {/* self-assignment */}
      left.i >>= right.i;
      return left;
   }
   Integer& operator<<=(Integer& left,
                       const Integer& right) {
      if(&left == &right) {/* self-assignment */}
      left.i <<= right.i;
```

```cpp
    return left;
}
// Conditional operators return true/false:
int operator==(const Integer& left,
               const Integer& right) {
    return left.i == right.i;
}
int operator!=(const Integer& left,
               const Integer& right) {
    return left.i != right.i;
}
int operator<(const Integer& left,
              const Integer& right) {
    return left.i < right.i;
}
int operator>(const Integer& left,
              const Integer& right) {
    return left.i > right.i;
}
int operator<=(const Integer& left,
               const Integer& right) {
    return left.i <= right.i;
}
int operator>=(const Integer& left,
               const Integer& right) {
    return left.i >= right.i;
}
int operator&&(const Integer& left,
               const Integer& right) {
    return left.i && right.i;
}
int operator||(const Integer& left,
               const Integer& right) {
    return left.i || right.i;
} ///:~

//: C12:IntegerTest.cpp
//{L} Integer
#include "Integer.h"
#include <fstream>
using namespace std;
ofstream out("IntegerTest.out");

void h(Integer& c1, Integer& c2) {
    // A complex expression:
```

```
  c1 += c1 * c2 + c2 % c1;
  #define TRY(OP) \
    out << "c1 = "; c1.print(out); \
    out << ", c2 = "; c2.print(out); \
    out << ";  c1 " #OP " c2 produces "; \
    (c1 OP c2).print(out); \
    out << endl;
  TRY(+) TRY(-) TRY(*) TRY(/)
  TRY(%) TRY(^) TRY(&) TRY(|)
  TRY(<<) TRY(>>) TRY(+=) TRY(-=)
  TRY(*=) TRY(/=) TRY(%=) TRY(^=)
  TRY(&=) TRY(|=) TRY(>>=) TRY(<<=)
  // Conditionals:
  #define TRYC(OP) \
    out << "c1 = "; c1.print(out); \
    out << ", c2 = "; c2.print(out); \
    out << ";  c1 " #OP " c2 produces "; \
    out << (c1 OP c2); \
    out << endl;
  TRYC(<) TRYC(>) TRYC(==) TRYC(!=) TRYC(<=)
  TRYC(>=) TRYC(&&) TRYC(||)
}

int main() {
  cout << "friend functions" << endl;
  Integer c1(47), c2(9);
  h(c1, c2);
} ///:~

//: C12:Byte.h
// Member overloaded operators
#ifndef BYTE_H
#define BYTE_H
#include "../require.h"
#include <iostream>
// Member functions (implicit "this"):
class Byte {
  unsigned char b;
public:
  Byte(unsigned char bb = 0) : b(bb) {}
  // No side effects: const member function:
  const Byte
    operator+(const Byte& right) const {
    return Byte(b + right.b);
  }
```

```
const Byte
  operator-(const Byte& right) const {
  return Byte(b - right.b);
}
const Byte
  operator*(const Byte& right) const {
  return Byte(b * right.b);
}
const Byte
  operator/(const Byte& right) const {
  require(right.b != 0, "divide by zero");
  return Byte(b / right.b);
}
const Byte
  operator%(const Byte& right) const {
  require(right.b != 0, "modulo by zero");
  return Byte(b % right.b);
}
const Byte
  operator^(const Byte& right) const {
  return Byte(b ^ right.b);
}
const Byte
  operator&(const Byte& right) const {
  return Byte(b & right.b);
}
const Byte
  operator|(const Byte& right) const {
  return Byte(b | right.b);
}
const Byte
  operator<<(const Byte& right) const {
  return Byte(b << right.b);
}
const Byte
  operator>>(const Byte& right) const {
  return Byte(b >> right.b);
}
// Assignments modify & return lvalue.
// operator= can only be a member function:
Byte& operator=(const Byte& right) {
  // Handle self-assignment:
  if(this == &right) return *this;
  b = right.b;
  return *this;
```

```
  }
  Byte& operator+=(const Byte& right) {
    if(this == &right) {/* self-assignment */}
    b += right.b;
    return *this;
  }
  Byte& operator-=(const Byte& right) {
    if(this == &right) {/* self-assignment */}
    b -= right.b;
    return *this;
  }
  Byte& operator*=(const Byte& right) {
    if(this == &right) {/* self-assignment */}
    b *= right.b;
    return *this;
  }
  Byte& operator/=(const Byte& right) {
    require(right.b != 0, "divide by zero");
    if(this == &right) {/* self-assignment */}
    b /= right.b;
    return *this;
  }
  Byte& operator%=(const Byte& right) {
    require(right.b != 0, "modulo by zero");
    if(this == &right) {/* self-assignment */}
    b %= right.b;
    return *this;
  }
  Byte& operator^=(const Byte& right) {
    if(this == &right) {/* self-assignment */}
    b ^= right.b;
    return *this;
  }
  Byte& operator&=(const Byte& right) {
    if(this == &right) {/* self-assignment */}
    b &= right.b;
    return *this;
  }
  Byte& operator|=(const Byte& right) {
    if(this == &right) {/* self-assignment */}
    b |= right.b;
    return *this;
  }
  Byte& operator>>=(const Byte& right) {
    if(this == &right) {/* self-assignment */}
```

```
    b >>= right.b;
    return *this;
  }
  Byte& operator<<=(const Byte& right) {
    if(this == &right) {/* self-assignment */}
    b <<= right.b;
    return *this;
  }
  // Conditional operators return true/false:
  int operator==(const Byte& right) const {
      return b == right.b;
  }
  int operator!=(const Byte& right) const {
      return b != right.b;
  }
  int operator<(const Byte& right) const {
      return b < right.b;
  }
  int operator>(const Byte& right) const {
      return b > right.b;
  }
  int operator<=(const Byte& right) const {
      return b <= right.b;
  }
  int operator>=(const Byte& right) const {
      return b >= right.b;
  }
  int operator&&(const Byte& right) const {
      return b && right.b;
  }
  int operator||(const Byte& right) const {
      return b || right.b;
  }
  // Write the contents to an ostream:
  void print(std::ostream& os) const {
    os << "0x" << std::hex << int(b) << std::dec;
  }
};
#endif // BYTE_H ///:~

//: C12:ByteTest.cpp
#include "Byte.h"
#include <fstream>
using namespace std;
ofstream out("ByteTest.out");
```

```
void k(Byte& b1, Byte& b2) {
  b1 = b1 * b2 + b2 % b1;

  #define TRY2(OP) \
    out << "b1 = "; b1.print(out); \
    out << ", b2 = "; b2.print(out); \
    out << ";  b1 " #OP " b2 produces "; \
    (b1 OP b2).print(out); \
    out << endl;

  b1 = 9; b2 = 47;
  TRY2(+)  TRY2(-)  TRY2(*)  TRY2(/)
  TRY2(%)  TRY2(^)  TRY2(&)  TRY2(|)
  TRY2(<<)  TRY2(>>)  TRY2(+=)  TRY2(-=)
  TRY2(*=)  TRY2(/=)  TRY2(%=)  TRY2(^=)
  TRY2(&=)  TRY2(|=)  TRY2(>>=)  TRY2(<<=)
  TRY2(=) // Assignment operator

  // Conditionals:
  #define TRYC2(OP) \
    out << "b1 = "; b1.print(out); \
    out << ", b2 = "; b2.print(out); \
    out << ";  b1 " #OP " b2 produces "; \
    out << (b1 OP b2); \
    out << endl;

  b1 = 9; b2 = 47;
  TRYC2(<)  TRYC2(>)  TRYC2(==)  TRYC2(!=)  TRYC2(<=)
  TRYC2(>=)  TRYC2(&&)  TRYC2(||)

  // Chained assignment:
  Byte b3 = 92;
  b1 = b2 = b3;
}

int main() {
  out << "member functions:" << endl;
  Byte b1(47), b2(9);
  k(b1, b2);
} ///:~
```

You can see that **operator=** is only allowed to be a member
function. This is explained later.

Notice that all of the assignment operators have code to check for self-assignment; this is a general guideline. In some cases this is not necessary; for example, with **operator+=** you often *want* to say **A+=A** and have it add **A** to itself. The most important place to check for self-assignment is **operator=** because with complicated objects disastrous results may occur. (In some cases it's OK, but you should always keep it in mind when writing **operator=**.)

All of the operators shown in the previous two examples are overloaded to handle a single type. It's also possible to overload operators to handle mixed types, so you can add apples to oranges, for example. Before you start on an exhaustive overloading of operators, however, you should look at the section on automatic type conversion later in this chapter. Often, a type conversion in the right place can save you a lot of overloaded operators.

Arguments & return values

It may seem a little confusing at first when you look at **OverloadingUnaryOperators.cpp**, **Integer.h** and **Byte.h** and see all the different ways that arguments are passed and returned. Although you *can* pass and return arguments any way you want to, the choices in these examples were not selected at random. They follow a logical pattern, the same one you'll want to use in most of your choices.

1. As with any function argument, if you only need to read from the argument and not change it, default to passing it as a **const** reference. Ordinary arithmetic operations (like + and −, etc.) and Booleans will not change their arguments, so pass by **const** reference is predominantly what you'll use. When the function is a class member, this translates to making it a **const** member function. Only with the operator-assignments (like +=) and the **operator=**, which change the left-hand argument, is the left argument *not* a constant, but it's still passed in as an address because it will be changed.

2. The type of return value you should select depends on the expected meaning of the operator. (Again, you can do anything you want with the arguments and return values.) If

the effect of the operator is to produce a new value, you will need to generate a new object as the return value. For example, **Integer::operator+** must produce an **Integer** object that is the sum of the operands. This object is returned by value as a **const**, so the result cannot be modified as an lvalue.

3.   All the assignment operators modify the lvalue. To allow the result of the assignment to be used in chained expressions, like **a=b=c**, it's expected that you will return a reference to that same lvalue that was just modified. But should this reference be a **const** or non**const**? Although you read **a=b=c** from left to right, the compiler parses it from right to left, so you're not forced to return a non**const** to support assignment chaining. However, people do sometimes expect to be able to perform an operation on the thing that was just assigned to, such as **(a=b).func( );** to call **func( )** on **a** after assigning **b** to it. Thus, the return value for all of the assignment operators should be a non**const** reference to the lvalue.

4.   For the logical operators, everyone expects to get at worst an **int** back, and at best a **bool**. (Libraries developed before most compilers supported C++'s built-in **bool** will use **int** or an equivalent **typedef**.)

The increment and decrement operators present a dilemma because of the pre- and postfix versions. Both versions change the object and so cannot treat the object as a **const**. The prefix version returns the value of the object after it was changed, so you expect to get back the object that was changed. Thus, with prefix you can just return ***this** as a reference. The postfix version is supposed to return the value *before* the value is changed, so you're forced to create a separate object to represent that value and return it. So with postfix you must return by value if you want to preserve the expected meaning. (Note that you'll sometimes find the increment and decrement operators returning an **int** or **bool** to indicate, for example, whether an object designed to move through a list is at the end of that list.) Now the question is: Should these be returned as **const** or non**const**? If you allow the object to be modified and someone writes **(++a).func( )**, **func( )** will be operating on **a** itself, but with **(a++).func( )**, **func( )** operates on the temporary object returned by the postfix **operator++**. Temporary objects are automatically **const**, so this would be flagged by the compiler, but for consistency's sake it may make more sense to make them both **const**, as was done here. Or you may choose to make the prefix version non-**const** and the postfix **const**. Because of the variety of meanings you may want to give the increment and decrement operators, they will need to be considered on a case-by-case basis.

Return by value as const

Returning by value as a **const** can seem a bit subtle at first, so it deserves a bit more explanation. Consider the binary **operator+**. If you use it in an expression such as **f(a+b)**, the result of **a+b** becomes a temporary object that is used in the call to **f( )**. Because it's a temporary, it's automatically **const**, so whether you explicitly make the return value **const** or not has no effect.

However, it's also possible for you to send a message to the return value of **a+b**, rather than just passing it to a function. For example, you can say **(a+b).g( )**, in which **g( )** is some member function of **Integer**, in this case. By making the return value **const**, you state that only a **const** member function can be called for that return value. This is **const**-correct, because it prevents you from storing potentially valuable information in an object that will most likely be lost.

The return optimization

When new objects are created to return by value, notice the form used. In **operator+**, for example:

```
return Integer(left.i + right.i);
```

This may look at first like a "function call to a constructor," but it's not. The syntax is that of a temporary object; the statement says "make a temporary **Integer** object and return it." Because of this, you might think that the result is the same as creating a named local object and returning that. However, it's quite different. If you were to say instead:

```
Integer tmp(left.i + right.i);
return tmp;
```

three things will happen. First, the **tmp** object is created including its constructor call. Second, the copy-constructor copies the **tmp** to the location of the outside return value. Third, the destructor is called for **tmp** at the end of the scope.

In contrast, the "returning a temporary" approach works quite differently. When the compiler sees you do this, it knows that you have no other need for the object it's creating than to return it. The compiler takes advantage of this by building the object *directly* into the location of the outside return value. This requires only a single ordinary constructor call (no copy-constructor is necessary) and there's no destructor call because you never actually create a local object. Thus, while it doesn't cost anything but programmer awareness, it's significantly more efficient. This is often called the *return value optimization.*

Unusual operators

Several additional operators have a slightly different syntax for overloading.

The subscript, **operator[ ]**, must be a member function and it requires a single argument. Because **operator[ ]** implies that the object it's being called for acts like an array, you will often return a reference from this operator, so it can be conveniently used on the left-hand side of an equal sign. This operator is commonly overloaded; you'll see examples in the rest of the book.

The operators **new** and **delete** control dynamic storage allocation and can be overloaded in a number of different ways. This topic is covered in the Chapter 13.

Operator comma

The comma operator is called when it appears next to an object of the type the comma is defined for. However, "**operator,**" is *not* called for function argument lists, only for objects that are out in the open, separated by commas. There doesn't seem to be a lot of practical uses for this operator; it's in the language for consistency. Here's an example showing how the comma function can be called when the comma appears *before* an object, as well as after:

```
//: C12:OverloadingOperatorComma.cpp
#include <iostream>
using namespace std;

class After {
public:
  const After& operator,(const After&) const {
    cout << "After::operator,()" << endl;
    return *this;
  }
};

class Before {};

Before& operator,(int, Before& b) {
  cout << "Before::operator,()" << endl;
  return b;
}

int main() {
  After a, b;
  a, b;  // Operator comma called

  Before c;
  1, c;  // Operator comma called
} ///:~
```

The global function allows the comma to be placed before the object in question. The usage shown is fairly obscure and questionable. Although you would probably use a comma-separated list as part of a more complex expression, it's too subtle to use in most situations.

Operator->

The **operator->** is generally used when you want to make an object appear to be a pointer. Since such an object has more "smarts" built into it than exist for a typical pointer, an object like this is often called a *smart pointer*. These are especially useful if you want to "wrap" a class around a pointer to make that pointer safe, or in the common usage of an *iterator*, which is an object that

---

moves through a *collection* /*container* of other objects and selects
them one at a time, without providing direct access to the
implementation of the container. (You'll often find containers and
iterators in class libraries, such as in the Standard C++ Library,
described in Volume 2 of this book.)

A pointer dereference operator must be a member function. It has
additional, atypical constraints: It must return an object (or
reference to an object) that also has a pointer dereference operator,
or it must return a pointer that can be used to select what the
pointer dereference operator arrow is pointing at. Here's a simple
example:

```
//: C12:SmartPointer.cpp
#include <iostream>
#include <vector>
#include "../require.h"
using namespace std;

class Obj {
  static int i, j;
public:
  void f() const { cout << i++ << endl; }
  void g() const { cout << j++ << endl; }
};

// Static member definitions:
int Obj::i = 47;
int Obj::j = 11;

// Container:
class ObjContainer {
  vector<Obj*> a;
public:
  void add(Obj* obj) { a.push_back(obj); }
  friend class SmartPointer;
};

class SmartPointer {
  ObjContainer& oc;
  int index;
public:
  SmartPointer(ObjContainer& objc) : oc(objc) {
```

```
      index = 0;
  }
  // Return value indicates end of list:
  bool operator++() { // Prefix
    if(index >= oc.a.size()) return false;
    if(oc.a[++index] == 0) return false;
    return true;
  }
  bool operator++(int) { // Postfix
    return operator++(); // Use prefix version
  }
  Obj* operator->() const {
    require(oc.a[index] != 0, "Zero value "
      "returned by SmartPointer::operator->()");
    return oc.a[index];
  }
};

int main() {
  const int sz = 10;
  Obj o[sz];
  ObjContainer oc;
  for(int i = 0; i < sz; i++)
    oc.add(&o[i]); // Fill it up
  SmartPointer sp(oc); // Create an iterator
  do {
    sp->f(); // Pointer dereference operator call
    sp->g();
  } while(sp++);
} ///:~
```

The class **Obj** defines the objects that are manipulated in this
program. The functions **f( )** and **g( )** simply print out interesting
values using **static** data members. Pointers to these objects are
stored inside containers of type **ObjContainer** using its **add( )**
function. **ObjContainer** looks like an array of pointers, but you'll
notice there's no way to get the pointers back out again. However,
SmartPointer is declared as a **friend** class, so it has permission
to look inside the container. The **SmartPointer** class looks very
much like an intelligent pointer – you can move it forward using
operator++ (you can also define an **operator– –**), it won't go
past the end of the container it's pointing to, and it produces (via
the pointer dereference operator) the value it's pointing to. Notice

that the **SmartPointer** is a custom fit for the container it's created for; unlike an ordinary pointer, there isn't a "general purpose" smart pointer. You will learn more about the smart pointers called "iterators" in the last chapter of this book and in Volume 2 (downloadable from *www.BruceEckel.com*).

In **main( )**, once the container **oc** is filled with **Obj** objects, a **SmartPointer sp** is created. The smart pointer calls happen in the expressions:

```
sp->f(); // Smart pointer calls
sp->g();
```

Here, even though **sp** doesn't actually have **f( )** and **g( )** member functions, the pointer dereference operator automatically calls those functions for the **Obj*** that is returned by **SmartPointer::operator–>**. The compiler performs all the checking to make sure the function call works properly.

Although the underlying mechanics of the pointer dereference operator are more complex than the other operators, the goal is exactly the same: to provide a more convenient syntax for the users of your classes.

A nested iterator

It's more common to see a "smart pointer" or "iterator" class nested within the class that it services. The previous example can be rewritten to nest **SmartPointer** inside **ObjContainer** like this:

```
//: C12:NestedSmartPointer.cpp
#include <iostream>
#include <vector>
#include "../require.h"
using namespace std;

class Obj {
  static int i, j;
public:
  void f() { cout << i++ << endl; }
  void g() { cout << j++ << endl; }
};
```

```cpp
// Static member definitions:
int Obj::i = 47;
int Obj::j = 11;

// Container:
class ObjContainer {
  vector<Obj*> a;
public:
  void add(Obj* obj) { a.push_back(obj); }
  class SmartPointer;
  friend SmartPointer;
  class SmartPointer {
    ObjContainer& oc;
    unsigned int index;
  public:
    SmartPointer(ObjContainer& objc) : oc(objc) {
      index = 0;
    }
    // Return value indicates end of list:
    bool operator++() { // Prefix
      if(index >= oc.a.size()) return false;
      if(oc.a[++index] == 0) return false;
      return true;
    }
    bool operator++(int) { // Postfix
      return operator++(); // Use prefix version
    }
    Obj* operator->() const {
      require(oc.a[index] != 0, "Zero value "
        "returned by SmartPointer::operator->()");
      return oc.a[index];
    }
  };
  // Function to produce a smart pointer that
  // points to the beginning of the ObjContainer:
  SmartPointer begin() {
    return SmartPointer(*this);
  }
};

int main() {
  const int sz = 10;
  Obj o[sz];
  ObjContainer oc;
  for(int i = 0; i < sz; i++)
```

```
    oc.add(&o[i]); // Fill it up
  ObjContainer::SmartPointer sp = oc.begin();
  do {
    sp->f(); // Pointer dereference operator call
    sp->g();
  } while(++sp);
} ///:~
```

Besides the actual nesting of the class, there are only two differences here. The first is in the declaration of the class so that it can be a **friend**:

```
class SmartPointer;
friend SmartPointer;
```

The compiler must first know that the class exists before it can be told that it's a **friend**.

The second difference is in the **ObjContainer** member function **begin( )**, which produces a **SmartPointer** that points to the beginning of the **ObjContainer** sequence. Although it's really only a convenience, it's valuable because it follows part of the form used in the Standard C++ Library.

Operator->*
The **operator->*** is a binary operator that behaves like all the other binary operators. It is provided for those situations when you want to mimic the behavior provided by the built-in *pointer-to-member* syntax, described in the previous chapter.

Just like **operator->**, the pointer-to-member dereference operator is generally used with some kind of object that represents a "smart pointer," although the example shown here will be simpler so it's understandable. The trick when defining **operator->*** is that it must return an object for which the **operator( )** can be called with the arguments for the member function you're calling.

The *function call* **operator( )** must be a member function, and it is unique in that it allows any number of arguments. It makes your object look like it's actually a function. Although you could define several overloaded **operator( )** functions with different arguments, it's often used for types that only have a single operation, or at least an especially prominent one. You'll see in Volume 2 that the Standard C++ Library uses the function call operator in order to create "function objects."

To create an **operator->*** you must first create a class with an **operator( )** that is the type of object that **operator->*** will return. This class must somehow capture the necessary information so that when the **operator( )** is called (which happens automatically), the pointer-to-member will be dereferenced for the object. In the following example, the **FunctionObject** constructor captures and stores both the pointer to the object and the pointer to the member function, and then the **operator( )** uses those to make the actual pointer-to-member call:

```
//: C12:PointerToMemberOperator.cpp
#include <iostream>
using namespace std;

class Dog {
public:
  int run(int i) const {
    cout << "run\n";
    return i;
  }
  int eat(int i) const {
    cout << "eat\n";
    return i;
  }
  int sleep(int i) const {
    cout << "ZZZ\n";
    return i;
  }
  typedef int (Dog::*PMF)(int) const;
  // operator->* must return an object
  // that has an operator():
  class FunctionObject {
    Dog* ptr;
    PMF pmem;
  public:
    // Save the object pointer and member pointer
    FunctionObject(Dog* wp, PMF pmf)
      : ptr(wp), pmem(pmf) {
```

```
      cout << "FunctionObject constructor\n";
    }
    // Make the call using the object pointer
    // and member pointer
    int operator()(int i) const {
      cout << "FunctionObject::operator()\n";
      return (ptr->*pmem)(i); // Make the call
    }
  };
  FunctionObject operator->*(PMF pmf) {
    cout << "operator->*" << endl;
    return FunctionObject(this, pmf);
  }
};

int main() {
  Dog· w;
  Dog::PMF pmf = &Dog::run;
  cout << (w->*pmf)(1) << endl;
  pmf = &Dog::sleep;
  cout << (w->*pmf)(2) << endl;
  pmf = &Dog::eat;
  cout << (w->*pmf)(3) << endl;
} ///:~
```

Dog has three member functions, all of which take an **int** argument and return an **int**. **PMF** is a **typedef** to simplify defining a pointer-to-member to **Dog**'s member functions.

A **FunctionObject** is created and returned by **operator->***. Notice that **operator->*** knows both the object that the pointer-to-member is being called for (**this**) and the pointer-to-member, and it passes those to the **FunctionObject** constructor that stores the values. When **operator->*** is called, the compiler immediately turns around and calls **operator( )** for the return value of **operator->***, passing in the arguments that were given to **operator->***. The **FunctionObject::operator( )** takes the arguments and then dereferences the "real" pointer-to-member using its stored object pointer and pointer-to-member.

Notice that what you are doing here, just as with **operator->**, is inserting yourself in the middle of the call to **operator->***. This allows you to perform some extra operations if you need to.

The **operator->*** mechanism implemented here only works for member functions that take an **int** argument and return an **int**. This is limiting, but if you try to create overloaded mechanisms for each different possibility, it seems like a prohibitive task. Fortunately, C++'s **template** mechanism (described in the last chapter of this book, and in Volume 2) is designed to handle just such a problem.

Operators you can't overload

There are certain operators in the available set that cannot be overloaded. The general reason for the restriction is safety. If these operators were overloadable, it would somehow jeopardize or break safety mechanisms, make things harder, or confuse existing practice.

- The member selection **operator..** Currently, the dot has a meaning for any member in a class, but if you allow it to be overloaded, then you couldn't access members in the normal way; instead you'd have to use a pointer and the arrow **operator->**.

- The pointer to member dereference **operator.***, for the same reason as **operator..**

- There's no exponentiation operator. The most popular choice for this was **operator**** from Fortran, but this raised difficult parsing questions. Also, C has no exponentiation operator, so C++ didn't seem to need one either because you can always perform a function call. An exponentiation operator would add a convenient notation, but no new language functionality to account for the added complexity of the compiler.

- There are no user-defined operators. That is, you can't make up new operators that aren't currently in the set. Part of the problem is how to determine precedence, and part of the problem is an insufficient need to account for the necessary trouble.

- You can't change the precedence rules. They're hard enough to remember as it is without letting people play with them.

Non-member operators

In some of the previous examples, the operators may be members or non-members, and it doesn't seem to make much difference. This usually raises the question, "Which should I choose?" In general, if it doesn't make any difference, they should be members, to emphasize the association between the operator and its class. When the left-hand operand is always an object of the current class, this works fine.

However, sometimes you want the left-hand operand to be an object of some other class. A common place you'll see this is when the operators << and >> are overloaded for iostreams. Since iostreams is a fundamental C++ library, you'll probably want to overload these operators for most of your classes, so the process is worth memorizing:

```
//: C12:IostreamOperatorOverloading.cpp
// Example of non-member overloaded operators
#include "../require.h"
#include <iostream>
#include <sstream> // "String streams"
#include <cstring>
using namespace std;

class IntArray {
  enum { sz = 5 };
  int i[sz];
public:
  IntArray() { memset(i, 0, sz* sizeof(*i)); }
  int& operator[](int x) {
    require(x >= 0 && x < sz,
      "IntArray::operator[] out of range");
    return i[x];
  }
  friend ostream&
    operator<<(ostream& os, const IntArray& ia);
  friend istream&
```

```
      operator>>(istream& is, IntArray& ia);
};

ostream&
operator<<(ostream& os, const IntArray& ia) {
  for(int j = 0; j < ia.sz; j++) {
    os << ia.i[j];
    if(j != ia.sz -1)
      os << ", ";
  }
  os << endl;
  return os;
}

istream& operator>>(istream& is, IntArray& ia){
  for(int j = 0; j < ia.sz; j++)
    is >> ia.i[j];
  return is;
}

int main() {
  stringstream input("47 34 56 92 103");
  IntArray I;
  input >> I;
  I[4] = -1; // Use overloaded operator[]
  cout << I;
} ///:~
```

This class also contains an overloaded **operator [ ]**, which returns a reference to a legitimate value in the array. Because a reference is returned, the expression

```
I[4] = -1;
```

not only looks much more civilized than if pointers were used, it also accomplishes the desired effect.

It's important that the overloaded shift operators pass and return *by reference*, so the actions will affect the external objects. In the function definitions, expressions like

```
os << ia.i[j];
```

cause the *existing* overloaded operator functions to be called (that is, those defined in **<iostream>**). In this case, the function called is **ostream& operator<<(ostream&, int)** because **ia.i[j]** resolves to an **int**.

Once all the actions are performed on the **istream** or **ostream**, it is returned so it can be used in a more complicated expression.

In **main( )**, a new type of **iostream** is used: the **stringstream** (declared in **<sstream>**). This is a class that takes a **string** (which it can create from a **char** array, as shown here) and turns it into an **iostream**. In the example above, this means that the shift operators can be tested without opening a file or typing data in on the command line.

The form shown in this example for the inserter and extractor is standard. If you want to create these operators for your own class, copy the function signatures and return types above and follow the form of the body.

Basic guidelines

Murray[1] suggests these guidelines for choosing between members and non-members:

Operator	Recommended use
All unary operators	member
= ( ) [ ] –> –>*	*must* be member
+= –= /= *= ^= &= |= %= >>= <<=	member
All other binary operators	non-member

---

[1] Rob Murray, *C++ Strategies & Tactics*, Addison-Wesley, 1993, page 47.

Overloading assignment

A common source of confusion with new C++ programmers is assignment. This is no doubt because the = sign is such a fundamental operation in programming, right down to copying a register at the machine level. In addition, the copy-constructor (described in Chapter 11) is also sometimes invoked when the = sign is used:

```
MyType b;
MyType a = b;
a = b;
```

In the second line, the object **a** is being *defined*. A new object is being created where one didn't exist before. Because you know by now how defensive the C++ compiler is about object initialization, you know that a constructor must always be called at the point where an object is defined. But which constructor? **a** is being created from an existing **MyType** object (**b**, on the right side of the equal sign), so there's only one choice: the copy-constructor. Even though an equal sign is involved, the copy-constructor is called.

In the third line, things are different. On the left side of the equal sign, there's a previously initialized object. Clearly, you don't call a constructor for an object that's already been created. In this case **MyType::operator=** is called for **a**, taking as an argument whatever appears on the right-hand side. (You can have multiple **operator=** functions to take different types of right-hand arguments.)

This behavior is not restricted to the copy-constructor. Any time you're initializing an object using an = instead of the ordinary function-call form of the constructor, the compiler will look for a constructor that accepts whatever is on the right-hand side:

```
//: C12:CopyingVsInitialization.cpp
class Fi {
public:
  Fi() {}
};
```

```
class Fee {
public:
  Fee(int) {}
  Fee(const Fi&) {}
};

int main() {
  Fee fee = 1; // Fee(int)
  Fi fi;
  Fee fum = fi; // Fee(Fi)
} ///:~
```

When dealing with the = sign, it's important to keep this distinction in mind: If the object hasn't been created yet, initialization is required; otherwise the assignment **operator=** is used.

It's even better to avoid writing code that uses the = for initialization; instead, always use the explicit constructor form. The two constructions with the equal sign then become:

```
Fee fee(1);
Fee fum(fi);
```

This way, you'll avoid confusing your readers.

Behavior of operator=

In **Integer.h** and **Byte.h**, you saw that **operator=** can be only a member function. It is intimately connected to the object on the left side of the '='. If it was possible to define **operator=** globally, then you might attempt to redefine the built-in '=' sign:

```
int operator=(int, MyType); // Global = not allowed!
```

The compiler skirts this whole issue by forcing you to make **operator=** a member function.

When you create an **operator=**, you must copy all of the necessary information from the right-hand object into the current object (that is, the object that **operator=** is being called for) to perform whatever you consider "assignment" for your class. For simple objects, this is obvious:

```cpp
//: C12:SimpleAssignment.cpp
// Simple operator=()
#include <iostream>
using namespace std;

class Value {
  int a, b;
  float c;
public:
  Value(int aa = 0, int bb = 0, float cc = 0.0)
    : a(aa), b(bb), c(cc) {}
  Value& operator=(const Value& rv) {
    a = rv.a;
    b = rv.b;
    c = rv.c;
    return *this;
  }
  friend ostream&
  operator<<(ostream& os, const Value& rv) {
    return os << "a = " << rv.a << ", b = "
      << rv.b << ", c = " << rv.c;
  }
};

int main() {
  Value a, b(1, 2, 3.3);
  cout << "a: " << a << endl;
  cout << "b: " << b << endl;
  a = b;
  cout << "a after assignment: " << a << endl;
} ///:~
```

Here, the object on the left side of the = copies all the elements of
the object on the right, then returns a reference to itself, which
allows a more complex expression to be created.

This example includes a common mistake. When you're assigning
two objects of the same type, you should always check first for self-
assignment: is the object being assigned to itself? In some cases,
such as this one, it's harmless if you perform the assignment
operations anyway, but if changes are made to the implementation
of the class, it can make a difference, and if you don't do it as a
matter of habit, you may forget and cause hard-to-find bugs.

Pointers in classes

What happens if the object is not so simple? For example, what if the object contains pointers to other objects? Simply copying a pointer means that you'll end up with two objects pointing to the same storage location. In situations like these, you need to do bookkeeping of your own.

There are two common approaches to this problem. The simplest technique is to copy whatever the pointer refers to when you do an assignment or a copy-construction. This is straightforward:

```
//: C12:CopyingWithPointers.cpp
// Solving the pointer aliasing problem by
// duplicating what is pointed to during
// assignment and copy-construction.
#include "../require.h"
#include <string>
#include <iostream>
using namespace std;

class Dog {
  string nm;
public:
  Dog(const string& name) : nm(name) {
    cout << "Creating Dog: " << *this << endl;
  }
  // Synthesized copy-constructor & operator=
  // are correct.
  // Create a Dog from a Dog pointer:
  Dog(const Dog* dp, const string& msg)
    : nm(dp->nm + msg) {
    cout << "Copied dog " << *this << " from "
        << *dp << endl;
  }
  ~Dog() {
    cout << "Deleting Dog: " << *this << endl;
  }
  void rename(const string& newName) {
    nm = newName;
    cout << "Dog renamed to: " << *this << endl;
  }
  friend ostream&
  operator<<(ostream& os, const Dog& d) {
```

```cpp
      return os << "[" << d.nm << "]";
  }
};

class DogHouse {
  Dog* p;
  string houseName;
public:
  DogHouse(Dog* dog, const string& house)
    : p(dog), houseName(house) {}
  DogHouse(const DogHouse& dh)
    : p(new Dog(dh.p, " copy-constructed")),
      houseName(dh.houseName
        + " copy-constructed") {}
  DogHouse& operator=(const DogHouse& dh) {
    // Check for self-assignment:
    if(&dh != this) {
      p = new Dog(dh.p, " assigned");
      houseName = dh.houseName + " assigned";
    }
    return *this;
  }
  void renameHouse(const string& newName) {
    houseName = newName;
  }
  Dog* getDog() const { return p; }
  ~DogHouse() { delete p; }
  friend ostream&
  operator<<(ostream& os, const DogHouse& dh) {
    return os << "[" << dh.houseName
      << "] contains " << *dh.p;
  }
};

int main() {
  DogHouse fidos(new Dog("Fido"), "FidoHouse");
  cout << fidos << endl;
  DogHouse fidos2 - fidos; // Copy construction
  cout << fidos2 << endl;
  fidos2.getDog()->rename("Spot");
  fidos2.renameHouse("SpotHouse");
  cout << fidos2 << endl;
  fidos = fidos2; // Assignment
  cout << fidos << endl;
  fidos.getDog()->rename("Max");
```

```
    fidos2.renameHouse("MaxHouse");
} ///:~
```

Dog is a simple class that contains only a **string** that holds the name of the dog. However, you'll generally know when something happens to a **Dog** because the constructors and destructors print information when they are called. Notice that the second constructor is a bit like a copy-constructor except that it takes a pointer to a **Dog** instead of a reference, and it has a second argument that is a message that's concatenated to the argument **Dog**'s name. This is used to help trace the behavior of the program.

You can see that whenever a member function prints information, it doesn't access that information directly but instead sends ***this** to **cout**. This in turn calls the **ostream operator<<**. It's valuable to do it this way because if you want to reformat the way that **Dog** information is displayed (as I did by adding the '[' and ']') you only need to do it in one place.

A **DogHouse** contains a **Dog*** and demonstrates the four functions you will always need to define when your class contains pointers: all necessary ordinary constructors, the copy-constructor, **operator=** (either define it or disallow it), and a destructor. The **operator=** checks for self-assignment as a matter of course, even though it's not strictly necessary here. This virtually eliminates the possibility that you'll forget to check for self-assignment if you *do* change the code so that it matters.

Reference Counting

In the example above, the copy-constructor and **operator=** make a new copy of what the pointer points to, and the destructor deletes it. However, if your object requires a lot of memory or a high initialization overhead, you may want to avoid this copying. A common approach to this problem is called *reference counting*. You give intelligence to the object that's being pointed to so it knows how many objects are pointing to it. Then copy-construction or assignment means attaching another pointer to an existing object and incrementing the reference count. Destruction means reducing the reference count and destroying the object if the reference count goes to zero.

But what if you want to write to the object (the **Dog** in the example above)? More than one object may be using this **Dog**, so you'd be modifying someone else's **Dog** as well as yours, which doesn't seem very neighborly. To solve this "aliasing" problem, an additional technique called *copy-on-write* is used. Before writing to a block of memory, you make sure no one else is using it. If the reference count is greater than one, you must make yourself a personal copy of that block before writing it, so you don't disturb someone else's turf. Here's a simple example of reference counting and copy-on-write:

```cpp
//: C12:ReferenceCounting.cpp
// Reference count, copy-on-write
#include "../require.h"
#include <string>
#include <iostream>
using namespace std;

class Dog {
  string nm;
  int refcount;
  Dog(const string& name)
    : nm(name), refcount(1) {
    cout << "Creating Dog: " << *this << endl;
  }
  // Prevent assignment:
  Dog& operator=(const Dog& rv);
public:
  // Dogs can only be created on the heap:
  static Dog* make(const string& name) {
    return new Dog(name);
  }
  Dog(const Dog& d)
    : nm(d.nm + " copy"), refcount(1) {
    cout << "Dog copy-constructor: "
         << *this << endl;
  }
  ~Dog() {
    cout << "Deleting Dog: " << *this << endl;
  }
  void attach() {
    ++refcount;
    cout << "Attached Dog: " << *this << endl;
```

```
    }
    void detach() {
      require(refcount != 0);
      cout << "Detaching Dog: " << *this << endl;
      // Destroy object if no one is using it:
      if(--refcount == 0) delete this;
    }
    // Conditionally copy this Dog.
    // Call before modifying the Dog, assign
    // resulting pointer to your Dog*.
    Dog* unalias() {
      cout << "Unaliasing Dog: " << *this << endl;
      // Don't duplicate if not aliased:
      if(refcount == 1) return this;
      --refcount;
      // Use copy-constructor to duplicate:
      return new Dog(*this);
    }
    void rename(const string& newName) {
      nm = newName;
      cout << "Dog renamed to: " << *this << endl;
    }
    friend ostream&
    operator<<(ostream& os, const Dog& d) {
      return os << "[" << d.nm << "], rc = "
        << d.refcount;
    }
};

class DogHouse {
  Dog* p;
  string houseName;
public:
  DogHouse(Dog* dog, const string& house)
    : p(dog), houseName(house) {
    cout << "Created DogHouse: "<< *this << endl;
  }
  DogHouse(const DogHouse& dh)
    : p(dh.p),
      houseName("copy-constructed " +
        dh.houseName) {
    p->attach();
    cout << "DogHouse copy-constructor: "
        << *this << endl;
  }
```

```
  DogHouse& operator=(const DogHouse& dh) {
    // Check for self-assignment:
    if(&dh != this) {
      houseName = dh.houseName + " assigned";
      // Clean up what you're using first:
      p->detach();
      p = dh.p; // Like copy-constructor
      p->attach();
    }
    cout << "DogHouse operator= : "
         << *this << endl;
    return *this;
  }
  // Decrement refcount, conditionally destroy
  ~DogHouse() {
    cout << "DogHouse destructor: "
         << *this << endl;
    p->detach();
  }
  void renameHouse(const string& newName) {
    houseName = newName;
  }
  void unalias() { p = p->unalias(); }
  // Copy-on-write. Anytime you modify the
  // contents of the pointer you must
  // first unalias it:
  void renameDog(const string& newName) {
    unalias();
    p->rename(newName);
  }
  // ... or when you allow someone else access:
  Dog* getDog() {
    unalias();
    return p;
  }
  friend ostream&
  operator<<(ostream& os, const DogHouse& dh) {
    return os << "[" << dh.houseName
      << "] contains " << *dh.p;
  }
};

int main() {
  DogHouse
    fidos(Dog::make("Fido"), "FidoHouse"),
```

```
    spots(Dog::make("Spot"), "SpotHouse");
  cout << "Entering copy-construction" << endl;
  DogHouse bobs(fidos);
  cout << "After copy-constructing bobs" << endl;
  cout << "fidos:" << fidos << endl;
  cout << "spots:" << spots << endl;
  cout << "bobs:" << bobs << endl;
  cout << "Entering spots = fidos" << endl;
  spots = fidos;
  cout << "After spots = fidos" << endl;
  cout << "spots:" << spots << endl;
  cout << "Entering self-assignment" << endl;
  bobs = bobs;
  cout << "After self-assignment" << endl;
  cout << "bobs:" << bobs << endl;
  // Comment out the following lines:
  cout << "Entering rename(\"Bob\")" << endl;
  bobs.getDog()->rename("Bob");
  cout << "After rename(\"Bob\")" << endl;
} ///:~
```

The class **Dog** is the object pointed to by a **DogHouse**. It contains a reference count and functions to control and read the reference count. There's a copy-constructor so you can make a new **Dog** from an existing one.

The **attach( )** function increments the reference count of a **Dog** to indicate there's another object using it. **detach( )** decrements the reference count. If the reference count goes to zero, then no one is using it anymore, so the member function destroys its own object by saying **delete this**.

Before you make any modifications (such as renaming a **Dog**), you should ensure that you aren't changing a **Dog** that some other object is using. You do this by calling **DogHouse::unalias( )**, which in turn calls **Dog::unalias( )**. The latter function will return the existing **Dog** pointer if the reference count is one (meaning no one else is pointing to that **Dog**), but will duplicate the **Dog** if the reference count is more than one.

The copy-constructor, instead of creating its own memory, assigns **Dog** to the **Dog** of the source object. Then, because there's now an additional object using that block of memory, it increments the reference count by calling **Dog::attach( )**.

The **operator=** deals with an object that has already been created on the left side of the =, so it must first clean that up by calling **detach( )** for that **Dog**, which will destroy the old **Dog** if no one else is using it. Then **operator=** repeats the behavior of the copy-constructor. Notice that it first checks to detect whether you're assigning the same object to itself.

The destructor calls **detach( )** to conditionally destroy the **Dog**.

To implement copy-on-write, you must control all the actions that write to your block of memory. For example, the **renameDog( )** member function allows you to change the values in the block of memory. But first, it uses **unalias( )** to prevent the modification of an aliased **Dog** (a **Dog** with more than one **DogHouse** object pointing to it). And if you need to produce a pointer to a **Dog** from within a **DogHouse**, you **unalias( )** that pointer first.

main( ) tests the various functions that must work correctly to implement reference counting: the constructor, copy-constructor, **operator=**, and destructor. It also tests the copy-on-write by calling **renameDog( )**.

Here's the output (after a little reformatting):

```
Creating Dog: [Fido], rc = 1
Created DogHouse: [FidoHouse]
  contains [Fido], rc = 1
Creating Dog: [Spot], rc = 1
Created DogHouse: [SpotHouse]
  contains [Spot], rc = 1
Entering copy-construction
Attached Dog: [Fido], rc = 2
DogHouse copy-constructor:
  [copy-constructed FidoHouse]
    contains [Fido], rc = 2
After copy-constructing bobs
fidos:[FidoHouse] contains [Fido], rc = 2
spots:[SpotHouse] contains [Spot], rc = 1
bobs:[copy-constructed FidoHouse]
```

```
    contains [Fido], rc = 2
Entering spots = fidos
Detaching Dog: [Spot], rc = 1
Deleting Dog: [Spot], rc = 0
Attached Dog: [Fido], rc = 3
DogHouse operator= : [FidoHouse assigned]
    contains [Fido], rc = 3
After spots = fidos
spots:[FidoHouse assigned] contains [Fido],rc = 3
Entering self-assignment
DogHouse operator= : [copy-constructed FidoHouse]
    contains [Fido], rc = 3
After self-assignment
bobs:[copy-constructed FidoHouse]
    contains [Fido], rc = 3
Entering rename("Bob")
After rename("Bob")
DogHouse destructor: [copy-constructed FidoHouse]
    contains [Fido], rc = 3
Detaching Dog: [Fido], rc = 3
DogHouse destructor: [FidoHouse assigned]
    contains [Fido], rc = 2
Detaching Dog: [Fido], rc = 2
DogHouse destructor: [FidoHouse]
    contains [Fido], rc = 1
Detaching Dog: [Fido], rc = 1
Deleting Dog: [Fido], rc = 0
```

By studying the output, tracing through the source code, and
experimenting with the program, you'll deepen your understanding
of these techniques.

Automatic operator= creation

Because assigning an object to another object *of the same type* is an
activity most people expect to be possible, the compiler will
automatically create a **type::operator=(type)** if you don't make
one. The behavior of this operator mimics that of the automatically
created copy-constructor; if the class contains objects (or is
inherited from another class), the **operator=** for those objects is
called recursively. This is called *memberwise assignment*. For
example,

```
//: C12:AutomaticOperatorEquals.cpp
```

```
#include <iostream>
using namespace std;

class Cargo {
public:
  Cargo& operator=(const Cargo&) {
    cout << "inside Cargo::operator=()" << endl;
    return *this;
  }
};

class Truck {
  Cargo b;
};

int main() {
  Truck a, b;
  a = b; // Prints: "inside Cargo::operator=()"
} ///:~
```

The automatically generated **operator=** for **Truck** calls
Cargo::operator=.

In general, you don't want to let the compiler do this for you. With
classes of any sophistication (especially if they contain pointers!)
you want to explicitly create an **operator=**. If you really don't want
people to perform assignment, declare **operator=** as a **private**
function. (You don't need to define it unless you're using it inside
the class.)

Automatic type conversion

In C and C++, if the compiler sees an expression or function call
using a type that isn't quite the one it needs, it can often perform an
automatic type conversion from the type it has to the type it wants.
In C++, you can achieve this same effect for user-defined types by
defining automatic type conversion functions. These functions
come in two flavors: a particular type of constructor and an
overloaded operator.

Constructor conversion

If you define a constructor that takes as its single argument an object (or reference) of another type, that constructor allows the compiler to perform an automatic type conversion. For example,

```
//: C12:AutomaticTypeConversion.cpp
// Type conversion constructor
class One {
public:
  One() {}
};

class Two {
public:
  Two(const One&) {}
};

void f(Two) {}

int main() {
  One one;
  f(one); // Wants a Two, has a One
} ///:~
```

When the compiler sees **f( )** called with a **One** object, it looks at the declaration for **f( )** and notices it wants a **Two**. Then it looks to see if there's any way to get a **Two** from a **One**, and it finds the constructor **Two::Two(One)**, which it quietly calls. The resulting **Two** object is handed to **f( )**.

In this case, automatic type conversion has saved you from the trouble of defining two overloaded versions of **f( )**. However, the cost is the hidden constructor call to **Two**, which may matter if you're concerned about the efficiency of calls to **f( )**.

Preventing constructor conversion

There are times when automatic type conversion via the constructor can cause problems. To turn it off, you modify the constructor by prefacing with the keyword **explicit** (which only works with constructors). Used to modify the constructor of class **Two** in the example above:

```
//: C12:ExplicitKeyword.cpp
// Using the "explicit" keyword
class One {
public:
  One() {}
};

class Two {
public:
  explicit Two(const One&) {}
};

void f(Two) {}

int main() {
  One one;
//!  f(one); // No auto conversion allowed
  f(Two(one)); // OK -- user performs conversion
} ///:~
```

By making **Two**'s constructor explicit, the compiler is told not to perform any automatic conversion using that particular constructor (other non-**explicit** constructors in that class can still perform automatic conversions). If the user wants to make the conversion happen, the code must be written out. In the code above, **f(Two(one))** creates a temporary object of type **Two** from **one**, just like the compiler did in the previous version.

Operator conversion

The second way to produce automatic type conversion is through operator overloading. You can create a member function that takes the current type and converts it to the desired type using the **operator** keyword followed by the type you want to convert to. This form of operator overloading is unique because you don't appear to specify a return type – the return type is the *name* of the operator you're overloading. Here's an example:

```
//: C12:OperatorOverloadingConversion.cpp
class Three {
  int i;
public:
  Three(int ii = 0, int = 0) : i(ii) {}
```

```
};

class Four {
   int x;
public:
   Four(int xx) : x(xx) {}
   operator Three() const { return Three(x); }
};

void g(Three) {}

int main() {
   Four four(1);
   g(four);
   g(1);    // Calls Three(1,0)
} ///:~
```

With the constructor technique, the destination class is performing the conversion, but with operators, the source class performs the conversion. The value of the constructor technique is that you can add a new conversion path to an existing system as you're creating a new class. However, creating a single-argument constructor *always* defines an automatic type conversion (even if it's got more than one argument, if the rest of the arguments are defaulted), which may not be what you want (in which case you can turn it off using **explicit**). In addition, there's no way to use a constructor conversion from a user-defined type to a built-in type; this is possible only with operator overloading.

Reflexivity

One of the most convenient reasons to use global overloaded operators instead of member operators is that in the global versions, automatic type conversion may be applied to either operand, whereas with member objects, the left-hand operand must already be the proper type. If you want both operands to be converted, the global versions can save a lot of coding. Here's a small example:

```
//: C12:ReflexivityInOverloading.cpp
class Number {
   int i;
public:
```

```
  Number(int ii = 0) : i(ii) {}
  const Number
  operator+(const Number& n) const {
    return Number(i + n.i);
  }
  friend const Number
    operator-(const Number&, const Number&);
};

const Number
  operator-(const Number& n1,
            const Number& n2) {
    return Number(n1.i - n2.i);
}

int main() {
  Number a(47), b(11);
  a + b; // OK
  a + 1; // 2nd arg converted to Number
//! 1 + a; // Wrong! 1st arg not of type Number
  a - b; // OK
  a - 1; // 2nd arg converted to Number
  1 - a; // 1st arg converted to Number
} ///:~
```

Class **Number** has both a member **operator+** and a **friend
operator−**. Because there's a constructor that takes a single **int**
argument, an **int** can be automatically converted to a **Number**, but
only under the right conditions. In **main( )**, you can see that
adding a **Number** to another **Number** works fine because it's an
exact match to the overloaded operator. Also, when the compiler
sees a **Number** followed by a + and an **int**, it can match to the
member function **Number::operator+** and convert the **int**
argument to a **Number** using the constructor. But when it sees an
int, a +, and a **Number**, it doesn't know what to do because all it
has is **Number::operator+**, which requires that the left operand
already be a **Number** object. Thus, the compiler issues an error.

With the **friend operator−**, things are different. The compiler
needs to fill in both its arguments however it can; it isn't restricted
to having a **Number** as the left-hand argument. Thus, if it sees

```
1 - a
```

---

it can convert the first argument to a **Number** using the constructor.

Sometimes you want to be able to restrict the use of your operators by making them members. For example, when multiplying a matrix by a vector, the vector must go on the right. But if you want your operators to be able to convert either argument, make the operator a friend function.

Fortunately, the compiler will not take **1 − 1** and convert both arguments to **Number** objects and then call **operator−**. That would mean that existing C code might suddenly start to work differently. The compiler matches the "simplest" possibility first, which is the built-in operator for the expression **1 − 1**.

Type conversion example

An example in which automatic type conversion is extremely helpful occurs with any class that encapsulates character strings (in this case, we will just implement the class using the Standard C++ **string** class because it's simple). Without automatic type conversion, if you want to use all the existing string functions from the Standard C library, you have to create a member function for each one, like this:

```cpp
//: C12:Strings1.cpp
// No auto type conversion
#include "../require.h"
#include <cstring>
#include <cstdlib>
#include <string>
using namespace std;

class Stringc {
  string s;
public:
  Stringc(const string& str = "") : s(str) {}
  int strcmp(const Stringc& S) const {
    return ::strcmp(s.c_str(), S.s.c_str());
  }
  // ... etc., for every function in string.h
```

```
};

int main() {
  Stringc s1("hello"), s2("there");
  s1.strcmp(s2);
} ///:~
```

Here, only the **strcmp( )** function is created, but you'd have to
create a corresponding function for every one in **<cstring>** that
might be needed. Fortunately, you can provide an automatic type
conversion allowing access to all the functions in **<cstring>**:

```
//: C12:Strings2.cpp
// With auto type conversion
#include "../require.h"
#include <cstring>
#include <cstdlib>
#include <string>
using namespace std;

class Stringc {
  string s;
public:
  Stringc(const string& str = "") : s(str) {}
  operator const char*() const {
    return s.c_str();
  }
};

int main() {
  Stringc s1("hello"), s2("there");
  strcmp(s1, s2); // Standard C function
  strspn(s1, s2); // Any string function!
} ///:~
```

Now any function that takes a **char*** argument can also take a
Stringc argument because the compiler knows how to make a
char* from a **Stringc**.

Pitfalls in automatic type conversion

Because the compiler must choose how to quietly perform a type
conversion, it can get into trouble if you don't design your
conversions correctly. A simple and obvious situation occurs with a

---

class **X** that can convert itself to an object of class **Y** with an **operator Y( )**. If class **Y** has a constructor that takes a single argument of type **X**, this represents the identical type conversion. The compiler now has two ways to go from **X** to **Y**, so it will generate an ambiguity error when that conversion occurs:

```
//: C12:TypeConversionAmbiguity.cpp
class Orange; // Class declaration

class Apple {
public:
  operator Orange() const; // Convert Apple to Orange
};

class Orange {
public:
  Orange(Apple); // Convert Apple to Orange
};

void f(Orange) {}

int main() {
  Apple a;
//! f(a); // Error: ambiguous conversion
} ///:~
```

The obvious solution to this problem is not to do it. Just provide a single path for automatic conversion from one type to another.

A more difficult problem to spot occurs when you provide automatic conversion to more than one type. This is sometimes called *fan-out*:

```
//: C12:TypeConversionFanout.cpp
class Orange {};
class Pear {};

class Apple {
public:
  operator Orange() const;
  operator Pear() const;
};
```

```
// Overloaded eat():
void eat(Orange);
void eat(Pear);

int main() {
  Apple c;
//! eat(c);
  // Error: Apple -> Orange or Apple -> Pear ???
} ///:~
```

Class **Apple** has automatic conversions to both **Orange** and **Pear**.
The insidious thing about this is that there's no problem until
someone innocently comes along and creates two overloaded
versions of **eat( )**. (With only one version, the code in **main( )**
works fine.)

Again, the solution – and the general watchword with automatic
type conversion – is to provide only a single automatic conversion
from one type to another. You can have conversions to other types;
they just shouldn't be *automatic*. You can create explicit function
calls with names like **makeA( )** and **makeB( )**.

Hidden activities

Automatic type conversion can introduce more underlying activities
than you may expect. As a little brain teaser, look at this
modification of **CopyingVsInitialization.cpp**:

```
//: C12:CopyingVsInitialization2.cpp
class Fi {};

class Fee {
public:
  Fee(int) {}
  Fee(const Fi&) {}
};

class Fo {
  int i;
public:
  Fo(int x = 0) : i(x) {}
  operator Fee() const { return Fee(i); }
};
```

```
int main() {
  Fo fo;
  Fee fee = fo;
} ///:~
```

There is no constructor to create the **Fee fee** from a **Fo** object.
However, **Fo** has an automatic type conversion to a **Fee**. There's no
copy-constructor to create a **Fee** from a **Fee**, but this is one of the
special functions the compiler can create for you. (The default
constructor, copy-constructor, **operator**=, and destructor can be
synthesized automatically by the compiler.) So for the relatively
innocuous statement

```
Fee fee = fo;
```

the automatic type conversion operator is called, and a copy-
constructor is created.

Use automatic type conversion carefully. As with all operator
overloading, it's excellent when it significantly reduces a coding
task, but it's usually not worth using gratuitously.

Summary

The whole reason for the existence of operator overloading is for
those situations when it makes life easier. There's nothing
particularly magical about it; the overloaded operators are just
functions with funny names, and the function calls happen to be
made for you by the compiler when it spots the right pattern. But if
operator overloading doesn't provide a significant benefit to you
(the creator of the class) or the user of the class, don't confuse the
issue by adding it.

Exercises

Solutions to selected exercises can be found in the electronic document *The Thinking in C++
Annotated Solution Guide*, available for a small fee from www.BruceEckel.com.

1. Create a simple class with an overloaded **operator++**. Try calling this operator in both pre- and postfix form and see what kind of compiler warning you get.

2. Create a simple class containing an **int** and overload the **operator+** as a member function. Also provide a **print( )** member function that takes an **ostream&** as an argument and prints to that **ostream&**. Test your class to show that it works correctly.

3. Add a binary **operator-** to Exercise 2 as a member function. Demonstrate that you can use your objects in complex expressions like
a + b − c.

4. Add an **operator++** and **operator--** to Exercise 2, both the prefix and the postfix versions, such that they return the incremented or decremented object. Make sure that the postfix versions return the correct value.

5. Modify the increment and decrement operators in Exercise 4 so that the prefix versions return a non-**const** reference and the postfix versions return a **const** object. Show that they work correctly and explain why this would be done in practice.

6. Change the **print( )** function in Exercise 2 so that it is the overloaded **operator<<** as in **IostreamOperatorOverloading.cpp**.

7. Modify Exercise 3 so that the **operator+** and **operator-** are non-member functions. Demonstrate that they still work correctly.

8. Add the unary **operator-** to Exercise 2 and demonstrate that it works correctly.

9. Create a class that contains a single **private char**. Overload the iostream operators << and >> (as in **IostreamOperatorOverloading.cpp**) and test them. You can test them with **fstreams**, **stringstream**s, and **cin** and **cout**.

10. Determine the dummy constant value that your compiler passes for postfix **operator++** and **operator--**.

11. Write a **Number** class that holds a **double**, and add overloaded operators for +, −, *, /, and assignment.

Choose the return values for these functions so that expressions can be chained together, and for efficiency. Write an automatic type conversion **operator double( )**.

12. Modify Exercise 11 so that the *return value optimization* is used, if you have not already done so.

13. Create a class that contains a pointer, and demonstrate that if you allow the compiler to synthesize the **operator=** the result of using that operator will be pointers that are aliased to the same storage. Now fix the problem by defining your own **operator=** and demonstrate that it corrects the aliasing. Make sure you check for self-assignment and handle that case properly.

14. Write a class called **Bird** that contains a **string** member and a **static int**. In the default constructor, use the **int** to automatically generate an identifier that you build in the **string**, along with the name of the class (**Bird #1**, **Bird #2**, etc.). Add an **operator<<** for **ostream**s to print out the **Bird** objects. Write an assignment **operator=** and a copy-constructor. In **main( )**, verify that everything works correctly.

15. Write a class called **BirdHouse** that contains an object, a pointer and a reference for class **Bird** from Exercise 14. The constructor should take the three **Bird**s as arguments. Add an **operator<<** for **ostream**s for **BirdHouse**. Disallow the assignment **operator=** and copy-constructor. In **main( )**, verify that everything works correctly. Make sure that you can chain assignments for **BirdHouse** objects and build expressions involving multiple operators.

16. Add an **int** data member to both **Bird** and **BirdHouse** in Exercise 15. Add member operators +, -, *, and / that use the **int** members to perform the operations on the respective members. Verify that these work.

17. Repeat Exercise 16 using non-member operators.

18. Add an **operator--** to **SmartPointer.cpp** and **NestedSmartPointer.cpp**.

19. Modify **CopyingVsInitialization.cpp** so that all of the constructors print a message that tells you what's going

on. Now verify that the two forms of calls to the copy-constructor (the assignment form and the parenthesized form) are equivalent.

20. Attempt to create a non-member **operator=** for a class and see what kind of compiler message you get.

21. Create a class with an assignment operator that has a second argument, a **string** that has a default value that says "op= call." Create a function that assigns an object of your class to another one and show that your assignment operator is called correctly.

22. In **CopyingWithPointers.cpp**, remove the **operator=** in **DogHouse** and show that the compiler-synthesized **operator=** correctly copies the **string** but simply aliases the **Dog** pointer.

23. In **ReferenceCounting.cpp**, add a **static int** and an ordinary **int** as data members to both **Dog** and **DogHouse**. In all constructors for both classes, increment the **static int** and assign the result to the ordinary **int** to keep track of the number of objects that have been created. Make the necessary modifications so that all the printing statements will say the **int** identifiers of the objects involved.

24. Create a class containing a **string** as a data member. Initialize the **string** in the constructor, but do not create a copy-constructor or **operator=**. Make a second class that has a member object of your first class; do not create a copy-constructor or **operator=** for this class either. Demonstrate that the copy-constructor and **operator=** are properly synthesized by the compiler.

25. Combine the classes in **OverloadingUnaryOperators.cpp** and **Integer.cpp**.

26. Modify **PointerToMemberOperator.cpp** by adding two new member functions to **Dog** that take no arguments and return **void**. Create and test an overloaded **operator->*** that works with your two new functions.

27. Add an **operator->*** to **NestedSmartPointer.cpp**.

28. Create two classes, **Apple** and **Orange**. In **Apple**, create a constructor that takes an **Orange** as an argument.

Create a function that takes an **Apple** and call that function with an **Orange** to show that it works. Now make the **Apple** constructor **explicit** to demonstrate that the automatic type conversion is thus prevented. Modify the call to your function so that the conversion is made explicitly and thus succeeds.

29. Add a global **operator*** to **ReflexivityInOverloading.cpp** and demonstrate that it is reflexive.

30. Create two classes and create an **operator+** and the conversion functions such that addition is reflexive for the two classes.

31. Fix **TypeConversionFanout.cpp** by creating an explicit function to call to perform the type conversion, instead of one of the automatic conversion operators.

32. Write simple code that uses the +, -, *, and / operators for **double**s. Figure out how your compiler generates assembly code and look at the assembly language that's generated to discover and explain what's going on under the hood.

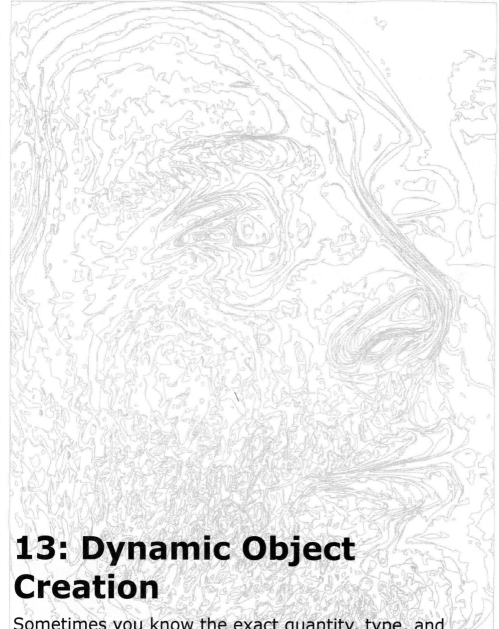

13: Dynamic Object Creation

Sometimes you know the exact quantity, type, and lifetime of the objects in your program. But not always.

How many planes will an air-traffic system need to handle? How many shapes will a CAD system use? How many nodes will there be in a network?

To solve the general programming problem, it's essential that you be able to create and destroy objects at runtime. Of course, C has always provided the *dynamic memory allocation* functions **malloc( )** and **free( )** (along with variants of **malloc( )**) that allocate storage from the *heap* (also called the *free store*) at runtime.

However, this simply won't work in C++. The constructor doesn't allow you to hand it the address of the memory to initialize, and for good reason. If you could do that, you might:

1.   Forget. Then guaranteed initialization of objects in C++ wouldn't be guaranteed.

2.   Accidentally do something to the object before you initialize it, expecting the right thing to happen.

3.   Hand it the wrong-sized object.

And of course, even if you did everything correctly, anyone who modifies your program is prone to the same errors. Improper initialization is responsible for a large portion of programming problems, so it's especially important to guarantee constructor calls for objects created on the heap.

So how does C++ guarantee proper initialization and cleanup, but allow you to create objects dynamically on the heap?

The answer is by bringing dynamic object creation into the core of the language. **malloc( )** and **free( )** are library functions, and thus outside the control of the compiler. However, if you have an *operator* to perform the combined act of dynamic storage allocation and initialization and another operator to perform the combined act of cleanup and releasing storage, the compiler can still guarantee that constructors and destructors will be called for all objects.

In this chapter, you'll learn how C++'s **new** and **delete** elegantly solve this problem by safely creating objects on the heap.

Object creation

When a C++ object is created, two events occur:

1.   Storage is allocated for the object.

2.   The constructor is called to initialize that storage.

By now you should believe that step two *always* happens. C++ enforces it because uninitialized objects are a major source of program bugs. It doesn't matter where or how the object is created – the constructor is always called.

Step one, however, can occur in several ways, or at alternate times:

1.   Storage can be allocated before the program begins, in the static storage area. This storage exists for the life of the program.

2.   Storage can be created on the stack whenever a particular execution point is reached (an opening brace). That storage is released automatically at the complementary execution point (the closing brace). These stack-allocation operations are built into the instruction set of the processor and are very efficient. However, you have to know exactly how many variables you need when you're writing the program so the compiler can generate the right code.

3.   Storage can be allocated from a pool of memory called the heap (also known as the free store). This is called dynamic memory allocation. To allocate this memory, a function is called at runtime; this means you can decide at any time that you want some memory and how much you need. You are also responsible for determining when to release the memory, which means the lifetime of that memory can be as long as you choose – it isn't determined by scope.

Often these three regions are placed in a single contiguous piece of physical memory: the static area, the stack, and the heap (in an order determined by the compiler writer). However, there are no rules. The stack may be in a special place, and the heap may be implemented by making calls for chunks of memory from the operating system. As a programmer, these things are normally shielded from you, so all you need to think about is that the memory is there when you call for it.

C's approach to the heap

To allocate memory dynamically at runtime, C provides functions in its standard library: **malloc( )** and its variants **calloc( )** and **realloc( )** to produce memory from the heap, and **free( )** to release the memory back to the heap. These functions are pragmatic but primitive and require understanding and care on the part of the programmer. To create an instance of a class on the heap using C's dynamic memory functions, you'd have to do something like this:

```
//: C13:MallocClass.cpp
// Malloc with class objects
// What you'd have to do if not for "new"
#include "../require.h"
#include <cstdlib> // malloc() & free()
#include <cstring> // memset()
#include <iostream>
using namespace std;

class Obj {
  int i, j, k;
  enum { sz = 100 };
  char buf[sz];
public:
  void initialize() { // Can't use constructor
    cout << "initializing Obj" << endl;
    i = j = k = 0;
    memset(buf, 0, sz);
  }
  void destroy() const { // Can't use destructor
    cout << "destroying Obj" << endl;
  }
};
```

```
int main() {
  Obj* obj = (Obj*)malloc(sizeof(Obj));
  require(obj != 0);
  obj->initialize();
  // ... sometime later:
  obj->destroy();
  free(obj);
} ///:~
```

You can see the use of **malloc( )** to create storage for the object in the line:

```
Obj* obj = (Obj*)malloc(sizeof(Obj));
```

Here, the user must determine the size of the object (one place for an error). **malloc( )** returns a **void*** because it just produces a patch of memory, not an object. C++ doesn't allow a **void*** to be assigned to any other pointer, so it must be cast.

Because **malloc( )** may fail to find any memory (in which case it returns zero), you must check the returned pointer to make sure it was successful.

But the worst problem is this line:

```
Obj->initialize();
```

If users make it this far correctly, they must remember to initialize the object before it is used. Notice that a constructor was not used because the constructor cannot be called explicitly[1] – it's called for you by the compiler when an object is created. The problem here is that the user now has the option to forget to perform the initialization before the object is used, thus reintroducing a major source of bugs.

It also turns out that many programmers seem to find C's dynamic memory functions too confusing and complicated; it's not

---

[1] There is a special syntax called *placement new* that allows you to call a constructor for a pre-allocated piece of memory. This is introduced later in the chapter.

uncommon to find C programmers who use virtual memory machines allocating huge arrays of variables in the static storage area to avoid thinking about dynamic memory allocation. Because C++ is attempting to make library use safe and effortless for the casual programmer, C's approach to dynamic memory is unacceptable.

operator new

The solution in C++ is to combine all the actions necessary to create an object into a single operator called **new**. When you create an object with **new** (using a *new-expression*), it allocates enough storage on the heap to hold the object and calls the constructor for that storage. Thus, if you say

```
MyType *fp = new MyType(1,2);
```

at runtime, the equivalent of **malloc(sizeof(MyType))** is called (often, it is literally a call to **malloc( )**), and the constructor for **MyType** is called with the resulting address as the **this** pointer, using **(1,2)** as the argument list. By the time the pointer is assigned to **fp**, it's a live, initialized object – you can't even get your hands on it before then. It's also automatically the proper **MyType** type so no cast is necessary.

The default **new** checks to make sure the memory allocation was successful before passing the address to the constructor, so you don't have to explicitly determine if the call was successful. Later in the chapter you'll find out what happens if there's no memory left.

You can create a new-expression using any constructor available for the class. If the constructor has no arguments, you write the new-expression without the constructor argument list:

```
MyType *fp = new MyType;
```

Notice how simple the process of creating objects on the heap becomes – a single expression, with all the sizing, conversions, and safety checks built in. It's as easy to create an object on the heap as it is on the stack.

---

operator delete

The complement to the new-expression is the *delete-expression*, which first calls the destructor and then releases the memory (often with a call to **free( )**). Just as a new-expression returns a pointer to the object, a delete-expression requires the address of an object.

```
delete fp;
```

This destructs and then releases the storage for the dynamically allocated **MyType** object created earlier.

delete can be called only for an object created by **new**. If you **malloc( )** (or **calloc( )** or **realloc( )**) an object and then **delete** it, the behavior is undefined. Because most default implementations of **new** and **delete** use **malloc( )** and **free( )**, you'd probably end up releasing the memory without calling the destructor.

If the pointer you're deleting is zero, nothing will happen. For this reason, people often recommend setting a pointer to zero immediately after you delete it, to prevent deleting it twice. Deleting an object more than once is definitely a bad thing to do, and will cause problems.

A simple example

This example shows that initialization takes place:

```cpp
//: C13:Tree.h
#ifndef TREE_H
#define TREE_H
#include <iostream>

class Tree {
  int height;
public:
  Tree(int treeHeight) : height(treeHeight) {}
  ~Tree() { std::cout << "*"; }
  friend std::ostream&
  operator<<(std::ostream& os, const Tree* t) {
    return os << "Tree height is: "
              << t->height << std::endl;
  }
```

```
};
#endif // TREE_H ///:~
//: C13:NewAndDelete.cpp
// Simple demo of new & delete
#include "Tree.h"
using namespace std;

int main() {
  Tree* t = new Tree(40);
  cout << t;
  delete t;
} ///:~
```

We can prove that the constructor is called by printing out the value of the **Tree**. Here, it's done by overloading the **operator<<** to use with an **ostream** and a **Tree***. Note, however, that even though the function is declared as a **friend**, it is defined as an inline! This is a mere convenience – defining a **friend** function as an inline to a class doesn't change the **friend** status or the fact that it's a global function and not a class member function. Also notice that the return value is the result of the entire output expression, which is an **ostream&** (which it must be, to satisfy the return value type of the function).

Memory manager overhead

When you create automatic objects on the stack, the size of the objects and their lifetime is built right into the generated code, because the compiler knows the exact type, quantity, and scope. Creating objects on the heap involves additional overhead, both in time and in space. Here's a typical scenario. (You can replace **malloc( )** with **calloc( )** or **realloc( )**.)

You call **malloc( )**, which requests a block of memory from the pool. (This code may actually be part of **malloc( )**.)

The pool is searched for a block of memory large enough to satisfy the request. This is done by checking a map or directory of some sort that shows which blocks are currently in use and which are available. It's a quick process, but it may take several tries so it might not be deterministic – that is, you can't necessarily count on **malloc( )** always taking exactly the same amount of time.

Before a pointer to that block is returned, the size and location of the block must be recorded so further calls to **malloc( )** won't use it, and so that when you call **free( )**, the system knows how much memory to release.

The way all this is implemented can vary widely. For example, there's nothing to prevent primitives for memory allocation being implemented in the processor. If you're curious, you can write test programs to try to guess the way your **malloc( )** is implemented. You can also read the library source code, if you have it (the GNU C sources are always available).

Early examples redesigned

Using **new** and **delete**, the **Stash** example introduced previously in this book can be rewritten using all the features discussed in the book so far. Examining the new code will also give you a useful review of the topics.

At this point in the book, neither the **Stash** nor **Stack** classes will "own" the objects they point to; that is, when the **Stash** or **Stack** object goes out of scope, it will not call **delete** for all the objects it points to. The reason this is not possible is because, in an attempt to be generic, they hold **void** pointers. If you **delete** a **void** pointer, the only thing that happens is the memory gets released, because there's no type information and no way for the compiler to know what destructor to call.

delete void* is probably a bug

It's worth making a point that if you call **delete** for a **void***, it's almost certainly going to be a bug in your program unless the destination of that pointer is very simple; in particular, it should not have a destructor. Here's an example to show you what happens:

```
//: C13:BadVoidPointerDeletion.cpp
// Deleting void pointers can cause memory leaks
```

```
#include <iostream>
using namespace std;

class Object {
  void* data; // Some storage
  const int size;
  const char id;
public:
  Object(int sz, char c) : size(sz), id(c) {
    data = new char[size];
    cout << "Constructing object " << id
         << ", size = " << size << endl;
  }
  ~Object() {
    cout << "Destructing object " << id << endl;
    delete []data; // OK, just releases storage,
    // no destructor calls are necessary
  }
};

int main() {
  Object* a = new Object(40, 'a');
  delete a;
  void* b = new Object(40, 'b');
  delete b;
} ///:~
```

The class **Object** contains a **void*** that is initialized to "raw" data (it doesn't point to objects that have destructors). In the **Object** destructor, **delete** is called for this **void*** with no ill effects, since the only thing we need to happen is for the storage to be released.

However, in **main( )** you can see that it's very necessary that **delete** know what type of object it's working with. Here's the output:

```
Constructing object a, size = 40
Destructing object a
Constructing object b, size = 40
```

Because **delete a** knows that **a** points to an **Object**, the destructor is called and thus the storage allocated for **data** is released. However, if you manipulate an object through a **void*** as in the case of **delete b**, the only thing that happens is that the storage for the **Object** is released – but the destructor is not called so there is no release of the memory that **data** points to. When this program compiles, you probably won't see any warning messages; the compiler assumes you know what you're doing. So you get a very quiet memory leak.

If you have a memory leak in your program, search through all the **delete** statements and check the type of pointer being deleted. If it's a **void*** then you've probably found one source of your memory leak (C++ provides ample other opportunities for memory leaks, however).

Cleanup responsibility with pointers

To make the **Stash** and **Stack** containers flexible (able to hold any type of object), they will hold **void** pointers. This means that when a pointer is returned from the **Stash** or **Stack** object, you must cast it to the proper type before using it; as seen above, you must also cast it to the proper type before deleting it or you'll get a memory leak.

The other memory leak issue has to do with making sure that **delete** is actually called for each object pointer held in the container. The container cannot "own" the pointer because it holds it as a **void*** and thus cannot perform the proper cleanup. The user must be responsible for cleaning up the objects. This produces a serious problem if you add pointers to objects created on the stack *and* objects created on the heap to the same container because a delete-expression is unsafe for a pointer that hasn't been allocated on the heap. (And when you fetch a pointer back from the container, how will you know where its object has been allocated?) Thus, you must be sure that objects stored in the following versions of **Stash** and **Stack** are made only on the heap, either through careful programming or by creating classes that can only be built on the heap.

It's also important to make sure that the client programmer takes responsibility for cleaning up all the pointers in the container. You've seen in previous examples how the **Stack** class checks in its destructor that all the **Link** objects have been popped. For a **Stash** of pointers, however, another approach is needed.

Stash for pointers

This new version of the **Stash** class, called **PStash**, holds *pointers* to objects that exist by themselves on the heap, whereas the old **Stash** in earlier chapters copied the objects by value into the **Stash** container. Using **new** and **delete**, it's easy and safe to hold pointers to objects that have been created on the heap.

Here's the header file for the "pointer **Stash**":

```
//: C13:PStash.h
// Holds pointers instead of objects
#ifndef PSTASH_H
#define PSTASH_H

class PStash {
  int quantity; // Number of storage spaces
  int next; // Next empty space
  // Pointer storage:
  void** storage;
  void inflate(int increase);
public:
  PStash() : quantity(0), storage(0), next(0) {}
  ~PStash();
  int add(void* element);
  void* operator[](int index) const; // Fetch
  // Remove the reference from this PStash:
  void* remove(int index);
  // Number of elements in Stash:
  int count() const { return next; }
};
#endif // PSTASH_H ///:~
```

The underlying data elements are fairly similar, but now **storage** is an array of **void** pointers, and the allocation of storage for that array is performed with **new** instead of **malloc( )**. In the expression

```
void** st = new void*[quantity + increase];
```

the type of object allocated is a **void***, so the expression allocates an array of **void** pointers.

The destructor deletes the storage where the **void** pointers are held rather than attempting to delete what they point at (which, as previously noted, will release their storage and not call the destructors because a **void** pointer has no type information).

The other change is the replacement of the **fetch( )** function with **operator[ ]**, which makes more sense syntactically. Again, however, a **void*** is returned, so the user must remember what types are stored in the container and cast the pointers when fetching them out (a problem that will be repaired in future chapters).

Here are the member function definitions:

```cpp
//: C13:PStash.cpp {O}
// Pointer Stash definitions
#include "PStash.h"
#include "../require.h"
#include <iostream>
#include <cstring> // 'mem' functions
using namespace std;

int PStash::add(void* element) {
  const int inflateSize = 10;
  if(next >= quantity)
    inflate(inflateSize);
  storage[next++] = element;
  return(next - 1); // Index number
}

// No ownership:
PStash::~PStash() {
  for(int i = 0; i < next; i++)
    require(storage[i] == 0,
      "PStash not cleaned up");
  delete []storage;
}

// Operator overloading replacement for fetch
void* PStash::operator[](int index) const {
```

```
      require(index >= 0,
        "PStash::operator[] index negative");
      if(index >= next)
        return 0; // To indicate the end
      // Produce pointer to desired element:
      return storage[index];
}

void* PStash::remove(int index) {
  void* v = operator[](index);
  // "Remove" the pointer:
  if(v != 0) storage[index] = 0;
  return v;
}

void PStash::inflate(int increase) {
  const int psz = sizeof(void*);
  void** st = new void*[quantity + increase];
  memset(st, 0, (quantity + increase) * psz);
  memcpy(st, storage, quantity * psz);
  quantity += increase;
  delete []storage; // Old storage
  storage = st; // Point to new memory
} ///:~
```

The **add( )** function is effectively the same as before, except that a pointer is stored instead of a copy of the whole object.

The **inflate( )** code is modified to handle the allocation of an array of **void*** instead of the previous design, which was only working with raw bytes. Here, instead of using the prior approach of copying by array indexing, the Standard C library function **memset( )** is first used to set all the new memory to zero (this is not strictly necessary, since the **PStash** is presumably managing all the memory correctly – but it usually doesn't hurt to throw in a bit of extra care). Then **memcpy( )** moves the existing data from the old location to the new. Often, functions like **memset( )** and **memcpy( )** have been optimized over time, so they may be faster than the loops shown previously. But with a function like **inflate( )** that will probably not be used that often you may not see a performance difference. However, the fact that the function calls are more concise than the loops may help prevent coding errors.

To put the responsibility of object cleanup squarely on the shoulders of the client programmer, there are two ways to access the pointers in the **PStash**: the **operator[]**, which simply returns the pointer but leaves it as a member of the container, and a second member function **remove( )**, which returns the pointer but also removes it from the container by assigning that position to zero. When the destructor for **PStash** is called, it checks to make sure that all object pointers have been removed; if not, you're notified so you can prevent a memory leak (more elegant solutions will be forthcoming in later chapters).

A test

Here's the old test program for **Stash** rewritten for the **PStash**:

```
//: C13:PStashTest.cpp
//{L} PStash
// Test of pointer Stash
#include "PStash.h"
#include "../require.h"
#include <iostream>
#include <fstream>
#include <string>
using namespace std;

int main() {
  PStash intStash;
  // 'new' works with built-in types, too. Note
  // the "pseudo-constructor" syntax:
  for(int i = 0; i < 25; i++)
    intStash.add(new int(i));
  for(int j = 0; j < intStash.count(); j++)
    cout << "intStash[" << j << "] = "
         << *(int*)intStash[j] << endl;
  // Clean up:
  for(int k = 0; k < intStash.count(); k++)
    delete intStash.remove(k);
  ifstream in ("PStashTest.cpp");
  assure(in, "PStashTest.cpp");
  PStash stringStash;
  string line;
  while(getline(in, line))
    stringStash.add(new string(line));
  // Print out the strings:
```

```
    for(int u = 0; stringStash[u]; u++)
      cout << "stringStash[" << u << "] = "
           << *(string*)stringStash[u] << endl;
    // Clean up:
    for(int v = 0; v < stringStash.count(); v++)
      delete (string*)stringStash.remove(v);
} ///:~
```

As before, **Stash**es are created and filled with information, but this
time the information is the pointers resulting from **new**-
expressions. In the first case, note the line:

```
intStash.add(new int(i));
```

The expression **new int(i)** uses the pseudo-constructor form, so
storage for a new **int** object is created on the heap, and the **int** is
initialized to the value **i**.

During printing, the value returned by **PStash::operator[ ]** must
be cast to the proper type; this is repeated for the rest of the
PStash objects in the program. It's an undesirable effect of using
void pointers as the underlying representation and will be fixed in
later chapters.

The second test opens the source code file and reads it one line at a
time into another **PStash**. Each line is read into a **string** using
getline( ), then a **new string** is created from **line** to make an
independent copy of that line. If we just passed in the address of
line each time, we'd get a whole bunch of pointers pointing to **line**,
which would only contain the last line that was read from the file.

When fetching the pointers, you see the expression:

```
*(string*)stringStash[v]
```

The pointer returned from **operator[ ]** must be cast to a **string***
to give it the proper type. Then the **string*** is dereferenced so the
expression evaluates to an object, at which point the compiler sees a
string object to send to **cout**.

The objects created on the heap must be destroyed through the use
of the **remove( )** statement or else you'll get a message at runtime

telling you that you haven't completely cleaned up the objects in the **PStash**. Notice that in the case of the **int** pointers, no cast is necessary because there's no destructor for an **int** and all we need is memory release:

```
delete intStash.remove(k);
```

However, for the **string** pointers, if you forget to do the cast you'll have another (quiet) memory leak, so the cast is essential:

```
delete (string*)stringStash.remove(k);
```

Some of these issues (but not all) can be removed using templates (which you'll learn about in Chapter 16).

new & delete for arrays

In C++, you can create arrays of objects on the stack or on the heap with equal ease, and (of course) the constructor is called for each object in the array. There's one constraint, however: There must be a default constructor, except for aggregate initialization on the stack (see Chapter 6), because a constructor with no arguments must be called for every object.

When creating arrays of objects on the heap using **new**, there's something else you must do. An example of such an array is

```
MyType* fp = new MyType[100];
```

This allocates enough storage on the heap for 100 **MyType** objects and calls the constructor for each one. Now, however, you simply have a **MyType***, which is exactly the same as you'd get if you said

```
MyType* fp2 = new MyType;
```

to create a single object. Because you wrote the code, you know that **fp** is actually the starting address of an array, so it makes sense to select array elements using an expression like **fp[3]**. But what happens when you destroy the array? The statements

```
delete fp2; // OK
```

```
delete fp;  // Not the desired effect
```

look exactly the same, and their effect will be the same. The destructor will be called for the **MyType** object pointed to by the given address, and then the storage will be released. For **fp2** this is fine, but for **fp** this means that the other 99 destructor calls won't be made. The proper amount of storage will still be released, however, because it is allocated in one big chunk, and the size of the whole chunk is stashed somewhere by the allocation routine.

The solution requires you to give the compiler the information that this is actually the starting address of an array. This is accomplished with the following syntax:

```
delete []fp;
```

The empty brackets tell the compiler to generate code that fetches the number of objects in the array, stored somewhere when the array is created, and calls the destructor for that many array objects. This is actually an improved syntax from the earlier form, which you may still occasionally see in old code:

```
delete [100]fp;
```

which forced the programmer to include the number of objects in the array and introduced the possibility that the programmer would get it wrong. The additional overhead of letting the compiler handle it was very low, and it was considered better to specify the number of objects in one place instead of two.

Making a pointer more like an array

As an aside, the **fp** defined above can be changed to point to anything, which doesn't make sense for the starting address of an array. It makes more sense to define it as a constant, so any attempt to modify the pointer will be flagged as an error. To get this effect, you might try

```
int const* q = new int[10];
```

or

```
const int* q = new int[10];
```

but in both cases the **const** will bind to the **int**, that is, what is being pointed *to*, rather than the quality of the pointer itself. Instead, you must say

```
int* const q = new int[10];
```

Now the array elements in **q** can be modified, but any change to **q** (like **q++**) is illegal, as it is with an ordinary array identifier.

Running out of storage

What happens when the **operator new( )** cannot find a contiguous block of storage large enough to hold the desired object? A special function called the *new-handler* is called. Or rather, a pointer to a function is checked, and if the pointer is nonzero, then the function it points to is called.

The default behavior for the new-handler is to *throw an exception*, a subject covered in Volume 2. However, if you're using heap allocation in your program, it's wise to at least replace the new-handler with a message that says you've run out of memory and then aborts the program. That way, during debugging, you'll have a clue about what happened. For the final program you'll want to use more robust recovery.

You replace the new-handler by including **new.h** and then calling **set_new_handler( )** with the address of the function you want installed:

```
//: C13:NewHandler.cpp
// Changing the new-handler
#include <iostream>
#include <cstdlib>
#include <new>
using namespace std;

int count = 0;

void out_of_memory() {
```

```
      cerr << "memory exhausted after " << count
        << " allocations!" << endl;
      exit(1);
}

int main() {
  set_new_handler(out_of_memory);
  while(1) {
    count++;
    new int[1000]; // Exhausts memory
  }
} ///:~
```

The new-handler function must take no arguments and have a **void**
return value. The **while** loop will keep allocating **int** objects (and
throwing away their return addresses) until the free store is
exhausted. At the very next call to **new**, no storage can be allocated,
so the new-handler will be called.

The behavior of the new-handler is tied to **operator new( )**, so if
you overload **operator new( )** (covered in the next section) the
new-handler will not be called by default. If you still want the new-
handler to be called you'll have to write the code to do so inside
your overloaded **operator new( )**.

Of course, you can write more sophisticated new-handlers, even one
to try to reclaim memory (commonly known as a *garbage
collector*). This is not a job for the novice programmer.

Overloading new & delete

When you create a new-expression, two things occur. First, storage
is allocated using the **operator new( )**, then the constructor is
called. In a delete-expression, the destructor is called, then storage
is deallocated using the **operator delete( )**. The constructor and
destructor calls are never under your control (otherwise you might
accidentally subvert them), but you *can* change the storage
allocation functions **operator new( )** and **operator delete( )**.

The memory allocation system used by **new** and **delete** is designed
for general-purpose use. In special situations, however, it doesn't

serve your needs. The most common reason to change the allocator is efficiency: You might be creating and destroying so many objects of a particular class that it has become a speed bottleneck. C++ allows you to overload **new** and **delete** to implement your own storage allocation scheme, so you can handle problems like this.

Another issue is heap fragmentation. By allocating objects of different sizes it's possible to break up the heap so that you effectively run out of storage. That is, the storage might be available, but because of fragmentation no piece is big enough to satisfy your needs. By creating your own allocator for a particular class, you can ensure this never happens.

In embedded and real-time systems, a program may have to run for a very long time with restricted resources. Such a system may also require that memory allocation always take the same amount of time, and there's no allowance for heap exhaustion or fragmentation. A custom memory allocator is the solution; otherwise, programmers will avoid using **new** and **delete** altogether in such cases and miss out on a valuable C++ asset.

When you overload **operator new( )** and **operator delete( )**, it's important to remember that you're changing only the way *raw storage is allocated*. The compiler will simply call your **new** instead of the default version to allocate storage, then call the constructor for that storage. So, although the compiler allocates storage *and* calls the constructor when it sees **new**, all you can change when you overload **new** is the storage allocation portion. (**delete** has a similar limitation.)

When you overload **operator new( )**, you also replace the behavior when it runs out of memory, so you must decide what to do in your **operator new( )**: return zero, write a loop to call the new-handler and retry allocation, or (typically) throw a **bad_alloc** exception (discussed in Volume 2, available at *www.BruceEckel.com*).

Overloading **new** and **delete** is like overloading any other operator. However, you have a choice of overloading the global allocator or using a different allocator for a particular class.

Overloading global new & delete

This is the drastic approach, when the global versions of **new** and **delete** are unsatisfactory for the whole system. If you overload the global versions, you make the defaults completely inaccessible – you can't even call them from inside your redefinitions.

The overloaded **new** must take an argument of **size_t** (the Standard C standard type for sizes). This argument is generated and passed to you by the compiler and is the size of the object you're responsible for allocating. You must return a pointer either to an object of that size (or bigger, if you have some reason to do so), or to zero if you can't find the memory (in which case the constructor is *not* called!). However, if you can't find the memory, you should probably do something more informative than just returning zero, like calling the new-handler or throwing an exception, to signal that there's a problem.

The return value of **operator new( )** is a **void***, *not* a pointer to any particular type. All you've done is produce memory, not a finished object – that doesn't happen until the constructor is called, an act the compiler guarantees and which is out of your control.

The **operator delete( )** takes a **void*** to memory that was allocated by **operator new**. It's a **void*** because **operator delete** only gets the pointer *after* the destructor is called, which removes the object-ness from the piece of storage. The return type is **void**.

Here's a simple example showing how to overload the global **new** and **delete**:

```
//: C13:GlobalOperatorNew.cpp
// Overload global new/delete
#include <cstdio>
#include <cstdlib>
using namespace std;

void* operator new(size_t sz) {
  printf("operator new: %d Bytes\n", sz);
  void* m = malloc(sz);
  if(!m) puts("out of memory");
  return m;
```

```
  }

  void operator delete(void* m) {
    puts("operator delete");
    free(m);
  }

  class S {
    int i[100];
  public:
    S() { puts("S::S()"); }
    ~S() { puts("S::~S()"); }
  };

  int main() {
    puts("creating & destroying an int");
    int* p = new int(47);
    delete p;
    puts("creating & destroying an s");
    S* s = new S;
    delete s;
    puts("creating & destroying S[3]");
    S* sa = new S[3];
    delete []sa;
  } ///:~
```

Here you can see the general form for overloading **new** and **delete**. These use the Standard C library functions **malloc( )** and **free( )** for the allocators (which is probably what the default **new** and **delete** use as well!). However, they also print messages about what they are doing. Notice that **printf( )** and **puts( )** are used rather than **iostreams**. This is because when an **iostream** object is created (like the global **cin**, **cout**, and **cerr**), it calls **new** to allocate memory. With **printf( )**, you don't get into a deadlock because it doesn't call **new** to initialize itself.

In **main( )**, objects of built-in types are created to prove that the overloaded **new** and **delete** are also called in that case. Then a single object of type **S** is created, followed by an array of **S**. For the array, you'll see from the number of bytes requested that extra memory is allocated to store information (inside the array) about the number of objects it holds. In all cases, the global overloaded versions of **new** and **delete** are used.

Overloading new & delete for a class

Although you don't have to explicitly say **static**, when you overload **new** and **delete** for a class, you're creating **static** member functions. As before, the syntax is the same as overloading any other operator. When the compiler sees you use **new** to create an object of your class, it chooses the member **operator new( )** over the global version. However, the global versions of **new** and **delete** are used for all other types of objects (unless they have their own **new** and **delete**).

In the following example, a primitive storage allocation system is created for the class **Framis**. A chunk of memory is set aside in the static data area at program start-up, and that memory is used to allocate space for objects of type **Framis**. To determine which blocks have been allocated, a simple array of bytes is used, one byte for each block:

```cpp
//: C13:Framis.cpp
// Local overloaded new & delete
#include <cstddef> // Size_t
#include <fstream>
#include <iostream>
#include <new>
using namespace std;
ofstream out("Framis.out");

class Framis {
  enum { sz = 10 };
  char c[sz]; // To take up space, not used
  static unsigned char pool[];
  static bool alloc_map[];
public:
  enum { psize = 100 };  // frami allowed
  Framis() { out << "Framis()\n"; }
  ~Framis() { out << "~Framis() ... "; }
  void* operator new(size_t) throw(bad_alloc);
  void operator delete(void*);
};
unsigned char Framis::pool[psize * sizeof(Framis)];
bool Framis::alloc_map[psize] = {false};

// Size is ignored -- assume a Framis object
```

```cpp
void*
Framis::operator new(size_t) throw(bad_alloc) {
  for(int i = 0; i < psize; i++)
    if(!alloc_map[i]) {
      out << "using block " << i << " ... ";
      alloc_map[i] = true; // Mark it used
      return pool + (i * sizeof(Framis));
    }
  out << "out of memory" << endl;
  throw bad_alloc();
}

void Framis::operator delete(void* m) {
  if(!m) return; // Check for null pointer
  // Assume it was created in the pool
  // Calculate which block number it is:
  unsigned long block = (unsigned long)m
    - (unsigned long)pool;
  block /= sizeof(Framis);
  out << "freeing block " << block << endl;
  // Mark it free:
  alloc_map[block] = false;
}

int main() {
  Framis* f[Framis::psize];
  try {
    for(int i = 0; i < Framis::psize; i++)
      f[i] = new Framis;
    new Framis; // Out of memory
  } catch(bad_alloc) {
    cerr << "Out of memory!" << endl;
  }
  delete f[10];
  f[10] = 0;
  // Use released memory:
  Framis* x = new Framis;
  delete x;
  for(int j = 0; j < Framis::psize; j++)
    delete f[j]; // Delete f[10] OK
} ///:~
```

The pool of memory for the **Framis** heap is created by allocating an array of bytes large enough to hold **psize Framis** objects. The allocation map is **psize** elements long, so there's one **bool** for every block. All the values in the allocation map are initialized to **false** using the aggregate initialization trick of setting the first element so the compiler automatically initializes all the rest to their normal default value (which is **false**, in the case of **bool**).

The local **operator new( )** has the same syntax as the global one. All it does is search through the allocation map looking for a **false** value, then sets that location to **true** to indicate it's been allocated and returns the address of the corresponding memory block. If it can't find any memory, it issues a message to the trace file and throws a **bad_alloc** exception.

This is the first example of exceptions that you've seen in this book. Since detailed discussion of exceptions is delayed until Volume 2, this is a very simple use of them. In **operator new( )** there are two artifacts of exception handling. First, the function argument list is followed by **throw(bad_alloc)**, which tells the compiler and the reader that this function may throw an exception of type **bad_alloc**. Second, if there's no more memory the function actually does throw the exception in the statement **throw bad_alloc**. When an exception is thrown, the function stops executing and control is passed to an *exception handler*, which is expressed as a **catch** clause.

In **main( )**, you see the other part of the picture, which is the *try-catch* clause. The **try** block is surrounded by braces and contains all the code that may throw exceptions – in this case, any call to **new** that involves **Framis** objects. Immediately following the **try** block is one or more **catch** clauses, each one specifying the type of exception that they catch. In this case, **catch(bad_alloc)** says that that **bad_alloc** exceptions will be caught here. This particular **catch** clause is only executed when a **bad_alloc** exception is thrown, and execution continues after the end of the last **catch** clause in the group (there's only one here, but there could be more).

In this example, it's OK to use iostreams because the global **operator new( )** and **delete( )** are untouched.

The **operator delete( )** assumes the **Framis** address was created in the pool. This is a fair assumption, because the local **operator new( )** will be called whenever you create a single **Framis** object on the heap – but not an array of them: global **new** is used for arrays. So the user might accidentally have called **operator delete( )** without using the empty bracket syntax to indicate array destruction. This would cause a problem. Also, the user might be deleting a pointer to an object created on the stack. If you think these things could occur, you might want to add a line to make sure the address is within the pool and on a correct boundary (you may also begin to see the potential of overloaded **new** and **delete** for finding memory leaks).

operator delete( ) calculates the block in the pool that this pointer represents, and then sets the allocation map's flag for that block to false to indicate the block has been released.

In **main( )**, enough **Framis** objects are dynamically allocated to run out of memory; this checks the out-of-memory behavior. Then one of the objects is freed, and another one is created to show that the released memory is reused.

Because this allocation scheme is specific to **Framis** objects, it's probably much faster than the general-purpose memory allocation scheme used for the default **new** and **delete**. However, you should note that it doesn't automatically work if inheritance is used (inheritance is covered in Chapter 14).

Overloading new & delete for arrays

If you overload operator **new** and **delete** for a class, those operators are called whenever you create an object of that class. However, if you create an *array* of those class objects, the global **operator new( )** is called to allocate enough storage for the array all at once, and the global **operator delete( )** is called to release that storage. You can control the allocation of arrays of objects by overloading the special array versions of **operator new[ ]** and **operator delete[ ]** for the class. Here's an example that shows when the two different versions are called:

```
//: C13:ArrayOperatorNew.cpp
// Operator new for arrays
#include <new> // Size_t definition
#include <fstream>
using namespace std;
ofstream trace("ArrayOperatorNew.out");

class Widget {
  enum { sz = 10 };
  int i[sz];
public:
  Widget() { trace << "*"; }
  ~Widget() { trace << "~"; }
  void* operator new(size_t sz) {
    trace << "Widget::new: "
          << sz << " bytes" << endl;
    return ::new char[sz];
  }
  void operator delete(void* p) {
    trace << "Widget::delete" << endl;
    ::delete []p;
  }
  void* operator new[](size_t sz) {
    trace << "Widget::new[]: "
          << sz << " bytes" << endl;
    return ::new char[sz];
  }
  void operator delete[](void* p) {
    trace << "Widget::delete[]" << endl;
    ::delete []p;
  }
};

int main() {
  trace << "new Widget" << endl;
  Widget* w = new Widget;
  trace << "\ndelete Widget" << endl;
  delete w;
  trace << "\nnew Widget[25]" << endl;
  Widget* wa = new Widget[25];
  trace << "\ndelete []Widget" << endl;
  delete []wa;
} ///:~
```

Here, the global versions of **new** and **delete** are called so the effect is the same as having no overloaded versions of **new** and **delete** except that trace information is added. Of course, you can use any memory allocation scheme you want in the overloaded **new** and **delete**.

You can see that the syntax of array **new** and **delete** is the same as for the individual object versions except for the addition of the brackets. In both cases you're handed the size of the memory you must allocate. The size handed to the array version will be the size of the entire array. It's worth keeping in mind that the *only* thing the overloaded **operator new( )** is required to do is hand back a pointer to a large enough memory block. Although you may perform initialization on that memory, normally that's the job of the constructor that will automatically be called for your memory by the compiler.

The constructor and destructor simply print out characters so you can see when they've been called. Here's what the trace file looks like for one compiler:

```
new Widget
Widget::new: 40 bytes
*
delete Widget
~Widget::delete

new Widget[25]
Widget::new[]: 1004 bytes
************************
delete []Widget
~~~~~~~~~~~~~~~~~~~~~~~~~Widget::delete[]
```

Creating an individual object requires 40 bytes, as you might expect. (This machine uses four bytes for an **int**.) The **operator new( )** is called, then the constructor (indicated by the *). In a complementary fashion, calling **delete** causes the destructor to be called, then the **operator delete( )**.

When an array of **Widget** objects is created, the array version of **operator new( )** is used, as promised. But notice that the size

---

requested is four more bytes than expected. This extra four bytes is where the system keeps information about the array, in particular, the number of objects in the array. That way, when you say

```
delete []Widget;
```

the brackets tell the compiler it's an array of objects, so the compiler generates code to look for the number of objects in the array and to call the destructor that many times. You can see that, even though the array **operator new( )** and **operator delete( )** are only called once for the entire array chunk, the default constructor and destructor are called for each object in the array.

Constructor calls

Considering that

```
MyType* f = new MyType;
```

calls **new** to allocate a **MyType**-sized piece of storage, then invokes the **MyType** constructor on that storage, what happens if the storage allocation in **new** fails? The constructor is not called in that case, so although you still have an unsuccessfully created object, at least you haven't invoked the constructor and handed it a zero **this** pointer. Here's an example to prove it:

```
//: C13:NoMemory.cpp
// Constructor isn't called if new fails
#include <iostream>
#include <new> // bad_alloc definition
using namespace std;

class NoMemory {
public:
  NoMemory() {
    cout << "NoMemory::NoMemory()" << endl;
  }
  void* operator new(size_t sz) throw(bad_alloc){
    cout << "NoMemory::operator new" << endl;
    throw bad_alloc(); // "Out of memory"
  }
};
```

```
int main() {
  NoMemory* nm = 0;
  try {
    nm = new NoMemory;
  } catch(bad_alloc) {
    cerr << "Out of memory exception" << endl;
  }
  cout << "nm = " << nm << endl;
} ///:~
```

When the program runs, it does not print the constructor message, only the message from **operator new( )** and the message in the exception handler. Because **new** never returns, the constructor is never called so its message is not printed.

It's important that **nm** be initialized to zero because the **new** expression never completes, and the pointer should be zero to make sure you don't misuse it. However, you should actually do more in the exception handler than just print out a message and continue on as if the object had been successfully created. Ideally, you will do something that will cause the program to recover from the problem, or at the least exit after logging an error.

In earlier versions of C++ it was standard practice to return zero from **new** if storage allocation failed. That would prevent construction from occurring. However, if you try to return zero from **new** with a Standard-conforming compiler, it should tell you that you ought to throw **bad_alloc** instead.

placement new & delete

There are two other, less common, uses for overloading **operator new( )**.

1. You may want to place an object in a specific location in memory. This is especially important with hardware-oriented embedded systems where an object may be synonymous with a particular piece of hardware.

2. You may want to be able to choose from different allocators when calling **new**.

Both of these situations are solved with the same mechanism: The overloaded **operator new( )** can take more than one argument. As you've seen before, the first argument is always the size of the object, which is secretly calculated and passed by the compiler. But the other arguments can be anything you want – the address you want the object placed at, a reference to a memory allocation function or object, or anything else that is convenient for you.

The way that you pass the extra arguments to **operator new( )** during a call may seem slightly curious at first. You put the argument list (*without* the **size_t** argument, which is handled by the compiler) after the keyword **new** and before the class name of the object you're creating. For example,

```
X* xp = new(a) X;
```

will pass **a** as the second argument to **operator new( )**. Of course, this can work only if such an **operator new( )** has been declared.

Here's an example showing how you can place an object at a particular location:

```
//: C13:PlacementOperatorNew.cpp
// Placement with operator new()
#include <cstddef> // Size_t
#include <iostream>
using namespace std;

class X {
  int i;
public:
  X(int ii = 0) : i(ii) {
    cout << "this = " << this << endl;
  }
  ~X() {
    cout << "X::~X(): " << this << endl;
  }
  void* operator new(size_t, void* loc) {
    return loc;
  }
};

int main() {
```

```
  int l[10];
  cout << "l = " << l << endl;
  X* xp = new(l) X(47); // X at location l
  xp->X::~X(); // Explicit destructor call
  // ONLY use with placement!
} ///:~
```

Notice that **operator new** only returns the pointer that's passed to
it. Thus, the caller decides where the object is going to sit, and the
constructor is called for that memory as part of the new-expression.

Although this example shows only one additional argument, there's
nothing to prevent you from adding more if you need them for
other purposes.

A dilemma occurs when you want to destroy the object. There's only
one version of **operator delete**, so there's no way to say, "Use my
special deallocator for this object." You want to call the destructor,
but you don't want the memory to be released by the dynamic
memory mechanism because it wasn't allocated on the heap.

The answer is a very special syntax. You can explicitly call the
destructor, as in

```
xp->X::~X(); // Explicit destructor call
```

A stern warning is in order here. Some people see this as a way to
destroy objects at some time before the end of the scope, rather
than either adjusting the scope or (more correctly) using dynamic
object creation if they want the object's lifetime to be determined at
runtime. You will have serious problems if you call the destructor
this way for an ordinary object created on the stack because the
destructor will be called again at the end of the scope. If you call the
destructor this way for an object that was created on the heap, the
destructor will execute, but the memory won't be released, which
probably isn't what you want. The only reason that the destructor
can be called explicitly this way is to support the placement syntax
for **operator new**.

There's also a placement **operator delete** that is only called if a
constructor for a placement **new** expression throws an exception

---

(so that the memory is automatically cleaned up during the exception). The placement **operator delete** has an argument list that corresponds to the placement **operator new** that is called before the constructor throws the exception. This topic will be explored in the exception handling chapter in Volume 2.

Summary

It's convenient and optimally efficient to create automatic objects on the stack, but to solve the general programming problem you must be able to create and destroy objects at any time during a program's execution, particularly to respond to information from outside the program. Although C's dynamic memory allocation will get storage from the heap, it doesn't provide the ease of use and guaranteed construction necessary in C++. By bringing dynamic object creation into the core of the language with **new** and **delete**, you can create objects on the heap as easily as making them on the stack. In addition, you get a great deal of flexibility. You can change the behavior of **new** and **delete** if they don't suit your needs, particularly if they aren't efficient enough. Also, you can modify what happens when the heap runs out of storage.

Exercises

Solutions to selected exercises can be found in the electronic document *The Thinking in C++ Annotated Solution Guide*, available for a small fee from www.BruceEckel.com.

1. Create a **class Counted** that contains an **int id** and a **static int count**. The default constructor should begin: **Counted( ) : id(count++) {**. It should also print its **id** and that it's being created. The destructor should print that it's being destroyed and its **id**. Test your class.

2. Prove to yourself that **new** and **delete** always call the constructors and destructors by creating an object of **class Counted** (from Exercise 1) with **new** and destroying it with **delete**. Also create and destroy an array of these objects on the heap.

3. Create a **PStash** object and fill it with **new** objects from Exercise 1. Observe what happens when this **PStash** object goes out of scope and its destructor is called.

4. Create a **vector< Counted*>** and fill it with pointers to **new Counted** objects (from Exercise 1). Move through the **vector** and print the **Counted** objects, then move through again and **delete** each one.

5. Repeat Exercise 4, but add a member function **f( )** to **Counted** that prints a message. Move through the **vector** and call **f( )** for each object.

6. Repeat Exercise 5 using a **PStash**.

7. Repeat Exercise 5 using **Stack4.h** from Chapter 9.

8. Dynamically create an array of objects of **class Counted** (from Exercise 1). Call **delete** for the resulting pointer, *without the square brackets*. Explain the results.

9. Create an object of **class Counted** (from Exercise 1) using **new**, cast the resulting pointer to a **void***, and delete that. Explain the results.

10. Execute **NewHandler.cpp** on your machine to see the resulting count. Calculate the amount of free store available for your program.

11. Create a class with an overloaded operator **new** and **delete**, both the single-object versions and the array versions. Demonstrate that both versions work.

12. Devise a test for **Framis.cpp** to show yourself approximately how much faster the custom **new** and **delete** run than the global **new** and **delete**.

13. Modify **NoMemory.cpp** so that it contains an array of **int** and so that it actually allocates memory instead of throwing **bad_alloc**. In **main( )**, set up a **while** loop like the one in **NewHandler.cpp** to run out of memory and see what happens if your **operator new** does not test to see if the memory is successfully allocated. Then add the check to your **operator new** and throw **bad_alloc**.

14. Create a class with a placement **new** with a second argument of type **string**. The class should contain a **static vector<string>** where the second **new**

---

argument is stored. The placement **new** should allocate storage as normal. In **main( )**, make calls to your placement **new** with **string** arguments that describe the calls (you may want to use the preprocessor's __**FILE**__ and __**LINE**__ macros).

15.   Modify **ArrayOperatorNew.cpp** by adding a **static vector<Widget*>** that adds each **Widget** address that is allocated in **operator new( )** and removes it when it is released via **operator delete( )**. (You may need to look up information about **vector** in your Standard C++ Library documentation or in the 2nd volume of this book, available at the Web site.) Create a second class called **MemoryChecker** that has a destructor that prints out the number of **Widget** pointers in your **vector**. Create a program with a single global instance of **MemoryChecker** and in **main( )**, dynamically allocate and destroy several objects and arrays of **Widget**. Show that **MemoryChecker** reveals memory leaks.

14: Inheritance & Composition

One of the most compelling features about C++ is code reuse. But to be revolutionary, you need to be able to do a lot more than copy code and change it.

That's the C approach, and it hasn't worked very well. As with most everything in C++, the solution revolves around the class. You reuse code by creating new classes, but instead of creating them from scratch, you use existing classes that someone else has built and debugged.

The trick is to use the classes without soiling the existing code. In this chapter you'll see two ways to accomplish this. The first is quite straightforward: You simply create objects of your existing class inside the new class. This is called *composition* because the new class is composed of objects of existing classes.

The second approach is subtler. You create a new class as a *type of* an existing class. You literally take the form of the existing class and add code to it, without modifying the existing class. This magical act is called *inheritance*, and most of the work is done by the compiler. Inheritance is one of the cornerstones of object-oriented programming and has additional implications that will be explored in Chapter 15.

It turns out that much of the syntax and behavior are similar for both composition and inheritance (which makes sense; they are both ways of making new types from existing types). In this chapter, you'll learn about these code reuse mechanisms.

Composition syntax

Actually, you've been using composition all along to create classes. You've just been composing classes primarily with built-in types (and sometimes **string**s). It turns out to be almost as easy to use composition with user-defined types.

Consider a class that is valuable for some reason:

```
//: C14:Useful.h
// A class to reuse
#ifndef USEFUL_H
#define USEFUL_H

class X {
```

```
  int i;
public:
  X() { i = 0; }
  void set(int ii) { i = ii; }
  int read() const { return i; }
  int permute() { return i = i * 47; }
};
#endif // USEFUL_H ///:~
```

The data members are **private** in this class, so it's completely safe to embed an object of type **X** as a **public** object in a new class, which makes the interface straightforward:

```
//: C14:Composition.cpp
// Reuse code with composition
#include "Useful.h"

class Y {
  int i;
public:
  X x; // Embedded object
  Y() { i = 0; }
  void f(int ii) { i = ii; }
  int g() const { return i; }
};

int main() {
  Y y;
  y.f(47);
  y.x.set(37); // Access the embedded object
} ///:~
```

Accessing the member functions of the embedded object (referred to as a *subobject*) simply requires another member selection.

It's more common to make the embedded objects **private**, so they become part of the underlying implementation (which means you can change the implementation if you want). The **public** interface functions for your new class then involve the use of the embedded object, but they don't necessarily mimic the object's interface:

```
//: C14:Composition2.cpp
// Private embedded objects
#include "Useful.h"
```

```
class Y {
  int i;
  X x; // Embedded object
public:
  Y() { i = 0; }
  void f(int ii) { i = ii; x.set(ii); }
  int g() const { return i * x.read(); }
  void permute() { x.permute(); }
};

int main() {
  Y y;
  y.f(47);
  y.permute();
} ///:~
```

Here, the **permute( )** function is carried through to the new class interface, but the other member functions of **X** are used within the members of **Y**.

Inheritance syntax

The syntax for composition is obvious, but to perform inheritance there's a new and different form.

When you inherit, you are saying, "This new class is like that old class." You state this in code by giving the name of the class as usual, but before the opening brace of the class body, you put a colon and the name of the *base class* (or base *classes*, separated by commas, for multiple inheritance). When you do this, you automatically get all the data members and member functions in the base class. Here's an example:

```
//: C14:Inheritance.cpp
// Simple inheritance
#include "Useful.h"
#include <iostream>
using namespace std;

class Y : public X {
  int i; // Different from X's i
```

```
public:
  Y() { i = 0; }
  int change() {
    i = permute(); // Different name call
    return i;
  }
  void set(int ii) {
    i = ii;
    X::set(ii); // Same-name function call
  }
};

int main() {
  cout << "sizeof(X) = " << sizeof(X) << endl;
  cout << "sizeof(Y) = "
       << sizeof(Y) << endl;
  Y D;
  D.change();
  // X function interface comes through:
  D.read();
  D.permute();
  // Redefined functions hide base versions:
  D.set(12);
} ///:~
```

You can see **Y** being inherited from **X**, which means that **Y** will contain all the data elements in **X** and all the member functions in **X**. In fact, **Y** contains a subobject of **X** just as if you had created a member object of **X** inside **Y** instead of inheriting from **X**. Both member objects and base class storage are referred to as subobjects.

All the **private** elements of **X** are still **private** in **Y**; that is, just because **Y** inherits from **X** doesn't mean **Y** can break the protection mechanism. The **private** elements of **X** are still there, they take up space – you just can't access them directly.

In **main( )** you can see that **Y**'s data elements are combined with **X**'s because the **sizeof(Y)** is twice as big as **sizeof(X)**.

You'll notice that the base class is preceded by **public**. During inheritance, everything defaults to **private**. If the base class were not preceded by **public**, it would mean that all of the **public** members of the base class would be **private** in the derived class.

This is almost never what you want[1]; the desired result is to keep all the **public** members of the base class **public** in the derived class. You do this by using the **public** keyword during inheritance.

In **change( )**, the base-class **permute( )** function is called. The derived class has direct access to all the **public** base-class functions.

The **set( )** function in the derived class *redefines* the **set( )** function in the base class. That is, if you call the functions **read( )** and **permute( )** for an object of type **Y**, you'll get the base-class versions of those functions (you can see this happen inside **main( )**). But if you call **set( )** for a **Y** object, you get the redefined version. This means that if you don't like the version of a function you get during inheritance, you can change what it does. (You can also add completely new functions like **change( )**.)

However, when you're redefining a function, you may still want to call the base-class version. If, inside **set( )**, you simply call **set( )** you'll get the local version of the function – a recursive function call. To call the base-class version, you must explicitly name the base class using the scope resolution operator.

The constructor initializer list

You've seen how important it is in C++ to guarantee proper initialization, and it's no different during composition and inheritance. When an object is created, the compiler guarantees that constructors for all of its subobjects are called. In the examples so far, all of the subobjects have default constructors, and that's what the compiler automatically calls. But what happens if your subobjects don't have default constructors, or if you want to change a default argument in a constructor? This is a problem because the new class constructor doesn't have permission to access the

---

[1] In Java, the compiler won't let you decrease the access of a member during inheritance.

private data elements of the subobject, so it can't initialize them directly.

The solution is simple: Call the constructor for the subobject. C++ provides a special syntax for this, the *constructor initializer list*. The form of the constructor initializer list echoes the act of inheritance. With inheritance, you put the base classes after a colon and before the opening brace of the class body. In the constructor initializer list, you put the calls to subobject constructors after the constructor argument list and a colon, but before the opening brace of the function body. For a class **MyType**, inherited from **Bar**, this might look like this:

```
MyType::MyType(int i) : Bar(i) { // ...
```

if **Bar** has a constructor that takes a single **int** argument.

Member object initialization

It turns out that you use this very same syntax for member object initialization when using composition. For composition, you give the names of the objects instead of the class names. If you have more than one constructor call in the initializer list, you separate the calls with commas:

```
MyType2::MyType2(int i) : Bar(i), m(i+1) { // ...
```

This is the beginning of a constructor for class **MyType2**, which is inherited from **Bar** and contains a member object called **m**. Note that while you can see the type of the base class in the constructor initializer list, you only see the member object identifier.

Built-in types in the initializer list

The constructor initializer list allows you to explicitly call the constructors for member objects. In fact, there's no other way to call those constructors. The idea is that the constructors are all called before you get into the body of the new class's constructor. That way, any calls you make to member functions of subobjects will always go to initialized objects. There's no way to get to the opening brace of the constructor without *some* constructor being

---

called for all the member objects and base-class objects, even if the compiler must make a hidden call to a default constructor. This is a further enforcement of the C++ guarantee that no object (or part of an object) can get out of the starting gate without its constructor being called.

This idea that all of the member objects are initialized by the time the opening brace of the constructor is reached is a convenient programming aid as well. Once you hit the opening brace, you can assume all subobjects are properly initialized and focus on specific tasks you want to accomplish in the constructor. However, there's a hitch: What about member objects of built-in types, which don't *have* constructors?

To make the syntax consistent, you are allowed to treat built-in types as if they have a single constructor, which takes a single argument: a variable of the same type as the variable you're initializing. Thus, you can say

```
//: C14:PseudoConstructor.cpp
class X {
  int i;
  float f;
  char c;
  char* s;
public:
  X() : i(7), f(1.4), c('x'), s("howdy") {}
};

int main() {
  X x;
  int i(100);   // Applied to ordinary definition
  int* ip = new int(47);
} ///:~
```

The action of these "pseudo-constructor calls" is to perform a simple assignment. It's a convenient technique and a good coding style, so you'll see it used often.

It's even possible to use the pseudo-constructor syntax when creating a variable of a built-in type outside of a class:

```
int i(100);
int* ip = new int(47);
```

This makes built-in types act a little bit more like objects.
Remember, though, that these are not real constructors. In
particular, if you don't explicitly make a pseudo-constructor call, no
initialization is performed.

Combining composition & inheritance

Of course, you can use composition & inheritance together. The
following example shows the creation of a more complex class using
both of them.

```
//: C14:Combined.cpp
// Inheritance & composition

class A {
  int i;
public:
  A(int ii) : i(ii) {}
  ~A() {}
  void f() const {}
};

class B {
  int i;
public:
  B(int ii) : i(ii) {}
  ~B() {}
  void f() const {}
};

class C : public B {
  A a;
public:
  C(int ii) : B(ii), a(ii) {}
  ~C() {} // Calls ~A() and ~B()
  void f() const {  // Redefinition
    a.f();
    B::f();
  }
};
```

```
int main() {
  C c(47);
} ///:~
```

C inherits from **B** and has a member object ("is composed of") of type **A**. You can see the constructor initializer list contains calls to both the base-class constructor and the member-object constructor.

The function **C::f( )** redefines **B::f( )**, which it inherits, and also calls the base-class version. In addition, it calls **a.f( )**. Notice that the only time you can talk about redefinition of functions is during inheritance; with a member object you can only manipulate the public interface of the object, not redefine it. In addition, calling **f( )** for an object of class **C** would not call **a.f( )** if **C::f( )** had not been defined, whereas it *would* call **B::f( )**.

Automatic destructor calls

Although you are often required to make explicit constructor calls in the initializer list, you never need to make explicit destructor calls because there's only one destructor for any class, and it doesn't take any arguments. However, the compiler still ensures that all destructors are called, and that means all of the destructors in the entire hierarchy, starting with the most-derived destructor and working back to the root.

It's worth emphasizing that constructors and destructors are quite unusual in that every one in the hierarchy is called, whereas with a normal member function only that function is called, but not any of the base-class versions. If you also want to call the base-class version of a normal member function that you're overriding, you must do it explicitly.

Order of constructor & destructor calls

It's interesting to know the order of constructor and destructor calls when an object has many subobjects. The following example shows exactly how it works:

```
//: C14:Order.cpp
// Constructor/destructor order
```

```cpp
#include <fstream>
using namespace std;
ofstream out("order.out");

#define CLASS(ID) class ID { \
public: \
  ID(int) { out << #ID " constructor\n"; } \
  ~ID() { out << #ID " destructor\n"; } \
};

CLASS(Base1);
CLASS(Member1);
CLASS(Member2);
CLASS(Member3);
CLASS(Member4);

class Derived1 : public Base1 {
  Member1 m1;
  Member2 m2;
public:
  Derived1(int) : m2(1), m1(2), Base1(3) {
    out << "Derived1 constructor\n";
  }
  ~Derived1() {
    out << "Derived1 destructor\n";
  }
};

class Derived2 : public Derived1 {
  Member3 m3;
  Member4 m4;
public:
  Derived2() : m3(1), Derived1(2), m4(3) {
    out << "Derived2 constructor\n";
  }
  ~Derived2() {
    out << "Derived2 destructor\n";
  }
};

int main() {
  Derived2 d2;
} ///:~
```

First, an **ofstream** object is created to send all the output to a file. Then, to save some typing and demonstrate a macro technique that will be replaced by a much improved technique in Chapter 16, a macro is created to build some of the classes, which are then used in inheritance and composition. Each of the constructors and destructors report themselves to the trace file. Note that the constructors are not default constructors; they each have an **int** argument. The argument itself has no identifier; its only reason for existence is to force you to explicitly call the constructors in the initializer list. (Eliminating the identifier prevents compiler warning messages.)

The output of this program is

```
Base1 constructor
Member1 constructor
Member2 constructor
Derived1 constructor
Member3 constructor
Member4 constructor
Derived2 constructor
Derived2 destructor
Member4 destructor
Member3 destructor
Derived1 destructor
Member2 destructor
Member1 destructor
Base1 destructor
```

You can see that construction starts at the very root of the class hierarchy, and that at each level the base class constructor is called first, followed by the member object constructors. The destructors are called in exactly the reverse order of the constructors – this is important because of potential dependencies (in the derived-class constructor or destructor, you must be able to assume that the base-class subobject is still available for use, and has already been constructed – or not destroyed yet).

It's also interesting that the order of constructor calls for member objects is completely unaffected by the order of the calls in the constructor initializer list. The order is determined by the order that the member objects are declared in the class. If you could change the order of constructor calls via the constructor initializer list, you could have two different call sequences in two different constructors, but the poor destructor wouldn't know how to properly reverse the order of the calls for destruction, and you could end up with a dependency problem.

Name hiding

If you inherit a class and provide a new definition for one of its member functions, there are two possibilities. The first is that you provide the exact signature and return type in the derived class definition as in the base class definition. This is called *redefining* for ordinary member functions and *overriding* when the base class member function is a **virtual** function (**virtual** functions are the normal case, and will be covered in detail in Chapter 15). But what happens if you change the member function argument list or return type in the derived class? Here's an example:

```cpp
//: C14:NameHiding.cpp
// Hiding overloaded names during inheritance
#include <iostream>
#include <string>
using namespace std;

class Base {
public:
  int f() const {
    cout << "Base::f()\n";
    return 1;
  }
  int f(string) const { return 1; }
  void g() {}
};

class Derived1 : public Base {
public:
  void g() const {}
};

class Derived2 : public Base {
public:
  // Redefinition:
```

```
    int f() const {
      cout << "Derived2::f()\n";
      return 2;
    }
};

class Derived3 : public Base {
public:
  // Change return type:
  void f() const { cout << "Derived3::f()\n"; }
};

class Derived4 : public Base {
public:
  // Change argument list:
  int f(int) const {
    cout << "Derived4::f()\n";
    return 4;
  }
};

int main() {
  string s("hello");
  Derived1 d1;
  int x = d1.f();
  d1.f(s);
  Derived2 d2;
  x = d2.f();
//!  d2.f(s); // string version hidden
  Derived3 d3;
//!  x = d3.f(); // return int version hidden
  Derived4 d4;
//!  x = d4.f(); // f() version hidden
  x = d4.f(1);
} ///:~
```

In **Base** you see an overloaded function **f( )**, and **Derived1** doesn't make any changes to **f( )** but it does redefine **g( )**. In **main( )**, you can see that both overloaded versions of **f( )** are available in **Derived1**. However, **Derived2** redefines one overloaded version of **f( )** but not the other, and the result is that the second overloaded form is unavailable. In **Derived3**, changing the return type hides both the base class versions, and **Derived4** shows that changing the argument list also hides both the base class versions.

In general, we can say that anytime you redefine an overloaded function name from the base class, all the other versions are automatically hidden in the new class. In Chapter 15, you'll see that the addition of the **virtual** keyword affects function overloading a bit more.

If you change the interface of the base class by modifying the signature and/or return type of a member function from the base class, then you're using the class in a different way than inheritance is normally intended to support. It doesn't necessarily mean you're doing it wrong, it's just that the ultimate goal of inheritance is to support *polymorphism*, and if you change the function signature or return type then you are actually changing the interface of the base class. If this is what you have intended to do then you are using inheritance primarily to reuse code, and not to maintain the common interface of the base class (which is an essential aspect of polymorphism). In general, when you use inheritance this way it means you're taking a general-purpose class and specializing it for a particular need – which is usually, but not always, considered the realm of composition.

For example, consider the **Stack** class from Chapter 9. One of the problems with that class is that you had to perform a cast every time you fetched a pointer from the container. This is not only tedious, it's unsafe – you could cast the pointer to anything you want.

An approach that seems better at first glance is to specialize the general **Stack** class using inheritance. Here's an example that uses the class from Chapter 9:

```
//: C14:InheritStack.cpp
// Specializing the Stack class
#include "../C09/Stack4.h"
#include "../require.h"
#include <iostream>
#include <fstream>
#include <string>
using namespace std;

class StringStack : public Stack {
```

```
public:
  void push(string* str) {
    Stack::push(str);
  }
  string* peek() const {
    return (string*)Stack::peek();
  }
  string* pop() {
    return (string*)Stack::pop();
  }
  ~StringStack() {
    string* top = pop();
    while(top) {
      delete top;
      top = pop();
    }
  }
};

int main() {
  ifstream in("InheritStack.cpp");
  assure(in, "InheritStack.cpp");
  string line;
  StringStack textlines;
  while(getline(in, line))
    textlines.push(new string(line));
  string* s;
  while((s = textlines.pop()) != 0) { // No cast!
    cout << *s << endl;
    delete s;
  }
} ///:~
```

Since all of the member functions in **Stack4.h** are inlines, nothing needs to be linked.

StringStack specializes **Stack** so that **push( )** will accept only **String** pointers. Before, **Stack** would accept **void** pointers, so the user had no type checking to make sure the proper pointers were inserted. In addition, **peek( )** and **pop( )** now return **String** pointers instead of **void** pointers, so no cast is necessary to use the pointer.

Amazingly enough, this extra type-checking safety is free in **push( )**, **peek( )**, and **pop( )**! The compiler is being given extra type information that it uses at compile-time, but the functions are inlined and no extra code is generated.

Name hiding comes into play here because, in particular, the **push( )** function has a different signature: the argument list is different. If you had two versions of **push( )** in the same class, that would be overloading, but in this case overloading is *not* what we want because that would still allow you to pass any kind of pointer into **push( )** as a **void***. Fortunately, C++ hides the **push(void*)** version in the base class in favor of the new version that's defined in the derived class, and therefore it only allows us to **push( ) string** pointers onto the **StringStack**.

Because we can now guarantee that we know exactly what kind of objects are in the container, the destructor works correctly and the ownership problem is solved – or at least, one approach to the ownership problem. Here, if you **push( )** a **string** pointer onto the **StringStack**, then (according to the semantics of the **StringStack**) you're also passing ownership of that pointer to the **StringStack**. If you **pop( )** the pointer, you not only get the pointer, but you also get ownership of that pointer. Any pointers that are left on the **StringStack** when its destructor is called are then deleted by that destructor. And since these are always **string** pointers and the **delete** statement is working on **string** pointers instead of **void** pointers, the proper destruction happens and everything works correctly.

There is a drawback: this class works *only* for **string** pointers. If you want a **Stack** that works with some other kind of object, you must write a new version of the class so that it works only with your new kind of object. This rapidly becomes tedious, and is finally solved using templates, as you will see in Chapter 16.

We can make an additional observation about this example: it changes the interface of the **Stack** in the process of inheritance. If the interface is different, then a **StringStack** really isn't a **Stack**, and you will never be able to correctly use a **StringStack** as a **Stack**. This makes the use of inheritance questionable here; if you're not creating a **StringStack** that *is-a* type of **Stack**, then why are you inheriting? A more appropriate version of **StringStack** will be shown later in this chapter.

Functions that don't automatically inherit

Not all functions are automatically inherited from the base class into the derived class. Constructors and destructors deal with the creation and destruction of an object, and they can know what to do with the aspects of the object only for their particular class, so all the constructors and destructors in the hierarchy below them must be called. Thus, constructors and destructors don't inherit and must be created specially for each derived class.

In addition, the **operator=** doesn't inherit because it performs a constructor-like activity. That is, just because you know how to assign all the members of an object on the left-hand side of the = from an object on the right-hand side doesn't mean that assignment will still have the same meaning after inheritance.

In lieu of inheritance, these functions are synthesized by the compiler if you don't create them yourself. (With constructors, you can't create *any* constructors in order for the compiler to synthesize the default constructor and the copy-constructor.) This was briefly described in Chapter 6. The synthesized constructors use memberwise initialization and the synthesized **operator=** uses memberwise assignment. Here's an example of the functions that are synthesized by the compiler:

```
//: C14:SynthesizedFunctions.cpp
// Functions that are synthesized by the compiler
#include <iostream>
using namespace std;

class GameBoard {
public:
  GameBoard() { cout << "GameBoard()\n"; }
  GameBoard(const GameBoard&) {
    cout << "GameBoard(const GameBoard&)\n";
```

```cpp
  }
  GameBoard& operator=(const GameBoard&) {
    cout << "GameBoard::operator=()\n";
    return *this;
  }
  ~GameBoard() { cout << "~GameBoard()\n"; }
};

class Game {
  GameBoard gb; // Composition
public:
  // Default GameBoard constructor called:
  Game() { cout << "Game()\n"; }
  // You must explicitly call the GameBoard
  // copy-constructor or the default constructor
  // is automatically called instead:
  Game(const Game& g) : gb(g.gb) {
    cout << "Game(const Game&)\n";
  }
  Game(int) { cout << "Game(int)\n"; }
  Game& operator=(const Game& g) {
    // You must explicitly call the GameBoard
    // assignment operator or no assignment at
    // all happens for gb!
    gb = g.gb;
    cout << "Game::operator=()\n";
    return *this;
  }
  class Other {}; // Nested class
  // Automatic type conversion:
  operator Other() const {
    cout << "Game::operator Other()\n";
    return Other();
  }
  ~Game() { cout << "~Game()\n"; }
};

class Chess : public Game {};

void f(Game::Other) {}

class Checkers : public Game {
public:
  // Default base-class constructor called:
  Checkers() { cout << "Checkers()\n"; }
```

```
    // You must explicitly call the base-class
    // copy constructor or the default constructor
    // will be automatically called instead:
    Checkers(const Checkers& c) : Game(c) {
      cout << "Checkers(const Checkers& c)\n";
    }
    Checkers& operator=(const Checkers& c) {
      // You must explicitly call the base-class
      // version of operator=() or no base-class
      // assignment will happen:
      Game::operator=(c);
      cout << "Checkers::operator=()\n";
      return *this;
    }
};

int main() {
  Chess d1;  // Default constructor
  Chess d2(d1); // Copy-constructor
//! Chess d3(1); // Error: no int constructor
  d1 = d2; // Operator= synthesized
  f(d1); // Type-conversion IS inherited
  Game::Other go;
//!  d1 = go; // Operator= not synthesized
          // for differing types
  Checkers c1, c2(c1);
  c1 = c2;
} ///:~
```

The constructors and the **operator=** for **GameBoard** and **Game**
announce themselves so you can see when they're used by the
compiler. In addition, the **operator Other( )** performs automatic
type conversion from a **Game** object to an object of the nested class
Other. The class **Chess** simply inherits from **Game** and creates no
functions (to see how the compiler responds). The function **f( )**
takes an **Other** object to test the automatic type conversion
function.

In **main( )**, the synthesized default constructor and copy-
constructor for the derived class **Chess** are called. The **Game**
versions of these constructors are called as part of the constructor-
call hierarchy. Even though it looks like inheritance, new
constructors are actually synthesized by the compiler. As you might

expect, no constructors with arguments are automatically created because that's too much for the compiler to intuit.

The **operator=** is also synthesized as a new function in **Chess** using memberwise assignment (thus, the base-class version is called) because that function was not explicitly written in the new class. And of course the destructor was automatically synthesized by the compiler.

Because of all these rules about rewriting functions that handle object creation, it may seem a little strange at first that the automatic type conversion operator *is* inherited. But it's not too unreasonable – if there are enough pieces in **Game** to make an **Other** object, those pieces are still there in anything derived from **Game** and the type conversion operator is still valid (even though you may in fact want to redefine it).

operator= is synthesized *only* for assigning objects of the same type. If you want to assign one type to another you must always write that **operator=** yourself.

If you look more closely at **Game**, you'll see that the copy-constructor and assignment operators have explicit calls to the member object copy-constructor and assignment operator. You will normally want to do this because otherwise, in the case of the copy-constructor, the default member object constructor will be used instead, and in the case of the assignment operator, *no* assignment at all will be done for the member objects!

Lastly, look at **Checkers**, which explicitly writes out the default constructor, copy-constructor, and assignment operators. In the case of the default constructor, the default base-class constructor is automatically called, and that's typically what you want. But, and this is an important point, as soon as you decide to write your own copy-constructor and assignment operator, the compiler assumes that you know what you're doing and *does not* automatically call the base-class versions, as it does in the synthesized functions. If you want the base class versions called (and you typically do) then you must explicitly call them yourself. In the **Checkers** copy-constructor, this call appears in the constructor initializer list:

```
Checkers(const Checkers& c) : Game(c) {
```

In the **Checkers** assignment operator, the base class call is the first line in the function body:

```
Game::operator=(c);
```

These calls should be part of the canonical form that you use whenever you inherit a class.

Inheritance and static member functions

static member functions act the same as non-**static** member functions:

1.   They inherit into the derived class.

2.   If you redefine a static member, all the other overloaded functions in the base class are hidden.

3.   If you change the signature of a function in the base class, all the base class versions with that function name are hidden (this is really a variation of the previous point).

However, **static** member functions cannot be **virtual** (a topic covered thoroughly in Chapter 15).

Choosing composition vs. inheritance

Both composition and inheritance place subobjects inside your new class. Both use the constructor initializer list to construct these subobjects. You may now be wondering what the difference is between the two, and when to choose one over the other.

Composition is generally used when you want the features of an existing class inside your new class, but not its interface. That is, you embed an object to implement features of your new class, but the user of your new class sees the interface you've defined rather than the interface from the original class. To do this, you follow the typical path of embedding **private** objects of existing classes inside your new class.

Occasionally, however, it makes sense to allow the class user to directly access the composition of your new class, that is, to make the member objects **public**. The member objects use access control themselves, so this is a safe thing to do and when the user knows you're assembling a bunch of parts, it makes the interface easier to understand. A **Car** class is a good example:

```
//: C14:Car.cpp
// Public composition

class Engine {
public:
  void start() const {}
  void rev() const {}
  void stop() const {}
};

class Wheel {
public:
  void inflate(int psi) const {}
};

class Window {
public:
  void rollup() const {}
  void rolldown() const {}
};

class Door {
public:
  Window window;
  void open() const {}
  void close() const {}
};

class Car {
public:
  Engine engine;
  Wheel wheel[4];
  Door left, right; // 2-door
};

int main() {
  Car car;
```

```
    car.left.window.rollup();
    car.wheel[0].inflate(72);
} ///:~
```

Because the composition of a **Car** is part of the analysis of the problem (and not simply part of the underlying design), making the members **public** assists the client programmer's understanding of how to use the class and requires less code complexity for the creator of the class.

With a little thought, you'll also see that it would make no sense to compose a **Car** using a "vehicle" object – a car doesn't contain a vehicle, it *is* a vehicle. The *is-a* relationship is expressed with inheritance, and the *has-a* relationship is expressed with composition.

Subtyping

Now suppose you want to create a type of **ifstream** object that not only opens a file but also keeps track of the name of the file. You can use composition and embed both an **ifstream** and a **string** into the new class:

```
//: C14:FName1.cpp
// An fstream with a file name
#include "../require.h"
#include <iostream>
#include <fstream>
#include <string>
using namespace std;

class FName1 {
  ifstream file;
  string fileName;
  bool named;
public:
  FName1() : named(false) {}
  FName1(const string& fname)
    : fileName(fname), file(fname.c_str()) {
    assure(file, fileName);
    named = true;
  }
  string name() const { return fileName; }
```

```
  void name(const string& newName) {
    if(named) return; // Don't overwrite
    fileName = newName;
    named = true;
  }
  operator ifstream&() { return file; }
};

int main() {
  FName1 file("FName1.cpp");
  cout << file.name() << endl;
  // Error: close() not a member:
//!  file.close();
} ///:~
```

There's a problem here, however. An attempt is made to allow the use of the **FName1** object anywhere an **ifstream** object is used by including an automatic type conversion operator from **FName1** to an **ifstream&**. But in main, the line

```
file.close();
```

will not compile because automatic type conversion happens only in function calls, not during member selection. So this approach won't work.

A second approach is to add the definition of **close( )** to **FName1**:

```
void close() { file.close(); }
```

This will work if there are only a few functions you want to bring through from the **ifstream** class. In that case you're only using part of the class, and composition is appropriate.

But what if you want everything in the class to come through? This is called *subtyping* because you're making a new type from an existing type, and you want your new type to have exactly the same interface as the existing type (plus any other member functions you want to add), so you can use it everywhere you'd use the existing type. This is where inheritance is essential. You can see that subtyping solves the problem in the preceding example perfectly:

```
//: C14:FName2.cpp
```

```
// Subtyping solves the problem
#include "../require.h"
#include <iostream>
#include <fstream>
#include <string>
using namespace std;

class FName2 : public ifstream {
  string fileName;
  bool named;
public:
  FName2() : named(false) {}
  FName2(const string& fname)
    : ifstream(fname.c_str()), fileName(fname) {
    assure(*this, fileName);
    named = true;
  }
  string name() const { return fileName; }
  void name(const string& newName) {
    if(named) return; // Don't overwrite
    fileName = newName;
    named = true;
  }
};

int main() {
  FName2 file("FName2.cpp");
  assure(file, "FName2.cpp");
  cout << "name: " << file.name() << endl;
  string s;
  getline(file, s); // These work too!
  file.seekg(-200, ios::end);
  file.close();
} ///:~
```

Now any member function available for an **ifstream** object is
available for an **FName2** object. You can also see that non-member
functions like **getline( )** that expect an **ifstream** can also work
with an **FName2**. That's because an **FName2** *is* a type of
ifstream; it doesn't simply contain one. This is a very important
issue that will be explored at the end of this chapter and in the next
one.

private inheritance

You can inherit a base class privately by leaving off the **public** in the base-class list, or by explicitly saying **private** (probably a better policy because it is clear to the user that you mean it). When you inherit privately, you're "implementing in terms of;" that is, you're creating a new class that has all of the data and functionality of the base class, but that functionality is hidden, so it's only part of the underlying implementation. The class user has no access to the underlying functionality, and an object cannot be treated as a instance of the base class (as it was in **FName2.cpp**).

You may wonder what the purpose of **private** inheritance is, because the alternative of using composition to create a **private** object in the new class seems more appropriate. **private** inheritance is included in the language for completeness, but if for no other reason than to reduce confusion, you'll usually want to use composition rather than **private** inheritance. However, there may occasionally be situations where you want to produce part of the same interface as the base class *and* disallow the treatment of the object as if it were a base-class object. **private** inheritance provides this ability.

Publicizing privately inherited members

When you inherit privately, all the **public** members of the base class become **private**. If you want any of them to be visible, just say their names (no arguments or return values) along with the **using** keyword in the **public** section of the derived class:

```
//: C14:PrivateInheritance.cpp
class Pet {
public:
  char eat() const { return 'a'; }
  int speak() const { return 2; }
  float sleep() const { return 3.0; }
  float sleep(int) const { return 4.0; }
};

class Goldfish : Pet { // Private inheritance
public:
  using Pet::eat; // Name publicizes member
  using Pet::sleep; // Both members exposed
```

```
};

int main() {
  Goldfish bob;
  bob.eat();
  bob.sleep();
  bob.sleep(1);
//! bob.speak();// Error: private member function
} ///:~
```

Thus, **private** inheritance is useful if you want to hide part of the functionality of the base class.

Notice that exposing the name of an overloaded function exposes all the versions of the overloaded function in the base class.

You should think carefully before using **private** inheritance instead of composition; **private** inheritance has particular complications when combined with runtime type identification (this is the topic of a chapter in Volume 2 of this book, downloadable from *www.BruceEckel.com*).

protected

Now that you've been introduced to inheritance, the keyword **protected** finally has meaning. In an ideal world, **private** members would always be hard-and-fast **private**, but in real projects there are times when you want to make something hidden from the world at large and yet allow access for members of derived classes. The **protected** keyword is a nod to pragmatism; it says, "This is **private** as far as the class user is concerned, but available to anyone who inherits from this class."

The best approach is to leave the data members **private** – you should always preserve your right to change the underlying implementation. You can then allow controlled access to inheritors of your class through **protected** member functions:

```
//: C14:Protected.cpp
// The protected keyword
#include <fstream>
```

```
using namespace std;

class Base {
  int i;
protected:
  int read() const { return i; }
  void set(int ii) { i = ii; }
public:
  Base(int ii = 0) : i(ii) {}
  int value(int m) const { return m*i; }
};

class Derived : public Base {
  int j;
public:
  Derived(int jj = 0) : j(jj) {}
  void change(int x) { set(x); }
};

int main() {
  Derived d;
  d.change(10);
} ///:~
```

You will find examples of the need for **protected** in examples later in this book, and in Volume 2.

protected inheritance

When you're inheriting, the base class defaults to **private**, which means that all of the public member functions are **private** to the user of the new class. Normally, you'll make the inheritance **public** so the interface of the base class is also the interface of the derived class. However, you can also use the **protected** keyword during inheritance.

Protected derivation means "implemented-in-terms-of" to other classes but "is-a" for derived classes and friends. It's something you don't use very often, but it's in the language for completeness.

Operator overloading & inheritance

Except for the assignment operator, operators are automatically inherited into a derived class. This can be demonstrated by inheriting from **C12:Byte.h**:

```
//: C14:OperatorInheritance.cpp
// Inheriting overloaded operators
#include "../C12/Byte.h"
#include <fstream>
using namespace std;
ofstream out("ByteTest.out");

class Byte2 : public Byte {
public:
  // Constructors don't inherit:
  Byte2(unsigned char bb = 0) : Byte(bb) {}
  // operator= does not inherit, but
  // is synthesized for memberwise assignment.
  // However, only the SameType = SameType
  // operator= is synthesized, so you have to
  // make the others explicitly:
  Byte2& operator=(const Byte& right) {
    Byte::operator=(right);
    return *this;
  }
  Byte2& operator=(int i) {
    Byte::operator=(i);
    return *this;
  }
};

// Similar test function as in C12:ByteTest.cpp:
void k(Byte2& b1, Byte2& b2) {
  b1 = b1 * b2 + b2 % b1;

  #define TRY2(OP) \
    out << "b1 = "; b1.print(out); \
    out << ", b2 = "; b2.print(out); \
    out << ";  b1 " #OP " b2 produces "; \
    (b1 OP b2).print(out); \
    out << endl;

  b1 = 9; b2 = 47;
```

```
    TRY2(+)  TRY2(-)  TRY2(*)  TRY2(/)
    TRY2(%)  TRY2(^)  TRY2(&)  TRY2(|)
    TRY2(<<)  TRY2(>>)  TRY2(+=)  TRY2(-=)
    TRY2(*=)  TRY2(/=)  TRY2(%=)  TRY2(^=)
    TRY2(&=)  TRY2(|=)  TRY2(>>=)  TRY2(<<=)
    TRY2(=) // Assignment operator

    // Conditionals:
    #define TRYC2(OP) \
      out << "b1 = "; b1.print(out); \
      out << ", b2 = "; b2.print(out); \
      out << ";  b1 " #OP " b2 produces "; \
      out << (b1 OP b2); \
      out << endl;

    b1 = 9; b2 = 47;
    TRYC2(<)  TRYC2(>)  TRYC2(==)  TRYC2(!=)  TRYC2(<=)
    TRYC2(>=)  TRYC2(&&)  TRYC2(||)

    // Chained assignment:
    Byte2 b3 = 92;
    b1 = b2 = b3;
}

int main() {
    out << "member functions:" << endl;
    Byte2 b1(47), b2(9);
    k(b1, b2);
} ///:~
```

The test code is identical to that in **C12:ByteTest.cpp** except that
Byte2 is used instead of **Byte**. This way all the operators are
verified to work with **Byte2** via inheritance.

When you examine the class **Byte2**, you'll see that the constructor
must be explicitly defined, and that only the **operator=** that
assigns a **Byte2** to a **Byte2** is synthesized; any other assignment
operators that you need you'll have to synthesize on your own.

Multiple inheritance

You can inherit from one class, so it would seem to make sense to
inherit from more than one class at a time. Indeed you can, but

---

whether it makes sense as part of a design is a subject of continuing debate. One thing is generally agreed upon: You shouldn't try this until you've been programming quite a while and understand the language thoroughly. By that time, you'll probably realize that no matter how much you think you absolutely must use multiple inheritance, you can almost always get away with single inheritance.

Initially, multiple inheritance seems simple enough: You add more classes in the base-class list during inheritance, separated by commas. However, multiple inheritance introduces a number of possibilities for ambiguity, which is why a chapter in Volume 2 is devoted to the subject.

Incremental development

One of the advantages of inheritance and composition is that these support *incremental development* by allowing you to introduce new code without causing bugs in existing code. If bugs do appear, they are isolated within the new code. By inheriting from (or composing with) an existing, functional class and adding data members and member functions (and redefining existing member functions during inheritance) you leave the existing code – that someone else may still be using – untouched and unbugged. If a bug happens, you know it's in your new code, which is much shorter and easier to read than if you had modified the body of existing code.

It's rather amazing how cleanly the classes are separated. You don't even need the source code for the member functions in order to reuse the code, just the header file describing the class and the object file or library file with the compiled member functions. (This is true for both inheritance and composition.)

It's important to realize that program development is an incremental process, just like human learning. You can do as much analysis as you want, but you still won't know all the answers when you set out on a project. You'll have much more success – and more immediate feedback – if you start out to "grow" your project as an organic, evolutionary creature, rather than constructing it all at once like a glass-box skyscraper[2].

Although inheritance for experimentation is a useful technique, at some point after things stabilize you need to take a new look at your class hierarchy with an eye to collapsing it into a sensible structure[3]. Remember that underneath it all, inheritance is meant to express a relationship that says, "This new class is a *type of* that old class." Your program should not be concerned with pushing bits around, but instead with creating and manipulating objects of various types to express a model in the terms given you from the problem space.

Upcasting

Earlier in the chapter, you saw how an object of a class derived from **ifstream** has all the characteristics and behaviors of an **ifstream** object. In **FName2.cpp**, any **ifstream** member function could be called for an **FName2** object.

The most important aspect of inheritance is not that it provides member functions for the new class, however. It's the relationship expressed between the new class and the base class. This relationship can be summarized by saying, "The new class *is a type of* the existing class."

This description is not just a fanciful way of explaining inheritance – it's supported directly by the compiler. As an example, consider a base class called **Instrument** that represents musical instruments and a derived class called **Wind**. Because inheritance means that all the functions in the base class are also available in the derived class, any message you can send to the base class can also be sent to the derived class. So if the **Instrument** class has a **play( )** member function, so will **Wind** instruments. This means we can accurately

---

[2] To learn more about this idea, see *Extreme Programming Explained*, by Kent Beck (Addison-Wesley 2000).
[3] See *Refactoring: Improving the Design of Existing Code* by Martin Fowler (Addison-Wesley 1999).

---

say that a **Wind** object is also a type of **Instrument**. The following example shows how the compiler supports this notion:

```
//: C14:Instrument.cpp
// Inheritance & upcasting
enum note { middleC, Csharp, Cflat }; // Etc.

class Instrument {
public:
  void play(note) const {}
};

// Wind objects are Instruments
// because they have the same interface:
class Wind : public Instrument {};

void tune(Instrument& i) {
  // ...
  i.play(middleC);
}

int main() {
  Wind flute;
  tune(flute); // Upcasting
} ///:~
```

What's interesting in this example is the **tune( )** function, which accepts an **Instrument** reference. However, in **main( )** the **tune( )** function is called by handing it a reference to a **Wind** object. Given that C++ is very particular about type checking, it seems strange that a function that accepts one type will readily accept another type, until you realize that a **Wind** object is also an **Instrument** object, and there's no function that **tune( )** could call for an **Instrument** that isn't also in **Wind** (this is what inheritance guarantees). Inside **tune( )**, the code works for **Instrument** and anything derived from **Instrument**, and the act of converting a **Wind** reference or pointer into an **Instrument** reference or pointer is called *upcasting*.

Why "upcasting?"

The reason for the term is historical and is based on the way class inheritance diagrams have traditionally been drawn: with the root at the top of the page, growing downward. (Of course, you can draw your diagrams any way you find helpful.) The inheritance diagram for **Instrument.cpp** is then:

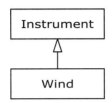

Casting from derived to base moves *up* on the inheritance diagram, so it's commonly referred to as upcasting. Upcasting is always safe because you're going from a more specific type to a more general type – the only thing that can occur to the class interface is that it can lose member functions, not gain them. This is why the compiler allows upcasting without any explicit casts or other special notation.

Upcasting and the copy-constructor

If you allow the compiler to synthesize a copy-constructor for a derived class, it will automatically call the base-class copy-constructor, and then the copy-constructors for all the member objects (or perform a bitcopy on built-in types) so you'll get the right behavior:

```
//: C14:CopyConstructor.cpp
// Correctly creating the copy-constructor
#include <iostream>
using namespace std;

class Parent {
  int i;
public:
  Parent(int ii) : i(ii) {
    cout << "Parent(int ii)\n";
  }
  Parent(const Parent& b) : i(b.i) {
    cout << "Parent(const Parent&)\n";
```

```
  }
  Parent() : i(0) { cout << "Parent()\n"; }
  friend ostream&
    operator<<(ostream& os, const Parent& b) {
    return os << "Parent: " << b.i << endl;
  }
};

class Member {
  int i;
public:
  Member(int ii) : i(ii) {
    cout << "Member(int ii)\n";
  }
  Member(const Member& m) : i(m.i) {
    cout << "Member(const Member&)\n";
  }
  friend ostream&
    operator<<(ostream& os, const Member& m) {
    return os << "Member: " << m.i << endl;
  }
};

class Child : public Parent {
  int i;
  Member m;
public:
  Child(int ii) : Parent(ii), i(ii), m(ii) {
    cout << "Child(int ii)\n";
  }
  friend ostream&
    operator<<(ostream& os, const Child& c){
    return os << (Parent&)c << c.m
             << "Child: " << c.i << endl;
  }
};

int main() {
  Child c(2);
  cout << "calling copy-constructor: " << endl;
  Child c2 = c; // Calls copy-constructor
  cout << "values in c2:\n" << c2;
} ///:~
```

The **operator<<** for **Child** is interesting because of the way that it calls the **operator<<** for the **Parent** part within it: by casting the **Child** object to a **Parent&** (if you cast to a base-class *object* instead of a reference you will usually get undesirable results):

```
return os << (Parent&)c << c.m
```

Since the compiler then sees it as a **Parent**, it calls the **Parent** version of **operator<<**.

You can see that **Child** has no explicitly-defined copy-constructor. The compiler then synthesizes the copy-constructor (since that is one of the four functions it will synthesize, along with the default constructor – if you don't create any constructors – the **operator=** and the destructor) by calling the **Parent** copy-constructor and the **Member** copy-constructor. This is shown in the output

```
Parent(int ii)
Member(int ii)
Child(int ii)
calling copy-constructor:
Parent(const Parent&)
Member(const Member&)
values in c2:
Parent: 2
Member: 2
Child: 2
```

However, if you try to write your own copy-constructor for **Child** and you make an innocent mistake and do it badly:

```
Child(const Child& c) : i(c.i), m(c.m) {}
```

then the *default* constructor will automatically be called for the base-class part of **Child**, since that's what the compiler falls back on when it has no other choice of constructor to call (remember that *some* constructor must always be called for every object, regardless of whether it's a subobject of another class). The output will then be:

```
Parent(int ii)
Member(int ii)
Child(int ii)
```

```
calling copy-constructor:
Parent()
Member(const Member&)
values in c2:
Parent: 0
Member: 2
Child: 2
```

This is probably not what you expect, since generally you'll want the base-class portion to be copied from the existing object to the new object as part of copy-construction.

To repair the problem you must remember to properly call the base-class copy-constructor (as the compiler does) whenever you write your own copy-constructor. This can seem a little strange-looking at first but it's another example of upcasting:

```
Child(const Child& c)
   : Parent(c), i(c.i), m(c.m) {
   cout << "Child(Child&)\n";
}
```

The strange part is where the **Parent** copy-constructor is called: **Parent(c)**. What does it mean to pass a **Child** object to a **Parent** constructor? But **Child** is inherited from **Parent**, so a **Child** reference *is* a **Parent** reference. The base-class copy-constructor call upcasts a reference to **Child** to a reference to **Parent** and uses it to perform the copy-construction. When you write your own copy constructors you'll almost always want to do the same thing.

Composition vs. inheritance (revisited)

One of the clearest ways to determine whether you should be using composition or inheritance is by asking whether you'll ever need to upcast from your new class. Earlier in this chapter, the **Stack** class was specialized using inheritance. However, chances are the **StringStack** objects will be used only as **string** containers and never upcast, so a more appropriate alternative is composition:

```
//: C14:InheritStack2.cpp
// Composition vs. inheritance
#include "../C09/Stack4.h"
```

```
#include "../require.h"
#include <iostream>
#include <fstream>
#include <string>
using namespace std;

class StringStack {
  Stack stack; // Embed instead of inherit
public:
  void push(string* str) {
    stack.push(str);
  }
  string* peek() const {
    return (string*)stack.peek();
  }
  string* pop() {
    return (string*)stack.pop();
  }
};

int main() {
  ifstream in("InheritStack2.cpp");
  assure(in, "InheritStack2.cpp");
  string line;
  StringStack textlines;
  while(getline(in, line))
    textlines.push(new string(line));
  string* s;
  while((s = textlines.pop()) != 0) // No cast!
    cout << *s << endl;
} ///:~
```

The file is identical to **InheritStack.cpp**, except that a **Stack** object is embedded in **StringStack**, and member functions are called for the embedded object. There's still no time or space overhead because the subobject takes up the same amount of space, and all the additional type checking happens at compile time.

Although it tends to be more confusing, you could also use **private** inheritance to express "implemented in terms of." This would also solve the problem adequately. One place it becomes important, however, is when multiple inheritance might be warranted. In that case, if you see a design in which composition can be used instead of inheritance, you may be able to eliminate the need for multiple inheritance.

Pointer & reference upcasting

In **Instrument.cpp**, the upcasting occurs during the function call – a **Wind** object outside the function has its reference taken and becomes an **Instrument** reference inside the function. Upcasting can also occur during a simple assignment to a pointer or reference:

```
Wind w;
Instrument* ip = &w; // Upcast
Instrument& ir = w; // Upcast
```

Like the function call, neither of these cases requires an explicit cast.

A crisis

Of course, any upcast loses type information about an object. If you say

```
Wind w;
Instrument* ip = &w;
```

the compiler can deal with **ip** only as an **Instrument** pointer and nothing else. That is, it cannot know that **ip** *actually* happens to point to a **Wind** object. So when you call the **play( )** member function by saying

```
ip->play(middleC);
```

the compiler can know only that it's calling **play( )** for an **Instrument** pointer, and call the base-class version of **Instrument::play( )** instead of what it should do, which is call **Wind::play( )**. Thus, you won't get the correct behavior.

This is a significant problem; it is solved in Chapter 15 by introducing the third cornerstone of object-oriented programming: polymorphism (implemented in C++ with **virtual** functions).

Summary

Both inheritance and composition allow you to create a new type from existing types, and both embed subobjects of the existing types inside the new type. Typically, however, you use composition to reuse existing types as part of the underlying implementation of the new type and inheritance when you want to force the new type to be the same type as the base class (type equivalence guarantees interface equivalence). Since the derived class has the base-class interface, it can be *upcast* to the base, which is critical for polymorphism as you'll see in Chapter 15.

Although code reuse through composition and inheritance is very helpful for rapid project development, you'll generally want to redesign your class hierarchy before allowing other programmers to become dependent on it. Your goal is a hierarchy in which each class has a specific use and is neither too big (encompassing so much functionality that it's unwieldy to reuse) nor annoyingly small (you can't use it by itself or without adding functionality).

Exercises

Solutions to selected exercises can be found in the electronic document *The Thinking in C++ Annotated Solution Guide*, available for a small fee from www.BruceEckel.com.

1.   Modify **Car.cpp** so that it also inherits from a class called **Vehicle**, placing appropriate member functions in **Vehicle** (that is, make up some member functions). Add a nondefault constructor to **Vehicle**, which you must call inside **Car**'s constructor.

2.   Create two classes, **A** and **B**, with default constructors that announce themselves. Inherit a new class called **C** from **A**, and create a member object of **B** in **C**, but do not create a constructor for **C**. Create an object of class **C** and observe the results.

3.   Create a three-level hierarchy of classes with default constructors, along with destructors, both of which announce themselves to **cout**. Verify that for an object of the most derived type, all three constructors and

---

destructors are automatically called. Explain the order in which the calls are made.

4. Modify **Combined.cpp** to add another level of inheritance and a new member object. Add code to show when the constructors and destructors are being called.

5. In **Combined.cpp**, create a class **D** that inherits from **B** and has a member object of class **C**. Add code to show when the constructors and destructors are being called.

6. Modify **Order.cpp** to add another level of inheritance **Derived3** with member objects of class **Member4** and **Member5**. Trace the output of the program.

7. In **NameHiding.cpp**, verify that in **Derived2**, **Derived3**, and **Derived4**, none of the base-class versions of **f( )** are available.

8. Modify **NameHiding.cpp** by adding three overloaded functions named **h( )** to **Base**, and show that redefining one of them in a derived class hides the others.

9. Inherit a class **StringVector** from **vector<void*>** and redefine the **push_back( )** and **operator[]** member functions to accept and produce **string***. What happens if you try to **push_back( )** a **void***?

10. Write a class containing a **long** and use the psuedo-constructor call syntax in the constructor to initialize the **long**.

11. Create a class called **Asteroid**. Use inheritance to specialize the **PStash** class in Chapter 13 (**PStash.h** & **PStash.cpp**) so that it accepts and returns **Asteroid** pointers. Also modify **PStashTest.cpp** to test your classes. Change the class so **PStash** is a member object.

12. Repeat Exercise 11 with a **vector** instead of a **PStash**.

13. In **SynthesizedFunctions.cpp**, modify **Chess** to give it a default constructor, copy-constructor, and assignment operator. Demonstrate that you've written these correctly.

14. Create two classes called **Traveler** and **Pager** without default constructors, but with constructors that take an argument of type **string**, which they simply copy to an internal **string** variable. For each class, write the correct

copy-constructor and assignment operator. Now inherit a class **BusinessTraveler** from **Traveler** and give it a member object of type **Pager**. Write the correct default constructor, a constructor that takes a **string** argument, a copy-constructor, and an assignment operator.

15. Create a class with two **static** member functions. Inherit from this class and redefine one of the member functions. Show that the other is hidden in the derived class.

16. Look up more of the member functions for **ifstream**. In **FName2.cpp**, try them out on the **file** object.

17. Use **private** and **protected** inheritance to create two new classes from a base class. Then attempt to upcast objects of the derived class to the base class. Explain what happens.

18. In **Protected.cpp**, add a member function in **Derived** that calls the **protected Base** member **read( )**.

19. Change **Protected.cpp** so that **Derived** is using **protected** inheritance. See if you can call **value( )** for a **Derived** object.

20. Create a class called **SpaceShip** with a **fly( )** method. Inherit **Shuttle** from **SpaceShip** and add a **land( )** method. Create a new **Shuttle**, upcast by pointer or reference to a **SpaceShip**, and try to call the **land( )** method. Explain the results.

21. Modify **Instrument.cpp** to add a **prepare( )** method to **Instrument**. Call **prepare( )** inside **tune( )**.

22. Modify **Instrument.cpp** so that **play( )** prints a message to **cout**, and **Wind** redefines **play( )** to print a different message to **cout**. Run the program and explain why you probably wouldn't want this behavior. Now put the **virtual** keyword (which you will learn about in Chapter 15) in front of the **play( )** declaration in **Instrument** and observe the change in the behavior.

23. In **CopyConstructor.cpp**, inherit a new class from **Child** and give it a **Member m**. Write a proper **constructor**, **copy-constructor**, **operator=**, and **operator<<** for ostreams, and test the class in **main( )**.

24. Take the example **CopyConstructor.cpp** and modify it by adding your own copy-constructor to **Child** *without* calling the base-class copy-constructor and see what happens. Fix the problem by making a proper explicit call to the base-class copy constructor in the constructor-initializer list of the **Child** copy-constructor.

25. Modify **InheritStack2.cpp** to use a **vector<string>** instead of a **Stack**.

26. Create a class **Rock** with a default constructor, a copy-constructor, an assignment operator, and a destructor, all of which announce to **cout** that they've been called. In **main( )**, create a **vector<Rock>** (that is, hold **Rock** objects by value) and add some **Rock**s. Run the program and explain the output you get. Note whether the destructors are called for the **Rock** objects in the **vector**. Now repeat the exercise with a **vector<Rock*>**. Is it possible to create a **vector<Rock&>**?

27. This exercise creates the design pattern called *proxy*. Start with a base class **Subject** and give it three functions: **f( )**, **g( )**, and **h( )**. Now inherit a class **Proxy** and two classes **Implementation1** and **Implementation2** from **Subject**. **Proxy** should contain a pointer to a **Subject**, and all the member functions for **Proxy** should just turn around and make the same calls through the **Subject** pointer. The **Proxy** constructor takes a pointer to a **Subject** that is installed in the **Proxy** (usually by the constructor). In **main( )**, create two different **Proxy** objects that use the two different implementations. Now modify **Proxy** so that you can dynamically change implementations.

28. Modify **ArrayOperatorNew.cpp** from Chapter 13 to show that, if you inherit from **Widget**, the allocation still works correctly. Explain why inheritance in **Framis.cpp** from Chapter 13 would *not* work correctly.

29. Modify **Framis.cpp** from Chapter 13 by inheriting from **Framis** and creating new versions of **new** and **delete** for your derived class. Demonstrate that they work correctly.

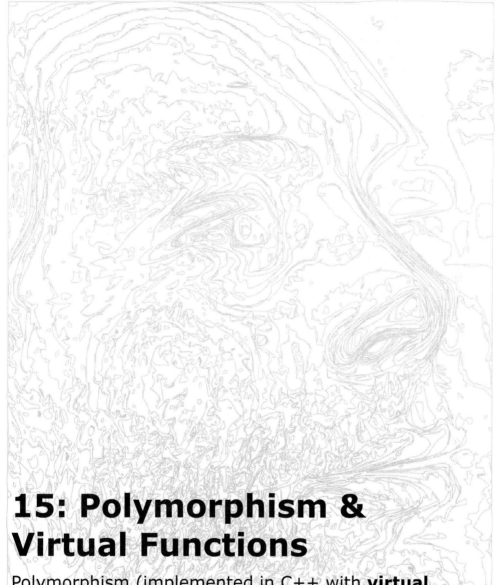

15: Polymorphism & Virtual Functions

Polymorphism (implemented in C++ with **virtual** functions) is the third essential feature of an object-oriented programming language, after data abstraction and inheritance.

It provides another dimension of separation of interface from implementation, to decouple *what* from *how*. Polymorphism allows improved code organization and readability as well as the creation of *extensible* programs that can be "grown" not only during the original creation of the project, but also when new features are desired.

Encapsulation creates new data types by combining characteristics and behaviors. Access control separates the interface from the implementation by making the details **private**. This kind of mechanical organization makes ready sense to someone with a procedural programming background. But virtual functions deal with decoupling in terms of *types*. In Chapter 14, you saw how inheritance allows the treatment of an object as its own type *or* its base type. This ability is critical because it allows many types (derived from the same base type) to be treated as if they were one type, and a single piece of code to work on all those different types equally. The virtual function allows one type to express its distinction from another, similar type, as long as they're both derived from the same base type. This distinction is expressed through differences in behavior of the functions that you can call through the base class.

In this chapter, you'll learn about virtual functions, starting from the basics with simple examples that strip away everything but the "virtualness" of the program.

Evolution of C++ programmers

C programmers seem to acquire C++ in three steps. First, as simply a "better C," because C++ forces you to declare all functions before using them and is much pickier about how variables are used. You can often find the errors in a C program simply by compiling it with a C++ compiler.

The second step is "object-based" C++. This means that you easily see the code organization benefits of grouping a data structure together with the functions that act upon it, the value of constructors and destructors, and perhaps some simple inheritance.

Most programmers who have been working with C for a while quickly see the usefulness of this because, whenever they create a library, this is exactly what they try to do. With C++, you have the aid of the compiler.

You can get stuck at the object-based level because you can quickly get there and you get a lot of benefit without much mental effort. It's also easy to feel like you're creating data types – you make classes and objects, you send messages to those objects, and everything is nice and neat.

But don't be fooled. If you stop here, you're missing out on the greatest part of the language, which is the jump to true object-oriented programming. You can do this only with virtual functions.

Virtual functions enhance the concept of type instead of just encapsulating code inside structures and behind walls, so they are without a doubt the most difficult concept for the new C++ programmer to fathom. However, they're also the turning point in the understanding of object-oriented programming. If you don't use virtual functions, you don't understand OOP yet.

Because the virtual function is intimately bound with the concept of type, and type is at the core of object-oriented programming, there is no analog to the virtual function in a traditional procedural language. As a procedural programmer, you have no referent with which to think about virtual functions, as you do with almost every other feature in the language. Features in a procedural language can be understood on an algorithmic level, but virtual functions can be understood only from a design viewpoint.

Upcasting

In Chapter 14 you saw how an object can be used as its own type or as an object of its base type. In addition, it can be manipulated through an address of the base type. Taking the address of an object (either a pointer or a reference) and treating it as the address of the base type is called *upcasting* because of the way inheritance trees are drawn with the base class at the top.

You also saw a problem arise, which is embodied in the following code:

```cpp
//: C15:Instrument2.cpp
// Inheritance & upcasting
#include <iostream>
using namespace std;
enum note { middleC, Csharp, Eflat }; // Etc.

class Instrument {
public:
  void play(note) const {
    cout << "Instrument::play" << endl;
  }
};

// Wind objects are Instruments
// because they have the same interface:
class Wind : public Instrument {
public:
  // Redefine interface function:
  void play(note) const {
    cout << "Wind::play" << endl;
  }
};

void tune(Instrument& i) {
  // ...
  i.play(middleC);
}

int main() {
  Wind flute;
  tune(flute); // Upcasting
} ///:~
```

The function **tune( )** accepts (by reference) an **Instrument**, but also without complaint anything derived from **Instrument**. In **main( )**, you can see this happening as a **Wind** object is passed to **tune( )**, with no cast necessary. This is acceptable; the interface in **Instrument** must exist in **Wind**, because **Wind** is publicly inherited from **Instrument**. Upcasting from **Wind** to

Instrument may "narrow" that interface, but never less than the full interface to **Instrument**.

The same arguments are true when dealing with pointers; the only difference is that the user must explicitly take the addresses of objects as they are passed into the function.

The problem

The problem with **Instrument2.cpp** can be seen by running the program. The output is **Instrument::play**. This is clearly not the desired output, because you happen to know that the object is actually a **Wind** and not just an **Instrument**. The call should produce **Wind::play**. For that matter, any object of a class derived from **Instrument** should have its version of **play( )** used, regardless of the situation.

The behavior of **Instrument2.cpp** is not surprising, given C's approach to functions. To understand the issues, you need to be aware of the concept of *binding*.

Function call binding

Connecting a function call to a function body is called *binding*. When binding is performed before the program is run (by the compiler and linker), it's called *early binding*. You may not have heard the term before because it's never been an option with procedural languages: C compilers have only one kind of function call, and that's early binding.

The problem in the program above is caused by early binding because the compiler cannot know the correct function to call when it has only an **Instrument** address.

The solution is called *late binding*, which means the binding occurs at runtime, based on the type of the object. Late binding is also called *dynamic binding* or *runtime binding*. When a language implements late binding, there must be some mechanism to determine the type of the object at runtime and call the appropriate member function. In the case of a compiled language, the compiler still doesn't know the actual object type, but it inserts code that finds out and calls the correct function body. The late-binding mechanism varies from language to language, but you can imagine that some sort of type information must be installed in the objects. You'll see how this works later.

virtual functions

To cause late binding to occur for a particular function, C++ requires that you use the **virtual** keyword when declaring the function in the base class. Late binding occurs only with **virtual** functions, and only when you're using an address of the base class where those **virtual** functions exist, although they may also be defined in an earlier base class.

To create a member function as **virtual**, you simply precede the declaration of the function with the keyword **virtual**. Only the declaration needs the **virtual** keyword, not the definition. If a function is declared as **virtual** in the base class, it is **virtual** in all the derived classes. The redefinition of a **virtual** function in a derived class is usually called *overriding*.

Notice that you are only required to declare a function **virtual** in the base class. All derived-class functions that match the signature of the base-class declaration will be called using the virtual mechanism. You *can* use the **virtual** keyword in the derived-class declarations (it does no harm to do so), but it is redundant and can be confusing.

To get the desired behavior from **Instrument2.cpp**, simply add the **virtual** keyword in the base class before **play( )**:

```
//: C15:Instrument3.cpp
// Late binding with the virtual keyword
#include <iostream>
using namespace std;
enum note { middleC, Csharp, Cflat }; // Etc.

class Instrument {
```

```
public:
  virtual void play(note) const {
    cout << "Instrument::play" << endl;
  }
};

// Wind objects are Instruments
// because they have the same interface:
class Wind : public Instrument {
public:
  // Override interface function:
  void play(note) const {
    cout << "Wind::play" << endl;
  }
};

void tune(Instrument& i) {
  // ...
  i.play(middleC);
}

int main() {
  Wind flute;
  tune(flute); // Upcasting
} ///:~
```

This file is identical to **Instrument2.cpp** except for the addition of the **virtual** keyword, and yet the behavior is significantly different: Now the output is **Wind::play**.

Extensibility

With **play( )** defined as **virtual** in the base class, you can add as many new types as you want without changing the **tune( )** function. In a well-designed OOP program, most or all of your functions will follow the model of **tune( )** and communicate only with the base-class interface. Such a program is *extensible* because you can add new functionality by inheriting new data types from the common base class. The functions that manipulate the base-class interface will not need to be changed at all to accommodate the new classes.

Here's the instrument example with more virtual functions and a number of new classes, all of which work correctly with the old, unchanged **tune( )** function:

```
//: C15:Instrument4.cpp
// Extensibility in OOP
#include <iostream>
using namespace std;
enum note { middleC, Csharp, Cflat }; // Etc.

class Instrument {
public:
  virtual void play(note) const {
    cout << "Instrument::play" << endl;
  }
  virtual char* what() const {
    return "Instrument";
  }
  // Assume this will modify the object:
  virtual void adjust(int) {}
};

class Wind : public Instrument {
public:
  void play(note) const {
    cout << "Wind::play" << endl;
  }
  char* what() const { return "Wind"; }
  void adjust(int) {}
};

class Percussion : public Instrument {
public:
  void play(note) const {
    cout << "Percussion::play" << endl;
  }
  char* what() const { return "Percussion"; }
  void adjust(int) {}
};

class Stringed : public Instrument {
public:
  void play(note) const {
    cout << "Stringed::play" << endl;
```

```
  }
  char* what() const { return "Stringed"; }
  void adjust(int) {}
};

class Brass : public Wind {
public:
  void play(note) const {
    cout << "Brass::play" << endl;
  }
  char* what() const { return "Brass"; }
};

class Woodwind : public Wind {
public:
  void play(note) const {
    cout << "Woodwind::play" << endl;
  }
  char* what() const { return "Woodwind"; }
};

// Identical function from before:
void tune(Instrument& i) {
  // ...
  i.play(middleC);
}

// New function:
void f(Instrument& i) { i.adjust(1); }

// Upcasting during array initialization:
Instrument* A[] = {
  new Wind,
  new Percussion,
  new Stringed,
  new Brass,
};

int main() {
  Wind flute;
  Percussion drum;
  Stringed violin;
  Brass flugelhorn;
  Woodwind recorder;
  tune(flute);
```

```
    tune(drum);
    tune(violin);
    tune(flugelhorn);
    tune(recorder);
    f(flugelhorn);
} ///:~
```

You can see that another inheritance level has been added beneath **Wind**, but the **virtual** mechanism works correctly no matter how many levels there are. The **adjust( )** function is *not* overridden for **Brass** and **Woodwind**. When this happens, the "closest" definition in the inheritance hierarchy is automatically used – the compiler guarantees there's always *some* definition for a virtual function, so you'll never end up with a call that doesn't bind to a function body. (That would be disastrous.)

The array **A[ ]** contains pointers to the base class **Instrument**, so upcasting occurs during the process of array initialization. This array and the function **f( )** will be used in later discussions.

In the call to **tune( )**, upcasting is performed on each different type of object, yet the desired behavior always takes place. This can be described as "sending a message to an object and letting the object worry about what to do with it." The **virtual** function is the lens to use when you're trying to analyze a project: Where should the base classes occur, and how might you want to extend the program? However, even if you don't discover the proper base class interfaces and virtual functions at the initial creation of the program, you'll often discover them later, even much later, when you set out to extend or otherwise maintain the program. This is not an analysis or design error; it simply means you didn't or couldn't know all the information the first time. Because of the tight class modularization in C++, it isn't a large problem when this occurs because changes you make in one part of a system tend not to propagate to other parts of the system as they do in C.

How C++ implements late binding

How can late binding happen? All the work goes on behind the scenes by the compiler, which installs the necessary late-binding mechanism when you ask it to (you ask by creating virtual functions). Because programmers often benefit from understanding the mechanism of virtual functions in C++, this section will elaborate on the way the compiler implements this mechanism.

The keyword **virtual** tells the compiler it should not perform early binding. Instead, it should automatically install all the mechanisms necessary to perform late binding. This means that if you call **play( )** for a **Brass** object *through an address for the base-class* **Instrument**, you'll get the proper function.

To accomplish this, the typical compiler[1] creates a single table (called the VTABLE) for each class that contains **virtual** functions. The compiler places the addresses of the virtual functions for that particular class in the VTABLE. In each class with virtual functions, it secretly places a pointer, called the *vpointer* (abbreviated as VPTR), which points to the VTABLE for that object. When you make a virtual function call through a base-class pointer (that is, when you make a polymorphic call), the compiler quietly inserts code to fetch the VPTR and look up the function address in the VTABLE, thus calling the correct function and causing late binding to take place.

All of this – setting up the VTABLE for each class, initializing the VPTR, inserting the code for the virtual function call – happens automatically, so you don't have to worry about it. With virtual functions, the proper function gets called for an object, even if the compiler cannot know the specific type of the object.

The following sections go into this process in more detail.

Storing type information

You can see that there is no explicit type information stored in any of the classes. But the previous examples, and simple logic, tell you that there must be some sort of type information stored in the

---

[1] Compilers may implement virtual behavior any way they want, but the way it's described here is an almost universal approach.

---

objects; otherwise the type could not be established at runtime. This is true, but the type information is hidden. To see it, here's an example to examine the sizes of classes that use virtual functions compared with those that don't:

```cpp
//: C15:Sizes.cpp
// Object sizes with/without virtual functions
#include <iostream>
using namespace std;

class NoVirtual {
  int a;
public:
  void x() const {}
  int i() const { return 1; }
};

class OneVirtual {
  int a;
public:
  virtual void x() const {}
  int i() const { return 1; }
};

class TwoVirtuals {
  int a;
public:
  virtual void x() const {}
  virtual int i() const { return 1; }
};

int main() {
  cout << "int: " << sizeof(int) << endl;
  cout << "NoVirtual: "
       << sizeof(NoVirtual) << endl;
  cout << "void* : " << sizeof(void*) << endl;
  cout << "OneVirtual: "
       << sizeof(OneVirtual) << endl;
  cout << "TwoVirtuals: "
       << sizeof(TwoVirtuals) << endl;
} ///:~
```

With no virtual functions, the size of the object is exactly what you'd expect: the size of a single[2] **int**. With a single virtual function in **OneVirtual**, the size of the object is the size of **NoVirtual** plus the size of a **void** pointer. It turns out that the compiler inserts a single pointer (the VPTR) into the structure if you have one *or more* virtual functions. There is no size difference between **OneVirtual** and **TwoVirtuals**. That's because the VPTR points to a table of function addresses. You need only one table because all the virtual function addresses are contained in that single table.

This example required at least one data member. If there had been no data members, the C++ compiler would have forced the objects to be a nonzero size because each object must have a distinct address. If you imagine indexing into an array of zero-sized objects, you'll understand. A "dummy" member is inserted into objects that would otherwise be zero-sized. When the type information is inserted because of the **virtual** keyword, this takes the place of the "dummy" member. Try commenting out the **int a** in all the classes in the example above to see this.

Picturing virtual functions

To understand exactly what's going on when you use a virtual function, it's helpful to visualize the activities going on behind the curtain. Here's a drawing of the array of pointers **A[ ]** in **Instrument4.cpp**:

---

[2] Some compilers might have size issues here but it will be rare.

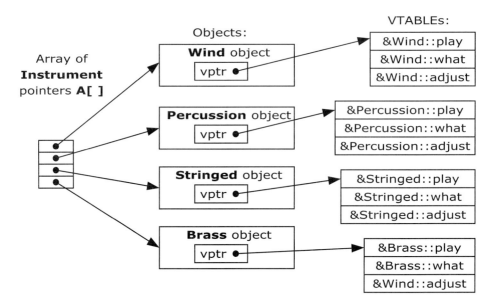

The array of **Instrument** pointers has no specific type information; they each point to an object of type **Instrument**. **Wind**, **Percussion**, **Stringed**, and **Brass** all fit into this category because they are derived from **Instrument** (and thus have the same interface as **Instrument**, and can respond to the same messages), so their addresses can also be placed into the array. However, the compiler doesn't know that they are anything more than **Instrument** objects, so left to its own devices it would normally call the base-class versions of all the functions. But in this case, all those functions have been declared with the **virtual** keyword, so something different happens.

Each time you create a class that contains virtual functions, or you derive from a class that contains virtual functions, the compiler creates a unique VTABLE for that class, seen on the right of the diagram. In that table it places the addresses of all the functions that are declared virtual in this class or in the base class. If you don't override a function that was declared virtual in the base class, the compiler uses the address of the base-class version in the derived class. (You can see this in the **adjust** entry in the **Brass** VTABLE.) Then it places the VPTR (discovered in **Sizes.cpp**) into the class. There is only one VPTR for each object when using simple inheritance like this. The VPTR must be initialized to point to the starting address of the appropriate VTABLE. (This happens in the constructor, which you'll see later in more detail.)

Once the VPTR is initialized to the proper VTABLE, the object in effect "knows" what type it is. But this self-knowledge is worthless unless it is used at the point a virtual function is called.

When you call a virtual function through a base class address (the situation when the compiler doesn't have all the information necessary to perform early binding), something special happens. Instead of performing a typical function call, which is simply an assembly-language **CALL** to a particular address, the compiler generates different code to perform the function call. Here's what a call to **adjust( )** for a **Brass** object looks like, if made through an **Instrument** pointer (An **Instrument** reference produces the same result):

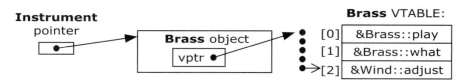

The compiler begins with the **Instrument** pointer, which points to the starting address of the object. All **Instrument** objects or objects derived from **Instrument** have their VPTR in the same place (often at the beginning of the object), so the compiler can pick the VPTR out of the object. The VPTR points to the starting address of the VTABLE. All the VTABLE function addresses are laid out in the same order, regardless of the specific type of the object. **play( )** is first, **what( )** is second, and **adjust( )** is third. The compiler knows that regardless of the specific object type, the **adjust( )** function is at the location VPTR+2. Thus, instead of saying, "Call the function at the absolute location **Instrument::adjust**" (early binding; the wrong action), it generates code that says, in effect, "Call the function at VPTR+2." Because the fetching of the VPTR and the determination of the actual function address occur at runtime, you get the desired late binding. You send a message to the object, and the object figures out what to do with it.

Under the hood

It can be helpful to see the assembly-language code generated by a virtual function call, so you can see that late-binding is indeed taking place. Here's the output from one compiler for the call

```
i.adjust(1);
```

inside the function **f(Instrument& i)**:

```
push   1
push   si
mov    bx, word ptr [si]
call   word ptr [bx+4]
add    sp, 4
```

The arguments of a C++ function call, like a C function call, are pushed on the stack from right to left (this order is required to support C's variable argument lists), so the argument **1** is pushed on the stack first. At this point in the function, the register **si** (part of the Intel X86 processor architecture) contains the address of **i**. This is also pushed on the stack because it is the starting address of the object of interest. Remember that the starting address corresponds to the value of **this**, and **this** is quietly pushed on the stack as an argument before every member function call, so the member function knows which particular object it is working on. So you'll always see one more than the number of arguments pushed on the stack before a member function call (except for **static** member functions, which have no **this**).

Now the actual virtual function call must be performed. First, the VPTR must be produced, so the VTABLE can be found. For this compiler the VPTR is inserted at the beginning of the object, so the contents of **this** correspond to the VPTR. The line

```
mov bx, word ptr [si]
```

fetches the word that **si** (that is, **this**) points to, which is the VPTR. It places the VPTR into the register **bx**.

The VPTR contained in **bx** points to the starting address of the VTABLE, but the function pointer to call isn't at location zero of the

VTABLE, but instead at location two (because it's the third function in the list). For this memory model each function pointer is two bytes long, so the compiler adds four to the VPTR to calculate where the address of the proper function is. Note that this is a constant value, established at compile time, so the only thing that matters is that the function pointer at location number two is the one for **adjust( )**. Fortunately, the compiler takes care of all the bookkeeping for you and ensures that all the function pointers in all the VTABLEs of a particular class hierarchy occur in the same order, regardless of the order that you may override them in derived classes.

Once the address of the proper function pointer in the VTABLE is calculated, that function is called. So the address is fetched and called all at once in the statement

```
call word ptr [bx+4]
```

Finally, the stack pointer is moved back up to clean off the arguments that were pushed before the call. In C and C++ assembly code you'll often see the caller clean off the arguments but this may vary depending on processors and compiler implementations.

Installing the vpointer

Because the VPTR determines the virtual function behavior of the object, you can see how it's critical that the VPTR always be pointing to the proper VTABLE. You don't ever want to be able to make a call to a virtual function before the VPTR is properly initialized. Of course, the place where initialization can be guaranteed is in the constructor, but none of the **Instrument** examples has a constructor.

This is where creation of the default constructor is essential. In the **Instrument** examples, the compiler creates a default constructor that does nothing except initialize the VPTR. This constructor, of course, is automatically called for all **Instrument** objects before you can do anything with them, so you know that it's always safe to call virtual functions.

The implications of the automatic initialization of the VPTR inside the constructor are discussed in a later section.

Objects are different

It's important to realize that upcasting deals only with addresses. If the compiler has an object, it knows the exact type and therefore (in C++) will not use late binding for any function calls – or at least, the compiler doesn't *need* to use late binding. For efficiency's sake, most compilers will perform early binding when they are making a call to a virtual function for an object because they know the exact type. Here's an example:

```
//: C15:Early.cpp
// Early binding & virtual functions
#include <iostream>
#include <string>
using namespace std;

class Pet {
public:
  virtual string speak() const { return ""; }
};

class Dog : public Pet {
public:
  string speak() const { return "Bark!"; }
};

int main() {
  Dog ralph;
  Pet* p1 = &ralph;
  Pet& p2 = ralph;
  Pet p3;
  // Late binding for both:
  cout << "p1->speak() = " << p1->speak() <<endl;
  cout << "p2.speak() = " << p2.speak() << endl;
  // Early binding (probably):
  cout << "p3.speak() = " << p3.speak() << endl;
} ///:~
```

In **p1–>speak( )** and **p2.speak( )**, addresses are used, which means the information is incomplete: **p1** and **p2** can represent the address of a **Pet** *or* something derived from **Pet**, so the virtual mechanism must be used. When calling **p3.speak( )** there's no ambiguity. The compiler knows the exact type and that it's an object, so it can't possibly be an object derived from **Pet** – it's *exactly* a **Pet**. Thus, early binding is probably used. However, if the compiler doesn't want to work so hard, it can still use late binding and the same behavior will occur.

Why virtual functions?

At this point you may have a question: "If this technique is so important, and if it makes the 'right' function call all the time, why is it an option? Why do I even need to know about it?"

This is a good question, and the answer is part of the fundamental philosophy of C++: "Because it's not quite as efficient." You can see from the previous assembly-language output that instead of one simple CALL to an absolute address, there are two – more sophisticated – assembly instructions required to set up the virtual function call. This requires both code space and execution time.

Some object-oriented languages have taken the approach that late binding is so intrinsic to object-oriented programming that it should always take place, that it should not be an option, and the user shouldn't have to know about it. This is a design decision when creating a language, and that particular path is appropriate for many languages.[3] However, C++ comes from the C heritage, where efficiency is critical. After all, C was created to replace assembly language for the implementation of an operating system (thereby rendering that operating system – Unix – far more portable than its predecessors). One of the main reasons for the invention of C++ was to make C programmers more efficient.[4] And the first question asked when C programmers encounter C++ is, "What kind of size and speed impact will I get?" If the answer were, "Everything's great

---

[3] Smalltalk, Java, and Python, for instance, use this approach with great success.

[4] At Bell Labs, where C++ was invented, there are a *lot* of C programmers. Making them all more efficient, even just a bit, saves the company many millions.

---

except for function calls when you'll always have a little extra overhead," many people would stick with C rather than make the change to C++. In addition, inline functions would not be possible, because virtual functions must have an address to put into the VTABLE. So the virtual function is an option, *and* the language defaults to nonvirtual, which is the fastest configuration. Stroustrup stated that his guideline was, "If you don't use it, you don't pay for it."

Thus, the **virtual** keyword is provided for efficiency tuning. When designing your classes, however, you shouldn't be worrying about efficiency tuning. If you're going to use polymorphism, use virtual functions everywhere. You only need to look for functions that can be made non-virtual when searching for ways to speed up your code (and there are usually much bigger gains to be had in other areas – a good profiler will do a better job of finding bottlenecks than you will by making guesses).

Anecdotal evidence suggests that the size and speed impacts of going to C++ are within 10 percent of the size and speed of C, and often much closer to the same. The reason you might get better size and speed efficiency is because you may design a C++ program in a smaller, faster way than you would using C.

Abstract base classes and pure virtual functions

Often in a design, you want the base class to present *only* an interface for its derived classes. That is, you don't want anyone to actually create an object of the base class, only to upcast to it so that its interface can be used. This is accomplished by making that class *abstract*, which happens if you give it at least one *pure virtual function*. You can recognize a pure virtual function because it uses the **virtual** keyword and is followed by = **0**. If anyone tries to make an object of an abstract class, the compiler prevents them. This is a tool that allows you to enforce a particular design.

When an abstract class is inherited, all pure virtual functions must be implemented, or the inherited class becomes abstract as well. Creating a pure virtual function allows you to put a member function in an interface without being forced to provide a possibly meaningless body of code for that member function. At the same time, a pure virtual function forces inherited classes to provide a definition for it.

In all of the instrument examples, the functions in the base class **Instrument** were always "dummy" functions. If these functions are ever called, something is wrong. That's because the intent of **Instrument** is to create a common interface for all of the classes derived from it.

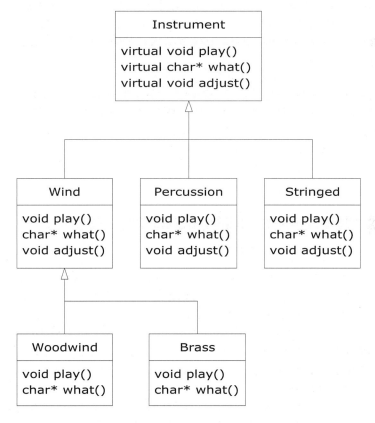

The only reason to establish the common interface is so it can be expressed differently for each different subtype. It creates a basic form that determines what's in common with all of the derived classes – nothing else. So **Instrument** is an appropriate candidate to be an abstract class. You create an abstract class when you only want to manipulate a set of classes through a common interface, but the common interface doesn't need to have an implementation (or at least, a full implementation).

If you have a concept like **Instrument** that works as an abstract class, objects of that class almost always have no meaning. That is, **Instrument** is meant to express only the interface, and not a particular implementation, so creating an object that is only an **Instrument** makes no sense, and you'll probably want to prevent the user from doing it. This can be accomplished by making all the virtual functions in **Instrument** print error messages, but that delays the appearance of the error information until runtime and it requires reliable exhaustive testing on the part of the user. It is much better to catch the problem at compile time.

Here is the syntax used for a pure virtual declaration:

```
virtual void f() = 0;
```

By doing this, you tell the compiler to reserve a slot for a function in the VTABLE, but not to put an address in that particular slot. Even if only one function in a class is declared as pure virtual, the VTABLE is incomplete.

If the VTABLE for a class is incomplete, what is the compiler supposed to do when someone tries to make an object of that class? It cannot safely create an object of an abstract class, so you get an error message from the compiler. Thus, the compiler guarantees the purity of the abstract class. By making a class abstract, you ensure that the client programmer cannot misuse it.

Here's **Instrument4.cpp** modified to use pure virtual functions. Because the class has nothing but pure virtual functions, we call it a *pure abstract class*:

```
//: C15:Instrument5.cpp
// Pure abstract base classes
#include <iostream>
using namespace std;
```

```
enum note { middleC, Csharp, Cflat }; // Etc.

class Instrument {
public:
  // Pure virtual functions:
  virtual void play(note) const = 0;
  virtual char* what() const = 0;
  // Assume this will modify the object:
  virtual void adjust(int) = 0;
};
// Rest of the file is the same ...

class Wind : public Instrument {
public:
  void play(note) const {
    cout << "Wind::play" << endl;
  }
  char* what() const { return "Wind"; }
  void adjust(int) {}
};

class Percussion : public Instrument {
public:
  void play(note) const {
    cout << "Percussion::play" << endl;
  }
  char* what() const { return "Percussion"; }
  void adjust(int) {}
};

class Stringed : public Instrument {
public:
  void play(note) const {
    cout << "Stringed::play" << endl;
  }
  char* what() const { return "Stringed"; }
  void adjust(int) {}
};

class Brass : public Wind {
public:
  void play(note) const {
    cout << "Brass::play" << endl;
  }
  char* what() const { return "Brass"; }
```

```
};

class Woodwind : public Wind {
public:
  void play(note) const {
    cout << "Woodwind::play" << endl;
  }
  char* what() const { return "Woodwind"; }
};

// Identical function from before:
void tune(Instrument& i) {
  // ...
  i.play(middleC);
}

// New function:
void f(Instrument& i) { i.adjust(1); }

int main() {
  Wind flute;
  Percussion drum;
  Stringed violin;
  Brass flugelhorn;
  Woodwind recorder;
  tune(flute);
  tune(drum);
  tune(violin);
  tune(flugelhorn);
  tune(recorder);
  f(flugelhorn);
} ///:~
```

Pure virtual functions are helpful because they make explicit the abstractness of a class and tell both the user and the compiler how it was intended to be used.

Note that pure virtual functions prevent an abstract class from being passed into a function *by value*. Thus, it is also a way to prevent *object slicing* (which will be described shortly). By making a class abstract, you can ensure that a pointer or reference is always used during upcasting to that class.

Just because one pure virtual function prevents the VTABLE from being completed doesn't mean that you don't want function bodies for some of the others. Often you will want to call a base-class version of a function, even if it is virtual. It's always a good idea to put common code as close as possible to the root of your hierarchy. Not only does this save code space, it allows easy propagation of changes.

Pure virtual definitions

It's possible to provide a definition for a pure virtual function in the base class. You're still telling the compiler not to allow objects of that abstract base class, and the pure virtual functions must still be defined in derived classes in order to create objects. However, there may be a common piece of code that you want some or all of the derived class definitions to call rather than duplicating that code in every function.

Here's what a pure virtual definition looks like:

```
//: C15:PureVirtualDefinitions.cpp
// Pure virtual base definitions
#include <iostream>
using namespace std;

class Pet {
public:
  virtual void speak() const = 0;
  virtual void eat() const = 0;
  // Inline pure virtual definitions illegal:
  //!  virtual void sleep() const = 0 {}
};

// OK, not defined inline
void Pet::eat() const {
  cout << "Pet::eat()" << endl;
}

void Pet::speak() const {
  cout << "Pet::speak()" << endl;
}
```

```
class Dog : public Pet {
public:
  // Use the common Pet code:
  void speak() const { Pet::speak(); }
  void eat() const { Pet::eat(); }
};

int main() {
  Dog simba;  // Richard's dog
  simba.speak();
  simba.eat();
} ///:~
```

The slot in the **Pet** VTABLE is still empty, but there happens to be a function by that name that you can call in the derived class.

The other benefit to this feature is that it allows you to change from an ordinary virtual to a pure virtual without disturbing the existing code. (This is a way for you to locate classes that don't override that virtual function.)

Inheritance and the VTABLE

You can imagine what happens when you perform inheritance and override some of the virtual functions. The compiler creates a new VTABLE for your new class, and it inserts your new function addresses using the base-class function addresses for any virtual functions you don't override. One way or another, for every object that can be created (that is, its class has no pure virtuals) there's always a full set of function addresses in the VTABLE, so you'll never be able to make a call to an address that isn't there (which would be disastrous).

But what happens when you inherit and add new virtual functions in the *derived* class? Here's a simple example:

```
//: C15:AddingVirtuals.cpp
// Adding virtuals in derivation
#include <iostream>
#include <string>
using namespace std;
```

```
class Pet {
  string pname;
public:
  Pet(const string& petName) : pname(petName) {}
  virtual string name() const { return pname; }
  virtual string speak() const { return ""; }
};

class Dog : public Pet {
  string name;
public:
  Dog(const string& petName) : Pet(petName) {}
  // New virtual function in the Dog class:
  virtual string sit() const {
    return Pet::name() + " sits";
  }
  string speak() const { // Override
    return Pet::name() + " says 'Bark!'";
  }
};

int main() {
  Pet* p[] = {new Pet("generic"),new Dog("bob")};
  cout << "p[0]->speak() = "
       << p[0]->speak() << endl;
  cout << "p[1]->speak() = "
       << p[1]->speak() << endl;
//! cout << "p[1]->sit() = "
//!      << p[1]->sit() << endl; // Illegal
} ///:~
```

The class **Pet** contains a two virtual functions: **speak( )** and **name( )**. **Dog** adds a third virtual function called **sit( )**, as well as overriding the meaning of **speak( )**. A diagram will help you visualize what's happening. Here are the VTABLEs created by the compiler for **Pet** and **Dog**:

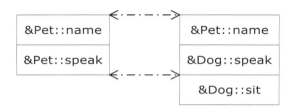

Notice that the compiler maps the location of the **speak( )** address into exactly the same spot in the **Dog** VTABLE as it is in the **Pet** VTABLE. Similarly, if a class **Pug** is inherited from **Dog**, its version of **sit( )** would be placed in its VTABLE in exactly the same spot as it is in **Dog**. This is because (as you saw with the assembly-language example) the compiler generates code that uses a simple numerical offset into the VTABLE to select the virtual function. Regardless of the specific subtype the object belongs to, its VTABLE is laid out the same way, so calls to the virtual functions will always be made the same way.

In this case, however, the compiler is working only with a pointer to a base-class object. The base class has only the **speak( )** and **name( )** functions, so those is the only functions the compiler will allow you to call. How could it possibly know that you are working with a **Dog** object, if it has only a pointer to a base-class object? That pointer might point to some other type, which doesn't have a **sit( )** function. It may or may not have some other function address at that point in the VTABLE, but in either case, making a virtual call to that VTABLE address is not what you want to do. So the compiler is doing its job by protecting you from making virtual calls to functions that exist only in derived classes.

There are some less-common cases in which you may know that the pointer actually points to an object of a specific subclass. If you want to call a function that only exists in that subclass, then you must cast the pointer. You can remove the error message produced by the previous program like this:

```
((Dog*)p[1])->sit()
```

Here, you happen to know that **p[1]** points to a **Dog** object, but in general you don't know that. If your problem is set up so that you must know the exact types of all objects, you should rethink it, because you're probably not using virtual functions properly. However, there are some situations in which the design works best (or you have no choice) if you know the exact type of all objects kept in a generic container. This is the problem of *run-time type identification* (RTTI).

RTTI is all about casting base-class pointers *down* to derived-class pointers ("up" and "down" are relative to a typical class diagram, with the base class at the top). Casting *up* happens automatically, with no coercion, because it's completely safe. Casting *down* is unsafe because there's no compile time information about the actual types, so you must know exactly what type the object is. If you cast it into the wrong type, you'll be in trouble.

RTTI is described later in this chapter, and Volume 2 of this book has a chapter devoted to the subject.

Object slicing

There is a distinct difference between passing the addresses of objects and passing objects by value when using polymorphism. All the examples you've seen here, and virtually all the examples you should see, pass addresses and not values. This is because addresses all have the same size[5], so passing the address of an object of a derived type (which is usually a bigger object) is the same as passing the address of an object of the base type (which is usually a smaller object). As explained before, this is the goal when using polymorphism – code that manipulates a base type can transparently manipulate derived-type objects as well.

If you upcast to an object instead of a pointer or reference, something will happen that may surprise you: the object is "sliced" until all that remains is the subobject that corresponds to the destination type of your cast. In the following example you can see what happens when an object is sliced:

---

[5] Actually, not all pointers are the same size on all machines. In the context of this discussion, however, they can be considered to be the same.

```
//: C15:ObjectSlicing.cpp
#include <iostream>
#include <string>
using namespace std;

class Pet {
  string pname;
public:
  Pet(const string& name) : pname(name) {}
  virtual string name() const { return pname; }
  virtual string description() const {
    return "This is " + pname;
  }
};

class Dog : public Pet {
  string favoriteActivity;
public:
  Dog(const string& name, const string& activity)
    : Pet(name), favoriteActivity(activity) {}
  string description() const {
    return Pet::name() + " likes to " +
      favoriteActivity;
  }
};

void describe(Pet p) { // Slices the object
  cout << p.description() << endl;
}

int main() {
  Pet p("Alfred");
  Dog d("Fluffy", "sleep");
  describe(p);
  describe(d);
} ///:~
```

The function **describe( )** is passed an object of type **Pet** *by value*.
It then calls the virtual function **description( )** for the **Pet** object.
In **main( )**, you might expect the first call to produce "This is
Alfred," and the second to produce "Fluffy likes to sleep." In fact,
both calls use the base-class version of **description( )**.

Two things are happening in this program. First, because **describe( )** accepts a **Pet** *object* (rather than a pointer or reference), any calls to **describe( )** will cause an object the size of **Pet** to be pushed on the stack and cleaned up after the call. This means that if an object of a class inherited from **Pet** is passed to **describe( )**, the compiler accepts it, but it copies only the **Pet** portion of the object. It *slices* the derived portion off of the object, like this:

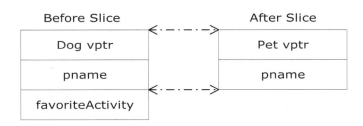

Now you may wonder about the virtual function call. **Dog::description( )** makes use of portions of both **Pet** (which still exists) and **Dog**, which no longer exists because it was sliced off! So what happens when the virtual function is called?

You're saved from disaster because the object is being passed by value. Because of this, the compiler knows the precise type of the object because the derived object has been forced to become a base object. When passing by value, the copy-constructor for a **Pet** object is used, which initializes the VPTR to the **Pet** VTABLE and copies only the **Pet** parts of the object. There's no explicit copy-constructor here, so the compiler synthesizes one. Under all interpretations, the object truly becomes a **Pet** during slicing.

Object slicing actually removes part of the existing object as it copies it into the new object, rather than simply changing the meaning of an address as when using a pointer or reference. Because of this, upcasting into an object is not done often; in fact, it's usually something to watch out for and prevent. Note that, in this example, if **description( )** were made into a pure virtual function in the base class (which is not unreasonable, since it doesn't really do anything in the base class), then the compiler would prevent object slicing because that wouldn't allow you to "create" an object of the base type (which is what happens when you upcast by value). This could be the most important value of pure virtual functions: to prevent object slicing by generating a compile-time error message if someone tries to do it.

Overloading & overriding

In Chapter 14, you saw that redefining an overloaded function in the base class hides all of the other base-class versions of that function. When **virtual** functions are involved the behavior is a little different. Consider a modified version of the **NameHiding.cpp** example from Chapter 14:

```cpp
//: C15:NameHiding2.cpp
// Virtual functions restrict overloading
#include <iostream>
#include <string>
using namespace std;

class Base {
public:
  virtual int f() const {
    cout << "Base::f()\n";
    return 1;
  }
  virtual void f(string) const {}
  virtual void g() const {}
};

class Derived1 : public Base {
public:
  void g() const {}
};

class Derived2 : public Base {
public:
  // Overriding a virtual function:
  int f() const {
    cout << "Derived2::f()\n";
    return 2;
  }
```

```
};

class Derived3 : public Base {
public:
  // Cannot change return type:
  //! void f() const{ cout << "Derived3::f()\n"; }
};

class Derived4 : public Base {
public:
  // Change argument list:
  int f(int) const {
    cout << "Derived4::f()\n";
    return 4;
  }
};

int main() {
  string s("hello");
  Derived1 d1;
  int x = d1.f();
  d1.f(s);
  Derived2 d2;
  x = d2.f();
//!  d2.f(s); // string version hidden
  Derived4 d4;
  x = d4.f(1);
//!  x = d4.f(); // f() version hidden
//!  d4.f(s); // string version hidden
  Base& br = d4; // Upcast
//!  br.f(1); // Derived version unavailable
  br.f(); // Base version available
  br.f(s); // Base version abailable
} ///:~
```

The first thing to notice is that in **Derived3**, the compiler will not allow you to change the return type of an overridden function (it will allow it if **f( )** is not virtual). This is an important restriction because the compiler must guarantee that you can polymorphically call the function through the base class, and if the base class is expecting an **int** to be returned from **f( )**, then the derived-class version of **f( )** must keep that contract or else things will break.

The rule shown in Chapter 14 still works: if you override one of the overloaded member functions in the base class, the other overloaded versions become hidden in the derived class. In **main( )** the code that tests **Derived4** shows that this happens even if the new version of **f( )** isn't actually overriding an existing virtual function interface – both of the base-class versions of **f( )** are hidden by **f(int)**. However, if you upcast **d4** to **Base**, then only the base-class versions are available (because that's what the base-class contract promises) and the derived-class version is not available (because it isn't specified in the base class).

Variant return type

The **Derived3** class above suggests that you cannot modify the return type of a virtual function during overriding. This is generally true, but there is a special case in which you can slightly modify the return type. If you're returning a pointer or a reference to a base class, then the overridden version of the function may return a pointer or reference to a class derived from what the base returns. For example:

```cpp
//: C15:VariantReturn.cpp
// Returning a pointer or reference to a derived
// type during ovverriding
#include <iostream>
#include <string>
using namespace std;

class PetFood {
public:
  virtual string foodType() const = 0;
};

class Pet {
public:
  virtual string type() const = 0;
  virtual PetFood* eats() = 0;
};

class Bird : public Pet {
public:
  string type() const { return "Bird"; }
```

```
  class BirdFood : public PetFood {
  public:
    string foodType() const {
      return "Bird food";
    }
  };
  // Upcast to base type:
  PetFood* eats() { return &bf; }
private:
  BirdFood bf;
};

class Cat : public Pet {
public:
  string type() const { return "Cat"; }
  class CatFood : public PetFood {
  public:
    string foodType() const { return "Birds"; }
  };
  // Return exact type instead:
  CatFood* eats() { return &cf; }
private:
  CatFood cf;
};

int main() {
  Bird b;
  Cat c;
  Pet* p[] = { &b, &c, };
  for(int i = 0; i < sizeof p / sizeof *p; i++)
    cout << p[i]->type() << " eats "
         << p[i]->eats()->foodType() << endl;
  // Can return the exact type:
  Cat::CatFood* cf = c.eats();
  Bird::BirdFood* bf;
  // Cannot return the exact type:
//!  bf = b.eats();
  // Must downcast:
  bf = dynamic_cast<Bird::BirdFood*>(b.eats());
} ///:~
```

The **Pet::eats( )** member function returns a pointer to a **PetFood**.
In **Bird**, this member function is overloaded exactly as in the base

---

class, including the return type. That is, **Bird::eats( )** upcasts the **BirdFood** to a **PetFood**.

But in **Cat**, the return type of **eats( )** is a pointer to **CatFood**, a type derived from **PetFood**. The fact that the return type is inherited from the return type of the base-class function is the only reason this compiles. That way, the contract is still fulfilled; **eats( )** always returns a **PetFood** pointer.

If you think polymorphically, this doesn't seem necessary. Why not just upcast all the return types to **PetFood***, just as **Bird::eats( )** did? This is typically a good solution, but at the end of **main( )**, you see the difference: **Cat::eats( )** can return the exact type of **PetFood**, whereas the return value of **Bird::eats( )** must be downcast to the exact type.

So being able to return the exact type is a little more general, and doesn't lose the specific type information by automatically upcasting. However, returning the base type will generally solve your problems so this is a rather specialized feature.

virtual functions & constructors

When an object containing virtual functions is created, its VPTR must be initialized to point to the proper VTABLE. This must be done before there's any possibility of calling a virtual function. As you might guess, because the constructor has the job of bringing an object into existence, it is also the constructor's job to set up the VPTR. The compiler secretly inserts code into the beginning of the constructor that initializes the VPTR. And as described in Chapter 14, if you don't explicitly create a constructor for a class, the compiler will synthesize one for you. If the class has virtual functions, the synthesized constructor will include the proper VPTR initialization code. This has several implications.

The first concerns efficiency. The reason for **inline** functions is to reduce the calling overhead for small functions. If C++ didn't provide **inline** functions, the preprocessor might be used to create these "macros." However, the preprocessor has no concept of access or classes, and therefore couldn't be used to create member function macros. In addition, with constructors that must have hidden code inserted by the compiler, a preprocessor macro wouldn't work at all.

You must be aware when hunting for efficiency holes that the compiler is inserting hidden code into your constructor function. Not only must it initialize the VPTR, it must also check the value of **this** (in case the **operator new** returns zero) and call base-class constructors. Taken together, this code can impact what you thought was a tiny inline function call. In particular, the size of the constructor may overwhelm the savings you get from reduced function-call overhead. If you make a lot of inline constructor calls, your code size can grow without any benefits in speed.

Of course, you probably won't make all tiny constructors non-inline right away, because they're much easier to write as inlines. But when you're tuning your code, remember to consider removing the inline constructors.

Order of constructor calls

The second interesting facet of constructors and virtual functions concerns the order of constructor calls and the way virtual calls are made within constructors.

All base-class constructors are always called in the constructor for an inherited class. This makes sense because the constructor has a special job: to see that the object is built properly. A derived class has access only to its own members, and not those of the base class. Only the base-class constructor can properly initialize its own elements. Therefore it's essential that all constructors get called; otherwise the entire object wouldn't be constructed properly. That's why the compiler enforces a constructor call for every portion of a derived class. It will call the default constructor if you don't explicitly call a base-class constructor in the constructor initializer list. If there is no default constructor, the compiler will complain.

The order of the constructor calls is important. When you inherit, you know all about the base class and can access any **public** and

protected members of the base class. This means you must be able to assume that all the members of the base class are valid when you're in the derived class. In a normal member function, construction has already taken place, so all the members of all parts of the object have been built. Inside the constructor, however, you must be able to assume that all members that you use have been built. The only way to guarantee this is for the base-class constructor to be called first. Then when you're in the derived-class constructor, all the members you can access in the base class have been initialized. "Knowing all members are valid" inside the constructor is also the reason that, whenever possible, you should initialize all member objects (that is, objects placed in the class using composition) in the constructor initializer list. If you follow this practice, you can assume that all base class members *and* member objects of the current object have been initialized.

Behavior of virtual functions inside constructors

The hierarchy of constructor calls brings up an interesting dilemma. What happens if you're inside a constructor and you call a virtual function? Inside an ordinary member function you can imagine what will happen – the virtual call is resolved at runtime because the object cannot know whether it belongs to the class the member function is in, or some class derived from it. For consistency, you might think this is what should happen inside constructors.

This is not the case. If you call a virtual function inside a constructor, only the local version of the function is used. That is, the virtual mechanism doesn't work within the constructor.

This behavior makes sense for two reasons. Conceptually, the constructor's job is to bring the object into existence (which is hardly an ordinary feat). Inside any constructor, the object may only be partially formed – you can only know that the base-class objects have been initialized, but you cannot know which classes are inherited from you. A virtual function call, however, reaches "forward" or "outward" into the inheritance hierarchy. It calls a function in a derived class. If you could do this inside a constructor, you'd be calling a function that might manipulate members that hadn't been initialized yet, a sure recipe for disaster.

The second reason is a mechanical one. When a constructor is called, one of the first things it does is initialize its VPTR. However, it can only know that it is of the "current" type – the type the constructor was written for. The constructor code is completely ignorant of whether or not the object is in the base of another class. When the compiler generates code for that constructor, it generates code for a constructor of that class, not a base class and not a class derived from it (because a class can't know who inherits it). So the VPTR it uses must be for the VTABLE of *that* class. The VPTR remains initialized to that VTABLE for the rest of the object's lifetime *unless* this isn't the last constructor call. If a more-derived constructor is called afterwards, that constructor sets the VPTR to *its* VTABLE, and so on, until the last constructor finishes. The state of the VPTR is determined by the constructor that is called last. This is another reason why the constructors are called in order from base to most-derived.

But while all this series of constructor calls is taking place, each constructor has set the VPTR to its own VTABLE. If it uses the virtual mechanism for function calls, it will produce only a call through its own VTABLE, not the most-derived VTABLE (as would be the case after *all* the constructors were called). In addition, many compilers recognize that a virtual function call is being made inside a constructor, and perform early binding because they know that late-binding will produce a call only to the local function. In either event, you won't get the results you might initially expect from a virtual function call inside a constructor.

Destructors and virtual destructors

You cannot use the **virtual** keyword with constructors, but destructors can and often must be virtual.

The constructor has the special job of putting an object together piece-by-piece, first by calling the base constructor, then the more derived constructors in order of inheritance (it must also call

---

member-object constructors along the way). Similarly, the destructor has a special job: it must disassemble an object that may belong to a hierarchy of classes. To do this, the compiler generates code that calls all the destructors, but in the *reverse* order that they are called by the constructor. That is, the destructor starts at the most-derived class and works its way down to the base class. This is the safe and desirable thing to do because the current destructor can always know that the base-class members are alive and active. If you need to call a base-class member function inside your destructor, it is safe to do so. Thus, the destructor can perform its own cleanup, then call the next-down destructor, which will perform *its* own cleanup, etc. Each destructor knows what its class is derived *from*, but not what is derived from it.

You should keep in mind that constructors and destructors are the only places where this hierarchy of calls must happen (and thus the proper hierarchy is automatically generated by the compiler). In all other functions, only *that* function will be called (and not base-class versions), whether it's virtual or not. The only way for base-class versions of the same function to be called in ordinary functions (virtual or not) is if you *explicitly* call that function.

Normally, the action of the destructor is quite adequate. But what happens if you want to manipulate an object through a pointer to its base class (that is, manipulate the object through its generic interface)? This activity is a major objective in object-oriented programming. The problem occurs when you want to **delete** a pointer of this type for an object that has been created on the heap with **new**. If the pointer is to the base class, the compiler can only know to call the base-class version of the destructor during **delete**. Sound familiar? This is the same problem that virtual functions were created to solve for the general case. Fortunately, virtual functions work for destructors as they do for all other functions except constructors.

```
//: C15:VirtualDestructors.cpp
// Behavior of virtual vs. non-virtual destructor
#include <iostream>
using namespace std;
```

```
class Base1 {
public:
  ~Base1() { cout << "~Base1()\n"; }
};

class Derived1 : public Base1 {
public:
  ~Derived1() { cout << "~Derived1()\n"; }
};

class Base2 {
public:
  virtual ~Base2() { cout << "~Base2()\n"; }
};

class Derived2 : public Base2 {
public:
  ~Derived2() { cout << "~Derived2()\n"; }
};

int main() {
  Base1* bp = new Derived1; // Upcast
  delete bp;
  Base2* b2p = new Derived2; // Upcast
  delete b2p;
} ///:~
```

When you run the program, you'll see that **delete bp** only calls the base-class destructor, while **delete b2p** calls the derived-class destructor followed by the base-class destructor, which is the behavior we desire. Forgetting to make a destructor **virtual** is an insidious bug because it often doesn't directly affect the behavior of your program, but it can quietly introduce a memory leak. Also, the fact that *some* destruction is occurring can further mask the problem.

Even though the destructor, like the constructor, is an "exceptional" function, it is possible for the destructor to be virtual because the object already knows what type it is (whereas it doesn't during construction). Once an object has been constructed, its VPTR is initialized, so virtual function calls can take place.

Pure virtual destructors

While pure virtual destructors are legal in Standard C++, there is an added constraint when using them: you must provide a function body for the pure virtual destructor. This seems counterintuitive; how can a virtual function be "pure" if it needs a function body? But if you keep in mind that constructors and destructors are special operations it makes more sense, especially if you remember that all destructors in a class hierarchy are always called. If you *could* leave off the definition for a pure virtual destructor, what function body would be called during destruction? Thus, it's absolutely necessary that the compiler and linker enforce the existence of a function body for a pure virtual destructor.

If it's pure, but it has to have a function body, what's the value of it? The only difference you'll see between the pure and non-pure virtual destructor is that the pure virtual destructor does cause the base class to be abstract, so you cannot create an object of the base class (although this would also be true if any other member function of the base class were pure virtual).

Things are a bit confusing, however, when you inherit a class from one that contains a pure virtual destructor. Unlike every other pure virtual function, you are *not* required to provide a definition of a pure virtual destructor in the derived class. The fact that the following compiles and links is the proof:

```
//: C15:UnAbstract.cpp
// Pure virtual destructors
// seem to behave strangely

class AbstractBase {
public:
  virtual ~AbstractBase() = 0;
};

AbstractBase::~AbstractBase() {}

class Derived : public AbstractBase {};
// No overriding of destructor necessary?

int main() { Derived d; } ///:~
```

Normally, a pure virtual function in a base class would cause the derived class to be abstract unless it (and all other pure virtual functions) is given a definition. But here, this seems not to be the case. However, remember that the compiler *automatically* creates a destructor definition for every class if you don't create one. That's what's happening here – the base class destructor is being quietly overridden, and thus the definition is being provided by the compiler and **Derived** is not actually abstract.

This brings up an interesting question: What is the point of a pure virtual destructor? Unlike an ordinary pure virtual function, you *must* give it a function body. In a derived class, you aren't forced to provide a definition since the compiler synthesizes the destructor for you. So what's the difference between a regular virtual destructor and a pure virtual destructor?

The only distinction occurs when you have a class that only has a single pure virtual function: the destructor. In this case, the only effect of the purity of the destructor is to prevent the instantiation of the base class. If there were any other pure virtual functions, they would prevent the instantiation of the base class, but if there are no others, then the pure virtual destructor will do it. So, while the addition of a virtual destructor is essential, whether it's pure or not isn't so important.

When you run the following example, you can see that the pure virtual function body is called after the derived class version, just as with any other destructor:

```
//: C15:PureVirtualDestructors.cpp
// Pure virtual destructors
// require a function body
#include <iostream>
using namespace std;

class Pet {
public:
  virtual ~Pet() = 0;
};

Pet::~Pet() {
```

```
    cout << "~Pet()" << endl;
  }

class Dog : public Pet {
public:
  ~Dog() {
    cout << "~Dog()" << endl;
  }
};

int main() {
  Pet* p = new Dog; // Upcast
  delete p; // Virtual destructor call
} ///:~
```

As a guideline, any time you have a virtual function in a class, you should immediately add a virtual destructor (even if it does nothing). This way, you ensure against any surprises later.

Virtuals in destructors

There's something that happens during destruction that you might not immediately expect. If you're inside an ordinary member function and you call a virtual function, that function is called using the late-binding mechanism. This is not true with destructors, virtual or not. Inside a destructor, only the "local" version of the member function is called; the virtual mechanism is ignored.

```
//: C15:VirtualsInDestructors.cpp
// Virtual calls inside destructors
#include <iostream>
using namespace std;

class Base {
public:
  virtual ~Base() {
    cout << "Base1()\n";
    f();
  }
  virtual void f() { cout << "Base::f()\n"; }
};

class Derived : public Base {
```

```
public:
  ~Derived() { cout << "~Derived()\n"; }
  void f() { cout << "Derived::f()\n"; }
};

int main() {
  Base* bp = new Derived; // Upcast
  delete bp;
} ///:~
```

During the destructor call, **Derived::f( )** is *not* called, even though
f( ) is virtual.

Why is this? Suppose the virtual mechanism *were* used inside the
destructor. Then it would be possible for the virtual call to resolve
to a function that was "farther out" (more derived) on the
inheritance hierarchy than the current destructor. But destructors
are called from the "outside in" (from the most-derived destructor
down to the base destructor), so the actual function called would
rely on portions of an object that have *already been destroyed*!
Instead, the compiler resolves the calls at compile-time and calls
only the "local" version of the function. Notice that the same is true
for the constructor (as described earlier), but in the constructor's
case the type information wasn't available, whereas in the
destructor the information (that is, the VPTR) is there, but is isn't
reliable.

Creating an object-based hierarchy

An issue that has been recurring throughout this book during the
demonstration of the container classes **Stack** and **Stash** is the
"ownership problem." The "owner" refers to who or what is
responsible for calling **delete** for objects that have been created
dynamically (using **new**). The problem when using containers is
that they need to be flexible enough to hold different types of
objects. To do this, the containers have held **void** pointers and so
they haven't known the type of object they've held. Deleting a **void**
pointer doesn't call the destructor, so the container couldn't be
responsible for cleaning up its objects.

One solution was presented in the example **C14:InheritStack.cpp**, in which the **Stack** was inherited into a new class that accepted and produced only **string** pointers. Since it knew that it could hold only pointers to **string** objects, it could properly delete them. This was a nice solution, but it requires you to inherit a new container class for each type that you want to hold in the container. (Although this seems tedious now, it will actually work quite well in Chapter 16, when templates are introduced.)

The problem is that you want the container to hold more than one type, but you don't want to use **void** pointers. Another solution is to use polymorphism by forcing all the objects held in the container to be inherited from the same base class. That is, the container holds the objects of the base class, and then you can call virtual functions – in particular, you can call virtual destructors to solve the ownership problem.

This solution uses what is referred to as a *singly-rooted hierarchy* or an *object-based hierarchy* (because the root class of the hierarchy is usually named "Object"). It turns out that there are many other benefits to using a singly-rooted hierarchy; in fact, every other object-oriented language but C++ enforces the use of such a hierarchy – when you create a class, you are automatically inheriting it directly or indirectly from a common base class, a base class that was established by the creators of the language. In C++, it was thought that the enforced use of this common base class would cause too much overhead, so it was left out. However, you can choose to use a common base class in your own projects, and this subject will be examined further in Volume 2 of this book.

To solve the ownership problem, we can create an extremely simple **Object** for the base class, which contains only a virtual destructor. The **Stack** can then hold classes inherited from **Object**:

```
//: C15:OStack.h
// Using a singly-rooted hierarchy
#ifndef OSTACK_H
#define OSTACK_H

class Object {
public:
```

```
    virtual ~Object() = 0;
};

// Required definition:
inline Object::~Object() {}

class Stack {
  struct Link {
    Object* data;
    Link* next;
    Link(Object* dat, Link* nxt) :
      data(dat), next(nxt) {}
  }* head;
public:
  Stack() : head(0) {}
  ~Stack(){
    while(head)
      delete pop();
  }
  void push(Object* dat) {
    head = new Link(dat, head);
  }
  Object* peek() const {
    return head ? head->data : 0;
  }
  Object* pop() {
    if(head == 0) return 0;
    Object* result = head->data;
    Link* oldHead = head;
    head = head->next;
    delete oldHead;
    return result;
  }
};
#endif // OSTACK_H ///:~
```

To simplify things by keeping everything in the header file, the
(required) definition for the pure virtual destructor is inlined into
the header file, and **pop( )** (which might be considered too large for
inlining) is also inlined.

Link objects now hold pointers to **Object** rather than **void**
pointers, and the **Stack** will only accept and return **Object**
pointers. Now **Stack** is much more flexible, since it will hold lots of

---

different types but will also destroy any objects that are left on the **Stack**. The new limitation (which will be finally removed when templates are applied to the problem in Chapter 16) is that anything that is placed on the **Stack** must be inherited from **Object**. That's fine if you are starting your class from scratch, but what if you already have a class such as **string** that you want to be able to put onto the **Stack**? In this case, the new class must be both a **string** and an **Object**, which means it must be inherited from both classes. This is called *multiple inheritance* and it is the subject of an entire chapter in Volume 2 of this book (downloadable from *www.BruceEckel.com*). When you read that chapter, you'll see that multiple inheritance can be fraught with complexity, and is a feature you should use sparingly. In this situation, however, everything is simple enough that we don't trip across any multiple inheritance pitfalls:

```cpp
//: C15:OStackTest.cpp
//{T} OStackTest.cpp
#include "OStack.h"
#include "../require.h"
#include <fstream>
#include <iostream>
#include <string>
using namespace std;

// Use multiple inheritance. We want
// both a string and an Object:
class MyString: public string, public Object {
public:
  ~MyString() {
    cout << "deleting string: " << *this << endl;
  }
  MyString(string s) : string(s) {}
};

int main(int argc, char* argv[]) {
  requireArgs(argc, 1); // File name is argument
  ifstream in(argv[1]);
  assure(in, argv[1]);
  Stack textlines;
  string line;
  // Read file and store lines in the stack:
  while(getline(in, line))
```

```
    textlines.push(new MyString(line));
  // Pop some lines from the stack:
  MyString* s;
  for(int i = 0; i < 10; i++) {
    if((s=(MyString*)textlines.pop())==0) break;
    cout << *s << endl;
    delete s;
  }
  cout << "Letting the destructor do the rest:"
    << endl;
} ///:~
```

Although this is similar to the previous version of the test program
for **Stack**, you'll notice that only 10 elements are popped from the
stack, which means there are probably some objects remaining.
Because the **Stack** knows that it holds **Object**s, the destructor can
properly clean things up, and you'll see this in the output of the
program, since the **MyString** objects print messages as they are
destroyed.

Creating containers that hold **Object**s is not an unreasonable
approach – *if* you have a singly-rooted hierarchy (enforced either by
the language or by the requirement that every class inherit from
Object). In that case, everything is guaranteed to be an **Object** and
so it's not very complicated to use the containers. In C++, however,
you cannot expect this from every class, so you're bound to trip over
multiple inheritance if you take this approach. You'll see in Chapter
16 that templates solve the problem in a much simpler and more
elegant fashion.

Operator overloading

You can make operators **virtual** just like other member functions.
Implementing **virtual** operators often becomes confusing,
however, because you may be operating on two objects, both with
unknown types. This is usually the case with mathematical
components (for which you often overload operators). For example,
consider a system that deals with matrices, vectors and scalar
values, all three of which are derived from class **Math**:

```
//: C15:OperatorPolymorphism.cpp
```

```
// Polymorphism with overloaded operators
#include <iostream>
using namespace std;

class Matrix;
class Scalar;
class Vector;

class Math {
public:
  virtual Math& operator*(Math& rv) = 0;
  virtual Math& multiply(Matrix*) = 0;
  virtual Math& multiply(Scalar*) = 0;
  virtual Math& multiply(Vector*) = 0;
  virtual ~Math() {}
};

class Matrix : public Math {
public:
  Math& operator*(Math& rv) {
    return rv.multiply(this); // 2nd dispatch
  }
  Math& multiply(Matrix*) {
    cout << "Matrix * Matrix" << endl;
    return *this;
  }
  Math& multiply(Scalar*) {
    cout << "Scalar * Matrix" << endl;
    return *this;
  }
  Math& multiply(Vector*) {
    cout << "Vector * Matrix" << endl;
    return *this;
  }
};

class Scalar : public Math {
public:
  Math& operator*(Math& rv) {
    return rv.multiply(this); // 2nd dispatch
  }
  Math& multiply(Matrix*) {
    cout << "Matrix * Scalar" << endl;
    return *this;
  }
```

```
  Math& multiply(Scalar*) {
    cout << "Scalar * Scalar" << endl;
    return *this;
  }
  Math& multiply(Vector*) {
    cout << "Vector * Scalar" << endl;
    return *this;
  }
};

class Vector : public Math  {
public:
  Math& operator*(Math& rv) {
    return rv.multiply(this); // 2nd dispatch
  }
  Math& multiply(Matrix*) {
    cout << "Matrix * Vector" << endl;
    return *this;
  }
  Math& multiply(Scalar*) {
    cout << "Scalar * Vector" << endl;
    return *this;
  }
  Math& multiply(Vector*) {
    cout << "Vector * Vector" << endl;
    return *this;
  }
};

int main() {
  Matrix m; Vector v; Scalar s;
  Math* math[] = { &m, &v, &s };
  for(int i = 0; i < 3; i++)
    for(int j = 0; j < 3; j++) {
      Math& m1 = *math[i];
      Math& m2 = *math[j];
      m1 * m2;
    }
} ///:~
```

For simplicity, only the **operator*** has been overloaded. The goal is
to be able to multiply any two **Math** objects and produce the
desired result – and note that multiplying a matrix by a vector is a
very different operation than multiplying a vector by a matrix.

The problem is that, in **main( )**, the expression **m1 * m2** contains two upcast **Math** references, and thus two objects of unknown type. A virtual function is only capable of making a single dispatch – that is, determining the type of one unknown object. To determine both types a technique called *multiple dispatching* is used in this example, whereby what appears to be a single virtual function call results in a second virtual call. By the time this second call is made, you've determined both types of object, and can perform the proper activity. It's not transparent at first, but if you stare at the example for awhile it should begin to make sense. This topic is explored in more depth in the Design Patterns chapter in Volume 2, which you can download at *www.BruceEckel.com*.

Downcasting

As you might guess, since there's such a thing as upcasting – moving up an inheritance hierarchy – there should also be *downcasting* to move down a hierarchy. But upcasting is easy since as you move up an inheritance hierarchy the classes always converge to more general classes. That is, when you upcast you are always clearly derived from an ancestor class (typically only one, except in the case of multiple inheritance) but when you downcast there are usually several possibilities that you could cast to. More specifically, a **Circle** is a type of **Shape** (that's the upcast), but if you try to downcast a **Shape** it could be a **Circle**, **Square**, **Triangle**, etc. So the dilemma is figuring out a way to safely downcast. (But an even more important issue is asking yourself why you're downcasting in the first place instead of just using polymorphism to automatically figure out the correct type. The avoidance of downcasting is covered in Volume 2 of this book.)

C++ provides a special *explicit cast* (introduced in Chapter 3) called **dynamic_cast** that is a *type-safe downcast* operation. When you use **dynamic_cast** to try to cast down to a particular type, the return value will be a pointer to the desired type only if the cast is proper and successful, otherwise it will return zero to indicate that this was not the correct type. Here's a minimal example:

```
//: C15:DynamicCast.cpp
```

```
#include <iostream>
using namespace std;

class Pet { public: virtual ~Pet(){}};
class Dog : public Pet {};
class Cat : public Pet {};

int main() {
  Pet* b = new Cat; // Upcast
  // Try to cast it to Dog*:
  Dog* d1 = dynamic_cast<Dog*>(b);
  // Try to cast it to Cat*:
  Cat* d2 = dynamic_cast<Cat*>(b);
  cout << "d1 = " << (long)d1 << endl;
  cout << "d2 = " << (long)d2 << endl;
} ///:~
```

When you use **dynamic_cast**, you must be working with a true polymorphic hierarchy – one with virtual functions – because **dynamic_cast** uses information stored in the VTABLE to determine the actual type. Here, the base class contains a virtual destructor and that suffices. In **main( )**, a **Cat** pointer is upcast to a **Pet**, and then a downcast is attempted to both a **Dog** pointer and a **Cat** pointer. Both pointers are printed, and you'll see when you run the program that the incorrect downcast produces a zero result. Of course, whenever you downcast you are responsible for checking to make sure that the result of the cast is nonzero. Also, you should not assume that the pointer will be exactly the same, because sometimes pointer adjustments take place during upcasting and downcasting (in particular, with multiple inheritance).

A **dynamic_cast** requires a little bit of extra overhead to run; not much, but if you're doing a lot of **dynamic_cast**ing (in which case you should be seriously questioning your program design) this may become a performance issue. In some cases you may know something special during downcasting that allows you to say for sure what type you're dealing with, in which case the extra overhead of the **dynamic_cast** becomes unnecessary, and you can use a **static_cast** instead. Here's how it might work:

```
//: C15:StaticHierarchyNavigation.cpp
// Navigating class hierarchies with static_cast
```

```cpp
#include <iostream>
#include <typeinfo>
using namespace std;

class Shape { public: virtual ~Shape() {}; };
class Circle : public Shape {};
class Square : public Shape {};
class Other {};

int main() {
  Circle c;
  Shape* s = &c; // Upcast: normal and OK
  // More explicit but unnecessary:
  s = static_cast<Shape*>(&c);
  // (Since upcasting is such a safe and common
  // operation, the cast becomes cluttering)
  Circle* cp = 0;
  Square* sp = 0;
  // Static Navigation of class hierarchies
  // requires extra type information:
  if(typeid(s) == typeid(cp)) // C++ RTTI
    cp = static_cast<Circle*>(s);
  if(typeid(s) == typeid(sp))
    sp = static_cast<Square*>(s);
  if(cp != 0)
    cout << "It's a circle!" << endl;
  if(sp != 0)
    cout << "It's a square!" << endl;
  // Static navigation is ONLY an efficiency hack;
  // dynamic_cast is always safer. However:
  // Other* op = static_cast<Other*>(s);
  // Conveniently gives an error message, while
  Other* op2 = (Other*)s;
  // does not
} ///:~
```

In this program, a new feature is used that is not fully described until Volume 2 of this book, where a chapter is given to the topic: C++'s *run-time type information* (RTTI) mechanism. RTTI allows you to discover type information that has been lost by upcasting. The **dynamic_cast** is actually one form of RTTI. Here, the **typeid** keyword (declared in the header file **<typeinfo>**) is used to detect the types of the pointers. You can see that the type of the upcast **Shape** pointer is successively compared to a **Circle** pointer and a

Square pointer to see if there's a match. There's more to RTTI than **typeid**, and you can also imagine that it would be fairly easy to implement your own type information system using a virtual function.

A **Circle** object is created and the address is upcast to a **Shape** pointer; the second version of the expression shows how you can use **static_cast** to be more explicit about the upcast. However, since an upcast is always safe and it's a common thing to do, I consider an explicit cast for upcasting to be cluttering and unnecessary.

RTTI is used to determine the type, and then **static_cast** is used to perform the downcast. But notice that in this design the process is effectively the same as using **dynamic_cast**, and the client programmer must do some testing to discover the cast that was actually successful. You'll typically want a situation that's more deterministic than in the example above before using **static_cast** rather than **dynamic_cast** (and, again, you want to carefully examine your design before using **dynamic_cast**).

If a class hierarchy has no **virtual** functions (which is a questionable design) or if you have other information that allows you to safely downcast, it's a tiny bit faster to do the downcast statically than with **dynamic_cast**. In addition, **static_cast** won't allow you to cast out of the hierarchy, as the traditional cast will, so it's safer. However, statically navigating class hierarchies is always risky and you should use **dynamic_cast** unless you have a special situation.

Summary

Polymorphism – implemented in C++ with virtual functions – means "different forms." In object-oriented programming, you have the same face (the common interface in the base class) and different forms using that face: the different versions of the virtual functions.

You've seen in this chapter that it's impossible to understand, or even create, an example of polymorphism without using data

---

abstraction and inheritance. Polymorphism is a feature that cannot be viewed in isolation (like **const** or a **switch** statement, for example), but instead works only in concert, as part of a "big picture" of class relationships. People are often confused by other, non-object-oriented features of C++, like overloading and default arguments, which are sometimes presented as object-oriented. Don't be fooled; if it isn't late binding, it isn't polymorphism.

To use polymorphism – and thus, object-oriented techniques – effectively in your programs you must expand your view of programming to include not just members and messages of an individual class, but also the commonality among classes and their relationships with each other. Although this requires significant effort, it's a worthy struggle, because the results are faster program development, better code organization, extensible programs, and easier code maintenance.

Polymorphism completes the object-oriented features of the language, but there are two more major features in C++: templates (which are introduced in Chapter 16 and covered in much more detail in Volume 2), and exception handling (which is covered in Volume 2). These features provide you as much increase in programming power as each of the object-oriented features: abstract data typing, inheritance, and polymorphism.

Exercises

Solutions to selected exercises can be found in the electronic document *The Thinking in C++ Annotated Solution Guide*, available for a small fee from www.BruceEckel.com.

1. Create a simple "shape" hierarchy: a base class called **Shape** and derived classes called **Circle**, **Square**, and **Triangle**. In the base class, make a virtual function called **draw( ),** and override this in the derived classes. Make an array of pointers to **Shape** objects that you create on the heap (and thus perform upcasting of the pointers), and call **draw( )** through the base-class pointers, to verify the behavior of the virtual function. If your debugger supports it, single-step through the code.

---

2. Modify Exercise 1 so **draw( )** is a pure virtual function. Try creating an object of type **Shape**. Try to call the pure virtual function inside the constructor and see what happens. Leaving it as a pure virtual, give **draw( )** a definition.

3. Expanding on Exercise 2, create a function that takes a **Shape** object *by value* and try to upcast a derived object in as an argument. See what happens. Fix the function by taking a reference to the **Shape** object.

4. Modify **C14:Combined.cpp** so that **f( )** is **virtual** in the base class. Change **main( )** to perform an upcast and a virtual call.

5. Modify **Instrument3.cpp** by adding a **virtual prepare( )** function. Call **prepare( )** inside **tune( )**.

6. Create an inheritance hierarchy of **Rodent: Mouse, Gerbil, Hamster**, etc. In the base class, provide methods that are common to all **Rodent**s, and redefine these in the derived classes to perform different behaviors depending on the specific type of **Rodent**. Create an array of pointers to **Rodent**, fill it with different specific types of **Rodent**s, and call your base-class methods to see what happens.

7. Modify Exercise 6 so that you use a **vector<Rodent*>** instead of an array of pointers. Make sure that memory is cleaned up properly.

8. Starting with the previous **Rodent** hierarchy, inherit **BlueHamster** from **Hamster** (yes, there is such a thing; I had one when I was a kid), override the base-class methods, and show that the code that calls the base-class methods doesn't need to change in order to accommodate the new type.

9. Starting with the previous **Rodent** hierarchy, add a non virtual destructor, create an object of class **Hamster** using **new**, upcast the pointer to a **Rodent***, and **delete** the pointer to show that it doesn't call all the destructors in the hierarchy. Change the destructor to be **virtual** and demonstrate that the behavior is now correct.

10. Starting with the previous **Rodent** hierarchy, modify **Rodent** so it is a pure abstract base class.

---

11. Create an air-traffic control system with base-class **Aircraft** and various derived types. Create a **Tower** class with a **vector<Aircraft*>** that sends the appropriate messages to the various aircraft under its control.

12. Create a model of a greenhouse by inheriting various types of **Plant** and building mechanisms into your greenhouse that take care of the plants.

13. In **Early.cpp**, make **Pet** a pure abstract base class.

14. In **AddingVirtuals.cpp**, make all the member functions of **Pet** pure virtuals, but provide a definition for **name( )**. Fix **Dog** as necessary, using the base-class definition of **name( )**.

15. Write a small program to show the difference between calling a virtual function inside a normal member function and calling a virtual function inside a constructor. The program should prove that the two calls produce different results.

16. Modify **VirtualsInDestructors.cpp** by inheriting a class from **Derived** and overriding **f( )** and the destructor. In **main( )**, create and upcast an object of your new type, then **delete** it.

17. Take Exercise 16 and add calls to **f( )** in each destructor. Explain what happens.

18. Create a class that has a data member and a derived class that adds another data member. Write a non-member function that takes an object of the base class *by value* and prints out the size of that object using **sizeof**. In **main( )** create an object of the derived class, print out its size, and then call your function. Explain what happens.

19. Create a simple example of a virtual function call and generate assembly output. Locate the assembly code for the virtual call and trace and explain the code.

20. Write a class with one virtual function and one non-virtual function. Inherit a new class, make an object of this class, and upcast to a pointer of the base-class type. Use the **clock( )** function found in **<ctime>** (you'll need to look this up in your local C library guide) to measure

the difference between a virtual call and non-virtual call. You'll need to make multiple calls to each function inside your timing loop in order to see the difference.

21. Modify **C14:Order.cpp** by adding a virtual function in the base class of the **CLASS** macro (have it print something) and by making the destructor virtual. Make objects of the various subclasses and upcast them to the base class. Verify that the virtual behavior works and that proper construction and destruction takes place.

22. Write a class with three overloaded virtual functions. Inherit a new class from this and override one of the functions. Create an object of your derived class. Can you call all the base class functions through the derived-class object? Upcast the address of the object to the base. Can you call all three functions through the base? Remove the overridden definition in the derived class. Now can you call all the base class functions through the derived-class object?

23. Modify **VariantReturn.cpp** to show that its behavior works with references as well as pointers.

24. In **Early.cpp**, how can you tell whether the compiler makes the call using early or late binding? Determine the case for your own compiler.

25. Create a base class containing a **clone( )** function that returns a pointer to a *copy* of the current object. Derive two subclasses that override **clone( )** to return copies of their specific types. In **main( )**, create and upcast objects of your two derived types, then call **clone( )** for each and verify that the cloned copies are the correct subtypes. Experiment with your **clone( )** function so that you return the base type, then try returning the exact derived type. Can you think of situations in which the latter approach is necessary?

26. Modify **OStackTest.cpp** by creating your own class, then multiply-inheriting it with **Object** to create something that can be placed into the **Stack**. Test your class in **main( )**.

27. Add a type called **Tensor** to **OperatorPolymorphism.cpp**.

28. (Intermediate) Create a base **class X** with no data members and no constructor, but with a virtual function. Create a **class Y** that inherits from **X**, but without an explicit constructor. Generate assembly code and examine it to determine if a constructor is created and called for **X**, and if so, what the code does. Explain what you discover. **X** has no default constructor, so why doesn't the compiler complain?

29. (Intermediate) Modify Exercise 28 by writing constructors for both classes so that each constructor calls a virtual function. Generate assembly code. Determine where the VPTR is being assigned inside each constructor. Is the virtual mechanism being used by your compiler inside the constructor? Establish why the local version of the function is still being called.

30. (Advanced) If function calls to an object passed by value *weren't* early-bound, a virtual call might access parts that didn't exist. Is this possible? Write some code to force a virtual call, and see if this causes a crash. To explain the behavior, examine what happens when you pass an object by value.

31. (Advanced) Find out exactly how much more time is required for a virtual function call by going to your processor's assembly-language information or other technical manual and finding out the number of clock states required for a simple call versus the number required for the virtual function instructions.

32. Determine the **sizeof** the VPTR for your implementation. Now multiply-inherit two classes that contain virtual functions. Did you get one VPTR or two in the derived class?

33. Create a class with data members and virtual functions. Write a function that looks at the memory in an object of your class and prints out the various pieces of it. To do this you will need to experiment and iteratively discover where the VPTR is located in the object.

34. Pretend that virtual functions don't exist, and modify **Instrument4.cpp** so that it uses **dynamic_cast** to

make the equivalent of the virtual calls. Explain why this is a bad idea.

35. Modify **StaticHierarchyNavigation.cpp** so that instead of using C++ RTTI you create your own RTTI via a virtual function in the base class called **whatAmI( )** and an **enum type { Circles, Squares };**.

36. Start with **PointerToMemberOperator.cpp** from Chapter 12 and show that polymorphism still works with pointers-to-members, even if **operator->*** is overloaded.

16: Introduction to Templates

Inheritance and composition provide a way to reuse object code. The *template* feature in C++ provides a way to reuse *source* code.

Although C++ templates are a general-purpose programming tool, when they were introduced in the language, they seemed to discourage the use of object-based container-class hierarchies (demonstrated at the end of Chapter 15). For example, the Standard C++ containers and algorithms (explained in two chapters of Volume 2 of this book, downloadable from *www.BruceEckel.com*) are built exclusively with templates and are relatively easy for the programmer to use.

This chapter not only demonstrates the basics of templates, it is also an introduction to containers, which are fundamental components of object-oriented programming and are almost completely realized through the containers in the Standard C++ Library. You'll see that this book has been using container examples – the **Stash** and **Stack** – throughout, precisely to get you comfortable with containers; in this chapter the concept of the *iterator* will also be added. Although containers are ideal examples for use with templates, in Volume 2 (which has an advanced templates chapter) you'll learn that there are many other uses for templates as well.

Containers

Suppose you want to create a stack, as we have been doing throughout the book. This stack class will hold **int**s, to keep it simple:

```
//: C16:IntStack.cpp
// Simple integer stack
//{L} fibonacci
#include "fibonacci.h"
#include "../require.h"
#include <iostream>
using namespace std;

class IntStack {
  enum { ssize = 100 };
  int stack[ssize];
  int top;
public:
  IntStack() : top(0) {}
```

```
  void push(int i) {
    require(top < ssize, "Too many push()es");
    stack[top++] = i;
  }
  int pop() {
    require(top > 0, "Too many pop()s");
    return stack[--top];
  }
};

int main() {
  IntStack is;
  // Add some Fibonacci numbers, for interest:
  for(int i = 0; i < 20; i++)
    is.push(fibonacci(i));
  // Pop & print them:
  for(int k = 0; k < 20; k++)
    cout << is.pop() << endl;
} ///:~
```

The class **IntStack** is a trivial example of a push-down stack. For
simplicity it has been created here with a fixed size, but you can also
modify it to automatically expand by allocating memory off the
heap, as in the **Stack** class that has been examined throughout the
book.

main( ) adds some integers to the stack, and pops them off again.
To make the example more interesting, the integers are created
with the **fibonacci( )** function, which generates the traditional
rabbit-reproduction numbers. Here is the header file that declares
the function:

```
//: C16:fibonacci.h
// Fibonacci number generator
int fibonacci(int n); ///:~
```

Here's the implementation:

```
//: C16:fibonacci.cpp {O}
#include "../require.h"

int fibonacci(int n) {
  const int sz = 100;
  require(n < sz);
```

```
static int f[sz]; // Initialized to zero
f[0] = f[1] = 1;
// Scan for unfilled array elements:
int i;
for(i = 0; i < sz; i++)
  if(f[i] == 0) break;
while(i <= n) {
  f[i] = f[i-1] + f[i-2];
  i++;
}
return f[n];
} ///:~
```

This is a fairly efficient implementation, because it never generates the numbers more than once. It uses a **static** array of **int**, and relies on the fact that the compiler will initialize a **static** array to zero. The first **for** loop moves the index **i** to where the first array element is zero, then a **while** loop adds Fibonacci numbers to the array until the desired element is reached. But notice that if the Fibonacci numbers through element **n** are already initialized, it skips the **while** loop altogether.

The need for containers

Obviously, an integer stack isn't a crucial tool. The real need for containers comes when you start making objects on the heap using **new** and destroying them with **delete**. In the general programming problem, you don't know how many objects you're going to need while you're writing the program. For example, in an air-traffic control system you don't want to limit the number of planes your system can handle. You don't want the program to abort just because you exceed some number. In a computer-aided design system, you're dealing with lots of shapes, but only the user determines (at runtime) exactly how many shapes you're going to need. Once you notice this tendency, you'll discover lots of examples in your own programming situations.

C programmers who rely on virtual memory to handle their "memory management" often find the idea of **new**, **delete,** and container classes disturbing. Apparently, one practice in C is to create a huge global array, larger than anything the program would appear to need. This may not require much thought (or awareness of **malloc( )** and **free( )**), but it produces programs that don't port well and that hide subtle bugs.

In addition, if you create a huge global array of objects in C++, the constructor and destructor overhead can slow things down significantly. The C++ approach works much better: When you need an object, create it with **new,** and put its pointer in a container. Later on, fish it out and do something to it. This way, you create only the objects you absolutely need. And usually you don't have all the initialization conditions available at the start-up of the program. **new** allows you to wait until something happens in the environment before you can actually create the object.

So in the most common situation, you'll make a container that holds pointers to some objects of interest. You will create those objects using **new** and put the resulting pointer in the container (potentially upcasting it in the process), pulling it out later when you want to do something with the object. This technique produces the most flexible, general sort of program.

Overview of templates

Now a problem arises. You have an **IntStack**, which holds integers. But you want a stack that holds shapes or aircraft or plants or something else. Reinventing your source code every time doesn't seem like a very intelligent approach with a language that touts reusability. There must be a better way.

There are three techniques for source code reuse in this situation: the C way, presented here for contrast; the Smalltalk approach, which significantly affected C++; and the C++ approach: templates.

The C solution. Of course you're trying to get away from the C approach because it's messy and error prone and completely inelegant. In this approach, you copy the source code for a **Stack** and make modifications by hand, introducing new errors in the process. This is certainly not a very productive technique.

The Smalltalk solution. Smalltalk (and Java, following its example) took a simple and straightforward approach: You want to reuse code, so use inheritance. To implement this, each container class holds items of the generic base class **Object** (similar to the example at the end of Chapter 15). But because the library in Smalltalk is of such fundamental importance, you don't ever create a class from scratch. Instead, you must always inherit it from an existing class. You find a class as close as possible to the one you want, inherit from it, and make a few changes. Obviously, this is a benefit because it minimizes your effort (and explains why you spend a lot of time learning the class library before becoming an effective Smalltalk programmer).

But it also means that all classes in Smalltalk end up being part of a single inheritance tree. You must inherit from a branch of this tree when creating a new class. Most of the tree is already there (it's the Smalltalk class library), and at the root of the tree is a class called **Object** – the same class that each Smalltalk container holds.

This is a neat trick because it means that every class in the Smalltalk (and Java[1]) class hierarchy is derived from **Object**, so every class can be held in every container (including that container itself). This type of single-tree hierarchy based on a fundamental generic type (often named **Object**, which is also the case in Java) is referred to as an "object-based hierarchy." You may have heard this term and assumed it was some new fundamental concept in OOP, like polymorphism. It simply refers to a class hierarchy with **Object** (or some similar name) at its root and container classes that hold **Object**.

Because the Smalltalk class library had a much longer history and experience behind it than did C++, and because the original C++ compilers had *no* container class libraries, it seemed like a good idea to duplicate the Smalltalk library in C++. This was done as an experiment with an early C++ implementation[2], and because it

---

[1] With the exception, in Java, of the primitive data types. These were made non-**Object**s for efficiency.

[2] The OOPS library, by Keith Gorlen while he was at NIH.

---

represented a significant body of code, many people began using it. In the process of trying to use the container classes, they discovered a problem.

The problem was that in Smalltalk (and most other OOP languages that I know of), all classes are automatically derived from a single hierarchy, but this isn't true in C++. You might have your nice object-based hierarchy with its container classes, but then you might buy a set of shape classes or aircraft classes from another vendor who didn't use that hierarchy. (For one thing, using that hierarchy imposes overhead, which C programmers eschew.) How do you insert a separate class tree into the container class in your object-based hierarchy? Here's what the problem looks like:

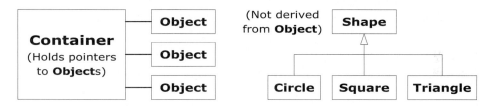

Because C++ supports multiple independent hierarchies, Smalltalk's object-based hierarchy does not work so well.

The solution seemed obvious. If you can have many inheritance hierarchies, then you should be able to inherit from more than one class: Multiple inheritance will solve the problem. So you do the following (a similar example was given at the end of Chapter 15):

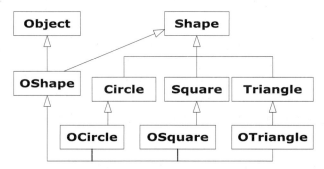

Now **OShape** has **Shape**'s characteristics and behaviors, but because it is also derived from **Object** it can be placed in

---

Container. The extra inheritance into **OCircle**, **OSquare**, etc. is necessary so that those classes can be upcast into **OShape** and thus retain the correct behavior. You can see that things are rapidly getting messy.

Compiler vendors invented and included their own object-based container-class hierarchies, most of which have since been replaced by template versions. You can argue that multiple inheritance is needed for solving general programming problems, but you'll see in Volume 2 of this book that its complexity is best avoided except in special cases.

The template solution

Although an object-based hierarchy with multiple inheritance is conceptually straightforward, it turns out to be painful to use. In his original book[3] Stroustrup demonstrated what he considered a preferable alternative to the object-based hierarchy. Container classes were created as large preprocessor macros with arguments that could be substituted with your desired type. When you wanted to create a container to hold a particular type, you made a couple of macro calls.

Unfortunately, this approach was confused by all the existing Smalltalk literature and programming experience, and it was a bit unwieldy. Basically, nobody got it.

In the meantime, Stroustrup and the C++ team at Bell Labs had modified his original macro approach, simplifying it and moving it from the domain of the preprocessor into the compiler. This new code-substitution device is called a **template**[4], and it represents a completely different way to reuse code. Instead of reusing object code, as with inheritance and composition, a template reuses *source code*. The container no longer holds a generic base class called **Object**, but instead it holds an unspecified parameter. When you

---

[3] *The C++ Programming Language* by Bjarne Stroustrup (1st edition, Addison-Wesley, 1986).

[4] The inspiration for templates appears to be ADA generics.

use a template, the parameter is substituted *by the compiler*, much like the old macro approach, but cleaner and easier to use.

Now, instead of worrying about inheritance or composition when you want to use a container class, you take the template version of the container and stamp out a specific version for your particular problem, like this:

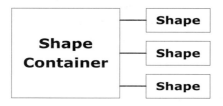

The compiler does the work for you, and you end up with exactly the container you need to do your job, rather than an unwieldy inheritance hierarchy. In C++, the template implements the concept of a *parameterized type*. Another benefit of the template approach is that the novice programmer who may be unfamiliar or uncomfortable with inheritance can still use canned container classes right away (as we've been doing with **vector** throughout the book).

Template syntax

The **template** keyword tells the compiler that the class definition that follows will manipulate one or more unspecified types. At the time the actual class code is generated from the template, those types must be specified so that the compiler can substitute them.

To demonstrate the syntax, here's a small example that produces a bounds-checked array:

```
//: C16:Array.cpp
#include "../require.h"
#include <iostream>
using namespace std;

template<class T>
class Array {
```

```
    enum { size = 100 };
    T A[size];
public:
    T& operator[](int index) {
        require(index >= 0 && index < size,
          "Index out of range");
        return A[index];
    }
};

int main() {
    Array<int> ia;
    Array<float> fa;
    for(int i = 0; i < 20; i++) {
        ia[i] = i * i;
        fa[i] = float(i) * 1.414;
    }
    for(int j = 0; j < 20; j++)
        cout << j << ": " << ia[j]
             << ", " << fa[j] << endl;
} ///:~
```

You can see that it looks like a normal class except for the line

```
template<class T>
```

which says that **T** is the substitution parameter, and that it represents a type name. Also, you see **T** used everywhere in the class where you would normally see the specific type the container holds.

In **Array**, elements are inserted *and* extracted with the same function: the overloaded **operator [ ]** . It returns a reference, so it can be used on both sides of an equal sign (that is, as both an *lvalue* and an *rvalue*). Notice that if the index is out of bounds, the **require( )** function is used to print a message. Since **operator[]** is an **inline**, you could use this approach to guarantee that no array-bounds violations occur, then remove the **require( )** for the shipping code.

In **main( )**, you can see how easy it is to create **Array**s that hold different types of objects. When you say

```
Array<int> ia;
Array<float> fa;
```

the compiler expands the **Array** template (this is called *instantiation*) twice, to create two new *generated classes*, which you can think of as **Array_int** and **Array_float**. (Different compilers may decorate the names in different ways.) These are classes just like the ones you would have produced if you had performed the substitution by hand, except that the compiler creates them for you as you define the objects **ia** and **fa**. Also note that duplicate class definitions are either avoided by the compiler or merged by the linker.

Non-inline function definitions

Of course, there are times when you'll want to have non-inline member function definitions. In this case, the compiler needs to see the **template** declaration before the member function definition. Here's the example above, modified to show the non-inline member definition:

```
//: C16:Array2.cpp
// Non-inline template definition
#include "../require.h"

template<class T>
class Array {
  enum { size = 100 };
  T A[size];
public:
  T& operator[](int index);
};

template<class T>
T& Array<T>::operator[](int index) {
  require(index >= 0 && index < size,
    "Index out of range");
  return A[index];
}

int main() {
  Array<float> fa;
  fa[0] = 1.414;
```

```
}  ///:~
```

Any reference to a template's class name must be accompanied by its template argument list, as in **Array<T>::operator[]**. You can imagine that internally, the class name is being decorated with the arguments in the template argument list to produce a unique class name identifier for each template instantiation.

Header files

Even if you create non-inline function definitions, you'll usually want to put all declarations *and* definitions for a template into a header file. This may seem to violate the normal header file rule of "Don't put in anything that allocates storage," (which prevents multiple definition errors at link time), but template definitions are special. Anything preceded by **template<...>** means the compiler won't allocate storage for it at that point, but will instead wait until it's told to (by a template instantiation), and that somewhere in the compiler and linker there's a mechanism for removing multiple definitions of an identical template. So you'll almost always put the entire template declaration *and* definition in the header file, for ease of use.

There are times when you may need to place the template definitions in a separate **cpp** file to satisfy special needs (for example, forcing template instantiations to exist in only a single Windows **dll** file). Most compilers have some mechanism to allow this; you'll have to investigate your particular compiler's documentation to use it.

Some people feel that putting all of the source code for your implementation in a header file makes it possible for people to steal and modify your code if they buy a library from you. This might be an issue, but it probably depends on the way you look at the problem: Are they buying a product or a service? If it's a product, then you have to do everything you can to protect it, and probably you don't want to give source code, just compiled code. But many people see software as a service, and even more than that, a subscription service. The customer wants your expertise, they want you to continue maintaining this piece of reusable code so that they don't have to – so they can focus on getting *their* job done. I personally think most customers will treat you as a valuable resource and will not want to jeopardize their relationship with you. As for the few who want to steal rather than buy or do original work, they probably can't keep up with you anyway.

IntStack as a template

Here is the container and iterator from **IntStack.cpp**, implemented as a generic container class using templates:

```
//: C16:StackTemplate.h
// Simple stack template
#ifndef STACKTEMPLATE_H
#define STACKTEMPLATE_H
#include "../require.h"

template<class T>
class StackTemplate {
  enum { ssize = 100 };
  T stack[ssize];
  int top;
public:
  StackTemplate() : top(0) {}
  void push(const T& i) {
    require(top < ssize, "Too many push()es");
    stack[top++] = i;
  }
  T pop() {
    require(top > 0, "Too many pop()s");
    return stack[--top];
  }
  int size() { return top; }
};
#endif // STACKTEMPLATE_H ///:~
```

Notice that a template makes certain assumptions about the objects it is holding. For example, **StackTemplate** assumes there is some sort of assignment operation for **T** inside the **push( )** function. You could say that a template "implies an interface" for the types it is capable of holding.

Another way to say this is that templates provide a kind of *weak typing* mechanism for C++, which is ordinarily a strongly-typed

---

language. Instead of insisting that an object be of some exact type in order to be acceptable, weak typing requires only that the member functions that it wants to call are *available* for a particular object. Thus, weakly-typed code can be applied to any object that can accept those member function calls, and is thus much more flexible[5].

Here's the revised example to test the template:

```
//: C16:StackTemplateTest.cpp
// Test simple stack template
//{L} fibonacci
#include "fibonacci.h"
#include "StackTemplate.h"
#include <iostream>
#include <fstream>
#include <string>
using namespace std;

int main() {
  StackTemplate<int> is;
  for(int i = 0; i < 20; i++)
    is.push(fibonacci(i));
  for(int k = 0; k < 20; k++)
    cout << is.pop() << endl;
  ifstream in("StackTemplateTest.cpp");
  assure(in, "StackTemplateTest.cpp");
  string line;
  StackTemplate<string> strings;
  while(getline(in, line))
    strings.push(line);
  while(strings.size() > 0)
    cout << strings.pop() << endl;
} ///:~
```

The only difference is in the creation of **is**. Inside the template argument list you specify the type of object the stack and iterator should hold. To demonstrate the genericness of the template, a

---

[5] All methods in both Smalltalk and Python are weakly typed, and so those languages do not need a template mechanism. In effect, you get templates without templates.

StackTemplate is also created to hold **string**. This is tested by reading in lines from the source-code file.

Constants in templates

Template arguments are not restricted to class types; you can also use built-in types. The values of these arguments then become compile-time constants for that particular instantiation of the template. You can even use default values for these arguments. The following example allows you to set the size of the **Array** class during instantiation, but also provides a default value:

```
//: C16:Array3.cpp
// Built-in types as template arguments
#include "../require.h"
#include <iostream>
using namespace std;

template<class T, int size = 100>
class Array {
  T array[size];
public:
  T& operator[](int index) {
    require(index >= 0 && index < size,
      "Index out of range");
    return array[index];
  }
  int length() const { return size; }
};

class Number {
  float f;
public:
  Number(float ff = 0.0f) : f(ff) {}
  Number& operator=(const Number& n) {
    f = n.f;
    return *this;
  }
  operator float() const { return f; }
  friend ostream&
    operator<<(ostream& os, const Number& x) {
      return os << x.f;
  }
```

```
};

template<class T, int size = 20>
class Holder {
  Array<T, size>* np;
public:
  Holder() : np(0) {}
  T& operator[](int i) {
    require(0 <= i && i < size);
    if(!np) np = new Array<T, size>;
    return np->operator[](i);
  }
  int length() const { return size; }
  ~Holder() { delete np; }
};

int main() {
  Holder<Number> h;
  for(int i = 0; i < 20; i++)
    h[i] = i;
  for(int j = 0; j < 20; j++)
    cout << h[j] << endl;
} ///:~
```

As before, **Array** is a checked array of objects and prevents you
from indexing out of bounds. The class **Holder** is much like **Array**
except that it has a pointer to an **Array** instead of an embedded
object of type **Array**. This pointer is not initialized in the
constructor; the initialization is delayed until the first access. This is
called *lazy initialization*; you might use a technique like this if you
are creating a lot of objects, but not accessing them all, and want to
save storage.

You'll notice that the **size** value in both templates is never stored
internally in the class, but it is used as if it were a data member
inside the member functions.

Stack and Stash
as templates

The recurring "ownership" problems with the **Stash** and **Stack** container classes that have been revisited throughout this book come from the fact that these containers haven't been able to know exactly what types they hold. The nearest they've come is the **Stack** "container of **Object**" that was seen at the end of Chapter 15 in **OStackTest.cpp**.

If the client programmer doesn't explicitly remove all the pointers to objects that are held in the container, then the container should be able to correctly delete those pointers. That is to say, the container "owns" any objects that haven't been removed, and is thus responsible for cleaning them up. The snag has been that cleanup requires knowing the type of the object, and creating a generic container class requires *not* knowing the type of the object. With templates, however, we can write code that doesn't know the type of the object, and easily instantiate a new version of that container for every type that we want to contain. The individual instantiated containers *do* know the type of objects they hold and can thus call the correct destructor (assuming, in the typical case where polymorphism is involved, that a virtual destructor has been provided).

For the **Stack** this turns out to be quite simple since all of the member functions can be reasonably inlined:

```
//: C16:TStack.h
// The Stack as a template
#ifndef TSTACK_H
#define TSTACK_H

template<class T>
class Stack {
  struct Link {
    T* data;
    Link* next;
    Link(T* dat, Link* nxt):
      data(dat), next(nxt) {}
  }* head;
```

```
public:
  Stack() : head(0) {}
  ~Stack(){
    while(head)
      delete pop();
  }
  void push(T* dat) {
    head = new Link(dat, head);
  }
  T* peek() const {
    return head ? head->data : 0;
  }
  T* pop(){
    if(head == 0) return 0;
    T* result = head->data;
    Link* oldHead = head;
    head = head->next;
    delete oldHead;
    return result;
  }
};
#endif // TSTACK_H ///:~
```

If you compare this to the **OStack.h** example at the end of Chapter 15, you will see that **Stack** is virtually identical, except that **Object** has been replaced with **T**. The test program is also nearly identical, except that the necessity for multiply-inheriting from **string** and **Object** (and even the need for **Object** itself) has been eliminated. Now there is no **MyString** class to announce its destruction, so a small new class is added to show a **Stack** container cleaning up its objects:

```
//: C16:TStackTest.cpp
//{T} TStackTest.cpp
#include "TStack.h"
#include "../require.h"
#include <fstream>
#include <iostream>
#include <string>
using namespace std;

class X {
public:
  virtual ~X() { cout << "~X " << endl; }
```

```
};

int main(int argc, char* argv[]) {
  requireArgs(argc, 1); // File name is argument
  ifstream in(argv[1]);
  assure(in, argv[1]);
  Stack<string> textlines;
  string line;
  // Read file and store lines in the Stack:
  while(getline(in, line))
    textlines.push(new string(line));
  // Pop some lines from the stack:
  string* s;
  for(int i = 0; i < 10; i++) {
    if((s = (string*)textlines.pop())==0) break;
    cout << *s << endl;
    delete s;
  } // The destructor deletes the other strings.
  // Show that correct destruction happens:
  Stack<X> xx;
  for(int j = 0; j < 10; j++)
    xx.push(new X);
} ///:~
```

The destructor for **X** is virtual, not because it's necessary here, but because **xx** could later be used to hold objects derived from **X**.

Notice how easy it is to create different kinds of **Stack**s for **string** and for **X**. Because of the template, you get the best of both worlds: the ease of use of the **Stack** class along with proper cleanup.

Templatized pointer Stash

Reorganizing the **PStash** code into a template isn't quite so simple because there are a number of member functions that should not be inlined. However, as a template those function definitions still belong in the header file (the compiler and linker take care of any multiple definition problems). The code looks quite similar to the ordinary **PStash** except that you'll notice the size of the increment (used by **inflate( )**) has been templatized as a non-class parameter with a default value, so that the increment size can be modified at the point of instantiation (notice that this means that the increment size is fixed; you may also argue that the increment size should be changeable throughout the lifetime of the object):

```
//: C16:TPStash.h
#ifndef TPSTASH_H
#define TPSTASH_H

template<class T, int incr = 10>
class PStash {
  int quantity; // Number of storage spaces
  int next; // Next empty space
  T** storage;
  void inflate(int increase = incr);
public:
  PStash() : quantity(0), next(0), storage(0) {}
  ~PStash();
  int add(T* element);
  T* operator[](int index) const; // Fetch
  // Remove the reference from this PStash:
  T* remove(int index);
  // Number of elements in Stash:
  int count() const { return next; }
};

template<class T, int incr>
int PStash<T, incr>::add(T* element) {
  if(next >= quantity)
    inflate(incr);
  storage[next++] = element;
  return(next - 1); // Index number
}

// Ownership of remaining pointers:
template<class T, int incr>
PStash<T, incr>::~PStash() {
  for(int i = 0; i < next; i++) {
    delete storage[i]; // Null pointers OK
    storage[i] = 0; // Just to be safe
  }
  delete []storage;
}

template<class T, int incr>
T* PStash<T, incr>::operator[](int index) const {
```

```
    require(index >= 0,
      "PStash::operator[] index negative");
    if(index >= next)
      return 0; // To indicate the end
    require(storage[index] != 0,
      "PStash::operator[] returned null pointer");
    // Produce pointer to desired element:
    return storage[index];
}

template<class T, int incr>
T* PStash<T, incr>::remove(int index) {
  // operator[] performs validity checks:
  T* v = operator[](index);
  // "Remove" the pointer:
  if(v != 0) storage[index] = 0;
  return v;
}

template<class T, int incr>
void PStash<T, incr>::inflate(int increase) {
  const int psz = sizeof(T*);
  T** st = new T*[quantity + increase];
  memset(st, 0, (quantity + increase) * psz);
  memcpy(st, storage, quantity * psz);
  quantity += increase;
  delete []storage; // Old storage
  storage = st; // Point to new memory
}
#endif // TPSTASH_H ///:~
```

The default increment size used here is small to guarantee that calls
to **inflate( )** occur. This way we can make sure it works correctly.

To test the ownership control of the templatized **PStash**, the
following class will report creations and destructions of itself, and
also guarantee that all objects that have been created were also
destroyed. **AutoCounter** will allow only objects of its type to be
created on the stack:

```
//: C16:AutoCounter.h
#ifndef AUTOCOUNTER_H
#define AUTOCOUNTER_H
#include "../require.h"
```

```cpp
#include <iostream>
#include <set> // Standard C++ Library container
#include <string>

class AutoCounter {
  static int count;
  int id;
  class CleanupCheck {
    std::set<AutoCounter*> trace;
  public:
    void add(AutoCounter* ap) {
      trace.insert(ap);
    }
    void remove(AutoCounter* ap) {
      require(trace.erase(ap) == 1,
        "Attempt to delete AutoCounter twice");
    }
    ~CleanupCheck() {
      std::cout << "~CleanupCheck()"<< std::endl;
      require(trace.size() == 0,
        "All AutoCounter objects not cleaned up");
    }
  };
  static CleanupCheck verifier;
  AutoCounter() : id(count++) {
    verifier.add(this); // Register itself
    std::cout << "created[" << id << "]"
              << std::endl;
  }
  // Prevent assignment and copy-construction:
  AutoCounter(const AutoCounter&);
  void operator=(const AutoCounter&);
public:
  // You can only create objects with this:
  static AutoCounter* create() {
    return new AutoCounter();
  }
  ~AutoCounter() {
    std::cout << "destroying[" << id
              << "]" << std::endl;
    verifier.remove(this);
  }
  // Print both objects and pointers:
  friend std::ostream& operator<<(
    std::ostream& os, const AutoCounter& ac){
```

```
      return os << "AutoCounter " << ac.id;
  }
  friend std::ostream& operator<<(
    std::ostream& os, const AutoCounter* ac){
    return os << "AutoCounter " << ac->id;
  }
};
#endif // AUTOCOUNTER_H ///:~
```

The **AutoCounter** class does two things. First, it sequentially numbers each instance of **AutoCounter**: the value of this number is kept in **id**, and the number is generated using the **static** data member **count**.

Second, and more complex, a **static** instance (called **verifier**) of the nested class **CleanupCheck** keeps track of all of the **AutoCounter** objects that are created and destroyed, and reports back to you if you don't clean all of them up (i.e. if there is a memory leak). This behavior is accomplished using a **set** class from the Standard C++ Library, which is a wonderful example of how well-designed templates can make life easy (you can learn about all the containers in the Standard C++ Library in Volume 2 of this book, available online).

The **set** class is templatized on the type that it holds; here it is instantiated to hold **AutoCounter** pointers. A **set** will allow only one instance of each distinct object to be added; in **add( )** you can see this take place with the **set::insert( )** function. **insert( )** actually informs you with its return value if you're trying to add something that's already been added; however, since object addresses are being added we can rely on C++'s guarantee that all objects have unique addresses.

In **remove( )**, **set::erase( )** is used to remove an **AutoCounter** pointer from the **set**. The return value tells you how many instances of the element were removed; in our case we only expect zero or one. If the value is zero, however, it means this object was already deleted from the **set** and you're trying to delete it a second time, which is a programming error that will be reported through **require( )**.

The destructor for **CleanupCheck** does a final check by making sure that the size of the **set** is zero – this means that all of the objects have been properly cleaned up. If it's not zero, you have a memory leak, which is reported through **require( )**.

The constructor and destructor for **AutoCounter** register and unregister themselves with the **verifier** object. Notice that the constructor, copy-constructor, and assignment operator are **private**, so the only way for you to create an object is with the **static create( )** member function – this is a simple example of a *factory*, and it guarantees that all objects are created on the heap, so **verifier** will not get confused over assignments and copy-constructions.

Since all of the member functions have been inlined, the only reason for the implementation file is to contain the static data member definitions:

```
//: C16:AutoCounter.cpp {O}
// Definition of static class members
#include "AutoCounter.h"
AutoCounter::CleanupCheck AutoCounter::verifier;
int AutoCounter::count = 0;
///:~
```

With **AutoCounter** in hand, we can now test the facilities of the **PStash**. The following example not only shows that the **PStash** destructor cleans up all the objects that it currently owns, but it also demonstrates how the **AutoCounter** class detects objects that haven't been cleaned up:

```
//: C16:TPStashTest.cpp
//{L} AutoCounter
#include "AutoCounter.h"
#include "TPStash.h"
#include <iostream>
#include <fstream>
using namespace std;

int main() {
  PStash<AutoCounter> acStash;
  for(int i = 0; i < 10; i++)
```

```
    acStash.add(AutoCounter::create());
  cout << "Removing 5 manually:" << endl;
  for(int j = 0; j < 5; j++)
    delete acStash.remove(j);
  cout << "Remove two without deleting them:"
       << endl;
  // ... to generate the cleanup error message.
  cout << acStash.remove(5) << endl;
  cout << acStash.remove(6) << endl;
  cout << "The destructor cleans up the rest:"
       << endl;
  // Repeat the test from earlier chapters:
  ifstream in("TPStashTest.cpp");
  assure(in, "TPStashTest.cpp");
  PStash<string> stringStash;
  string line;
  while(getline(in, line))
    stringStash.add(new string(line));
  // Print out the strings:
  for(int u = 0; stringStash[u]; u++)
    cout << "stringStash[" << u << "] = "
         << *stringStash[u] << endl;
} ///:~
```

When **AutoCounter** elements 5 and 6 are removed from the
PStash, they become the responsibility of the caller, but since the
caller never cleans them up they cause memory leaks, which are
then detected by **AutoCounter** at run time.

When you run the program, you'll see that the error message isn't
as specific as it could be. If you use the scheme presented in
AutoCounter to discover memory leaks in your own system, you
will probably want to have it print out more detailed information
about the objects that haven't been cleaned up. Volume 2 of this
book shows more sophisticated ways to do this.

Turning ownership on and off

Let's return to the ownership problem. Containers that hold objects
by value don't usually worry about ownership because they clearly
own the objects they contain. But if your container holds pointers
(which is more common with C++, especially with polymorphism),

---

then it's very likely those pointers may also be used somewhere else in the program, and you don't necessarily want to delete the object because then the other pointers in the program would be referencing a destroyed object. To prevent this from happening, you must consider ownership when designing and using a container.

Many programs are much simpler than this, and don't encounter the ownership problem: One container holds pointers to objects that are used only by that container. In this case ownership is very straightforward: The container owns its objects.

The best approach to handling the ownership problem is to give the client programmer a choice. This is often accomplished by a constructor argument that defaults to indicating ownership (the simplest case). In addition there may be "get" and "set" functions to view and modify the ownership of the container. If the container has functions to remove an object, the ownership state usually affects that removal, so you may also find options to control destruction in the removal function. You could conceivably add ownership data for every element in the container, so each position would know whether it needed to be destroyed; this is a variant of reference counting, except that the container and not the object knows the number of references pointing to an object.

```
//: C16:OwnerStack.h
// Stack with runtime conrollable ownership
#ifndef OWNERSTACK_H
#define OWNERSTACK_H

template<class T> class Stack {
  struct Link {
    T* data;
    Link* next;
    Link(T* dat, Link* nxt)
      : data(dat), next(nxt) {}
  }* head;
  bool own;
public:
  Stack(bool own = true) : head(0), own(own) {}
  ~Stack();
  void push(T* dat) {
    head = new Link(dat,head);
```

```
  }
  T* peek() const {
    return head ? head->data : 0;
  }
  T* pop();
  bool owns() const { return own; }
  void owns(bool newownership) {
    own = newownership;
  }
  // Auto-type conversion: true if not empty:
  operator bool() const { return head != 0; }
};

template<class T> T* Stack<T>::pop() {
  if(head == 0) return 0;
  T* result = head->data;
  Link* oldHead = head;
  head = head->next;
  delete oldHead;
  return result;
}

template<class T> Stack<T>::~Stack() {
  if(!own) return;
  while(head)
    delete pop();
}
#endif // OWNERSTACK_H ///:~
```

The default behavior is for the container to destroy its objects but
you can change this by either modifying the constructor argument
or using the **owns( )** read/write member functions.

As with most templates you're likely to see, the entire
implementation is contained in the header file. Here's a small test
that exercises the ownership abilities:

```
//: C16:OwnerStackTest.cpp
//{L} AutoCounter
#include "AutoCounter.h"
#include "OwnerStack.h"
#include "../require.h"
#include <iostream>
#include <fstream>
```

```
#include <string>
using namespace std;

int main() {
  Stack<AutoCounter> ac; // Ownership on
  Stack<AutoCounter> ac2(false); // Turn it off
  AutoCounter* ap;
  for(int i = 0; i < 10; i++) {
    ap = AutoCounter::create();
    ac.push(ap);
    if(i % 2 == 0)
      ac2.push(ap);
  }
  while(ac2)
    cout << ac2.pop() << endl;
  // No destruction necessary since
  // ac "owns" all the objects
} ///:~
```

The **ac2** object doesn't own the objects you put into it, thus **ac** is the "master" container which takes responsibility for ownership. If, partway through the lifetime of a container, you want to change whether a container owns its objects, you can do so using **owns( )**.

It would also be possible to change the granularity of the ownership so that it is on an object-by-object basis, but that will probably make the solution to the ownership problem more complex than the problem.

Holding objects by value

Actually creating a copy of the objects inside a generic container is a complex problem if you don't have templates. With templates, things are relatively simple – you just say that you are holding objects rather than pointers:

```
//: C16:ValueStack.h
// Holding objects by value in a Stack
#ifndef VALUESTACK_H
#define VALUESTACK_H
#include "../require.h"
```

```
template<class T, int ssize = 100>
class Stack {
  // Default constructor performs object
  // initialization for each element in array:
  T stack[ssize];
  int top;
public:
  Stack() : top(0) {}
  // Copy-constructor copies object into array:
  void push(const T& x) {
    require(top < ssize, "Too many push()es");
    stack[top++] = x;
  }
  T peek() const { return stack[top]; }
  // Object still exists when you pop it;
  // it just isn't available anymore:
  T pop() {
    require(top > 0, "Too many pop()s");
    return stack[--top];
  }
};
#endif // VALUESTACK_H ///:~
```

The copy constructor for the contained objects does most of the
work by passing and returning the objects by value. Inside **push( )**,
storage of the object onto the **Stack** array is accomplished with
T::operator=. To guarantee that it works, a class called
SelfCounter keeps track of object creations and copy-
constructions:

```
//: C16:SelfCounter.h
#ifndef SELFCOUNTER_H
#define SELFCOUNTER_H
#include "ValueStack.h"
#include <iostream>

class SelfCounter {
  static int counter;
  int id;
public:
  SelfCounter() : id(counter++) {
    std::cout << "Created: " << id << std::endl;
  }
  SelfCounter(const SelfCounter& rv) : id(rv.id){
```

```cpp
      std::cout << "Copied: " << id << std::endl;
    }
    SelfCounter operator=(const SelfCounter& rv) {
      std::cout << "Assigned " << rv.id << " to "
                << id << std::endl;
      return *this;
    }
    ~SelfCounter() {
      std::cout << "Destroyed: "<< id << std::endl;
    }
    friend std::ostream& operator<<(
      std::ostream& os, const SelfCounter& sc){
      return os << "SelfCounter: " << sc.id;
    }
};
#endif // SELFCOUNTER_H ///:~

//: C16:SelfCounter.cpp {O}
#include "SelfCounter.h"
int SelfCounter::counter = 0; ///:~

//: C16:ValueStackTest.cpp
//{L} SelfCounter
#include "ValueStack.h"
#include "SelfCounter.h"
#include <iostream>
using namespace std;

int main() {
  Stack<SelfCounter> sc;
  for(int i = 0; i < 10; i++)
    sc.push(SelfCounter());
  // OK to peek(), result is a temporary:
  cout << sc.peek() << endl;
  for(int k = 0; k < 10; k++)
    cout << sc.pop() << endl;
} ///:~
```

When a **Stack** container is created, the default constructor of the
contained object is called for each object in the array. You'll initially
see 100 **SelfCounter** objects created for no apparent reason, but
this is just the array initialization. This can be a bit expensive, but
there's no way around it in a simple design like this. An even more
complex situation arises if you make the **Stack** more general by

allowing the size to grow dynamically, because in the implementation shown above this would involve creating a new (larger) array, copying the old array to the new, and destroying the old array (this is, in fact, what the Standard C++ Library **vector** class does).

Introducing iterators

An *iterator* is an object that moves through a container of other objects and selects them one at a time, without providing direct access to the implementation of that container. Iterators provide a standard way to access elements, whether or not a container provides a way to access the elements directly. You will see iterators used most often in association with container classes, and iterators are a fundamental concept in the design and use of the Standard C++ containers, which are fully described in Volume 2 of this book (downloadable from *www.BruceEckel.com*). An iterator is also a kind of *design pattern*, which is the subject of a chapter in Volume 2.

In many ways, an iterator is a "smart pointer," and in fact you'll notice that iterators usually mimic most pointer operations. Unlike a pointer, however, the iterator is designed to be safe, so you're much less likely to do the equivalent of walking off the end of an array (or if you do, you find out about it more easily).

Consider the first example in this chapter. Here it is with a simple iterator added:

```
//: C16:IterIntStack.cpp
// Simple integer stack with iterators
//{L} fibonacci
#include "fibonacci.h"
#include "../require.h"
#include <iostream>
using namespace std;

class IntStack {
  enum { ssize = 100 };
  int stack[ssize];
```

```
    int top;
public:
  IntStack() : top(0) {}
  void push(int i) {
    require(top < ssize, "Too many push()es");
    stack[top++] = i;
  }
  int pop() {
    require(top > 0, "Too many pop()s");
    return stack[--top];
  }
  friend class IntStackIter;
};

// An iterator is like a "smart" pointer:
class IntStackIter {
  IntStack& s;
  int index;
public:
  IntStackIter(IntStack& is) : s(is), index(0) {}
  int operator++() { // Prefix
    require(index < s.top,
      "iterator moved out of range");
    return s.stack[++index];
  }
  int operator++(int) { // Postfix
    require(index < s.top,
      "iterator moved out of range");
    return s.stack[index++];
  }
};

int main() {
  IntStack is;
  for(int i = 0; i < 20; i++)
    is.push(fibonacci(i));
  // Traverse with an iterator:
  IntStackIter it(is);
  for(int j = 0; j < 20; j++)
    cout << it++ << endl;
} ///:~
```

The **IntStackIter** has been created to work only with an **IntStack**. Notice that **IntStackIter** is a **friend** of **IntStack**, which gives it access to all the **private** elements of **IntStack**.

Like a pointer, **IntStackIter**'s job is to move through an **IntStack** and retrieve values. In this simple example, the **IntStackIter** can move only forward (using both the pre- and postfix forms of the **operator++**). However, there is no boundary to the way an iterator can be defined, other than those imposed by the constraints of the container it works with. It is perfectly acceptable (within the limits of the underlying container) for an iterator to move around in any way within its associated container and to cause the contained values to be modified.

It is customary that an iterator is created with a constructor that attaches it to a single container object, and that the iterator is not attached to a different container during its lifetime. (Iterators are usually small and cheap, so you can easily make another one.)

With the iterator, you can traverse the elements of the stack without popping them, just as a pointer can move through the elements of an array. However, the iterator knows the underlying structure of the stack and how to traverse the elements, so even though you are moving through them by pretending to "increment a pointer," what's going on underneath is more involved. That's the key to the iterator: It is abstracting the complicated process of moving from one container element to the next into something that looks like a pointer. The goal is for *every* iterator in your program to have the same interface so that any code that uses the iterator doesn't care what it's pointing to – it just knows that it can reposition all iterators the same way, so the container that the iterator points to is unimportant. In this way you can write more generic code. All of the containers and algorithms in the Standard C++ Library are based on this principle of iterators.

To aid in making things more generic, it would be nice to be able to say "every container has an associated class called **iterator**," but this will typically cause naming problems. The solution is to add a nested **iterator** class to each container (notice that in this case, "**iterator**" begins with a lowercase letter so that it conforms to the style of the Standard C++ Library). Here is **IterIntStack.cpp** with a nested **iterator**:

```
//: C16:NestedIterator.cpp
// Nesting an iterator inside the container
//{L} fibonacci
#include "fibonacci.h"
#include "../require.h"
#include <iostream>
#include <string>
using namespace std;

class IntStack {
  enum { ssize = 100 };
  int stack[ssize];
  int top;
public:
  IntStack() : top(0) {}
  void push(int i) {
    require(top < ssize, "Too many push()es");
    stack[top++] = i;
  }
  int pop() {
    require(top > 0, "Too many pop()s");
    return stack[--top];
  }
  class iterator;
  friend class iterator;
  class iterator {
    IntStack& s;
    int index;
  public:
    iterator(IntStack& is) : s(is), index(0) {}
    // To create the "end sentinel" iterator:
    iterator(IntStack& is, bool)
      : s(is), index(s.top) {}
    int current() const { return s.stack[index]; }
    int operator++() { // Prefix
      require(index < s.top,
        "iterator moved out of range");
      return s.stack[++index];
    }
    int operator++(int) { // Postfix
      require(index < s.top,
```

```
        "iterator moved out of range");
      return s.stack[index++];
    }
    // Jump an iterator forward
    iterator& operator+=(int amount) {
      require(index + amount < s.top,
        "IntStack::iterator::operator+=() "
        "tried to move out of bounds");
      index += amount;
      return *this;
    }
    // To see if you're at the end:
    bool operator==(const iterator& rv) const {
      return index == rv.index;
    }
    bool operator!=(const iterator& rv) const {
      return index != rv.index;
    }
    friend ostream&
    operator<<(ostream& os, const iterator& it) {
      return os << it.current();
    }
  };
  iterator begin() { return iterator(*this); }
  // Create the "end sentinel":
  iterator end() { return iterator(*this, true); }
};

int main() {
  IntStack is;
  for(int i = 0; i < 20; i++)
    is.push(fibonacci(i));
  cout << "Traverse the whole IntStack\n";
  IntStack::iterator it = is.begin();
  while(it != is.end())
    cout << it++ << endl;
  cout << "Traverse a portion of the IntStack\n";
  IntStack::iterator
    start = is.begin(), end = is.begin();
  start += 5, end += 15;
  cout << "start = " << start << endl;
  cout << "end = " << end << endl;
  while(start != end)
    cout << start++ << endl;
} ///:~
```

When making a nested **friend** class, you must go through the process of first declaring the name of the class, then declaring it as a **friend**, then defining the class. Otherwise, the compiler will get confused.

Some new twists have been added to the iterator. The **current( )** member function produces the element in the container that the iterator is currently selecting. You can "jump" an iterator forward by an arbitrary number of elements using **operator+=**. Also, you'll see two overloaded operators: **==** and **!=** that will compare one iterator with another. These can compare any two **IntStack::iterator**s, but they are primarily intended as a test to see if the iterator is at the end of a sequence in the same way that the "real" Standard C++ Library iterators do. The idea is that two iterators define a range, including the first element pointed to by the first iterator and up to but *not* including the last element pointed to by the second iterator. So if you want to move through the range defined by the two iterators, you say something like this:

```
while(start != end)
  cout << start++ << endl;
```

where **start** and **end** are the two iterators in the range. Note that the **end** iterator, which we often refer to as the *end sentinel*, is not dereferenced and is there only to tell you that you're at the end of the sequence. Thus it represents "one past the end."

Much of the time you'll want to move through the entire sequence in a container, so the container needs some way to produce the iterators indicating the beginning of the sequence and the end sentinel. Here, as in the Standard C++ Library, these iterators are produced by the container member functions **begin( )** and **end( )**. **begin( )** uses the first **iterator** constructor that defaults to pointing at the beginning of the container (this is the first element pushed on the stack). However, a second constructor, used by **end( )**, is necessary to create the end sentinel **iterator**. Being "at the end" means pointing to the top of the stack, because **top** always indicates the next available – but unused – space on the stack. This **iterator** constructor takes a second argument of type **bool**, which is a dummy to distinguish the two constructors.

The Fibonacci numbers are used again to fill the **IntStack** in
main( ), and **iterator**s are used to move through the whole
IntStack and also within a narrowed range of the sequence.

The next step, of course, is to make the code general by templatizing
it on the type that it holds, so that instead of being forced to hold
only **int**s you can hold any type:

```
//: C16:IterStackTemplate.h
// Simple stack template with nested iterator
#ifndef ITERSTACKTEMPLATE_H
#define ITERSTACKTEMPLATE_H
#include "../require.h"
#include <iostream>

template<class T, int ssize = 100>
class StackTemplate {
  T stack[ssize];
  int top;
public:
  StackTemplate() : top(0) {}
  void push(const T& i) {
    require(top < ssize, "Too many push()es");
    stack[top++] = i;
  }
  T pop() {
    require(top > 0, "Too many pop()s");
    return stack[--top];
  }
  class iterator; // Declaration required
  friend class iterator; // Make it a friend
  class iterator { // Now define it
    StackTemplate& s;
    int index;
  public:
    iterator(StackTemplate& st): s(st),index(0){}
    // To create the "end sentinel" iterator:
    iterator(StackTemplate& st, bool)
      : s(st), index(s.top) {}
    T operator*() const { return s.stack[index]; }
    T operator++() { // Prefix form
      require(index < s.top,
        "iterator moved out of range");
      return s.stack[++index];
```

```
    }
    T operator++(int) { // Postfix form
      require(index < s.top,
        "iterator moved out of range");
      return s.stack[index++];
    }
    // Jump an iterator forward
    iterator& operator+=(int amount) {
      require(index + amount < s.top,
        " StackTemplate::iterator::operator+=() "
        "tried to move out of bounds");
      index += amount;
      return *this;
    }
    // To see if you're at the end:
    bool operator==(const iterator& rv) const {
      return index == rv.index;
    }
    bool operator!=(const iterator& rv) const {
      return index != rv.index;
    }
    friend std::ostream& operator<<(
      std::ostream& os, const iterator& it) {
      return os << *it;
    }
  };
  iterator begin() { return iterator(*this); }
  // Create the "end sentinel":
  iterator end() { return iterator(*this, true); }
};
#endif // ITERSTACKTEMPLATE_H ///:~
```

You can see that the transformation from a regular class to a **template** is reasonably transparent. This approach of first creating and debugging an ordinary class, then making it into a template, is generally considered to be easier than creating the template from scratch.

Notice that instead of just saying:

```
friend iterator; // Make it a friend
```

This code has:

```
friend class iterator; // Make it a friend
```

This is important because the name "iterator" is already in scope, from an included file.

Instead of the **current( )** member function, the **iterator** has an **operator*** to select the current element, which makes the **iterator** look more like a pointer and is a common practice.

Here's the revised example to test the template:

```
//: C16:IterStackTemplateTest.cpp
//{L} fibonacci
#include "fibonacci.h"
#include "IterStackTemplate.h"
#include <iostream>
#include <fstream>
#include <string>
using namespace std;

int main() {
  StackTemplate<int> is;
  for(int i = 0; i < 20; i++)
    is.push(fibonacci(i));
  // Traverse with an iterator:
  cout << "Traverse the whole StackTemplate\n";
  StackTemplate<int>::iterator it = is.begin();
  while(it != is.end())
    cout << it++ << endl;
  cout << "Traverse a portion\n";
  StackTemplate<int>::iterator
    start = is.begin(), end = is.begin();
  start += 5, end += 15;
  cout << "start = " << start << endl;
  cout << "end = " << end << endl;
  while(start != end)
    cout << start++ << endl;
  ifstream in("IterStackTemplateTest.cpp");
  assure(in, "IterStackTemplateTest.cpp");
  string line;
  StackTemplate<string> strings;
  while(getline(in, line))
    strings.push(line);
  StackTemplate<string>::iterator
```

```
    sb = strings.begin(), se = strings.end();
  while(sb != se)
    cout << sb++ << endl;
} ///:~
```

The first use of the iterator just marches it from beginning to end
(and shows that the end sentinel works properly). In the second
usage, you can see how iterators allow you to easily specify a range
of elements (the containers and iterators in the Standard C++
Library use this concept of ranges almost everywhere). The
overloaded **operator+=** moves the **start** and **end** iterators to
positions in the middle of the range of the elements in **is**, and these
elements are printed out. Notice in the output that the end sentinel
is *not* included in the range, thus it can be one past the end of the
range to let you know you've passed the end – but you don't
dereference the end sentinel, or else you can end up dereferencing a
null pointer. (I've put guarding in the **StackTemplate::iterator**,
but in the Standard C++ Library containers and iterators there is no
such code – for efficiency reasons – so you must pay attention.)

Lastly, to verify that the **StackTemplate** works with class objects,
one is instantiated for **string** and filled with the lines from the
source-code file, which are then printed out.

Stack with iterators

We can repeat the process with the dynamically-sized **Stack** class
that has been used as an example throughout the book. Here's the
Stack class with a nested iterator folded into the mix:

```
//: C16:TStack2.h
// Templatized Stack with nested iterator
#ifndef TSTACK2_H
#define TSTACK2_H

template<class T> class Stack {
  struct Link {
    T* data;
    Link* next;
    Link(T* dat, Link* nxt)
      : data(dat), next(nxt) {}
  }* head;
```

```
public:
  Stack() : head(0) {}
  ~Stack();
  void push(T* dat) {
    head = new Link(dat, head);
  }
  T* peek() const {
    return head ? head->data : 0;
  }
  T* pop();
  // Nested iterator class:
  class iterator; // Declaration required
  friend class iterator; // Make it a friend
  class iterator { // Now define it
    Stack::Link* p;
  public:
    iterator(const Stack<T>& tl) : p(tl.head) {}
    // Copy-constructor:
    iterator(const iterator& tl) : p(tl.p) {}
    // The end sentinel iterator:
    iterator() : p(0) {}
    // operator++ returns boolean indicating end:
    bool operator++() {
      if(p->next)
        p = p->next;
      else p = 0; // Indicates end of list
      return bool(p);
    }
    bool operator++(int) { return operator++(); }
    T* current() const {
      if(!p) return 0;
      return p->data;
    }
    // Pointer dereference operator:
    T* operator->() const {
      require(p != 0,
        "PStack::iterator::operator->returns 0");
      return current();
    }
    T* operator*() const { return current(); }
    // bool conversion for conditional test:
    operator bool() const { return bool(p); }
    // Comparison to test for end:
    bool operator==(const iterator&) const {
      return p == 0;
```

```
    }
    bool operator!=(const iterator&) const {
      return p != 0;
    }
  };
  iterator begin() const {
    return iterator(*this);
  }
  iterator end() const { return iterator(); }
};

template<class T> Stack<T>::~Stack() {
  while(head)
    delete pop();
}

template<class T> T* Stack<T>::pop() {
  if(head == 0) return 0;
  T* result = head->data;
  Link* oldHead = head;
  head = head->next;
  delete oldHead;
  return result;
}
#endif // TSTACK2_H ///:~
```

You'll also notice the class has been changed to support ownership, which works now because the class knows the exact type (or at least the base type, which will work assuming virtual destructors are used). The default is for the container to destroy its objects but you are responsible for any pointers that you **pop( )**.

The iterator is simple, and physically very small – the size of a single pointer. When you create an **iterator**, it's initialized to the head of the linked list, and you can only increment it forward through the list. If you want to start over at the beginning, you create a new iterator, and if you want to remember a spot in the list, you create a new iterator from the existing iterator pointing at that spot (using the iterator's copy-constructor).

To call functions for the object referred to by the iterator, you can use the **current( )** function, the **operator***, or the pointer dereference **operator->** (a common sight in iterators). The latter

---

has an implementation that *looks* identical to **current( )** because it returns a pointer to the current object, but is different because the pointer dereference operator performs the extra levels of dereferencing (see Chapter 12).

The **iterator** class follows the form you saw in the prior example. **class iterator** is nested inside the container class, it contains constructors to create both an iterator pointing at an element in the container and an "end sentinel" iterator, and the container class has the **begin( )** and **end( )** methods to produce these iterators. (When you learn the more about the Standard C++ Library, you'll see that the names **iterator**, **begin( )**, and **end( )** that are used here were clearly lifted standard container classes. At the end of this chapter, you'll see that this enables these container classes to be used as if they were Standard C++ Library container classes.)

The entire implementation is contained in the header file, so there's no separate **cpp** file. Here's a small test that exercises the iterator:

```
//: C16:TStack2Test.cpp
#include "TStack2.h"
#include "../require.h"
#include <iostream>
#include <fstream>
#include <string>
using namespace std;

int main() {
  ifstream file("TStack2Test.cpp");
  assure(file, "TStack2Test.cpp");
  Stack<string> textlines;
  // Read file and store lines in the Stack:
  string line;
  while(getline(file, line))
    textlines.push(new string(line));
  int i = 0;
  // Use iterator to print lines from the list:
  Stack<string>::iterator it = textlines.begin();
  Stack<string>::iterator* it2 = 0;
  while(it != textlines.end()) {
    cout << it->c_str() << endl;
    it++;
```

```
    if(++i == 10) // Remember 10th line
       it2 = new Stack<string>::iterator(it);
  }
  cout << (*it2)->c_str() << endl;
  delete it2;
} ///:~
```

A **Stack** is instantiated to hold **string** objects and filled with lines
from a file. Then an iterator is created and used to move through
the sequence. The tenth line is remembered by copy-constructing a
second iterator from the first; later this line is printed and the
iterator – created dynamically – is destroyed. Here, dynamic object
creation is used to control the lifetime of the object.

PStash with iterators

For most container classes it makes sense to have an iterator.
Here's an iterator added to the **PStash** class:

```
//: C16:TPStash2.h
// Templatized PStash with nested iterator
#ifndef TPSTASH2_H
#define TPSTASH2_H
#include "../require.h"
#include <cstdlib>

template<class T, int incr = 20>
class PStash {
  int quantity;
  int next;
  T** storage;
  void inflate(int increase = incr);
public:
  PStash() : quantity(0), storage(0), next(0) {}
  ~PStash();
  int add(T* element);
  T* operator[](int index) const;
  T* remove(int index);
  int count() const { return next; }
  // Nested iterator class:
  class iterator; // Declaration required
  friend class iterator; // Make it a friend
  class iterator { // Now define it
    PStash& ps;
```

```
    int index;
public:
  iterator(PStash& pStash)
    : ps(pStash), index(0) {}
  // To create the end sentinel:
  iterator(PStash& pStash, bool)
    : ps(pStash), index(ps.next) {}
  // Copy-constructor:
  iterator(const iterator& rv)
    : ps(rv.ps), index(rv.index) {}
  iterator& operator=(const iterator& rv) {
    ps = rv.ps;
    index = rv.index;
    return *this;
  }
  iterator& operator++() {
    require(++index <= ps.next,
      "PStash::iterator::operator++ "
      "moves index out of bounds");
    return *this;
  }
  iterator& operator++(int) {
    return operator++();
  }
  iterator& operator--() {
    require(--index >= 0,
      "PStash::iterator::operator-- "
      "moves index out of bounds");
    return *this;
  }
  iterator& operator--(int) {
    return operator--();
  }
  // Jump interator forward or backward:
  iterator& operator+=(int amount) {
    require(index + amount < ps.next &&
      index + amount >= 0,
      "PStash::iterator::operator+= "
      "attempt to index out of bounds");
    index += amount;
    return *this;
  }
  iterator& operator-=(int amount) {
    require(index - amount < ps.next &&
      index - amount >= 0,
```

```
        "PStash::iterator::operator-= "
        "attempt to index out of bounds");
      index -= amount;
      return *this;
    }
    // Create a new iterator that's moved forward
    iterator operator+(int amount) const {
      iterator ret(*this);
      ret += amount; // op+= does bounds check
      return ret;
    }
    T* current() const {
      return ps.storage[index];
    }
    T* operator*() const { return current(); }
    T* operator->() const {
      require(ps.storage[index] != 0,
        "PStash::iterator::operator->returns 0");
      return current();
    }
    // Remove the current element:
    T* remove(){
      return ps.remove(index);
    }
    // Comparison tests for end:
    bool operator==(const iterator& rv) const {
      return index == rv.index;
    }
    bool operator!=(const iterator& rv) const {
      return index != rv.index;
    }
  };
  iterator begin() { return iterator(*this); }
  iterator end() { return iterator(*this, true);}
};

// Destruction of contained objects:
template<class T, int incr>
PStash<T, incr>::~PStash() {
  for(int i = 0; i < next; i++) {
    delete storage[i]; // Null pointers OK
    storage[i] = 0; // Just to be safe
  }
  delete []storage;
}
```

```
template<class T, int incr>
int PStash<T, incr>::add(T* element) {
  if(next >= quantity)
    inflate();
  storage[next++] = element;
  return(next - 1); // Index number
}

template<class T, int incr> inline
T* PStash<T, incr>::operator[](int index) const {
  require(index >= 0,
    "PStash::operator[] index negative");
  if(index >= next)
    return 0; // To indicate the end
  require(storage[index] != 0,
    "PStash::operator[] returned null pointer");
  return storage[index];
}

template<class T, int incr>
T* PStash<T, incr>::remove(int index) {
  // operator[] performs validity checks:
  T* v = operator[](index);
  // "Remove" the pointer:
  storage[index] = 0;
  return v;
}

template<class T, int incr>
void PStash<T, incr>::inflate(int increase) {
  const int tsz = sizeof(T*);
  T** st = new T*[quantity + increase];
  memset(st, 0, (quantity + increase) * tsz);
  memcpy(st, storage, quantity * tsz);
  quantity += increase;
  delete []storage; // Old storage
  storage = st; // Point to new memory
}
#endif // TPSTASH2_H ///:~
```

Most of this file is a fairly straightforward translation of both the
previous **PStash** and the nested **iterator** into a template. This

---

time, however, the operators return references to the current iterator, which is the more typical and flexible approach to take.

The destructor calls **delete** for all contained pointers, and because the type is captured by the template, proper destruction will take place. You should be aware that if the container holds pointers to a base-class type, that type should have a **virtual** destructor to ensure proper cleanup of derived objects whose addresses have been upcast when placing them in the container.

The **PStash::iterator** follows the iterator model of bonding to a single container object for its lifetime. In addition, the copy-constructor allows you to make a new iterator pointing at the same location as the existing iterator that you create it from, effectively making a bookmark into the container. The **operator+=** and **operator-=** member functions allow you to move an iterator by a number of spots, while respecting the boundaries of the container. The overloaded increment and decrement operators move the iterator by one place. The **operator+** produces a new iterator that's moved forward by the amount of the addend. As in the previous example, the pointer dereference operators are used to operate on the element the iterator is referring to, and **remove( )** destroys the current object by calling the container's **remove( )**.

The same kind of code as before (*a la* the Standard C++ Library containers) is used for creating the end sentinel: a second constructor, the container's **end( )** member function, and **operator==** and **operator!=** for comparison.

The following example creates and tests two different kinds of **Stash** objects, one for a new class called **Int** that announces its construction and destruction and one that holds objects of the Standard library **string** class.

```
//: C16:TPStash2Test.cpp
#include "TPStash2.h"
#include "../require.h"
#include <iostream>
#include <vector>
#include <string>
using namespace std;
```

```cpp
class Int {
  int i;
public:
  Int(int ii = 0) : i(ii) {
    cout << ">" << i << ' ';
  }
  ~Int() { cout << "~" << i << ' '; }
  operator int() const { return i; }
  friend ostream&
    operator<<(ostream& os, const Int& x) {
      return os << "Int: " << x.i;
  }
  friend ostream&
    operator<<(ostream& os, const Int* x) {
      return os << "Int: " << x->i;
  }
};

int main() {
  { // To force destructor call
    PStash<Int> ints;
    for(int i = 0; i < 30; i++)
      ints.add(new Int(i));
    cout << endl;
    PStash<Int>::iterator it = ints.begin();
    it += 5;
    PStash<Int>::iterator it2 = it + 10;
    for(; it != it2; it++)
      delete it.remove(); // Default removal
    cout << endl;
    for(it = ints.begin();it != ints.end();it++)
      if(*it) // Remove() causes "holes"
        cout << *it << endl;
  } // "ints" destructor called here
  cout << "\n------------------\n";
  ifstream in("TPStash2Test.cpp");
  assure(in, "TPStash2Test.cpp");
  // Instantiate for String:
  PStash<string> strings;
  string line;
  while(getline(in, line))
    strings.add(new string(line));
  PStash<string>::iterator sit = strings.begin();
  for(; sit != strings.end(); sit++)
```

```
    cout << **sit << endl;
  sit = strings.begin();
  int n = 26;
  sit += n;
  for(; sit != strings.end(); sit++)
    cout << n++ << ": " << **sit << endl;
} ///:~
```

For convenience, **Int** has an associated **ostream operator<<** for both an **Int&** and an **Int***.

The first block of code in **main( )** is surrounded by braces to force the destruction of the **PStash<Int>** and thus the automatic cleanup by that destructor. A range of elements is removed and deleted by hand to show that the **PStash** cleans up the rest.

For both instances of **PStash**, an iterator is created and used to move through the container. Notice the elegance produced by using these constructs; you aren't assailed with the implementation details of using an array. You tell the container and iterator objects *what* to do, not how. This makes the solution easier to conceptualize, to build, and to modify.

Why iterators?

Up until now you've seen the mechanics of iterators, but understanding why they are so important takes a more complex example.

It's common to see polymorphism, dynamic object creation, and containers used together in a true object-oriented program. Containers and dynamic object creation solve the problem of not knowing how many or what type of objects you'll need. And if the container is configured to hold pointers to base-class objects, an upcast occurs every time you put a derived-class pointer into the container (with the associated code organization and extensibility benefits). As the final code in Volume 1 of this book, this example will also pull together various aspects of everything you've learned so far – if you can follow this example, then you're ready for Volume 2.

Suppose you are creating a program that allows the user to edit and produce different kinds of drawings. Each drawing is an object that contains a collection of **Shape** objects:

```
//: C16:Shape.h
#ifndef SHAPE_H
#define SHAPE_H
#include <iostream>
#include <string>

class Shape {
public:
  virtual void draw() = 0;
  virtual void erase() = 0;
  virtual ~Shape() {}
};

class Circle : public Shape {
public:
  Circle() {}
  ~Circle() { std::cout << "Circle::~Circle\n"; }
  void draw() { std::cout << "Circle::draw\n";}
  void erase() { std::cout << "Circle::erase\n";}
};

class Square : public Shape {
public:
  Square() {}
  ~Square() { std::cout << "Square::~Square\n"; }
  void draw() { std::cout << "Square::draw\n";}
  void erase() { std::cout << "Square::erase\n";}
};

class Line : public Shape {
public:
  Line() {}
  ~Line() { std::cout << "Line::~Line\n"; }
  void draw() { std::cout << "Line::draw\n";}
  void erase() { std::cout << "Line::erase\n";}
};
#endif // SHAPE_H ///:~
```

This uses the classic structure of virtual functions in the base class that are overridden in the derived class. Notice that the **Shape** class includes a **virtual** destructor, something you should automatically add to any class with **virtual** functions. If a container holds pointers or references to **Shape** objects, then when the **virtual** destructors are called for those objects everything will be properly cleaned up.

Each different type of drawing in the following example makes use of a different kind of templatized container class: the **PStash** and **Stack** that have been defined in this chapter, and the **vector** class from the Standard C++ Library. The "use'" of the containers is extremely simple, and in general inheritance might not be the best approach (composition could make more sense), but in this case inheritance is a simple approach and it doesn't detract from the point made in the example.

```cpp
//: C16:Drawing.cpp
#include <vector> // Uses Standard vector too!
#include "TPStash2.h"
#include "TStack2.h"
#include "Shape.h"
using namespace std;

// A Drawing is primarily a container of Shapes:
class Drawing : public PStash<Shape> {
public:
  ~Drawing() { cout << "~Drawing" << endl; }
};

// A Plan is a different container of Shapes:
class Plan : public Stack<Shape> {
public:
  ~Plan() { cout << "~Plan" << endl; }
};

// A Schematic is a different container of Shapes:
class Schematic : public vector<Shape*> {
public:
  ~Schematic() { cout << "~Schematic" << endl; }
};

// A function template:
template<class Iter>
void drawAll(Iter start, Iter end) {
```

```
    while(start != end) {
      (*start)->draw();
      start++;
    }
}

int main() {
  // Each type of container has
  // a different interface:
  Drawing d;
  d.add(new Circle);
  d.add(new Square);
  d.add(new Line);
  Plan p;
  p.push(new Line);
  p.push(new Square);
  p.push(new Circle);
  Schematic s;
  s.push_back(new Square);
  s.push_back(new Circle);
  s.push_back(new Line);
  Shape* sarray[] = {
    new Circle, new Square, new Line
  };
  // The iterators and the template function
  // allow them to be treated generically:
  cout << "Drawing d:" << endl;
  drawAll(d.begin(), d.end());
  cout << "Plan p:" << endl;
  drawAll(p.begin(), p.end());
  cout << "Schematic s:" << endl;
  drawAll(s.begin(), s.end());
  cout << "Array sarray:" << endl;
  // Even works with array pointers:
  drawAll(sarray,
    sarray + sizeof(sarray)/sizeof(*sarray));
  cout << "End of main" << endl;
} ///:~
```

The different types of containers all hold pointers to **Shape** and
pointers to upcast objects of classes derived from **Shape**. However,
because of polymorphism, the proper behavior still occurs when the
virtual functions are called.

Note that **sarray**, the array of **Shape***, can also be thought of as a container.

Function templates

In **drawAll( )** you see something new. So far in this chapter, we have been using only *class templates*, which instantiate new classes based on one or more type parameters. However, you can as easily create *function templates*, which create new functions based on type parameters. The reason you create a function template is the same reason you use for a class template: You're trying to create generic code, and you do this by delaying the specification of one or more types. You just want to say that these type parameters support certain operations, not exactly what types they are.

The function template **drawAll( )** can be thought of as an *algorithm* (and this is what most of the function templates in the Standard C++ Library are called). It just says how to do something given iterators describing a range of elements, as long as these iterators can be dereferenced, incremented, and compared. These are exactly the kind of iterators we have been developing in this chapter, and also – not coincidentally – the kind of iterators that are produced by the containers in the Standard C++ Library, evidenced by the use of **vector** in this example.

We'd also like **drawAll( )** to be a *generic algorithm*, so that the containers can be any type at all and we don't have to write a new version of the algorithm for each different type of container. Here's where function templates are essential, because they automatically generate the specific code for each different type of container. But without the extra indirection provided by the iterators, this genericness wouldn't be possible. That's why iterators are important; they allow you to write general-purpose code that involves containers without knowing the underlying structure of the container. (Notice that, in C++, iterators and generic algorithms require function templates in order to work.)

You can see the proof of this in **main( )**, since **drawAll( )** works unchanged with each different type of container. And even more interesting, **drawAll( )** also works with pointers to the beginning and end of the array **sarray**. This ability to treat arrays as containers is integral to the design of the Standard C++ Library, whose algorithms look much like **drawAll( )**.

Because container class templates are rarely subject to the inheritance and upcasting you see with "ordinary" classes, you'll almost never see **virtual** functions in container classes. Container class reuse is implemented with templates, not with inheritance.

Summary

Container classes are an essential part of object-oriented programming. They are another way to simplify and hide the details of a program and to speed the process of program development. In addition, they provide a great deal of safety and flexibility by replacing the primitive arrays and relatively crude data structure techniques found in C.

Because the client programmer needs containers, it's essential that they be easy to use. This is where the **template** comes in. With templates the syntax for source-code reuse (as opposed to object-code reuse provided by inheritance and composition) becomes trivial enough for the novice user. In fact, reusing code with templates is notably easier than inheritance and composition.

Although you've learned about creating container and iterator classes in this book, in practice it's much more expedient to learn the containers and iterators in the Standard C++ Library, since you can expect them to be available with every compiler. As you will see in Volume 2 of this book (downloadable from *www.BruceEckel.com*), the containers and algorithms in the Standard C++ Library will virtually always fulfill your needs so you don't have to create new ones yourself.

The issues involved with container-class design have been touched upon in this chapter, but you may have gathered that they can go much further. A complicated container-class library may cover all sorts of additional issues, including multithreading, persistence and garbage collection.

Exercises

Solutions to selected exercises can be found in the electronic document *The Thinking in C++ Annotated Solution Guide*, available for a small fee from www.BruceEckel.com.

1. Implement the inheritance hierarchy in the **OShape** diagram in this chapter.

2. Modify the result of Exercise 1 from Chapter 15 to use the **Stack** and **iterator** in **TStack2.h** instead of an array of **Shape** pointers. Add destructors to the class hierarchy so you can see that the **Shape** objects are destroyed when the **Stack** goes out of scope.

3. Modify **TPStash.h** so that the increment value used by **inflate( )** can be changed throughout the lifetime of a particular container object.

4. Modify **TPStash.h** so that the increment value used by **inflate( )** automatically resizes itself to reduce the number of times it needs to be called. For example, each time it is called it could double the increment value for use in the next call. Demonstrate this functionality by reporting whenever an **inflate( )** is called, and write test code in **main( )**.

5. Templatize the **fibonacci( )** function on the type of value that it produces (so it can produce **long**, **float**, etc. instead of just **int**).

6. Using the Standard C++ Library **vector** as an underlying implementation, create a **Set** template class that accepts only one of each type of object that you put into it. Make a nested **iterator** class that supports the "end sentinel" concept in this chapter. Write test code for your **Set** in **main( )**, and then substitute the Standard C++ Library **set** template to verify that the behavior is correct.

7. Modify **AutoCounter.h** so that it can be used as a member object inside any class whose creation and destruction you want to trace. Add a **string** member to hold the name of the class. Test this tool inside a class of your own.

8. Create a version of **OwnerStack.h** that uses a Standard C++ Library **vector** as its underlying implementation. You may need to look up some of the member functions

of **vector** in order to do this (or just look at the **<vector>** header file).

9. Modify **ValueStack.h** so that it dynamically expands as you **push( )** more objects and it runs out of space. Change **ValueStackTest.cpp** to test the new functionality.

10. Repeat Exercise 9 but use a Standard C++ Library **vector** as the internal implementation of the **ValueStack**. Notice how much easier this is.

11. Modify **ValueStackTest.cpp** so that it uses a Standard C++ Library **vector** instead of a **Stack** in **main( )**. Notice the run-time behavior: Does the **vector** automatically create a bunch of default objects when it is created?

12. Modify **TStack2.h** so that it uses a Standard C++ Library **vector** as its underlying implementation. Make sure that you don't change the interface, so that **TStack2Test.cpp** works unchanged.

13. Repeat Exercise 12 using a Standard C++ Library **stack** instead of a **vector** (you may need to look up information about the **stack**, or hunt through the **<stack>** header file).

14. Modify **TPStash2.h** so that it uses a Standard C++ Library **vector** as its underlying implementation. Make sure that you don't change the interface, so that **TPStash2Test.cpp** works unchanged.

15. In **IterIntStack.cpp**, modify **IntStackIter** to give it an "end sentinel" constructor, and add **operator==** and **operator!=**. In **main( )**, use an iterator to move through the elements of the container until you reach the end sentinel.

16. Using **TStack2.h**, **TPStash2.h**, and **Shape.h**, instantiate **Stack** and **PStash** containers for **Shape***, fill them each with an assortment of upcast **Shape** pointers, then use iterators to move through each container and call **draw( )** for each object.

17. Templatize the **Int** class in **TPStash2Test.cpp** so that it holds any type of object (feel free to change the name of the class to something more appropriate).

18. Templatize the **IntArray** class in
    IostreamOperatorOverloading.cpp from Chapter
    12, templatizing both the type of object that is contained
    and the size of the internal array.

19. Turn **ObjContainer** in **NestedSmartPointer.cpp**
    from Chapter 12 into a template. Test it with two different
    classes.

20. Modify **C15:OStack.h** and **C15:OStackTest.cpp** by
    templatizing **class Stack** so that it automatically
    multiply inherits from the contained class and from
    Object. The generated **Stack** should accept and produce
    only pointers of the contained type.

21. Repeat Exercise 20 using **vector** instead of **Stack**.

22. Inherit a class **StringVector** from **vector<void*>** and
    redefine the **push_back( )** and **operator[]** member
    functions to accept and produce only **string*** (and
    perform the proper casting). Now create a template that
    will automatically make a container class to do the same
    thing for pointers to any type. This technique is often
    used to reduce code bloat from too many template
    instantiations.

23. In **TPStash2.h**, add and test an **operator-** to
    PStash::iterator, following the logic of **operator+**.

24. In **Drawing.cpp**, add and test a function template to call
    erase( ) member functions.

25. (Advanced) Modify the **Stack** class in **TStack2.h** to
    allow full granularity of ownership: Add a flag to each
    link indicating whether that link owns the object it points
    to, and support this information in the **push( )** function
    and destructor. Add member functions to read and
    change the ownership for each link.

26. (Advanced) Modify **PointerToMemberOperator.cpp**
    from Chapter 12 so that the **FunctionObject** and
    operator->* are templatized to work with any return
    type (for **operator->***, you'll have to use *member
    templates*, described in Volume 2). Add and test support
    for zero, one and two arguments in **Dog** member
    functions.

A: Coding Style

This appendix is not about indenting and placement of parentheses and curly braces, although that will be mentioned. It is about the general guidelines used in this book for organizing the code listings.

Although many of these issues have been introduced throughout the book, this appendix appears at the end so it can be assumed that every topic is fair game, and if you don't understand something you can look it up in the appropriate section.

All the decisions about coding style in this book have been deliberately considered and made, sometimes over a period of years. Of course, everyone has their reasons for organizing code the way they do, and I'm just trying to tell you how I arrived at mine and the constraints and environmental factors that brought me to those decisions.

General

In the text of this book, identifiers (function, variable, and class names) are set in **bold**. Most keywords will also be set in bold, except for those keywords that are used so much that the bolding can become tedious, such as "class" and "virtual."

I use a particular coding style for the examples in this book. It was developed over a number of years, and was partially inspired by Bjarne Stroustrup's style in his original *The C++ Programming Language*.[1] The subject of formatting style is good for hours of hot debate, so I'll just say I'm not trying to dictate correct style via my examples; I have my own motivation for using the style that I do. Because C++ is a free-form programming language, you can continue to use whatever style you're comfortable with.

That said, I will note that it is important to have a consistent formatting style within a project. If you search the Internet, you will find a number of tools that can be used to reformat all the code in your project to achieve this valuable consistency.

The programs in this book are files that are automatically extracted from the text of the book, which allows them to be tested to ensure that they work correctly. Thus, the code files printed in the book

---

[1] Ibid.

should all work without compile-time errors when compiled with an implementation that conforms to Standard C++ (note that not all compilers support all language features). The errors that *should* cause compile-time error messages are commented out with the comment **//!** so they can be easily discovered and tested using automatic means. Errors discovered and reported to the author will appear first in the electronic version of the book (at *www.BruceEckel.com*) and later in updates of the book.

One of the standards in this book is that all programs will compile and link without errors (although they will sometimes cause warnings). To this end, some of the programs, which demonstrate only a coding example and don't represent stand-alone programs, will have empty **main( )** functions, like this

```
int main() {}
```

This allows the linker to complete without an error.

The standard for **main( )** is to return an **int**, but Standard C++ states that if there is no **return** statement inside **main( )**, the compiler will automatically generate code to **return 0**. This option (no **return** statement in **main( )**) will be used in this book (some compilers may still generate warnings for this, but those are not compliant with Standard C++).

File names

In C, it has been traditional to name header files (containing declarations) with an extension of **.h** and implementation files (that cause storage to be allocated and code to be generated) with an extension of **.c**. C++ went through an evolution. It was first developed on Unix, where the operating system was aware of upper and lower case in file names. The original file names were simply capitalized versions of the C extensions: **.H** and **.C**. This of course didn't work for operating systems that didn't distinguish upper and lower case, such as DOS. DOS C++ vendors used extensions of **hxx** and **cxx** for header files and implementation files, respectively, or **hpp** and **cpp**. Later, someone figured out that the only reason you needed a different extension for a file was so the compiler could determine whether to compile it as a C or C++ file. Because the compiler never compiled header files directly, only the implementation file extension needed to be changed. The custom, across virtually all systems, has now become to use **cpp** for implementation files and **h** for header files. Note that when including Standard C++ header files, the option of having no file name extension is used, i.e.: **#include <iostream>**.

Begin and end comment tags

A very important issue with this book is that all code that you see in the book must be verified to be correct (with at least one compiler). This is accomplished by automatically extracting the files from the book. To facilitate this, all code listings that are meant to be compiled (as opposed to code fragments, of which there are few) have comment tags at the beginning and end. These tags are used by the code-extraction tool **ExtractCode.cpp** in Volume 2 of this book (which you can find on the Web site *www.BruceEckel.com*) to pull each code listing out of the plain-ASCII text version of this book.

The end-listing tag simply tells **ExtractCode.cpp** that it's the end of the listing, but the begin-listing tag is followed by information about what subdirectory the file belongs in (generally organized by chapters, so a file that belongs in Chapter 8 would have a tag of **C08**), followed by a colon and the name of the listing file.

Because **ExtractCode.cpp** also creates a **makefile** for each subdirectory, information about how a program is made and the command-line used to test it is also incorporated into the listings. If a program is stand-alone (it doesn't need to be linked with anything else) it has no extra information. This is also true for header files. However, if it doesn't contain a **main( )** and is meant to be linked with something else, then it has an **{O}** after the file name. If this listing is meant to be the main program but needs to be linked with other components, there's a separate line that begins with **//{L}** and continues with all the files that need to be linked (without extensions, since those can vary from platform to platform).

You can find examples throughout the book.

If a file should be extracted but the begin- and end-tags should not be included in the extracted file (for example, if it's a file of test data) then the begin-tag is immediately followed by a '!'.

Parentheses, braces, and indentation

You may notice the formatting style in this book is different from many traditional C styles. Of course, everyone thinks their own style is the most rational. However, the style used here has a simple logic behind it, which will be presented here mixed in with ideas on why some of the other styles developed.

The formatting style is motivated by one thing: presentation, both in print and in live seminars. You may feel your needs are different because you don't make a lot of presentations. However, working code is read much more than it is written, and so it should be easy for the reader to perceive. My two most important criteria are "scannability" (how easy it is for the reader to grasp the meaning of a single line) and the number of lines that can fit on a page. This latter may sound funny, but when you are giving a live presentation, it's very distracting for the audience if the presenter must shuffle back and forth between slides, and a few wasted lines can cause this.

Everyone seems to agree that code inside braces should be indented. What people don't agree on – and the place where there's the most inconsistency within formatting styles – is this: Where does the opening brace go? This one question, I think, is what causes such variations among coding styles (For an enumeration of coding styles, see C++ Programming Guidelines, by Tom Plum and Dan Saks, Plum Hall 1991.) I'll try to convince you that many of today's coding styles come from pre-Standard C constraints (before function prototypes) and are thus inappropriate now.

First, my answer to that key question: the opening brace should always go on the same line as the "precursor" (by which I mean "whatever the body is about: a class, function, object definition, if statement, etc."). This is a single, consistent rule I apply to all of the code I write, and it makes formatting much simpler. It makes the "scannability" easier – when you look at this line:

```
int func(int a);
```

you know, by the semicolon at the end of the line, that this is a declaration and it goes no further, but when you see the line:

```
int func(int a) {
```

you immediately know it's a definition because the line finishes with an opening brace, not a semicolon. By using this approach, there's no difference in where you place the opening parenthesis for a multi-line definition:

```
int func(int a) {
  int b = a + 1;
  return b * 2;
}
```

and for a single-line definition that is often used for inlines:

```
int func(int a) { return (a + 1) * 2; }
```

Similarly, for a class:

```
class Thing;
```

is a class name declaration, and

```
class Thing {
```

is a class definition. You can tell by looking at the single line in all cases whether it's a declaration or definition. And of course, putting the opening brace on the same line, instead of a line by itself, allows you to fit more lines on a page.

So why do we have so many other styles? In particular, you'll notice that most people create classes following the style above (which Stroustrup uses in all editions of his book *The C++ Programming Language* from Addison-Wesley) but create function definitions by putting the opening brace on a single line by itself (which also engenders many different indentation styles). Stroustrup does this except for short inline functions. With the approach I describe here, everything is consistent – you name whatever it is (**class**, function, **enum**, etc.) and on that same line you put the opening brace to indicate that the body for this thing is about to follow. Also, the opening brace is the same for short inlines and ordinary function definitions.

I assert that the style of function definition used by many folks comes from pre-function-prototyping C, in which you didn't declare the arguments inside the parentheses, but instead between the closing parenthesis and the opening curly brace (this shows C's assembly-language roots):

```
void bar()
  int x;
  float y;
{
  /* body here */
}
```

Here, it would be quite ungainly to put the opening brace on the same line, so no one did it. However, they did make various decisions about whether the braces should be indented with the body of the code or whether they should be at the level of the "precursor." Thus, we got many different formatting styles.

There are other arguments for placing the brace on the line immediately following the declaration (of a class, struct, function, etc.). The following came from a reader, and is presented here so you know what the issues are:

> Experienced 'vi' (vim) users know that typing the ']' key twice will take the user to the next occurrence of '{' (or ^L) in column 0. This feature is extremely useful in navigating code (jumping to the next function or class definition). [My comment: when I was initially working under Unix, GNU Emacs was just appearing and I became enmeshed in that. As a result, 'vi' has never made sense to me, and thus I do not think in terms of "column 0 locations." However, there is a fair contingent of 'vi' users out there, and they are affected by this issue.]

Placing the '{' on the next line eliminates some confusing code in complex conditionals, aiding in the scannability. Example:

```
if(cond1
    && cond2
    && cond3) {
    statement;
}
```

The above [asserts the reader] has poor scannability. However,

```
if (cond1
&& cond2
&& cond3)
{
statement;
}
```

breaks up the 'if' from the body, resulting in better readability. [Your opinions on whether this is true will vary depending on what you're used to.]

Finally, it's much easier to visually align braces when they are aligned in the same column. They visually "stick out" much better. [End of reader comment]

The issue of where to put the opening curly brace is probably the most discordant issue. I've learned to scan both forms, and in the end it comes down to what you've grown comfortable with. However, I note that the official Java coding standard (found on Sun's Java Web site) is effectively the same as the one I present here – since more folks are beginning to program in both languages, the consistency between coding styles may be helpful.

The approach I use removes all the exceptions and special cases, and logically produces a single style of indentation as well. Even within a function body, the consistency holds, as in:

```
for(int i = 0; i < 100; i++) {
  cout << i << endl;
  cout << x * i << endl;
}
```

The style is easy to teach and to remember – you use a single, consistent rule for all your formatting, not one for classes, two for functions (one-line inlines vs. multi-line), and possibly others for **for** loops, **if** statements, etc. The consistency alone, I think, makes it worthy of consideration. Above all, C++ is a newer language than C, and although we must make many concessions to C, we shouldn't be carrying too many artifacts with us that cause problems in the future. Small problems multiplied by many lines of code become big problems. For a thorough examination of the subject, albeit in C, see *C Style: Standards and Guidelines*, by David Straker (Prentice-Hall 1992).

The other constraint I must work under is the line width, since the book has a limitation of 50 characters. What happens when something is too long to fit on one line? Well, again I strive to have a consistent policy for the way lines are broken up, so they can be easily viewed. As long as something is part of a single definition, argument list, etc., continuation lines should be indented one level in from the beginning of that definition, argument list, etc.

Identifier names

Those familiar with Java will notice that I have switched to using the standard Java style for all identifier names. However, I cannot be completely consistent here because identifiers in the Standard C and C++ libraries do not follow this style.

The style is quite straightforward. The first letter of an identifier is only capitalized if that identifier is a class. If it is a function or variable, then the first letter is lowercase. The rest of the identifier consists of one or more words, run together but distinguished by capitalizing each word. So a class looks like this:

```
class FrenchVanilla : public IceCream {
```

an object identifier looks like this:

```
FrenchVanilla myIceCreamCone(3);
```

and a function looks like this:

```
void eatIceCreamCone();
```

(for either a member function or a regular function).

The one exception is for compile-time constants (**const** or **#define**), in which all of the letters in the identifier are uppercase.

The value of the style is that capitalization has meaning – you can see from the first letter whether you're talking about a class or an object/method. This is especially useful when **static** class members are accessed.

Order of header inclusion

Headers are included in order from "the most specific to the most general." That is, any header files in the local directory are included first, then any of my own "tool" headers, such as **require.h**, then any third-party library headers, then the Standard C++ Library headers, and finally the C library headers.

The justification for this comes from John Lakos in *Large-Scale C++ Software Design* (Addison-Wesley, 1996):

> *Latent usage errors can be avoided by ensuring that the .h file of a component parses by itself – without externally-provided declarations or definitions... Including the .h file as the very first line of the .c file ensures that no critical piece of information intrinsic to the physical interface of the component is missing from the .h file (or, if there is, that you will find out about it as soon as you try to compile the .c file).*

If the order of header inclusion goes "from most specific to most general," then it's more likely that if your header doesn't parse by itself, you'll find out about it sooner and prevent annoyances down the road.

Include guards on header files

Include guards are always used inside header files to prevent multiple inclusion of a header file during the compilation of a single **.cpp** file. The include guards are implemented using a preprocessor **#define** and checking to see that a name hasn't already been defined. The name used for the guard is based on the name of the header file, with all letters of the file name uppercase and replacing the '.' with an underscore. For example:

```
// IncludeGuard.h
#ifndef INCLUDEGUARD_H
#define INCLUDEGUARD_H
// Body of header file here...
#endif // INCLUDEGUARD_H
```

The identifier on the last line is included for clarity. Although some preprocessors ignored any characters after an **#endif**, that isn't standard behavior and so the identifier is commented.

Use of namespaces

In header files, any "pollution" of the namespace in which the header is included must be scrupulously avoided. That is, if you change the namespace outside of a function or class, you will cause that change to occur for any file that includes your header, resulting in all kinds of problems. No **using** declarations of any kind are allowed outside of function definitions, and no global **using** directives are allowed in header files.

In **cpp** files, any global **using** directives will only affect that file, and so in this book they are generally used to produce more easily-readable code, especially in small programs.

Use of require( ) and assure( )

The **require( )** and **assure( )** functions defined in **require.h** are used consistently throughout most of the book, so that they may properly report problems. If you are familiar with the concepts of

---

preconditions and *postconditions* (introduced by Bertrand Meyer) you will recognize that the use of **require( )** and **assure( )** more or less provide preconditions (usually) and postconditions (occasionally). Thus, at the beginning of a function, before any of the "core" of the function is executed, the preconditions are checked to make sure everything is proper and that all of the necessary conditions are correct. Then the "core" of the function is executed, and sometimes some postconditions are checked to make sure that the new state of the data is within defined parameters. You'll notice that the postcondition checks are rare in this book, and **assure( )** is primarily used to make sure that files were opened successfully.

B: Programming Guidelines

This appendix is a collection of suggestions for C++ programming. They've been assembled over the course of my teaching and programming experience and also from the insights of friends including Dan Saks (co-author with Tom Plum of *C++ Programming Guidelines*, Plum Hall, 1991), Scott Meyers (author of *Effective C++*, 2nd edition, Addison-Wesley, 1998), and Rob Murray (author of *C++ Strategies & Tactics*, Addison-Wesley, 1993). Also, many of the tips are summarized from the pages of *Thinking in C++*.

1. First make it work, then make it fast. This is true even if you are certain that a piece of code is really important and that it will be a principal bottleneck in your system. Don't do it. Get the system going first with as simple a design as possible. Then if it isn't going fast enough, profile it. You'll almost always discover that "your" bottleneck isn't the problem. Save your time for the really important stuff.

2. Elegance always pays off. It's not a frivolous pursuit. Not only does it give you a program that's easier to build and debug, but it's also easier to understand and maintain, and that's where the financial value lies. This point can take some experience to believe, because it can seem that while you're making a piece of code elegant, you're not being productive. The productivity comes when the code seamlessly integrates into your system, and even more so when the code or system is modified.

3. Remember the "divide and conquer" principle. If the problem you're looking at is too confusing, try to imagine what the basic operation of the program would be, given the existence of a magic "piece" that handles the hard parts. That "piece" is an object – write the code that uses the object, then look at the object and encapsulate *its* hard parts into other objects, etc.

4. Don't automatically rewrite all your existing C code in C++ unless you need to significantly change its functionality (that is, don't fix it if it isn't broken). *Recompiling* C in C++ is a valuable activity because it may reveal hidden bugs. However, taking C code that works fine and rewriting it in C++ may not be the best use of your time, unless the C++ version will provide a lot of opportunities for reuse as a class.

5. If you do have a large body of C code that needs changing, first isolate the parts of the code that will not be modified, possibly wrapping those functions in an "API class" as static member functions. Then focus on the code that will be changed, refactoring it into classes to facilitate easy modifications as your maintenance proceeds.

6. Separate the class creator from the class user (*client programmer*). The class user is the "customer" and doesn't need or want to know what's going on behind the scenes of the class. The class creator must be the expert in class design and write the class so that it can be used by the most novice programmer possible, yet still work robustly in the application. Library use will be easy only if it's transparent.

7. When you create a class, make your names as clear as possible. Your goal should be to make the client programmer's interface conceptually simple. Attempt to make your names so clear that comments are unnecessary. To this end, use function overloading and default arguments to create an intuitive, easy-to-use interface.

8. Access control allows you (the class creator) to change as much as possible in the future without damaging client code in which the class is used. In this light, keep everything as **private** as possible, and make only the class interface **public**, always using functions rather than data. Make data **public** only when forced. If class users don't need to access a function, make it **private**. If a part of your class must be exposed to inheritors as **protected**, provide a function interface rather than expose the actual data. In this way, implementation changes will have minimal impact on derived classes.

9. Don't fall into analysis paralysis. There are some things that you don't learn until you start coding and get some kind of system working. C++ has built-in firewalls; let them work for you. Your mistakes in a class or set of classes won't destroy the integrity of the whole system.

10. Your analysis and design must produce, at minimum, the classes in your system, their public interfaces, and their relationships to other classes, especially base classes. If your design methodology produces more than that, ask yourself if all the pieces produced by that methodology have value over the lifetime of the program. If they do not, maintaining them will cost you. Members of development teams tend not to maintain anything that does not contribute to their productivity; this is a fact of life that many design methods don't account for.

11. Write the test code first (before you write the class), and keep it with the class. Automate the running of your tests through a makefile or similar tool. This way, any changes can be automatically verified by running the test code, and you'll immediately discover errors. Because you know that you have the safety net of your test framework, you will be bolder about making sweeping changes when you discover the need. Remember that the greatest improvements in languages come from the built-in testing that type checking, exception handling, etc., provide, but those features take you only so far. You must go the rest of the way in creating a robust system by filling in the tests that verify features that are specific to your class or program.

12. Write the test code first (before you write the class) in order to verify that your class design is complete. If you can't write test code, you don't know what your class looks like. In addition, the act of writing the test code will often flush out additional features or constraints that you need in the class – these features or constraints don't always appear during analysis and design.

13. Remember a fundamental rule of software engineering[1]: *All software design problems can be simplified by introducing an extra level of conceptual indirection*. This one idea is the

---

[1] Explained to me by Andrew Koenig.

basis of abstraction, the primary feature of object-oriented programming.

14.   Make classes as atomic as possible; that is, give each class a single, clear purpose. If your classes or your system design grows too complicated, break complex classes into simpler ones. The most obvious indicator of this is sheer size: if a class is big, chances are it's doing too much and should be broken up.

15.   Watch for long member function definitions. A function that is long and complicated is difficult and expensive to maintain, and is probably trying to do too much all by itself. If you see such a function, it indicates that, at the least, it should be broken up into multiple functions. It may also suggest the creation of a new class.

16.   Watch for long argument lists. Function calls then become difficult to write, read and maintain. Instead, try to move the member function to a class where it is (more) appropriate, and/or pass objects in as arguments.

17.   Don't repeat yourself. If a piece of code is recurring in many functions in derived classes, put that code into a single function in the base class and call it from the derived-class functions. Not only do you save code space, you provide for easy propagation of changes. You can use an inline function for efficiency. Sometimes the discovery of this common code will add valuable functionality to your interface.

18.   Watch for **switch** statements or chained **if-else** clauses. This is typically an indicator of *type-check coding*, which means you are choosing what code to execute based on some kind of type information (the exact type may not be obvious at first). You can usually replace this kind of code with inheritance and polymorphism; a polymorphic function call will perform the type checking for you, and allow for more reliable and easier extensibility.

19.   From a design standpoint, look for and separate things that change from things that stay the same. That is, search for the

elements in a system that you might want to change without forcing a redesign, then encapsulate those elements in classes. You can learn significantly more about this concept in the Design Patterns chapter in Volume 2 of this book, available at *www.BruceEckel.com.*

20. Watch out for *variance.* Two semantically different objects may have identical actions, or responsibilities, and there is a natural temptation to try to make one a subclass of the other just to benefit from inheritance. This is called variance, but there's no real justification to force a superclass/subclass relationship where it doesn't exist. A better solution is to create a general base class that produces an interface for both as derived classes – it requires a bit more space, but you still benefit from inheritance and will probably make an important discovery about the design.

21. Watch out for *limitation* during inheritance. The clearest designs add new capabilities to inherited ones. A suspicious design removes old capabilities during inheritance without adding new ones. But rules are made to be broken, and if you are working from an old class library, it may be more efficient to restrict an existing class in its subclass than it would be to restructure the hierarchy so your new class fits in where it should, above the old class.

22. Don't extend fundamental functionality by subclassing. If an interface element is essential to a class it should be in the base class, not added during derivation. If you're adding member functions by inheriting, perhaps you should rethink the design.

23. Less is more. Start with a minimal interface to a class, as small and simple as you need to solve the problem at hand, but don't try to anticipate all the ways that your class *might* be used. As the class is used, you'll discover ways you must expand the interface. However, once a class is in use you cannot shrink the interface without disturbing client code. If you need to add more functions, that's fine; it won't disturb code, other than forcing recompiles. But even if new member

functions replace the functionality of old ones, leave the existing interface alone (you can combine the functionality in the underlying implementation if you want). If you need to expand the interface of an existing function by adding more arguments, leave the existing arguments in their current order, and put default values on all of the new arguments; this way you won't disturb any existing calls to that function.

24. Read your classes aloud to make sure they're logical, referring to the relationship between a base class and derived class as "is-a" and member objects as "has-a."

25. When deciding between inheritance and composition, ask if you need to upcast to the base type. If not, prefer composition (member objects) to inheritance. This can eliminate the perceived need for multiple inheritance. If you inherit, users will think they are supposed to upcast.

26. Sometimes you need to inherit in order to access **protected** members of the base class. This can lead to a perceived need for multiple inheritance. If you don't need to upcast, first derive a new class to perform the protected access. Then make that new class a member object inside any class that needs to use it, rather than inheriting.

27. Typically, a base class will be used primarily to create an interface to classes derived from it. Thus, when you create a base class, default to making the member functions pure virtual. The destructor can also be pure virtual (to force inheritors to explicitly override it), but remember to give the destructor a function body, because all destructors in a hierarchy are always called.

28. When you put a **virtual** function in a class, make all functions in that class **virtual**, and put in a **virtual** destructor. This approach prevents surprises in the behavior of the interface. Only start removing the **virtual** keyword when you're tuning for efficiency and your profiler has pointed you in this direction.

29. Use data members for variation in value and **virtual** functions for variation in behavior. That is, if you find a class that uses state variables along with member functions that switch behavior based on those variables, you should probably redesign it to express the differences in behavior within subclasses and overridden **virtual** functions.

30. If you must do something nonportable, make an abstraction for that service and localize it within a class. This extra level of indirection prevents the non-portability from being distributed throughout your program.

31. Avoid multiple inheritance. It's for getting you out of bad situations, especially repairing class interfaces in which you don't have control of the broken class (see Volume 2). You should be an experienced programmer before designing multiple inheritance into your system.

32. Don't use **private** inheritance. Although it's in the language and seems to have occasional functionality, it introduces significant ambiguities when combined with run-time type identification. Create a private member object instead of using private inheritance.

33. If two classes are associated with each other in some functional way (such as containers and iterators), try to make one a **public** nested **friend** class of the other, as the Standard C++ Library does with iterators inside containers (examples of this are shown in the latter part of Chapter 16). This not only emphasizes the association between the classes, but it allows the class name to be reused by nesting it within another class. The Standard C++ Library does this by defining a nested **iterator** class inside each container class, thereby providing the containers with a common interface. The other reason you'll want to nest a class is as part of the **private** implementation. Here, nesting is beneficial for implementation hiding rather than the class association and prevention of namespace pollution noted above.

34. Operator overloading is only "syntactic sugar:" a different way to make a function call. If overloading an operator doesn't make the class interface clearer and easier to use, don't do it. Create only one automatic type conversion operator for a class. In general, follow the guidelines and format given in Chapter 12 when overloading operators.

35. Don't fall prey to premature optimization. That way lies madness. In particular, don't worry about writing (or avoiding) **inline** functions, making some functions non**virtual**, or tweaking code to be efficient when you are first constructing the system. Your primary goal should be to prove the design, unless the design requires a certain efficiency.

36. Normally, don't let the compiler create the constructors, destructors, or the **operator=** for you. Class designers should always say exactly what the class should do and keep the class entirely under control. If you don't want a copy-constructor or **operator=**, declare them as **private**. Remember that if you create any constructor, it prevents the default constructor from being synthesized.

37. If your class contains pointers, you must create the copy-constructor, **operator=**, and destructor for the class to work properly.

38. When you write a copy-constructor for a derived class, remember to call the base-class copy-constructor explicitly (also the member-object versions). (See Chapter 14.) If you don't, the default constructor will be called for the base class (or member object) and that probably isn't what you want. To call the base-class copy-constructor, pass it the derived object you're copying from:
    ```
    Derived(const Derived& d) : Base(d) { // ...
    ```

39. When you write an assignment operator for a derived class, remember to call the base-class version of the assignment operator explicitly. (See Chapter 14.) If you don't, then nothing will happen (the same is true for the member

objects). To call the base-class assignment operator, use the base-class name and scope resolution:

```
Derived& operator=(const Derived& d) {
  Base::operator=(d);
```

40. If you need to minimize recompiles during development of a large project, use the handle class/Cheshire cat technique demonstrated in Chapter 5, and remove it only if runtime efficiency is a problem.

41. Avoid the preprocessor. Always use **const** for value substitution and **inline**s for macros.

42. Keep scopes as small as possible so the visibility and lifetime of your objects are as small as possible. This reduces the chance of using an object in the wrong context and hiding a difficult-to-find bug. For example, suppose you have a container and a piece of code that iterates through it. If you copy that code to use with a new container, you may accidentally end up using the size of the old container as the upper bound of the new one. If, however, the old container is out of scope, the error will be caught at compile time.

43. Avoid global variables. Always strive to put data inside classes. Global functions are more likely to occur naturally than global variables, although you may later discover that a global function may fit better as a **static** member of a class.

44. If you need to declare a class or function from a library, always do so by including a header file. For example, if you want to create a function to write to an **ostream**, never declare **ostream** yourself using an incomplete type specification like this,

```
class ostream;
```

This approach leaves your code vulnerable to changes in representation. (For example, **ostream** could actually be a **typedef**.) Instead, always use the header file:

```
#include <iostream>
```

When creating your own classes, if a library is big, provide your users an abbreviated form of the header file with incomplete type specifications (that is, class name declarations) for cases in which they need to use only pointers. (It can speed compilations.)

45. When choosing the return type of an overloaded operator, consider what will happen if expressions are chained together. Return a copy or reference to the lvalue (**return *this**) so it can be used in a chained expression (**A = B = C**). When defining **operator=**, remember **x=x**.

46. When writing a function, pass arguments by **const** reference as your first choice. As long as you don't need to modify the object being passed, this practice is best because it has the simplicity of pass-by-value syntax but doesn't require expensive constructions and destructions to create a local object, which occurs when passing by value. Normally you don't want to be worrying too much about efficiency issues when designing and building your system, but this habit is a sure win.

47. Be aware of temporaries. When tuning for performance, watch out for temporary creation, especially with operator overloading. If your constructors and destructors are complicated, the cost of creating and destroying temporaries can be high. When returning a value from a function, always try to build the object "in place" with a constructor call in the return statement:
```
return MyType(i, j);
```
rather than
```
MyType x(i, j);
return x;
```
The former return statement (the so-called *return-value optimization*) eliminates a copy-constructor call and destructor call.

48. When creating constructors, consider exceptions. In the best case, the constructor won't do anything that throws an exception. In the next-best scenario, the class will be composed and inherited from robust classes only, so they will automatically clean themselves up if an exception is thrown. If you must have naked pointers, you are responsible for

---

catching your own exceptions and then deallocating any resources pointed to before you throw an exception in your constructor. If a constructor must fail, the appropriate action is to throw an exception.

49. Do only what is minimally necessary in your constructors. Not only does this produce a lower overhead for constructor calls (many of which may not be under your control) but your constructors are then less likely to throw exceptions or cause problems.

50. The responsibility of the destructor is to release resources allocated during the lifetime of the object, not just during construction.

51. Use exception hierarchies, preferably derived from the Standard C++ exception hierarchy and nested as public classes within the class that throws the exceptions. The person catching the exceptions can then catch the specific types of exceptions, followed by the base type. If you add new derived exceptions, existing client code will still catch the exception through the base type.

52. Throw exceptions by value and catch exceptions by reference. Let the exception-handling mechanism handle memory management. If you throw pointers to exception objects that have been created on the heap, the catcher must know to destroy the exception, which is bad coupling. If you catch exceptions by value, you cause extra constructions and destructions; worse, the derived portions of your exception objects may be sliced during upcasting by value.

53. Don't write your own class templates unless you must. Look first in the Standard C++ Library, then to vendors who create special-purpose tools. Become proficient with their use and you'll greatly increase your productivity.

54. When creating templates, watch for code that does not depend on type and put that code in a non-template base class to prevent needless code bloat. Using inheritance or composition, you can create templates in which the bulk of

the code they contain is type-dependent and therefore essential.

55. Don't use the **<cstdio>** functions, such as **printf( )**. Learn to use iostreams instead; they are type-safe and type-extensible, and significantly more powerful. Your investment will be rewarded regularly. In general, always use C++ libraries in preference to C libraries.

56. Avoid C's built-in types. They are supported in C++ for backward compatibility, but they are much less robust than C++ classes, so your bug-hunting time will increase.

57. Whenever you use built-in types as globals or automatics, don't define them until you can also initialize them. Define variables one per line along with their initialization. When defining pointers, put the '*' next to the type name. You can safely do this if you define one variable per line. This style tends to be less confusing for the reader.

58. Guarantee that initialization occurs in all aspects of your code. Perform all member initialization in the constructor initializer list, even built-in types (using pseudo-constructor calls). Using the constructor initializer list is often more efficient when initializing subobjects; otherwise the default constructor is called, and you end up calling other member functions (probably **operator**=) on top of that in order to get the initialization you want.

59. Don't use the form **MyType a = b;** to define an object. This one feature is a major source of confusion because it calls a constructor instead of the **operator=**. For clarity, always be specific and use the form **MyType a(b);** instead. The results are identical, but other programmers won't be confused.

60. Use the explicit casts described in Chapter 3. A cast overrides the normal typing system and is a potential error spot. Since the explicit casts divide C's one-cast-does-all into classes of well-marked casts, anyone debugging and maintaining the code can easily find all the places where logical errors are most likely to happen.

61. For a program to be robust, each component must be robust. Use all the tools provided by C++: access control, exceptions, const-correctness, type checking, and so on in each class you create. That way you can safely move to the next level of abstraction when building your system.

62. Build in **const**-correctness. This allows the compiler to point out bugs that would otherwise be subtle and difficult to find. This practice takes a little discipline and must be used consistently throughout your classes, but it pays off.

63. Use compiler error checking to your advantage. Perform all compiles with full warnings, and fix your code to remove all warnings. Write code that utilizes the compile-time errors and warnings rather than that which causes runtime errors (for example, don't use variadic argument lists, which disable all type checking). Use **assert( )** for debugging, but use exceptions for runtime errors.

64. Prefer compile-time errors to runtime errors. Try to handle an error as close to the point of its occurrence as possible. Prefer dealing with the error at that point to throwing an exception. Catch any exceptions in the nearest handler that has enough information to deal with them. Do what you can with the exception at the current level; if that doesn't solve the problem, rethrow the exception. (See Volume 2 for more details.)

65. If you're using exception specifications (see Volume 2 of this book, downloadable from *www.BruceEckel.com*, to learn about exception handling), install your own **unexpected( )** function using **set_unexpected( )**. Your **unexpected( )** should log the error and rethrow the current exception. That way, if an existing function gets overridden and starts throwing exceptions, you will have a record of the culprit and can modify your calling code to handle the exception.

66. Create a user-defined **terminate( )** (indicating a programmer error) to log the error that caused the exception, then release system resources, and exit the program.

67. If a destructor calls any functions, those functions might throw exceptions. A destructor cannot throw an exception (this can result in a call to **terminate( )**, which indicates a programming error), so any destructor that calls functions must catch and manage its own exceptions.

68. Don't create your own "decorated" private data member names (prepending underscores, Hungarian notation, etc.), unless you have a lot of pre-existing global values; otherwise, let classes and namespaces do the name scoping for you.

69. Watch for overloading. A function should not conditionally execute code based on the value of an argument, default or not. In this case, you should create two or more overloaded functions instead.

70. Hide your pointers inside container classes. Bring them out only when you are going to immediately perform operations on them. Pointers have always been a major source of bugs. When you use **new**, try to drop the resulting pointer into a container. Prefer that a container "own" its pointers so it's responsible for cleanup. Even better, wrap a pointer inside a class; if you still want it to look like a pointer, overload **operator->** and **operator***. If you must have a free-standing pointer, always initialize it, preferably to an object address, but to zero if necessary. Set it to zero when you delete it to prevent accidental multiple deletions.

71. Don't overload global **new** and **delete**; always do this on a class-by-class basis. Overloading the global versions affects the entire client programmer project, something only the creators of a project should control. When overloading **new** and **delete** for classes, don't assume that you know the size of the object; someone may be inheriting from you. Use the provided argument. If you do anything special, consider the effect it could have on inheritors.

72. Prevent object slicing. It virtually never makes sense to upcast an object by value. To prevent upcasting by value, put pure virtual functions in your base class.

73. Sometimes simple aggregation does the job. A "passenger comfort system" on an airline consists of disconnected elements: seat, air conditioning, video, etc., and yet you need to create many of these in a plane. Do you make private members and build a whole new interface? No – in this case, the components are also part of the public interface, so you should create public member objects. Those objects have their own private implementations, which are still safe. Be aware that simple aggregation is not a solution to be used often, but it does happen.

C: Recommended Reading

Resources for further study.

C

Thinking in C: Foundations for Java & C++, by Chuck Allison (a MindView, Inc. Seminar-on-CD ROM, ©2000, bound into the back of this book and also available at *www.BruceEckel.com*). This is a course including lectures and slides in the foundations of the C Language to prepare you to learn Java or C++. This is not an exhaustive course in C; only the necessities for moving on to the other languages are included. Additional language-specific sections introduce features for the C++ or Java programmer-to-be. Recommended prerequisite: some experience with a high-level programming language, such as Pascal, BASIC, Fortran, or LISP (it's possible to struggle through the CD without this background, but the course isn't designed to be an introduction to the basics of programming).

General C++

The C++ Programming Language, 3rd edition, by Bjarne Stroustrup (Addison-Wesley 1997). To some degree, the goal of the book that you're currently holding is to allow you to use Bjarne's book as a reference. Since his book contains the description of the language by the author of that language, it's typically the place where you'll go to resolve any uncertainties about what C++ is or isn't supposed to do. When you get the knack of the language and are ready to get serious, you'll need it.

C++ Primer, 3rd Edition, by Stanley Lippman and Josee Lajoie (Addison-Wesley 1998). Not that much of a primer anymore; it's evolved into a thick book filled with lots of detail, and the one that I reach for along with Stroustrup's when trying to resolve an issue. *Thinking in C++* should provide a basis for understanding the *C++ Primer* as well as Stroustrup's book.

C & C++ Code Capsules, by Chuck Allison (Prentice-Hall, 1998). This book assumes that you already know C and C++, and covers some of the issues that you may be rusty on, or that you may not have gotten right the first time. This book fills in C gaps as well as C++ gaps.

The C++ Standard. This is the document that the committee worked so hard on for all those years. This is *not* free, unfortunately. But at least you can buy the electronic form in PDF for only $18 at *www.cssinfo.com*.

My own list of books

Listed in order of publication. Not all of these are currently available.

Computer Interfacing with Pascal & C (Self-published via the Eisys imprint, 1988. Only available via *www.BruceEckel.com*). An introduction to electronics from back when CP/M was still king and DOS was an upstart. I used high-level languages and often the parallel port of the computer to drive various electronic projects. Adapted from my columns in the first and best magazine I wrote for, *Micro Cornucopia* (To paraphrase Larry O'Brien, long-time editor of *Software Development Magazine*: the best computer magazine ever published – they even had plans for building a robot in a flower pot!) Alas, Micro C became lost long before the Internet appeared. Creating this book was an extremely satisfying publishing experience.

Using C++ (Osborne/McGraw-Hill 1989). One of the first books out on C++. This is out of print and replaced by its second edition, the renamed **C++ Inside & Out**.

C++ Inside & Out (Osborne/McGraw-Hill 1993). As noted, actually the 2nd edition of **Using C++**. The C++ in this book is reasonably accurate, but it's circa 1992 and *Thinking in C++* is intended to replace it. You can find out more about this book and download the source code at *www.BruceEckel.com*.

Thinking in C++, 1st edition (Prentice-Hall 1995).

Black Belt C++, the Master's Collection, Bruce Eckel, editor (M&T Books 1994). Out of print. A collection of chapters by various

C++ luminaries based on their presentations in the C++ track at the Software Development Conference, which I chaired. The cover on this book stimulated me to gain control over all future cover designs.

Thinking in Java, 2nd edition (Prentice-Hall, 2000). The first edition of this book won the *Software Development Magazine* Productivity Award and the *Java Developer's Journal* Editor's Choice Award in 1999. Downloadable from *www.BruceEckel.com*.

Depth & dark corners

These books go more deeply into language topics, and help you avoid the typical pitfalls inherent in developing C++ programs.

Effective C++ (2nd Edition, Addison-Wesley 1998) and **More Effective C++** (Addison-Wesley 1996), by Scott Meyers. The classic, must-have texts for serious problem-solving and code design in C++. I've tried to capture and express many of the concepts from these books in *Thinking in C++*, but I don't fool myself in thinking that I've succeeded. If you spend any serious time with C++ you'll end up with these books. Also available on CD ROM.

Ruminations on C++, by Andrew Koenig and Barbara Moo (Addison-Wesley, 1996). Andrew worked directly with Stroustrup on many aspects of the C++ language and is an extremely reliable authority. I've also found the incisiveness of his insights to be refreshing, and have learned much from him, both in print and in person, over the years.

Large-Scale C++ Software Design, by John Lakos (Addison-Wesley, 1996). Covers issues and answers questions you will encounter during the creation of big projects, but often smaller ones as well.

C++ Gems, Stan Lippman, editor (SIGS publications, 1996). A selection of articles from *The C++ Report*.

The Design & Evolution of C++, by Bjarne Stroustrup (Addison-Wesley 1994). Insights from the inventor of C++ about why he made various design decisions. Not essential, but interesting.

Analysis & design

Extreme Programming Explained by Kent Beck (Addison-Wesley 2000). I *love* this book. Yes, I tend to take a radical approach to things but I've always felt that there could be a much different, much better program development process, and I think XP comes pretty darn close. The only book that has had a similar impact on me was *PeopleWare* (described below), which talks primarily about the environment and dealing with corporate culture. *Extreme Programming Explained* talks about programming, and turns most things, even recent "findings," on their ear. They even go so far as to say that pictures are OK as long as you don't spend too much time on them and are willing to throw them away. (You'll notice that this book does *not* have the "UML stamp of approval" on its cover.) I could see deciding whether to work for a company based solely on whether they used XP. Small book, small chapters, effortless to read, exciting to think about. You start imagining yourself working in such an atmosphere and it brings visions of a whole new world.

UML Distilled by Martin Fowler (2nd edition, Addison-Wesley, 2000). When you first encounter UML, it is daunting because there are so many diagrams and details. According to Fowler, most of this stuff is unnecessary so he cuts through to the essentials. For most projects, you only need to know a few diagramming tools, and Fowler's goal is to come up with a good design rather than worry about all the artifacts of getting there. A nice, thin, readable book; the first one you should get if you need to understand UML.

The Unified Software Development Process by Ivar Jacobsen, Grady Booch, and James Rumbaugh (Addison-Wesley 1999). I went in fully prepared to dislike this book. It seemed to have all the makings of a boring college text. I was pleasantly surprised – only pockets of the book contain explanations that seem as if those concepts aren't clear to the authors. The bulk of the book is not only clear, but enjoyable. And best of all, the process makes a lot of practical sense. It's not Extreme Programming (and does not have their clarity about testing) but it's also part of the UML juggernaut – even if you can't get XP adopted, most people have climbed aboard the "UML is good" bandwagon (regardless of their *actual* level of experience with it) and so you can probably get it adopted. I think this book should be the flagship of UML, and the one you can read after Fowler's *UML Distilled* when you want more detail.

Before you choose any method, it's helpful to gain perspective from those who are not trying to sell one. It's easy to adopt a method without really understanding what you want out of it or what it will do for you. Others are using it, which seems a compelling reason. However, humans have a strange little psychological quirk: If they want to believe something will solve their problems, they'll try it. (This is experimentation, which is good.) But if it doesn't solve their problems, they may redouble their efforts and begin to announce loudly what a great thing they've discovered. (This is denial, which is not good.) The assumption here may be that if you can get other people in the same boat, you won't be lonely, even if it's going nowhere (or sinking).

This is not to suggest that all methodologies go nowhere, but that you should be armed to the teeth with mental tools that help you stay in experimentation mode ("It's not working; let's try something else") and out of denial mode ("No, that's not really a problem. Everything's wonderful, we don't need to change"). I think the following books, read *before* you choose a method, will provide you with these tools.

Software Creativity, by Robert Glass (Prentice-Hall, 1995). This is the best book I've seen that discusses *perspective* on the whole methodology issue. It's a collection of short essays and papers that Glass has written and sometimes acquired (P.J. Plauger is one contributor), reflecting his many years of thinking and study on the subject. They're entertaining and only long enough to say what's necessary; he doesn't ramble and bore you. He's not just blowing smoke, either; there are hundreds of references to other papers and studies. All programmers and managers should read this book before wading into the methodology mire.

Software Runaways: Monumental Software Disasters, by Robert Glass (Prentice-Hall 1997). The great thing about this book is that it brings to the forefront what we don't talk about: how many projects not only fail, but fail spectacularly. I find that most of us still think "That can't happen to me" (or "That can't happen *again*") and I think this puts us at a disadvantage. By keeping in mind that things can always go wrong, you're in a much better position to make them go right.

Object Lessons by Tom Love (SIGS Books, 1993). Another good "perspective" book.

Peopleware, by Tom Demarco and Timothy Lister (Dorset House, 2nd edition 1999). Although they have backgrounds in software development, this book is about projects and teams in general. But the focus is on the *people* and their needs rather than the technology and its needs. They talk about creating an environment where people will be happy and productive, rather than deciding what rules those people should follow to be adequate components of a machine. This latter attitude, I think, is the biggest contributor to programmers smiling and nodding when XYZ method is adopted and then quietly doing whatever they've always done.

Complexity, by M. Mitchell Waldrop (Simon & Schuster, 1992). This chronicles the coming together of a group of scientists from different disciplines in Santa Fe, New Mexico, to discuss real problems that the individual disciplines couldn't solve (the stock market in economics, the initial formation of life in biology, why people do what they do in sociology, etc.). By crossing physics, economics, chemistry, math, computer science, sociology, and others, a multidisciplinary approach to these problems is developing. But more importantly, a different way of *thinking* about these ultra-complex problems is emerging: Away from mathematical determinism and the illusion that you can write an equation that predicts all behavior and toward first *observing* and looking for a pattern and trying to emulate that pattern by any means possible. (The book chronicles, for example, the emergence of genetic algorithms.) This kind of thinking, I believe, is useful as we observe ways to manage more and more complex software projects.

Index

B

C

D

declaration syntax · 83; point of declaration & scope · 145; virtual · 632; base-class declarations · 632; derived-class declarations · 632

decoration, name · 230, 231, 237, 442; overloading · 311

decoupling · 628; via polymorphism · 39

decrement · 128, 164; and increment operators · 506; overloading operator · 493

default: argument · 310, 311, 321; as a flag · 329; vs. overloading · 324; constructor · 304, 327, 408, 470, 563; inheritance · 663; copy-constructor · 468; default values in templates · 703; keyword · 124

defining: function pointer · 198; initializing at the same time · 290; initializing variables · 130; variable · 145; anywhere in the scope · 145

definition · 81; array · 338; block · 289; class · 277; complex function definitions · 198; const · 340; declaration · 243; duplicate class definitions and templates · 699; formatting pointer definitions · 342; function · 83; non-inline template member function definitions · 699; object · 285; pure virtual function definitions · 651; storage for static data members · 424; structure definition in a header file · 234

delete · 164, 223, 553; calling delete for zero · 327; delete-expression · 553, 566; keyword · 42; multiple deletions of the same object · 553; new; and containers · 692; for arrays · 563; overloading new and delete · 566; array · 573; class · 570; global · 568; void*, deleting is a bug · 555; zero pointer · 553

Demarco, Tom · 781

dependency: makefile · 204; static initialization · 432

deprecation, of ++ with a bool flag · 131

dereference: * · 164; dereferencing function pointers · 200; pointer · 137

derived: adding new virtual functions in the derived class · 652; types · 32; virtual keyword in derived-class declarations · 632

design: analysis and design, object-oriented · 44; book; cover · 17; design and production · 18; consulting, mentoring, and design and code walkthroughs from MindView · 16; five stages of object design · 54; inlines · 380; mistakes · 279; pattern, iterator · 719; patterns · 59, 70

destructor · 287; automatic destructor calls · 297; with inheritance and composition · 592; doesn't automatically inherit · 600; explicit destructor call · 579; initialization and cleanup on the heap · 548; inlines · 392; order of constructor and destructor calls · 592; pure virtual destructor · 668; scope · 288; static objects · 410; tracking creations and destructions · 709; virtual destructor · 665, 707, 736, 740; virtual function calls in destructors · 670

development, incremental · 614

diagram: class inheritance diagrams · 617; inheritance · 40; use case · 49

directive: preprocessor · 79; using, namespaces · 92, 418; header files · 247

directly accessing structure · 240

disallowing assignment · 533

dispatching, double/multiple · 675

division (/) · 156

double · 155; dispatching, and multiple dispatching · 675; double precision floating point · 130; internal format · 189

do-while · 120

downcast: static_cast · 681; type-safe · 678

duplicate class definitions and templates · 699

dynamic: binding · 631; memory allocation · 223, 548; object creation · 42, 547, 732, 738; type checking · 80

dynamic_cast · 678

E

early binding · 38, 631, 641, 644

edition, 2nd, what's new in · 2

efficiency · 371; C++ · 66; constructor · 663; creating and returning objects · 507; inlines · 392; memory allocation · 567; references · 455; trap of premature optimization · 329; virtual functions · 645

elegance, in programming · 60

Ellis, Margaret · 433

else · 118
embedded: object · 585; systems · 577
encapsulation · 239, 270
end sentinel, iterator · 724, 728, 736
enum: and const in classes · 353; clarifying
    programs with · 179; hack · 358;
    incrementing · 180; keyword · 179; type
    checking · 180; untagged · 320, 358
equivalence · 166; == · 158
error: exception handling · 43; off-by-one ·
    301; preventing with common header
    files · 244; reporting errors in book · 16;
    structure redeclaration · 245
escape sequences · 94
evaluation order, inline · 391
evolution, in program development · 58
exception handling · 43, 565; simple use ·
    572
executing code: after exiting main( ) · 411;
    before entering main( ) · 411
execution: controlling · 117; point · 549
exercise solutions · 12
exit( ) · 397, 409
explicit: cast · 678; C++ · 167; for
    upcasting · 681; keyword to prevent
    automatic type conversion · 534
exponential · 154; notation · 130
exponentiation, no operator · 517
expressions, complicated, and operator
    overloading · 488
extending a class during inheritance · 34
extensible program · 633
extern · 84, 147, 151, 335, 339, 412; const ·
    335, 340; to link C code · 442
external: linkage · 152, 338, 339, 412;
    references, during linking · 228
extractor and inserter, overloading for
    iostreams · 518
Extreme Programming (XP) · 61, 615, 779

F

factory, design pattern · 712
false · 158, 163, 246; and true, in
    conditionals · 117; bool, true and false ·
    131
fan-out, automatic type conversion · 540
Fibonacci · 725
fibonacci( ) · 691
file: header · 233, 242, 323; code
    organization · 248; const · 335;

namespaces · 423; names · 749; reading
    and writing · 100; scope · 150, 152, 412;
    static · 150, 244, 414; structure
    definition in a header file · 234
flags, debugging · 194
floating point: float · 130, 155; float.h · 129;
    internal format · 189; number size
    hierarchy · 132; numbers · 130, 154;
    true and false · 159
for: defining variables inside the control
    expression · 145; loop · 106, 121; loop
    counter, defined inside control
    expression · 291; variable lifetime in for
    loops · 292
formatting pointer definitions · 342
forward: declaration · 151; reference, inline
    · 391
Fowler, Martin · 45, 58, 779
fragile base-class problem · 276
fragmentation, heap · 225, 567
free store · 549
free( ) · 223, 550, 553, 555, 569
free-standing reference · 451
friend · 263, 554; declaration of a nested
    friend class · 514; global function · 264;
    injection into namespace · 417; member
    function · 264; nested structure · 266;
    structure · 264
fstream · 100
function · 81; abstract base classes and
    pure virtual functions · 646; access ·
    379; adding more to a design · 280;
    adding new virtual functions in the
    derived class · 652; address · 198, 391;
    argument · 138; const · 344; const
    reference · 351; reference · 451; array of
    pointers to · 201; assembly-language
    code generated; function call · 456;
    virtual function call · 642; binding, for a
    function call · 631, 641; body · 83; C
    library · 116; call operator( ) · 514; call
    overhead · 372, 377; called for side
    effect · 313; complicated function
    definitions · 198; constructors, behavior
    of virtual functions inside · 664;
    creating · 112; declaration · 116, 245,
    313; not essential in C · 228; required ·
    233; syntax · 82; definition · 83; empty
    argument list, C vs. C++ · 114;
    expanding the function interface · 330;
    global · 234; friend · 264; helper,
    assembly · 457; inline · 372, 377, 646;

header files · 396; local class (class defined inside a function) · 428; member function · 28, 230; calling; a member function · 239; another member function from within a member function · 234; base-class functions · 588; const · 352, 359; friend · 264; inheritance and static member functions · 604; overloaded operator · 487; selection · 234; objects · 515; overloading · 310; operator · 486; using declaration, namespaces · 421; overriding · 35; pass-by reference & temporary objects · 453; pointer; defining · 198; to member function · 475; using a function pointer · 200; polymorphic function call · 637; prototyping · 113; pure virtual function definitions · 651; redefinition during inheritance · 588; return value; by reference · 451; returning a value · 115; type · 597; void · 115; signature · 597; stack frame for a function call · 458; static; class objects inside functions · 408; member · 366, 429, 465; objects inside functions · 437; variables inside functions · 406; templates · 742; type · 390; unique identifier for each · 310; variable argument list · 114; virtual function · 627, 629; constructor · 662; overriding · 632; picturing · 639

guaranteed initialization · 294, 548
guards, include, on header files · 757
guidelines: argument passing · 455; C++ programming guidelines · 760; object development · 56

iteration, in program development · 57
iterator · 509, 719, 730; containers · 690;
motivation · 738; nested class · 512;
Standard C++ Library · 724

J

Jacobsen, Ivar · 779
Java · 3, 15, 65, 71, 74, 588, 645, 694, 816

K

K&R C · 112
keywords: #define · 245, 335; #endif · 245,
757; #ifdef · 245; #include · 85; & · 134;
( ), function call operator overloading ·
514; * · 136, 164; .* · 474; :: · 232, 253; '.'
(member selection operator) · 237; = ·
156; overloading · 505, 521; -> · 164;
overloading · 509; struct member
selection via pointer · 178; ->* · 474;
overloading · 514; asm, for in-line
assembly language · 173; auto · 149,
414; bool · 125; true and false · 131;
break · 122; case · 124; catch · 572; char
· 96, 130, 132; class · 25, 31, 271; const ·
153, 333, 453; const_cast · 170;
continue · 122; default · 124; delete · 42,
223; do · 120; double · 130, 132;
dynamic_cast · 678; else · 118; enum ·
179, 358; untagged · 320; explicit · 534;
extern · 84, 147, 151, 335, 339, 412; for
alternate linkage · 442; false · 117, 131;
float · 130, 132; for · 106, 121; friend ·
263; goto · 125, 288, 293; if · 118; inline
· 394, 662; int · 130; long · 132; long
double · 132; long float (not legal) · 132;
mutable · 363; namespace · 91, 414,
757; new · 42, 223; operator · 486;
private · 262, 270, 380, 610; protected ·
263, 270, 610; public · 261; register ·
149, 414; reinterpret_cast · 171; return ·
115; short · 132; signed · 132; signed
char · 132; sizeof · 132, 172, 587; with
struct · 240; static · 149, 350, 406;
static_cast · 169, 679; struct · 175, 260;
switch · 123, 293; template · 689, 696;
this · 234, 286, 363, 380, 429; throw ·
572; true · 117, 131; try · 572; typedef ·

174; typeid · 680; union · 181, 318;
anonymous · 320; unsigned · 132; using
· 92, 417; virtual · 39, 595, 627, 632,
637, 646, 665; void · 114; void& (illegal)
· 143; void* · 142, 450; volatile · 155;
while · 101, 119
Koenig, Andrew · 376, 762, 778

L

Lajoie, Josee · 776
Lakos, John · 756, 778
language: C++ is a more strongly typed
language · 450; C++, hybrid object-
oriented language, and friend · 269;
hybrid object-oriented programming
language · 7
large programs, creation of · 78
late binding · 38, 631; implementing · 636
layout, object, and access control · 269
lazy initialization · 704
leading underscore, on identifiers
(reserved) · 381
leaks, memory · 224, 300
left-shift operator << · 160
less than: < · 158; or equal to <= · 158
library · 76, 80, 88, 218; C · 219; code · 78;
creating your own with the librarian ·
117; issues with different compilers ·
312; Standard C function; abort( ) ·
409; atexit( ) · 409; exit( ) · 409
lifetime: for loop variables · 292; object ·
42, 547; temporary objects · 468
limits.h · 129
linkage · 152, 406; alternate linkage
specification · 442; controlling · 412;
external · 338, 339, 412; internal · 335,
339, 412; no linkage · 153, 412; type-
safe · 313
linked list · 248, 275, 298
linker · 78, 79, 87; collision · 244; external
references · 228; object file order · 88;
pre-empting a library function · 89;
searching libraries · 88, 117; unresolved
references · 88
Lippman, Stanley · 776
list: constructor initializer · 353, 589;
linked · 248, 275, 298
Lister, Timothy · 781
local: array · 186; classes · 428; static
object · 410; variable · 138, 149

logarithm · 466

logical: *and* && · 166; const · 362; explicit bitwise and logical operators · 173; *not* ! · 163; operators · 158, 505; *or* || · 166

long · 132, 135

long double · 132, 155

longjmp( ) · 288

loop: for · 106; loop counter, defined inside control expression · 291; variable lifetime in for loops · 292; while · 101

Love, Tom · 781

lvalue · 156, 346, 698

M

machine instructions · 76

macro: argument · 374; makefile · 205; preprocessor · 158, 192, 372; macros for parameterized types, instead of templates · 696; unsafe · 399; to generate classes · 594

magic numbers, avoiding · 334

main( ): basic form · 93; executing code after exiting · 411; executing code before entering · 411

maintenance, program · 58

make · 202; dependencies · 204; macros · 205; suffix rules · 205; SUFFIXES · 206

makefile · 203, 750

malloc( ) · 223, 550, 552, 554, 569; behavior, not deterministic in time · 555

management obstacles · 71

mangling, name · 230, 231, 237; and overloading · 311

mathematical operators · 156

Matson, Kris C. · 126

member: defining storage for static data member · 424; initializing const data members · 355; member function · 28, 230; calling · 239; calling another member function from within a member function · 234; const · 352, 359; four member functions the compiler synthesizes · 619; friend · 264; non-inline template member function definitions · 699; return type · 597; selection · 234; signature · 597; static · 366, 429, 465; and inheritance · 604; object · 30; object initialization · 589; overloaded member operator · 487;

pointers to members · 473; selection operator · 237; static data member inside a class · 423; vs. non-member operators · 518

memberwise: assignment · 532, 600; const · 362; initialization · 471, 600

memcpy( ) · 560; standard C library function · 326

memory · 133; allocation and efficiency · 566; dynamic memory allocation · 223, 548; leak · 224, 300; finding with overloaded new and delete · 573; from delete void* · 557; management; example of · 324; reference counting · 526; memory manager overhead · 554; read-only (ROM) · 364; simple storage allocation system · 570

memset( ) · 269, 326, 356, 560

mentoring: and training · 71, 73; consulting, mentoring, and design and code walkthroughs from MindView · 16

message, sending · 25, 239, 636

methodology, analysis and design · 44

Meyers, Scott · 28, 760, 778

MindView: public hands-on training seminars · 16; seminars-on-CD-ROM · 16

minimum size of a struct · 241

mission statement · 47

mistakes, and design · 279

modulus (%) · 156

Moo, Barbara · 778

Mortensen, Owen · 477

multiparadigm programming · 24

multiple: dispatching · 675; inclusion of header files · 244; inheritance · 586, 613, 621, 673, 695; multiple-declaration problem · 244

multiplication (*) · 156

multitasking and volatile · 365

multi-way selection · 124

Murray, Rob · 520, 760

mutable · 363; bitwise vs. logical const · 362

mutators · 380

N

name: clashes · 229; collisions, in C · 68; decoration · 230, 231, 237, 442; no standard for · 312; overloading and ·

P

re-entrant · 458
refactoring · 58
reference · 153, 450, 451; C++ · 140; const · 345, 453; and operator overloading · 505; for argument passing · 351; efficiency · 455; external, during linking · 228; free-standing · 451; function · 452; NULL · 451, 479; passing const · 473; pointer & reference upcasting · 622; pointer, reference to a pointer · 454; reference counting · 526, 714; rules · 451; upcasting · 630; void reference (illegal) · 143; vs. pointer when modifying outside objects · 472
reflexivity, in operator overloading · 536
register · 414; variables · 149
reinterpret_cast · 171
relational operators · 158
reporting errors in book · 16
request, in OOP · 25
require( ) · 698, 711, 757
require.h · 237, 252, 756, 757; function definitions · 396
requireArgs( ), from require.h · 252
requirements analysis · 48
resolution, scope: global · 253; nested structures · 278; operator :: · 232
resolving references · 80
return: by value · 450; by value as const, and operator overloading · 507; const value · 345; constructor return value · 287; efficiency when creating and returning objects · 507; function return values, references · 451; keyword · 115; operator; overloaded return type · 488; overloading arguments and return values · 505; overloading on return values · 312; passing and returning by value, C · 455; passing and returning large objects · 457; references to local objects · 452; type · 597; value · 81; from a function · 115; optimization · 507; semantics · 350; void · 115
RETURN, assembly-language · 458
reusability · 29
reuse · 55; code reuse · 583; existing class libraries · 70; source code reuse with templates · 696; templates · 689
right-shift operator (>>) · 160
ROM, read-only memory, ROMability · 364
rotate · 162; bit manipulation · 162

RTTI, run-time type identification · 655, 680
rule, makefile · 204
Rumbaugh, James · 779
run-time: access control · 275; binding · 631; debugging flags · 195; type identification (RTTI) · 655, 680
rvalue · 156, 698

S

safe union · 319
Saks, Dan · 66, 394, 751, 760
scenario · 49
scheduling · 51
Schwarz, Jerry · 434
scope · 143, 288, 339, 554; consts · 337; file · 339, 412; going out of · 143; hide variables from the enclosing scope · 292; preprocessor · 376; resolution, global · 253; nested structures · 278; operator :: · 232, 429; and namespaces · 417; for calling base-class functions · 588; scoped variable · 42; static member initialization · 425; storage allocation · 549; use case · 57
second edition, what's new · 2
security · 276
selection: member function · 234; multi-way · 124
self-assignment, checking for in operator overloading · 505, 523
semantics, return value · 350
seminars: on CD-ROM, from MindView · 16; public · 5; training seminars from MindView · 16
sending a message · 25, 239, 636
sentinel, end · 728, 736
separate compilation · 78, 80; and make · 202
separation of interface and implementation · 29, 261, 271
sequence point · 286, 293
set: <set> standard header file · 711; and get functions · 381; container class from the Standard C++ Library · 711
setf( ), iostreams · 466
setjmp( ) · 288
SGI (Silicon Graphics) STL project · 103
shape: example · 32; hierarchy · 682
shift operators · 160

minimum size · 241; pointer selection of member with -> · 178; size of · 240

structure: aggregate initialization and structures · 302; declaration · 245, 265; definition in a header file · 234; friend · 264; nested · 248; redeclaring · 245

subobject · 585, 587, 588, 604

substitutability, in OOP · 24

substitution: principle · 35; value · 334

subtraction (-) · 156

subtyping · 606

suffix rules, makefile · 205

SUFFIXES, makefile · 206

sugar, syntactic · 485

switch · 123, 293; defining variables inside the selector statement · 145

syntax: function declaration syntax · 82; operator overloading · 487; sugar, with operator overloading · 485; variable declaration syntax · 83

synthesized: default constructor, behavior of · 305; member functions that are automatically created by the compiler · 600, 619

system specification · 48

system() · 98

T

tab · 95

table-driven code · 201

tag name · 220

tag, comment for linking · 148

template · 689, 696; argument list · 700; basic usage · 104; class · 742; constants and default values in templates · 703; container class templates and virtual functions · 743; function · 742; generated classes · 699; header file · 700, 707; implies an interface · 701; inline · 707; instantiation · 699; multiple definitions · 700; non-inline template member function definitions · 699; preprocessor macros for parameterized types, instead of templates · 696; Standard Template Library (STL) · 103; Stash and Stack examples as templates · 705; weak typing · 701

temporary object · 347, 468, 535; bugs · 348; function references · 453; passing a temporary object to a function · 351; return value · 508

ternary operator · 164

testing: automated · 62; Extreme Programming (XP) · 61

Thinking in C: Foundations for Java and C++ CD ROM · 2, 112, 776

Thinking in C++ Volume 2, what's in it and how to get it · 3

this · 286, 363, 380, 429, 468, 552, 642; address of current object · 234

throw · 572

time, Standard C library · 384

time_t · 384

token pasting, preprocessor · 395

toupper( ), unexpected results · 376

trailing arguments only can be defaults · 322

training · 69; and mentoring · 71, 73; seminars from MindView · 16

translation unit · 228, 432

true · 158, 163, 166, 246; and false, in conditionals · 117; bool, true and false · 131

try block · 572

type: abstract data type · 239; automatic type conversion · 533; preventing with the keyword explicit · 534; with operator overloading · 535; base · 32; basic built-in · 129; cast · 135; checking · 80, 83, 153, 167; stricter in C++ · 227; conversion · 228; implicit · 154; creation, composite · 174; data type equivalence to class · 26; derived · 32; function type · 390; improved type checking · 236; incomplete type specification · 265, 277; inheritance, is-a · 615; initialization of built-in types with 'constructors' · 354; run-time type identification (RTTI) · 655, 680; storing type information · 637; type checking; for enumerations · 180; for unions · 181; type-safe linkage · 313; user-defined · 76, 239; weak typing · 38, 702; C++ via templates · 701

typedef · 174, 177, 220, 231, 414

typefaces, book · 18

typeid · 680

typeinfo standard header file · 680

type-safe downcast · 678

799

U

UML · 54; indicating composition · 30; Unified Modeling Language · 27, 779

unary: examples of all overloaded unary operators · 489; minus - · 163; operators · 159, 163; overloaded · 487; plus + · 163

underscore, leading, on identifiers (reserved) · 381

Unified Modeling Language (UML) · 27, 779

union: additional type checking · 181; anonymous · 320; file scope · 321; difference between a union and a class · 319; member functions and access control · 318; safe · 319; saving memory with · 181

unit, translation · 228

unnamed: arguments · 114; namespace · 416

unresolved references, during linking · 88

unsigned · 132

untagged enum · 320, 358

unusual operator overloading · 508

upcasting · 40, 615, 629, 636, 678, 738; by value · 644; copy-constructor · 617; explicit cast for upcasting · 681; pointer · 631; and reference upcasting · 622; reference · 630; type information, lost · 622

use case · 49; iteration · 57; scope · 57

user interface · 51

user-defined data type · 76, 129, 239

using keyword, for namespaces · 92, 417; declaration · 421, 757; directive · 92, 418, 757; header files · 247; namespace std · 247

V

value: constant · 154; minimum and maximum for built-in types · 129; pass-by-value · 137; preprocessor value substitution · 334; return · 81; returning by value · 352

varargs · 243; variable argument list · 243

variable: argument list · 114; varargs · 243; automatic · 42, 149, 153; declaration syntax · 83; defining · 145; file scope · 150; global · 147; going out of scope · 143; hide from the enclosing scope · 292; initializer for a static variable of a built-in type · 408; lifetime, in for loops · 292; local · 138, 149; point of definition · 289; register · 149; scoped · 42; stack · 225; turning name into a string · 196

vector · 740; assignment · 108; of change · 59; push_back( ) · 104; Standard C++ Library · 102

virtual destructor · 665, 707, 736, 740; pure virtual destructor · 668

virtual function · 595, 627, 629, 646, 741; adding new virtual functions in the derived class · 652; and dynamic_cast · 679; assembly-language code generated by a virtual function · 642; constructors, behavior of virtual functions inside · 662, 664; destructors, behavior of virtual functions inside · 670; efficiency · 645; late binding · 637; operator overloading and virtual functions · 675; overriding · 632; picturing virtual functions · 639; pure virtual function; and abstract base classes · 646; definitions · 651; size overhead of virtual functions · 637; virtual keyword · 39, 632; in base-class declarations · 632; in derived-class declarations · 632

virtual memory · 552

visibility · 406

void: argument list · 114; casting void pointers · 235; keyword · 114; pointer · 220, 450, 555, 559, 562; reference (illegal) · 143

void* · 142, 170, 220; bugs · 235; containers and ownership · 671; delete, a bug · 555

volatile · 155, 365; casting with const_cast · 170

Volume 2, Thinking in C++ · 3

vpointer, abbreviated as VPTR · 637

VPTR · 637, 640, 642, 662, 665; installation by the constructor · 643

VTABLE · 637, 640, 642, 648, 653, 662, 665; inheritance and the VTABLE · 652

W

Waldrop, M. Mitchell · 781
weak: typing · 702; in C++ via templates · 701; weakly typed language · 38
while loop · 101, 119; defining variables inside the control expression · 145
width( ), iostreams · 466
wild-card · 46
Will-Harris, Daniel · 17, 18
word size · 133
writing files · 100

X

xor ^ bitwise exclusive-or · 159, 173
xor_eq, ^= bitwise exclusive-*or*-assignment · 173
XP, Extreme Programming · 61

Z

zero indexing · 183

Public
C++ Seminars

Check **www.BruceEckel.com**
for in-depth details and the date
and location of the next:

Hands-On C++ Seminar
- Based on this book
- Get a solid grounding in Standard C++ fundamentals
- Includes in-class programming exercises
- Personal attention during exercises

Intermediate C++ Seminar
- Based on Volume 2 of this book (downloadable at www.BruceEckel.com)
- In-depth coverage of the Standard C++ Library
- Strings, containers, iterators, algorithms
- In-depth templates & exception handling

Advanced C++ Topics
- Based on advanced topics in Volume 2 of this book
- Design patterns
- Building robust systems
- Creating testing & debugging frameworks

**Subscribe to the free newsletter
to be automatically informed
of upcoming seminars**

Also visit www.BrucEckel.com for:

■ **Consulting Services**

■ **Exercise solutions for this book**

End-User License Agreement for Microsoft Software

IMPORTANT-READ CAREFULLY: This Microsoft End-User License Agreement ("EULA") is a legal agreement between you (either an individual or a single entity) and Microsoft Corporation for the Microsoft software product included in this package, which includes computer software and may include associated media, printed materials, and "online" or electronic documentation ("SOFTWARE PRODUCT"). The SOFTWARE PRODUCT also includes any updates and supplements to the original SOFTWARE PRODUCT provided to you by Microsoft. By installing, copying, downloading, accessing or otherwise using the SOFTWARE PRODUCT, you agree to be bound by the terms of this EULA. If you do not agree to the terms of this EULA, do not install, copy, or otherwise use the SOFTWARE PRODUCT.

SOFTWARE PRODUCT LICENSE

The SOFTWARE PRODUCT is protected by copyright laws and international copyright treaties, as well as other intellectual property laws and treaties. The SOFTWARE PRODUCT is licensed, not sold.

1. GRANT OF LICENSE. This EULA grants you the following rights:

1.1 License Grant. Microsoft grants to you as an individual, a personal nonexclusive license to make and use copies of the SOFTWARE PRODUCT for the sole purposes of evaluating and learning how to use the SOFTWARE PRODUCT, as may be instructed in accompanying publications or documentation. You may install the software on an unlimited number of computers provided that you are the only individual using the SOFTWARE PRODUCT.

1.2 Academic Use. You must be a "Qualified Educational User" to use the SOFTWARE PRODUCT in the manner described in this section. To determine whether you are a Qualified Educational User, please contact the Microsoft Sales Information Center/One Microsoft Way/Redmond, WA 98052-6399 or the Microsoft subsidiary serving your country. If you are a Qualified Educational User, you may either:

(i) exercise the rights granted in Section 1.1, OR

(ii) if you intend to use the SOFTWARE PRODUCT solely for instructional purposes in connection with a class or other educational program, this EULA grants you the following alternative license models:

(A) Per Computer Model. For every valid license you have acquired for the SOFTWARE PRODUCT, you may install a single copy of the SOFTWARE PRODUCT on a single computer for access and use by an unlimited number of student end users at your educational institution, provided that all such end users comply with all other terms of this EULA, OR

(B) Per License Model. If you have multiple licenses for the SOFTWARE PRODUCT, then at any time you may have as many copies of the SOFTWARE PRODUCT in use as you have licenses, provided that such use is limited to student or faculty end users at your educational institution and provided that all such end users comply with all other terms of this EULA. For purposes of this subsection, the SOFTWARE PRODUCT is "in use" on a computer when it is loaded into the temporary memory (i.e., RAM) or installed into the permanent memory (e.g., hard disk, CD ROM, or other storage device) of that computer, except that a copy installed on a network server for the sole purpose of distribution to other computers is not "in use". If the anticipated number of users of the SOFTWARE PRODUCT will exceed the number of applicable licenses, then you must have a reasonable mechanism or process in place to ensure that the number of persons using the SOFTWARE PRODUCT concurrently does not exceed the number of licenses.

2. DESCRIPTION OF OTHER RIGHTS AND LIMITATIONS.

• Limitations on Reverse Engineering, Decompilation, and Disassembly. You may not reverse engineer, decompile, or disassemble the SOFTWARE PRODUCT, except and only to the extent that such activity is expressly permitted by applicable law notwithstanding this limitation.

• Separation of Components. The SOFTWARE PRODUCT is licensed as a single product. Its component parts may not be separated for use on more than one computer.

• Rental. You may not rent, lease or lend the SOFTWARE PRODUCT.

• Trademarks. This EULA does not grant you any rights in connection with any trademarks or service marks of Microsoft.

• Software Transfer. The initial user of the SOFTWARE PRODUCT may make a one-time permanent transfer of this EULA and SOFTWARE PRODUCT only directly to an end user. This transfer must include all of the SOFTWARE PRODUCT (including all component parts, the media and printed materials, any upgrades, this EULA, and, if applicable, the Certificate of Authenticity). Such transfer may not be by way of consignment or any other indirect transfer. The transferee of such one-time transfer must agree to comply with the terms of this EULA, including the obligation not to further transfer this EULA and SOFTWARE PRODUCT.

• No Support. Microsoft shall have no obligation to provide any product support for the SOFTWARE PRODUCT.

• Termination. Without prejudice to any other rights, Microsoft may terminate this EULA if you fail to comply with the terms and conditions of this EULA. In such event, you must destroy all copies of the SOFTWARE PRODUCT and all of its component parts.

3. COPYRIGHT. All title and intellectual property rights in and to the SOFTWARE PRODUCT (including but not limited to any images, photographs, animations, video, audio, music, text, and "applets" incorporated into the SOFTWARE PRODUCT), the accompanying printed materials, and any copies of the SOFTWARE PRODUCT are owned by Microsoft or its suppliers. All title and intellectual property rights in and to the content which may be accessed through use of the SOFTWARE PRODUCT is the property of the respective content owner and may be protected by applicable copyright or other intellectual property laws and treaties. This EULA grants you no rights to use such content. All rights not expressly granted are reserved by Microsoft.

4. BACKUP COPY. After installation of one copy of the SOFTWARE PRODUCT pursuant to this EULA, you may keep the original media on which the SOFTWARE PRODUCT was provided by Microsoft solely for backup or archival purposes. If the original media is required to use the SOFTWARE PRODUCT on the COMPUTER, you may make one copy of the SOFTWARE PRODUCT solely for backup or archival purposes. Except as expressly provided in this EULA, you may not otherwise make copies of the SOFTWARE PRODUCT or the printed materials accompanying the SOFTWARE PRODUCT.

5. U.S. GOVERNMENT RESTRICTED RIGHTS. The SOFTWARE PRODUCT and documentation are provided with RESTRICTED RIGHTS. Use, duplication, or disclosure by the Government is subject to restrictions as set forth in subparagraph (c)(1)(ii) of the Rights in Technical Data and Computer Software clause at DFARS 252.227-7013 or subparagraphs (c)(1) and (2) of the Commercial Computer Software-Restricted Rights at 48 CFR 52.227-19, as applicable. Manufacturer is Microsoft Corporation/One Microsoft Way/Redmond, WA 98052-6399.

6. EXPORT RESTRICTIONS. You agree that you will not export or re-export the SOFTWARE PRODUCT, any part thereof, or any process or service that is the direct product of the SOFTWARE PRODUCT (the foregoing collectively referred to as the "Restricted Components"), to any country, person, entity or end user subject to U.S. export restrictions. You specifically agree not to export or re-export any of the Restricted Components (i) to any country to which the U.S. has embargoed or restricted the export of goods or services, which currently include, but are not necessarily limited to Cuba, Iran, Iraq, Libya, North Korea, Sudan and Syria, or to any national of any such country, wherever located, who intends to transmit or transport the Restricted Components back to such country; (ii) to any end-user who you know or have reason to know will utilize the Restricted

Components in the design, development or production of nuclear, chemical or biological weapons; or (iii) to any end-user who has been prohibited from participating in U.S. export transactions by any federal agency of the U.S. government. You warrant and represent that neither the BXA nor any other U.S. federal agency has suspended, revoked, or denied your export privileges.

7. NOTE ON JAVA SUPPORT. THE SOFTWARE PRODUCT MAY CONTAIN SUPPORT FOR PROGRAMS WRITTEN IN JAVA. JAVA TECHNOLOGY IS NOT FAULT TOLERANT AND IS NOT DESIGNED, MANUFACTURED, OR INTENDED FOR USE OR RESALE AS ON-LINE CONTROL EQUIPMENT IN HAZARDOUS ENVIRONMENTS REQUIRING FAIL-SAFE PERFORMANCE, SUCH AS IN THE OPERATION OF NUCLEAR FACILITIES, AIRCRAFT NAVIGATION OR COMMUNICATION SYSTEMS, AIR TRAFFIC CONTROL, DIRECT LIFE SUPPORT MACHINES, OR WEAPONS SYSTEMS, IN WHICH THE FAILURE OF JAVA TECHNOLOGY COULD LEAD DIRECTLY TO DEATH, PERSONAL INJURY, OR SEVERE PHYSICAL OR ENVIRONMENTAL DAMAGE.

MISCELLANEOUS

If you acquired this product in the United States, this EULA is governed by the laws of the State of Washington.

If you acquired this product in Canada, this EULA is governed by the laws of the Province of Ontario, Canada. Each of the parties hereto irrevocably attorns to the jurisdiction of the courts of the Province of Ontario and further agrees to commence any litigation which may arise hereunder in the courts located in the Judicial District of York, Province of Ontario.

If this product was acquired outside the United States, then local law may apply.

Should you have any questions concerning this EULA, or if you desire to contact Microsoft for any reason, please contact Microsoft, or write: Microsoft Sales Information Center/One Microsoft Way/Redmond, WA 98052-6399.

LIMITED WARRANTY

LIMITED WARRANTY. Microsoft warrants that (a) the SOFTWARE PRODUCT will perform substantially in accordance with the accompanying written materials for a period of ninety (90) days from the date of receipt, and (b) any Support Services provided by Microsoft shall be substantially as described in applicable written materials provided to you by Microsoft, and Microsoft support engineers will make commercially reasonable efforts to solve any problem. To the extent allowed by applicable law, implied warranties on the SOFTWARE PRODUCT, if any, are limited to ninety (90) days. Some states/jurisdictions do not allow limitations on duration of an implied warranty, so the above limitation may not apply to you.

CUSTOMER REMEDIES. Microsoft's and its suppliers' entire liability and your exclusive remedy shall be, at Microsoft's option, either (a) return of the price paid, if any, or (b) repair or replacement of the SOFTWARE PRODUCT that does not meet Microsoft's Limited Warranty and that is returned to Microsoft with a copy of your receipt. This Limited Warranty is void if failure of the SOFTWARE PRODUCT has resulted from accident, abuse, or misapplication. Any replacement SOFTWARE PRODUCT will be warranted for the remainder of the original warranty period or thirty (30) days, whichever is longer. Outside the United States, neither these remedies nor any product support services offered by Microsoft are available without proof of purchase from an authorized international source.

NO OTHER WARRANTIES. TO THE MAXIMUM EXTENT PERMITTED BY APPLICABLE LAW, MICROSOFT AND ITS SUPPLIERS DISCLAIM ALL OTHER WARRANTIES AND CONDITIONS, EITHER EXPRESS OR IMPLIED, INCLUDING, BUT NOT LIMITED TO, IMPLIED WARRANTIES OR CONDITIONS OF MERCHANTABILITY, FITNESS FOR A PARTICULAR PURPOSE, TITLE AND NON-INFRINGEMENT, WITH REGARD TO THE SOFTWARE PRODUCT, AND THE PROVISION OF OR FAILURE TO PROVIDE SUPPORT SERVICES. THIS LIMITED WARRANTY GIVES YOU SPECIFIC LEGAL RIGHTS. YOU MAY HAVE OTHERS, WHICH VARY FROM STATE/JURISDICTION TO STATE/JURISDICTION.

LIMITATION OF LIABILITY. TO THE MAXIMUM EXTENT PERMITTED BY APPLICABLE LAW, IN NO EVENT SHALL MICROSOFT OR ITS SUPPLIERS BE LIABLE FOR ANY SPECIAL, INCIDENTAL, INDIRECT, OR CONSEQUENTIAL DAMAGES WHATSOEVER (INCLUDING, WITHOUT LIMITATION, DAMAGES FOR LOSS OF BUSINESS PROFITS, BUSINESS INTERRUPTION, LOSS OF BUSINESS INFORMATION, OR ANY OTHER PECUNIARY LOSS) ARISING OUT OF THE USE OF OR INABILITY TO USE THE SOFTWARE PRODUCT OR THE FAILURE TO PROVIDE SUPPORT SERVICES, EVEN IF MICROSOFT HAS BEEN ADVISED OF THE POSSIBILITY OF SUCH DAMAGES. IN ANY CASE, MICROSOFT'S ENTIRE LIABILITY UNDER ANY PROVISION OF THIS EULA SHALL BE LIMITED TO THE GREATER OF THE AMOUNT ACTUALLY PAID BY YOU FOR THE SOFTWARE PRODUCT OR U.S.$5.00; PROVIDED, HOWEVER, IF YOU HAVE ENTERED INTO A MICROSOFT SUPPORT SERVICES AGREEMENT, MICROSOFT'S ENTIRE LIABILITY REGARDING SUPPORT SERVICES SHALL BE GOVERNED BY THE TERMS OF THAT AGREEMENT. BECAUSE SOME STATES/JURISDICTIONS DO NOT ALLOW THE

EXCLUSION OR LIMITATION OF LIABILITY, THE ABOVE LIMITATION
MAY NOT APPLY TO YOU.
0495 Part No. 64358

LICENSE AGREEMENT FOR MindView, Inc.'s
Thinking in C: Foundations for C++ & Java CD-ROM
by Chuck Allison
This CD is provided together with the book "Thinking in C++ 2nd
edition, Volume 1."

READ THIS AGREEMENT BEFORE USING THIS "Thinking in C:
Foundations for C++ & Java" (Hereafter called "CD"). BY USING THE
CD YOU AGREE TO BE BOUND BY THE TERMS AND CONDITIONS OF
THIS AGREEMENT. IF YOU DO NOT AGREE TO THE TERMS AND
CONDITIONS OF THIS AGREEMENT, IMMEDIATELY RETURN THE
UNUSED CD FOR A FULL REFUND OF MONIES PAID, IF ANY.

SOFTWARE REQUIREMENTS
The purpose of this CD is to provide the Content, not the associated
software necessary to view the Content. The Content of this CD is in
HTML for viewing with Microsoft Internet Explorer 4 or newer, and uses
Microsoft Sound Codecs available in Microsoft's Windows Media Player
for Windows. It is your responsibility to correctly install the appropriate
Microsoft software for your system.

The text, images, and other media included on this CD ("Content") and
their compilation are licensed to you subject to the terms and
conditions of this Agreement by MindView Inc., having a place of
business at 5343 Valle Vista, La Mesa, CA 91941. Your rights to use
other programs and materials included on the CD are also governed by
separate agreements distributed with those programs and materials on
the CD (the "Other Agreements"). In the event of any inconsistency
between this Agreement and the Other Agreements, this Agreement
shall govern. By using this CD, you agree to be bound by the terms
and conditions of this Agreement. MindView Inc. owns title to the
Content and to all intellectual property rights therein, except insofar as
it contains materials that are proprietary to third-party suppliers. All
rights in the Content except those expressly granted to you in this
Agreement are reserved to MindView Inc. and such suppliers as their
respective interests may appear.

1. LIMITED LICENSE
MindView Inc. grants you a limited, nonexclusive, nontransferable
license to use the Content on a single dedicated computer (excluding
network servers). This Agreement and your rights hereunder shall
automatically terminate if you fail to comply with any provisions of this

Agreement or any of the Other Agreements. Upon such termination, you agree to destroy the CD and all copies of the CD, whether lawful or not, that are in your possession or under your control.

2. ADDITIONAL RESTRICTIONS

a. You shall not (and shall not permit other persons or entities to) directly or indirectly, by electronic or other means, reproduce (except for archival purposes as permitted by law), publish, distribute, rent, lease, sell, sublicense, assign, or otherwise transfer the Content or any part thereof.

b. You shall not (and shall not permit other persons or entities to) use the Content or any part thereof for any commercial purpose or merge, modify, create derivative works of, or translate the Content.

c. You shall not (and shall not permit other persons or entities to) obscure MindView's or its suppliers copyright, trademark, or other proprietary notices or legends from any portion of the Content or any related materials.

3. PERMISSIONS

a. Except as noted in the Contents of the CD, you must treat this software just like a book. However, you may copy it onto a computer to be used and you may make archival copies of the software for the sole purpose of backing up the software and protecting your investment from loss. By saying, "just like a book," MindView, Inc. means, for example, that this software may be used by any number of people and may be freely moved from one computer location to another, so long as there is no possibility of its being used at one location or on one computer while it is being used at another. Just as a book cannot be read by two different people in two different places at the same time, neither can the software be used by two different people in two different places at the same time.

b. You may show or demonstrate the un-modified Content in a live presentation, live seminar, or live performance as long as you attribute all material of the Content to MindView, Inc.

c. Other permissions and grants of rights for use of the CD must be obtained directly from MindView, Inc. at http://www.MindView.net. (Bulk copies of the CD may also be purchased at this site.)

DISCLAIMER OF WARRANTY

The Content and CD are provided "AS IS" without warranty of any kind, either express or implied, including, without limitation, any warranty of merchantability and fitness for a particular purpose. The entire risk as to the results and performance of the CD and Content is assumed by you. MindView Inc. and its suppliers assume no responsibility for defects in the CD, the accuracy of the Content, or omissions in the CD or the Content. MindView Inc. and its suppliers do not warrant, guarantee, or make any representations regarding the use, or the results of the use, of the product in terms of correctness, accuracy, reliability, currentness, or otherwise, or that the Content will meet your needs, or that operation of the CD will be uninterrupted or error-free, or that any defects in the CD or Content will be corrected. MindView Inc. and its suppliers shall not be liable for any loss, damages, or costs arising from the use of the CD or the interpretation of the Content. Some states do not allow exclusion or limitation of implied warranties or limitation of liability for incidental or consequential damages, so all of the above limitations or exclusions may not apply to you.

In no event shall MindView Inc. or its suppliers' total liability to you for all damages, losses, and causes of action (whether in contract, tort, or otherwise) exceed the amount paid by you for the CD.

MindView, Inc., and Prentice-Hall, Inc. specifically disclaim the implied warrantees of merchantability and fitness for a particular purpose. No oral or written information or advice given by MindView, Inc., Prentice-Hall, Inc., their dealers, distributors, agents or employees shall create a warrantee. You may have other rights, which vary from state to state.

Neither MindView, Inc., Bruce Eckel, Chuck Allison, Prentice Hall, nor anyone else who has been involved in the creation, production or delivery of the product shall be liable for any direct, indirect, consequential, or incidental damages (including damages for loss of business profits, business interruption, loss of business information, and the like) arising out of the use of or inability to use the product even if MindView, Inc., has been advised of the possibility of such damages. Because some states do not allow the exclusion or limitation of liability for consequential or incidental damages, the above limitation may not apply to you.

This CD is provided as a supplement to the book "Thinking in C++ 2nd edition." The sole responsibility of Prentice-Hall will be to provide a replacement CD in the event that the one that came with the book is defective. This replacement warrantee shall be in effect for a period of sixty days from the purchase date. MindView, Inc. does not bear any additional responsibility for the CD.

NO TECHNICAL SUPPORT IS PROVIDED WITH THIS CD ROM

The following are trademarks of their respective companies in the U.S. and may be protected as trademarks in other countries: Sun and the Sun Logo, Sun Microsystems, Java, all Java-based names and logos and the Java Coffee Cup are trademarks of Sun Microsystems; Internet Explorer, the Windows Media Player, DOS, Windows 95, and Windows NT are trademarks of Microsoft.

Thinking in C: Foundations for Java & C++

Multimedia Seminar-on-CD ROM

WARNING: BEFORE OPENING THE DISC PACKAGE, CAREFULLY READ THE TERMS AND CONDITIONS OF THE LICENSE AGREEMENT & WARANTEE LIMITATION ON THE PREVIOUS PAGES.

The CD ROM packaged with this book is a multimedia seminar consisting of synchronized slides and audio lectures. The goal of this seminar is to introduce you to the aspects of C that are necessary for you to move on to C++ or Java, leaving out the unpleasant parts that C programmers must deal with on a day-to-day basis but that the C++ and Java languages steer you away from. The CD also contains this book in HTML form along with the source code for the book.

This CD ROM will work with Windows (with a sound system). However, you must:

1. Install the most recent version of Microsoft's Internet Explorer. Because of the features provided on the CD, it will NOT work with Netscape Navigator. **The Internet Explorer software for Windows 9X/NT is included on the CD.**

2. Install Microsoft's *Windows Media Player*. Unfortunately this is only allowed to be distributed directly from Microsoft's Web site, so it is NOT included on the CD. You will need to go to **http://www.microsoft.com/windows/mediaplayer** and follow the instructions or links there to download and install the Media Player for your particular platform. Please note that Microsoft sometimes changes the location of Web pages on their site and in that case you'll need to use their searching capability to find the media player.

At this point you should be able to play the lectures on the CD. Using the Internet Explorer Web browser, open the file **Install.html** that you'll find on the CD. This will introduce you to the CD and provide further instructions about the use of the CD.